International Business

International Business provides students with a balanced perspective on business in a global environment, exploring implications for multinational companies in developed and emerging markets. It is the first text of its kind to emphasize strategic decision making as the cornerstone of its approach while focusing on emerging markets.

Traditional topics, like foreign exchange markets and global competition, are contrasted with emerging operations, like Chinese market intervention and Islamic finance, to provide students with an understanding of successful business strategy. Readers learn to develop and implement these strategies across cultures, and across economic, legal, and religious institutions in order to cope with competitive players in the global landscape. Application-based chapters open with reading goals and conclude with case studies and discussion questions to encourage a practical understanding of strategy.

With in-depth analyses and recommended strategies, this edition equips students of international business with the skills they need for success on the global stage. A companion website features an instructor's manual, test bank, PowerPoint slides, and useful tips for instructors as well as in-class exercises and web resources for students.

K. Praveen Parboteeah is the inaugural COBE Distinguished Professor and Director of the Doctorate of Business Administration at the University of Wisconsin–Whitewater, USA.

John B. Cullen is Professor of Management and Huber Chair of Entrepreneurial Studies at Washington State University, USA.

"Parboteeah and Cullen do a great job of covering traditional international business topics like the environment, institutions, and culture. They also cover all of the operational and organizational materials, so it is a complete book. The focus on emerging markets is particularly timely and important."

Len J. Treviño, *Florida Atlantic University, USA*

"In today's volatile, uncertain world, global firms are looking for employees who have a global view as well as special skills to manage uncertainties across world markets. This book strives to bridge the gap between domestic and global skill sets. It is an excellent resource for students, faculty, and corporates who want to learn about international business from an analytical, logical framework, and knowledge point of view."

Prashant Salwan, *Indian Institute of Management Indore, India*

International Business

Perspectives from Developed and Emerging Markets

SECOND EDITION

K. Praveen Parboteeah & John B. Cullen

Routledge
Taylor & Francis Group

NEW YORK AND LONDON

First published 2018
by Routledge
711 Third Avenue, New York, NY 10017

and by Routledge
2 Park Square, Milton Park, Abingdon, Oxon OX14 4RN

Routledge is an imprint of the Taylor & Francis Group, an informa business

Library of Congress Cataloging in Publication Data
Names: Cullen, John B. (John Brooks), 1948- author. | Parboteeah, Praveen, author.
Title: International business : perspectives from developed and emerging markets / by K. Praveen Parboteeah & John B. Cullen.
Description: Second edition. | New York, NY : Routledge, 2017. | Includes bibliographical references and index.
Identifiers: LCCN 2016050586| ISBN 9781138122413 (hbk) | ISBN 9781138122420 (pbk) | ISBN 9781315650517 (ebk) | ISBN 9781317307228 (mobi/kindle)
Subjects: LCSH: International business enterprises--Management. | Business planning.
Classification: LCC HD62.4 .C847 2017| DDC 658.4/012--dc23
LC record available at https://lccn.loc.gov/2016050586

ISBN: 978-1-138-12241-3 (hbk)
ISBN: 978-1-138-12242-0 (pbk)
ISBN: 978-1-31565-051-7 (ebk)

Typeset in Sabon
by Saxon Graphics Ltd, Derby

Visit the companion website: www.routledge.com/cw/parboteeah

To
Kyong, Alisha, and Davin
and
Jean and Jaye

Brief Contents

Detailed Contents

Feature Topics

Examples from real companies that give information on the strategic implications for international businesses in emerging markets that relate to the current discussion in the text.

EMERGING MARKET ETHICAL CHALLENGE

Examples from the popular press that show ethical issues relevant to the chapter content within the context of emerging markets.

BRIC INSIGHT

Examples of material particularly relevant to the BRIC bloc; namely, Brazil, Russia, India, and China.

EMERGING MARKET BRIEF

Examples of emerging market situations in brief.

Chapter Introductory and Concluding Material

Preview IB Emerging Market Strategic Insight

Brief case to add realistic context to chapter material and serve as early referent to the strategic implications of the material in the context of emerging markets.

Concluding Case Study with Case Discussion Points

Similar to Preview Emerging Market IB Strategic Insight.

International Business Skill Builder

Experiential exercise relevant to chapter content.

Chapter Internet Activity

Key Concepts

Discussion Questions

List of Photographs and Exhibits

Preface

The globalization of markets and companies, the impact of the possible recession, the sustained performance of the emerging markets economic bloc, and the pressures for companies to become more environmentally sustainable define international business today. No companies are immune to such environmental forces. To cope adequately with this complex global environment, international managers need to be able to develop and implement successful strategies. *International Business: Perspectives From Developed and Emerging Markets* is designed to provide students with the latest insights into the complexity of managing multinationals and domestic operations across borders. The text uses a strategic perspective as the dominant theme to explore international business and its implications for the multinational company (MNC). This text also is among the first international business texts to acknowledge the critical roles played by emerging markets. The book's central theme is to expose students to critical challenges facing multinationals as they operate in such markets. This text thus informs students of the environment in emerging markets in comparison to developed markets through an emphasis on strategic decision making as the cornerstone of its approach.

Pedagogical Approach

International Business: Perspectives From Developed and Emerging Markets provides a thorough review and analysis of international business using several learning tools:

Strategy as the Theme   All chapters have been written using strategy as a unifying theme that is highlighted for the learner through the relevance of the material. This theme provides the students with the ability to see how the various functional areas of international business contribute to the overall strategy of the MNC.

Emerging Markets Compared to Developed Markets   All chapters have ample examples of situations and challenges in emerging markets in comparison to developed markets. Such an approach helps the students to see the unique circumstances facing any international business manager as they operate in such critical markets. The text therefore provides deep insights into emerging markets—something that most other international texts do not do.

Application-based   All chapters give the learner three opportunities to apply the knowledge gained from reading the chapter—an International Business Skill Builder, Chapter Internet Activity, and an end-of-chapter Case Study. These exercises provide deeper insights into the challenges faced by international business managers.

Current   The text contains the latest international business information and examples. It is the first to address the issue of emerging markets in depth in the international business area.

Key Features

Chapter Case Studies, Internet Activities, and International Business Skill Builders   End-of-chapter projects include cases and activities, which give the learner the opportunity to apply text material to real-life international business problems.

Extensive Examples   Throughout, many examples enhance the text material by showing actual international management situations. These examples are illustrated in six different formats:

- *Preview IB Emerging Market Strategic Insight* show you how real MNCs handle issues in emerging markets to be discussed in the chapter.
- *IB Emerging Market Strategic Insight* give information on the strategic implications for international businesses in emerging markets that relate to the current discussion in the text.
- *BRIC Insights* highlight chapter material of particular relevance to the BRIC bloc; namely, Brazil, Russia, China, and India.
- *Emerging Market Ethical Challenges* are examples of situations faced by multinational managers in dealing with ethical issues in emerging markets being discussed in the chapter.
- *Emerging Market Briefs* discuss emerging market situations in less detail.

Learning Aids   The companion website (**www.routledge.com/cw/parboteeah**) also contains an extensive selection of Internet links to resources and information that are updated regularly.

Current Data   All chapters have been updated to include the latest research, examples, and statistics in multinational management, creating the most accurate and current presentation possible.

Contents

The book is divided into five major sections. Each section contains chapters that provide information on essential topics of international business as they apply to emerging markets. The intent is to give you an overview of the complex and exciting world of international business and the challenges facing multinationals as they operate globally with a special emphasis on emerging markets.

The first section provides an introduction to the field of international business, including background on globalization and how MNCs compete strategically. It is important that you first understand the strategic choices open to MNCs. With that understanding, you will have a better appreciation of the information provided in later chapters that gives essential material for understanding international business in emerging markets.

Part Two of your text is intended to provide you with an understanding of the global context in which MNCs compete. Chapter 1, in Part One, touched on the issue of how growing international trade and investment combined with global economic integration is changing the competitive landscape for MNCs. These are illustrated within the context of emerging markets. Two additional chapters will show you how money moves across borders to make international transactions possible. One chapter overviews the basics of foreign exchange. There you learn what affects the varying values of currencies from different countries and how international managers manage cross-border money transactions. A second chapter discusses how MNCs, in today's global financial systems, get capital from bond and stock markets outside of their own countries.

Part Three looks inside the countries (with a special focus on emerging markets) where MNCs do business. Here you will learn how MNCs adjust their strategies and operations to the local context. One chapter looks at how culture influences the conduct of international business. The other chapter focuses on social institutions such as the legal and political systems. It also considers the effects of religion on an MNC's operations and strategies when doing business in countries or areas of the world with particular religious institutions.

Part Four of your text brings you inside the MNC to look at the functional and operational strategies that support the broader multinational strategies that you learned about in Chapter 2. This is the largest part of the book because there are many issues that an MNC must consider in conducting its international businesses in emerging markets. One chapter shows how MNCs actually set up operations in different countries through techniques such as joint ventures or licensing. The second chapter in this part looks at how companies adjust their marketing and supply-chain management strategies to support operations in varied countries. The third and fourth chapters show how MNCs develop specialized accounting systems and manage their financial systems to conduct cross-border activities successfully.

Because running an MNC is an organizational challenge, Part Four contains a chapter devoted to organizational structures for international operations. Similarly, because of the complexities of dealing with managers and workers located anywhere in the world, a full chapter is also dedicated to international human resource management. Part Four concludes with a chapter on e-commerce for the MNC. This chapter focuses on the unique challenges of running an international operation via the Internet.

Part Five, the final part of your text, contains only one chapter, "Managing Ethical and Social Responsibility in an MNC." However, the challenges of managing ethical issues in varied cultural and institutional contexts cannot be overestimated. This becomes especially challenging in emerging markets where local environmental conditions bring on additional difficulties. While you will not learn how to be ethical by reading this chapter, you will be introduced to the basics of ethical reasoning and some of the issues you need to consider when faced with ethically challenging decisions in all markets.

Support Materials

International Business offers a website for both students and instructors at **www.routledge.com/cw/parboteeah**. This site contains supplements to the text that give students and instructors many options for learning and teaching the text content.

For Instructors
Web support is available with the following features:

Instructor's Manual Chapter-by-chapter outlines with teaching tips, web and in-class excercises, and video resources.

Test Bank A full test bank for each chapter, with multiple choice and true/false questions, available as Word documents or in a format compatible with uploading to Blackboard or WebCT.

PowerPoint® Slide Presentations   Instructors can access more than 40 slides per chapter illustrating the main points of each text.

Weblinks   Useful links are provided as instructional resources, including all the links in the Instructor's Manual.

For Students

Web support is available with the following features:

Practice Quizzes   Self-tests for each chapter provide students with instant feedback on their answers.

Flashcards   Interactive flashcards allow students to test their knowledge of the book's key concepts.

Weblinks   All the book's informational links are provided to give students easy access to online resources.

Acknowledgments

Numerous individuals helped make this book possible. Most of all, we must thank our families for giving us the time and quiet to accomplish this task:

- Jean Johnson, Professor of Marketing at Washington State University, John's wife, read and commented on all chapters. Her suggestions improved both the content and the writing, and resulted in a better product. She also authored Chapter 10 on international marketing.
- Kyong Pyun, Praveen's wife, is always supportive during such projects. She allowed uninterrupted blocks of time to finish the project. She also worked on the instructor's manual, completing the teaching outline, presentations, and other support material. Alisha, Praveen's daughter, now in high school was unaffected by the project! Davin, Praveen's 10-year-old son retains the 'best son in the world' title.

This text would not be possible without the support of a professional editorial team. In particular, our thanks go to Routledge editor Sharon Golan, who encouraged us to write a second edition of the text on international business and supported the emerging markets perspectives. She was also very patient with the delays in the project. Editorial Assistant Erin Arata worked us on track for a very tight writing schedule. Our thanks also go to several other professionals who contributed to this project, including Charles A. Rarick, who contributed to the cases in the book.

We also appreciate the efforts of individuals involved in marketing and production.

The authors would like to thank the many reviewers from a wide array of colleges and universities who provided valuable feedback in crafting the manuscript.

K. Praveen Parboteeah
John B. Cullen

About the Authors

K. Praveen Parboteeah is the COBE Distinguished Professor and Director of the Doctorate of Business Administration in the College of Business and Economics at the University of Wisconsin–Whitewater. He received his PhD from Washington State University, and holds an MBA from California State University–Chico and a BSc (Honors) in Management Studies from the University of Mauritius.

Parboteeah regularly teaches international management, business ethics, and strategic management at both undergraduate and graduate levels. He also teaches doctoral level classes such as scientific inquiry in business administration and other doctoral seminars. He has received numerous teaching awards and is included in multiple editions of *Who's Who Among America's Teachers* and is a University of Wisconsin–Whitewater Master Teacher and Teaching Scholar.

Parboteeah's research interests include international management, ethics, and technology and innovation management. He has published over 45 articles in leading journals such as the *Academy of Management Journal, Organization Science, Decision Sciences, Journal of Business Ethics, Journal of International Business Studies, Journal of World Business*, and *Management International Review*. He has received numerous awards for his research, including the Western Academy of Management Ascendant Scholar award. He is also one of two faculty members at the University of Wisconsin–Whitewater who has won the university's Research Award twice. He is also on the editorial boards of the major journals including *Journal of International Business Studies, Journal of World Business, Management International Review*, and *Journal of Business Ethics*.

Parboteeah has been involved in many aspects of international business education at the University of Wisconsin–Whitewater. He is the exchange faculty coordinator for the exchange programs in France, namely ESC Rouen and the Burgundy School of Business in Dijon. He was part of the team that received grants from the US Department of Agriculture to further agricultural exchanges between the US markets and emerging markets such as China and India. For these efforts, the emerging markets program was awarded the Small Business/Export Assistance Governor's Award. He has also been a visiting professor at universities such as WHU–Otto Beisheim School of Business, Indian Institute of Management in Indore, and Ludwig Maximilian University among many others.

Of Indian ancestry, Parboteeah grew up on the African island of Mauritius and speaks Creole, French, and English. He currently lives in Whitewater with his South Korean wife Kyong, daughter Alisha and son Davin.

John B. Cullen is in phased retirement as Professor of Management at the Carson College of Business at Washington State University, where he teaches courses on international management, business ethics, organizational theory, and strategic management. Previously, he held the Huber Chair of Entrepreneurial Studies and was Director of the PhD Program. He received his PhD from Columbia University.

In addition to numerous presentations at Asian and European universities, Professor Cullen has been a visiting professor at l'Université Catholique de Lille in France and, as a Fulbright Scholar, at Waseda and Keio Universities in Japan. More recently, Professor Cullen was Professor of Strategy at the Amsterdam Business School, University of Amsterdam.

Professor Cullen is a senior editor at the *Journal of World Business* and the author or co-author of five books, including *International Management: Strategy and the Multinational Company*, and over 80 journal publications. His research has appeared in journals such as *Administrative Science Quarterly*, *Journal of International Business Studies*, *Academy of Management Journal*, *Organization Science*, *Decision Sciences*, *American Journal of Sociology*, *Journal of Management*, *Organizational Studies*, *Management International Review*, *Journal of Vocational Behavior*, *Journal of Business Ethics*, *Organizational Dynamics*, and the *Journal of World Business*.

Professor Cullen's major research interests include the effects of social institutions and national culture on ethical outcomes and work values; the management of entrepreneurial firms in changing environments, trust, and commitment in international strategic alliances; ethical climates in multinational organizations; and the dynamics of organizational structure.

Professor Cullen has consulted with both private and public organizations in the US and elsewhere in the areas of international management, organizational design, and ethics management.

Chapters in Part One

CHAPTER 1

Competing in the Global Marketplace

After reading this chapter you should be able to:

- Define international business.

- Understand the critical importance of emerging markets in today's international business environment.

- Understand the nature of an MNC.

- Understand the key forces that drive globalization and the current global economy.

- Know the basic types of economies that make up the world's competitive landscape.

- Appreciate the role that low-cost countries and rapidly emerging economies play in today's world.

- Appreciate the importance of sustainability in the new global environment.

International Business   *Preview IB Emerging Market Strategic Insight*

Emerging Markets: The Wave of the Future

The popular business press abounds with stories of emerging markets and emerging market multinationals. Emerging markets is an umbrella term referring to countries that have traditionally been seen as less developed but have markets that have grown rapidly recently. Prominent examples of emerging markets include the BRIC countries or Brazil, Russia, India, and China. Despite an economic slowdown recently, emerging markets continue to present tremendous potential.

Within these emerging markets, new multinationals have emerged and they are taking the business world by storm. Such emerging market multinationals are rewriting the rules of the game. Consider the emerging market multinationals such as Bimbo from Mexico, Tata from India, and Orascom from Egypt and how they are all rewriting the rules of business. These emerging market multinationals shy away from long-term planning typical of multinationals based in more developed economies. Rather, they strive on chaos and have an insatiable hunger for global expansion. Such multinationals have undeniable advantages based on their knowledge of extremely volatile local environments and their ability to deal with chaos.

Many factors have impacted the development of such emerging market multinationals. Emerging markets have typically faced markets for labor, capital, goods, and services that are imperfect or incomplete. Additionally, emerging markets have also included governments that have been ready to have heavy intervention. Some emerging markets also have unstable currencies.

Despite such challenges, emerging market multinationals have experienced success and have achieved tremendous learning in the process. They have been able to imitate developed world multinationals in some areas such as strategy and organizational structure. However, they have also developed their own innovative capabilities based on the unique characteristics of the markets they operate in. Such local challenges and chaotic environments have enabled emerging market multinationals to develop uniquely innovative products that can potentially help in developed markets. Consider, for instance, the case of the Tata Nano, the Indian giant's effort to develop a very low-cost car. Such advances are helping Tata develop products for low-income countries that will soon have more individuals in the middle class. These individuals will be interested in cheap transportation options in the future.

Source: Based on D. Currell and T. D. Bradley, 2013, "Greased palms, giant headaches," *Harvard Business Review*, September, pp. 21–23; M. F. Guillén and E. García-Canal, 2011, "The rise of emerging market multinationals," *IESE Insight*, Third Quarter, issue 10, pp. 13–19; C. Nettesheim, L. Faeste, D. Khanna, B. Waltermann and P. Ullrich, 2016, "Transformation in emerging markets," Boston Consulting Group, February, http://bcg.perspectives; M. Sako, 2015, "Competing in emerging markets," *Communications of the ACM*, 58(4), 27–29.

As the Preview IB Emerging Market Strategic Insight shows, emerging markets and emerging market multinationals will continue playing a critical role in the international business arena. Often, in today's competitive world, the only opportunity to grow a business and its profitability is when a company leaves its home country. Established multinationals have traditionally looked to developed market economies for such opportunities. However, as the above examples show, emerging markets present significant opportunities. Nevertheless, with these opportunities come the challenges of running a multinational operation in an emerging market. To help you understand and meet the challenges of international business, the objective of this text is to show you how companies such as Shoprite succeed in the global marketplace and how they cope with the many complexities of running an international operation.

Whether a business is large or small or located in whatever continent, the pressures to think global continue to grow. Consider just a few examples: if you look at the clothes you wear, the cars you drive, or the computers that sit on your desk, or keep track of your money in the bank, all have some components produced or sold by companies engaged in international business. Why? The major reason is the unrelenting pressures of globalization.

Globalization is the worldwide trend of the economies of the world becoming borderless and interlinked—companies are no longer limited by their domestic boundaries and may conduct any business activity anywhere in the world. Globalization means that companies are more

globalization
the worldwide trend of economic integration across borders allowing businesses to expand beyond their domestic boundaries

likely to compete anywhere. Many companies now sell anywhere, source their raw materials or conduct research and development (R&D) anywhere, and produce anywhere.

Trade barriers are falling, and world trade among countries in goods and services is growing faster than domestic production. Money is flowing more freely across national borders as companies seek the best rates for financing anywhere in the world, and investors look for the best returns anywhere in the world. The Internet crosses national boundaries with the click of a mouse, allowing even the smallest of businesses to go global immediately. Consequently, companies can no longer afford the luxury of assuming that success in their home market equates to long-term profitability—or even survival.

Globalization is perhaps the major reason why you should study international business. In today's Internet-connected world, you may have little choice. With companies increasingly looking at global rather than domestic markets, managers must become international in outlook and strategies. Your suppliers, your research and development, your manufacturing facilities, your strategic alliance partners, and your customers increasingly come from beyond your national borders. Foreign competition and doing business in foreign markets are daily facts of life for today's managers. Successful managers must become international in outlook. These are executives with the ability and motivation to meet and beat the challenges of international business. The study of international business helps prepare you to deal with this evolving global economy and to develop the skills necessary to succeed in business in a globalizing world.

To provide you with a basic background in international business, this book introduces you to the latest information on how managers respond to the challenges of globalization and conduct competitive international operations. Throughout the text, you will also learn about the importance of emerging markets and the critical influence they are having on global business. You will see how businesses both large and small deal with the complexities of national differences in cultural, economic, legal, ethical, religious, and political systems. You will learn how multinational managers use their understanding of these national differences to formulate strategies that maximize their companies' success in globalizing industries. You will also learn how multinational managers implement international strategies with supporting marketing, financial, organizational, and human resource management systems.

To help you better understand the real world of international business, you will find several types of real business examples in this and the following chapters. **Preview IB Emerging Market Strategic Insight** show you how real **multinational companies** handle issues in emerging markets to be discussed in the chapter. **IB Emerging Market Strategic Insight** give information on the strategic implications for international businesses in emerging markets that relate to the current discussion in the text. **BRIC Insights** highlight chapter material of particular relevance to the BRIC bloc, namely Brazil, Russia, China, and India. **Emerging Market Ethical Challenges** are examples of situations faced by multinational managers in dealing with ethical issues in emerging markets as pertaining to the areas being discussed in the chapter. Finally, **Emerging Market Briefs** discuss emerging market situations in less detail.

multinational company (MNC)
any company that engages in business functions beyond its domestic borders

The Nature of International Business

A company engages in **international business** when it conducts any business functions beyond its domestic borders. What kinds of business activities might make a company international? The most apparent activity, of course, is international sales. When a company produces in its own country and sells in another, it engages in the simplest level of international activity. However, as you will see in much more detail later in the book, crossing national borders opens up more international options than simply selling internationally.

international business
when a company conducts any business functions beyond its domestic borders

In this text, we refer to any company engaging in international business as a multinational company or MNC. This is a broad definition, which includes all types of companies, large and small, that engage in international business. Most multinational companies, however, are also multinational corporations—the companies are publicly owned through stocks. Most often, when you see references to MNCs in the popular business press, the reference is to multinational corporations.

As mentioned in the Preview IB Emerging Market Strategic Insight, the importance of emerging markets has also seen the rise of **emerging market multinationals**. Emerging market multinationals are influential multinationals from emerging markets that are changing the traditional rules of competition and establishing new business models. These multinationals are competing head-to-head with established developed world multinationals. Other prominent examples include Mexico's cement manufacturer CEMEX and bakery company Bimbo, Brazil's aircraft manufacturer Embraer, and India's software companies Wipro and Infosys. These multinationals have had dramatic impact on how business is being done worldwide. To give you further insights on an African emerging market multinational, consider the following IB Emerging Market Strategic Insight.

emerging market multinationals are influential multinationals from emerging markets that are changing the traditional rules of competition and establishing new business models

South Africa's Shoprite: The Next Walmart?

IB EMERGING MARKET STRATEGIC INSIGHT

Already operating with over 1855 corporate and 359 franchise outlets in 15 countries such as Mauritius and Madagascar, Shoprite (www.shoprite.co.za), the South African Walmart wannabe, now has revenues of $9.9 billion a year. Only given the opportunity to go international in 1994 after the fall of apartheid, Shoprite now gets over half its revenue outside of South Africa. Shoprite is now the largest retailer in Africa.

Because Shoprite operates mostly in poorer developing nations, its target customers are low- to middle-income customers. Most traditional multinational retailers have ignored this niche. However, by focusing on value, the company has been able to build a strong customer base from this income group. Because this group continues to grow, Shoprite is poised to continue outcompeting rival multinationals as it continues its expansion in the future.

In spite of its success, Shoprite also faces many challenges in running its multinational operations. It is very dependent on the African continent and that has been problematic. African currencies are highly volatile making the costs of supplies and value of sales very unpredictable. Additionally, economic growth in Africa has fallen from 7 percent in 2007 to around 4 percent in 2014. This suggests that Shoprite will need to look into other markets to succeed in the future.

Also, with over 138,000 employees speaking many different languages and complex differences in local laws regarding health, employment, taxes, etc., organizational challenges are constant. Like many multinationals, Shoprite uses technology to help manage these complex operations. A satellite system tracks shipping and sales, and suppliers and local stores are linked with an ecommerce system.

Source: Based on A. Brown, 2016, "Africa's Sam Walton," *Forbes*, March 21, pp. 66–75; *The Economist*, 2005, "Africa's Walmart heads east," www.economist.com, January 13; www.shoprite.co.za/

As you can see above, emerging market multinationals have had significant influence on how business is conducted worldwide. They will likely keep growing in stature in the future. Furthermore, many of the top largest multinationals today come from emerging markets. Exhibit 1.1 lists the top MNCs in the world.

Company	Revenues (US$ million)	Country
1. Walmart	482,130	USA
2. State Grid	329,601	China
3. China National Petroleum	299,271	China
4. Sinopec Group	294,344	China
5. Royal Dutch Shell	272,156	Holland
6. Exxon Mobil	246,204	USA
7. Volkswagen	236,600	Germany
8. Toyota Motor	236,592	Japan
9. Apple	233,715	USA
10. BP	225,982	UK
11. Berkshire Hathaway	210,821	USA
12. McKesson	192,487	USA
13. Samsung Electronics	177,440	South Korea
14. Glencore	170,497	Anglo-Swiss
15. Industrial & Commercial Bank of China	167,227	China

Exhibit 1.1 Top 15 Companies in the World Based on Revenues, 2015
Source: Adapted from Fortune Global 500, http://beta.fortune.com/global500/

As you can see from the above, emerging market multinationals feature prominently on the list of top multinationals worldwide. Additionally, examination of the top 500 companies shows that there are many such multinationals in that list. This confirms the importance and clout of these emerging market multinationals.

To introduce some of the international options, consider the following hypothetical company that produces PCs. As a domestic-only company it can manufacture the chips and other electronic components, build the cases, assemble the components, and sell the computers, all in its home country. However, the firm might not be able to compete successfully using this approach. The local market may be stagnant, with competitive pricing and lower profit margins. Even in a growing market, competitors like Dell Computer might source high-quality, low-cost components from anywhere in the world. Competitors might also find lower production costs in low-cost countries, allowing them to offer lower prices. What can this company do?

As an MNC, the firm might sell PCs to overseas buyers in countries with less competition and higher prices. Several other international activities might increase its competitive strength. For example, this company might locate any of the steps in obtaining components or completing production in other countries. It might buy the highest-quality chips from Taiwan, use the lowest-cost assemblers in Vietnam, and sell primarily in Europe and the US. For any of these steps, the company might outsource the activity to local companies in another country or own its own factories within another country. As you will see in later chapters, MNCs must develop strategies and systems to accomplish all or some of these international business tasks.

Next, we will consider the forces that drive the new economic reality facing the next generation of international managers and MNCs.

Globalization: A Dynamic Context for International Business

Globalization is not a simple uniform evolutionary process. Not all economies of the world benefit equally or participate equally. In the recent past, financial crises, terrorism, wars, increased border security, and a worldwide economic stagnation have limited, or in some cases even reversed, some of the aspects of globalization. You will see below, in the context of the discussion of the major drivers of globalization, some of the effects produced by political, economic, and sociocultural upheavals. Consider Exhibit 1.2, which shows the history of globalization's major events.

The financial crisis of 2008 demonstrated just how interconnected the global economy has become in the last few decades. When failures and bad debt in the home mortgage industry forced some US banks and other financial institutions out of business, the US stock market declined quickly and precipitously. Almost immediately, financial institutions around the world followed the US market. Before discussing the key globalization trends that affect international business, it is useful to look at some commonly used classifications of the world's countries. The classifications roughly indicate a country's gross domestic product (GDP) and the growth in GDP. The classifications are not exact but they simplify discussions of world trade and investments.

Time	Economic	Political	Technological
1940s	• Establishment of the Bretton Woods System, a new international monetary system (1944–1971) • Establishment of GATT (1947) entering into force in January 1948 • Soviet Union establishes the Council for Mutual Economic Assistance (CMEA) for economic cooperation among communist countries (1949–1991)	• Foundation of the United Nations (1945) • Launch of the Marshall Plan (1948–1957), a European recovery program • Founding of the Organization for European Economic Cooperation (1948) • Decolonization starts (1948–1962). Independence of India, Indonesia, Egypt, for example • China becomes a socialist republic in 1949	• Expansion of plastics and fiber products e.g. first nylon stockings for women (1940) • Discovery of large oilfields in the Middle East, especially in Saudi Arabia (1948)
1950s	• Treaty of Rome establishes the European Community (1957). EC and the European Free Trade Association (1959) favor West European integration • Major currencies become convertible (1958–1964) • Development of the Eurodollar Market in London, which contributed to the expansion of international liquidity	• Korean war (1950–1953) • Suez crisis (1956) • Decolonization in Africa (15 countries become independent between 1958 and 1962)	• Increased use of oil from the Middle East in Europe and Japan • "Just-in-time" production implemented by Toyota • Increasing usage of jet engines in air transport (1957–1972) • Offshore oil and gas production developed
1960s	• Foundation of the Organization of the Petroleum Exporting Countries (OPEC) (1960) • Kennedy Round, 6th session of the GATT (1964–1967)	• Erection of Berlin Wall (1961) and Cuban missile crisis (1962) highlight sharp confrontation between East and West	• Green Revolution— transforming agricultural production in developing countries (1960s onwards) • Integrated circuits become commercially available (1961)

Exhibit 1.2 Globalization Chronology

Time	Economic	Political	Technological
1960s cont'd	• Rapid spread of automobiles and highways in the North accelerates demand and shift in fuels consumption (from coal to oil) • Trade politics of East Asian countries put more emphasis on export-led development than on import substitution • Elimination of last customs duties within EC (1968)		• First person in space (Yuri Gagarin, 1961) and the first man on the moon (Neil Armstrong, 1969) • First line of Japan's high-speed train system (*shinkansen*) opened in 1964 • Mont Blanc Road Tunnel (1965) • Increasing usage of containerization in ocean transport (1968 onwards)
1970s	• Departure from US dollar exchange rate gold standard (1971) • Tokyo Round of the GATT (1973–1979) • Oil price "shocks" (1973–1974 and 1979) reverse decades of real oil price declines • Rise of Asian newly industrialized countries • China's economic reform (1978)	• Yom Kippur war (1973) helps to trigger oil price hike • EU enlargement to nine members (1973)	• First single chip microprocessor (Intel 4004) is introduced (1971)
1980s	• Volcker Fed successfully extinguishes US inflation • Developing country debt crisis • Mexico starts market reforms and joins the GATT in 1986 • Louvre Accord promotes stabilization of major exchange rates (1987)	• Enlargement of the EU to 12 members • Fall of the Berlin Wall (1989)	• IBM introduces first personal computer (1981) • Microsoft Windows introduced (1985) • Invention of the World Wide Web by Tim Berners-Lee (1989)
1990s	• Indian economic reforms launched in 1991 • Establishment of the North American Free Trade Agreement (1994) • Establishment of the WTO (1995) • Asian financial crisis (1997) • Adoption of the euro by 11 European countries (1999)	• Dissolution of the Soviet Union (1991) leads to the formation of 13 independent states • Maastricht Treaty (formally, the Treaty on European Union) signed (1992)	• First website put online in 1991 • Launch of the first 2G-GSM network by Radiolinja in Finland (1991) • Eurotunnel opens in 1994 linking the United Kingdom to the continent • The number of mobile phones increases due to the introduction of second-generation (2G) networks using digital technology
2000s	• Dotcom crisis (2001) • China joins WTO (2001) • End of the Multi-fiber Agreement in 2005 (quantitative restrictions of textiles lifted) • Increased importance of emerging markets to global economy • Global value chains become critical	• European Union has 28 members (as of 2016) • Millions out of poverty in emerging nations • Number of multinationals increase to 111,000 from only 24,000 in 1990s	• Number of Internet users in 2016 rises to 3.5 billion from 800 million in 2005 • Container ships transport more than 70 percent of the seaborne trade in value terms • All types of transport and communication technologies continue serious improvement

Exhibit 1.2 Globalization Chronology

Source: UNCTAD, 2007, *World Investment Report*, New York and Geneva: United Nations, pp. 22–23; World Trade Report, 2015, www.wto.org/english/res_e/booksp_e/world_trade_report15_e.pdf

Types of Economies in the Global Marketplace: The Arrived, the Coming, and the Struggling

developed economies
mature economies with
substantial per capita
GDPs and international
trade and investments

developing economies
economies that have
grown extensively over
the past two decades

transition economies
countries in the process
of changing from
government-controlled
economic systems to
capitalistic systems

**least developed
countries (LDCs)**
the poorest nations,
often plagued with
unstable political
regimes, high
unemployment, and low
worker skills

Understanding how economies have traditionally been classified can provide important insights on these economies. **Developed economies** have mature economies with substantial per capita GDPs and international trade and investments. Prominent examples include the USA, Canada, and Australia and most European nations such as Germany, Belgium, and the UK. The **developing economies**, such as Hong Kong, Singapore, South Korea, and Taiwan, have economies that have grown extensively over the past two decades yet have sometimes struggled recently, especially during the setbacks of the Asian crisis in the late 1990s. Other developing economies to watch are what the UN calls the **transition economies** of the Czech Republic, Hungary, Poland, and Russia, and the developing economies of Indonesia, Malaysia, the Philippines, Vietnam, and Thailand.

Transition economies are countries that have changed from government-controlled, mostly communist economic systems to market or capitalistic systems. The former systems relied on state-owned organizations and centralized government control to run the economy. In the transition to free market and capitalistic systems, many government-owned companies were converted to private ownership. The market and not the government then determined the success of companies. Several of these transition economies, such as Hungary, Poland, Slovakia, and the Czech Republic, developed market economies that allowed them to join the European Union. Furthermore, many multinationals are deciding to locate in transition economies for various reasons. Another important aspect of the international business environment is **least developed countries (LDCs)**, which have yet to show much progress in the evolving global economy. They are the poorest nations and are often plagued with unstable political regimes, high unemployment, and unskilled workers. Most of these countries are located in Central and South America, Africa, and the Middle East.

| Developed Countries | Developing Countries | | | |
	Asia	Transition Economies	Low-cost Countries (LCCs)	Least Developed Countries (LDCs)
Australia	China	Czech Republic	Brazil	Afghanistan
Austria	Hong Kong	Hungary	China	Cambodia
Belgium	India	Poland	India	Chad
Britain	Indonesia	Russia	Mexico	Congo
Canada	Malaysia		Russia	Ethiopia
Denmark	Singapore			Niger
France	South Korea			Sudan
Germany	Taiwan			Yemen
Ireland	Thailand			
Italy				
Japan				
Netherlands				
Spain				
Sweden				
Switzerland				
United States				

Exhibit 1.3 Types of Economies in the Globe (example countries)
Source: Adapted from UNCTD, 2016, www.un.org

Over the past decade, many of the developing countries have enjoyed tremendous growth and large numbers of people have been lifted out of poverty in these countries. This has led experts to term such countries as **emerging countries** or **emerging markets**. Many of what were considered developing markets or transition economies have now become emerging markets.

While these emerging markets have enjoyed tremendous growth over the last decade, more recent evidence suggests that growth in many of these countries has slowed down.[1] For example, members of the BRICS group (Brazil, Russia, India, China, and South Africa) have also seen growth drop from solid percentages (7–10 percent) to much slower growth such as 6.5 percent in China and flat growth in Brazil. However, despite this slowdown, experts agree that emerging markets will stay extremely critical to global business. Consider the following IB Emerging Market Strategic Insight.

Potential of Emerging Markets

IB EMERGING MARKET STRATEGIC INSIGHT

Although growth in most emerging markets has either slowed down or even contracted, most experts agree that emerging markets will continue to remain critical for multinationals worldwide. Reasons for such importance include:

- Although economic growth has slowed down, experts predict that emerging markets will grow around 2.2 percent points faster than developed economies in 2016. Most industries in such countries will continue growing.
- Despite the slowdown, economic growth in emerging markets accounted for 68 percent of global growth. This growth will continue to remain strong in the future.
- In terms of infrastructure, demand for investment will be around $25 trillion through 2025. This will also mean that multinationals in such areas will have significant potential.
- Incomes will continue rising substantially in emerging markets. For example, 37 percent of the 60 million households will enter the middle class in Brazil by 2020 compared to only 20 percent now. Middle-class consumers in India and China will represent $1.2 trillion in buying power. Additionally, around 300 million households will enter the consuming class.
- Population of emerging markets is growing four times faster than populations in developed economies. This also signals tremendous opportunities.
- By 2020, 6.4 billion people (out of 7.5 billion people worldwide) or 85 percent of the world's population will be living in emerging markets.

Source: Adapted from C. Nettesheim, L. Faeste., D. Khanna., B. Waltermann and P. Ullrich, 2016, "Transformation in emerging markets," Boston Consulting Group, February, http://bcg.perspectives; B. Waltermann, D. C. Michael and D. Khanna, 2014, "Time to reengage with, not retreat from, emerging markets," Boston Consulting Group, May 19, www.bcgperspectives.com/content/articles/globalization_growth_time_reengage_retreat_emerging_markets/

As you can see from the above IB Emerging Market Strategic Insight, emerging markets will remain critical in the future. Such markets will also present challenges. But given this importance, this book will discuss international business issues in the light of such markets. You will read more later about the importance of such markets.

With this overview of the major economies of the world, we can now look more closely at the driving forces of the new world economy.

Globalization Drivers

Several key trends drive the globalization of the world economy and, in turn, force businesses to consider international operations to survive and prosper. Some of the most important trends include falling borders, growing cross-border trade and investment, the rise of global products and global customers, the growing use of the Internet and sophisticated information technology (IT), the role of emerging markets in the world market, and the rise of global standards of quality and production. Exhibit 1.4 illustrates these important forces. Each of these driving forces is discussed below.

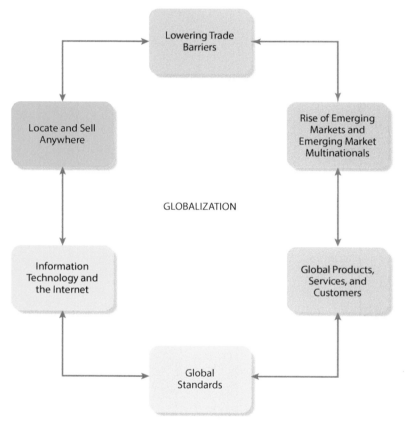

Exhibit 1.4 The Drivers of Globalization

Lowering the Barriers of National Borders: Making Trade and Cross-border Investment Easier

In the mid-1900s, worldwide tariffs averaged 45 percent. By the early 2000s, tariffs on industrial products fell to 3.8 percent.[2] Tariffs are taxes most often charged to goods imported into a country. They have the effect of raising the price of an imported good. As you will see in more detail in Chapters 4 and 9, tariffs tend to make foreign goods more expensive and less competitive with local goods. Trade is reduced because companies cannot compete with domestic producers. After several rounds of tariff negotiations, known as the **General Agreement on Tariffs and Trade (GATT)**, worldwide tariffs on manufactured goods declined from 45 percent to less than 7 percent.

General Agreement on Tariffs and Trade (GATT) tariff negotiations between several nations that reduced the average worldwide tariff on manufactured goods

Later negotiations in Uruguay ended with agreements to reduce tariffs even further from 7 percent, liberalize trade in agriculture and services, and eliminate some nontariff barriers to international trade, such as excessive use of health regulations to keep out imports.[3] The Uruguay talks ended in 1993 and established the **World Trade Organization (WTO)**. The WTO now provides a formal organization that promotes continued negotiations and settles trade disputes among nations. In 2016 there were 164 members in the WTO, up from the original 92 in 1994. Over 90 percent of world trade takes place among countries that are WTO members. In 2016 at least 22 more countries including Algeria, Bhutan, and Sudan are seeking WTO membership.

The WTO is not the only organization that seeks to eliminate trade barriers. Other organizations based on **regional trade agreements**, such as the **European Union (EU)** and **North American Free Trade Agreement (NAFTA)**, also attempt to reduce tariffs and develop similar technical and economic standards. These regional organizations lead to more trade among the member nations, and some scholars argue that regional agreements are the first step toward complete globalization. Others, however, argue that regional agreements benefit only the trade-group members and often harm poorer nations that are left out of the agreements (such as the Caribbean countries that are not members of NAFTA).[4] From a practical point of view, although they do benefit member countries the most, regional agreements contribute to world trade more than they restrict such trade. Also, the regional agreements, with fewer countries, are more politically achievable than worldwide trade agreements that include many countries.[5] In Chapter 3 you will find out much more about these agreements.

It is important to note that emerging markets have also started working on regional agreements to encourage trade. For instance, the Association of Southeast Asian Nations (ASEAN) was created in 1967 by Indonesia, Malaysia, Philippines, Thailand, and Singapore to promote trade and economic cooperation among these countries. It now has 10 members and the group has been successful in encouraging trade among themselves.[6] Additionally, the ASEAN members recently started negotiations with six other partner countries such as Australia, China, and Japan to propose a new trade agreement known as the Regional Comprehensive Economic Partnership (RCEP) to promote trade.[7] Such new trade agreements are created with the intention to facilitate trade worldwide.

Is free trade a success? The WTO argues that the answer is yes, and the data seem to support their position. Following the early GATT agreements, world trade exceeded the output of the world's gross domestic product by over fourfold. However, the policies of the WTO do have critics. Some argue that the WTO favors the developed nations, because the developed nations have the resources to outcompete poorer nations in a non-regulated world. Environmentalists also criticize free trade because it allows MNCs to skirt regulations in many of the developed countries by moving environmentally damaging production to poorer countries that often have weaker protection laws. Ethicists argue that such actions give commercial interests priority over the environment, health, and safety. Organized labor sees free trade as a source of job loss and pressure to reduce wages for remaining jobs as MNCs move or threaten to move production from higher-wage countries to low-cost countries. You can see the WTO's response to these criticisms on their website at www.wto.org.

Locate and Sell Anywhere to Anybody: It's No Longer Only for Manufacturing but Services as Well

The September 11, 2001, attack on the United States and the resulting worldwide economic stagnation led to a major setback for world trade. For example, double-digit growth in worldwide exporting of merchandise in 2000 was followed by a more than 4 percent decline in the following two years. However, most of the world's trade rebounded in 2003 and 2004 and

World Trade Organization (WTO)
a formal structure for continued negotiations to reduce trade barriers and to act as a mechanism for settling trade disputes

regional trade agreements
agreements among nations in a particular region to reduce tariffs and develop similar technical and economic standards

European Union (EU)
Austria, Belgium, Britain, Bulgaria, Croatia, Cyprus, Czech Republic, Denmark, Estonia, Finland, France, Germany, Greece, Hungary, Ireland, Italy, Latvia, Lithuania, Luxembourg, Malta, the Netherlands, Poland, Portugal, Romania, Slovakia, Slovenia, Spain, and Sweden, plus Norway and Switzerland in the related European Free Trade Area

North American Free Trade Agreement (NAFTA)
a multilateral treaty that links the United States, Canada, and Mexico in an economic bloc that allows freer exchange of goods and services

trade growth neared double digits again by 2007. Some countries, particularly China, have benefited substantially during the post 9/11 period. 2007 was some of the highest global trade in the past decade. However, the 2008–2009 economic crisis brought a decline in trade. Things started improving again in 2009 and 2015 saw some of the highest trade levels since 2009.[8]

Exhibit 1.5 shows the current leading countries in terms of import and export total volume. This suggests that the world's economies are increasingly more intertwined and mutually stimulated.

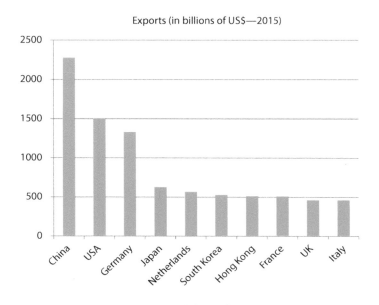

Exports (in billions of US$—2015)

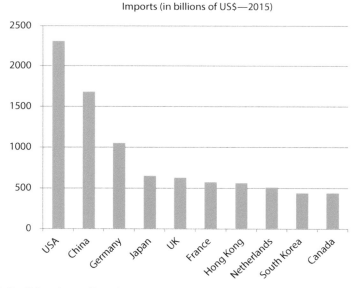

Imports (in billions of US$—2015)

Exhibit 1.5 World's Top 10 Exporters and Importers
Source: Based on www.statista.com/statistics/264623/leading-export-countries-worldwide/ and www.statista.com/statistics/268184/leading-import-countries-worldwide/

What does Exhibit 1.5 show? The Exhibit again confirms the importance of emerging markets to the world. As you can see, emerging markets such as China, Hong Kong, and South Korea feature prominently on the list of both the top 10 importers and exporters. This suggests that trade with these markets will continue growing.

Not only do MNCs trade across borders with exports and imports, but they also build global networks that connect different worldwide locations for R&D, supply, support services like call centers, production, and sales. Setting up and owning your own operations in another country is known as **foreign direct investment (FDI)**. That is, FDI occurs when an MNC from one country owns an organizational unit located in another country. Multinationals often build their own units in foreign countries but they also use cross-border mergers and acquisitions, such as the acquisition of the European company Arcelor for $32 billion by the Indian company Mittal Steel in 2006. This was also the largest acquisition ever by a company from a developing nation.[9]

Which countries give and get these cross-border investments in the global economy? The competitive landscape is changing, with the developing nations taking a more active role.

FDI soared to record levels, increasing by over 36 percent between 1996 and 2000 and ultimately topping $1.5 trillion in 2000.[10] However, following a pattern similar to international trade, FDI declined to $735 billion in 2001, less than half of the previous year, and declined another 25 percent in the following two years. Since that time, however, and again like world trade, FDI has regained its steam, growing nearly 40 percent a year until 2007.[11] FDI again fell in line with the economic recession of 2008–2009 but started growing again. The most recent data suggest that FDI has been strong at $1.76 trillion in 2015. This is the highest level since the global economic crisis of 2008–2009.[12]

In terms of inflow FDI (FDI coming to countries or regions), the emerging markets remain significant destinations. Inward FDI in 2015 to emerging/developing economies was at $765 billion, an increase of 9 percent from 2014. Furthermore, Asian emerging markets remained the most important FDI recipient of emerging markets. Exhibit 1.6 below shows the top 15 recipients of FDI inflows.

foreign direct investment (FDI) a multinational firm's ownership, in part or in whole, of an operation in another country

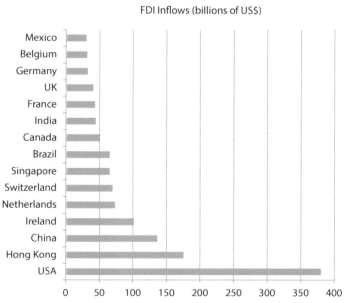

FDI Inflows (billions of US$)

Exhibit 1.6 FDI Inflows, 2015

Source: Based on UNCTAD, 2016, *World Investment Report, 2016*, http://unctad.org/en/pages/PublicationWebflyer. aspx?publicationid=1555

As Exhibit 1.6 shows, many of the world's biggest emerging markets were in the top 15 recipients of FDI inflows. Emerging markets such as Brazil, China, India, and Mexico feature on the list. However, it is important to note that developed markets such as the USA, Canada, etc. were also among the top recipients of FDI. In fact, data suggest that FDI flows to Europe and North America experienced tremendous increase recently rising 160 percent from 2014 to 2015. This large increase was mainly due to an increase in mergers and acquisitions whereby companies from developed markets acquired multinationals from other developed markets. Examples include Merck of Germany acquiring Sigma of the USA for $17 billion and Actavis of Ireland acquiring Allergan of the USA for $68 billion.[13]

What does this mean for individual companies? Perhaps the most important implication is that companies engaging in international business now more easily locate and sell anywhere that makes the most sense for their business. However, most importantly, emerging markets will continue presenting multinationals with tremendous opportunities.

The Rise of Emerging Markets and Emerging Market Multinationals

Emerging markets and emerging market multinationals have played important roles as drivers of globalization. Traditionally, emerging markets fueled trade and investments by MNCs looking for low-cost platforms to manufacture goods or secure services such as information technology and call centers. The cost savings of locating in an emerging market for a typical manufacturing organization are shown in Exhibit 1.7. This significant cost difference between emerging markets and the developed world encourages companies such as GE to set up operations in countries like China, or companies such as Walmart (previously Wal-Mart) to source their goods or services from local companies, or others such as IBM to locate in India. As you will see in later chapters, although a traditional trade theory suggests that we all benefit from moving jobs where the work can be done best or cheapest, there are those who are hurt by the shifting of jobs from the developed economies to the emerging markets.

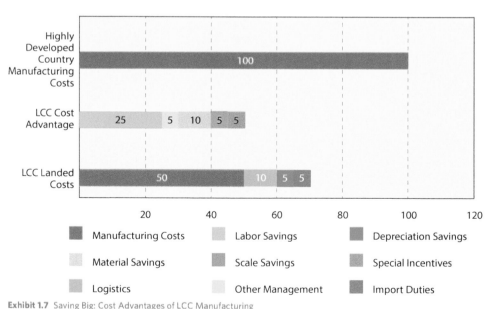

Exhibit 1.7 Saving Big: Cost Advantages of LCC Manufacturing

Source: Adapted from Boston Consulting Group, 2005, *BCG Focus, Navigating the Five Currents of Globalization*, Boston, MA: Boston Consulting Group, p. 5.

However, simply looking at many emerging markets as low-cost production sites is flawed. Most emerging markets have an expanding market for multinational sales. Although growth rates in emerging markets have slowed down recently, they are still critically important for multinationals as destinations to sell products and services. Experts mention that around 300 million additional households will enter the consuming class this decade. Coupled with the growth of people moving into the middle-income category, emerging markets will continue presenting tremendous potential.

Another aspect of emerging markets that remains enticing is the rural areas. While urban markets in more developed economies have remained sluggish, demand in rural markets have developed at an astonishingly high rate. In India, for instance, the $12 billion consumer good market is expected to grow to $100 billion by 2025.[14] Additionally, many of these rural consumers are starting to pay attention to more branded products and multinationals need to be early movers to build brand awareness.

In addition to seeing emerging markets as sources of new customers, many companies are finding that they can also use emerging markets as the innovation platform to develop new products that they can then sell in more developed markets. New products such as Tata's Nano car and GE's portable ultrasound have been developed thanks to emerging market insights. These products were developed in emerging markets because companies operating in such markets were faced with unique and difficult situations that required novel approaches to the problem. Similarly, Tata developed a water filter using straw and other cheap ingredients because of the demand from India's low-income group for an affordable product. Emerging market multinationals have thus played important roles in the race to innovation. Consider the following BRIC Insight.

Emerging Market Multinationals and Innovation

BRIC INSIGHT

As mentioned earlier in this chapter, emerging market multinationals are formidable competitors that have changed how business is done for most developed world multinationals. They have been developing innovative new business models as a result of facing the realities of their home environments. These multinationals are coming from countries in Africa, Asia, and Latin America. Their experiences provide important implications for developed world multinationals.

Consider the case of Bharti Airtel, India's cell phone provider. While most companies assess demand using average revenue per minute, Bharti Airtel emphasized the "more for less" principle. It developed its business model by outsourcing most of the activities that have high fixed costs. For instance, it worked with Vodafone and others to build towers. To increase availability of their products, they worked with companies such as Godrej and Unilever that already have around 10,000 distributors in India. Finally, to make the product accessible to rural consumers, it worked with microfinance organizations to allow consumers to pay for the equipment in installments. This has allowed Bharti Airtel to focus on growing its customer base and not worry about what are typically high fixed costs.

China's Haier, a leader in major appliances such as washing machines, fridges, etc., is another example of an emerging market multinational that has been very innovative. While most Western multinationals have approached emerging markets with standardized global products, Haier has found solutions to the unique problems facings its customers. For example, when they found that mud was clogging their washing machines, they discovered that rural farmers were using the machines to wash vegetables. They quickly modified their product to accommodate the possibility of mud clogging in the machines.

Additionally, they also found that customers needed to wash their clothes regularly in the humid larger cities and hence they also developed a small model that worked with less electricity and less water and these small new machines were instant hits. These small machines also worked well because they fitted more easily in the tiny and cramped apartments found in many of China's largest cities.

Source: Based on P. Dupoux, L. Ivers, A. Abouzied, A. Chraïti, F. Dia, H. Maher and S. Niavas, 2015, "Dueling with lions," www.bcgperspectives.com/content/articles/globalization-growth-dueling-with-lions-playing-new-game-business-success-africa/; S. A. Nonis and C. Relyea, 2012, "Business innovations from emerging markets into developed countries: Implications for multinationals from developed countries," *Thunderbird International Business Review*, 54(3), May/June, 291–298.

As the above BRIC Insight shows, emerging market multinationals will continue to be sources of new business models. Any developed world multinational ignoring such new multinationals will likely be in trouble. Why are emerging market multinationals so effective? As mentioned earlier, many of them grew in very difficult environmental conditions. Their ability to tackle such difficult challenges has allowed them to become very successful. Consider the earlier example of Haier. Haier's ability to develop unique appliances that cater to customers' needs at low prices has allowed them to apply such lessons to other markets. For instance, its low-cost fridges have opened doors in developed markets. They have been able to appeal to college students who are cost conscious. Furthermore, they have also been able to address the needs of the hotel industry that requires a refrigerator in each room.[15]

In Africa, local multinationals have benefitted from a number of recent changes that have enabled them to succeed.[16] First, most African multinationals now have easier access to both capital and technology. This has allowed them the means to invest as needed while also getting access to much needed expertise and know-how. Additionally, although African multinationals suffered from the small-scale problem, many of them have expanded significantly in recent decades to take advantage of large-scale economies. Finally, they have also benefitted from improvement in local conditions such as better economic and political environments.

The above discussion shows that emerging market multinationals will continue to excel and develop significant competitive advantages relative to developed world multinationals. But how do they differ from developed world multinationals? Exhibit 1.8 shows some of the main differences between developed world multinationals and emerging market multinationals.

As Exhibit 1.8 shows, there are clear differences between emerging market multinationals and developed world multinationals. Emerging market multinationals have succeeded because they have often operated successfully in chaotic local conditions and have used such flexibility to leverage into other new markets. Additionally, they have not shied away from engaging in alliances and joint ventures with developed world multinationals to get access to new technology and expertise. Starting as mostly distributors or suppliers, they have morphed into sophisticated organizations involved in all aspects of production and sales. Consider the following BRIC Insight.

Activity/Strategy	Emerging Market Multinationals	Developed World Multinationals
Environment they face	Chaotic, unpredictable, existence of voids	More predictable and organized
How they expand in new markets	Simultaneous entrance in emerging and developed markets	From developed markets to emerging markets
How fast they go international	Very quickly	More measured and gradual
Experiences in emerging markets	Extensive as they have extensive on-the-ground experience	Limited but growing
Access to factual information and other data about markets	Very limited statistics available	Much more extensive
Political knowledge/expertise	Extensive as they have dealt with local governments	Much more limited as political knowledge not as necessary
Preferred modes of entry in international markets	Alliances and other joint efforts	Much more solitary through wholly owned subsidiaries
Organizational flexibility	High because of the need to tackle challenges in local markets	More limited because of ingrained cultures and structures

Exhibit 1.8 Differences Between Emerging Market Multinationals and Developed World Multinationals

Source: Based on P. Dupoux, L. Ivers, A. Abouzied, A. Chraïti, F. Dia, H. Maher and S. Niavas, 2015, "Dueling with lions," www.bcgperspectives.com/content/articles/globalization-growth-dueling-with-lions-playing-new-game-business-success-africa/; M. F. Guillén and E. García-Canal, 2011, "The rise of emerging market multinationals," IESE Insight, Third Quarter, *10*, pp. 13–19.

Competitors on the Move: The Case of Infosys

BRIC INSIGHT

Indian information technology (IT) services firms such as Wipro and Infosys want to be more than low-cost sources of IT outsourcing for major US and European firms. They want to take on the IBMs and Accentures by becoming the Walmart of IT, turning software engineering and business processes such as running call centers into commodities that can be produced cheaply and sold in great volume around the world. In India, where top engineers cost significantly less a year than in most developed economies and top companies meet or exceed global standards, this might be the future.

Infosys remains a prime example of an emerging market multinational that is constantly scanning its environment and responding as needed. It is seen today as the model multinational that started as a global start-up and that took the world by surprise. And although some emerging market multinationals were beset by ethical problems, Infosys remains one of the icons of Indian companies guided by values emphasizing fairplay and transparency. Infosys is now facing major environmental changes influenced by the disruption of the IT services by digital, cloud, and Internet of Things business models. Additionally, it faced internal turmoil because of the departure of many top managers and low employee morale.

In 2014 Infosys named a new CEO, Vishal Sikka, who has implemented many changes to ensure Infosys' success. He has changed the organizational structure from an industry focused organization to one based on consolidation of delivery to achieve better economies of scale. He has also set a goal of achieving $20 billion revenue in 2020 (from $8.7 billion revenue in 2016). CEO Sikka believes they can achieve such an ambitious goal and has provided many avenues to reach the goal. He is now encouraging the company to automate and make software to replace humans. He has also pioneered the 'zero distance' principle with clients where employees work very closely with clients to understand their needs. Finally, he is also encouraging the designing of artificial intelligence tools to help clients improve research productivity.

Results show that these efforts are paying off. While competitors' revenue growth have been either very slow or have slowed down, Infosys saw its economic growth increase from 3.2 percent to 8.5 percent most recently.

Source: Based on V. Babu, 2016, "Life after Infosys," *Business Today*, May 8, pp. 76–81; R. Dubey, 2016, "Re-imagining Infosys," *Business Today*, April 10, pp. 53–61; *The Economist*, 2004, "The latest in remote control," www.economist.com, September 9; *The Economist*, 2004, "Faster, cheaper, better," www.economist. com, November 11.

As the above shows, emerging market multinationals will continue playing critical roles in influencing the business environment. Another type of emerging market multinational that has been influential is the state-owned enterprise. **State-owned enterprises (SOEs)** are legal entities that are created and governed by the government to engage in business activities. SOEs tend to be in strategic sectors such as petroleum, defense, and electricity[17] and can be found in most emerging markets worldwide. Prominent examples include Brazil's airplane manufacturing giant Embraer, South African diamond miner Alexkor, and China's refiner Sinopec.

SOEs are important global players as they have significant size. Consider the case of Chinese SOEs. As of 2015, China had an impressive 76 SOEs on Fortune's Global 500 companies. Exhibit 1.9 shows the Top 10 Chinese SOEs, their revenues, and their rank in Fortune's Global 500 Companies.

state-owned enterprises (SOEs)
legal entities that are created and governed by the government to engage in business activities

Company Name	Revenues in 2014 (US$ billion)	Fortune Global 500 Rank
1. Sinopec Group	446.8	2
2. China National Petroleum	428.6	4
3. State Grid	339.4	7
4. Industrial and Commercial Bank of China	163.2	18
5. China Construction Bank	139.9	29
6. Agricultural Bank of China	130.0	36
7. China State Construction Engineering	129.9	37
8. Bank of China	120.9	45
9. China Mobile Communications	107.5	55
10. SAIC Motor	102.2	60

Exhibit 1.9 China's SOEs: Revenues and Fortune Global 500 Rankings
Source: Adapted from S. Cendrowski, 2015, "China's Global 500 Companies are bigger than ever—and mostly state-owned," *Fortune*, http://fortune.com/2015/07/22/china-global-500-government-owned/

As Exhibit 1.9 shows, in China, SOEs are giants that have had significant impact on industries. This is true in many other emerging nations. In fact, the reason for the large size of many of the Chinese SOEs is because there has been significant consolidation recently. Such consolidation has meant the combination of smaller SOEs into larger monopolies or oligarchies. Such larger entities have resulted in organizations with significant power in their industries. Critics argue that SOEs have other unfair advantages over private multinationals: Anti-trust authorities are often willing to overlook the use of monopolistic power; SOEs are often able to get loans at a fraction of what private firms get charged; they are also often the preferred recipients of state contracts for products; and they also tend to typically receive various forms of state aid and subsidies.

Given all of the above, what can multinationals do to benefit from emerging markets while also competing successfully with each other? Experts agree that multinationals will have to transform to succeed in such markets. Emerging markets no longer pose the same advantages as they did in the past. Countries such as China and India no longer provide cost advantages as they used to because of rising labor costs and higher energy costs. Additionally, as mentioned earlier, many of these emerging nations see challenges related to slowing economic growth and increased competition from local companies. Multinationals will therefore have to make critical changes if they are to succeed in these markets and compete successfully with emerging market multinationals. Experts therefore suggest the following:[18]

- Transform local operations—multinationals can no longer approach emerging markets with global products. Local conditions require customized approaches and those multinationals that can provide such products are more likely to succeed.
- Focus on competitiveness rather than growth—multinationals need to realize that they do not need to enter all emerging markets. It is now much more critical for them to focus on how they can achieve competitiveness against local competitors.
- Do not focus only on the high-income segment—multinationals are finding that concentrating only on the high-income segment is problematic. They often face strong competition and consumers are very price sensitive. While this may work in developed countries, it may not necessarily work in emerging markets. It therefore makes sense to focus on lower and middle-income segments that present much more potential for growth.
- Do not shy away from mergers and acquisitions—evidence suggests that the quickest way to gain access to distribution networks and economies of scale is through some form of partnership with local companies. Experts therefore suggest that multinationals should not be afraid to buy or to team up with local firms.
- Send talented individuals and give emerging markets the importance they deserve—multinationals often underestimate emerging markets and are reluctant to send the appropriate talented individuals. To succeed, multinationals will need to improve their recruitment and training programs to ensure that they send the best individuals or teams of individuals for the challenging tasks in emerging markets.

Information Technology and the Internet: A Necessary Tool for Globally Dispersed Companies

The explosive growth in the capabilities of information technology and the Internet increases the MNC's ability to reach customers in a global economy and to manage operations throughout the world. Since any website can be accessed by anyone with a computer and Internet access, the Internet makes it easy for companies to go global. That is, with a global online population exceeding 3.4 billion (or 46.1 percent of the world's population),[19] individuals can shop anywhere and companies can sell anywhere.

Growth of potential Internet users in emerging markets remains very strong. Consider the following IB Emerging Market Strategic Insight.

Internet Users in Emerging Markets

Emerging markets such as India and China will see impressive growth in the number of online customers. China saw growth of 600 percent between 2010 and 2014 making it the largest e-commerce market today. Much of this growth can be attributed to indigenous companies that had a better understanding of local market realities. Consider the case of Alibaba, China's e-commerce giant that was started in 1999. When it started operations, it realized that a big barrier to e-commerce was trust in the transaction. It therefore created Alipay, which holds the buyer's money until the purchased product is received. Alipay has now evolved into a financial services company providing loans to small businesses and other entrepreneurs.

According to experts, the next emerging market that will attract significant attention is India. In the next 15 years, it is predicted that India will see more people come online than in any other country. While e-commerce sales in 2015 were about $16 billion, it is expected that it will be around $112 billion in 2020 (or 7 times larger). Though there are significant challenges such as poorer customers and worse infrastructure than China, many companies want to take advantage of such growth and are investing in all aspects of e-commerce. Amazon, the US-based e-commerce giant, is hopeful that India will be its second biggest market and has been investing in the market.

The potential in India is also resulting in new start-ups with innovative business models. Consider the case of Zomato, a restaurant listing service. It initially started by uploading pictures and menus of restaurants in Delhi, services that many of them were unable to do. Zomato employees would visit the restaurants once every three months to get updates and new pictures. Posting on Zomato allowed these restaurants to generate new foodie customers and they are therefore more than willing to advertise. Zomato is now hoping to expand this business model worldwide. Whereas competitors such as Trip Advisor rely on reviews of users, Zomato's services are driven more by their employees.

Source: *The Economist*, 2016, "The great race," March 5, pp. 19–21; *The Economist*, 2016, "Global appetites," April 9, pp. 66–67.

As the above IB Emerging Market Strategic Insight shows, investing in emerging markets is critical. Furthermore, electronic communication (e-mail, the World Wide Web, Twitter, Facebook, etc.) allows MNCs to communicate with company locations throughout the world. Information technology expands the global reach of an organization. MNCs can now monitor worldwide operations to an extent never before possible. Text and graphic information can flow to any part of the world nearly instantaneously. Headquarters, research and development, manufacturing, or sales can be located anywhere there is a computer. Because employees, suppliers, and customers are geographically dispersed, organizations are becoming virtual— linked by networks of computers. Information technology makes it all happen.

Information technology is also spurring a borderless financial market. Investors are going global, and companies of the future will get their financing not in local stock or bond markets but in global markets that seek the best companies worldwide.

The decreasing price and increasing sophistication of computer systems also affects globalization. Small companies can now have computer power that only the largest multinationals could have afforded just a few years ago. Similarly, cheap and readily available computer power allows companies in poorer nations to make technological gains previously reserved for the rich.

The use of information technology and the Internet is also speeding up another globalization driver. Since many companies now use the Web to search for suppliers, it is easier to be a global customer. Because of the importance of this growing trend, Chapter 15 in this book discusses the impact of the Internet on **multinational management** in detail.

Increasing Global Products, Services, and Customers

Even though countries differ in national cultures, political, and economic systems, customers in different countries increasingly want similar products and services. For example, aircraft manufacturers such as Boeing and Airbus and fast-food chains such as Kentucky Fried Chicken offer the same or similar products in many different markets. When companies can sell the same product or deliver the same service regardless of the nationality of the customer, the industry has a **global product**. When industries have mostly global products, global competition is more likely.

Perhaps driven by the rise of similar customer needs worldwide, customers are also crossing borders and becoming **global customers**. Global customers look for products or services ignoring national boundaries, seeking instead the best price and quality rather than national location. Companies making industrial purchases are more likely than individuals to become global customers. However, with the increased use of web stores for purchasing consumer goods, any site is available for customers worldwide so anyone with a computer can be a global customer. Many of you seeking better prices may have already become global customers by purchasing books or computer equipment from outside of your home country.

Increasingly, similar customer needs and the willingness of customers to shop globally encourage the speed of globalization because companies are more likely to offer one product for everybody, allowing any customer to buy anything from anywhere. These trends will continue as developing nations move beyond simply serving as low-cost production sites and, instead, become the centers of consumer growth.

Can I Buy it in Germany and Use it in India? The Need for Global Standards

Increasingly, especially for technical products, global design standards are common. That is, for example, you can buy a pin drive for your computer in Paris and use it in Nebraska. Why is this so? Probably the most important reason is that, once a product standard is accepted globally or regionally, manufacturers need only produce one or a few versions of a product and still can sell worldwide. Because this is cheaper than making dozens of different versions, one for each country, everyone benefits with a lower-cost product and companies face fewer obstacles to selling outside of their own country. Component makers also become more efficient with fewer product designs. The competitive pressure to save money by developing one product for everyone will likely increase as products are introduced into the world market. A tremendous strategic advantage exists for those companies that can establish their standards as dominant either regionally or worldwide. For example, the company that develops and deploys the next generation standards for video downloads on cell phones will have a dominant position in the market.

However, although global standardization has progressed substantially, it should be noted that it will take a long time for such standards to be adopted. As you saw earlier, many emerging markets have unique local circumstances that make standardization difficult to adopt. In such cases, multinationals are advised to follow the guidelines discussed earlier.

The above provides an understanding of the many factors making the business environment global. However, as more multinationals are entering the world of international trade and investment, they are being pressured to be more ethical and to implement more environmentally friendly practices. Next we discuss issues pertinent to business ethics and environmental responsibility.

multinational management
the formulation of strategies and the design of management systems that successfully take advantage of international opportunities and respond to international threats

global product
the same product or service regardless of the nationality of the customer

global customers
global customers search the world for products or services without regard for national boundaries

Business Ethics and Environmental Sustainability

business ethics
approach used by
companies when they
face ethical dilemmas

Most companies, domestic and international alike, are being pressured to implement ethical and sustainable practices. **Business ethics** refers to the approach used by companies when they face ethical dilemmas. As you will see in Chapter 16, multinationals often face situations that have ethical implications. Deciding what safety features to include in a product or whether children can be employed are both examples of ethical dilemmas where the multinational needs to decide what strategy to implement and how it affects others. Multinationals are being increasingly pressured to behave in an ethical manner. Because of their size and clout, they are often scrutinized for their actions and unethical behaviors are often highlighted. It therefore becomes imperative for multinationals to be ethical.

Experts agree that emerging markets are especially fraught with ethical dilemmas. Emerging market multinationals are also often involved in unethical actions. Consider the following Emerging Market Ethical Challenge.

Business Ethics of Emerging Markets and Emerging Market Multinationals

EMERGING MARKET
ETHICAL CHALLENGE

Despite the huge potential offered by emerging markets, they also pose immense challenges. Established multinationals have found that they often have to deal with local officials who require illegal payments to 'resolve' regulatory obstacles. Because of unclear regulations or other obscure laws, a multinational manager at the negotiating table may find that such issues have to be resolved before business can proceed. Paying a local official such bribes may allow the multinational to be able to start operations much faster, thereby gaining in revenues. Consider the case of Walmart in Mexico and the bribery scandal where they paid local officials to change zoning to allow them to build a store close to a major city. In fact, it has been claimed that Walmart was involved in numerous bribery scandals around Mexico.

Such bribery scandals end up costing multinationals millions of dollars in fines. In fact, as you will see in Chapter 16, most countries are becoming stricter about correcting ethical violations. Many governments have implemented more strict regulations and are also more likely to go after multinationals involved in ethical violations.

While the above shows that developed world multinationals are not unlikely to engage in unethical behavior, such activities also affect emerging market multinationals. Consider the case of Alexkor, the South African stated-owned diamond miner. Despite mining in areas with huge reserves, Alexkor has more than often experienced losses than profits. A big problem is that many of the diamonds that are mined do not make it to the income statement. Some have claimed that around half of the mined diamonds are stolen. Those involved in such activities sometimes use pigeons that are smuggled in the mines and are then sent home with rough diamonds. Many of the South African state-owned multinationals are plagued by losses resulting from corruption and incompetent management. Such behaviors end up costing the South African economy significantly through frequent bailouts and lost revenues because of corruption.

Source: D. Currell and T. D. Bradley, 2013, "Greased palms, giant headaches," *Harvard Business Review*, September, 21–23; *The Economist*, 2015, "Commanding plights," August 29, www.economist.com

As the above Emerging Market Ethical Challenge shows, multinationals will continue to face scrutiny with regards to decisions with ethical consequences. It will therefore be critical for such multinationals to implement ethical practices. Another related aspect of ethics are **sustainable practices**, which refer to the business practices that minimize the impact of business operations on the earth's environment, thereby enhancing the ability of the earth's ecosystems to stay healthy and to continue functioning indefinitely.[20] Consider, for example, that Walmart has been working closely with suppliers for the past decade to reduce packaging waste, while Nike has been removing toxic chemicals from its shoes. Furthermore, many other multinationals are working hard to reduce the impact of their activities on the natural environment.

A recent study of executives by the McKinsey group shows that the environment has become one of the top priorities for most executives around the world. In fact, most executives consider sustainability as one of the top priorities to consider when crafting their overall strategy.[21] Exhibit 1.10 shows the percentage of executives who felt sustainability to be one of the top three priorities over the years.

> sustainable practices business practices that minimize the impact of business operations on the earth's environment, thereby enhancing the ability of the earth's ecosystems to stay healthy and to continue functioning indefinitely

Percentage of CEOs Who See Sustainability as a top CEO Priority

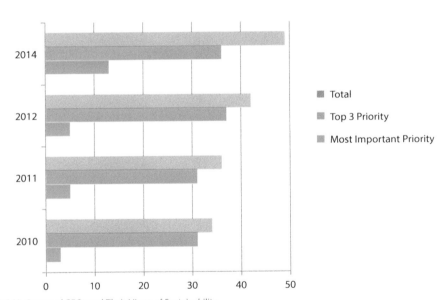

Exhibit 1.10 Survey of CEOs and Their Views of Sustainability
Source: Based on McKinsey & Company, 2014, "Sustainability's strategic worth: McKinsey global survey results," www.mckinsey.com/business-functions/sustainability-and-resource-productivity/our-insights/sustainabilitys-strategic-worth-mckinsey-global-survey-results

As Exhibit 1.10 shows, over the years, a higher percentage of CEOs have seen sustainability as the most important priority. Furthermore, in 2014, a total of 49 percent see sustainability as one of the top priorities (including 36 percent who see it as a top 3 priority and 13 percent as the top priority). Why have environmental and sustainable issues become so important? As most societies become concerned about global warming and greenhouse gas emissions, managers are becoming increasingly concerned about the impact of their actions on shareholders, as well as how such actions are portrayed in the media. However, the McKinsey report also suggests that many executives feel that going green can also present a company with significant market opportunities through reputation management efforts.[22] Many companies are seeing increased customer demand for their environmentally friendly products. However, beyond economic drivers, many multinationals are engaging in sustainable practices for other reasons. Some multinationals are proactive and are implementing sustainable practices to avoid future governmental legislation. Other companies are implementing sustainable practices to reduce costs.

This introduction gives you just a brief taste of the exciting world of international business. Before we go on to other chapters, the next section gives you a brief outline of what to expect in this text.

Plan of the Book

The book is divided into five major sections. Each section contains chapters that provide information on essential topics of international business with a special emphasis on emerging markets. The intent is to give you an overview of the complex and exciting world of international business. Throughout the different parts of the book, you will be exposed to the exciting but challenging environments characterizing emerging markets. You will also have a chance to read about some of the potential solutions to the challenges of emerging markets.

Part One provides an introduction to the field of international business, including background on globalization and how MNCs compete strategically. It is important that you first understand the strategic choices open to MNCs. With that understanding you will have a better appreciation of the information presented in later chapters that provides essential material for understanding international business.

Part Two of your text is intended to provide you with an understanding of the global context in which MNCs compete. Chapter 1 touched on the issue of how growing international trade and investment, combined with global economic integration, is changing the competitive landscape for MNCs. In this part, two chapters, Chapter 3 on economic integration and Chapter 4 on global trade and investment, will give you more detail on how and why these trends are driving international business throughout the world. Chapters 5 and 6 will show you how money moves across borders to make international transactions possible. Chapter 5 overviews the basics of foreign exchange: that is, what affects the varying values of currency from different countries and how multinational managers manage cross-border money transactions. Chapter 6 discusses how MNCs, in today's global financial systems, get capital from bond and stock markets outside of their own countries.

Part Three looks inside the countries where MNCs do business. Here you will learn how MNCs adjust their strategies and operations to the local context. Chapter 7 looks at how culture influences the conduct of international business. Chapter 8 focuses on social institutions such as the legal and political systems. This chapter also considers the effects of religion on an MNC's operations and strategies when doing business in countries or areas of the world with particular religious institutions. The chapter also discusses the many voids that plague emerging markets.

Part Four of your text brings you inside the MNC to look at the functional and operational strategies that support the broader multinational strategies that you learned about in Chapter 2. This is the largest part of the book because there are many issues that an MNC must consider in conducting its international businesses in emerging markets and elsewhere. Chapter 9 shows how MNCs actually set up operations in different countries through techniques such as joint ventures or licensing. Chapter 10 looks at how companies adjust their marketing and supply-chain management strategies to support operations in varied countries. The third and fourth chapters in this part, Chapters 11 and 12, show how MNCs develop specialized accounting systems and manage their financial systems to conduct cross-border activities successfully.

Because running an MNC is an organizational challenge, Chapter 13 is devoted to organizational structures for international operations. Similarly, because of the complexities of dealing with managers and workers located anywhere in the world, Chapter 14 is also dedicated to international human resource management (IHRM). You will also learn about the complexities of IHRM in emerging markets. Part Four concludes with Chapter 15 on e-commerce for the MNC. This chapter focuses on the unique challenges of running an international operation via the Internet.

Part Five, the final part of your text, contains only one chapter, "Managing Ethical and Social Responsibility in an MNC." The challenges of managing ethical issues in varied cultural and institutional contexts cannot be underestimated. While you will not learn how to be ethical by reading this chapter, you will be introduced to the basics of ethical reasoning and some of the issues you need to consider when faced with ethically challenging decisions. You will also learn about approaches to manage ethics operations in emerging markets.

International Business: A Strategic Approach

This book takes a strategic approach to international business. Why? Because strategy focuses on how to compete successfully in the global economy.

Strategy is defined here as the activities that managers use to outcompete other companies by increasing and then sustaining superior organizational performance. Strategy formulation is the process managers use to craft a strategy. Strategy implementation includes all the activities that managers and an organization must perform to achieve strategic objectives.

From the perspective of the MNC and its managers, strategies must include maneuvers and tactics that deal with operating and competing in more than one country, each with its unique culture and political, legal, religious, and financial systems. In turn, more complex strategies require that multinational strategy implementation deal with added challenges, including the need to understand different economic, cultural, legal, financial, and ethical systems. Thus, not only do you need to understand the complex systems in which you conduct international business but also, as potential international managers, you must develop the management systems to carry out strategies that reach beyond domestic boundaries into emerging markets.

Chapter Review

This chapter has provided you with key background information that supports the study of international management. The chapter defined international management and the MNC. Because we exist in a globalizing world, considerable attention has been devoted to the forces that drive globalization. These are key environmental issues that affect every MNC and its managers. World trade and investments are growing rapidly but not always consistently, making all economies more linked and creating both opportunities and threats for both domestic and multinational companies. New competitors, strong and motivated, are coming from emerging markets in Asia, the Americas, and Eastern Europe. Customers, products, and standards are becoming more global. The increasing sophistication and lower cost of information technology fuel the development of global companies that can more easily manage worldwide operation.

Multinational managers of the next generation will need skills not always considered necessary for domestic-only managers. Perhaps the most encompassing characteristic is the global mindset. Managers with a global mindset understand the rapidly changing business and economic environment. They can see the world as an integrated market, yet appreciate and understand the wide array of differences in the world cultures and social institutions.

After reading this text, you should have the foundation for understanding the latest challenges and practices of international business. However, the world is dynamic and your learning will never be complete, as the challenges of international business will continue to the distant future. Additionally, you should get a good understanding of the potential but challenges presented by emerging markets.

Discussion Questions

1   Discuss how any company can become an MNC. What are some of the options available to companies that allow them to use international markets and locations competitively?

2   Discuss some reasons why reductions in world trade barriers are driving the world toward a global economy.

3   Consider how wars, terrorist acts, SARS, etc., might alter the progression of globalization. What should a multinational manager do to deal with these situations?

4   Discuss the differences between foreign trade and foreign direct investment.

5   Identify some of the major differences between emerging market multinationals and developed world multinationals.

6   Discuss the ethics of operating in emerging markets.

7   Discuss some of the advantages and disadvantages of setting up production in emerging markets. Consider the benefits of market growth and the risk of an example venture.

8   Where do you think the next generation of world-class competitors will come from? Why?

International Business Skill Builder

Pros and Cons of Globalization

Step 1: Do an Internet search on the pros and cons of globalization. You will find thousands of sites. Start your search in the year 2000 and end in the present. See if you observe any trends in different pros or cons. Do people from different countries or regions have different perceptions of globalization? Do people from different groups (age, gender, job type, race, etc.) view globalization differently?

Step 2: Pair up with a fellow student. One student should take the pro side and the other the con side. Discuss and argue the merits of your position. Alternatively, discuss globalization from the perspective of different groups.

Step 3: Share your positions with your class.

Chapter Internet Activity

As you will see, throughout this text there are Internet Activities at the end of each chapter. These activities are designed to expand on important information as well as to enhance your knowledge and understanding of the management resources on the Web. Your instructor may assign these activities or you may choose to complete them on your own. However, while every effort has been made to ensure that the sites you are directed to are stable and live, the Internet is a rapidly changing environment in which it is hard to always keep pace.

For the Internet Activity for this chapter, simply familiarize yourself with the Internet sites identified in this chapter. Many contain valuable up-to-date information on the changing nature of international business and multinational management. Log onto the Web and spend 30–60 minutes searching for multinational management information or resources. What did you find? Was it difficult to locate the information? Compile a list of resources for future use in this class or others.

Key Concepts

- business ethics
- developed economies
- developing economies
- emerging market multinationals
- European Union (EU)
- foreign direct investment (FDI)
- General Agreement on Tariffs and Trade (GATT)
- global customers
- global product
- globalization
- international business

- least developed countries (LDCs)
- low-cost countries (LCCs)
- multinational company (MNC) multinational management
- North American Free Trade Agreement (NAFTA)
- rapidly developing economies (RDEs)
- regional trade agreements
- state-owned enterprises (SOEs)
- sustainable practices
- transition economies
- World Trade Organization (WTO)

CASE 1 BUSINESS > INTERNATIONAL

McDonald's in India: No Hamburgers Please

In 1954, a milkshake mixer salesman named Ray Kroc traveled to San Bernardino, California, to see why one restaurant had ordered so many of his Multimixers. The McDonald brothers had invented a new concept in the restaurant business and Kroc wanted to see for himself why the business was so popular. Dick and Mac McDonald had pioneered fast food based on high volume, low prices, limited menu, and quick service. The restaurant was a success, and Ray Kroc wanted it. He negotiated an agreement with the McDonald brothers in which he would become the exclusive franchiser of the McDonald name.

In 1955, the first McDonald's franchise opened in Des Plaines, Illinois. The McDonald's empire would be based on four core values providing customers with *quality, service, cleanliness*, and *value* (QSCV). Kroc believed that consistency in these core values would allow McDonald's to build a strong brand image throughout the United States. He was right. The concept was a success, and by 1963 McDonald's was selling 1 million hamburgers a day.

The first international McDonald's opened in Canada in 1967. McDonald's continued its international expansion into Japan, Germany, Australia, France, and England in the 1970s. Additional outlets were established in Latin America, the Middle East, Central and Eastern Europe, Russia, and China. The motive for McDonald's international expansion was the realization that most potential sales existed outside the United States. As Kroc had said in 1954, when he witnessed the McDonald brothers' original restaurant concept, "This idea can sell anywhere." Based on the need for additional sales growth and the belief that the concept could be exported, McDonald's embarked on an aggressive international expansion effort beginning in the 1970s. Today, McDonald's has restaurants in 119 countries and derives over 60 percent of its profits from sales overseas. On average, the company opens a new restaurant somewhere in the world every five hours, and McDonald's can be found on every continent, except Antarctica.

Prior to 1996, McDonald's did not have a restaurant anywhere on the Indian subcontinent. With a population of over 1 billion, India is viewed by many as a market with an enormous potential. India's population is second only to that of China, and, with differing birth rates, India will become the most populated country in the world by 2020, according to some estimates.

India represented a big challenge to McDonald's because most Indians could not eat the main menu item: the beef hamburger. Over 80 percent of the Indian population is Hindu and this religion prohibits the consumption of cow products. Also, approximately 40 percent of Indians are strict vegetarians and eat no meat of any kind. A significant percentage of the Indian population is Muslim, which also prohibits the consumption of pork products.

CASE 1
cont'd

India is a federal republic, which gained its independence from Great Britain in 1947. After many years of British rule, Mahatma Gandhi led a mass movement for independence. Since that time, India has been as its constitution states, a "sovereign, socialist, secular, democratic republic." The economic self-reliance or "swadeshi" begun under Gandhi influenced public policy in India for over 40 years. India finally began to liberalize economic policy after experiencing a severe foreign currency crisis. In 1991, major changes occurred that made foreign investment easier, including reduced tariffs, removal of non-tariff barriers to trade, and loosened foreign investment restrictions and currency controls.

India still remains a poor country and a difficult market for Western companies. Per capita GDP is $1,498, and many Indians live on less than a dollar a day. Yet, the economy with a high growth rate in recent years has raised many out of poverty and produced widespread income gains. The government recognizes eighteen languages, with Hindi being the most widely spoken. English is also spoken, especially in urban areas and among the better-educated component of the population. Violent religious clashes occur between Hindus and Christians and between Hindus and Muslims, and there is a current movement to establish an all-Hindu India. The religious and social class tolerances advocated by Gandhi do not seem to be as well accepted by many in India today. India is a country divided by languages, religion, and caste.

In 1996, McDonald's opened its first restaurant in India. The first McDonald's in India was located in Delhi and was the only McDonald's outlet worldwide not to offer beef on its menu. Due to dietary restrictions imposed by religion, McDonald's had to be creative in its product offerings. Without the possibility of serving beef or pork, McDonald's offered the lamb patty and a veggie burger. The Big Mac was named the Maharaja Mac and substituted ground lamb for beef. After opening its second restaurant in India, this one in Mumbai, McDonald's had invested $14 million, yet the company was not completely sure of the potential of the Indian market. Although business was brisk at both locations, some concerns were raised.

Some consumers complained about the bland taste of the food. Accustomed to the spicy traditional Indian food, McDonald's meals seemed too plain for some consumers. There was also a concern about the political stability of the country and long-term acceptance of McDonald's in India. The Indian government did not support the entry of McDonald's into the country and some Indians protested the arrival of the American multinational. Previous American franchises have been the target of vandalism in India in the past. KFC, Dominos Pizza, and Pizza Hut all have several locations in India, and some of the restaurants have experienced difficulties with political mobs. McDonald's is perhaps in an even more vulnerable position because its primary product worldwide (beef) is viewed by many Hindus as not appropriate for consumption. As one protestor remarked "They are the chief killers of the cow." Other protestors see McDonald's as a symbol of the exploitation of the world's poor by rich American multinationals. In 2005, McDonald's settled a $10 million lawsuit

CASE 1
cont'd

brought by vegetarians in the United States who had charged McDonald's with misleading advertising. McDonald's had been using a beef flavoring for its French fries without telling consumers. The news of this culinary process caused protest in India and some store vandalism, however, McDonald's had been careful not to use the beef flavoring in India.

McDonald's of India is a 50/50 partnership between the McDonald's Corp. and two Indian businessmen, who have divided the market into North and East, and West and South markets of India. McDonald's faces stiff competition from Yum! Brands Inc., which operates KFC, Pizza Hut, and Taco Bell. Yum has the advantage of having its product offerings more consistent with the requirements of a Hindi diet. At present there more than 250 McDonald's restaurants in India and there is a plan to double that number by 2020. McDonald's of India continues to experiment with different product offering to satisfy local tastes and preferences and has developed a McDonald's delivery phone app to bring meals to consumers.

Faced with the difficulties of product acceptance, low purchasing power among consumers, and the ever-present potential of political conflict, McDonald's, nevertheless, hopes to grow this emerging market in the coming decades. With a large and growing population, and increasing incomes, McDonald's feels that Indians will embrace the product offerings and make India a very good growth market for the company.

CASE DISCUSSION POINTS:

1   What approach to international business is McDonald's following: ethnocentric, polycentric, or geocentric? Explain.
2   Does the movement into the Indian market represent any risks for McDonald's? Explain your answer.
3   What lessons can be learned by other MNCs from McDonald's experience in India?

Source: McDonald's corporate web site, www.mcdonalds.com; S. Mohanty, 1996, "India's Maharaja Mac has no beef," *Reuters Business Report*, October 11; S. Mohanty, 1996, "Where's the beef: India's McDonald's eschews chuck," *Reuters*, October 11; *Dallas Morning News*, 1996, "McDonald's goes to India without beef," October 12; K. Cooper, 1996, "Where's the beef: McDonald's menu in India culturally correct, but company's presence cooks up controversy," *Dallas Morning News*, November 10; L. S. Kadaba, 1998, "Big in Bombay: The Maharaja Mac is one hot item," *The Philadelphia Inquirer*, April 22; US Department of State, 2009, "Background notes: India," January 20; S. Dutta, 2000, "Domino theory," *Business India*, May 1; L. Kadaba and D. Gardner, 2000, "India's elusive reforms," *Financial Times*, August 4; C. Raghatta, 2005, "McDonald's pays up Hindu veggie group in US," *The New Times of India*, July 12; M. Caggeso, 2007, "McDonald's finds unique way to beef up its presence in India," www.moneymorning.com. October, 27; www.mcdonaldsinindia.net accessed on July 18, 2016; *The Hindu*, 2015, "McDonald's India hopes to double outlets by 2020," September 15.

Case prepared by Charles A. Rarick

Notes

1   C. Nettesheim, L. Faeste, D. Khanna, B. Waltermann and P. Ullrich, 2016, "Transformation in emerging markets," Boston Consulting Group, February, http://bcg.perspectives

2   WTO (World Trade Organization), 2002, *World Trade Organization: Trading into the Future*, Geneva: World Trade Organization; *The Economist*, 2003, "Heading east," www.economist.com, March 27; *The Economist*, 2003, "All aboard the Euro-train!" www.economist.com, April 3.

3   *The Economist*, 1996, "All free traders now?" December 7, pp. 23–25.

4   *The Economist*, 2002, "United we fall," www.economist.com, September 26; *The Economist*, 1996, "Spoiling world trade," December 7, pp. 15–16.

5   R. F. M. Lubbers, 1996, "Globalization: An exploration," *Nijenrode Management Review*, 1.

6   http://asean.org/

7   UNCTAD, 2016, *World Investment Report, 2016*, http://unctad.org/en/pages/PublicationWebflyer. aspx?publicationid=1555

8   UNCTAD, 2016, *World Investment Report, 2016*, http://unctad.org/en/pages/PublicationWebflyer. aspx?publicationid=1555

9   UNCTAD, 2007, *World Investment Report*, New York and Geneva: United Nations.

10 UNCTAD, 2000, *World Investment Report*, New York and Geneva: United Nations; UNCTAD, 2000, "World FDI flows exceed US$ 1.1 trillion in 2000," UNCTAD Press Release, December 7; UNCTAD, 2002, *World Investment Report*, New York and Geneva: United Nations.

11 UNCTAD, 2007, *World Investment Report*, New York and Geneva: United Nations.

12 UNCTAD, 2016, *World Investment Report, 2016*, http://unctad.org/en/pages/PublicationWebflyer. aspx?publicationid=1555

13 UNCTAD, 2016, *World Investment Report, 2016*, http://unctad.org/en/pages/PublicationWebflyer. aspx?publicationid=1555

14 N. Kapur, S. Dawar and V. R. Ahuja, 2014, "Unlocking the wealth in rural markets," *Harvard Business Review*, June, pp. 113–117

15 S. A. Nonis and C. Relyea, 2012, "Business innovations from emerging markets into developed countries: Implications for multinationals from developed countries," *Thunderbird International Business Review*, 54(3), May/June, pp. 291–298.

16 P. Dupoux, L. Ivers, A. Abouzied, A. Chraïti, F. Dia, H. Maher and S. Niavas, 2015, "Dueling with lions," www.bcgperspectives.com/content/articles/globalization-growth-dueling-with-lions-playing-new-game-business-success-africa/

17 W. Leuter, 2016, "Challenges ahead in China's reform of state-owned organizations," *Asia Policy*, 21, pp. 83–99.

18 S. Ichii, S. Hattori and D. Michael, 2012, "How to win in emerging markets: Lessons from Japan," *Harvard Business Review*, May, pp. 126–130; C. Nettesheim, L. Faeste, D. Khanna, B. Waltermann and P. Ullrich, 2016, "Transformation in emerging markets," Boston Consulting Group, February, http://bcg.perspectives

19 www.internetlivestats.com/internet-users/

20 G. C. Unruh, 2008, "The biosphere rules," *Harvard Business Review*, February, pp. 111–117.

21 McKinsey & Company, 2014, "Sustainability's strategic worth: McKinsey global survey results," www. mckinsey.com/business-functions/sustainability-and-resource-productivity/our-insights/sustainabilitys-strategic-worth-mckinsey-global-survey-results

22 McKinsey & Company, 2014, "Sustainability's strategic worth: McKinsey global survey results," www. mckinsey.com/business-functions/sustainability-and-resource-productivity/our-insights/sustainabilitys-strategic-worth-mckinsey-global-survey-results

CHAPTER 2

Strategy and the MNC

After reading this chapter you should be able to:

- Understand the benefits MNCs can achieve using global integration or local adaptation.

- Understand the conflicting pressures of the global–local dilemma faced by international managers in MNCs.

- Know the content of the basic multinational strategies: transnational, international, multidomestic, and regional.

- Choose a multinational strategy by using the diagnostic questions that help MNCs to cope with the global–local dilemma.

- Understand the unique challenges faced by emerging market MNCs when executing multinational strategies.

- Understand the unique challenges faced by MNCs when executing multinational strategies in emerging markets.

International Business *Preview IB Emerging Market Strategic Insight*

Starbucks' Emerging Market Challenge

It's hard to walk a couple of city blocks in any US city without encountering the green-and-white Starbucks logo. After its phenomenal growth in the US, Starbucks went international in 1996, first with two stores in Japan and another 125 in Canada. Starbucks is the leading seller of specialty coffee in the world, with nearly 22,000 outlets in 71 countries but, more recently, has focused on emerging markets to provide the opportunities for expansion. Building on success and lessons learned in China, Starbucks opened stores in South Africa, South Korea, and Vietnam. Although a positive indicator for Starbucks' future the company faces challenges in emerging markets.

Starbucks greatest success is in China where it has more than 1,100 stores. CEO Howard Schultz sees China as a big opportunity where his goal is to have thousands of stores. "We're highly profitable there" he notes.

However, Schultz notes, "not everything from Starbucks in China should be invented in Starbucks in Seattle." While, emerging market customers, like customers all around the world, do not want a watered-down Starbucks, the company must still be sensitive to the cultural differences in every market, as for example its recent release of Asian Dolce Latte in Ho Chi Minh City.

However, as Starbucks' bottom line suggests, coffee-drinking culture varies widely and local regulations can be a challenge. "Some countries present more challenges than others," notes Herman Uscategui, who has the responsibility of developing Starbucks' international stores.

Source: Adapted from *Knight Ridder/Tribune Business News*, 2004, "Starbucks offers glimpse of global strategy," June 12; *Business Wire*, 2006, "Starbucks outlines international growth strategy for fiscal 2007," October 5; *Business Wire*, 2004, "Starbucks outlines international growth strategy; focus on retail expansion and profitability;" October 14; 2014, "Starbucks expands coffeehouse experience to Hanoi, Vietnam," www.starbucks.com, July 23; Trefes Team, 2016, "How significant is the South African market for Starbucks?" *Forbes*, May 12; A. Webb, 2011, "Starbucks' quest for healthy growth: An interview with Howard Schultz," McKinsey & Company.

The Preview IB Emerging Market Strategic Insight describes a situation showing how even very successful companies such as Starbucks must carefully choose the best strategies to take their products or services international. There are many options for an MNC to take advantage of international opportunities for growth and profits. In this chapter you will find a review of the essential strategies that MNCs use to succeed in this endeavor, especially when entering emerging markets.

This chapter contains two major sections. In the first section, you are introduced to general strategies regarding international operations. In the second section, you are introduced to some of the questions international managers must answer to choose their best multinational strategies. After reading this chapter you should understand how the choice of a multinational strategy depends on differences in global markets, products, competition, and risks. You should also understand that international management is more complex and challenging than domestic-only management.

Strategic Choices for MNCs

Companies engaged in international business, like all businesses, face pressures to respond to the unique needs of their customers. However, when your customers come from different countries and regions of the world, they often have different needs and desires for products and services. When a company decides to focus on meeting customer needs based on national and regional differences, it adopts a **local responsiveness strategy**. Alternatively, when a company decides to de-emphasize local differences and locate its operations anywhere in the world where it is advantageous, it adopts what is known as a **global integration strategy**.

local responsiveness strategy
responding to differences in the markets in all the countries in which a company operates

global integration strategy
conducting business similarly throughout the world, and locating company units wherever there is high quality and low cost

Companies that adopt a local responsiveness strategy stress customizing their organizations and products to accommodate country or regional differences. They focus on satisfying local customer needs by tailoring products or services to meet those needs. Forces that favor a local responsiveness strategy come primarily from cultural differences in consumer tastes and variations in customer needs, as well as differences driven by social institutions such as religion and the political system. For example, government regulations can require a company to share ownership with a local company. Some governments also require companies to produce their products in the countries in which they sell.[1]

MNCs that lean toward a global integration strategy reduce their costs by using standardized products, promotional strategies, and distribution channels in every country. In addition, such globally oriented multinationals seek sources of lower costs or higher quality by locating their operations anywhere in the world. For example, in such companies, headquarters, R&D, production, or distribution centers may be located where they provide the best value added with quality or lower cost.[2] With products like athletic shoes, for example, companies such as Nike and Reebok use low-cost Asian manufacturing sites for all of their manufacturing while keeping most research and design at their headquarters.

However, neither responding to local customer needs nor selling the same product worldwide is a guarantee of success. For example, customers may be willing to pay a higher price for products or services that are tailored to their needs. Alternatively, if customers see no value in unique products or services, they will be more attracted to a product or service that is sourced in low-cost countries and can be priced for less. Multinational firms must choose carefully for each product or business how globally or locally they orient their strategies. The problem of which strategic orientation to choose is called **global–local dilemma**. Later in the chapter you will see some of the questions that managers must answer before selecting an appropriate multinational strategy. Before that, however, consider the Emerging Market Brief below, which stories how Sweden's IKEA struggles to get the right balance in an emerging market.

The Emerging Market Brief below shows how IKEA works to perfect its multinational strategies. For most firms, this is an ongoing process that requires continuous refinements and adjustments to changing competitive conditions. Before we consider more specific applications of the basic multinational strategies, one needs a basic understanding of the value chain. Much of multinational strategy concerns decisions regarding what activities such as production or research and development, for example, should be located in different parts of the world. Such activities are part of a firm's value chain, and the next section gives a basic explanation of this concept.

global–local dilemma choice between a local responsiveness or global approach to a multinational's strategies

IKEA Adapts to Emerging Markets

EMERGING MARKET BRIEF

IKEA, a low-cost furniture company, entered China in the late 1990s. Now the world's leading furniture retailer, IKEA is aggressively expanding in emerging markets. Despite recent market turmoil, revenue in China and Russia grew over 11 percent in 2015. As such, the company opened three new Chinese stores in Guangzhou, Suzhou, and Chengdu, giving the company 18 stores in China and 14 in Russia. India is next on the horizon. The company store count reached 328 in 28 countries, including its first location in South Korea, the largest in the world.

IKEA sells its 10,000 products in all countries but it changes store layouts to match local sensibilities. In China, it focuses on living rooms since the Chinese consumer gives that room more priority, and even has the balconies typical of Chinese apartments in the stores. Such experience in China helped IKEA understand local markets and adapt its strategies to match local needs.

IKEA's global branding based on low prices did not work in China. Furniture made by local competitors was priced lower as companies had access to cheaper labor and raw materials. As a result, IKEA's low-price strategy created confusion among Chinese consumers. IKEA's reaction was to cut its prices by more than 60 percent. IKEA also decided to target young professionals because of their higher incomes, better education, and more openness to Western furniture styles. In contrast to targeting mass markets in other countries, this represented a major change in strategy.

One of the main problems for IKEA was that its prices, considered low in Europe and North America, were higher than the average in China. High prices were one of the biggest barriers in China for people to purchase IKEA products.

In adapting to the Chinese market IKEA learned that doing business in emerging markets changes the game for a multinational company. Adapting to China was not easy taking IKEA 12 years to become profitable and numerous changes to its strategies.

IKEA expects its China experiences will come in handy in India. In particular, IKEA has learned that global brands may not replicate their success in emerging markets by using the low-price strategy that they employ in developed markets. As in China, in India there will likely be local manufacturers with a lower cost structure that can undercut IKEA's prices. Therefore, somewhat similar to China, IKEA hopes to attract India's urban middle-class buyers who find stylish international brands attractive.

Source: Based on Valerie Chu, Alka Girdhar and Rajal Sood, 2013, "Couching tiger tames the dragon," *Business Today*, July 21; Niklas Magnusson, 2015, "Ikea to keep investing in emerging markets as China fuels growth," *Bloomberg News*, September 10; Paula M. Miller, 2004, "Ikea with Chinese characteristics," *China Business Review*, July/August, *31*(4), pp. 36–38.

The Value Chain and Competitive Advantage for the Multinational Company

A firm can gain a competitive advantage over other firms by finding sources of lower cost or added value in any of its activities. This means that companies can make more money than competitors can by doing things more cheaply or by delivering better value to customers for which they can charge a higher price or provide at lower costs to the company. Such activities range from getting necessary raw materials, through production, to sales, and to eventual follow-up with after-sales service. For example, a company may find cost savings sourcing cheaper raw materials or cheaper labor in emerging market countries. Taking advantage of the low-cost clothing production in India and the reduction of import quotas into the US and the EU, Sears and the British department store Marks & Spencer invest in Indian factories to produce their garments.

One convenient way of thinking about the activities multinational companies can use to create competitive advantage is called the **value chain**. That is, the value chain identifies the areas in a multinational company's input, throughput, and output processes where the firm can find sources of differentiation or lower costs.

value chain
a way of identifying all the areas where a firm can create value for customers

Harvard University's Michael Porter, a leading scholar and consultant in strategic management, uses the term "value chain" to represent all the activities that a firm uses "to design, produce, market, deliver, and support its product."[3] The value chain identifies areas where a firm can create value for customers. Better designs, more efficient production, and better service all represent value added in the value chain. Ultimately, the value a company produces represents what customers will pay for a product or service. Exhibit 2.1 shows a picture of the value chain. Later you will see that the value chain provides a useful way of thinking about how MNCs operate.

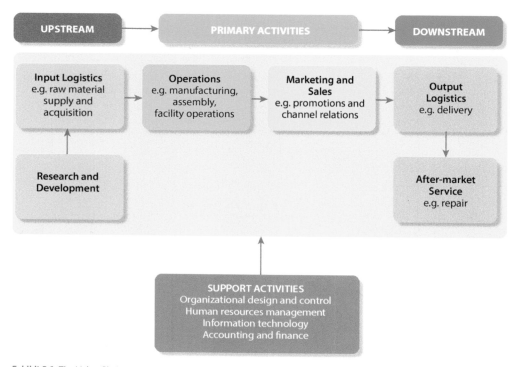

Exhibit 2.1 The Value Chain
Source: Adapted from Michael E. Porter, 1985, *Competitive Advantage*, New York: The Free Press, pp. 35, 37.

Porter divides the value chain into primary and support activities. These activities represent (1) the processes of creating goods or services, and (2) the organizational mechanisms necessary to support the creative activities. *Primary activities* involve the physical actions of creating (or serving), selling, and after-sales service of products. Early activities in the value chain, such as R&D and managing the supply chain, are called *upstream*. Later value-chain activities, such as sales and dealing with distribution channels, represent *downstream* activities. *Support activities* include systems for human resources management (e.g. recruitment and selection procedures), information technology, organizational design and control (e.g. structural form and accounting procedures), and a firm's basic technology.

One of the advantages of being an MNC over domestic-only companies is the use of country locations outside of the headquarters country to conduct value-chain activities. MNCs have the potential to gain advantages over rivals by basing value activities in many countries. How they configure these activities is really the basis of multinational strategy.

In addition to dispersing in part or in whole value-chain operations to other countries, MNCs often use the option of outsourcing. **Outsourcing** is the deliberate decision to use other companies to perform certain activities in the value chain. Since MNCs often outsource across borders, this is also known as **offshoring**. However, an MNC can also offshore by moving its own units into other countries. When should an MNC offshore? In general, offshoring makes sense if a company can perform a value-chain task better or more cheaply than in the MNC's home operations. This might occur through foreign direct investment to have a unit in another country or by contracting with local companies. In the BRIC Insight below, you can see BRIC and other emerging market countries provide attractive contexts for outsourcing via offshoring. In the following Emerging Market Ethical Challenge you can see that this MNC tactic has some disadvantages for the MNC's home country.

outsourcing
contracting with other companies to perform certain activities in the value chain

offshoring
outsourcing to a foreign company or using foreign direct investment to move company operations to a foreign country

Outsourcing/Offshoring Value-chain Activities to BRIC Countries

BRIC INSIGHT

Many MNCs have offshored value-chain activities to emerging markets such as the BRIC countries—Brazil, Russia, India, and China—largely but not exclusively because of the cost savings. China provides many multinational companies with a location for low-cost manufacturing. India, with its large supply of engineers, is often the country of choice for MNCs seeking IT outsourcing/offshoring. The top 10 Indian IT companies, including Infosys and Satyam, make up nearly 45 percent of the global IT market.

There are numerous factors to consider when an MNC looks for an outsourcing location.

The consulting and research firm, A.T. Kearney, rates the outsourcing potential for numerous countries using dozens of key statistics representing three broad areas: Financial Attractiveness, People Skills and Availability, and Business Environment. In the most recent data on services outsourcing India ranked first based on the best mix of factors. But it did not lead in all dimensions. For services outsourcing, English language skills and a large skill base make India attractive for MNC offshoring, but wages in India are rising making other emerging markets attractive locations. The table below shows selected BRIC and other emerging market countries as the top locations for services outsourcing based on their respective resources.

Country	Top Rated Outsourcing Countries for Services—A.T. Kearney Global Services Location Index			
	Overall Rating	Financial Attractiveness	People Skills and Availability	Business Environment
India	7.0	3.2	2.6	1.1
China	6.5	2.3	2.7	1.5
Malaysia	6.1	2.8	1.4	1.9
Brazil	6.0	2.3	2.0	1.6
Indonesia	5.9	3.2	1.5	1.2

Exhibit 2.2 Top Rated Outsourcing Countries for Services

Source: Based on www.atkearney.com/strategic-it/global-services-location-index, 2016.

The Specter of Job Loss

EMERGING MARKET ETHICAL CHALLENGE

Offshoring is often controversial in the MNC's home country as it often means a loss of local jobs. Take the United States, for example. In 2015 alone over 2.3 million jobs were offshored to foreign countries. Jobs were lost in all value-chain activities, including manufacturing (53 percent), IT services (43 percent), R&D (38 percent), distribution (26 percent), and call/help centers (12 percent). The most common reason MNC managers cited for offshoring was cost control or cost reduction. However, it is not the sole or the majority rationale. Managers noted other factors, such as better quality labor and access to resources not available in the home country as additional reasons to offshore.

Source: Based on www.statisticbrain.com/outsourcing-statistics-by-country/; https://www. outsource2india.com/why_outsource/articles/ethics_outsourcing.asp

Exhibit 2.3 Multinational Strategy Orientations

With a basic knowledge of the value chain you will now see how the global integration and local responsiveness strategies can be refined further.

Exhibit 2.3 shows a graphical presentation of the basic orientations of the global integration and local responsiveness strategies.

Global Integration: Where Can We Do Things Best or Cheapest?

We can think of the global integration strategy as a box representing a company's value-chain activities. In the most extreme global integration strategy, all activities from all corners of the box are spread around the globe based on strategic advantages.

The Transnational Strategy

The more inclusive version of global integration is known as the **transnational strategy**. Its top priorities are seeking location advantages and gaining economic efficiencies from operating worldwide.[4] **Location advantages** mean that the transnational company disperses or locates its value-chain activities (e.g. manufacturing, R&D, and sales) anywhere in the world where the company can "do it best or cheapest" as the situation requires. For example, Intel has manufacturing and testing facilities located in five countries outside of the US, its headquarters. These production facilities offer cheaper but also high-quality labor. Michael Porter argues that, for global competition, firms must look at countries not only as potential markets but also as

---

transnational strategy
two goals get top priority: seeking location advantages and gaining economic efficiencies from operating worldwide

location advantages
dispersing value-chain activities anywhere in the world where the company can do them best or cheapest

"global platforms."[5] A **global platform** is a country location where a firm can outperform competitors in some, but not necessarily all, of its value-chain activities.

Like companies, nations have advantages in costs, quality, or other resources available to local and MNCs. Economists call this **absolute advantage**. Later, in Chapter 4, you will learn more about how the advantages associated with a particular nation influence trade patterns. For example, countries with cheaper and better-educated labor have absolute advantages over other nations. Germany, for example, is generally considered to have an excellent educational system and thus has an advantage over other nations in the availability of a technical workforce. Absolute advantage is important to local organizations because they can use their nation's advantages to gain competitive advantages over rivals from other nations. Germany is known for producing high-quality technical products such as luxury automobiles (BMW) and appliances (Bosch dishwashing machines). Most emerging market countries have absolute advantages in labor costs when compared with countries such as the US.

Traditionally, many international business experts viewed absolute advantage as something from which only the indigenous or local organizations could benefit in world competition. Many Japanese and Korean organizations, for example, built their early competitive advantages on the cheap, high-quality, and motivated labor available in their countries. However, the transnational strategy has made this view out of date. Absolute advantages no longer give competitive advantages to local companies only. That is, in a globalizing world, any resources available in different nations such as educated workers or raw materials provide the transnational firm with the global platforms to boost location-based competitive advantages in costs and quality. The transnational views *any country* as a global platform where it can perform *any value-chain activity*. Thus, the absolute advantage of a nation is no longer just for locals. With increasingly free and open borders, any firm, regardless of the nationality of ownership, can turn any national absolute advantage into a competitive advantage for the whole company—if the firm has the flexibility and willingness to locate anywhere.

Examples of such transnational strategic activities in emerging and developed markets include:

- Locate upstream supply units near cheap sources of high-quality raw material— approximately 18 multinational oil companies are in Nigeria.
- Locate research and development centers near centers of research and innovation—in 2005 Motorola opened its new R&D center in Bangalore, a growing center of IT development in India.
- Locate manufacturing subunits near sources of high-quality or low-cost labor—Intel has five sites where labor is relatively cheap and well educated.
- Share discoveries and innovations made in any unit regardless of location with operations in other parts of the world—Ford's Taiwan-based design center, named Ford Lio, is working on the next-generation Tierra medium-sized sedan, which shares a chassis platform with the Mazda 323, for the Asia-Pacific market.
- Locate supporting value-chain activities such as accounting in low-cost countries—GE Capital uses Indian employees to do support activities such as checking eligibility of payments on health plans.
- Operate close to key customers—BMW produces a sport utility vehicle in the US, which is the major market for this type of vehicle.
- Offshore aftermarket support such as call centers to low-cost countries—if you call American Express, Sprint, Citibank, or IBM it is likely your call will be answered in India.

Location advantages provide the transnational company with cost or quality gains for different value-chain activities. To reduce costs even further, transnational strategists strive for uniform

global platform
country location where a firm can best perform some, but not necessarily all, of its value-chain activities

absolute advantage
that arising from cost, quality, or resource advantages associated with a particular nation

marketing and promotional activities throughout the world; these companies use the same brand names, advertisements, and promotional brochures wherever they sell their products or services. The soft-drink companies, such as Coca-Cola, have been among the most successful in taking their brands worldwide. When a company can do things similarly throughout the world, it can take advantage of economies of scale. Thus, for example, it is most efficient to have one package of the same color and size produced worldwide in centralized production facilities.

Of course, it does not always make good business sense to move value-chain activities to other countries even if there are apparent savings in costs or other possible benefits. For example, because wages tend to rise when multinationals enter a country, low-cost local labor is often a temporary advantage. Perhaps more important is that when subunits are spread all over the world the coordination and control of the international operations becomes a significant challenge for international managers.

What happens if the advantages of a global platform location are based in part in opportunities that may endanger the people in a country of operation? The Emerging Market Ethical Challenge below confronts this issue for oil companies operating in Nigeria.

International Strategy

international strategies selling global products and using similar marketing techniques worldwide

The international strategy is a partial global integration strategy. That is, companies pursuing **international strategies**, such as Toys "R" Us, Boeing, Apple, and IBM, take a middle ground regarding the global–local dilemma. Like the transnational strategist, the international strategist prefers, to the degree possible, to use global products and similar marketing techniques everywhere. To the degree that local customs, culture, and laws allow, they limit adaptations to minor adjustments in product offerings and marketing strategies. However, international-strategist MNCs differ from transnational companies in that they keep as many value-chain activities as possible located at home. In particular, the international strategist concentrates its R&D and manufacturing units at home to gain economies of scale and quality that are more difficult to achieve with the dispersed activities of the transnational. For example, Boeing keeps most of its R&D and production in the United States while selling its planes worldwide with a similar marketing approach focusing on price and technology. However, for its most recent plane, the Dreamliner, Boeing became a little more transnational, outsourcing production and design of some components to Japan and other countries but leaving final assembly in the US.

Getting Oil Cheaply but with Increased Environmental Controls: A Report from the US Government

EMERGING MARKET
ETHICAL CHALLENGE

An early 2002 US government report on oil companies and sustainability practices in Nigeria noted the following:

> The perceived indifference of both the Nigerian federal government and the oil companies to the environment in the Niger Delta has been exacerbated by Nigeria's lack of coherent pollution control policy. Until recently, there was little incentive for power plants to implement pollution abatement strategies or for oil companies to undertake environmental remediation efforts, as the Nigerian federal government was unwilling or unable to enforce environmental laws. However, the Nigerian federal government has indicated that it is no longer willing to tolerate oil companies absolving themselves of their responsibility to reduce pollution.

The Nigerian government has ordered oil companies operating in the country to comply with the Environmental Guidelines and Standards for the Oil Industry, published by the Department of Petroleum Resources (DPR), the monitoring arm of the Nigeria National Petroleum Corporation (NNPC), or risk paying a fine. The 300-page guidelines provide rules to reduce pollution and procedures for environmental monitoring. The DPR also has been tasked with conducting regular health, safety, and environment audits of the oil companies.

Recently, the Nigerian subsidiary of Shell was ordered to pay $1.5 billion to the Ijaw tribe for the company's actions in the state of Bayelsa over a 50-year period. A government committee that investigated Shell ruled that the company was responsible for a number of oil spills and environmental incidents, including an epidemic in which 1,400 people were killed that was blamed on a Shell oil spill. The government committee blamed the prevalence of cancer in the region on exposure to the company's oil spills, noting that Shell continually refused to pay compensation for these spills, and where it had, the payment was inadequate.

Over a decade later a report by Amnesty International, and Friends of The Earth Europe, Center for Environment, Human Rights and Development, Environmental Rights Action charged that little action has been taken to clean up pollution by oil production in Nigeria's Niger Delta region, either by the government or Shell Oil.

The United Nations Environment Program produced a detailed assessment of pollution in the oil-producing area in 2011. The report gave several examples of contaminated water and land, noting "Families are drinking water from wells that is contaminated with benzene, a known carcinogen, at levels over 900 times above World Health Organization guidelines."

Oil companies like Shell blame gangs that break into pipelines to steal crude oil for causing oil spills in the region. Three years after the UN report, the activist groups noted above accused Shell of falsely blaming spills on oil theft, and thus avoiding responsibility and acting on the findings of the UN report. Now facing a lawsuit in the United Kingdom arguing that the company does not do enough to maintain and protect its pipelines from oil thief sabotage, Shell continues to insist that it follows international best practice in its operations in Nigeria.

Oil companies such as Shell have profited substantially by operations in developing countries. Lax environmental regulations often provide an opportunity to lower costs. Are these companies responsible for the negative consequences of their actions, even if they are consistent with the laws in operation at this time?

Source: US Government, 2003, "Country analysis briefs: Nigeria: environmental issues," eia.doe.gov; *The Guardian*, 2014, "Shell and Nigeria have failed on oil pollution cleanup, Amnesty says," www.theguardian. com/environment/2014/aug/04/shell-nigeria-oil-pollution-clean-up-amnesty; UNEP, 2011, *Environmental Assessment of Ogoniland*, http://postconflict.unep.ch/publications/OEA/UNEP_OEA.pdf

When necessary for economic or political reasons, companies with international strategies frequently do set up sales and production units in major countries of operation. However, home-country headquarters retain control of local strategies, marketing, R&D, finances, and production. Local facilities become only "mini-replicas" of production and sales facilities at home.[6]

The Local Responsiveness Strategy: How Far to Go?

The local responsiveness strategy is in many respects a form of differentiation strategy. That is, a company attempts to differentiate itself from competitors by giving its products or services an extra value that attracts customers by closely satisfying their cultural needs and expectations. For example, advertisements, packaging, sales outlets, and pricing are adapted to local practices, with the hope that customers will find this more attractive than something produced similarly for the whole world. Even if a product might seem similar in different countries, there are often local adaptations required to serve local needs. For example, Kentucky Fried Chicken sells tempura crispy strips in Japan and potato-and-onion croquettes in Holland, and its Dutch chicken produce becomes spicier as one goes further inland from the seacoast cities.

Although recently losing some market share in China, Kentucky Fried Chicken has proven a master in adapting to emerging markets. The company now has over 4,500 stores in China and is the leading fast food restaurant. KFC learned quickly to adapt and offers menus with nearly twice as many products as US stores. Typical offerings include rice dishes, spicy chicken, fried dough sticks, soymilk drinks, wraps with local sauces, egg tarts, and fish and shrimp burgers.[7]

As with most uses of a differentiation strategy, it usually costs more for MNCs to produce and sell unique or special products for different countries throughout the world. There are extra costs to adapt each product to local requirements, such as different package sizes and colors. Thus, to succeed, a local responsiveness strategy usually requires charging higher prices to recoup the costs of tailoring a product for local needs. Customers, like the Chinese KFC patrons discussed above, will pay a higher price than offered by street vendors if they perceive an extra value in having a company's products adapted to their tastes, distribution systems, and industry structures.

A local responsive strategy is not limited to large multinationals that can afford to set up overseas subsidiaries. Even a small firm that only exports its products may use a local responsive strategy by extensively adapting its product line to different countries and cultures. However, for larger organizations with production and sales units in many countries, using a local responsive strategy often means treating foreign subsidiaries as independent businesses. Headquarters focuses on the bottom line, viewing each country as a profit center. Each country's subsidiary is free to manage its own operations following local customs, but it must generate a profit to get resources from headquarters. Besides having its own local production facilities, marketing strategy, sales staff, and distribution system, the subsidiary of the local responsive company often uses local sources of raw materials and employs mostly local people.

Multidomestic and Regional Strategies

One important problem for a locally responsive strategist is the question of how fine-grained one should focus. The extreme approach is called the **multidomestic strategy**, which means each country where you do business is treated differently. A similar but more broadly targeted approach is called the **regional strategy**. This strategy attempts to gain some of the economic efficiency and location advantages of the more global strategies combined with some of the local-adaptation advantages of the multidomestic strategy. Rather than having worldwide products and a worldwide value chain, the regional strategist manages raw material sourcing, production, marketing, and some support activities within a particular region. For example, a regional strategist might have one set of products for North America and another for Mexico and South America. Not only does this allow some cost savings similar to those of the transnational and international strategists, but it also gives the firm flexibility for regional responsiveness. Managers have the opportunity to deal regionally with regional problems, such as competitive position, product mix, promotional strategy, and sources of capital.[8]

Regional trading blocs such as the EU and NAFTA have led to more uniformity of customer needs and expectations within member nations. Trading blocs also reduce differences in government- and industry-required specifications for products. As a result, within the trading bloc, companies can use regional products and regional location advantages for all value-chain

multidomestic strategy
emphasizing local responsiveness issues at the country level

regional strategy
managing raw-material sourcing, production, marketing, and support activities within a particular region

activities. The rise of trading blocs has forced some former multidomestic strategists, especially in Europe and the US, to adopt regional strategies. For example, Procter & Gamble and DuPont have combined their subunits in Mexico, the US, and Canada into one regional organization. With this strategy, these companies gain some of the advantages of local adaptation and some of the advantages of transnationalization.

For practical considerations, many companies mix regional and country focus. There are simply too many countries, many of which are small markets, for MNCs to treat each one separately as a different market. Consequently, some companies focus on larger market countries such as the US or Japan with a multidomestic approach while treating regions such as Southeast Asia with a regional approach. The IB Emerging Market Strategic Insight below shows how a regional strategy grew beyond its borders, even creating a new French word, *delocalization*.

Romania

IB EMERGING MARKET
STRATEGIC INSIGHT

A marketplace of 22 million, a well-educated workforce, and an expanding economy with access to the Black Sea and Asia has made Romania an attractive location for investment by MNCs. As in most East European countries, the wages in Romania are quite low in comparison to Western Europe. As such, countries like Romania are also often considered as low-cost production platforms for MNCs. However, as with other former communist countries, some of the products produced during the communist years can retain a negative image. Such is or at least was the case for Dacia, a company born during the communist era but with help from Renault. In Romania, the Dacia always had a positive image. However, in the rest of Eastern Europe people remember the brand from communist times, but with a tremble.

Once Renault owned Dacia (bought in 2004) its plan was to build a cheap car for local use in Eastern Europe and perhaps sell to emerging markets—at best a domestic or regional strategy. The new model was called the Logan, although Romanian workers at the Dacia factory built it. Gérard Detourbet, the Renault CEO, notes that building a no-frills inexpensive car "would not make sense paying French or Spanish wages."

Then something interesting happened. Renault discovered that the car was being sold in France as an unofficial import. It met EU standards, so some entrepreneurs decided to see if the car would sell in Western Europe as well. The result: Renault started selling the Logan in France with sales quickly exceeding over 80,000 units. Although in North Africa and the EU the Logan is still named as a Dacia brand, it is sold through Renault dealers. With a price of €7,600 for the basic model, Mr. Detourbet notes that, even though most French buyers know that it is made in Romania, "they don't really think it's a Dacia." Now it is a stable product of Renault in France and hence the new French word, *delocalization*.

There are benefits to the Romanian Dacia factory workers as well. Their salaries were raised an average of 20 percent to about €450 a month.

Source: Adapted from www.buyusa.gov/romania; *The Economist*, 2008, "The logic of the Logan," www. economist.com, May 29.

A Brief Summary and Caveat

Exhibit 2.4 summarizes the content of the four basic multinational strategies. Students of international business should realize, however, that these strategies are general descriptions of multinational strategic options. Seldom do companies adopt a pure form of a multinational strategy. Companies with more than one business may adopt different multinational strategies for each business. Even single-business companies may alter strategies to adjust for product differences. In addition, governmental regulations regarding trade, the historical evolution of the company, and the cost of switching strategies may prevent a firm from fully implementing a particular strategy.

Given the choice, strategic options for international operations means that international managers must carefully analyze the situation for their company and its products or businesses when formulating or choosing a multinational strategy. The next section gives some diagnostic questions that international managers use to help select the best strategy for their company. These diagnostic questions guide MNCs in resolving the global–local dilemma.

Content Areas	Adaptation Strategy Content		Global Strategy Content	
	Multidomestic	**Regional**	**International**	**Transnational**
Markets	Treat each country as a separate market	Treat regions (e.g. EU) as markets	Maintain flexibility for local adaptation directed from headquarters	Maintain flexibility for local adaptation based on local learning
Products	Tailor products to best serve local customer needs in the country of location	Use similar products within major economic regions but different between regions	Use minimal local adaptation and rely on worldwide brand recognition	Use minimal local adaptation and rely on worldwide brand recognition
Marketing	Focus on local country customers using local practices of advertising, promotion, and sales	Focus on customers in the region using regional practices of advertising, promotion, and sales	Use similar marketing tactics worldwide	Use similar marketing tactics worldwide
Location of Value-chain Activities	Locate all or most value-chain activities in each country of operation	Locate all or most value-chain activities in the region which can include best sites in different countries	Limit mostly to sales and where necessary use local production replicating home country organization	Locate anywhere based on best value to company—lowest cost for highest quality

Exhibit 2.4 The Content of Multinational Strategies: From Local Adaptation to Global Integration
Source: Adapted from John B. Cullen and K. Praveen Parboteeah, 2008, *Multinational Management*, Mason, OH: Thomson South-Western, p. 265.

Choosing a Multinational Strategy: How to Solve the Global–Local Dilemma

Choosing a multinational strategy, be it transnational, multidomestic, international, regional, or some combination of these options, depends to a large degree on the balance of pressures for local adaptation and potential advantages of cost and quality from global integration. Exhibit 2.5 shows where the basic multinational strategies fall in meeting these often conflicting demands.

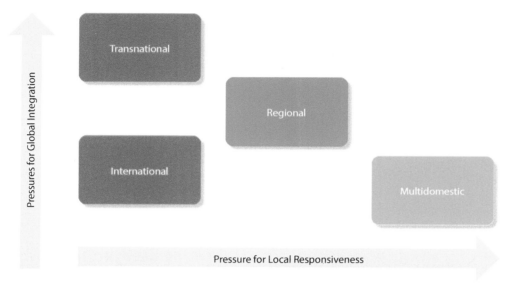

Exhibit 2.5 Solutions to the Global-Local Dilemma

One of the best ways to determine whether local adaptation pressures or global integration pressures are more important is to understand the degree of globalization of the industry in which your company competes. According to the multinational strategy expert George Yip, international managers can tell how globalized their industry is by looking at the industry's degree of globalization. You can tell how global your industry is by looking at its globalization drivers.

What are globalization drivers? **Globalization drivers** define the industry characteristics that suggest when an MNC will likely be more successful adopting more globally oriented transnational or international strategies over the MNCs that choose more locally oriented multidomestic or regional strategies.[9] The globalization drivers come from the nature of markets, cost structure of the industry, government policies in countries of operation, and what the competition is doing. For each of these areas the international strategist can ask diagnostic questions that help assess the degree of globalization of the industry and in turn suggest different multinational strategies.[10] The next section outlines these questions.

globalization drivers
conditions in an industry
that favor transnational
or international
strategies over
multidomestic or
regional strategies

Global Markets

Do Your Customers From Different Countries Have Similar Needs?   Increasingly, the needs of customers are becoming more similar around the world. However, this convergence is not the same in all industries and for all products. The consumer electronics and pharmaceutical industries tend to have customers with similar needs. For example, antibiotics are needed throughout the world. If you wear soft contact lenses, you have a need for saline solution whether you live in Moscow, Idaho, USA, or Moscow, Russia. Bausch & Lomb can provide you with this solution almost anywhere in the world.

However, in industries where cultural differences, government requirements, income, and physical climate are important, common customer needs are less likely. For example, in spite of the worldwide love of the automobile, no company has succeeded in developing one car for all markets. Difference in income levels, fuel prices, roads and highways, government regulations, and consumer preferences for styles and options have made this a difficult challenge.

Are There Global Customers?   Global customers are organizations or people who shop for their goods or services anywhere in the world. Global customers are usually organizations (not individual consumers). They search the world market for suppliers. PC manufacturers are perhaps some of the most global customers for PC components. If you looked inside your PC you would find that the components come from companies located all over the world. As we saw in Chapter 1, an important trend is that many businesses are not only acting as global customers for components but are also shopping for business services such as IT and customer service centers.

Although more rare, individual consumers can be global customers. If you have ever bought software or music from a site outside your country, you are a global customer. Many people are global customers when they fly internationally, picking a carrier based on price and convenient service rather than nationality.

Although soft contact lens wearers may not shop for saline solution worldwide, shoppers in the EU often cross borders to find lower-cost medical supplies.

Can You Transfer Marketing Activities to Other Countries?   If you can use the same brand name, advertising, packaging, and channels of distribution, the industry is more global. Brand names like Coke and Microsoft are certainly recognized worldwide and need little adaptation. Although conventional wisdom would suggest that advertisements need adjustments to local cultures, if customers respond similarly regardless of nationality, globally oriented companies can efficiently and effectively use the same strategies worldwide. Some companies like Exxon purposely developed world brands not based on any specific language to benefit from a single global advertising strategy.[11]

Marketing channels represent how products get from the producer to the ultimate consumer. Business-to-business sales (e.g. Boeing or Airbus selling to an airline) are often direct and the channel is similar worldwide. Other channels may be more complex and differ by country.

Take, for example, our example of Bausch & Lomb saline solution for soft contact lenses. Basically just salt water, it is a global product; however, in the US one can purchase saline in grocery stores and a variety of other outlets. In most European countries, saline must be sold through pharmacies so companies like Bausch & Lomb must make local adaptations in distribution. More consistent with the image of a medicine, bottles are also smaller than one might find in a US grocery store. In such cases, the more local adaptation required in the industry, the less it is globalized.

Globalization Cost Drivers

Are There Global Economies of Scale?   In some industries, such as the aircraft industry, no one country's market is sufficiently large to buy all the products of efficient production runs. To be cost-competitive, firms in this industry must go global and sell worldwide. Industries where individual unit costs drop substantially with more volume tend to be more globalized. For example, Airbus hopes to sell over 700 A380s, its super jumbo jet. Just to break even, it must sell over 500, something not achieved in the ten years since launch. The only way to do this is to sell to airlines all over the world. No one country could produce a demand of 500. Not surprisingly, as a result the civil aircraft industry is one of the most globalized.

Are There Global Sources of Low-cost Raw Materials or Components?   Usually it pays to procure your raw materials or components in low-cost countries with absolute cost advantages. The trade-off is that the supplies must be sufficiently less expensive to offset the additional costs of shipping and administration. India's Tata Steel is one of the lowest-cost producers in the world and is a source of steel material for a variety of MNCs. Tata also has access to a native iron ore that is low in phosphorus content, making it ideal for steel used in automobiles, household appliances, and computers.[12]

Are There Cheaper Sources of Skilled Labor?   Similar to the case for raw materials, the cost advantage is for companies to manufacture in low-cost countries. The move of many manufacturing plants to Eastern Europe by European companies and the move of many US manufacturing operations to China represent examples of companies seeking global sources of lower costs. Take Tower Automotive, for example. Tower is a supplier of truck frames for both Dodge and Ford. To be closer to Dodge assembly plants in Mexico and to get a much cheaper labor force, Tower moved its Dodge Ram production to Monterrey. Over 500 jobs left Ohio and were transferred to Mexico at a significant cost saving.

Are Product Development Costs High?   When product development costs are high, companies often find it more efficient to produce a few products that they can sell worldwide. Sometimes a single country or even regional market is not sufficiently large to absorb the development costs of a unique product produced for that market even if sales are high. For instance, Toyota's sales volume for its higher-end Camry sedan can recover development costs because Toyota sells the car throughout the world using a different name and standard internal components. To be sure, they vary the exterior in different countries to meet local consumer tastes and local regulations. Similarly, the major aircraft manufacturers Boeing and Airbus must sell the same products worldwide to recover the billions of dollars it takes to develop a new plane model.

Governments

Do Many Countries Have Favorable Trade Policies for the Industry?   As you read in Chapter 1, barriers are falling to trade and investment, encouraging globalization and global strategies. That is, the WTO and trading blocs such as NAFTA and the EU encourage the use of more transnational and international strategies by lowering governmental investment and trade restrictions, at least among member nations. The US government keeps a close watch on trade barriers that directly affect US companies.[13] However, government policies that allow tariffs, quotas, and subsidized local companies still exist and restrict global strategies. Rice farmers in Japan, for example, benefit from import restrictions and heavy subsidies of rice that keep foreign competition out of Japan and allow domestic prices over four times the world market price.

Do Many Countries Have Regulations that Restrict Operations in the Industry?   Government regulations regarding foreign ownership on the use of foreign components, on the ability of foreign managers and workers to work in the country, and on advertising and promotional content, make the full implementation of a transnational strategy or an international strategy more difficult. Although the general trend of globalization is reducing these regulations, they still exist in many countries for certain industries. Particularly, many countries restrict foreign ownership in defense-related industries or other industries such as agriculture when they are considered essential to the survival of the country. For instance, majority ownership by local citizens is required by airlines in the EU and most North American countries, as well as in the telecommunications industry in Japan. Additionally, foreign ownership is forbidden in the oil industry in Mexico and energy industries in Iceland.[14]

The Competition

What Strategies Do Your Competitors Use?   When transnational or international MNCs outcompete multidomestic and local competitors, it suggests two reasons to follow the more global strategists. First, if uniform products and marketing strategies are successful in a variety of different countries then the pressure is on all firms to follow similar practices. Second, since more global firms are more likely to use low-cost-country sources of raw materials and labor and can price lower than other competitors, others are forced to source from similar locations. For example, the low-cost production facilities in Asia have driven athletic shoe companies such as Nike and Germany's Adidas to move production to match competitors' costs.

What is the Volume of Imports and Exports in the Industry?   A high volume of trade in an industry is a strong indicator of a globalized industry and suggests that success is related to cross-borders. That is, it shows an already existing high level of international competition and acceptance of products from different countries. It also suggests that many companies have already taken advantage of strategies that are more global.

A Caveat

Although MNCs are finding the more global strategies increasingly popular and successful, cultural and national differences remain and the astute international manager remains sensitive to these differences. The important thing is to find a proper balance. Managing the degree of local adaptation can also be a challenge, though. The IB Emerging Market Strategic Insight below describes how Metro, the German warehouse company, tries to find the right levels of local adaptation.

A Warehouse Store in India

IB EMERGING MARKET
STRATEGIC INSIGHT

Although almost unknown in the US, Metro operates in 30 countries besides its home country, Germany. Resembling in style the US-headquartered Costco or Sam's Club, Metro stores have a bare-bones look. Metro, however, is a warehouse store that sells just to businesses. The typical store carries 50,000 items compared to the 4,000 of a Costco. Metro's business model is to source locally, especially for food.

Metro has a cash-and-carry format that works well for small entrepreneurs in emerging markets. In places like India and China, where small enterprises are everywhere, it provides a centralized alternative to traditional specialized markets. The breadth of its product offerings and the cash-and-carry format serve the emerging markets exceptionally well. Most of Metro's recent growth is in Asia and the transition economies in Eastern Europe. In addition, as a wholesaler it often avoids prohibitions on foreign retailers.

Although the business model seems to work for most emerging market nations, local adaptations are usually required. When Metro opened a store in Saigon, local manager James Scott, a British expatriate, tried to set up Metro's standard procurement systems: sign a contract, send orders by fax, take payments by checks. What he found was that farmers didn't have fax machines, didn't have bank accounts, and had never seen contracts. After fax lessons, he convinced the farmers to open accounts and sign the contracts. With his sourcing set up, Scott still had more to learn. Customers ripped open shrink-wrapped tomatoes. "They thought we were hiding rotten fruit underneath," noted Scott. Fruit is re-stacked in open stalls.

Even with success in a variety of emerging market countries, Hans-Joachim Körber, CEO of Metro and the force behind Metro's international strategy, admits "We were a bit naïve" when they set up shop in Shanghai. For example, Körber notes that Metro had to quickly install tanks for live snakes, snails, and frogs. "We learned that in China fresh means alive."

Recently, Metro has struggled in some markets not because of its strategies but because of socio-political upheavals. Turmoil around the world battered the company and forced the chain to retrench and focus on Europe. One major hit was a €1 billion exchange-rate loss based on the Russian ruble's slide due to Western country sanctions. Recent crises in many markets including Russia, Greece, and Egypt severely hurt results. The Metro case shows that emerging markets have great potential but often great risks.

Source: Adapted from Deborah Orr, 2005, "Don't wrap the veggies," *Forbes*, April 18; Ellen Emmerentze Jervell, 2016, "German supermarket Metro finds growth at home: Company scales back from emerging nations to focus on Europe," *Wall Street Journal*, January 21.

How to Make the Transnational or International Choice

When companies compete in more globalized industries, transnational and international MNCs usually are more successful than multidomestic or regional strategists. They can usually offer cheaper or higher-quality products or services by using uniform product/services and marketing, or lower-cost or higher-quality sourcing. How then do international managers decide whether to be more transnational or international in strategy?

To select a more transnational strategy over a more international strategy, the international manager must believe that the benefits of dispersing value-chain activities worldwide offset the costs of coordinating a more complex organization. For example, with a more transnational approach, a company may do R&D in one country, parts manufacturing in another, final assembly in another, and sales in a fourth. Coordination of these activities across national borders and in different parts of the world is costly and difficult. The transnational strategist, however, anticipates that the benefits of these dispersed activities in low-cost or high-quality labor and raw materials will offset the difficulties and costs of coordination to produce better or cheaper products.

In contrast to the transnational strategist, the international business manager adopting a more international strategy believes that centralizing key activities such as R&D reduces coordination costs and gives economies of scale. An economy of scale means that it is more efficient to do all of one activity in one place. The cost savings from economies of scale then offset the lower costs or high-quality raw materials or labor that the transnationalist can find by locating worldwide. Traditionally, Boeing adopted more of an international strategy, doing research and development for commercial aircraft and most manufacturing in its plants in the US.

In the reality of the world's competitive landscape, most major multinational corporations, such as IBM, GE, and Siemens, do not adopt a pure international or transnational strategy. Instead, they blend both approaches depending on the businesses they own or the products they are producing. However, as information systems and communications systems become more sophisticated, many of the traditional international firms are developing more transnational characteristics. For example, with the Dreamliner—a high-tech plane built from new composite material and new engine technologies—Boeing moved away from its purer international strategy and is manufacturing the majority of the plane's components using supplier composite production expertise located in Japan and China.

Company-Situation Analysis and the Multinational Strategy Choice

Each company faces its own unique situation in the competitive business world. In addition to looking at the globalization of their industry, managers must understand what *their* particular company can and cannot do best, realistically assessing their company's resources and strategic capabilities. In addition, in formulating their multinational strategies, they must identify the opportunities or threats that globalization poses to their company's unique position in the industry. The globalization drivers represent a balance sheet of forces in an industry that suggests the potential success of more transnational or international strategies or more regional or multidomestic strategies. Thus, the diagnostic questions based on the globalization drivers help international managers formulate better strategies to compete globally or locally.

In addition to the globalization drivers external to the MNC, the location of the firm's competitive advantage in the value chain influences the choice of a multinational strategy.

When an MNC has competitive advantages from primarily upstream in the value chain, as for example from low-cost or high-quality design, engineering, and manufacturing, it can often generalize these advantages to many markets with similar high-quality products. A transnational strategy or an international strategy usually follows. For example, Mercedes-Benz and BMW use their world-class designs to sell similar products in all major markets. In contrast, other types of MNCs generally focus most of their value downstream—in marketing, sales, and service. Such MNCs have natural local adaptation strengths and are more likely to adopt a more multidomestic or regional strategy, serving each market uniquely.

Of course, competing internationally is complex and a company's competitive strengths may not align directly with the degree of globalization in the industry. Some firms may compete in industries with strong globalization drivers, yet their competitive strengths are in downstream

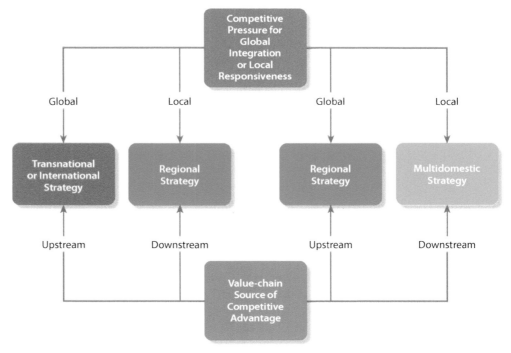

Exhibit 2.6 Pressure for Global Integration or Local Responsiveness, Value-chain Sources of Competitive Advantage, and Multinational Strategy Choices

value-chain activities, such as after-market service. Other MNCs may compete in industries with weak globalization drivers and thus weaker pressures, yet be stronger in manufacturing and R&D rather than in customer service. When facing such misaligned situations, MNCs often select a regional strategy as a compromise. For the MNC with upstream strengths, such as high-quality production that faces pressure for local adaptation, a more regional strategy allows: (1) some use of similar products, and (2) some downstream adaptation to regional differences. For the MNC with downstream competitive strengths, such as after-market service, facing pressure for globalization, a more regional strategy allows: (1) some adaptation of customer interactions to more local markets, and (2) some ability to respond to the globalization driver of lower costs by the economies of scale produced by activities such as centralized purchasing and uniform products.

Exhibit 2.6 shows how the location of strengths within the value chain combine with the pressures for globalization or local responsiveness and lead to different multinational strategies.

Successful firms monitor not only their industry, which is usually called the operating environment, but also the broader environment, which is usually called the general environment. The general environment includes all the social institutions (e.g. economy, political system) and cultural context discussed earlier as the national context. It also includes broad issues of technological change, such as the evolution of the Internet that has provided opportunities for many new business forms as well as threats to established organizations.

Chapter Review

Beyond the traditional strategic questions facing all managers, the international manager, in both large and small companies, must confront the global–local dilemma. Markets, costs, governments, and the competition drive the choice of a solution. As the world becomes more globalized (see Chapter 1), we are seeing more companies choosing transnational or international strategies to compete with low cost and high quality. However, cultural and other national differences remain, and these will continue to provide opportunities to companies with more local or regional orientations.

As a form of differentiation—meeting unique customer needs—there are benefits to favoring the more local responsiveness-oriented strategies. That is, the multidomestic or regional strategy tailors the product or service to meet the unique needs of customers in a country or region. Because you deliver unique products or services for each country, the pure multidomestic strategy is the most costly. However, it allows an MNC the most latitude to handle differences in culture, language, and political and legal systems. The regional strategy is less costly as it is only a partial adaptation to local differences, allowing the use of more similar products and lower-cost or higher-quality production within the region. In this way, adaptation to regional differences is balanced against the efficiencies of doing things similarly within the region.

The goal for international and transnational strategists is to produce high-quality products as efficiently as possible. Typically, MNCs using these strategies or a mix of the two try to have global products with global marketing. Differing from the international strategist, the MNC with a more transnational strategy uses worldwide locations or platforms for its value-chain activities to maximize efficiency and quality. That is, the more transnational strategies will look to do anything anywhere if it makes good business sense. They are particularly attracted to offshoring activities to the low-cost countries.

The complexities of choosing multinational strategies in an ever-globalizing economy represent considerable challenges to international managers. To name only a few issues, for example, in choosing a multinational strategy the international manager must consider the type of the product or service (e.g. can it be global?), the government and political systems where the MNC has units (e.g. how safe are the assets?), the financial risk of the investment (e.g. what are the expected returns?), and the needs of the company to control operations (e.g. can we really do it right 2,000 miles away?). The IB Emerging Market Strategic Insight in this chapter have shown you several examples of how practicing international managers in real companies faced and responded to the challenges of formulating multinational strategies.

MNCs execute multinational strategies in a dynamic global context related to relationships among governments, patterns of trade and investments, foreign exchange markets, and global capital markets. This chapter dealt very briefly with some of these issues in terms of multinational strategy formulation and content. In the next section, you will see in much more detail how this dynamic global context influences the playing field in which companies compete internationally.

Discussion Questions

1   Discuss the conditions where a multidomestic or regional strategy might perform better than a transnational or international strategy. Consider if emerging market countries are more suitable for a multidomestic strategy.

2   Explain how global integration and local responsiveness might be successful in the same industry.

3   Contrast the transnational and international strategies in their approach to location advantages.

4   Using the diagnostic questions in the chapter, analyze the globalization potential of the "big box" (e.g. Walmart, Costco, Metro) retail trade industry.

5   Do the same as in Question 4 but for an industry of your choice.

6   Discuss how a small manufacturing company might adopt some aspects of international and transnational strategies.

International Business Skill Builder

Identifying the Value-chain and Multinational Strategies

Step 1: Choose a global industry such as the automobile industry or the cell-phone industry and identify two major competitors in the industry.

Step 2: Research the selected companies in the popular business press and make a list of their major value-chain activities.

Step 3: For each company, using the matrix below, identify the major geographical locations of these value-chain activities. Are they in the home country? Or are they dispersed around the globe? How are emerging market countries used in the strategies?

Value-chain Activity	Home Country	Location 1	Location 2	Location 3
R&D				
Input Logistics				
Global Products				
Operations				
Marketing and Sales				
Output Logistics				
After-market Service				

Step 4: For each company, write an analysis showing how the company attempts to gain a competitive advantage by its choice of value-chain locations. What is its predominant multinational strategy?

Chapter Internet Activity

Explore the Internet sites of three companies noted in the chapter. Go to the investor relations section in the sites and look for information on their multinational strategies. Often, the annual report contains a description of the company's strategy. See if you can tell the degree to which the company uses primarily a local responsiveness or global integration strategy.

Key Concepts

- absolute advantage
- global integration strategy
- global platform
- global–local dilemma
- globalization drivers
- international strategies
- local responsiveness strategy

- location advantages
- multidomestic strategy
- offshoring
- outsourcing
- regional strategy
- transnational strategy
- value chain

CASE 2

BUSINESS > INTERNATIONAL

Jollibee Foods Corporation

Jollibee Foods Corporation operates a number of different concept restaurants in the Philippines, and beyond. From its core business, a McDonald's-like concept restaurant, Jollibee has expanded into a pizza chain, fast food Chinese restaurants, bakeries, and grilled chicken. The company has been keen to experiment with new food concepts, yet all have been successful. Jollibee competes well with multinationals in the Philippines, and has begun a large expansion into the international market, including the United States. The flagship brand, Jollibee, with its distinctive company mascot, a large red and yellow bumble bee, and additional product concepts dreams of becoming a global powerhouse in the global restaurant industry.

THE PHILIPPINES

The Republic of the Philippines is a country in Southeast Asia consisting of over 7,000 islands. The Philippines was "discovered" by Ferdinand Magellan in 1521, who claimed the islands for Spain. While Magellan met his death soon after arriving in the Philippines, the country was under

CASE 2
cont'd

Spanish control for a number of years. The Philippines came under the rule of the United States in 1898, when Admiral Dewey defeated the Spanish, and Spain ceded the islands under the Treaty of Paris. While Tagalog, or Filipino, is the official language of the Philippines, English is widely spoken, especially among educated Filipinos. In 1935 the Philippines became a self-governing commonwealth, and gained complete independence in 1946. After a number of different administrations, strongman Ferdinand Marcos ruled the country for a number of years and maintained strong ties with the United States. With increasing discontentment of the Filipino people, a "people's revolution" occurred, and Marcos was forced to leave the country. Political instability resulted for a time, however, democracy quickly took a firm hold in the Philippines. The democracy could be described as somewhat fragile, suffering from a number of cases of political corruption and attempted coups.

The population of the Philippines is approximately 94 million, with an estimated population growth rate of 2 percent per year. The Filipino people are a mix of Malay, Indonesian, and Spanish, with a significant Chinese ancestry population. The ethnic Chinese have been very influential in the Filipino economy. Filipino culture is a mix of Asian, Spanish, and American cultural values. The economy of the Philippines has been one of the fasting growing economies in Asia with a GDP growth for 2015 of 6 percent. Per capita GDP is $2,920 (PPP). The currency of the Philippines is the peso (PHP) and has traded in an approximate range of 47 to 41 PHP per US dollar during the past five years.

HISTORY AND MISSION OF JOLLIBEE

What would eventually become Jollibee Foods was an ice cream parlor named Magnolia, started by Tony Tan in 1975 as a family-based business. Eventually the company began offering hot meals and sandwiches, and from this operation the concept of a fast food hamburger business was developed. From these humble beginnings, Jollibee has expanded over the years, both in terms of revenue, and concentric diversification. In 1978 the company began a bakery, and by 1986 Jollibee opened its first international operation in Taiwan. With the acquisition and development of additional restaurant concepts, Jollibee moved into the pizza business, breakfast cafés, Chinese fast food, and the teahouse business. Much of this diversification has come in recent years. While mostly known for its Jollibee hamburger franchise, the company has diversified into many additional fast food areas, and expanded significantly in terms of outlets and geographical coverage.

The mission of Jollibee Foods is stated as: *To serve great tasting food, bringing the joy of eating to everyone.* Jollibee has a vision statement which not only expresses its current values, but also addresses its aspirations.

CASE 2
cont'd

VISION

We excel in providing great tasting food that meets local preferences better than anyone.

We provide superior dining experience, through FSC (Food, Service, Cleanliness) excellence in every encounter.

We are the most cost efficient restaurant company in our business segments, allowing us to price at the most popular levels.

Our people are passionate about their work and thrive in a high performance culture.

We strive to become a model corporate citizen by being relevant to the communities we serve.

Our brands are either #1 or #2 in each of our market segments.

It is the vision of JFC to become one of the three largest and most profitable restaurant companies in the world by 2020.

Jollibee makes itself well-known in the Philippines through extensive advertising, hiring of celebrity endorsers with wholesome images, and through its charitable works.

STRATEGIC BUSINESS UNITS AND EXPANSION

Jollibee Foods Corporation (JFC) consists of a number of SBUs which cut across different food groups. At the core of JFC is Jollibee, the McDonald's-like hamburger restaurant. The unit sells a standard fare of lunch and breakfast items, but adds a local touch with products such as the Amazing Aloha Burger (slice of pineapple on top of a burger), the Jolly Hotdog Taco Style, Chickjoy with Rice, and Palabok (noodles with a spicy sauce, boiled egg, shrimp, ground pork). Jollibee competes with McDonald's on the basis of price, local product offerings, and national identity. JFC also owns Chow King, a Chinese fast food restaurant chain with operations in a number of countries. The firm has a pizza restaurant chain called Greenwich. In addition, JFC owns a bakery chain called Red Ribbon, and a grilled chicken and fish restaurant called Mang Inasal. In 2011 JFC purchased the Burger King Franchise for the Philippines and operates a number of Burger King restaurants throughout the Philippines. In addition JFC is experimenting with various restaurant concepts and joint ventures in a number of neighboring countries including China, Vietnam, Cambodia, and Indonesia.

JFC is looking internationally to increase sales. JFC operates restaurants in the Philippines, Bahrain, Brunei, Vietnam, Hong Kong, China, Macau, Saudi Arabia, Qatar, Dubai, Kuwait, and the United States. The units in the USA are located in areas with large Filipino-American populations. JFC feels that international expansion is important not only to grow the company, but because: "Being open to different cultures widens one's spectrum of tastes, styles, and ways of

CASE 2
cont'd

seeing food." JFC feels that international expansion provides for organizational learning, and the leveraging of this learning into new markets. JFC is always searching for new product concepts, including a failed attempt with a store called Tio Pepe Karinderia. This restaurant concept served very low-priced typical Filipino dishes, and sought to compete with street vendors by offering a more hygienic and cost-efficient operation. JFC could be called a firm with a "bias for action" in that the company moves quickly when it sees an opportunity and isn't afraid of failure.

LOOKING AHEAD

As Jollibee looks to the future it seeks greater expansion opportunities. The company plans on opening more stores, and in more markets. Jollibee has experienced great success in its relatively short history. In 2015 JFC reported sales of 130.7 billion (PHP), an increase of 10.9 percent over the previous year. The company continues to open new stores both domestically and abroad. Although inflation has dropped to around 2–3 percent in the Philippines, and the country's credit rating was recently upgraded, JFC operates in a somewhat volatile and politically risky environment. In addition, the flagship brand must compete with McDonald's as both continue to open more new stores in the Philippines. According to Tony Lopez of the *Manila Times*, McDonald's beats Jollibee in revenue per store, and has been gaining ground through better customer service, better kid's meals, and better cost and supply chain management. McDonald's has the advantage of being an American company and having a degree of status over Jollibee in the Philippines. Jollibee remains the largest fast food chain in the Philippines and has high hopes of capturing the international market in the years ahead.

CASE DISCUSSION POINTS:

1   What advantages does a domestic firm have over an MNC in its local market?
2   Can Jollibee Foods Corporation continue to leverage its brands and products in other geographic markets successfully? Explain.
3   What strategic direction would you suggest for Jollibee Foods Corporation?

Source: S. Chae, 2007, "Jollibee serves up fast food, Filipino-style: Chicken, rice noodles a nice change," *Tribune Business News*, November 8; L. Cuevas-Miel, 2008, "Fast-food giant plans new round of price hikes," *Tribune Business News*, May 15; Jollibee Foods Corporation Annual Report 2012; T. Lopez, 2007, "McDo vs. Jollibee," *The Manila Times*, August 14; R. Rubio, 2007, "Jollibee ventures into karinderia concept," *Business World*, July 25; www.jollibee.com.ph, accessed on June 23, 2016; www.state.gov. "Country background notes: Philippines," accessed on June 3, 2016; www.economywatch.com, January 3, 2014.

Case prepared by Charles A. Rarick

Notes

1 Sumatra Ghoshal, 1987, "Global strategy: An organizing framework," *Strategic Management Journal*, 8, pp. 424–440.

2 Michael E. Porter, 1986, "Changing patterns of international competition," *California Management Review*, 28, p. 2; Michael E. Porter, 1990, *Competitive Advantage of Nations*, New York: Free Press.

3 Michael E. Porter, 1985, *Competitive Advantage: Creating and Sustaining Superior Performance*, New York: Free Press.

4 C. A. Bartlett and S. Ghoshal, 1990, *Managing Across Borders: The Transnational Solution*, Boston, MA: Harvard Business School Press.

5 Michael E. Porter, 1985, *Competitive Advantage: Creating and Sustaining Superior Performance*, New York: Free Press.

6 Charles Hill, 2005, *International Business: Competing in the Global Marketplace*, Burr Ridge, IL: Irwin.

7 "Managing brands in global markets: One size doesn't fit all," http://knowledge.wharton.upenn.edu/article/1206.cfm, 2005.

8 Allen J. Morrison, David A. Ricks and Kendall Roth, 1991, "Globalization versus regionalization: Which way for the multinational?" *Organizational Dynamics*, Winter, pp. 17–29.

9 George S. Yip, 2002, *Total Global Strategy II*, Englewood Cliffs, NJ: Prentice Hall.

10 George S. Yip, 2002, *Total Global Strategy II*, Englewood Cliffs, NJ: Prentice Hall.

11 George S. Yip, 2002, *Total Global Strategy II*, Englewood Cliffs, NJ: Prentice Hall.

12 www.tata.com

13 www.ustr.gov

14 OECD, 2003, "Foreign direct investment restrictions in OECD countries," *OECD Economic Outlook*, June.

THE GLOBAL CONTEXT OF MULTINATIONAL COMPETITIVE STRATEGY

CHAPTER 3

Global and Regional Economic Integration

An Evolving Competitive Landscape

After reading this chapter you should be able to:

- Know the history of GATT and the WTO.

- Understand how WTO agreements can influence your company and its multinational strategies.

- Understand the possible trade implications of regional trade agreements.

- Know the types of regional trade agreements.

- Be familiar with the nature and structure of the major regional trade agreements in the world.

- Be aware of how the WTO and regional trade agreements affect emerging economies in positive and negative ways.

International Business   *Preview IB Emerging Market Strategic Insight*

Let the Wines Pour In: Trade Agreements with China Open the Bottles

Prior to its joining the World Trade Organization, selling wine in China was difficult. Changyu, Dynasty, Great Wall, and Tonghua, the top Chinese wine brands, controlled over 60 percent of the wine market. Why? Import tariffs on foreign wine were 65 percent, making it very difficult for foreign wine makers to sell wine at a price the Chinese consumers could afford. Although there are still some tariffs for imports, they are drastically lower now.

Although wine making in China can be traced back over 8,000 years, the oldest in the world, and alcoholic drinks are a ritual part of Chinese celebrations, wine now makes up only a small percentage of the alcoholic drinks market. However, in the booming Chinese economy wine is becoming a fashionable drink for the emerging affluent Chinese. The reduction in tariffs combined with the growing Chinese attraction to wine is encouraging foreign vintners to go to China. For example, marketing and sales director Doyle Hinman of Henry Estate Winery in Roseburg, Oregon, notes, "If we can get just a fraction of a fraction of a fraction of their 1.3 billion people to buy our wines, it will be huge business for us." There are an estimated 2+ billion customers for the import wine market. However, convincing consumers to spend high prices for top-quality wine remains a challenge in a country where the average bottle costs less than two dollars and a culture of wine drinking is a novelty.

Currently the wine import business into China is booming reaching $1 billion in just the first half of 2016. The most rapidly growing channel for importing wine into China is with Internet sales, considering that over half of Chinese wine purchases are done online. Tmall, the Alibaba cross-border shopping site held it first wine-specific sale on September 9, 2016. The US industry was represented by Gallo and Mondavi. In spite of Tmall's 9-9 International Global Wine and Spirits Festival Day, China remains a challenge for US winemakers as Chinese consumers are more familiar with French wines, with over 42 percent of imports being French, and US wines are still hit with a 14 percent tariff. Based on a free trade agreement, China will abolish all tariffs for Australian wine in 2019.

Source: Adapted from Yilu Zhao, 2003, "Inroads in China for wine importers," *New York Times*, December 28, pp. 3, 5; *Columbian*, 2004, "Oregon wine hits China," December 12, p. E2; Zhang Lu, 2004, "Low tariffs help foreign wines pour in," *China Daily*, December 23, p. 11; Justine Lau, 2005, "Domestic wines hit the spot: Changing tastes have opened up the market for Western-style wines," *Financial Times*, January 19, p. 9; Jeannie Cho Lee, 2016, "Alibaba's Jack Ma bets big on China's first online wine festival," September 8, *Forbes*, www.forbes.com; Elizabeth Weise, 2016, "Alibaba makes case for a wine sale with a good Chinese pun," *USA Today*, September 9, www.usatoday.com; www.decanterchina.com/en/news/china-wine-imports-rise-strongly-in-2015

The Preview IB Emerging Market Strategic Insight shows how changes in trade barriers can open up new markets for different products. Of course, as you learned in Chapter 1, trade has never been as open as it is today. However, not all products or services are free from government restrictions regarding importing or exporting. Some governments use trade regulations to protect key or emerging industries such as defense contracting. Not all countries, including some big countries such as Russia, participate fully in the efforts to reduce world trade barriers. As such, since trade regulations change frequently, international managers must monitor and understand how evolving government trade policies affect their operations. In this chapter you will see some of the history of how we arrived at our present system and how world trade negotiations are structured and continue to evolve.

Dropping Barriers to World Trade: GATT and the WTO

tariffs
taxes applied to imported or exported goods

In 1947, faced with the prospect of rebuilding world trade after World War II, several nations began negotiating to limit worldwide tariffs and to encourage free trade. **Tariffs** are taxes applied to imported or exported goods. A tariff is also known as a customs duty. The word "tariff" comes from Tenerife, which is the name of an island in the Canary Islands. Folklore suggests that local Tenerife pirates forced passing ships to pay a fee to sail in the local waters around the island.[1]

Immediately after World War II, tariffs averaged 45 percent worldwide, adding a huge price increase for goods from other countries and severely limiting world trade. Eight rounds of tariff negotiations reduced the average worldwide tariffs on manufactured goods from 45 percent to less than 7 percent. These negotiations were known as the **General Agreement on Tariffs and Trade (GATT)**.

During this time, world trade grew dramatically. That is, much like the entry of import wine companies into China, as shown in the Preview IB Emerging Market Strategic Insight, reduced tariffs prompted more companies to see opportunities to enter foreign markets where they could compete on an equal footing with domestic companies.

GATT created the basic principle of nondiscrimination, with the intent to put all the signing nations on an equal footing for trade and to reduce trade barriers. The **principle of nondiscrimination** requires that trade agreements between any two nations apply to all GATT signers. That is, signing nations must give to all other GATT members the same favorable treatment that they give to any other nation. This favorable treatment is now called normal trade relations, although it was once called most favored nation treatment. Nondiscrimination also means that participants must treat industries from other nations no differently than the same industries in one's own country. Once foreign products enter the market they must be treated the same as domestic products.

Exhibit 3.1 shows the chronology of the GATT negotiations and the subjects covered at each stage.

After the initial success of the Geneva round of negotiations, progress on tariff reductions slowed considerably. This occurred because many tariff negotiations became bilateral. Bilateral trade negotiations take place between pairs of countries agreeing to reduce tariffs on particular products. An important change occurred in the Kennedy round, so named after President Kennedy, who was the driving force behind the negotiations. At the Kennedy round, negotiations became multilateral, meaning several countries at once. Multilateral trade negotiations are more efficient because all the group members agree at once to reduce tariffs on broad categories of goods.

Prior to the Tokyo round of negotiations, the GATT countries worked only on reducing trade barriers based on tariffs. A significant change with this negotiation round was the reduction in trade barriers of other forms. Tariffs are not the only barriers countries use to protect domestic industries. Non-tariff barriers to trade include, for example:

- State subsidies that give some companies an advantage in the international market. Boeing accuses Airbus of having unfair subsidies from European countries to design new aircraft.
- Quotas that limit the amount of imports and/or exports. The US has often used quotas to limit the amount of imports of certain product types. As a strategy to avoid more restrictive trade barriers, the Japanese with automobiles in the 1970s and more recently the Chinese with textiles used voluntary quotas to restrict their imports into the US.
- National regulations related to health and safety. The European Union restricts the sale of genetically modified foods or beef treated with growth hormones. This prevents the sale of many US-produced agricultural goods.
- "Buy national" policies. These can require governments to procure from own-country suppliers and can also be nationalistic campaigns to encourage citizens to buy local.
- These and other trade-restricting techniques were addressed in the Tokyo round.

General Agreement on Tariffs and Trade (GATT) eight rounds of tariff negotiations that reduced the average worldwide tariffs on manufactured goods from 45 percent to less than 7 percent

principle of nondiscrimination requires that trade agreements between any two nations apply to all GATT signers

Name of Round	Year	Countries Participating	Major Focus of Negotiations
Geneva	1947	23	Tariffs
Annecy	1949	13	Tariffs
Torquay	1951	38	Tariffs
Geneva	1956	26	Tariffs
Dillon	1960–1961	26	Tariffs
Kennedy	1964–1967	62	Tariffs and anti-dumping measures
Tokyo	1973–1979	102	Tariffs, non-tariff measures, partial agreements by some countries on more general frameworks for trade
Uruguay	1986–1993	123	Tariffs, non-tariff measures, rules, services, intellectual property, dispute settlement, textiles, agriculture, creation of WTO, etc.
Doha	2001–present	153	Tariffs, agriculture, services, intellectual property, government procurement, anti-dumping, regional trade agreements, e-commerce, trade and environment, small economies

Exhibit 3.1 A Chronology of GATT and the WTO

Source: Adapted from www.wto.org/english/thewto_e/whatis_e/tif_e/fact4_e.htm#rounds

The final round of the GATT was the Uruguay round. Negotiations in Uruguay began in 1986 and ended in 1993 with agreements to reduce tariffs even further, liberalize trade in agriculture and services, and eliminate some non-tariff barriers to international trade, such as excessive use of health regulations to keep out imports.[2] Most importantly, the Uruguay talks also established the **World Trade Organization (WTO)** to succeed GATT.

Differing from GATT, which, as we have seen, is a series of governmental agreements, the WTO is a formal organizational structure for continued negotiations and for settling trade disputes among member nations. There are now 164 nations in the WTO, up from 92 when the 1986 GATT talks began, including nearly all emerging economies. Nineteen more countries seek WTO membership, called "ascension" in WTO terminology.[3] Nearly all of the world's trade occurs among WTO member countries.

As an organization, the WTO has several objectives.[4] These include:

- administering trade agreements based on GATT and those negotiated later;
- cooperating with other international organizations such as the UN and the World Bank;
- providing technical assistance and training for developing countries;
- monitoring the trade policies of member nations;
- providing a forum for current and future trade negotiations;
- adjudicating trade disputes.

Exhibits 3.2 and 3.3 show, respectively, descriptions of the basic functions and agreements of the WTO and its organizational structure.

The most recent series of talks began in 2001. Members met in Doha, Qatar, in what are now called the Doha talks, with the wide-ranging objectives of trade reduction, but with particular emphasis on reducing trade barriers for food and reducing the developed world's subsidies for farmers. The talks are ongoing. However, the goal of reducing agricultural subsidies has proven difficult to attain as the developed nations such as the US have resisted eliminating subsidies to farmers, a sensitive political issue in many countries.

The US pays farmers approximately $20 billion in subsidies per year. The subsidies peaked in 2000 at $32.3 billion, according to the US Department of Agriculture. The EU is an even bigger

World Trade Organization (WTO) a formal structure for continued negotiations and for settling trade disputes among nations

spender, paying out farmers roughly $59 billion. Japan is another big farm subsidizer, particularly in rice. In the early 2000s, Brazil and a host of other countries took the issue of US cotton subsidies to the WTO, arguing that the United States exceeds allowable subsidy levels. According to the International Food Policy Research Institute, a Washington DC group funded partly by the World Bank, subsidies by industrialized nations cost developing countries about $24 billion annually in lost income. It took until 2014 for the issue to be finally settled and the US agreed to cap its cotton subsidies.[5] However, as the BRIC Insight below shows it is not just the developed world that uses farm subsidies to benefit their local agricultural industry.[6]

The US Challenges China's Farm Subsidies in the WTO

BRIC INSIGHT

In September 2016 the US launched a complaint to the WTO accusing China of unfair agricultural subsidies for three crops—wheat, corn, and rice. The complaint alleged that China's "excessive government support" hurts US farmers. Such support encourages farmers to overproduce beyond market demand and raises prices above market levels. US officials claim that China exceeded its allowable limits on subsidies in the three crops by over $100 billion in 2015. The subsidies work by the Chinese government buying rice, wheat, and corn at inflated minimum prices during harvest season. Since 2009 this is just one of 29 complaints to the WTO regarding China's trade policies.

Paradoxically, China is projected to pass Canada as the largest export market for agricultural commodities. As the leading agricultural exporter in the world, the US typically exports over $20 billion worth of agricultural products to China a year. But the US Department of Agriculture Secretary Tom Vilsack said "But we could be doing much better, particularly if our grain exports could compete in China on a level playing field."

Source: Adapted from Jeff Daniels, 2016, "US files trade complaint over China's 'excessive' ag subsidies," www.cnbc.com/2016/09/13/us-files-trade-complaint-over-chinas-excessive-ag-subsidies.html; Shawn Donnan, 2016, "US takes China to WTO over farm subsidies," *Financial Times*, September 13, www.ft.com/content/8f791bfe-79c6-11e6-97ae-647294649b28

WTO Functions	Goods	Services	Intellectual Property
Basic Agreements	GATT	GATS	TRIPS
	General Agreements on Tariffs and Trade	General Agreement on Trade in Services	Trade Related Aspects of Intellectual Property Rights
Dispute Settlement	DISPUTE SETTLEMENT BODY		
Transparency	TRADE POLICY REVIEWS OF COUNTRY COMPLIANCE		

Exhibit 3.2 WTO Agreements and Functions
Source: Adapted from www.wto.org/english/thewto_e/whatis_e/tif_e/agrm1_e.htm, 2016.

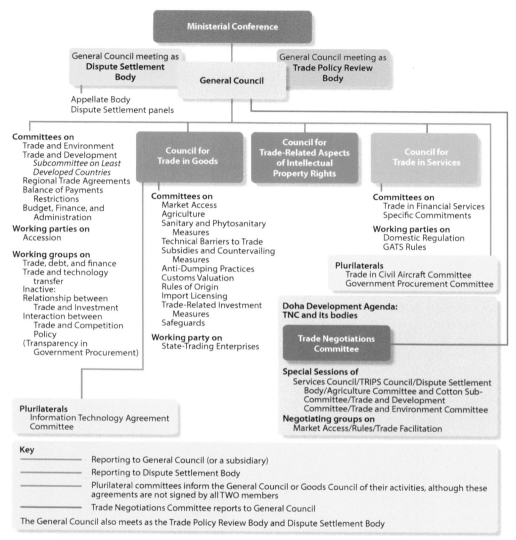

Exhibit 3.3 WTO Structure

All WTO members may participate in all councils, committees, etc., except Appellate Body, Dispute Settlement panels, and plurilateral committees.

Source: www.wto.org/english/thewto_e/whatis_e/tif_e/organigram_e.pdf

Quotas on textiles (fabrics for clothing and other cloth goods), in contrast to the continuing battle over agricultural products, ended on January 1, 2005. The result was an immediate surge in textile imports into the US and the EU. However, so large was this growth that both the EU and the US negotiated or imposed import limitations under WTO rules that allow temporary controls to avoid extreme market disruption.[7]

The IB Emerging Market Strategic Insight below shows how countries such as India can follow WTO rules and still affect the strategic choices of domestic and foreign pharmaceuticals.

How the WTO Can Influence Your Strategy

IB EMERGING MARKET
STRATEGIC INSIGHT

Prior to entering the WTO India did not have patent protection for pharmaceutical products. The result was the Indian pharmaceutical companies were free to copy expensive drugs developed and patented by leading pharmaceutical companies from around the world. Indian companies became the leading generic drug producers in the world providing cheaper drugs for their own people and for many developing countries.

When India did join the WTO it agreed to following WTO rules and became subject to the TRIPS (Trade Related Aspects of Intellectual Property Rights) agreement. This required patent protection for pharmaceuticals in India and other emerging economies. With the TRIPS agreement coming online in 2005, Big Pharma essentially had worldwide protection for its products. Wealthy countries like the US and Switzerland were proponents of the agreement and most experts agree they benefited to the detriment of poorer countries.

Playing within the WTO rules India developed laws that changed the game for the foreign MNCs. The result: Novartis lost a six-year court case disallowing them to make small changes to a drug and hence get a new 20-year patent, called an "ever greening" strategy. Around the same time, Bayer's cancer drug Nexavar was required to take the status of a compulsory license. This status withdraws patent protection for drugs deemed necessary for public health and prohibitively expensive and allows copying of such drugs.

Source: Adapted from William Bennett, 2014, "Indian pharmaceutical patent law and the effects of Novartis Ag v. Union of India," *Washington University Global Studies Law Review*, *13*(3); Tim Smedley, 2013, "Patent wars: Has India taken on Big Pharma and won?" *The Guardian*, May 14.

Is free trade working? The WTO thinks so and the data seem to support its conclusion. Since the early GATT agreements, world trade has grown at more than four times the output of the world's gross domestic product. This suggests that the world's economies are increasingly more intertwined and mutually stimulated.

There are, however, critics. Some argue that the WTO favors the developed nations, because it is more difficult for poorer nations to compete in a non-regulated world. Environmentalists note that free trade encourages large MNCs to move environmentally damaging production to poorer and often environmentally sensitive countries. That is, commercial interests have priority over the environment, health, and safety. Labor unions see free trade leading to the migration of jobs from higher-wage countries to lower-wage countries. You can see the WTO's counter-arguments on their website at www.wto.org.

The WTO trade agreements alter the competitive landscape for MNCs. International managers must be aware of how trade policies influence their industries and companies. The IB Emerging Market Strategic Insights above and below show how the WTO influences the strategies of Big Pharma and Indian pharmaceutical companies.

Free trade also brings into conflict different policies on the protection of the environment and sustainability practices. In the Emerging Market Ethical Challenge box you will see how different perspectives on the environmental and human safety of genetically modified organisms come into conflict in a WTO trade dispute.

Trade and the Environmental Threat of Genetically Modified Organisms (GMOs)

Often called genetic engineering or biotechnology, GMOs are created by taking genetic material from one organism and merging it with another. This is different from selective breeding that people have used for centuries to allow us to have different varieties of food and animals. It is different because it is possible to take genetic material from one species and merge it with another: for example, put a plant gene into a fish. In traditional selective breeding, only closely related species can be interbred.

Because GMOs are relatively new, countries disagree on how to protect the environment and health from potential and perhaps yet unknown dangers that might occur as these organisms enter the food chain and our diets. When countries have different regulations to test and approve procedures to take GMOs and their products on the market, trade problems can occur. Companies from countries who hope to sell GMO plants, food, and animals argue that blocking GMOs is just another form of trade protection. Some emerging market countries resent the power of the EU to block potential sales of GMO products. Although the US has the largest proportion of GMO crops, China and Argentina are increasing their production.

In a recent case, Argentina joined Canada and the United States to sue the European Union at the WTO, after the WTO ruled that a de facto EU ban on imports of genetically modified foods between 1984 and 2004 was illegal. In particular, Austria has refused to allow imports of two genetically modified corn types produced by Monsanto of the United States, a leading GMO producer in the world. More recently, EU Environment Commissioner Stavros Dimas was potentially starting another conflict with the United States when he proposed a European ban on the cultivation of modified corn made by Dow Agrosciences, Pioneer Hi-Bred, and Syngenta. Dimas claims that the products potentially harm the environment. This is in spite of US claims that EU scientists found that the corn had no impact. In addition to the GMO companies, US farmers claim that the EU ban cost them $300 million a year in lost sales.

In spite of the favorable WTO ruling in 2006, the EU continues to restrict the import of US GMO goods. The tactic used by several EU countries is to apply the SPS agreement (Sanitary and Phytosanitary measures). This is based on Article 2.1, which defines WTO member nations' basic rights: "Members have the right to take sanitary and phytosanitary measures necessary for the protection of human, animal or plant life or health, provided that such measures are not inconsistent with the provisions of this Agreement." Technically, application of this agreement requires scientific backing but there remains a strong debate regarding the safety of GMO products. However, the US position is that the EU is in violation of trade agreements.

Source: Adapted from: GM WATCH daily, 2006, "EU steadfast in rejecting genetically engineered food, despite WTO pressure," www.gmwatch.org, February 7; James Kanter, 2007, "WTO gives EU more time on genetically modified foods," *International Herald Tribune*, November 22; www.wto.org; Andrew Porterfield, 2015, "Is Europe's opposition to importing GMOs violating trade agreements?" Genetic Literacy Project, November 30, www.geneticliteracyproject.org/2015/11/30/europes-opposition-importing-gmos-violating-trade-agreements/

Regional Trade Agreements (RTAs)

Are RTAs Friend or Foe to World Trade?

The WTO is not the only group encouraging the elimination of trade barriers. **Regional trade agreements** (RTAs) are agreements among groups of nations to reduce tariffs and develop similar technical and economic standards. Such agreements have usually led to more trade among the member nations. Some argue that these agreements are the first step toward complete globalization. Others criticize the agreements as benefiting only trade-group members and harmful for the poorer nations left out of the agreements (such as the Caribbean countries that are not members of NAFTA).[8] From a practical point of view, regional agreements benefit world trade more than they hurt it. Although they do benefit member countries the most, such agreements are more politically manageable than worldwide trade agreements.[9]

Technically, the WTO is not fully comfortable with regional trade agreements. While many regional agreements have paved the way for later WTO multilateral agreements (agreements among all WTO members), the fear is that regional agreements can lead to unequal treatment of nations that are not members of the region. Because of this, under Article XXIV of the GATT, members of the WTO are required to notify the WTO when they enter into an agreement. These agreements must be notified to the WTO to be checked for compliance with the GATT–WTO regulations. Not all nations follow this rule, so not all agreements are notified, but most of the major agreements have WTO approval.[10]

Within the last few years, the number of regional trade agreements notified to the WTO has expanded significantly.[11] By 2016 there were 635 notified agreements with 423 still active.[12] In addition, many potential agreements are under consideration for approval by the WTO.[13] Most new negotiations are bilateral, that is between two countries. Others involve several WTO members. Regarding agreement in development, WTO identifies the following: the Trans-Pacific Partnership (TPP) Agreement in the Asia-Pacific Region (between 12 countries); ASEAN members and six other WTO members; the Pacific Alliance in Latin America (including Chile, Colombia, Mexico, and Peru); and the Tripartite Agreement among parties to COMESA, EAC, and SADC agreements in Africa. Such agreements among several countries likely will reduce the number of bilateral agreements.[14]

Exhibit 3.4 looks at the trends in notified agreements since the founding of GATT.

Not all regional trade agreements have the same form or structure. In the next section you will see the types in use today and the consequences for trading or doing business within and between these types.

Types of Regional Trade Agreements

Typically, experts look at the types of agreements as a hierarchy, with each level involving more complex relationships and economic integration. Exhibit 3.5 summarizes the various options.

regional trade agreements (RTAs) agreements among groups of nations to reduce tariffs and develop similar technical and economic standards

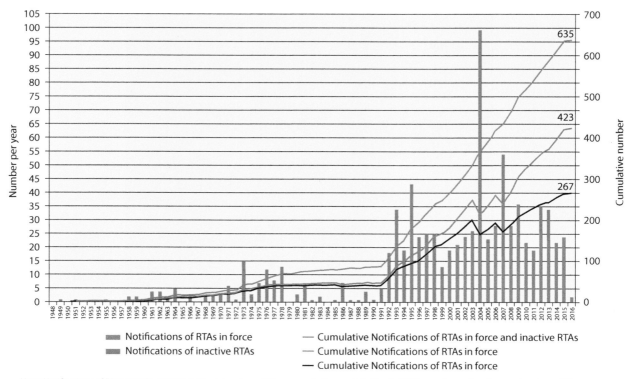

Note: Notifications of RTAs: goods, services & accessions to an RTA are counted separately. Physical RTAs goods, services & accessions to an RTA are counted together. The cumulative lines show the number of notifications/physical RTAs that were in force for a given year.
Source: WTO Secretariat.

Exhibit 3.4 The Evolution of Regional Trade Agreements
Source: WTO Secretariat, www.wto.org/english/tratop_e/region_e/regfac_e.htm

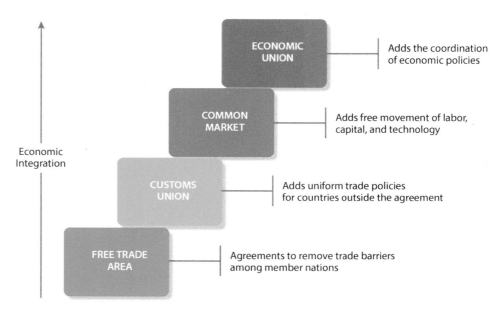

Exhibit 3.5 The Steps of Economic Integration

The most basic agreement is called a **preferential trade agreement**. With this type, nations grant preferential trade to a group of nations. These are not necessarily reciprocal. One example, called the "Bolivarian alternative," is an agreement between Bolivia and Cuba to eliminate tariffs on imports and allow state-owned companies unrestricted operations in both countries. Already, Bolivia sells Cuba, with preferential treatment, nearly a quarter of the oil consumed in the island.[15] Part of the motivation for this "alternative" is the US-backed Free Trade Area of the Americas.

Free trade areas are reciprocal agreements among a group of nations, usually from one region of the world, to remove tariffs and other trade barriers (e.g. quotas) affecting trade with each other. Each nation, however, remains free to impose any barriers or preferential treatments to other nations outside of the area. The most famous free trade area is the North American Free Trade Agreement (NAFTA) between the United States, Canada, and Mexico. Later in this chapter you will get more information on how this and other major regional trade agreements operate.

One weakness of a free trade area is called **trade deflection**. Trade deflection often occurs in free trade areas when companies from nonmember countries enter the free trade area through a member country with low trade barriers. They then can re-export their goods to the other countries in the area and avoid the other countries' trade restrictions. This is an attractive strategy for companies located outside the area because they can price their goods much more cheaply in their target countries.

To prevent trade deflection, countries often agree to **rules of origin**. Rules of origin specify how much of the content or valued added of a product must be produced in a member country to count as "produced" in the country. Specifying how these rules work can be quite complex. For example, in NAFTA, the rules of origin for textiles require that fabrics or clothing be spun from yarns or fibers produced in NAFTA countries. Rules also require that they and the fabrics or clothing be cut and sewn within the NAFTA area.[16] Such rules of origin prevent trade deflection of third-country goods from one NAFTA country to other NAFTA countries.

The next level of regional trade integration is called the **customs union**. The oldest customs union in the world is the Southern African Customs Union (SACU), which includes the countries of South Africa, Botswana, Lesotho, Namibia, and Swaziland.

Customs unions are similar to free trade areas regarding relationships among members. All members get the same benefits of reduced tariffs and other trade barriers with each other. What makes customs unions different from regional trade agreements is that country members also agree to use uniform treatment of outsiders with regard to trade policies. This means, for example, that South Africa and Botswana in the SACU must impose the same tariff rates or other import restrictions on goods imported from the US or EU.

From an international manager's point of view, this means that the company from a country outside the union will pay the same tariffs regardless of which country is chosen as the entry into the union. That is, unlike the free trade area, there is no possibility of a back-door low-tariff entry point into the union. Although customs unions have free trade among members and treat outsiders with similar trade policies, there are still barriers between the countries. To take the next step in the economic integration ladder, countries form **common markets**. Common markets allow free movement of labor, capital, and technology across member nations' borders. From the strategic point of view, this allows companies to locate any value-chain activity in any fellow common market country without restrictions. For example, the best available managers and workers can be hired from anywhere within the common market and be stationed at any of the company's locations. Ideally, as you learned from the discussion of transnational activities in

preferential trade agreement preferential trade relations granted to a group of nations, not necessarily reciprocal

free trade areas reciprocal agreements among groups of nations to remove tariffs and other trade barriers among members, but each nation is free to impose any barriers or preferential treatments to other nations

trade deflection occurs in free trade areas when companies from nonmember countries enter the free trade area through a member country with low trade barriers

rules of origin specify how much of the content or valued added of a product must be produced in a member country to count as "produced" in the country

customs union a free trade area with the additional provision that members use uniform treatment of outsiders with regard to trade policies

common markets add to the customs union the free movement of labor, capital, and technology among member nations

Chapter 2, this increases the efficiency and effectiveness of companies because they can use the best platforms in their market in terms of price of quality. The European Union moved to a common market status in 1992.

The final step typically achieved in economic integration without becoming a new country is called the **economic union**. The economic union includes all of the integration mechanisms of a common market but goes a step further. Member countries agree to coordinate economic policies, which include such factors as monetary policies, taxation, and currencies. The European Union is making strides toward becoming an economic union as member countries adopt the use of a single currency, called the euro (€). You will see more detail about the euro in the discussion of the European Union, below.

economic union
adds to the common market the agreement to coordinate economic policies, which include such factors as monetary policies, taxation, and currencies

Motivations for Regional Trade Agreements

Countries seek to join RTAs not only for economic reasons associated with trade and investment growth possibilities but also for political reasons. In addition, regional trade agreements are often easier to create than the multilateral trade agreements favored by the WTO. That is, fewer countries, especially when they are located close to each other, have less trouble finding common trading grounds.

The major motivation is economic growth with access to larger markets, more foreign investment, and more efficient use of local resources. Smaller nations such as Mexico are also attracted to agreements that lock in trade relationships with large countries such as the US. Political gains from joining regional trade areas can include benefits such as solidifying support for local reforms. For example, many of the transition economies of Eastern Europe used the requirements of regional agreements to lock in reforms such as the privatization of government-owned businesses that moved them toward more capitalistic economies. Political considerations also relate to enhanced security in the region. That is, some governments seek regional trade agreements to strengthen relationships among nations as a basis for increased security. Many experts point to the history of conflicts among European countries and note that economic integration reduces political friction among partners. Governments use agreements as rewards to other countries that conform to political goals. Some of the rationale for the US entering agreements such as the Free Trade Area of the Americas and the Central American Free Trade Agreement is to use access to the US market as a reward for economic liberalization and democratization.

Are Regional Trade Agreements Good for Business?

In general, experts see RTAs as having both positive and negative effects on trade. These two opposing forces are called **trade creation** and **trade diversion**.

Once member nations eliminate protectionist barriers such as tariffs, quotas, and non-tariff barriers such as subsidies, there are economic incentives to increase trade among the members based on the advantages member nations have in the production of certain goods or services. That is, trade creation occurs because the lower-cost or higher-quality production from one member country can now be exported freely to replace the higher-cost or lower-quality production in other member countries. Consumers benefit by getting better products or services at lower prices. For individual companies, enhanced trade increases the competitive environment as all companies must compete against the most efficient and effective producers from any member country.

However, the increased trade among RTA partners can also lead to potentially higher prices and less efficient use of resources and capabilities. As you will see in Chapter 4, economic theory suggests that if we all traded freely, nations would produce what they do most efficiently or best

trade creation
occurs when higher-cost production in one member country is replaced with lower-cost production from another member country

trade diversion
occurs when high-cost trade among member nations replaces trade with lower-cost producers who are outside of the agreement

and would trade this output with other nations in exchange for what the other nations do cheapest or best. Because RTAs promote free trade only with their members and not with outsiders, there is a chance that trade barriers with outsiders may block what might otherwise be the most beneficial trade relations. This is called trade diversion: the trade among member nations replaces trade with lower-cost or higher-quality producers who are outside of the agreement. In general, economists see the net effect of trade creation and trade diversion as an indication of how the regional trade agreement contributes to world trade.

Regional Trade Agreements: A Look Inside

There are many regional trade agreements and most nations belong to more than one. Exhibit 3.6 shows the membership of major agreements. However, new agreements are being created all of the time.

Next, to look more closely at how free trade agreements work, we will look at the structure and organization of three groups. These groups are: the European Union, the North American Free Trade Agreement, and Asia-Pacific Economic Cooperation. These three largest free trade groups account for nearly half of the world's trade.

European Union

Initially, the **European Union** (**EU**) included just six countries. By 1995 the EU totaled 15 countries: Austria, Belgium, United Kingdom, Denmark, Finland, France, Germany, Greece, Ireland, Italy, Luxembourg, the Netherlands, Portugal, Spain, and Sweden. In 2004, with its biggest expansion, the EU added ten new countries and nearly doubled in population served. It now represents more than 508 million people, which would make it the third largest nation after China and India. These newer member countries included many from the former Eastern Bloc, including Poland, the Czech Republic, Hungary, Slovakia, Lithuania, Latvia, Slovenia, Estonia, Cyprus, and Malta. Additional countries in the process or considering joining the EU include Bosnia and Herzegovina, Montenegro, Iceland, Kosovo, Macedonia, Albania, Serbia, and Turkey. Norway and Switzerland are closely aligned with the EU countries by their membership of the related European Free Trade Area.

In 2016 the people of the UK voted to leave the EU. The UK is the first country to do this and the process is not clear. As such, how long this process will take remains unknown at the time of this writing and when executed it is unknown if the UK can remain a member of the EFTA.

Note the map in Exhibit 3.7 shows the current make-up of the EU and the location of its countries.

Since 1992, the EU countries have allowed goods and services to move across borders without customs duties and quotas, and more recently, as noted above, some of the countries have adopted the euro as their national currency. All European Union Member States are part of Economic and Monetary Union (EMU) and have agreed to coordinate their economic policy-making activities. When the euro was first introduced 11 of the then 15 EU countries adopted the new currency. Currently, there are 19 of the 28 EU countries using the euro and are part of the **Eurozone**. Later adopters included Greece in 2001, Slovenia in 2007, Cyprus and Malta in 2008, Slovakia in 2009, Estonia in 2011, Latvia in 2014, and Lithuania in 2015.[17] Eventually, all countries in the EU, with the exception of the UK and Denmark, which have "opt-out" clauses in their treaties, are required to join the Eurozone and will have the euro as their national currency. Britain and Denmark chose to stay out of the Eurozone prior to it becoming a requirement.

European Union
a group of 28 countries (27 when the UK exit is completed) that act as a common market with the goal of being a complete economic union

Eurozone
the EU countries that use the euro as a common currency

African Growth and Opportunity Act (AGOA)
Angola, Benin, Botswana, Burkina Faso, Burundi, Cameroon, Cape Verde, Chad, Comoros, Republic of Congo, Democratic Republic of Congo, Djibouti, Ethiopia, Gabon, The Gambia, Ghana, Guniea, Guinea-Bissau, Kenya, Lesotho, Liberia, Madagascar, Malawi, Mali, Mauritius, Mozambique, Namibia, Niger, Nigeria, Rwanda, Sao Tome and Principe, Senegal, Seychelles, Sierra Leone, South Africa, Swaziland, Tanzania, Togo, Uganda, Zambia

Asia Pacific Economic Cooperation (APEC)
Australia, Brunei Darussalam, Canada, Chile, People's Republic of China, Hong Kong, Indonesia, Japan, Republic of Korea, Malaysia, Mexico, New Zealand, Papua New Guinea, Peru, Philippines, Russian Federation, Singapore, Taiwan, Thailand, United States, Vietnam

Association of South East Asian Nations (ASEAN)
Brunei Darussalam, Burma (Myanmar), Cambodia, Indonesia, Laos, Malaysia, Philippines, Singapore, Thailand, Vietnam

Central America-Dominican Republic Free Trade Agreement (CAFTA-DR)
Costa Rica, Dominican Republic, El Salvador, Guatemala, Honduras, Nicaragua, United States

Andean Community (CAN)
Bolivia, Colombia, Ecuador, Peru

Caribbean Community and Common Market (CARICOM)
Antigua and Barbuda, Bahamas, Barbados, Belize, Dominica, Grenada, Guyana, Haiti, Jamaica, Montserrat, St. Kitts and Nevis, St. Lucia, St. Vincent and the Grenadines, Suriname, Trinidad and Tobago

Economic and Monetary Community of Central Africa (CEMAC)
Cameroon, Central African Republic, Chad, Republic of Congo, Equatorial Guinea, Gabon

Commonwealth of Independent States (CIS)
Armenia, Azerbaijan, Belarus, Georgia, Kazakhstan, Kyrgyz Republic, Moldova, Russian Federation, Tajikistan, Turkmenistan, Ukraine, Uzbekistan

Common Market for Eastern and Southern Africa (COMESA)
Burundi, Comoros, Democratic Republic of Congo, Djibouti, Egypt, Eritrea, Ethiopia, Kenya, Libya, Madagascar, Malawi, Mauritius, Rwanda, Seychelles, Sudan, Swaziland, Uganda, Zambia, Zimbabwe

Economic Cooperation Organization (ECO)
Afghanistan, Azerbaijan, Iran, Kazakhstan, Kyrgyz Republic, Pakistan, Tajikistan, Turkey, Turkmenistan, Uzbekistan

European Free Trade Association (EFTA)
Iceland, Liechtenstein, Norway, Switzerland

European Union – 25 (EU-25)
Austria, Belgium, Cyprus, Czech Republic, Denmark, Estonia, Finland, France, Germany, Greece, Hungary, Ireland, Italy, Latvia, Lithuania, Luxembourg, Malta, Netherlands, Poland, Portugal, Slovakia, Slovenia, Spain, Sweden, United Kingdom

European Union – 27 (EU-27)
Austria, Belgium, Bulgaria, Cyprus, Czech Republic, Denmark, Estonia, Finland, France, Germany, Greece, Hungary, Ireland, Italy, Latvia, Lithuania, Luxembourg, Malta, Netherlands, Poland, Portugal, Romania, Slovakia, Slovenia, Spain, Sweden, United Kingdom

European Union – 28 (EU-28)
Austria, Belgium, Bulgaria, Croatia, Cyprus, Czech Republic, Denmark, Estonia, Finland, France, Germany, Greece, Hungary, Ireland, Italy, Latvia, Lithuania, Luxembourg, Malta, Netherlands, Poland, Portugal, Romania, Slovakia, Slovenia, Spain, Sweden, United Kingdom

Free Trade Area of the Americas (FTAA)
Antigua and Barbuda, Argentina, Bahamas, Barbados, Belize, Bolivia, Brazil, Canada, Chile, Colombia, Costa Rica, Dominica, Dominican Republic, Ecuador, El Salvador, Grenada, Guatemala, Guyana, Haiti, Honduras, Jamaica, Mexico, Nicaragua, Panama, Paraguay, Peru, Saint Kitts and Nevis, Saint Lucia, Saint Vincent and the Grenadines, Suriname, Trinidad and Tobago, United States, Uruguay, Venezuela

Gulf Cooperation Council (GCC)
Bahrain, Kuwait, Oman, Qatar, Saudi Arabia, United Arab Emirates

Global System of Trade Preferences among Developing Countries (GSTP)
Algeria, Argentina, Bangladesh, Benin, Bolivia, Brazil, Cameroon, Chile, Colombia, Cuba, Democratic People's Republic of Korea, Ecuador, Egypt, Ghana, Guinea, Guyana, India, Indonesia, Islamic Republic of Iran, Iraq, Libya, Malaysia, Mexico, Morocco, Mozambique, Burma (Myanmar), Nicaragua, Nigeria, Pakistan, Paraguay, Peru, Philippines, Republic of Korea, Singapore, Sri Lanka, Sudan, Thailand, Trinidad and Tobago, Tunisia, United Republic of Tanzania, Uruguay, Venezuela, Vietnam, Zimbabwe

Exhibit 3.6 Selected Regional Trade Agreements and Member Nations

Southern Common Market (MERCOSUR)
Argentina, Brazil, Paraguay, Uruguay

North American Free Trade Agreement (NAFTA)
Canada, Mexico, United States

Organization of the Petroleum Exporting Countries (OPEC)
Algeria, Angola, Ecuador, Iran, Iraq, Kuwait, Libya, Nigeria, Qatar, Saudi Arabia, United Arab Emirates, Venezuela

South Asian Association for Regional Cooperation (SAARC)
Bangladesh, Bhutan, India, Maldives, Nepal, Pakistan, Sri Lanka

South African Customs Union (SACU)
Botswana, Lesotho, Namibia, South Africa, Swaziland

South African Development Community (SADC)
Angola, Botswana, Democratic Republic of Congo, Lesotho, Madagascar, Malawi, Mauritius, Mozambique, Namibia, Seychelles, South Africa, Swaziland, Tanzania, Zambia, Zimbabwe

West African Economic and Monetary Union (UEMOA/WAEMU)
Benin, Burkina Faso, Côte d'Ivoire, Guinea Bissau, Mali, Niger, Senegal, Togo

Exhibit 3.6 Selected Regional Trade Agreements and Member Nations
Source: www.trade.gov/mas/ian/referenceinfo/tg_ian_001874.asp

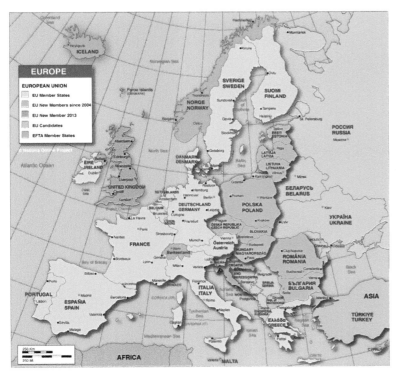

Exhibit 3.7   The Countries of the European Union
Source: www.nationsonline.org/oneworld/europe_map.htm
Contact: mail2@nationsonline.org. Copyright © 1998–2016: nationsonline.org

Not only must all new EU member countries eventually use the euro but they also must manage their economies to satisfy the preconditions to adopt the euro, as spelled out in the Maastricht Treaty.[18] One important precondition is that the accession countries must achieve exchange-rate stability between the value of their current national currencies and the euro for at least two years.

Full integration including adopting the euro or common currency may not occur for some time. However, the EU has an economy generating a GDP of €16.2 trillion making it the largest or second largest in the world depending on the source.[19]

The use of a common currency can have different impacts on countries and business. International managers must be aware of how such forms of economic integration can affect their companies and industries now and in the future. A big benefit is that the risk associated with changing exchange rates among euro countries is gone. For individual companies this can really pay off. Rick Simonson, the chief financial officer of Nokia, the Finnish cell-phone company, estimates that they have substantial savings by not having currency transaction costs in the Eurozone. He also estimates that "It makes the whole supply chain more efficient," because Nokia's suppliers also benefit. In Italy, even upscale fashion designers such as Giorgio Armani are looking to China to produce their lower-level items such as jeans. However, in spite of the difficulties of inflexible work arrangements and a highly valued currency, some companies still thrive. The innovative fitness-equipment maker Technogym is a $285 million company growing at nearly 15 percent a year. Eighty percent of its sales are from exports. Nerio Alessandri, founder and president, notes, "If you have an innovative product, the strong euro and the Asians [low-cost competitors] are not a problem ... change [cut costs or innovate] or die."[20]

In addition to a common currency, another important step in the economic integration of the EU was the creation of the European Central Bank. This bank took over the role of the central banks in euro countries that previously managed local currencies and monetary policies such as interest rates. The European Central Bank now manages euro and monetary policy for the Union. As more members take on the euro and if EU members can ever agree on a common constitution, the European Union will move even closer to becoming a true economic union.

History and Organization of the EU   French Foreign Minister Robert Schuman proposed the seeds for the idea of a European Union in a speech on May 9, 1950. Although May 9 is now considered the birthday of the EU, Mr. Schuman's proposal was modest. He only suggested that coal and steel industries be integrated. The result was the European Coal and Steel Community (ECSC), which included six members: Belgium, West Germany, Luxembourg, France, Italy, and the Netherlands. Further integration followed and the original six countries signed the Treaties of Rome, creating the European Atomic Energy Community (EURATOM) and the European Economic Community (EEC).

To simplify managing these agreements, in 1967 participating countries created a Commission, a Council of Ministers, and the European Parliament. By the late 1970s, the Parliament became a legislative body elected directly by the citizens of member states every five years.

Originally, the members of the European Parliament were chosen by the national parliaments. But in 1979 this changed and the first direct elections were held, allowing the citizens of the member states to vote for the candidate of their choice. Since then, direct elections have been held every five years.

Continuous political and economic integration led eventually to the formal creation of the EU with the Treaty of Maastricht in 1992 and the creation of a common market. During the 1990s most countries abolished customs borders and more and more products and services crossed borders freely. As noted above, the Maastricht Treaty also created the EMU and the introduction of the euro.[21]

Perhaps because the EU is the most integrated of the regional trade agreements its governing structures are complex and resemble those of parliamentary democracies with legislative and executive branches of government. There are three major organizational units used to govern EU activities: the European Parliament, the Council of the European Union, and the European Commission.

The *European Commission* is somewhat like an executive branch (law-enforcing and daily management) of government, with the exception that it is appointed. The European Commission proposes legislation to the legislative (law-making) branches of the organization, which include the *Parliament* and the *Council*. It also manages and implements EU policies and the budget, enforces European law (jointly with the Court of Justice), and represents the EU in its dealings with other countries.

The European Parliament is the one legislative branch elected directly by the people. It shares its legislative authority with the Council. The Parliament and the Council legislate laws and rules that have EU-wide applications. The Parliament also has the authority to approve or reject the nomination of Commissioners and, somewhat like the US House of Representatives, it shares with the Council the authority over the EU budget. Exhibit 3.8 shows the number of elected representatives from each EU country during different time periods.

In addition to its legislative functions shared with the Parliament, the Council co-ordinates the broad economic policies of the EU, develops the EU's Common Foreign and Security Policy, and coordinates legal issues with the member states. Ministers in the Council are appointed by their governments and not elected directly. They also have the power to commit their government to EU actions without further consultations.

You can check the current status of the EU at https://europa.eu/european-union/index_en.

North American Free Trade Agreement

The **North American Free Trade Agreement (NAFTA)** links the United States, Canada, and Mexico in an economic bloc that allows freer exchange of goods and services. After the agreement went into effect in the early 1990s, all three countries saw immediate increases in trade. However, the Mexican economy soon went into a tailspin, with inflation running as high as 45 percent. Emergency loans from the United States helped stabilize the situation, and by 1996 Mexico had paid back the loans—before the due date. The next step for NAFTA may be to expand, as we have seen with the EU. However, the FTAA or the Free Trade Area of the Americas includes not only the United States, Canada, and Mexico, but also most other Caribbean, Central American, and South American nations.

> **North American Free Trade Agreement (NAFTA)** links the United States, Canada, and Mexico in an economic bloc that allows freer exchange of goods and services

Governance of NAFTA   NAFTA has two major governing bodies, the Free Trade Commission and the NAFTA Coordinators, and one major dispute resolution body, the NAFTA Secretariat.

The *Free Trade Commission* consists of cabinet-level representatives from the three member countries. It meets annually. The Commission supervises the implementation of the NAFTA agreement by subordinate committees and working groups.

The *NAFTA Coordinators* are in charge of day-to-day management of NAFTA. This is a shared leadership role among three senior trade department officials assigned by Canada, Mexico, and the US. NAFTA also uses over 30 working groups and committees to manage specific areas of the agreement. These include, for example, trade in goods, rules of origin, customs, agricultural trade and subsidies, standards, government procurement, investment and services, and cross-border movement of business people (e.g. visa standards and work permits).

	1999–2004	2004–2007	2007–2009	2009–2016
Austria	21	18	18	19
Belgium	25	24	24	26
Bulgaria	—	—	18	18
Croatia	—	—	—	11
Cyprus	—	6	6	7
Czech Republic	—	24	24	22
Denmark	16	14	14	14
Estonia	—	6	6	7
Finland	16	14	14	15
France	87	78	78	74
Germany	99	99	99	96
Greece	25	24	24	23
Hungary	—	24	24	21
Ireland	15	13	13	11
Italy	87	78	78	76
Latvia	—	9	9	9
Lithuania	—	13	13	12
Luxembourg	6	6	6	6
Malta	—	5	5	6
Netherlands	31	27	27	27
Poland	—	54	54	54
Portugal	25	24	24	22
Romania	—	—	36	34
Slovakia	—	14	14	13
Slovenia	—	7	7	8
Spain	64	54	54	63
Sweden	22	19	19	23
United Kingdom	87	78	78	74
(MAX) TOTAL	626	732	786	791

Exhibit 3.8 Number of Elected Representatives to the European Parliament
Source: http://europarl.europa.eu

Two Canadian Companies Succeed Because of NAFTA

IB EMERGING MARKET
STRATEGIC INSIGHT

KDM Electronics Inc. (www.octasound.com) of Scarborough, Ontario, is a family-owned company with only six employees. It produces speaker systems and music sound systems for commercial use in gymnasiums, convention centers, sports arenas, shopping malls, warehouses, and factories. "Being highly specialized and niche-oriented, we need a sizable market," says Ron Bull, president of KDM. He notes, "With an industrial and commercial market eight times the size of Canada's, the United States fits the bill. And it's all one level playing field, due to NAFTA."

Since the signing of NAFTA, KDM's exports to the US have increased to 85 percent of the company's total production. Bull says, "And as long as you're competitive, the border is transparent. For KDM that's crucial, as we often deal with small, family-owned businesses who don't want the hassles of regulations and tariffs. What they do require is a stable trading relationship, and with NAFTA that's what we have."

Like KDM, the Quebec-based freight carrier SGT Inc. (www.sgt.qu.ca) saw a boom in business after NAFTA. Fleet size grew to 1,600 vehicles, up from 100, and the company now employs 750 people, up from 30. SGT ships from Alaska to the Yucatan. It has terminals and sales offices throughout Canada, the US, and Mexico.

SGT President Denis Coderre notes, "Since NAFTA came into effect, we have a lot more traffic from Mexico to Canada and the US. By easing restrictions and reducing tariffs, the agreement has facilitated the transportation of all kinds of products. For us, it has meant a boost in volume and more jobs."

Source: Adapted from www.itcan-cican.gc.ca/menu-en.asp

The *NAFTA Secretariat* is responsible for dispute settlement between member nations. The Secretariat has Canadian, US, and Mexican sections. They coordinate the investigation and resolution of disputes under NAFTA. Information on the Secretariat is available from www.nafta-sec-alena.org.

As with all types of trade agreements, from the WTO to the regional trade agreements, some gain from the openness while others lose. In the IB Emerging Market Strategic Insight above you can see two different perspectives on the effects of NAFTA. Both show the positive effects for two Canadian companies.

Having seen how NAFTA benefited KDM and SGT, consider the Emerging Market Ethical Challenge on the following page, which takes a more negative position on the effects of NAFTA.

The final example of a regional trade agreement considered in this chapter looks at the major agreement for countries in the Asia and Pacific region. It also shows a type of relationship that is less structured than the EU or NAFTA.

Asia-Pacific Economic Cooperation

When compared with the EU or NAFTA, the **Asia-Pacific Economic Cooperation (APEC)** is a looser confederation of 21 nations with less specific agreements on trade facilitation. However, ultimate goals call for total free trade in the Pacific region by 2020.[22] Member nations in APEC include: Australia; Brunei Darussalam; Canada; Chile; the People's Republic of China; Hong Kong, China; Indonesia; Japan; the Republic of Korea; Malaysia; Mexico; New Zealand; Papua New Guinea; Peru; the Republic of the Philippines; the Russian Federation; Singapore; Chinese Taipei; Thailand; the United States of America; and Vietnam.

Asia-Pacific Economic Cooperation (APEC)
a loose confederation of 21 nations with nonbinding free trade area agreements

Public Citizen's Global Trade Watch Takes a Negative Position on NAFTA   EMERGING MARKET ETHICAL CHALLENGE

Not all people support multilateral trade agreements and regional trade agreements because they believe that certain groups are particularly hurt. Below is a quote from *Public Citizen's Global Trade Watch*, which looks at the downside of NAFTA for many Mexican workers:

> Mexico suffered many negative economic effects as a result of NAFTA. Sharp cuts in farm subsidy programs combined with the near-elimination of import restrictions on corn and other commodities resulted in dumped US corn flooding the Mexican market, forcing over 1.5 million *campesinos* or peasant farmers whose livelihoods were based on small-scale farming off their land. Many US agribusiness multinationals also used NAFTA investment and service sector rules to buy corn-processing and tortilla-making factories in Mexico. Yet instead of falling (as "free" trade theory predicts), retail prices for food products increased sharply. The cost of tortillas rose by 50 percent in Mexico City and more in the countryside, even as prices paid to Mexican farmers for corn plummeted. At the same time, the purchasing power of the average Mexican worker has also dropped. Since NAFTA, a combination of factors—including the migration of so many *campesinos* to the cities—has caused Mexican industrial wages to decline by approximately 10 percent. The economic fallout from NAFTA has also been shown to have had particularly harsh consequences for Mexican women; a recent study found that the poverty rate for female-headed households in Mexico has increased by 50 percent since NAFTA went into effect.

In a twenty year review the *Public Citizen's Global Trade Watch* concluded this effect on Mexican farmers:

> The agricultural provisions of NAFTA, which removed Mexican tariffs on corn imports and eliminated programs supporting small farmers but did not discipline U.S. subsidies, led to widespread dislocation in the Mexican countryside. Amidst a NAFTA-spurred influx of cheap U.S. corn, the price paid to Mexican farmers for the corn that they grew fell by 66 percent after NAFTA, forcing many to abandon farming.

Source: Labor Council for Latin American Advancement, 2004, "Another Americas is possible: The impact of NAFTA on the US Latino community and lessons for future trade agreements," *Public Citizen's Global Trade Watch*, August, p. 4; www.citizen.org/documents/naftas-mexico-legacy.pdf.

In addition, other trade groups in the Pacific region often participate in APEC activities as observers. These include the Association of South East Asian Nations (ASEAN) Secretariat, the Pacific Economic Cooperation Council (PECC), and the Pacific Islands Forum Secretariat (PIF).

APEC is unique when compared to other regional trade agreements. It operates on the basis of non-binding commitments. That is, unlike the WTO or other RTAs, APEC has no treaty obligations that govern member nations. Instead, trade agreements are voluntary and are reached by consensus.

Although APEC does not have the treaty authority to enforce compliance with trade rules that are part of other treaty-based agreements, it is important because of its coverage of major sections of the world's economy. APEC nations have more than a third of the world's population (2.8 billion people) and produce 57 percent of the world's GDP and nearly half of world trade.[23] Moreover, in spite of the lack of binding agreements, it seems that APEC has, at least in part, helped the growth of trade and investment in the region. Since its founding, exports for APEC countries have increased by 113 percent to over $2.5 trillion, and FDI grew by 210 percent overall and by 475 percent in lower-income APEC countries.[24]

A summary of the structure and activities of APEC is shown in Exhibit 3.9. You can see that its organization is somewhat similar to other RTAs even without the formal binding agreements among members.

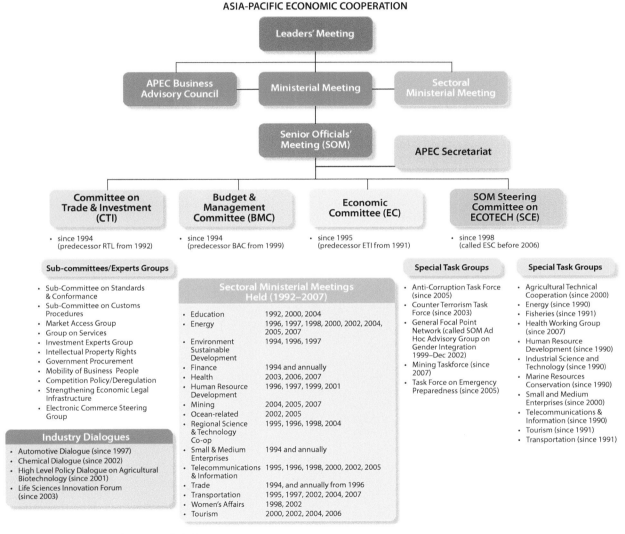

Exhibit 3.9 The Structure and Activities of APEC
Source: www.apec.org

Chapter Review

This chapter provided you with an overview of the existing mechanisms for global and regional integration. These agreements are important for international business people because they define the context of international competition and the extent of globalization. As barriers to trade drop, MNCs are more likely to adopt transnational, international, or regional multinational strategies because crossing borders becomes easier. Companies can source raw material or sell anywhere more advantageous when barriers to trade fall.

The chapter began with a history of GATT and how this basic agreement led eventually to the creation of a permanent organization, the WTO, to manage the reduction in trade barriers around the world. Importantly, the WTO also added a mechanism for dispute resolution when countries came into conflict over violations of agreements. Prior to GATT and the WTO, most trade agreements were bilateral, that is just between two countries. Now such agreements tend to be multilateral, agreements between groups of countries who are members of the WTO or of the many regional trade agreements.

The goal of the WTO is to reduce trade barriers worldwide. However, there are many other groups involved in trade barriers reduction. These regional trade agreements vary widely in membership and structure. Most countries belong to several groups in addition to the WTO. The RTAs range from simple agreements for preferential treatment to the more complex agreements of the customs union and economic union. The customs union not only treats members preferentially but also treats all outsiders with a uniform trade policy. The economic union goes even further by combining under one monetary policy.

To look inside the operations of RTAs in action, the chapter described the history and structure of the EU, NAFTA, and APEC. The EU is the most integrated of all RTAs and is now approaching a true economic union with the use of the euro as a common currency at least among some members. NAFTA is a less integrated preferential trade agreement but may at some time become more like the EU, with new agreements such as the Central American Free Trade Agreement. APEC is a loosely configured preferential trade agreement where members do not sign binding treaties. Nevertheless, APEC seemingly has succeeded in reducing trade barriers among its member nations.

In all cases, the astute international manager will understand the implications of the various agreements for the types of goods or services produced by his or her company. Each new agreement creates both opportunities and threats for companies in different countries and different industries.

Discussion Questions

1   Describe how GATT evolved into the WTO. What are the major differences between these agreements?

2   What are the differences between multilateral and bilateral trade agreements?

3   Describe how a company might use trade deflection or trade diversion to gain a strategic advantage over competitors.

4   Describe the basic types of regional trade agreements. Discuss some of the advantages and disadvantages of MNCs doing business in each type.

5   Discuss some of the implications (costs and benefits) of a common currency for companies operating in countries that formerly had their own currencies.

International Business Skill Builder

Understanding the WTO Debate

Not everyone agrees that the WTO is beneficial for the people of the world, particularly the emerging economies. The WTO is founded on the economic belief that free trade is more efficient and that on aggregate most people will be better served in a free trade environment. Critics argue that the multinational corporations and the developed nations are the prime beneficiaries with an array of negative effects for some countries and people.

For this exercise, consider both sides of the debate.

Step 1: Investigate some of the organizations that are critical of the WTO and most other trade agreements. Some examples are:
www.globalexchange.org/campaigns/wto/
www.citizen.org/trade/wto/
www.globalissues.org/TradeRelated/Seattle.asp

Step 2: Consider the WTO's positions regarding many of these criticisms. You can find the WTO's perspective on their website, www.wto.org. Search the WTO site and read Chapter 1 of *The Future of the WTO*. Also look at *Ten Benefits of the WTO Trading System* and *Ten Common Misunderstandings about the WTO*. These publications can be downloaded in PDF or read online.

Step 3: Consider the merits of each side and be prepared to defend and debate your position.

Step 4: Form teams of pro and con WTO positions and debate the issue in class.

Chapter Internet Activity

In this project you will get to explore the effects of different tariffs on different products. As an international manager considering exporting:

1   Pick a product that you intend to export. Imagine that you will export that product to one of the APEC nations.

2   Explore the APEC tariff database at www.apectariff.org/ to see what trade barriers exist. You will need to register but registration is free.

3   Identify the countries with the lowest and highest tariff barriers.

4   Write or present a report dealing with your findings.

Key Concepts

- Asia-Pacific Economic Cooperation (APEC)
- common markets
- customs unions
- economic union
- Eurozone
- European Union
- free trade areas
- General Agreement on Tariffs and Trade (GATT)
- North American Free Trade Agreement (NAFTA)

- preferential trade agreement
- principle of nondiscrimination
- regional trade agreements (RTAs)
- rules of origin
- tariffs
- trade creation
- trade deflection
- trade diversion
- World Trade Organization (WTO)

CASE 3

BUSINESS > INTERNATIONAL

What Happens to Emerging Markets if the Euro Crashes?

Created on January 1, 1999 with great fanfare, a single currency was created which was to unify most, if not all European countries. While not introduced as an actual physical currency until 2002, currency values among the member states were locked and the value of the euro set at $1.17USD. Originally 11 members of the European Union adopted the euro in place of their own national currency. These countries were Austria, Belgium, Finland, France, Germany, Ireland, Italy, Luxembourg, the Netherlands, Portugal, and Spain. Greece soon followed making it the 12th member of the Eurozone. Since the initial issuance, five other member countries have adopted the euro as their official currency— Cyprus, Estonia, Malta, Slovakia, and Slovenia. The euro became the world's second most important currency, just behind the United States dollar, and at one point was predicted by some to become the reserve currency of the world. As of 2016 the euro had fallen from grace and its future was being questioned.

The history of the euro can be traced back to Robert Schuman, the French politician who first called for greater economic integration in Europe in 1950, which led to the founding of the European Coal and Steel Community. The Treaty of Rome in 1957 established the European Community (common market) and the Single European Act moved Europe further creating greater integration and the removal of trade barriers among members of the Community. The Treaty of Maastricht in 1991 created the single European currency. Not all members of the European Union chose to adopt the euro as their national currency. The UK and Denmark opted out of joining the Eurozone. The Treaty of

**CASE 3
cont'd**

Maastricht also established the European Central Bank (ECB) with authority to determine monetary policy within the Eurozone. Within two years the euro had fallen significantly against the US dollar but regained its strength over time. Its main challenges were ahead.

When the original 6 countries established the European Union, there was a lot of talk about unity and solidarity, and the concept of "One Europe." The original motive for economic integration was that of peace. Europe has seen more than its share of wars, and the idea that economic integration and dependence would bring peace was a strong and desirable motive. A common European citizenry and identity and acting for the common good were also strong motives for integration. In giving up their national currencies, member states made great sacrifices for the good of the European Continent. One of the most powerful aspects of a sovereign state is the ability to print its own currency.

While the main goal of economic integration was peace, there were economic gains that would hopefully be achieved through a single currency, including reduced or eliminated transaction costs on currency, greater price transparency and competition, easier access to global capital markets, and greater economic and political clout in the world community. In addition, the formation and expansion of the European Union would hopefully bring a more competitive Europe by reducing trade barriers and allowing countries to capitalize on their comparative advantages.

While optimism reigned in Europe over the increasingly powerful and influential economic block, with its combined membership greater in population and GDP than the United States, not everyone was expecting success. The European Union and the euro represented a large, in fact very large, social experiment. Not many in Europe seemed to recognize this fact, and the thought of the experiment not working, the "unthinkable," was quickly dismissed as foolish speculation.

Not all thought the single currency was a good idea. Many Germans for example were reluctant to give up their deutsche marks, but perhaps having the European Central Bank located in Frankfurt was comforting. The monetary theorist and Nobel Laureate, Milton Friedman predicted the demise of the euro stating in 2001:

> There is no historical precedent for such an arrangement. It involves each country's giving up power over its internal monetary policy to an entity not under its political control. Such a system has economic advantages and disadvantages, but I believe that its real Achilles heel will prove to be political; a system under which the political and currency boundaries do not match is bound to be unstable." *

The problem Dr. Friedman was pointing out in his statement was that a single currency without a single economy and fiscal union would face major difficulties. The problems were not as great when the original 6 member states formed a union. Most of the economies were doing well, with the exception of Greece, and all were somewhat alike economically. With the expansion of the EU into less-developed parts of Europe, the

CASE 3
cont'd

disparity in economies grew. The concept of an "optimal currency area" seemed to be violated. An optimal currency area develops when countries have similar enduring economic conditions and levels of development. A single currency would appear to work well there. When economic conditions are much different among countries, a single currency doesn't work as well. This appeared to be the case with the 2004 expansion and the addition of Romania and Bulgaria in 2007.

With the addition of more divergent economies, each pursuing its own fiscal policies it became more difficult for one monetary policy to be effective. The main problems, however, developed in some of the original 6 member states who began to spend more than they took through tax revenue. Productivity rates varied among member states and with a single currency some countries were competitive and others not. Portugal, Ireland, Greece, and Spain (PIGS) began to experience high levels of unemployment and low levels of economic growth.

Members of the Eurozone have been operating on a two-track path for some time, with Northern Europe doing relatively well and Southern Europe performing poorly. With a single currency and economically strong cousin states like Germany, some Eurozone countries borrowed heavily to pay for social spending. The PIGS developed sovereign debt problems with Greece being the worst. Greece was forced to accept a financial bailout from the EU and the IMF in exchange for austerity measures. The fiscal discipline imposed by Germany revived some anti-German sentiment, and in some cases an ugly display of nationalist feeling and biases. By 2012 the era of unity and goodwill among Europeans had eroded. In June 2016 the United Kingdom voted to leave the EU.

CASE DISCUSSION POINTS:

1   Why is a fiscal union an important consideration in the development of an economic union?
2   There are a number of forms of economic integration in emerging market countries. What lessons can be learned from the European Union?
3   If the euro collapses what effects do you predict on emerging markets? Are all the effects bad? Explain.

Source: J. Bowyer, 2012, "Happy birthday Milton Friedman, the European crisis is your latest vindication," Forbes, August 1; P. Coy, 2012, "Greece needs Europe, as the latest numbers show," BusinessWeek, May 23; P. Coy, N. Malkoutzis, C. Matlack and G. Thesing, 2012, "What a return to the drachma really looks like," *BusinessWeek*, May 24; P. Coy, 2012, "Europe could benefit from less, not more, commonality," *BusinessWeek*, December 20; C. Crook, 2012, "Who lost the euro?" *BusinessWeek*, May 24; H. Dixon, 2012, "Can the euro omelette be unscrambled?" *Reuters*, April 16; B. Eichengreen, 2012, "Keep the European Union, scrap the euro," *Business Insider*, December 15; C. Hill, 2013, *International Business: Competing in the Global Marketplace*, New York: McGraw-Hill/Irwin; T. Judah, 2012, "Croatia joins the club," The World in 2013, November 8; N. Lewis, 2011, "Europe's economic crisis is not a euro

<table>
<tr><td>CASE 3
cont'd</td><td>crisis," Forbes, October 24; J. Lichfield, 2012, "Review of the Eurozone in 2012:
A crisis of debt and identity," The Independent, December 22; The Economist,
2011, "Northern lights, southern cross," May 19; T. Pettinger, 2012, "Will the
Eurozone breakup?" www.economicshelp.org/5223/economics/will-the-eurozone-
breakup/; The Econ Review, 2011, www.econreview.com/events/euro1999b.htm;
www.economist.com/brexit, 2016.

*Friedman quote is from the J. Bowyer's Forbes article referenced above.

 Case prepared by Charles A. Rarick </td></tr>
</table>

Notes

1   www.explore-law.com/law/T/Tariff.html

2   *The Economist*, 1996, "All free traders now?" December 7, pp. 23–25.

3   WTO, 2015, *Understanding the WTO*, Geneva: World Trade Organization; *The Economist*, 2003, "Heading east," www.economist.com, March 27.

4   WTO, 2015, *Understanding the WTO*, Geneva: World Trade Organization; www.wto.org/english/ thewto_e/whatis_e/tif_e/tif_e.htm

5   Jeffrey Sparshott, 2003, "Agricultural subsidies targeted," *Washington Times*, www.washtimes.com/ business/20031 207-114046-8545r.htm; Dan Charles, 2016, "Farm subsidies persist and grow, despite talk of reform," www.npr.org/sections/thesalt/2016/02/01/465132866/farm-subsidies-persist-and-grow-despite-talk-of-reform, http://farmsubsidy.openspending.org/

6   https://ustr.gov/about-us/policy-offices/press-office/press-releases/2014/October/United-States-and-Brazil-Reach-Agreement-to-End-WTO-Cotton-Dispute

7   BBC News, 2005, "US limits Chinese imports," May 15, http://news.bbc.co.uk/2/hi/business/4546373.stm

8   *The Economist*, 1996, "Spoiling world trade," December 7, pp. 15–16; *The Economist*, 2000, "Responsible regionalism," www.economist.com, December 2.

9   R. F. M. Lubbers, 1996, "Globalization: An exploration," *Nijenrode Management Review*, 1.

10 WTO, 2015, *Understanding the WTO*, Geneva: World Trade Organization.

11 WTO, 2015, *Understanding the WTO*, Geneva: World Trade Organization.

12 https://www.wto.org/english/tratop_e/region_e/region_e.htm

13 WTO, 2015, *Understanding the WTO*, Geneva: World Trade Organization.

14 www.wto.org/english/tratop_e/region_e/regfac_e.htm

15 *The Economist*, 2005, "With help from oil and friends," January 13.

16 Ram Upendra Das, 2004, "Rules of origin need proper perspective under trade pacts," *Financial Express*, May 10.

17 http://ec.europa.eu/economy_finance/euro/adoption/euro_area/index_en.htm

18 Peter B. Kenen and Ellen E. Meade, 2003, "EU accession and the Euro: Close together or far apart?" International Policy Briefs, Institute for International Economics, October.

19 World Economic Outlook, *International Monetary Fund*.

20 *BusinessWeek Online*, 2005, "Italy: The Euro-zone's sickest patient," www.businessweek.com, June 6; *BusinessWeek Online*, 2005, "Squeezed by the euro," www.businessweek.com, June 6; Neil Williams, 2016, "The Eurozone's winners and losers—and how to close the gap," June 13, www.cityam.com/ profile/neil-williams

21 https://europa.eu/european-union/about-eu/history_en; European Commission, 2000, *Enlargement Strategy Paper*, Brussels: EC.

22 www.apec.org/apec.html.

23 www.apec.org/About-Us/About-APEC/Achievements%20and%20Benefits.aspx

24 www.apec.org/apec.html

CHAPTER 4

Global Trade and Foreign Direct Investment

After reading this chapter you should be able to:

- Understand the history of trade theory.

- Appreciate how the knowledge of trade theory can help you select better multinational strategies.

- Understand the concepts of absolute and comparative advantage.

- Appreciate the benefits and costs of international trade.

- Be familiar with the basic theories that explain foreign direct investment.

- Understand the costs and benefits for emerging nations engaged in international trade and investments.

International Business   *Preview IB Emerging Market Strategic Insight*

Boeing's 787 Dreamliner is 70 Percent Imported!

At the heart of globalization is increasing trade between companies from different countries. Companies use world trade to find both suppliers and customers. No company probably illustrates this trend more than the US aircraft manufacturer, Boeing. For Boeing, things have changed drastically in the world of commercial jet manufacturing and sales. In the 1960s, the Boeing 727 was the company's prize product. Only 2 percent of its components came from outside the US. By the mid-1990s, components for Boeing's 777 were 30 percent foreign. The 787 is 70 percent foreign and most of that Japanese. Japan's three major aerospace manufacturers, Fuji, Kawasaki, and Mitsubishi, will build approximately 35 percent of the plane. These companies also subcontract component manufacturing to other Asian countries, particularly China.

Exhibit 4.1 below shows the international component suppliers Boeing uses for the 787.

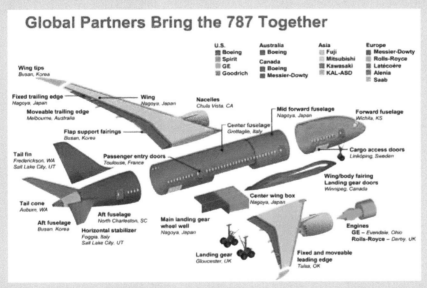

Exhibit 4.1 International Component Suppliers Used by Boeing for the 787

Although not as extensive as with the Dreamliner, importing components for commercial aircraft production is common. Even the European Airbus planes often have nearly 50 percent of US-produced components. One-third of Boeing's 3,500 world fleet of planes has major parts and assemblies built in China. Boeing has contracts valued at $1.6 billion with the Chinese aviation industry for components for all of its major models. Boeing also plans to build a production facility in China.

Boeing's 787 Dreamliner represents a radical departure in commercial aircraft production. Built almost entirely of ultra-light composite materials, the plane is lighter and more efficient than contemporary aircraft.

Another radical shift in Boeing's strategy is that suppliers are not just building components based on exact specified designs delivered to suppliers in final form. Boeing is using the talents and money of suppliers to produce components from the design to final production. This makes Boeing more of a virtual company coordinating the design and production process remotely.

Source: Adapted from *Flight International*, 2005, "787 suppliers sign deal," May 31–6 June, p. 8; www.boeing.com; *The Economist*, 2005, "How Japan learned to fly," June 25, p. 68; Stephen Joiner, 2012, "Inside Boeing's 787 factory: The Dreamliner's quiet revolution," *Air & Space Magazine*, July; Jon Ostrower, 2014, "Boeing to build stretched 787-10 in South Carolina," *Wall Street Journal*, July 30; Loren Thompson, 2015, "Boeing to build its first offshore plane factory in China as Ex-IM Bank withers," *Forbes*, September 23; Steve Wilhelm, 2016, "As Airbus starts work on second China factory, Boeing remains hush on its China plans," *Puget Sound Business Journal*, March 18.

The Preview IB Emerging Market Strategic Insight shows how Boeing uses the international trade system to benefit from global supply sources. Boeing takes advantage of the engineering and manufacturing strengths located in countries like Japan to build an entirely new airplane quicker and more efficiently than doing it completely in the US. This is only possible because trade occurs between countries.

In this chapter, you will see why such international trade as well as cross-border investments often make sense and work to the general benefit of most people. The chapter begins this exploration by a look at the history of trade theories.

History of Trade Theory

Although trade between countries is as old as the existence of nation-states, the development of modern trade theory came much later. Below you will see some of the important historical developments in our understanding of how trade works.

Mercantilism: Early Thinking

zero-sum game
when one side loses, another side gains

mercantilism
the objective of between-country trade is for a country to win by exporting more than it imports

favorable trade balance
a surplus of exports over imports overall or applied to a particular country

specie-flow mechanism
when the supply or amount of money in a country increases, the prices in that country tend to go up as well

During the seventeenth and early eighteenth centuries, the common belief was that trade between countries was a **zero-sum game**. A zero-sum game is like a tennis match: when one person wins a point, the other person loses. In the **mercantilism** philosophy, the objective of between-country trade was for a country to win by exporting more than it imported.

This trade philosophy prospered at a period of nation building and the expectation that each state would accumulate as much gold and silver as possible. Gold and silver was the currency of trade, and nations that exported more than they imported accumulated more gold and silver. One nation's gain was another nation's loss. Economists call this surplus of exports over imports a **favorable trade balance**. The belief was that there was a fixed amount of gold and silver in the world and the nation that had the most of these precious metals would be the most powerful.

By the mid-1700s, the mercantilists were under attack. David Hume pointed out the basic flaws in the mercantilism reasoning.[1] He noted two problems. The first was a very practical one. How would you like to live in a country that has lots of gold and silver buried deeply in secure areas like Fort Knox in the US, but fewer goods or services to buy? Hume argued that most people want the things that gold or silver or any other form of money can buy.

The second problem relates to what economists call the **specie-flow mechanism**. What this means is that when the supply or amount of money in a country increases, the prices in that country tend to go up as well. Since gold and silver represent the money supply, this means that more of these metals that a country accumulates from exporting, the higher prices become in the country. As people generally get more affluent, they purchase more goods and services. Thus, as the demands for these goods and services go up, so do the prices.

But what is the impact on trade? Consider if France and Germany were trading partners, with France having a favorable trade balance with Germany (France exports more to Germany than Germany does to France). As France accumulates gold and silver, its money supply, and hence prices, will go up in France. This has two effects. It makes French goods more expensive for Germans, reducing French imports into Germany, and it makes German goods cheaper for the French, increasing German imports into France. The result is that, in the end, trade surpluses disappear and mercantilist policies provide a country only a short-term advantage. Despite the evidence that the mercantilism approach does not work, it does receive some support. See the IB Emerging Market Strategic Insight below.

Neo-mercantilism: Should the US Protect the US Tire from Chinese Imports?

IB EMERGING MARKET
STRATEGIC INSIGHT

In spite of the efforts of the WTO and the general opinion of economists that mercantilism does not work, variants of the mercantile position are often popular for the companies in industries hurt by international competition and with politicians who support those industries.

One popular argument is that the developed economies such as the US need to protect jobs from low-cost manufacturers in emerging market countries such as China and Vietnam. The logic is that applying tariffs to products produced less expensively in low-cost labor countries makes local companies more competitive and protects local jobs that otherwise would disappear as domestic companies lose market share or abandon the US and move manifesting to low-cost countries.

	Protected Industry	Jobs Saved	Total Cost (in $ millions)	Annual Cost per Job Saved ($)
1	Benzenoid chemicals	216	297	1,376,435
2	Luggage	226	290	1,285,078
3	Softwood lumber	605	632	1,044,271
4	Sugar	2,261	1,868	826,104
5	Polyethylene resins	298	242	812,928
6	Dairy products	2,378	1,630	685,323
7	Frozen concentrate orange juice	609	387	635,103
8	Ball bearings	146	88	603,368
9	Maritime services	4,411	2,522	571,668
10	Ceramic tiles	347	191	551,367
11	Machine tools	1,556	746	479,452
12	Ceramic articles	418	140	335,876
13	Women's handbags	773	204	263,535
14	Canned tuna	390	100	257,640
15	Glassware	1,477	366	247,889
16	Apparel and textiles	168,786	33,629	199,241
17	Peanuts	397	74	187,223
18	Rubber footwear	1,701	286	168,312
19	Women's nonathletic footwear	3,702	518	139,800
20	Costume jewelry	1,067	142	132,870
	Total	191,764	44,352	
	Average (weighted)			231,289

Exhibit 4.2 The Cost of Protection

How much does it cost to protect a job? An average of $231,289, figured across just 20 of the many protected industries. Costs range from $132,870 per job saved in the costume jewelry business to $1,376,435 in the benzenoid chemical industry. Protectionism costs US consumers nearly $100 billion annually. It increases the cost not just of the protected items but of downstream products as well. Protecting sugar raises candy and soft-drink prices; protecting lumber raises home-building costs; protecting steel makes car prices higher; and so forth. Then there are the job losses in downstream industries. Workers in steel-using industries outnumber those in steel-producing industries by 57 to 1. And the protection may not even work. Decades old subsidies to steel-producing industries have exceeded $23 billion; yet industry employment has declined by nearly two-thirds.

However, there is a flip side. Those companies that use or sell the cheaper imports as components in their products can be more competitive, domestically and internationally, with less expensive supplies. Thus, if we restrict imports, companies that make products from such imports pass along those price increases to consumers. Additionally, when companies that sell the restricted products pay higher prices for such protected goods due to tariffs, then they pass those costs along to consumers.

For example, early in his presidency, with the objective of saving US jobs, President Obama imposed safeguard tariffs on Chinese car and light truck tires. Estimates are that these tariffs saved a maximum of 1,200 jobs. However, the total cost to US consumers from the higher prices that resulted from safeguard tariffs on Chinese tires was around $1.1 billion. That works out as a cost per tire job manufacturing saved as approximately $900,000 in one year. Additionally, since more expensive tires reduced spending on other retail goods, which costs jobs in the retail industry, there was a loss of around 2,500 jobs in the retail sector that offset the gains in tire manufacturing. Perhaps more importantly, the Chinese retaliated and imposed antidumping duties on imports of US chicken parts that cost that industry nearly $1 billion in sales.

Look at Exhibit 4.2 to see additional estimates of the costs in higher prices paid by society as a whole to save jobs. They are often more expensive than the wages of the jobs saved and consider the costs and benefits of saving jobs that must be borne by the society as a whole.

Source: Adapted from; Laura D'Andrea Tyson, 2005, "Stop scapegoating China—before it's too late," *BusinessWeek*, May 2, p. 26; C. P. Chandrasekhar and Jayati Ghosh, 2005, "The Chinese bogeyman in US clothing," *Macroscan*, May 25; *The Economist*, 2005, "The great stitch-up," www.economist.com, May 26; Gary Clyde Hufbauer and Sean Lowry, 2012, "US tire tariffs: Saving few jobs at high cost," Peterson Institute for International Economics, April.

Foundations of Modern Trade Theory

Absolute Advantage: The World According to Adam Smith

In 1776, Adam Smith published his famous book, *The Wealth of Nations*.[2] In this book, he attacked the mercantilism belief that the amount of wealth in the world is fixed and trade surpluses or deficits are a zero-sum game where one trading partner must win at the other's expense. Smith argued that the world's wealth is not fixed because when nations engage in international trade world productivity increases (everyone is wealthier). This happens because individual nations do what they do most efficiently and pass on the gains from this efficiency to all trading partners. Next, we can see how this works.

For Smith, the organizations in each nation should specialize in producing those things that they can do at the lowest cost. In Smith's view, costs are based on the value of labor, and the cost to produce a good depends on the amount of labor to produce the good. Thus, country A has an **absolute advantage** in the production of a good when it takes fewer units of labor to produce the good than in country B. According to Smith, for the world to benefit from absolute advantages, a country should produce goods for which it has absolute advantage and import those goods in which it has absolute disadvantage.

For a personal example, let us imagine that you and one other person (call her Jane) are marooned on an island. You do not trust each other very much so both of you try to survive on your own. The island has fertile soil so you can grow fruits and vegetables, and it has a good supply of fish so you can also fish for your food. You come from a family of farmers and have been successful at growing all the fruit and vegetables you need. Unfortunately, you are not very

absolute advantage
when the production of a good in country A takes fewer units of labor than production of the good in country B

good at fishing and it takes a lot of time and effort for you to catch any fish. Jane has just the opposite problem. She comes from a fishing family and is very good at fishing but has trouble getting her fruits and vegetables to grow.

What should you do? According to Smith you should specialize in what you do best—farming—and the other person should specialize in what she does best—fishing—and you should trade. If things work as Smith predicts both of you will have more fish and fruit and vegetables than you did before. Now we can look at a more formal example of how these numbers work out.

You can see the benefits from trade using absolute advantage in labor costs in a simple example of a two-nation, two-product world. Exhibit 4.3 shows an example of French wine production and US wheat production. For a unit of labor, French wineries produce 15 liters of wine, three times the 5 liters produced by US wineries. The French have an absolute advantage in wine production. US farmers, however, are more efficient than French farmers at producing wheat. They produce twice as many bushels of wheat for a unit of labor as do the French farmers. As you can see in Exhibit 4.3, if countries simply produce for their own consumption of wheat and wine, the total worldwide production in our example "world" is 20 liters of wine and 30 bushels of wheat with two units of labor.

What happens when we specialize? That is, what happens if US farmers just produce wheat and French farmers just produce wine? When the French shift their inefficient wheat production to wine, for every freed-up unit of labor that previously produced wheat they get 15 liters of wine. Similarly, when the US shifts its inefficient wine production to wheat, it gets another 20 bushels of wheat. The result of this shift in production to specialize in areas of absolute advantage is shown in the bottom part of Exhibit 4.3. Without using any more labor, total world production increases, and if the US imports wine and the French wheat, everyone in those countries can drink more wine and eat more bread than they did before.

Of course, this example makes many simplifying assumptions to show how trading based on absolute advantage can be beneficial to all trading partners. For example, in the real world it is not always possible to shift agricultural production from one product to another. For example, even if soil and climate conditions are best for a particular crop other factors such as investments in crop-specific equipment and tacit knowledge regarding raising the crop may encourage otherwise inefficient production. As we will see in our journey through the history of trade theory, scholars have expanded on these basic ideas to explain better what happens in the real world of international trade.

Absolute Advantage with No Specialization Output from Units of Labor				
Nation	**Wine**	**Units of Labor Input**	**Wheat**	**Units of Labor Input**
France	15 liters	1	10 bushels	1
United States	5 liters	1	20 bushels	1
World totals	20 liters	2	30 bushels	2
Absolute Advantage with Total Specialization				
	Output from Units of Labor			
Nation	Wine	Units of Labor Input	Wheat	Units of Labor Input
France	30 liters	2	0 bushels	0
United States	0 liters	0	40 bushels	2
World totals	30 liters	2	40 bushels	2

Exhibit 4.3 Two-nation Wine and Wheat Production Possibilities Under Conditions of Absolute Advantage in a Hypothetical Two-nation World

One of the problems of trading based on absolute advantage is that it eliminates many potential trading partners. For our small two-product, two-country world, what happens if one country has absolute advantage in both products? Although it does not seem to make as much intuitive sense as Adam Smith's view on trade based on absolute advantage, David Ricardo made the insightful observation that trade can benefit both partners even if one is more efficient in producing both goods.[3] In the next section, we will see how this is possible.

Comparative Advantage: The World According to David Ricardo

Within any particular nation the companies and industries do some things better than they do other things. That is, for example, one nation may be twice as good at making computers as it is at growing corn. Another nation may be better at growing corn than at producing computers. The principle of **comparative advantage** explains how these relative differences within countries can lead to beneficial trade between partners.

comparative advantage the relative advantage in production efficiency that a nation has internally over another

Returning to our example of the island, imagine that you and Jane both are still fishing and farming to survive. She spends half a day fishing and one day farming and she gets all the food she needs for a week. Since you do not fish very well it takes you a whole day to get a week's fish. It takes you a day and half to get your farming done. Jane is more efficient than you are in both tasks since she spends less time in both tasks. She has absolute advantage in both tasks. However, because Jane is better at fishing than farming she spends twice as much of her time farming as she does fishing. Because you are better at farming than fishing, you spend 1.5 times as much time fishing as farming.

Because both Jane and you are relatively better at one task than another task, there are comparative advantages. Jane's is fishing and yours is farming. Does it make sense for you to specialize in what you do best and for Jane to specialize in what she does best, and trade fish for fruits and vegetables? Let us look at a simple example as given in Exhibit 4.4 to show how trade in such a situation can work for both sides' benefit.

In this example, we compare US and Chinese production of computers and bicycles. Many people in the US and Europe now fear that production of many goods will go to emerging market nations, with their low-cost labor and increasingly sophisticated production technologies. However, even if, for example, the Chinese can do most things more cheaply, the theory of comparative advantage suggests that trade can still be beneficial to the world's trading partners.

To illustrate the point, we arbitrarily make the Chinese computer and bicycle manufacturers more efficient than their US counterparts. For the example of absolute advantage shown in Exhibit 4.4, we considered only labor costs and input, but since we know that much more than labor goes into producing something, we generalize in this example to consider broadly the input of resources. Thus, in this illustration, the Chinese use 10 units of resources (e.g. labor, materials, capital, machinery, etc.) to produce one computer and 2 units of resources to produce a bicycle. In comparison, the US producers use 100 resource units for a computer and 4 units for a bicycle. The Chinese have absolute advantage in the production of both products because they use fewer resources.

	Resource Inputs		Opportunity Costs	
	Computer	Bicycle	Computer	Bicycle
China	10	2	5	0.2
United States	100	4	25	0.04

Exhibit 4.4 Comparative Advantage and Opportunity Costs When One Country has Absolute Advantage in Both Goods

Comparative advantage relates to the idea of **opportunity costs**. Opportunity costs mean that when you choose to produce one good, you have to give up the opportunity to produce another good. Thus, there is a trade-off each country makes when it decides to produce one good in place of another. A country has comparative advantage in good A if it has to give up producing fewer units of good B than does another country. This means that within that country it is relatively more efficient to produce one product than another product.

We estimate opportunity costs by comparing the relative resource inputs into producing a good. That is, how many resources would you have to switch from one product to produce another product? In our example, you can see that if the Chinese want to produce another computer with the required 10 units of resources, they must give up production of five bicycles. The opportunity costs are 10/2, or 5. That is, for every computer produced instead of bicycles they lose about five bicycles. US manufacturers must give up 25 bicycles for each computer since they are comparatively less efficient than are the Chinese in computer production. For the US producers, however, an additional bicycle costs only a very small fraction of the resources that produce a computer (4/100 = 0.04). This is relatively better than the Chinese output (2/10 = 0.2). Thus, although the Chinese have absolute advantage in both products, the US has comparative advantage in bicycle production and the Chinese have comparative advantage in computer production.

Comparative Advantage and Production Gains   The theory of comparative advantage suggests that countries should specialize not only in those products for which they have absolute advantage but also in those products for which they have comparative advantage. With specialization and trade it becomes possible with comparative advantage for both trading partners to gain.

Exhibit 4.4 shows how it works out. In this Exhibit, we show how each country could use 10,000 resource units in the production of bicycles and computers.

With no trade between the US and China, which economists call the state of **autarky** or lack of trade, each country would have to produce and consume its own output. Each country would then produce a mixture of computers and bicycles by allocating its 10,000 resource units between the two products. The Chinese could produce up to 1,000 computers with no bicycles or up to 5,000 bicycles with no computers. US manufacturers could produce up to 100 computers with no bicycles or 2,500 bicycles without any computers. These are the extremes of the production possibilities; more realistically, each country would produce a mix of products depending on consumer tastes. It is unlikely that there would be no demand for at least some bicycles or some computers in each country.

For the sake of illustration, let us assume that each country divides its 10,000 resource units equally between bicycle production and computer production. Using the required resource units per computer and per bicycle, Exhibit 4.5 shows the production from 10,000 resource units spread equally between products based on the required resource inputs for each country (see Exhibit 4.4 for the resource units required to produce each product). Chinese manufacturers can produce 500 computers (5,000/10) and 2,500 bicycles (5,000/2) in China and 50 computers (5,000/100) and 1,250 bicycles (5,000/4) in the US.

If each country specializes in its area of comparative advantage, as shown in Exhibit 4.5, production becomes greater in both bicycles and computers! Unlike for absolute advantage, total specialization by each country does not always produce more in both products. Had the Chinese completely specialized in computers and the US in bicycles, the world would have many more computers and slightly fewer bicycles than before specialization. However, the Chinese could increase world production output using only 70 percent of their resources and still allocate the remaining 30 percent to bicycle production. With the US totally specializing in bicycle production, worldwide production is now higher than before in both products.

opportunity costs
the choice to produce one good requires you to give up the opportunity to produce another good

autarky
the absence of trade

Production Gains from Trade	Before Specialization		After Specialization		Net Gain (Loss)	
	Computers	Bicycles	Computers	Bicycles	Computers	Bicycles
China	500	2,500	700	1,500	200	−1,000
US	50	1,250	0	2,500	−50	1,250
Total	550	3,750	700	4,000	150	250

Consumption Gains from Trade	Before Trade		After Trade		Net Gain (Loss)	
	Computers	Bicycles	Computers	Bicycles	Computers	Bicycles
China	500	2,500	575	2,625	75	125
US	50	1,250	125	1,375	75	125
Total	550	3,750	700	4,000	150	250

Exhibit 4.5 Production and Consumption Possibilities for Computers and Bicycles Using 10,000 Resource Units in China and the US

Comparative Advantage and Consumption Gains   With the production gains, there are now 150 more computers and 250 more bicycles available for Chinese and US American consumers. However, in order to get these goods, China and the US must trade.

Without trade, Chinese and US consumers were limited in what they could purchase by the range of production possibilities in the trade-offs between computers and bicycles. Exhibit 4.5 shows the net gains in consumption possibilities for the two-country world assuming they were divided equally between China and the US. With trade and the right forms of specialization, consumers in both countries now can consume more than would be possible in a world without trade. Theoretically, at least, everyone benefits.

Free trade advocates rely heavily on the theory of comparative advantage to offset arguments that low-cost countries such as China will eventually produce everything, leaving the developed world with nothing but local service industries and many lost jobs. The argument is that no country can have comparative advantage in everything.

Ricardo's theory of comparative advantage looks at the efficiency of production primarily through labor costs as the basis of comparative advantage. For example, it is easy to see in today's world that countries like Mexico, China, and the Czech Republic have lower wages than the US or Germany, and thus are more efficient at producing some products. However, there are other sources of comparative advantage besides the efficiency of resource inputs. In the next section, we consider other sources of comparative advantage as outlined by two Swedish economists, Eli Heckscher[4] and the Nobel prizewinner Bertil Ohlin.[5]

The Heckscher–Ohlin Theory and the Role of Factor Endowments

Heckscher–Ohlin theory (HO)
a nation's comparative advantage comes from the relative abundance of its factor endowments

The **Heckscher–Ohlin theory** (**HO**) argues that a nation's comparative advantage comes from the relative abundance of its factor endowments. Factor endowments are resources that a nation's businesses use to produce their products or services. There are two basic types of factor endowments. One is capital, which in trade theory refers to inputs that go into making a product or delivering a service, such as land, energy, machines, buildings, or tools. The other is labor. Not all nations have equal factor endowments. For example, the US has abundant supplies of natural resources such as land and energy. Japan has limited factor endowments in land and natural resources such as coal.

As in traditional views of comparative advantage based on the *relative* costs of inputs to production, the HO theory uses the *relative* abundance of capital versus labor to define comparative advantage. That is, a nation would have a comparative advantage in labor if it has more labor available than capital, even if it has less labor and capital than another nation. Like the theories of Ricardo and Smith, the HO theory argues that free trade is beneficial to all partners. However, for HO theory, international trade is driven not by relative differences in production efficiency but by relative differences in the factor endowments of countries.

With unrestricted trade, nations will export goods that require factors in which they have comparative advantage and import goods that require factors in which they are relatively less endowed. For example, Brazil exports coffee and France exports wine because they have the factor endowment of the right soil and climate conditions for growing coffee beans and grapes. China exports huge numbers of garments and textiles to the US and Europe because it has comparative advantage in cheaper labor.

Consider again our example of your lost island. When your ship sank, not only you but also your friend managed to swim to shore on the same island. When Jane's ship sank, she was the only one to swim to the same island as you. However, her boat's fishing equipment washed ashore. On your half of the island, with two people, you have more factor endowments in labor. On Jane's half of the island, with her fishing gear, Jane has more factor endowments in capital. Even if Jane were a great farmer, HO theory would predict that Jane should use her superior factor endowments and specialize in fishing while you use your superior labor force and do farming. You can then trade.

One additional prediction of the HO theory is that trade will lead to factor price equality among partners. What this means is that the prices of the capital and labor that go into producing something in both countries will gradually become equal. Prior to trade, the price of goods produced from the rarer factor—say, for example, industrial products in agricultural countries—would cost more. This makes sense because we usually have to pay more for things that are in short supply. After trading with nations endowed with industrial production capacity, the supply of industrial goods in the agricultural nation goes up. Again, based on simple supply and demand, we would expect prices for industrial products in the agricultural nation to decline. Thus, for example, HO theory would predict the reduction of wages for unskilled workers (a reduction in labor costs) in the US when the types of goods produced by these workers are imported from countries like China or Mexico with high endowments of unskilled labor. As you will see from some of the strategic insights in this chapter, the likelihood of this happening is one reason why many unskilled workers look to the government to protect their industries from low-cost country competition.

Exhibit 4.6 shows the Penn World Table statistics on the capital per worker endowments of various countries. Based on the HO theory, which countries would you predict to export and import goods that involve capital-intensive production?

For approximately two decades after the introduction of the HO theory, most economists took intuitive examples like capital-intensive Germany exporting technical machinery as evidence that the HO theory was correct. In the early 1950s, Wassily Leontief produced the first comprehensive test of the HO theory and found some unusual results.[6] The next section details the findings of this study.

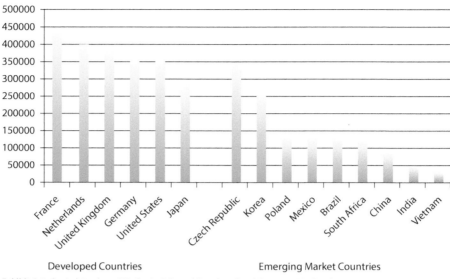

Exhibit 4.6 Capital Stock per Worker in Selected Developed and Emerging Market Countries
Source: Penn World Table, International Comparisons of Production, Income and Prices 9.0.

The Leontief Paradox According to the HO theory, a capital-intensive country such as the United States should export capital-intensive goods and import labor-intensive goods. To test this hypothesis, Leontief looked at 200 industries in the US. Contrary to expectations, he found that the US was exporting relatively more labor-intensive goods and importing capital-intensive goods. Much to the surprise of economists, the US exports were about 30 percent more labor-intensive than its imports. This result was so contrary to expectations that this finding became known as the **Leontief Paradox**.

Updating the HO Theory Although the Leontief Paradox showed that the simple form of HO theory could not fully explain world trade, economists up to the present time have continued to modify and update the theory. Current empirical tests of the theory show that, in its updated versions, the HO theory can explain many aspects of trade quite well.[7]

One assumption of the HO theory is that tastes in countries are identical. That is, people in different countries enjoy the same products. Given equal tastes, countries will import goods for which they have a comparative disadvantage. But what happens if a capital-intensive country, for example like Germany, has consumers that have strong preferences for capital-intensive goods such as high technology cars? Such a taste bias may completely offset the German comparative advantage in capital-intensive goods and result in Germany importing more capital-intensive goods even in areas of its comparative advantage. For example, Germany still imports luxury cars from Japan. However, research also suggests that most countries have a "home bias" in tastes and prefer to consume goods made in their own country. Adjusting the HO theory for taste differences can partially explain the Leontief Paradox, but these differences are not enough to offset the Paradox completely.

A second assumption of the original HO theory was that the companies in different nations used similar technologies to produce their goods. A look at the US and Japanese automobile producers in the 1970s and 1980s shows this as untrue. Using innovative production and supply technologies, the Japanese car makers outcompeted their US rivals with cheaper and higher-quality vehicles. Their imports into the US rose so fast that the US government convinced the Japanese to adopt voluntary quotas to limit Japanese competition. Eventually, US manufacturers

Leontief Paradox
when a capital-intensive country exports more labor-intensive goods and imports capital-intensive goods

managed to increase quality and efficiency of production to compete with their Japanese rivals and both US and Japanese companies now face increasing competition from South Korean automobile manufacturers. Most recent economics research suggests that trade is best explained by both Ricardo's comparative advantage in efficiency of production (in part due to superior technologies) and the relative factor endowments identified by HO theory.

Another advance in the HO theory is a refinement of the two factors of capital and labor into more detailed classifications. Most economists now consider factor endowments as farmland, raw materials or natural resources, human capital or skilled labor, manmade capital such as transportation systems, and unskilled labor. The HO theory works much better with a more precise breakdown of resources. For example, it then makes more sense that the US is a big exporter of agricultural products (based on the large endowment of arable land) and also outputs like super-computers (based on large endowments in university and industry research and development).

Exhibit 4.7 shows the relative factor endowments of selected countries. Capital factor endowments relate to structures and equipment. Human capital endowments indicate the levels of skilled labor based on education. Note that the US and the EU countries are highly endowed with physical capital and skilled labor (human capital). India and China have less skilled labor, but the Chinese have significant physical capital endowments. Recent US trade data suggest a pattern consistent with the HO theory. The US exports more goods and services requiring skilled labor than it imports, and it imports more low-skilled labor-intensive manufactured goods such as athletic shoes and textiles. For a specific case, look at Exhibit 4.8 to see if this pattern holds for the trade between the US and China. This Exhibit shows the trade balance of exports and imports of the US with China. The positive numbers show the top ten product categories in which the US exports more to China than it imports. The negative numbers show the top ten product categories in which the US imports more than it exports to China, hence a negative trade balance.

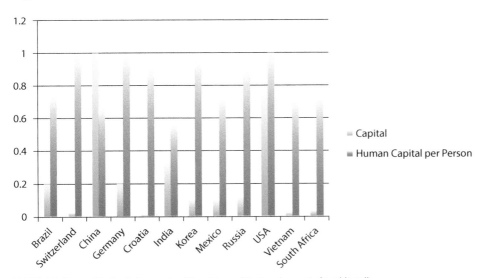

Exhibit 4.7 Types of Factor Endowments of Countries and Regions (percent of world total)
Source: Penn World Table, International Comparisons of Production, Income and Prices 9.0.
Note: Relative capital computed from Capital stock using prices for structures and equipment in constant US$ across countries; Relative human capital per person computed from the Index of Human Capital per Person based on years of schooling and returns to education.

Positive Categories		Negative Categories	
Aircraft & Associated Equipment	14,954,061	Automatic Data Processing Machines	−49,533,070
Oil Seeds and Oleaginous Fruit	10,507,564	Toys and Sporting Goods	−25,199,371
Motor Vehicles	8,810,257	Furniture and Bedding Accessories	−21,021,136
Pulp and Waste Paper	3,412,425	Footwear	−17,194,236
Nonferrous Base Metal Waste & Scrap	3,014,425	Clothing	−11,964,421
Animal Food	2,114,598	Electrical Machinery and Apparatus	−11,349,329
Cereals	2,114,785	Televisions	−11,050,281
Raw Hides and Skins	1,143,785	Office Machine Parts	−10,535,082
Liquefied Propane and Butane	961,288	Articles of Plastics	−10,541,363
Wood	900,214	Household Electric and Nonelectric Equipment	−10,360,468

Exhibit 4.8 The US Trade Balance with China by Top Ten Positive and Negative Product Categories: Exports − Imports ($,000) 2015

Source: Data reported in Trade Stats Express, Office of Trade and Industry Information, http://tse.export.gov/tse/TSEOptions.aspx?ReportID=2&Referrer=TSEReports.aspx&DataSource=NTD

Most economists believe that the continuing modifications to the HO theory produce a reasonable explanation of a significant amount of world trade. However, the model is still not a complete explanation and one needs to understand alternative models to grasp more completely the complexities of world trade. We now turn to examine some of these complementary and alternative views.

Other Views of Trade

In this section, we consider three additional views of the drivers of world trade, product life cycle theory, **new trade theory**, and Michael Porter's view of national advantages.

new trade theory countries gain comparative advantage through the cost-saving gains from specialization and economies of scale

The Product Life Cycle: A Technology Innovation View

As we noted above, the HO theory assumed that all nations used the same technology. Of course, there are many examples that show this simplifying assumption as incorrect. For example, in the US and especially the western states, the availability of many large rivers allows US companies to take advantage of hydroelectric power at a very low cost. This technology is not available in Saudi Arabia or other desert countries. Nations keep other technologies secret for security reasons. The US government restricts the exportation of technological equipment or computer software, such as the encryption programs designed by Microsoft, which may have military applications. Interestingly, the Dutch satellite company New Skies Satellites NV lobbied the US Congress to ease rules that limit exports of satellite technology to companies outside the US. New Skies wants to obtain US satellite technology that is not readily accessible to foreign-based companies such as them. New Skies argues that companies from North Atlantic Treaty Organization (NATO) countries should be exempt from the US Export Control Act. Similarly, patent and copyright laws attempt to restrict the flow of technologies across borders and can be a source of competitive advantage for companies in particular nations.

One aspect of technology that may determine trade patterns is not what the technology is but who gets it first and who eventually produces it most efficiently. This viewpoint, first proposed by Raymond Vernon, focuses on the life cycle of a product from its initial innovation and introduction to its eventual standardization. For an example of a product life cycle, consider the history of electronic calculators. When first introduced, even with simple functions such as square root, they were quite expensive (often over $1,000) and innovative products. This was the new product stage. After a period, many companies learned to produce calculators with increasing efficiency. As competition drove down prices, more and more people could afford a calculator. This was the growth product stage. Of course, now one can have that once-$1,000 calculator for a few dollars or even free on the Internet. Calculators are now a mature product. Can you think of any other products going through this life cycle? Flat screen TVs seem to be in the growth stage now. Why should this relate to trade?

In what became known as **product life cycle theory**, Vernon[8] proposed that the major industrial economies, such as the US, Japan, and Germany, focus on new product development and innovation. Such countries with their highly skilled workforce and large capital resources provide the fertile ground for companies to develop new and innovative products. Typically, companies like Apple begin small and gradually refine the production process and the product. Apple began with the Apple I prototype in a garage. This was soon followed by the Apple II, which became the first commercially successful personal computer. Apple has maintained its very profitable operation by leading the industry in new product developments, striving continuously to stay ahead of the lower cost imitations that soon follow new releases often from emerging economies like China and Korea.

> **product life cycle theory** major industrial economies focus on new product development and innovation and less-developed countries focus on production of mature products

If the product is successful, companies first serve domestic markets and then move to export markets. As long as the innovating company controls the technology, it has little fear of competition from companies from other nations. Eventually, as the production of the product becomes standardized, companies consider moving production of the entire product or its components to other countries such as China. No longer are the companies willing to pay for the highly skilled labor needed initially in the product's early development. Once production of a product becomes routine, it makes sense to replace higher-paid, higher-skilled workers with lower-skilled and lower-paid workers in other countries. At the same time, foreign competitors in the low-cost countries begin to develop the skills necessary to produce the product.

Eventually imports from foreign companies rather than domestic production serve the innovating countries' markets. In summary, many manufactured products go through the following stages:

1. Introduction into the home market.
2. Export sales are added to domestic sales.
3. Foreign production begins in lower-cost countries.
4. Domestic industry loses its competitive advantage in price and innovation.
5. Foreign competition serves the domestic market with imports.

Exhibit 4.9 shows how these processes work over time.

Products that seemingly have followed Vernon's hypothesis include the pocket calculator, radios, televisions, personal computers, and cell phones. Initially producers from the major industrialized countries dominated the production of these products. Eventually, through standardized production and the movement of the technologies first to Japan (when it was a low-cost country) and then to other low-cost countries, the US now imports most of these goods. For example, consider the history of the TV. Prior to 1970, single manufacturers designed, produced, and assembled each component of their TVs. Most TVs came from the US, Japan, and Germany, at the time among the top industrialized nations. Now almost all TVs purchased in the US come from other low-cost emerging market countries, such as China. Even Japanese imports into the US are manufactured in low-cost emerging market countries under Japanese brand names.

Although the product life cycle theory seems to explain the post-World War II product development innovations in the US and the eventual migration of the production of these products to low-cost countries, its application to today's more integrated global economy may be less strong. MNCs often introduce new products simultaneously in many countries. In addition, MNCs such as Dell Computer may still produce in developed countries using highly automated assembly plants. Yet, Dell sources its PC components worldwide from manufacturers in lower-cost countries such as China and Taiwan.

Product life cycle theory adds another consideration regarding how to look at specialization of production based on absolute or comparative advantage. That is, according to this view, some countries are more likely to develop companies that are good at creating new products when other countries are more likely to develop companies that are efficient at producing mature products. Next, we will look at an additional explanation of trade that considers specialization in production based on a different type of efficiency.

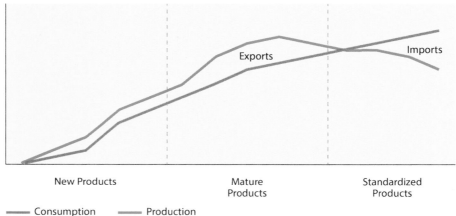

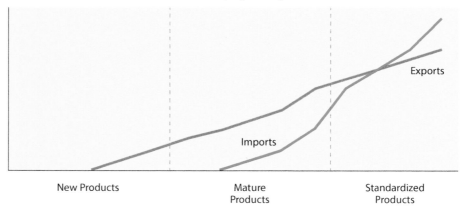

Exhibit 4.9 Vernon's Product Life Cycle Theory

Source: Adapted from R. Vernon and L. T. Wells, 1986, *The Economic Environment of International Business* (4th edn), Upper Saddle River, NJ: Pearson Education.

New Trade Theory

One limitation of traditional views of comparative advantage is their failure to explain why nations with similar resources engage in so much trade. The US, for example, imports and exports more to Canada and the EU than any other country or region. During the 1980s, several economists developed what is now called new trade theory.[9]

New trade theory looks at how companies and industries in a nation can take advantage of **economies of scale**. Economies of scale mean that each additional unit of production costs less to produce than did the previous unit. Companies gain economies of scale most often when they can spread large fixed costs over more units of output. For example, the Airbus super jumbo jet required huge investments in development costs. Airbus must sell over 500 planes just to break even, but after that the development cost per plane gets progressively smaller. Pharmaceutical companies face similar problems. It often takes years of research and development and millions of dollars to bring a drug to market. As with commercial airplanes, when companies spread these costs over a larger volume of sales, the cost per unit drops. Not only do larger production runs allow companies to spread fixed costs over more units, but they also allow workers to learn the production skills, both of which lead to reduced costs.

Firms can also get economies of scale from the nature of the industry. These are often called external scale economies. As industry output increases, suppliers get larger and can pass on some of their economies to the producer. In addition, the pool of skilled labor grows with the industry and companies can gain efficiencies from this labor pool. Many experts link the availability of skilled labor in an industry to what experts call industrial agglomeration. This means the tendency of companies in an industry to cluster in one location. Some examples of industrial agglomeration include the movie industry in Hollywood, the financial industry in London and New York, and computer-related industries in Silicon Valley and Bangalore, India. Although, to some extent, historical accident has led to this clustering, the benefits are often apparent. Once the clustering begins, new companies in an industry locate closer to competitors to take advantage of the local supply of skilled labor. In addition to skilled labor, companies in industrial clusters sometimes benefit from lower transportation from suppliers and to customers. Clusters can also increase competition, which forces companies to be more innovative and technologically advanced. Close proximity also seems to increase the amount of learning that companies can get from each other. People move from one company to another, shared projects are more likely, and the competition encourages related companies (e.g. supplier and manufacturer) to share more information.

How do economies of scale, whether internal or external to the company, relate to trade? The basic answer points to the cost-saving gains from specialization. If a nation, by accident or through the encouragement of government policy, can develop an industry that can produce in great quantities, then it can produce at lower costs and trade the excess production beyond domestic needs to other countries. Thus, two nations with equal endowments of resources who, based on other trade theories, would have no reason to trade, may specialize in products they produce with economies of scale. They can then trade with each other, and consumers in both countries will get access to less expensive goods.

Next, we will see an alternative view of trade offered by the renowned Harvard University strategy professor Michael Porter.

Michael Porter and the Competitive Advantage of Nations

Porter asks the question, "Why does a nation become the home base for successful international competitors in an industry?"[10] For example, he asks, "Why is Switzerland a leader in pharmaceuticals and chocolates?" "Why is Germany a leader in luxury cars and chemical production?" "Why is Japan a leader in automobile production?"

economies of scale
each additional unit of production costs less to produce than did the previous unit

Porter rejects the notion that comparative advantage is sufficient to explain world trade. More importantly, he sees trade theories based on existing endowments as assuming away what managers do to compete: strategize, improve technology and management practices, and differentiate products. As such, he is more concerned with what makes industries competitive in different national settings and how companies can take advantage of these conditions.

Porter sees four broad areas in a nation that lead to international competitive companies in different industries. These include:

- *Firm strategy, structure, and rivalry*: how a company is run and how it competes.
- *Related and supporting industries*: the existence of suppliers and related talents.
- *Demand conditions*: the home country demand for the industry's output.
- *Factor endowments*: similar to HO theory but with additional possibilities.

national diamond
includes: firm strategy, structure, and rivalry; related and supporting industries; demand conditions; and, factor endowments

He argues that these areas form a **national diamond** of interrelated factors, and that an industry must have advantages in most or all to achieve and maintain competitive success. Exhibit 4.10 shows a picture of the national diamond as illustrated by Porter.

Firm Strategy, Structure, and Rivalry   No one management system is appropriate for all industries, and different countries support different types of management. For example, in Germany, many top executives hold PhDs in technical areas and this produces a superior ability to improve product designs and production processes. Porter contrasts this with the US management emphasis on finance, to which he attributes the US decline in some manufacturing industries.

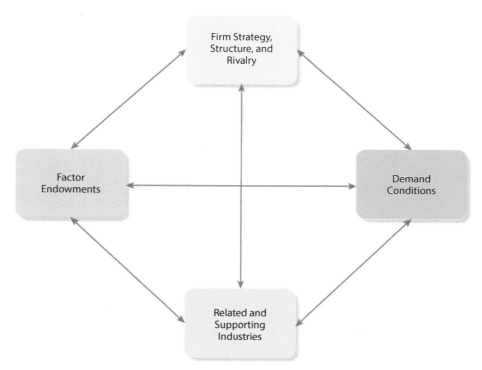

Exhibit 4.10 Porter's National Diamond: Determinants of National Competitive Advantage
Source: Michael E. Porter, 1990, *The Competitive Advantage of Nations*, New York: The Free Press.

Also important for developing internationally competitive companies is the existence of high levels of rivalry in a domestic industry. This competition drives companies to achieve superior performance just to compete locally. For Porter, national competition is a driver of innovation, and this innovation makes these companies better international competitors. Without such rivalry, companies are more likely to stay in their domestic market. For example, the local competition in Japan for flat-panel TV displays is fierce. Four companies dominate the Japanese market: NEC, the Fujitsu/Hitachi consortium, Pioneer, and Matsushita Electric, Japan's largest consumer electronics company. This competition at home helps drive innovations in flat-panel display technologies and manufacturing efficiencies. In turn, it makes these companies better competitors in the world market.

Related and Supporting Industries   When suppliers are superior and more innovative, companies in the industry are more likely to gain knowledge about the processes of innovation and upgrading from these relationships. That is, suppliers help companies see new methods of operations and perceive opportunities to use new technologies. This is a spin-off of ideas and innovations from one industry to another. For example, Italian firms produce the majority of the jewelry-making machinery in the world. Italian jewelry-manufacturing companies such as New Silver in Vicenza, Italy, are leaders in the gold and silver jewelry industry in part because they have more ready access to the latest jewelry-producing machines.

A Look at the Seoul Digital Industrial Complex in Korea: Building World-class Competitive Advantage in an Emerging Market

IB EMERGING MARKET
STRATEGIC INSIGHT

What began in the 1970s as an export development complex focusing on textile and sewing for the export market is now a cluster of resident uses that focus on high-value operations in the information technology and knowledge-creating industries. No longer dominated by the textile and sewing companies, now nearly 60 percent of the companies in the cluster are non-manufacturing.

The Seoul Digital Industrial Complex has four miniclusters—digital contents, ICT (information and communications technology), green IT, and IT-convergence medical clusters, based on the types of businesses. The miniclusters provide the networks among businesses (497), universities, research centers (33), and other support organizations. ICT and digital contents are the major businesses in the complex, with 209 members and 176 members, respectively. Supporting organizations focus on technology development and marketing and also include global marketing support for export of resident companies.

A recent entrepreneurial success story is CMMC, which manufactures a nearly pain free injection device for diabetes patients. In two years this born global company captured 5 percent of the world market selling 10 million units of injectors a year with a value of $1 million a year in exports. It was able to compete globally because of clusters of suppliers, subcontractors, and associated human resource talents.

Source: Adapted from Korea Industrial Complex Corporation, 2015, *Industrial Complex Clusters in Korea: Achievements and Challenges.*

Porter discovered that internationally competitive industries in a country tend to cluster into groups of related industries. Often this cluster is in one geographical area. Related industries transfer knowledge and innovation to each other. For example, many Japanese companies are world leaders in the production of synthetic textile fibers. The technologies used in producing these synthetic fibers are similar to those used in the production of textiles made from silk. This just happens to be another industry in which the Japanese are internationally competitive.

The IB Emerging Market Strategic Insight above shows how the situation in Seoul, Korea, gives an example of how related and supporting industries allow Korea to be a major competitor in the world market.

Demand Conditions   The core design of products usually first reflects the nature of the home country's demand. For example, to accommodate highly congested areas, high fuel costs, and a strong cultural value for quality, Japanese consumers have demanded smaller, high-quality, and highly efficient automobiles. For example, when Toyota introduced its hybrid (gas and electric) sedan Prius, its success set the stage for world competition with hybrid technology. Not surprisingly, Japanese automobile manufacturers are among the world leaders in many areas of automobile production, including hybrid technology. Porter argues that companies gain competitive advantage when the demand in the home country gives them a clearer or earlier picture of buyer needs from other nations.

Factor Endowments   Porter also argues that created and not inherited factors are the most important for competitive success. He calls these created factors the specialized factors of production, and they include skilled labor, capital, and the country's infrastructure. Non-key or general-use factors are unskilled labor and raw materials. He does not see these factors as leading to competitive advantage because companies can easily get these inputs. For example, although Japan, Taiwan, and Korea have little natural endowments of raw materials such as iron ore or coal, they get these on the world market. Instead, they use their endowments of skilled and motivated labor to produce worldwide competitive products. Because specialized factors such as educating a skilled workforce require heavy and sustained investments, they are difficult to imitate. Hence, countries like Germany, even with the most highly paid workers in the world, can have competitive companies because the German educational system does an excellent job at producing technologically skilled workers. Approximately 70 percent of German secondary school graduates continue in some type of specialized occupational training. Often this combines with on-the-job training paid for by companies with part-time vocational education paid for by the government.

Evaluating Trade Theories: What Do They Tell Us?

The economic theories of trade generally tell us that free trade between nations is, on average, beneficial for all of the involved countries. Although limited by simplifying assumptions, the theories of absolute and comparative advantage provide the mathematical logic that trade works to produce more products and give consumers more options.

The world is not as simple as the two-country, two-product examples typically used to illustrate absolute and comparative advantage. When applied to the real world that is multi-country, multi-product, culturally diverse in tastes, and diverse in economic structures and affluence, we see that the fundamental trade theories are incomplete. Contemporary theories of trade attempt to fill in the blanks by providing explanations of the missing links in explaining the growing world trade phenomena.

Traditional theories of trade focused on explaining the importing and exporting of goods. In today's global economy, international business people are also concerned with the exporting and importing of services. Although we have no reason to assume that trade in services will not follow similar patterns to trade in goods, we do not have the extensive scientific research to know for sure.

Trade theories, with the partial exception of Porter's diamond, tend to look at the nation as the unit of analysis. However, individual companies make the strategic decisions to import or export. Later chapters in the text will deal more thoroughly with the strategic rationale and decision-making processes regarding how and when to procure or sell your products or services in other nations.

At this point, we can note that the prime strategic reasons to import are to get cheaper or otherwise unavailable services or supplies for a company. For example, in the computer industry, companies like Dell source their chips, LCDs, and keyboards from all over the world. Similarly, the global automobile industry imports automotive components from all over the world. Although we seldom can track the sources of all the components of our cars, some might come from companies such as Hella KGaA Hueck located in Lippstadt, Germany. Tomas Hedenborg, Hella's former president and CEO, notes that they are "the only company worldwide specializing in front-end modules." They supply components to VW's plant in Puebla, Mexico; to Ford's plant in Hermosillo (the Ford Fusion, Mercury Milan, and Lincoln Zephyr); and for Chrysler in St Louis and Windsor, Canada. According to Hedenborg, Hella is the world leader with 23 percent of the global market share for outsourced front-end modules.[11]

From the company's perspective, exporting is an opportunity to increase sales and revenues. Besides this obvious motivation, companies may export because of saturated markets at home, unused production capacity, or difficulty in overcoming the advantages of a market leader at home. For example, AMD, the computer chip manufacturer and competitor of market leader Intel, exports more products to South America, where it gained an early advantage over Intel.

An important strategic concern of all international companies is to understand the impact of government policies regarding trade on their industry's position in the world economy. When governments choose to join free trade areas or choose to impose tariffs or other barriers to trade, particular industries may benefit or be hurt. For example, big box retailers like Walmart benefit greatly from clothing, television, and other electronics imports from China. Alternatively, leaders in some industries are calling for restrictions on imports to protect their local companies and jobs. In the next section, we will consider some other anti-free trade arguments.

The anti-free trade arguments associated with the political environment in Europe and the US did reduce world trade and investment. Although most economists believe that restricting free trade hurts all in the long run it seems that emerging market countries are more vulnerable. Their economies tend to be built not on internal consumption as with the US but on external trade such as China with the world.[12]

Arguments Against Free Trade

While most economists are free trade advocates, there are counter-arguments to a system based mostly on efficiency and less on political and socio-cultural considerations. Those who hold these positions typically call on their governments to impose tariffs or other import restrictions on foreign imports. Several of these arguments follow.

Free Trade as a Threat to National Sovereignty
This position, often adopted by anti-free trade politicians such as Pat Buchanan in the US, reflects the worry that if a nation loses its production capacity in key products it may be in danger of

losing its core national identity. Sometimes this position reflects a challenge to the unique nature of a national culture. In France, for example, there exists a concern for protecting the uniqueness of French culture and language. In particular, there is a concern for the use of English in advertising, the naming of products, and workplace terms. For example, labor unions at General Electric Medical Systems in France challenged in court the company's right to use a technical manual published only in English. The unions won their case—French law requires that all workplace manuals be translated into French.[13] MNCs that work in France must be aware of the laws regarding language use. Consider the IB Emerging Market Strategic Insight below.

Other areas of concern related to national sovereignty focus on security. Leaders often believe that some industries are too important for national security to allow a reliance on imports. For example, the US government supports industries essential for the military, such as fighter aircraft production, because many consider it bad policy to become reliant on other countries for military-related equipment. An arms supplier could become a future enemy or be conquered by an enemy. In Japan, consumers pay several times the world market price for rice because the Japanese government believes that rice is essential for Japanese survival.

Protecting Infant Industries

The basic point of this argument is that new industries need a temporary shield from foreign competition. This position is not totally against free trade but holds that an infant industry will never develop if the government allows more mature and efficient foreign companies into a country without some tariff or other trade barrier. Similar arguments are often used to temporarily protect industries with aging technologies.

Fair Trade

The fair trade argument proposes that free trade takes advantage of cheap labor that does not have the protection of minimum wages, child labor prohibitions, and worker safety protections. Advocates of fair trade or, as it is sometimes called, the trade justice approach often promote voluntary standards so that consumers can know that the product was produced according to minimum standards for workers' protection. Coffee imported from South and Central America to the US often has fair trade labeling. Starbucks offers fair trade coffee in its selections.

A Temporary Protection of the Steel Industry in Egypt	IB EMERGING MARKET STRATEGIC INSIGHT

The Egyptian Minister of Trade and Industry, Mounir Fakhry Abdel Nour, recently announced a 7.3 percent temporary tariff to protect domestic steel manufacturers. The plan is to limit the duration of the tariff to 200 days. The motivation for the tariff was complaints from Egyptian steel manufacturers regarding increasing imports from Turkey, which is the world's top exporter of reinforcing steel.

Local steel manufacturers were charging 5,200 EGP a ton as compared to imported steel at 4,900 EGP per ton. Unfortunately for local steel producers the success of this temporary protection from lower priced Turkish steel seem unlikely to succeed. Steel importers in Egypt found other suppliers in China and contracted to buy large quantities from the Chinese.

Source: *The Cairo Post*, 2014, "Egypt imposes temporary tariff on steel imports to protect local industry," October 14.

Protecting the Environment

This argument is related in some respects to the fair trade argument, in that companies in countries with stronger environmental protection laws are often more costly producers than are companies in countries with weak protection laws. From a broader perspective, the "green" argument is that decisions made for pure economic efficiency push production to countries with less concern for the environment, often because they have little choice if they wish to attract business. The conclusion is that the world will eventually pay the price. Economists call this a social cost that is often not borne by the seller. For example, when factories in China produce goods under less strict pollution controls than in the US or Europe, they save money. Consumers around the world get these goods at cheaper prices. However, the pollution also adds to global warming and potentially costly climate changes such as a reduced ozone layer (more cancer) and possibly more violent and damaging weather. As such, although it is not part of the original exchange, pollution is not free and the world must pay such social costs.

The Emerging Market Ethical Challenge box opposite gives an example of the environmental costs and benefits of transferring operations to a low-cost country.

Job Loss

Probably the most emotional appeal against free trade is the job-loss argument. Even the most supportive of free trade accept that some jobs will be lost to a country when another country can produce the product or service with absolute or comparative advantage. The US has lost approximately one in six manufacturing jobs since the year 2000. Proponents of the job-loss argument see most of these jobs lost to imports that outcompete local companies, forcing them to close or reduce production, or US companies moving production to the low-cost countries. The Emerging Market Ethical Challenge below gives one poignant example of this situation.

As you saw earlier in the chapter, free traders counter that protecting jobs costs the society generally. They also argue that manufacturing job loss is not all attributable to trade. Automation probably has cost more US manufacturing jobs than offshoring.

Exporting Absolute Advantage While Reducing the Local Carbon Footprint

EMERGING MARKET
ETHICAL CHALLENGE

In the northern Chinese city of Handan, residents often complain that clothes hung out to dry end up covered in black fallout from pollution generated from nearby Handan Iron and Steel. Although separated by 5,000 miles and a decade in time, neighbors of a former ThyssenKrupp steel mill in Dortmund, Germany, used to have similar complaints.

Not so in Germany any more. In the late 1990s ThyssenKrupp's hulking blast furnace was plucked from the heartland of Germany's old industrial district, the Ruhr Valley, disassembled and shipped to Handan in Hebei Province, China's now equivalent of the German Ruhr Valley. This transfer was just one of dozens which have made China a steel producer that exceeds the combined output of Germany, Japan, and the United States. Chinese mills now provide about 55 percent of the world's total steel output.

Why the growth? Chen Kexin, an economist from the Ministry of Commerce, notes that, perhaps even more than cheap labor, weak environmental laws and cheap power allow Chinese steel producers to have the lowest prices. Mr. Chen notes, "The shortfall of environmental protection is one of the main reasons why our exports are cheaper." As the *New York Times* points out, "China has become the world's factory, but also its smokestack."

Exporting jobs to China has been costly to Dortmund and other Ruhr cities. These cities still face high unemployment rates because of the migration of jobs to lower-cost countries like China. Dortmund's unemployment rate is 15 percent, which is 50 percent higher than the national average. Dortmund now has barely 3,000 working in steel mills; in 1960, there were 40,000. However, switching to what is often seen as a comparative or absolute advantage of German technology, the region now has 12,000 new jobs in information technology and 2,300 in nanotechnology. Where once there were no universities, there are now six universities and eight technical colleges.

There is also a cost to the residents of Handan. While Germany has reduced its annual carbon emissions by 19 percent, China's coal-fired power plants contribute heavily to the country's rising emissions of sulfur dioxide and carbon dioxide. In Handan, residents live in a sea of smoke and dust that spills from the steel plant, which even Chinese authorities acknowledge contains carcinogens. Only after public protests did Handan Iron and Steel agree to pay an annual "pollution fee" as compensation to its neighbors.

A paradox for the world and increasing carbon levels is that China's steel mills emit three times as much carbon dioxide per ton of steel as did the German producers. This is in a significant degree because about 85 percent of even the newer Chinese plants burn coal as their fuel.

Recently however the Chinese government has started enforcing stricter environmental regulations on steel companies. Coinciding with a glut of steel on the world market and reduced prices this has forced some of the more offending Chinese plants to go out of business. A recent survey by the Hebei Province Metallurgical Industry Association, noted that as many as 26 blast furnaces in Tangshan were closed for several months for overhauls. In addition, they reported that many steel processing plants in Hebei either shut down or halved production in response to weak prices and environmental pressures.

Source: Adapted from Joseph Kahn and Mark Landler, 2007, "China grabs West's smoke-spewing factories," *New York Times*, www.nytimes.com/2007/12/21/world/asia/21transfer.html?_r=3&hp &oref=slogin&oref=slogin&oref=slogin, December 21; David Stanway, 2015, "China's steel city feels impact of pollution regulations," *Reuters*, August 5; Cecilia Jamasmie, 2016, "Extreme pollution forces China to shut down hundreds of coal, steel operations," Mining.com, September 27; Peter Pham, 2016, "China's steel industry is dominating the global market—But will it last?" *Forbes*, April 27.

To this point, we have considered the incentives for trade between companies from different countries. However, companies can achieve many of the same benefits by setting up operations in another country. The next section explores broadly the rationale for investing in assets in other countries.

Foreign Direct Investment

foreign direct investment (FDI) having ownership or control of at least 10 percent or more of an enterprise in another country

The US Department of Commerce defines **foreign direct investment** (**FDI**, as it is commonly referred to) as having ownership or control of at least 10 percent or more of an enterprise in another country.

As you remember from Chapter 2, a major issue in formulating a multinational strategy is using location advantages to find lower-cost or higher-quality inputs (supplies or labor) and to expand sales and service to customers. Later, in Chapter 10, you will see how international managers make the strategic choice to export/import or to engage in FDI, or to do both. Consequently, this chapter will provide only a brief overview of some of the theoretical reasons to engage in FDI.

One general observation is that worldwide FDI, like international trade, has grown substantially over the last few decades. Exhibits in Chapter 1 give the latest worldwide statistics on both the growth of FDI and international trade. Although the tragedy of 9/11 affected both trade and investment after the year 2001, statistics that are more recent suggest a return to higher levels of FDI. In any case, in spite of a large drop in the post-2001 years, worldwide FDI remains higher than that of the previous decade. Similar to the situation for world trade, where companies seek to buy exports from low-cost countries, FDI in low-cost countries is also growing for similar reasons. Exhibit 4.11 shows recent levels of FDI for the BRIC countries. Note that there is much more investment going into the BRIC countries than coming out and that China leads the way.

As noted above, some of the same drivers of exporting and importing influence the choice of companies to engage in FDI. Next, we review briefly some contemporary theories of FDI.

Monopolistic advantage theory is an economic view of FDI that argues that FDI should occur only when foreign companies have unique competitive advantages over local companies.[14] That is, FDI occurs when the foreign company is superior in areas such as technology, management, economies of scale, brand name, or financial assets. The prime motivation for FDI

monopolistic advantage theory

argues that FDI should occur only when foreign companies have unique competitive advantages over local companies

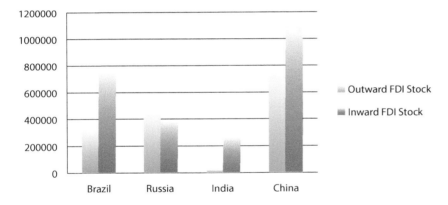

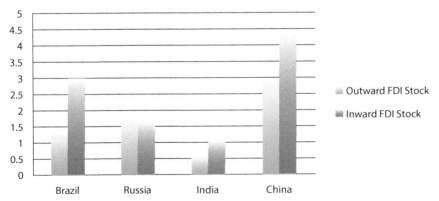

Exhibit 4.11 Recent FDI Inflows and Outflows for Brazil, Russia, India, and China

Note: Outward FDI stock is the value of a country's equity in and net loans to enterprises in foreign economies. The inward FDI stock is the value of foreign investors' equity in and net loans to the receiving country.

Source: UNCTADStat, United Nations Conference on Trade and Development.

then is to keep control of these competitive advantages while using them in other countries. Intel, the computer chip manufacturer, is a good example of this type of FDI motivation. Intel has superior knowledge of chip-manufacturing technology. For its assembly and testing facilities, Intel uses only a few carefully selected sites in low-cost countries, but always as fully owned operations. Intel has a hierarchical and integrated international production system based on tightly controlled subsidiaries. This means that Intel not only produces computer chips but also owns the companies that supply the raw materials for chips, such as silicon wafers. Recently, the company said it was investing US$1.6 billion over 15 years in a China plant for mobile chip development and manufacturing in an effort to remain in complete control.[15]

Internalization theory also asks the question of why FDI exists. Internalization theory begins with the assumption that operating in a foreign country is likely more costly than operating at home. Foreign companies are unlikely to have the local contacts and same knowledge of local customs, cultures, and business practices as local competitors. If a company has something of value, why not export the product or license the production process to local companies to take advantage of their local expertise?[16]

Exporting and licensing are types of market relationships that usually require contracts. Internalization theory uses the concept of **transaction costs** to point out that contracts are not free. To make market transactions one must negotiate, monitor, and enforce contracts. Some companies decide that the transaction costs are too high to use the market to sell their goods, services, and procedures. Instead, they adopt the strategy that it makes more sense (in terms of costs) to internalize (do it yourself) the international operation.

Internalization theory would further explain the rationale for Intel's FDI. With its proprietary technology of chip development and manufacturing, Intel would need to invest considerable effort in monitoring any contracted manufacturer of its chips. It would also face great risk if future foreign competition appropriated its advanced design and production technology.

Dunning's eclectic theory focuses on three advantages that a company must have to succeed with FDI.[17] These advantages consider both the internal characteristics of the MNC and the local environment in which it operates. They also combine the ideas suggested by earlier FDI theories.

1. *Ownership advantages* As with monopolistic advantage theory, the eclectic theory argues that a company must have some strategic competitive advantages over local companies. Otherwise, without something like a superior technology or internationally recognized brand name, a foreign competitor could not compete with the locals. Toyota has an internationally recognized brand name for quality and has superior manufacturing technologies to its competitors. These are two reasons why Toyota owns production facilities throughout the world.
2. *Internalization advantages* A company must gain some cost savings over exporting its product or service or licensing its production processes or brand name.
3. *Location advantages* This means that there must be some profit motive to produce in another country. Usually, this comes from lower-cost production that can serve either local or home markets. Cost saving, and thus higher profits, can also come from reduced transportation costs in serving local markets. BMW, for example, manufactures its X5 sport utility and Z4 roadster in the US. Profits are higher because transportation costs to serve the US market are lower than if these products were shipped from Germany or other BMW plants in England or South Africa. This is important because of the strong demand for sport utility vehicles in the US. However, because US wages are lower than the

---

internalization theory asks the question of when it is less costly to do something yourself in another country rather than selling your product or service

transaction costs the costs associated with negotiating, monitoring, and enforcing contracts

Dunning's eclectic theory focuses on three advantages that a company must have to succeed with FDI: ownership, internalization, and location

approximately $40/hour paid to German workers, the US plant produces all of BMW's X5s and Z4s not only for the US market but also for exporting to the rest of the world.

These theories broadly explain some of the motivations for FDI. However, the strategic decision on how to enter a market is quite complex, and you will see more detail later in the text. Among the many factors that companies take into account when considering FDI include better local image, availability of required natural resources, closer access to customers, and closer access to suppliers.

Chapter Review

Traditional theories of trade help explain the importing and exporting of goods among nations.

The economic theories of trade generally tell us that free trade between nations is, on average, beneficial for all of the involved countries. However, the gains from trade are not distributed equally in all industries. Undoubtedly, some people and industries suffer. Trade theories suggest that if you are in an industry that is less efficient than that same industry in another country, your company will face stiff international competition. However, trade does not occur in a vacuum and government interventions are common. As such, an important strategic concern for international managers is to understand the impact of government policies regarding trade on their industry's position in the world economy.

Modern trade theories began as reaction to mercantilism. In the mercantilism philosophy, the objective of between-country trade was for a country to win by exporting more than it imported. One nation's gain was another nation's loss. Economists call this surplus of exports over imports a favorable balance of trade. Although limited by simplifying assumptions, and counter to the mercantilist view, the theories of absolute and comparative advantage provide the mathematical logic that trade works to produce more products and give consumers more options.

Adam Smith argued that the world's wealth is not fixed because, when nations engage in international trade, world productivity increases (everyone is wealthier). According to Smith, for the world to benefit from absolute advantages, a country should produce goods for which it has absolute advantage and import those goods in which it has absolute disadvantage.

The theory of comparative advantage suggests that countries should specialize not only in those products for which they have absolute advantage but also for those products in which they have comparative advantage. With specialization and trade, it becomes possible with comparative advantage for both trading partners to gain.

The Heckscher–Ohlin theory argues that a nation's comparative advantage comes from the relative abundance of its factor endowments. Like Ricardo and Smith, the HO theory argues that free trade is beneficial to all partners. However, international trade is driven not only by relative differences in production efficiency but also by relative differences in the factor endowments of countries. Most recent economics research suggests that trade is best explained by both Ricardo's comparative advantage in efficiency of production (in part due to superior technologies) and the relative factor endowments identified by HO theory.

Product life cycle theory adds another consideration regarding how to look at specialization of production based on absolute or comparative advantage. That is, according to this view, some countries are more likely to develop companies that are good at creating new products, while other countries are more likely to develop companies that are efficient at producing mature products. Once a production of a product becomes routine, it makes sense to replace higher-paid, higher-skilled workers with lower-skilled and lower-paid workers in other countries. At the same time, foreign competitors in the low-cost countries begin to develop the skills necessary to produce the product. Eventually imports from foreign companies rather than domestic production serve the innovating countries' markets.

During the 1980s, several economists developed what is now called new trade theory. New trade theory looks at how companies and industries in a nation can take advantage of economies of scale. Economies of scale mean that each additional unit of production costs less to produce than did the previous unit. Economies of scale are another form of comparative advantage.

Harvard strategic management professor Michael Porter rejects the notion that comparative advantage is sufficient to explain world trade. His diamond model notes that local demand, the existence of related and supporting industries, as well as factor endowments, give industries in certain countries an international competitive advantage.

The chapter considered several arguments against free trade. These included free trade as a threat to national sovereignty, the need to protect infant industries, the argument that trade must be fair, and the protection of local jobs and the environment. Different interest groups and industries hurt by international competition often appeal to governments for protection based on these arguments.

Exporting and importing are not the only strategies for companies to engage in international operations. Foreign direct investment (FDI) is another option. This chapter considered some of the theoretical reasons for FDI. In later chapters, you will see more information on how to use FDI as a strategic option for an international company.

Monopolistic advantage theory is an economic view of FDI that argues that FDI should occur only when foreign companies have unique competitive advantages over local companies. Internalization theory looks at the relative efficiency of using the market (e.g. import or export) to go international contrasted with building or acquiring your own organization in another country. Dunning's eclectic theory focuses on three advantages that a company must have to succeed with FDI. Ownership advantage means that a company must have some strategic competitive advantages over local companies. Internalization advantage means that a company must gain some cost savings over exporting its product or service or licensing its production processes or brand name. Location advantage means that there must be some profit reason to go into a foreign location.

Discussion Questions

1   Compare and contrast the theories of absolute and comparative advantage.

2   How does the Heckscher–Ohlin (HO) theory build on the earlier work of absolute and comparative advantage?

3   The Leontief Paradox finds opposite trading patterns for the US to those predicted by the HO theory. How can you resolve this paradox?

4   Although economists generally discredit mercantilism, can you find any examples in the popular press where politicians or business leaders use similar arguments to protect an industry?

5   Identify some products initially produced in the US, Germany, or Japan that followed the product life cycle theory. Can you trace the sales and production of such products to any emerging market countries?

6   Present arguments that saving jobs in one industry is a cost that should be shared by everyone in a society.

7   Present alternative arguments about saving jobs, looking at how saving jobs in one industry might eventually hurt another industry.

8   Based on your knowledge of trade theory, discuss the usefulness of limiting imports from China and other emerging market countries into the US.

9   In deciding whether to export to another country or build their own sales or production site, based on your knowledge of trade theory and theories of FDI what are the major considerations for international managers making this choice?

10 Boeing is using world-class manufacturing facilities in Japan to supply components for its new Dreamliner. Should Boeing consider building production plants in countries like India and China, where there are many excellent lower-wage engineers? What factors should they take into account?

International Business Skill Builder

A Simulation of International Trade

Step 1: Review the theory of comparative advantage.

Step 2: Go to the website http://desertislandgame.com/.

Step 3: Play the simple and advanced trade games.

Step 4: Compare your performance with other students and discuss the implications for world trade.

Chapter Internet Activity

In this project, you will explore the absolute advantage of labor costs.

1. Go to the International Labor Organization's website (**www.ilo.org/ilostat/**) and look at the wages of manufacturing workers in your own country and two or three others. Note whether these countries have lower or higher wages.

2. Now go the World Trade Organization's statistics website (**www.wto.org/english/res_e/statis_e/wts2016_e/ wts2016_e.pdf**) and examine the trade patterns in manufactured goods between your country and the other countries.

3. Write a brief report or prepare a presentation that examines whether the trade flows make sense in terms of which countries have the absolute advantage in terms of labor costs. If the trade patterns do not reflect trade based on absolute advantage, consider why this might not be working. For example, there may be cultural, political, manufacturing capacity, or other factors involved.

Key Concepts

- absolute advantage
- autarky
- comparative advantage
- Dunning's eclectic theory
- economies of scale
- favorable trade balance
- foreign direct investment (FDI)
- Heckscher–Ohlin theory (HO)
- internalization theory
- Leontief Paradox

- mercantilism
- monopolistic advantage theory
- national diamond
- new trade theory
- opportunity costs
- product life cycle theory
- specie-flow mechanism
- transaction costs
- zero-sum game

BUSINESS > INTERNATIONAL

Vietnam: The New China?

On February 28, 2006 Intel Corporation announced its decision to invest $300 million to create a semiconductor assembly and testing facility in Vietnam. Intel's Chairman at the time, Craig Barrett, while in Ho Chi Minh City (formerly known as Saigon) stated, "We applaud the progress the country has made in building up their technology infrastructure and support of education programs to advance the capabilities of the local workforce." The initial plan to invest $300 million would grow to a billion dollars by the opening of the plant in 2010. The Vietnamese plant, built to make and test chipsets for computers and mobile devices is the largest Intel plant in the world.

The Intel investment represented the largest US non-oil investment in Vietnam. Prior investments from the United States had mainly been in low-tech manufacturing such as shoes, food processing, and textiles. Vietnam had experienced a sizable increase in FDI in recent years, and political leaders planned to expand the economy and improve living standards shattered by wars and prior poor economic decision making. With wage rates rising in China, this emerging Southeast Asian country could emerge as a major manufacturing country by draining foreign investment away from China.

Located in Southeast Asia, Vietnam has attracted the attention of Western governments since at least the 19th century. In 1858 the French colonized Vietnam. After internal fighting in an eight-year war, the French signed the Geneva Agreement in 1954 which led to their withdrawal from the country and the division of Vietnam into the communist north and noncommunist south. The Geneva Agreement required elections to be held for unification, however, the government in the south refused to participate and proclaimed itself the Republic of Vietnam. Armed conflict between the communist north and noncommunist south started shortly thereafter and intensified as the decade progressed.

US involvement began in 1961 as President Kennedy sent US military advisors to Vietnam. In 1965 President Johnson sent military combat forces to Vietnam. The war in Vietnam escalated, and without a clear sign of victory the American public grew increasingly tired of the conflict. In 1973 a peace agreement was reached and the US withdrew its military forces. Within two years the communist government from the north invaded the south and unified the country into the Socialist Republic of Vietnam. Many Americans felt the United States had lost the war in Vietnam and some still harbor negative views and sentiments about the country.

With its population and economy suffering under the strains of a socialist economic system, the Communist Party of Vietnam—the only political party permitted in the country—instituted a program of economic liberalization and structural reforms in 1986. The program, referred to as *doi moi* (renovation) signaled the country was ready to move towards a market economy.

The cornerstone of *doi moi* was an export-led economic growth strategy, a strategy that had already been pursued with reasonable success by the so-called "Asian Tigers." Vietnam sought to position itself for targeted manufacturing and assembly operations as a lower-cost location than countries such as Taiwan, Hong Kong, and Singapore. Under *doi moi*, economic sectors and industries with potential for significant export growth were targeted and given preferential treatment in the forms of tax breaks and subsidies. Foreign investment was steered to the preferential sectors to provide the capital necessary to support expansion. Finally, Vietnam instituted a controlled, fixed exchange rate policy designed to maintain an undervalued currency in order to promote exports.

While the country has moved towards a market economy, Vietnam still remains a communist country. The Propaganda and Training Department still control newspapers, books, and even tourism companies to insure that the political ideology of the communist party is maintained. Although the government of Vietnam is still communist, the economy has become more capitalistic. The government, however, still maintains significant control over the economy and operates many state-owned enterprises (SOEs). While providing employment to the citizens of Vietnam, the SOEs tend to be inefficient operations and represent a drain on the economy.

In the late 1980s foreign investment began to flow into Vietnam as economic liberalization began to take shape. Lured by the prospects of cheap labor and untapped markets for consumer and industrial goods, foreign investors made their way to Vietnam in hopes of finding a new Asian Tiger. The initial inflow of foreign capital was motivated by economic reform (*doi moi*) and the prospects of an underdeveloped market. Vietnam also benefited from a trend in FDI being directed towards emerging markets and increased intra-regional investment and trade in Southeast Asia. The enthusiasm for FDI in Vietnam, however, didn't last long as communist bureaucracy and corruption began to make the country a less attractive market. Many early investors retreated from Vietnam in 1996. The Asian financial crisis of 1997 further dampened foreign investor interest. Subsequent to the liberalization of the economy, Vietnam began to experience significant inflows of foreign direct investment and rapid economic growth. Real GDP expanded at a robust nine percent annual rate from 1993 to 1997. Per capita income more than doubled, rising from about $810 in 1987 to roughly $1750 in 1997. Many Western companies raced into Vietnam during this period due to its low labor costs, the preferential treatment provided by the government, and the view that Vietnam was an untapped market for industrial and consumer goods. With the sudden drop in foreign investment in 1997, Vietnamese leaders knew a different direction in policy was needed. In order to regain its standing as one of the most attractive host countries for FDI, change was needed.

CASE 4
cont'd

Vietnam responded to the problems experienced by foreign investors and made some necessary changes. These changes re-affirmed its commitment to economic liberalization and international integration, and allowed it to become a member of the ASEAN Free Trade Area. In December, 2001 Vietnam signed a bilateral trade agreement with the United States and started the process of applying for membership in the World Trade Organization. Once again, FDI had begun to make its way back into Vietnam. With rising labor costs in China, increased trade agreements with the United States and the EU, and the expected entry into the World Trade Organization (which occurred in 2007), beginning in 2005 Vietnam's FDI inflows once again started to rise. In the first two months of 2006 Vietnam gained a record $1.3 billion in FDI, and at the time, the country attracted more FDI as a percent of GDP than China. Foreign direct investment in Vietnam continued to rise and peaked in 2008 with $11.5 billion in invested capital. After 2008 FDI flows remained steady (for the most part) but previous growth rates were nowhere to be seen.

Per capita income in Vietnam has risen to $3,400 and workers earn on average $68–92 a month. They are considered to be hard working and reasonably dedicated employees. Vietnam has a young population, with over two-thirds of its 92 million inhabitants in the prime working ages of 16 to 64. It has a literacy rate of 94 percent, and a growing middle class. English is favored as a second language, although not widely spoken. Vietnam offers lower production costs, not only due to low labor rates, but also because of additional lower operating costs including land, rents, and electricity.

International investors consider Vietnam's political environment to be a stable one. Although Vietnam has a communist form of government, it has provided stability, unlike its neighbor Thailand which experienced a bloodless coup in 2006 and further political protests in following years. Vietnam has not suffered from the internal Islamic terrorist attacks which have occurred in Indonesia, Thailand, and the Philippines. Vietnam also offers an attractive alternative to firms who seek to diversify their supply sources in the region (China + 1 policy). These and other factors have prompted A.T. Kearney, the international consulting firm, to rank Vietnam 12th in its ranking of desirable locations for foreign direct investment in 2010.

The decision by Intel to invest in Vietnam was seen by some as confirmation that Vietnam had arrived as a major international player in the global sourcing game. Intel chose Vietnam over Thailand, the Philippines, Malaysia, and China mainly due to its low production costs. As Chairman Barrett stated, when responding to why Intel chose Vietnam, "Cost is always a driving force." Intel continues to operate manufacturing facilities in China, Malaysia, the Philippines, and Costa Rica. It appears likely that Intel will continue to invest in Vietnam. According to Barrett, "We consider this to be a small step in a long journey of involvement in Vietnam."

CASE 4
cont'd

While Vietnam is still seen as an attractive location for foreign investment, the country still has a number of difficulties that may make the future less certain. Vietnam remains a one-party communist country, and some of the problems that early investors experienced are still present. Although the country has become more capitalistic, the government maintains significant control over the economy and operates many state-owned enterprises. Corruption and government bureaucracy continue to be problems, as well as a poor infrastructure, and restrictive laws concerning business operations.

The stability and supply of electricity is a concern. Vietnam's electrical infrastructure is insufficient for the country's growing needs. Electricity of Vietnam, the state-owned source of power, sells electricity at a loss in order to keep rates low. While lower rates for electricity are desirable for foreign investment, they prevent the needed private investment required to build an adequate infrastructure. Electricity rates are a politically sensitive issue and the government has been unwilling to raise them to levels found in neighboring countries such as Thailand or Cambodia.

On the international front, heated tensions with China over ownership of islands in the South China Sea have brought an added element of political risk to Vietnam. China has made some aggressive moves over disputed ownership of land in the Spratly Islands. Up until recently the land was considered unimportant, but with the recent discovery of huge oil and gas reserves a number of countries have begun to claim ownership. While a number of countries are in the dispute, such as the Philippines, Malaysia, and Taiwan, the tensions have been especially high between Vietnam and China.

Foreign direct investment in Vietnam has had its ups and downs in recent years. By 2012 it appeared that Vietnam was losing some appeal to international investors. High-profile corruption scandals and a shaky banking system rocked the country at the same time economic growth was beginning to slow. Government deficits were becoming a concern, and after many devaluations of the dong, Vietnam still experienced deficits in international trade. The devaluation of the dong was helping to fuel inflation in Vietnam, which was also becoming a growing concern.

Vietnam imposes export taxes on some products and maintains high import tariffs on products that the government desires to be produced locally. Both export and import taxes have been reduced or eliminated in recent years, however, the government has a history of making policy changes quickly in order to achieve its objectives in international trade. The government maintains tight control over FDI, and this regulation is fragmented and sometimes ambiguous. Vietnam still is a developing country and its rule of law is considered weak by many observers. Vietnam ranks 98th out of 183 countries tracked by the World Bank in terms of the ease of doing business. Particular concerns include restrictions on hiring and firing employees, protection of foreign assets,

CASE 4
cont'd

and contract enforcement. Transparency International ranks Vietnam 112th out of 182 countries studied in terms of corruption (with a lower number representing lower levels of corruption). Foreign direct investment flow moves from country to country and Vietnam must consider its competition in the region. Compared to Thailand for example, Vietnam is considered to be more corrupt, maintains more restrictions on foreign investment, and has a weaker rule of law and contract enforcement, a weaker currency, and a less desirable quality of life for expatriate managers. If Vietnam relies too heavily on low wage rates to attract foreign direct investment then international investors may soon become more interested in Myanmar, Cambodia, or perhaps Laos. With the easing of US and European sanctions on Myanmar due to movement towards political reform, this "frontier market" may represent a challenge to Vietnam. With an abundance of natural resources and extremely low wage rates, Myanmar could be an attractive FDI host country. High inflation, high interest rates, increasing labor unrest and demands for higher wages, power outages, and a lack of skilled workers make Vietnam a challenge. Vietnam is still a competitive country with low wage rates and a sizable population with potential market, yet it remains to be seen if Vietnam can continue to attract high-value FDI and compete with neighboring countries.

CASE DISCUSSION POINTS:

1   Compare the attractiveness of Vietnam as a host country for FDI with China. What factors make it more and less attractive compared to its large northern neighbor?
2   Do some forms or types of FDI in Vietnam make more sense than others for international investors?
3   If you were advising a firm considering investing directly in Vietnam, what suggestions would you offer?

Source: *Vietnam Business Forum*, 2006, "Merrill Lynch upbeat on investing in Vietnam," February 9; *EIU News Wire*, 2005, "Vietnam: investment regulations," May 9; F. Balfour, 2006, "Good morning Vietnam: Intel's deal to build a factory is likely to spur more Western investment," *BusinessWeek*, March 13; B. Bland, 2012, "Vietnam offers companies China alternatives," *Financial Times*, March 14; B. Buchel and T. Lai Xuan, 2001, "Measures of joint venture performance from multiple perspectives: An evaluation of local and foreign managers in Vietnam," *Asian Pacific Journal of Management*, 18(1), pp. 101–111; N. Freeman, 2002, "Foreign direct investment in Vietnam: An overview," DFI Workshop on Globalization and Poverty in Vietnam, September 13–14; M. Goonan, 2011, "Half-free trade in Vietnam," *Asian Times*, November 16; P. Hirschberg, 2011, "Vietnam power outages risk harming foreign investment as prices loom," *Bloomberg News*, February 15; J. Hookway and A. Frangos, 2012, "Vietnam loses glow as a market darling," *The Wall Street Journal*, September 10; "IBM sets up 'innovation center' in Vietnam," Phys.org.com, May 22, 2009; R. Jennings, 2011, "Vietnam loses appeal to foreign investment amid economic

**CASE 4
cont'd**

woes," *The Christian Science Monitor*, August 2; K. Johnson, 2006, "Vietnam trades up: By joining the WTO, Asia's second fastest growing economy is poised to kick its exports into high gear," *Time Asia*, November 13; A. Kazmin, 2006, "Intel to spend $300M on chip plant in Vietnam," *Financial Times*, February 28; A. Minh, 2006, "It's high time for FDI," *Vietnam Economic News*, 49(6); H. Minh, 2012, "Vietnam Jan–July FDI slips, longer term pledges down sharply," *Reuters*, July 26; "Myanmar: White elephant or new tiger economy?" Economist Intelligence Unit, April 2012; S. Phang, 2012, "Vietnam swings to trade deficit for first time in three months," *Bloomberg News*, August 26; S. Prasso, 1999, "Vietnam: Welcome back?" *BusinessWeek*, August, 16; M. Stone, 2006, "Battle for the history of the Vietnam War," *Vietnam*, June; I. Timberlake, 2010, "Intel opens biggest ever chip plant in Vietnam," *The Age*, October 30; B. Venard, 1998, "Vietnam in mutation: Will it be the next tiger or a future jaguar?" *Asian Pacific Journal of Management*, 15(1), pp. 77–95; L. Webster, 1999, "The new breed," *Vietnam Business Journal*, 8(4), pp. 1–8; www.state.gov/p/eap/ci/vm/, accessed on September 26, 2012; www.business-in-china.com/investment. comparison.html, accessed on March 15, 2006; www.cia.gov/publications/ factbook/geos/vm.html, accessed on May 22, 2006; www.china-asean.net/ asean_biz/vietnam/investment, accessed on March 15, 2006; www.fraserinstitute. ca/admin/books/chapterfiles/EFW2005ch1, accessed on May 22, 2006; www.intel. com, accessed on March 14, 2016; www.transparency.org, accessed on September 28, 2016; www.wto.org, accessed on May 15, 2016.

Case written by Charles A. Rarick

Notes

1 David Hume, 1752 [1912], "Of money," *Essays*, Vol. 1, London: Green.
2 Adam Smith, 1776 [1937], *The Wealth of Nations*, New York: Modern Library.
3 David Ricardo, 1817 [1966], *The Principles of Political Economy and Taxation*, London: Cambridge University Press.
4 Eli Heckscher, 1919, "The effects of foreign trade on the distribution of income," *Economisk Tidskrift*, 21, pp. 497–512.
5 Bertil Ohlin, 1933, *Interregional and International Trade*, Cambridge, MA: Harvard University Press.
6 Wassily Leontief, 1954, "Domestic production and foreign trade: The American capital position re-examined," *Economia Internazionale*, February, pp. 3–32; Wassily Leontief, 1956, "Factor proportions and the structure of American trade: Further theoretical and empirical analysis," *Review of Economics and Statistics*, November, pp. 386–407.
7 Wenli Cheng, Jeffrey Sachs, and Xiaokai Yang, 2004, "An extended Heckscher–Ohlin model with transaction costs and technological comparative advantage," *Economic Theory*, 23, pp. 671–688.
8 Raymond Vernon, 1966, "International investment and international trade in the product life cycle," *Quarterly Journal of Economics*, 80, pp. 190–207.
9 Paul Krugman, 1983, "New theories of trade among industrial countries," *American Economic Review*, 73, pp. 343–347; Elhanan Helpman, 1999, "The structure of foreign trade," *Journal of Economic Perspectives*, 2, pp. 121–144.
10 Michael E. Porter, 1990, *The Competitive Advantage of Nations*, New York: Free Press, p. 1.
11 Gary S. Vasilash, 2005, "Bright strategies: Hella's independent approach," *Automotive Design and Production*, www.autofield guide.com, May.
12 Isobel Finkel, 2016, "The new protectionism will hit emerging markets right where it hurts, says HSBC," HSBC Holdings PLC, May 12.

13   Eleanor Beardsley, 2005, "When it comes to French business, the accent is on English," *The Christian Science Monitor*, www.csmonitor.com, August 11.

14   Stephen Hymer, 1990 [1968], "The large multinational 'corporation'," in M. Casson (ed.), *Multinational Corporations*, Hants: Edward Elgar, pp. 6–31.

15   Agam Shah, 2014, "Intel plunks down billions to expand in mobile market," *IT World*, December 5.

16   J.-F. Hennart, 2000, "Transaction costs theory and the multinational enterprise," in C. Pitelis and R. Sugden (eds), *The Nature of the Transnational Firm*, London: Routledge, pp. 72–118.

17   John H. Dunning, 1988, "The eclectic paradigm of international production: A restatement and some possible extensions," *Journal of International Business Studies*, 19, pp. 1–31.

CHAPTER 5

Foreign Exchange Markets

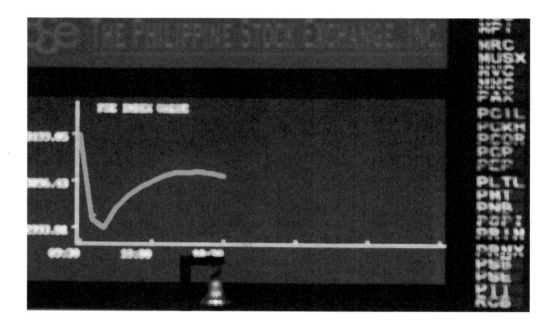

After reading this chapter you should be able to:

- Understand the nature of the foreign exchange market with a special focus on emerging markets.

- Know the history of financial exchange systems.

- Understand the impact of appreciation or depreciation on multinationals.

- Appreciate the reasons and impact of government intervention in the foreign exchange market.

- Understand what determines exchange rates.

- Know how MNCs manage exchange-rate risks.

- Be familiar with the nature of foreign exchange arbitrage.

International Business *Preview IB Emerging Market Strategic Insight*

The Chinese Yuan and Market Intervention

China today accounts for 17 percent of the world's Gross Domestic Product (GDP). Given that, it is undeniable that China plays a significant role in the global business environment. It is therefore not surprising that significant attention is paid to the Chinese currency, the Renminbi or yuan. Significant trade occurs on a daily basis using the yuan. Multinationals around the world purchase products from China. Consider that Walmart makes significant trades with companies based in China. Furthermore, as the Chinese government works to provide international investors with increased access to domestic capital markets, significantly more trade is occurring through the yuan.

An important component of the attention paid to the yuan is whether the Chinese government is artificially manipulating its currency to keep the value low. For example, the recent **currency devaluation** (reduction of the value of the home currency with respect to a foreign currency) of the yuan has taken the world by surprise. However, the Chinese economy has recently experienced an economic slowdown driven by decreased orders of goods from foreign markets. Coupled with a potential fall in real estate, the Chinese government decided to devalue the currency to make sure it stays competitive worldwide. A currency devaluation means that exports are cheaper while imports become more expensive.

Despite these criticisms, others have argued that China is not a currency manipulator. For instance, the Renminbi has actually appreciated 33 percent with respect to the US dollar. Additionally, other experts suggest that it is a good time to buy Chinese stocks. They argue that the low Renminbi means that one can buy Chinese stocks at lower prices. These experts believe that the Chinese government will take every step to stabilize the economy and that there will be long-term growth.

Source: Based on R. Katz, 2015, "The myth of currency manipulation," *International Economy*, Summer, pp. 40–43, 63–64; D. Paolo, 2016, "Do not adjust your set: time to buy China," *Global Capital*, February 1, p. 1; D. Paolo, 2015, "Time for China to get a grip," Global Capital, September 21, p. 81.

> **currency devaluation** reduction of the value of the home currency relative to a foreign currency

The Preview IB Emerging Market Strategic Insight shows the implications of foreign exchange markets on international business. Changes in exchange rates can have large effects on the value of purchases or sales made across borders or even fulfilling debt obligations. MNCs worldwide must deal with such issues because. Furthermore, as this case shows, governmental intervention can have dramatic effects on individuals worldwide. While multinationals purchasing products are affected, the Preview shows that the average investor also needs to be aware of the foreign exchange markets.

In this chapter, you will see how exchange-rate systems operate, and you will see how MNCs can use this knowledge to mitigate the dangers fluctuating rates have on international commerce. As has been the case in previous chapters, the discussion will focus on the many unique situations presented by emerging markets.

What is the Foreign Exchange Market?

Because each country, or group of countries in the case of the EU, has its own currency, cross-border business requires that companies exchange their home currency for the currencies of other countries in which they do business. If, for example, a Brazilian company wants to invest in a factory in Japan or buy supplies from Japanese companies, it will usually acquire Japanese currency (yen) to make its purchases. It is the foreign exchange market that provides the Brazilian company with the ability to exchange real for yen and then use the yen to do business in Japan. Similarly, if Japanese companies were to accept payment in the Brazilian currency real, they would not have much use for real in Japan and would need to use the foreign exchange market to replace this foreign currency with yen.

Thus, international trade and investment requires that people and companies from one country can convert their currencies into the currencies of another country. Rather than buying and selling currencies to each other, tourists, investors, exporters, and importers buy and sell

foreign exchange
market
a combination of
national central banks,
private banks, and
foreign exchange dealers
and brokers through
which people and
companies can sell or buy
foreign currencies

foreign currencies primarily through banks. The **foreign exchange market** is a combination of national central banks, private banks, and foreign exchange dealers and brokers through which people and companies can sell or buy foreign currencies.

It is important to note that foreign exchange markets are increasingly intertwined today. Because of globalization and the amount of cross-border trading, economies increasingly depend on each other. As such, if a foreign exchange market fails, it will be felt around the world. In fact, a recent study found that around 11 percent of the volatility of the foreign exchange could be explained by external factors.[1]

The foreign exchange market is the biggest market in the world, with transactions exceeding US$5.3 trillion a day. Consider that the transactions amounted to around $1.5 trillion a day in 2007. As you can see, the transactions have risen dramatically over the years. Exhibit 5.1 below shows the progression of foreign exchange transactions over the years.

As Exhibit 5.1 shows, global transactions have grown rapidly over the years. This is not surprising as the sharp rise in global transactions coincides with the global rise in prominence of emerging markets. As global trades have increased among trading groups, foreign exchanges have also experienced tremendous growth.

Unlike a stock market, the foreign exchange market is not an organized structure with a centralized meeting place. Rather, exchanges in currencies take place all over the world and some exchange is open nearly every hour of the day. London, Tokyo, and New York are the biggest markets. The market opens in Hong Kong on Monday morning (which is Sunday evening in New York) and progresses across the world via Tokyo, Frankfurt, London, New York, Chicago, and San Francisco. An hour after banks on the US west coast close on Monday, Hong Kong is opening for business on Tuesday morning.

exchange rate
represents the prices of
foreign currencies in
terms of other currencies

An **exchange rate** represents the price of one currency in terms of the value of another currency. Every exchange rate has two sides, the value of currency X in terms of Y, and value of currency Y in terms of X. For example, a US dollar might buy or be worth 17.91 Mexican pesos, whereas, at the same rate, the Mexican peso be worth US$0.06. This is called a bilateral exchange rate. When multiple currencies are considered in terms of each other's values, this is called currency cross rates.

Exhibit 5.2 shows example currency cross rates among often-traded currencies.

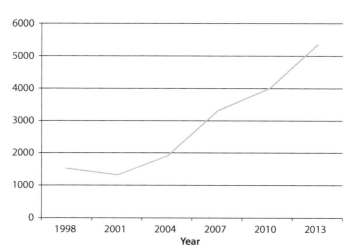

Exhibit 5.1 Foreign Exchange Transactions (billions of US dollars)
Source: Bank for International Settlements, 2013, *Foreign Exchange Turnover in April 2013—Preliminary Global Results.*

Currency	USD	EUR	AUD	BRL	GBP	CNY	INR	HKD	MXN	ZAR	RUB
EUR	0.88		0.64	0.25	1.29	0.14	0.01	0.11	0.05	0.06	0.01
AUD	1.37	1.55		0.39	2.01	0.21	0.02	0.18	0.08	0.09	0.02
BRL	3.51	4.00	2.57		5.09	0.54	0.05	0.45	0.19	0.22	0.05
GBP	0.69	0.78	0.50	0.20		0.11	0.01	0.09	0.04	0.04	0.01
CNY	6.52	7.37	4.75	1.86	9.48		0.10	0.84	0.36	0.42	0.10
INR	66.84	75.54	48.68	19.19	97.59	10.29		8.69	3.67	4.31	1.01
HKD	7.76	8.75	5.64	2.21	11.24	1.19	0.12		0.42	0.50	0.12
MXN	18.30	20.79	13.39	5.24	26.63	2.81	0.27	2.37		1.18	0.27
ZAR	15.67	17.89	11.53	4.45	22.65	2.39	0.23	2.02	0.85		0.23
RUB	65.03	73.78	47.53	18.44	97.03	10.24	0.99	8.64	3.64	4.29	

Exhibit 5.2 A Sample of Currency Cross Rates

USD = US dollar; EUR = Euro; AUD = Australian dollar; BRL = Brazilian Real; GBP = Great Britain pound; CNY = Chinese Yuan; INR = Indian Rupee; HKD = Hong Kong dollar; MXN = Mexican Peso; ZAR = South African Rand; and RUB = Russian Ruble.

Like any market, the value of currencies in terms of other currencies changes continuously, often up to 20 times a minute. Currencies may depreciate or appreciate against each other. For example, when it takes more US dollars to buy Indian Rupees (INRs), one would say that the dollar has depreciated against the Indian Rupee. Imagine yesterday's exchange rates are in the table in Exhibit 5.2; yesterday one dollar could buy 66.84 Indian Rupees. Today, however, the US dollar can buy only 60.16 Indian Rupees. This means that the dollar has depreciated roughly by 10 percent (66.84 – 60.16/66.84 = 0.1). Conversely, since an Indian Rupee can buy more dollars today than yesterday, we say the Indian rupee has appreciated relative to the dollar. You can check current trends in exchange rates at *The Economist* website, www.economist.com/markets/currency/map.cfm.

What are the implications of appreciation or depreciation for multinationals? Consider the following IB Emerging Market Strategic Insight.

As the IB Emerging Market Strategic Insight shows, exchange rate changes can have a dramatic impact on multinationals. Furthermore, the exchange rates you see in Exhibit 5.2 and reported daily in the business press such as *The Wall Street Journal* or the *Financial Times* are the midpoints between what banks and other exchange dealers call **the bid and the ask spread.** Banks and others dealing with currency exchange often do not charge for their services but make money by buying at one price, the bid price, and selling currency at a higher price, the ask price.

Economists often look at the foreign exchange market as a tiered system.[2] First is the wholesale tier, which includes the commercial banks that directly serve the businesses and individuals who wish to buy or sell a foreign currency. Second is the retail tier, which consists of the small agents who buy and sell foreign exchange.

The wholesale tier is an informal, geographically dispersed network of about 2,000 banks and currency brokerage firms. Approximately three-quarters of the $5.3 trillion a day in exchanges is between banks. SWIFT (Society for Worldwide Interbank Financial Telecommunication) is the primary clearing system for international transactions. Banks involved in a foreign currency transaction transfer bank deposits through SWIFT to settle a transaction.[3] Occasionally, banks use brokers who provide a wholesale interbank market for foreign exchange. Brokers buy and sell currencies to banks that may not have enough of a desired currency in their possession to conduct a transaction. The broker would receive a commission for their services.

the bid and the ask spread
the difference between the price a bank buys a currency, the bid price, and price a bank sells a currency, the ask price

Emerging Market Companies in Latin America and Debt

IB EMERGING MARKET
STRATEGIC INSIGHT

Recent reports on emerging markets indicate that the level of debt in such countries is very high. Furthermore, the IMF reported that around $18 million of emerging market corporate debt is outstanding. If companies in emerging markets are unable to meet their debt obligations, such defaults can have catastrophic effects on both the local economies as well as the world business environment. The world is so intertwined today that any financial disasters in one part of the world can send ripple effects in other parts. A strong appreciation of these challenges is therefore an important component of managing businesses in a global environment.

Why have the risks of corporate defaults in emerging markets risen so much? An important factor explaining such risks are the exchange rate changes over the last few years. Consider emerging market companies in Latin America. Many of them hold debt in US dollars. In fact, a recent estimate suggests there to be around US$3 trillion worth of debt. Over the last few years, the US dollar has appreciated considerably relative to emerging market currencies. In fact, for the 18 months preceding January 2016, the US dollar appreciated by around 20 percent. Furthermore, because of the relatively strong US economy and recent instability in China, many have resorted to the safety of the US treasury bond market. This has fueled the rise in the value of the US dollar.

Why do exchange rate changes fuel the possibility of default? Consider the case of a Mexican company that has borrowed US$10 million and is paying a rate of interest of 3.5 percent per year. For each year, the interest that the company has to pay is $350,000. However, the Mexican company has to pay in the local currency. In February of 2015, the Mexican peso was worth 14.89 per US dollar. When converted into Mexican pesos, the Mexican company owes US$350,000 ×14.89 or 5,211,500 Mexican pesos as interest to banks in February of 2015. However, consider the exchange rate in February 2016 when the US$ is equivalent to 18.28 Mexican pesos. In 2016, the interest payment of US$350,000 is now US$350,000 × 18.28 or 6,398,000 Mexican pesos. Simply because of exchange rate changes, the Mexican company now has to come up with an additional 1,186,500 Mexican pesos to meet its obligations. When considering the other difficulties facing emerging markets (declining demand, housing bubbles, etc.), one can see how meeting such additional obligations can be so difficult.

Source: Based on J. Gallup and M. Fitzgerald, 2016, "Time bombs in emerging market debt," *International Financial Law Review*, April 4.

Tourists, exporters, importers, and foreign investors usually do not have stores of foreign currency to purchase products or services, or to make investments in other countries. Similarly, when companies and individuals receive foreign currencies, they usually wish to convert those currencies to their own currencies for use in their home countries. For example, if you returned to your home in France with ¥200,000 remaining from your trip to Japan, your money would not be very useful in the land of the euro and you would likely want to exchange your yen for euros.

Most often, MNCs buy and sell the foreign currencies they use to conduct their cross-national businesses from large commercial banks such as Citibank. This allows them to buy and sell goods and services in other countries in the local currency. However, despite these intermediaries, such free flow of currency is not the case in all emerging markets. Consider the following Emerging Market Brief.

Currency Flows in Selected Countries

Most developed nations allow foreign currency to be exchanged or traded without any restrictions. However, this is not the case in all countries. Consider the case of Venezuela. The Venezuelan government is now rationing the use of scarce US dollars. For instance, the governmental agency in charge of foreign currency disbursements actually reduced the amount available to travelers by 70 percent. Additionally, the Venezuelan government used to subsidize the selling of US dollars to its citizens. Although the free market suggests that the price of a US$ is 190 bolivars, the government was selling the US$ for only 12 bolivars. Recently, it also decided to reduce paying such subsidy.

Why is the Venezuelan government placing such restrictions on the flow of foreign currency? With the price of oil falling, the revenues for the Venezuelan government have fallen dramatically. However, the government is still trying to maintain policies aimed at helping the average Venezuelan. Programs such as subsidies for electricity and subsidies for imported foods are still in place despite the heavy losses the government experiences every year on these subsidies. To save US$ to import food and other items, the government is resorting to more drastic foreign currency control.

Such control has a very significant impact on the local companies as well as multinationals. Local companies find it difficult to acquire the necessary foreign currency to import raw materials and other products. For example, Polar, a local conglomerate that produces around 80 percent of Venezuelan beer had to stop production. The Venezuelan government denied the company's requests for the dollars it needs to import malted barley. Multinationals also suffer from such restrictions. They will find it harder to repatriate profits as the government restricts the movement of the dollar.

Source: Based on *The Economist*, 2016, "Lights out," May 7, pp. 31–32; Stratfor Analysis, 2015, "In Venezuela, spending cuts are not enough," April, p. 1.

As the above Emerging Market Brief shows, the artificial control of currency can place significant hardships on both local companies as well as multinationals[4]. Later we discuss governmental intervention for other economic reasons. Nevertheless, multinationals operating in such emerging markets need to be aware of such restrictions or the potential of such future restrictions. Next, we consider the types of foreign exchange transactions.

Types of Foreign Exchange Transactions

Foreign exchange transactions can take different forms. The **spot transaction** is an immediate transaction at a specific exchange rate. By convention, when banks engage in spot transactions two business days are allowed to complete the transaction. This allows time to debit and credit bank accounts in the countries involved. The exchange rates reported in the popular business press represent the spot rates. They also usually are for transactions of a million dollars or more, so the exchange rate the individual tourist is going to receive is not as favorable.

International businesses have other options regarding their transactions. Say, for example, a manufacturing company wants to buy raw materials from China in August. The manufacturer believes that she will need approximately $1.5 million worth of Chinese Yuan on September 15, when she will receive a major shipment of the material. Fearing that the Yuan might appreciate

spot transaction
an immediate transaction at a specific exchange rate

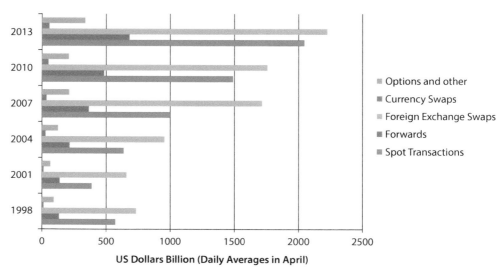

Exhibit 5.3 Types of Transactions in the Global Market (in billions of US dollars/year)
Source: Bank for International Settlements, 2013, *Foreign Exchange Turnover in April 2013—Preliminary Global Results.*

in terms of dollars over the next month (and thus cost her more dollars to buy the material), she contracts with a bank to buy the necessary Yuan on September 15 at an agreed-upon exchange rate. She and the bank then know the exchange rate, and she takes delivery of the Yuan on September 15. This is known as a **forward transaction**. Later we will see how MNCs use forward transactions to cover the risk of exchange-rate changes.

A third type of transaction, which typically occurs between banks, is called a **currency swap**. A swap involves two exchanges. First, the banks agree to exchange a certain amount of currency for another currency at a set exchange rate. Second, they agree to re-swap the currencies back in the future at a set exchange rate. Banks do this to make sure they have enough of a particular currency to serve their customers. For example, if the Bank of China is running short of dollars needed by its Chinese customers to pay for US imports, it may arrange a dollar–Yuan currency swap with Citibank. Citibank sells the Bank of China dollars for Yuan and then later buys the dollars back with its accumulated Yuan. Exhibit 5.3 shows the relative extent of spot, forward, and currency swaps in the global market.

forward transaction
an agreed-upon future exchange rate

currency swap
banks agree to exchange and then re-swap the currency at a future date

The History of Exchange-rate Systems

There is a variety of rules that countries can use to govern the value of their currencies relative to the values of other nations' currencies. These rules are called the **exchange-rate system**.[5] Historically, there have been three major exchange-rate systems: the gold standard, the Bretton Woods system, and the floating system.

exchange-rate system
a variety of rules that countries can use to govern the value of their currencies relative to the values of other nations' currencies

The Gold Standard
Starting in the mid-1800s and lasting to the 1930s, many countries established the value of their currencies relative to one ounce of gold. An ounce of gold for the US dollar, for example, was valued at $20.646 until 1933. During the same period, one ounce of gold cost 86.672 German marks or 107.008 French francs. Thus, national policies stabilized the values of currencies needed to purchase gold from each nation's stocks of gold. That is, countries guaranteed to exchange gold for their currencies at a specific rate. Theoretically, at least, one could exchange

the gold "coin" note for $100 worth of gold in 1923. Thus, the term "gold standard" means a standard value of a currency in terms of gold.

How did this result in an exchange-rate system? The reason that this established an exchange-rate system is that all countries adopting the gold standard established a value of the currency relative to the same commodity: gold. Thus, for example, if you know that one ounce of gold = $20.646 = DM 86.672 = Ffr 107.008, you also know that $1 = (DM 86.672/$20.646) or $1= DM 4.198. Similarly, $1 = (Ffr 107.008/$20.646) = Ffr 5.183. Thus, using this system, you know that you could buy the same amount of gold in any of the countries by exchanging your home country's currency at the set price of gold.

One important point about a commodity-based exchange rate such as gold is that a nation must hold substantial amounts of gold in reserve to legitimate the value of its currency in gold. This means that to have more money in a country's economy you must mine or otherwise secure more gold. The value of the money in circulation and the value of the gold need not match exactly, but must remain stable. For example, during early 1900s, the US had approximately eight times more money in circulation than the value of the gold held by the government.

Although the gold standard resulted in a stability of prices and exchange rates, after the beginning of World War I most European nations prevented their currencies from being converted to gold. When the war ended, some nations tried to return to the earlier fixed exchange rates based on the gold standard. However, the value of the currencies did not reflect the post-World War I economic realities and the ensuing depression that began in 1929. Most industrialized nations began to pursue polices such as increasing employment levels rather than maintaining the value of their currency. An overvalued currency can make the goods and services in a country costly, reducing demand from outside and thus lowering employment. For example, when the United Kingdom attempted to return to earlier gold standard currency values, the price of goods produced in the UK became artificially high relative to other countries. This led to a decrease in demand for UK products and an accompanying rise in unemployment. By 1931, the UK abandoned the gold standard. When the value of a country's currency depreciates relative to other currencies, the country's products become cheaper on the world market. This often leads to increased international and domestic sales because foreign goods become more expensive to local consumers, and local goods become cheaper on the international market. In turn, employment levels tend to rise.

The Bretton Woods Agreement

After World War II, most governments realized that rebuilding the economies of Europe and Japan would require stable exchange rates. With this realization, representatives from over 40 nations met in 1940 at a small resort in Bretton Woods, New Hampshire. The agreement on exchange rates that emerged from this conference is called the **Bretton Woods Agreement**.

To help keep currency exchange rates stable, the Bretton Woods participants agreed to adopt a **pegged exchange-rate system**. When nations participate in a pegged exchange-rate system, they agree to fix the value of their currencies relative to another currency rather than to a commodity such as gold. Specifically, the exchange-rate system allows for minor deviations within a specific range. A country therefore fixes the value of its currency within a range called the target zone.[6]

The US dollar was chosen as the base currency and all the countries agreed to keep the value of their currency within plus or minus 1 percent of a specific value of the dollar. The German mark was pegged to the dollar at DM 4.20 per dollar and the British pound was pegged to the dollar at £2.80 to the dollar. In contrast to all the other nations, the US currency maintained a relationship with gold fixed at $35/ounce. Thus, because the US dollar remained fixed to gold, this was an indirect gold standard, but nations used US dollars rather than gold to settle international transactions. The US, on the other hand, still agreed to exchange dollars for gold at the $35/ounce value.

Bretton Woods Agreement
the agreement on exchange rates to peg currencies to the US dollar that emerged from the conference at a small resort in Bretton Woods

pegged exchange-rate system
fixing the value of a currency relative to another currency rather than to a commodity such as gold

International Monetary Fund (IMF)
an international organization that helps manage international money exchanges

The Bretton Woods Agreement also created the **International Monetary Fund (IMF)**. The IMF is a multination organization that helps manage international money exchanges. Members agreed to follow specific exchange-rate policies such as the pegged exchange-rate system.

By the early 1970s, speculators and some governments were exchanging dollars for the US-held gold at increasing rates. Speculators noted that the US's trade imbalance (the US was buying more from other countries than other countries were from the US) was increasing the supply of dollars abroad. This suggested that the US might devalue the dollar by requiring more dollars to buy an ounce of gold. The dollar would have less value because it would require more dollars to buy the same amount of gold. Thus, speculators tried to buy gold at $35 an ounce with the hope of selling back the gold later for more dollars and a profit.

With gold outflows increasing daily, President Nixon suspended the convertibility of the dollar into gold on August 15, 1971. This effectively ended the Bretton Woods Agreement and the world's exchange-rate system was in turmoil. Various attempts to re-establish a pegged exchange-rate system met with little success and a floating-rate system emerged.[7] This was eventually formalized at the Jamaica Accords in 1976. There, IMF member nations agreed to change the IMF constitution to allow the new system. A **floating-rate system** allows each nation to use market forces to determine the value of its currency. Today, most major economies use a floating-rate system, but it is certainly not the only system encountered by MNCs.

floating-rate system
allows each nation to use market forces to determine the value of its currency

What is the nature of exchange-rate systems in emerging markets? Consider the following IB Emerging Market Strategic Insight.

As the IB Emerging Market Strategic Insight shows, local governments can intervene for a variety of reasons. Exhibit 5.4 below shows the various reasons and the percentage of respondents who felt that the motives for intervention were of high importance in 2005 and 2013.

Exchange-rate Systems in Emerging Markets

IB EMERGING MARKET STRATEGIC INSIGHT

Foreign Exchange Market Government Intervention
local government intervention to buy or sell foreign currency

While most of the developed world has an exchange rate that is free floating, most emerging markets tend to have an exchange rate system that is between a free floating and a fixed exchange rate. This is reflected in the emerging markets' **Foreign Exchange Market Government Intervention**. Because many emerging economies tend to hold most of the foreign currency nowadays, their central banks are more likely to intervene. Central banks in such countries may decide to either buy or sell foreign currency in an attempt to stabilize markets. As such, these interventions mean that exchange rates in many emerging markets are neither a pegged-exchange system nor a floating-rate system. Rather, these economies see a combination of both approaches.

Why do central banks intervene and transact in foreign currencies? Empirical evidence suggests that governments often believe that intervention is necessary to ensure stability of the exchange rate. As you saw earlier, exchange rates have major influences on the volume of exports and, consequently, growth and employment. If exchange rates go unchecked, exports may become too expensive and economic growth may slow down. However, exchange rates also have influences on imports. Exchange-rate volatility impacts import prices and can even result in inflation. As such, foreign exchange intervention is seen as necessary to keep rates stable and to also correct any perceived move away from some targets or the natural equilibrium. Additionally, central banks may also decide to buy foreign currency in an attempt to build up reserves.

Despite anecdotal evidence of the generally negative effects of governmental intervention, a recent study shows that foreign market intervention may not be necessarily detrimental. The authors argue that many emerging markets often face exchange rate instability because of cyclical factors. Analyzing a sample of 18 emerging markets, the researchers do find that such foreign market intervention is actually effective in keeping foreign market exchange going in the desired direction.

Source: Based on C. Daude, E. L. Yeyati and A. J. Nagengast, 2016, "On the effectiveness of exchange rates in emerging markets," *Journal of International Money and Finance*, *64*, pp. 239–261; L. Menkhoff, 2013, "Foreign exchange intervention in emerging markets: A survey of empirical studies," *The World Economy*, *36*(9), pp. 1187–1208.

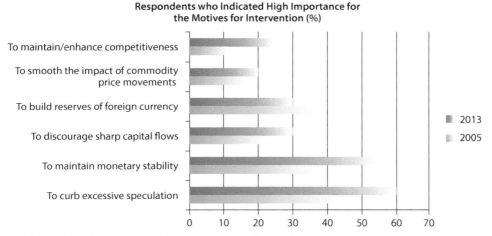

Exhibit 5.4 Motives for Foreign Market Exchange Government Intervention

Source: Based on C. Daude, E. L. Yeyati and A. J. Nagengast, 2016, "On the effectiveness of exchange rates in emerging markets," *Journal of International Money and Finance*, *64*, pp. 239–261.

Other Currency Exchange-rate Systems

The above IB Emerging Market Strategic Insight shows the type of exchange rates currently in many emerging markets. In addition to the floating-rate system and the pegged-rate system, emerging markets have a managed-float system. In the managed-float system, countries reserve the right to intervene to influence the value of their currency on the open market. Remember that the independent-float system allows the market to determine the value of a currency relative to another currency. As you will see later in this chapter, the value of a currency is determined in part by the supply of the currency in the market. For example, if the national banks of many countries hold many dollars, the supply is plentiful and the value of the dollar faces downward pressure. One way the US can influence the supply of dollars is to buy dollars from other countries with different currencies. The result is that the supply will decrease and the value will increase.

We saw earlier that the Bretton Woods Agreement resulted in many currencies pegged to the US dollar at a fixed rate. Many smaller nations still peg their currencies to other currencies, often because they are close trading partners or interact via tourism. For example, many of the Caribbean island nations peg their currencies to the US dollar, including Antigua, the Bahamas,

crawling-peg system
system in which the
currency peg is allowed
to adjust within
boundaries over time

currency-basket peg
to peg currencies to an
average of several
currencies

dollarization
to adopt the currency of
another country

Barbados, Grenada, the Netherlands Antilles, and St Vincent and the Grenadines. Pegging currencies reduces the volatility of exchange rates and encourages trade. However, economic conditions often differ between countries and this leads to difficulties in maintaining the peg. To adjust for these differences some countries adopt a **crawling-peg system**. With this system, the peg is allowed to adjust within boundaries over time. Nicaragua, for example, allows its currency to adjust in value by 1 percent a month relative to the US dollar.

Rather than pegging their currencies to a single country, some nations choose to peg their currencies to an average of several currencies, usually six or fewer. This approach is called the **currency-basket peg**. To visualize a currency basket, imagine you have a basket with five coins, each from a different country. The sum value of the coins in the basket should equal a unit of your currency. That is, the exchange is based on a combination of the exchange rates for each currency. All of the five currency exchange rates can be given equal weighting. However, similar to selecting one currency for pegging, some currency exchange rates might be more important to your country because of economic relationships. In that case, these currencies are often given added weight.

One final way a nation can manage its exchange rate is to adopt the currency of another country.[8] Since the US dollar is most often the currency of choice, this practice is called **dollarization**. The IMF reports that over 20 percent of its members use the currency of another nation as their own. Exhibit 5.5 shows a list of countries that use the dollarization approach to managing their currencies.

Nation	Political status	Currency	Since
American Samoa	US territory	US dollar	1899
Andorra	Independent	Euro (formerly French franc, Spanish peseta), own coins	1278
British Virgin Islands	British dependency	US dollar	1973
Cocos (Keeling) Islands	Australian external territory	Australian dollar	1955
Cook Islands	New Zealand self-governing territory	New Zealand dollar	1995
Cyprus, Northern	De facto independent	Turkish lira	1974
East Timor	Independent	US dollar	2000
Ecuador	Independent	US dollar	2000
El Salvador	Independent	US dollar	2001
Greenland	Danish self-governing region	Danish krone	before 1800
Guam	US territory	US dollar	1898
Kiribati	Independent	Australian dollar, own coins	1943
Kosovo	UN administration	Euro	1999
Lichtenstein	Independent	Swiss franc	1921
Marshall Islands	Independent	US dollar	1944
Micronesia	Independent	US dollar	1944
Monaco	Independent	Euro (formerly French franc)	1865
Montenegro	Semi-independent	Euro (partly "DM-ized" since 1999)	2002
Nauru	Independent	Australian dollar	1914

Exhibit 5.5 Dollarization Around the World

Nation	Political status	Currency	Since
Niue	New Zealand self-governing territory	New Zealand dollar	1901
Norfolk Island	Australian external territory	Australian dollar	before 1900?
Northern Mariana Islands	US commonwealth	US dollar	1944
Palau	Independent	US dollar	1944
Panama	Independent	US dollar, own balboa coins	1904
Pitcairn Island	British dependency	New Zealand, US dollars	1800s
Puerto Rico	US commonwealth	US dollar	1899
San Marino	Independent	Euro (formerly Italian lira), own coins	1897
Tokelau	New Zealand territory	New Zealand dollar	1926
Turks and Caicos Islands	British colony	US dollar	1973
Tuvalu	Independent	Australian dollar, own coins	1892
US Virgin Islands	US territory	US dollar	1934
Vatican City	Independent	Euro (formerly Italian lira), own coins	1929

Exhibit 5.5 Dollarization Around the World

Source: K. Chibber, 2014., Here are all the countries that don't have a currency of their own, http://qz.com/260980/
meet-the-countries-that-dont-use-their-own-currency/; CIA World Factbook 2016; press reports.

Why do countries decide to dollarize? Often countries decide to dollarize because they are not able to borrow in the local currency. Additionally, some research suggests that dollarization occurs because countries also want to fight inflation. Other reasons include as a way to ward off foreign exchange instability as well as local monetary policy instability. However, despite these advantages, experts argue that dollarization is not necessarily beneficial. Studies have shown that dollarization often leads to higher inflation[9] as well as depreciation of the local currency.[10] Such effects have led some countries to de-dollarize. Consider the following Emerging Market Brief.

De-dollarization in Angola

EMERGING
MARKET BRIEF

Despite the popularity of dollarization, some evidence suggests that it is not always beneficial. Dollarization can result in higher inflation through the exchange pass-through effect. This occurs because banks in such countries will typically issue debts in the foreign currency. This also means that as the local currency depreciates, local firms need to pay more to service their debts. This also implies that they have to increase domestic prices to meet higher debt servicing.

Angola, an emerging post-war nation in Africa, is now enjoying strong economic growth and has seen a boom in construction. It decided to de-dollarize its currency to deal with the detrimental effects of dollarization. Locals argue that it does not make sense to trade in a currency that is not theirs. Furthermore, the local currency, the Angolan Kwanza, is now being accepted by all. Other local experts argue that de-dollarization is also making them less dependent on the swings of the foreign exchange market. Local companies will no longer go bankrupt because of depreciation.

Source: K. Saigal, 2015, "Angola's de-dollarization drive," *Euromoney*, September, pp. 209–213.

What Determines Exchange Rates

Purchasing Power Parity

Purchasing Power
Parity (PPP)
ignoring tax differences,
transportation costs, and
trade restrictions, goods
and other services in any
two countries should
have the same prices
after converting each of
their currencies into a
common currency

Purchasing power parity (PPP) means that, ignoring tax differences, transportation costs, and trade restrictions, goods and services in any two countries should have the same prices *after converting each of their currencies into a common currency.*[11] This is also called the Law of One Price. The theory argues that exchange-rate movements will depend on the differences between domestic and foreign prices and that exchange rates will achieve equilibrium in the long run. If there are differences in prices, buyers or other market participants will take advantage of the price differences and exchange rates will thus reach some equilibrium in the long-run.

For example, you buy your favorite tennis racquet in Los Angeles for $200. Your friend, who is studying in India for the year, buys the same racquet for 13,540 Indian Rupees at a Delhi sporting goods store. Applying the logic of PPP, these prices should be the same when we factor in the exchange rate between the dollar and the Indian Rupee. Assume that the exchange rate = $/67.70 Indian Rupees. Your friend can then convert the price you paid in dollars for your racquet to the price she should pay in Indian Rupees as $200 × 67.70 = 13,540 Indian Rupees.

Some studies have found support for the purchasing power parity theory.[12,13] However, because currencies can be "overvalued" or "undervalued," the Law of One Price does not always hold. Overvalued means that the currency is worth more than would be predicted by an economic model. Undervalued means the currency is worth less than would be predicted by an economic model. The use of PPP since the sixteenth century makes it perhaps the oldest economic model used to estimate how over- or undervalued is a currency.

Big Mac Index
an index of currency
overvaluation or
undervaluation based on
the price of a McDonald's
Big Mac, published by *The
Economist* each year

Based on the theory of PPP, *The Economist* publishes each year an index of currency overvaluation and undervaluation based on the price of a McDonald's Big Mac. This has become known as the **Big Mac Index**. The logic is that the price of a Big Mac should be the same everywhere if exchange rates are correct. However, as you can see from the recent index in Exhibit 5.6, and based on what you must pay for a Big Mac in many countries, most currencies are over- or undervalued relative to the US dollar.

Look at the price of a Big Mac in China. It is around two thirds of the price in the US. This suggests that the Chinese currency is undervalued by around 33 percent.

Of course, the Big Mac Index is a simple way of looking at currency values regarding PPP. Numerous other factors that come into play determine exchange rates. We discuss some of those drivers below.

Market Factors

Exchange rates reflect the price of money bought and sold in a market. As such, like most markets, the supply and demand for a currency affects its price in terms of other currencies. Of course, not all exchange rates are allowed to respond to market forces (see the history of exchange rates in this chapter) and governments often intervene by buying or selling currencies to influence their value. However, supply and demand remain the major drivers of currency value.

derived demand
demand that comes from
the demand for goods
and services

The demand for a currency is based on **derived demand**. That means, for example, that demand for the pesos comes from the degree to which people from other countries wish to purchase Mexican products or services or invest in Mexican companies. That is, for example, if US consumers buy Mexican cement (a demand for a Mexican good) then US dollars must be converted into pesos to buy cement. Consequently, the demand for pesos increases.

Country	Local Price	Price (US$)	Exchange Rate	US$ (PPP)	US$ Valuation
Argentina	33.00	2.39	13.81	6.69	−52
Australia	5.30	3.74	1.42	1.08	−24
Brazil	13.50	3.35	4.02	2.74	−32
Britain	2.89	4.22	0.68	0.59	−14
Canada	5.84	4.14	1.41	1.18	−16
Chile	2100.00	2.94	715.22	425.96	−40
China	17.60	2.68	6.56	3.57	−46
Colombia	7900.00	2.43	3253.90	1602.43	−51
Denmark	30.00	4.32	6.94	6.09	−12
Egypt	16.93	2.16	7.83	3.43	−56
Euro area	3.72	4.00	0.93	0.75	−19
Hong Kong	19.20	2.48	7.75	3.89	−50
India	127.00	1.90	66.80	25.76	−61
Indonesia	30500.00	2.19	13947.50	6186.61	−56
Malaysia	8.00	1.82	4.39	1.62	−63
Mexico	49.00	2.81	17.44	9.94	−43
New Zealand	5.90	3.91	1.51	1.20	−21
Norway	46.80	5.21	8.97	9.49	6
Pakistan	300.00	2.86	104.89	60.85	−42
Peru	10.00	2.93	3.42	2.03	−41
Philippines	131.00	2.79	47.02	26.57	−43
Poland	9.60	2.37	4.05	1.95	−52
Russia	114.00	1.53	74.66	23.12	−69
South Africa	28.00	1.77	15.81	5.68	−64
South Korea	4300.00	3.59	1197.75	872.21	−27
Sri Lanka	350.00	2.43	144.05	70.99	−51
Sweden	45.00	5.23	8.60	9.13	6
Switzerland	6.50	6.44	1.01	1.32	31
Taiwan	69.00	2.08	33.23	14.00	−58
Thailand	112.00	3.09	36.22	22.72	−37
Turkey	10.25	3.41	3.01	2.08	−31
UAE	13.00	3.54	3.67	2.64	−28
Ukraine	36.00	1.54	23.35	7.30	−69
USA	4.93	4.93	1.00	1.00	0
Uruguay	113.00	3.74	30.19	22.92	−24
Vietnam	60000.00	2.67	22467.50	12170.39	−46

Exhibit 5.6 The Big Mac Index

Source: Economist.com, 2016, Big Mac Index, www.economist.com/content/big-mac-index

Exhibit 5.7 shows the relationship between the exchange rate and the demand for pesos. The *x*-axis on this chart shows the quantity of pesos demanded and the *y*-axis shows hypothetical exchange rates. Note, as the number of dollars it takes to buy pesos drops, there is an increase in the quantity of pesos demanded. This occurs because US consumers and companies are encouraged to buy more Mexican goods when it takes fewer dollars to do so. Demand goes up, because to buy more Mexican goods, people and companies need to purchase more pesos.

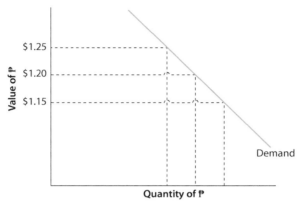

Exhibit 5.7 Demand Curve for Pesos

The foreign exchange market also includes the supply of, for our example, pesos available for sale or for exchange with US dollars. Similar to the US demand curve for pesos, we can look at a supply curve for the sale of pesos in the foreign exchange market relative to the exchange rate with US dollars.

As shown in Exhibit 5.8, as the ability of pesos to buy more US dollars increases, the supply of pesos for sale increases. The supply of pesos increases when pesos can buy more US dollars because US goods and services become cheaper and Mexican consumers and companies do not have to use as many pesos to satisfy their needs. That is, because they use fewer pesos, there are more pesos available.

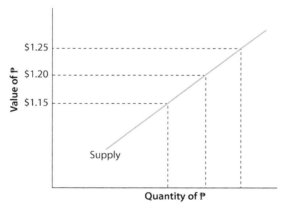

Exhibit 5.8 Supply Curve for Pesos

The point where demand and supply curves intersect is the equilibrium point. As shown in Exhibit 5.9, this is the point where the demand for pesos equals the supply of pesos, and the result is the price of each currency in terms of the other: namely, the exchange rate. This simple supply/demand view of exchange-rate determination begins with the logic of international trade activities determining the demand or attractiveness of the products and services in another country, and shows how changes in price (exchange rates) increase the demand and supply of currencies to complete these transactions. Of course, many other factors influence the nature of these demand and supply curves and we will consider some of these factors below.

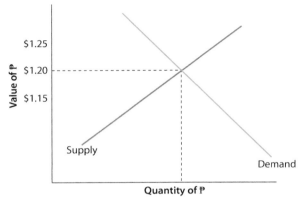

Exhibit 5.9 Equilibrium Point for the Exchange Rate

Effects of Other Factors on Exchange Rates

Inflation   Imagine that the US economy is experiencing a period of inflation. That means that prices are increasing rapidly. In Mexico, however, inflation is low so prices are rising more slowly. These price differences make Mexican goods cheaper and more attractive to US businesses and consumers and, conversely, make US goods more expensive and thus less attractive to Mexican companies and consumers. Exhibit 5.10 shows a shift in the demand curve reflecting the increased demand from the US to purchase Mexican goods and thus demand more pesos. This increase in demand due to differences in inflation rates brings a new equilibrium point that reflects a higher price (exchange rate) in dollars/pesos.

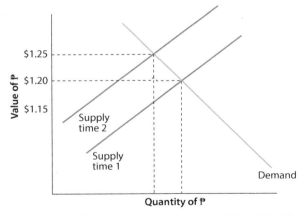

Exhibit 5.10 Equilibrium Points for Exchange Rates with Rising US Inflation

Relative Interest Rates   Another factor that influences the demand and supply for currencies is the interest rate. The interest rate is important because investors tend to put their money into countries where they can get the highest rate of return. Thus, if interest rates in the US are higher than in Mexico, both Mexican and US investors would find the potentially higher returns a motivation to buy US stocks and bonds. For example, imagine that a typical US company must issue bonds paying 8 percent when it needs to finance its operations with debt. Companies issue or sell bonds to raise money, with the promise to pay back the money with interest in the future to those who buy the bonds. However, similar Mexican companies need only pay 4 percent for their bond issues. US bonds are more attractive because the return is higher.

Attracted by the differences in returns, investors will demand fewer pesos than dollars, since they will need dollars to invest in the US. As shown in Exhibit 5.11, when investors seek fewer pesos to invest in Mexico, the demand for pesos drops. Also, in this example, because Mexican investors exchange pesos for dollars to take advantage of the higher US interest rates, the supply of pesos increases, and the supply curve shifts to the right (more pesos are available) while the demand curve shifts to the left (fewer pesos are sought by investors). The situation reduces or depreciates the value of the pesos relative to the dollar.

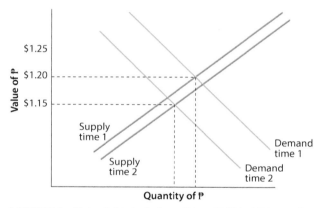

Exhibit 5.11 Equilibrium Points for Exchange Rates with Rising US Interest Rates

Because an increasing interest rate often accompanies an increasing inflation rate, the effects on the value of a currency can be offset. Rising interest rates attract investors and increase the demand for a currency. Rising inflation increases prices and reduces the demand for a currency. To consider these effects in combination, economists often look at the **real interest rate**. Sometimes called the Fisher effect, the real interest rate is represented as:

real interest rate
the inflation rate subtracted from the interest rate

Real interest rate = interest rate – inflation rate

Income Levels   Of course, not all countries have similar income levels so the relative income levels between trading partners can affect the amount of imports from a country. When a country's income levels rise relative to a trading partner's (assuming this is not just inflation but also a real rise in purchasing power), that country will likely buy more goods from its partner. For example, if US incomes levels rise, US consumers are likely to buy more European automobiles. Like all the other factors that can increase the demand for a currency, this would make the price of the European euros rise.

Government Controls   As was mentioned earlier, governments can and often do intervene with the market forces that determine exchange rates. Governments and their central banks have several tools to influence exchange rates. The choice of an exchange-rate policy that is not free-floating limits the effects of market forces.

Trade-related Factors

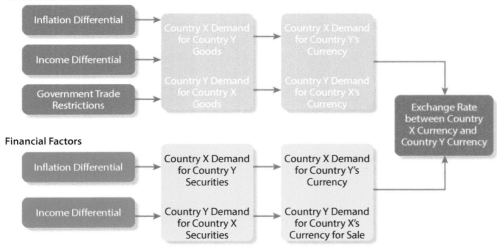

Financial Factors

Exhibit 5.12 Factors Influencing Exchange Rates

Other options include barriers on foreign trade and investments. Tariffs or restrictions on imports reduce the demand for a foreign currency. Similarly, a government can tax foreign investments at a high rate, offsetting the effects of higher interest rates in other countries. As we saw in an earlier example, the Venezuelan government has imposed significant limits on foreign exchanges. Finally, governments often purchase or sell currencies in the exchange market for the sole purpose of influencing supply and demand and thus the exchange rates. Exhibit 5.12 gives a graphic summary of the major factors affecting exchange rates.

Exchange-rate Risks and Hedging

Because exchange rates vary continuously, MNCs necessarily face continuous uncertainties regarding how to value in their own currency what they own in other countries, what they buy from other countries, and what they sell to other countries. As you saw in many examples earlier, being engaged in international trade means that companies are subject to the risks associated with fluctuations in exchange rates. Changes in exchange rates may affect future cash flows and the value of the firm.[14] In some cases, a company can go bankrupt because of the firm's inability to service its debt.

The type of exchange-rate risk discussed above is called **transaction exposure**. Formally, transaction exposure occurs when the MNC agrees to a transaction in a foreign currency—selling or buying—in the future.

A second problem dealing with exchange rates for MNCs is how they value foreign assets (e.g. an asset might be a factory owned in Munich, Germany, by an Australian company) and liabilities (e.g. debt owed to a Swiss bank by an Australian company) in their home country currency, in this case Australian dollars. As the relationships among these currencies change, the worth of the company changes in its home currency. For example, if the Australian dollar depreciates against the Swiss franc, the Australian company's debt, in Australian dollars, increases because it will take more dollars to pay off the debt. For publicly owned companies, US law requires that assets and liabilities be translated into US dollars at the existing exchange rate at the end of the reporting period. If you look at annual reports for MNCs, you can see how companies do this in their financial statements. Since foreign currencies are translated into

transaction exposure
a risk that MNCs face that involves uncertainty regarding: the value of their own currency for what they own in other countries, what they buy from other countries, and what they sell to other countries

the home currency for financial statements, this type of risk is called **translation exposure**. The risk is that the financial characteristics of an MNC with assets and liabilities in different currencies can look quite different, depending on the exchange rates.

What can companies do to offset these risks? Companies attempt to offset exchange-rate risk by hedging. **Hedging** offsets risk by making future exchange rates predictable. Hedging is used by both multinationals operating in a foreign country and local companies involved in international trade. Do companies see hedging as a beneficial activity? A recent study of 50 Indian exporting countries shows that hedging is clearly seen as a robust way to protect the company from risks associated with foreign exchange markets.[15] In fact, as Exhibit 5.13 shows, only 15 percent of the Indian companies felt that they did not benefit from using hedging as a way to manage currency risks.

Clearly, Exhibit 5.13 shows that the majority of the local Indian export companies benefitted from hedging activities. How can companies do this? There are several mechanisms.

Imagine that you are working for a company that buys a lot of land for a greenfield investment in Poland. A greenfield investment means that you are going to start the company from scratch (imagine building a factory in a green field). Your company agrees to the sale price of 39,650,500 Polish zloty, which on the day of the contract is worth approximately US$10 million. The problem for your company is that real-estate transactions often take a few months to complete and, in the meantime, the exchange rate between the zloty and the dollar will likely change. One way to reduce your uncertainty is to buy a **forward exchange contract** from a commercial bank. The forward exchange contract is an agreement to purchase a foreign currency in the future, say three months for this example, at a specified exchange rate.

In this hypothetical contract, your company agrees to purchase Polish zloty in three months at the exchange rate of 1 Polish zloty = 0.252 US$. Now you know that your cost for the property is $10 million (39,650,500 Polish zloty × 0.252 = $10,000,000) regardless of what happens to the exchange rate. Forward exchange rates for major currencies are available from major banks and business publications. Unlike the example above, forward rates are seldom the same as current or spot rates. To a large degree, forward rates are based on anticipated economic conditions in the countries involved and may be less (a discount) or greater (a premium) than the current rate.

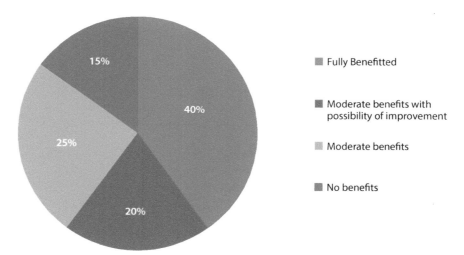

Exhibit 5.13 Percentage of Indian Companies that Perceived Benefits of Hedging
Source: Based on H. Maniar, 2016, "Hedging practices used by Indian companies in managing foreign exchange risks," *IUP Journal of Financial Risk Management*, 8(2), pp. 41–62.

Another way to hedge on the future changes in exchange rates, similar to a forward contract, is called the **currency futures contracts**. Like the forward exchange contract, the MNC locks into an exchange rate to purchase foreign currency in the future. For the forward contract, the agreement is usually between two parties such as a bank and an MNC, with size and delivery date.

For the futures contract, contracts to buy or sell currencies in the future at a fixed exchange rate are traded in a regulated market with standardized lots, delivery dates, and only in major currencies. The world's largest currency futures market is the International Monetary Market of the Chicago Mercantile Exchange. Large MNCs with close relationships with banks usually use forward contracts to tailor the exchange to their exact currency needs. Smaller operations prefer the futures market.

Forward contracts make exchange rates predictable for MNCs. However, there is always a chance that exchange rates will move in a direction favorable to the company. Because of this, many companies attempt to forecast future exchange rates to anticipate whether the rates will move in a favorable direction. For example, if a company anticipates that the dollar will appreciate against the yen, it may be willing to agree to a price in yen for a future delivery, hoping that the future price in dollars will be less.

If a company tries to anticipate the price of a currency and feels comfortable about its forecasting, the company may also engage in the **options hedging method**. In this case, the buyer contracts with a seller and pays a premium price to have the ability to pay a specific price for a currency by a certain date. In this hedging approach, the buying company has a right to buy the currency but is not obligated to do so. In contrast, the seller has a binding contract to sell the currency at the agreed price if the buyer decides to exercise its buying right.

The techniques of forecasting exchange rates are complex and beyond the scope of this text. However, you can see forecasts available from various services on the Web, such as www. forecasts.org/exchange-rate/index.htm.

Finally, another hedging method is currency swaps. You already learned about how this method worked earlier in this chapter.

Which methods are preferred by companies? Consider the following BRIC Insight.

There are also opportunities to make money on small differences in exchange rates. This is called foreign exchange arbitrage and it is covered in the next section.

currency futures contracts
an agreement to purchase a foreign currency in the future based on contracts traded in a market tailored to the parties' needs

options hedging method
contract where buyer pays premium to have the option but no obligation to buy foreign currency at set prices by a specific date

Hedging by Indian Companies
BRIC INSIGHT

India used to follow a very tightly controlled foreign exchange market prior to economic reforms in 1991. During this regulated exchange regime, there were very strict import and other foreign exchange controls. Such controls resulted in a very vibrant black market for currency exchanges. However, the government initiated many major economic reforms in 1991. Now local companies face a liberated exchange market where the value of the Indian rupee is determined by the forces of demand and supply. Consequently, Indian companies now face many of the same foreign currency exchange risks as most multinationals worldwide.

How do Indian companies deal with such foreign currency risks? A recent study of 50 Indian export-oriented companies provides some insights on the hedging approach used. These companies have been very active raising finances from foreign sources. Additionally, these companies are also involved in many forms of cross-border transactions.

Exhibit 5.14 shows the types of hedging preferred by these companies.

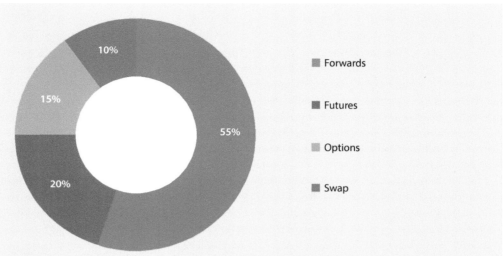

Exhibit 5.14 Preferred Hedging Approach by Indian Export-oriented Companies

As can be seen, the Indian companies studied clearly preferred the forwards method as the best hedging approach (55 percent). However, 20 percent of the companies preferred the futures approach. The least preferred approaches were the options method (15 percent) and the swap approach (10 percent).

Source: Based on H. Maniar, 2016, "Hedging practices used by Indian companies in managing foreign exchange risks," *IUP Journal of Financial Risk Management*, 8(2), pp. 41–62.

Foreign Exchange Arbitrage

Because currencies trade in markets all over the world, exchange rates may differ in different markets. When exchange rates do differ, there is an opportunity to make money by buying lower and selling higher. In fact, the word "arbitrage" means buy low and sell high.

Suppose the exchange rate for the Mexican peso and the US dollar was 40.5 peso/dollar in New York. However, in Tokyo the exchange rate was 40.75 peso/dollar. If both markets are open and there are no restrictions on trade, there is an arbitrage opportunity. Arbitrageurs with substantial dollars or with substantial credit lines in dollars can purchase more pesos per dollar in Tokyo and then immediately sell the pesos in New York for more dollars than they paid. For example, $1,000,000 would buy 40,750,000 pesos in Tokyo. These pesos could then buy $1,006,173 in New York (40,750,000 pesos/40.5 = $1,006,173) for a profit of $6,173.

Of course, when arbitrage opportunities exist, currency traders move quickly to take advantage of the exchange-rate difference. Because an increase in demand for the cheaper currency will cause its value to rise, markets quickly adjust, eliminating arbitrage opportunities. Because rates often differ by a very small amount, it takes very large transactions to show a profit. Although it is mostly currency speculators that try to take advantage of arbitrage, MNCs also do so when opportunities arise.

Chapter Review

To buy, sell, or invest across national borders, MNCs must be able to exchange their home currencies for the currencies of the nations in which they do business. The foreign exchange market is where these currency exchanges take place. The foreign exchange market is the biggest in the world. The dollar value of daily exchanges exceeds $5.3 trillion. Thus, having a basic understanding of how currency exchange works is an important step in conducting international business.

The price of one currency in terms of another represents the exchange rate between the two currencies. Major business publications publish the ending daily exchange rates among major currencies each day. However, the values of currencies change continuously, often up to 20 times a minute.

Early efforts to manage and stabilize exchange rates among currencies led to the development of the gold standard. When countries used the gold standard, they set the value of their currency in terms of an ounce of gold. The US set the price of gold at $20.646, and technically you could buy an ounce of gold from the US Treasury at that price. This system broke down after World War II and many countries then fixed the value of their currencies to the US dollar. Although some countries still fix the value of their money to the US dollar or to several other currencies, most major economies in the world now use a floating-rate system. Market forces set the value of currencies.

People and companies tend to buy and invest in other countries where their own currency has greater buying power, so they need more of the foreign currency to do this. This is the demand side of the currency market. The supply of a currency is also influenced by the exchange rate since if you need less of currency X to buy currency Y then the supply of currency available increases. When the demand and supply curves of a currency cross, that is the equilibrium point and reflects the exchange rate. However, other market forces that determine the value of currencies include a country's inflation rate, interest rates, income levels, and government controls. These factors shift the supply and demand curves and thus change the exchange rates.

Emerging markets tend to see higher levels of governmental intervention in the foreign exchange markets. Such governments intervene for a variety of reasons ranging from the desire to control the market for foreign currency. However, some governments also intervene for economic reasons such as preserving stability of exchange rates or to control prices.

Because exchange rates change so much, MNCs face exchange-rate risks. When a company buys or sells something and gives or takes payments in the future, costs or income from these exchanges are often different from those existing at the time of the initial agreement. This is called transaction exposure. Similarly, the values of investments and debts in other countries vary with the exchange rates. This is called translation exposure. To hedge against these variations, MNCs can fix the rates of exchange in the future by buying forward exchange contracts or currency futures contracts.

Because the foreign exchange market is a worldwide operation and because markets do not always value currencies at the same rates, there exist opportunities for foreign exchange arbitrage. This means that one buys the currency in one market at a cheaper price and then sells in another market at a higher price. Since currency values change continuously, arbitrage opportunities are often fleeting and companies must move very fast with large amounts of money to succeed before the markets adjust.

All international business people must keep a vigil on the foreign exchange market as it affects all cross-border transactions as well as the value of one's company. Tactics such as hedging allow managers to have some reducibility in their transnational operations. However, in parts of the world where currencies are highly unstable, the exchange-rate risks can make international business a challenging financial management problem.

Discussion Questions

1   Describe the foreign exchange market. Discuss why it exists and why it is necessary for international trade and commerce.

2   What is an exchange rate and how does it relate to the bid and the ask spread?

3   Compare and contrast the basic types of foreign exchange transactions.

4   Explain how the gold standard worked and why it led to stable exchange rates. What might be some advantages and disadvantages of returning to the gold standard?

5   Describe the relationship between purchasing power parity and the Big Mac Index.

6   What is derived demand and how does this relate to the value of one currency in terms of another?

7   What are the advantages of hedging for an MNC? How do MNCs hedge?

8   Why do governments intervene in foreign exchange markets? What are the specific reasons for such actions?

International Business Skill Builder

Formulating a Hedging Strategy

Step 1: Find a local small business that buys or sells internationally.

Step 2: Interview the manager/owner to find out how they manage their exchange-rate risk. If you cannot contact a real business, create a simulated company that engages in foreign transactions. See www.forecasts.org/exchange-rate.

Step 3: Create a hypothetical (or real, if you have the information) anticipated purchase or sale a few months into the future.

Step 4: Recommend to the company whether to hedge on exchange rates or to trust forecasts that may show beneficial exchange rates in the future. In formulating your strategy, check the future rates at Chicago Mercantile Exchange, www.cme.com/trading/dta/del/globex.html and compare with forecasted rates from sites such as www.forecasts.org/exchange-rate

Chapter Internet Activity

Open a practice account at **https://fxtrade.oanda.com/** and explore the world of currency trading. Explore this site for all kinds of currency exchange information, including current and historical rates.

Key Concepts

- Big Mac Index
- Bretton Woods Agreement
- crawling-peg system
- currency-basket peg
- currency devaluation
- currency futures contracts
- currency swaps
- derived demand
- dollarization
- exchange rate
- exchange-rate system
- floating-rate system
- foreign exchange market

- Foreign Exchange Market Government Intervention
- forward exchange contract
- forward transaction
- hedging
- International Monetary Fund (IMF)
- options heading method
- pegged exchange-rate system
- Purchasing Power Parity (PPP)
- real interest rate
- spot transaction
- the bid and the ask spread
- transaction exposure
- translation exposure

CASE 5   BUSINESS > INTERNATIONAL

Weak or Strong Dollar Which is Better for Emerging Markets?

A mighty economy with a strong dollar and a lot of purchasing power for consumers is the stuff of politicians. A strong dollar represents economic strength and stability. A strong dollar makes Americans proud. A strong dollar just sounds right. Why shouldn't the world's largest economy with the most powerful military force in history have a strong currency? While it may sound right, or be intuitively appealing, the idea of a strong currency does not necessarily represent sound economic policy and may not be in the best interest of a country.

It may be the terms themselves that produce the misguided judgments. Strong is preferred over weak in most situations. It is better to have a strong heart than a weak one. When building a tall structure, strong steel beams would be preferred over weak ones. A strong bond between a parent and a child is generally perceived as being better than a weak relationship. So, it seems correct that a country should also have a strong currency. Some have proposed changing the terminology from strong and weak to "import" and "export" in order to avoid a natural preference. With the US dollar (USD), it would be called an export dollar when the USD is weak and an import dollar when it is strong. When the dollar is weak American goods become cheaper for foreign buyers and when the dollar is strong, American exports are more expensive. Changing the way we refer to a currency might change the view in which a strong currency is perceived as better.

Putting aside the question of the merits of a strong dollar for now, it is clear that a dollar doesn't buy what it did in the past. The purchasing power of the US dollar has eroded for many years. While the relative economic strength of the American economy relative to the rest of the world can be debated, especially as much of the world has made significant economic gains since the end of the War, the driving force in the decline of the purchasing power of the dollar is inflation. One would have to consider wage levels to get a more accurate view. In 1948 the minimum wage was 40 cents an hour. The current federal minimum wage is $7.25 per hour, with some states having an even higher minimum wage requirement. While the cost of a loaf of bread may have been around 14 cents in 1948, with a 40 cent minimum wage, it took 21 minutes of working to buy one. At the current federal minimum wage, 21 minutes of work earns $2.54. Inflation eroding the value of a currency is not unique to the United States. Even small levels of inflation over time greatly erode the purchasing power of a currency. As long as wage levels keep up with inflation, the situation is not too problematic.

CASE 5
cont'd

Putting purchasing power aside, the strength of the US dollar can be compared to other currencies using the US Dollar Index, or DXY. Created in 1973 by J.P. Morgan, the index compares the value of the USD to a basket of weighted currencies which include the Japanese yen, the British pound, the Canadian dollar, the Swiss franc, the Swedish krona, and the euro (the index was altered when the euro was introduced). The euro is very heavily weighted in the index representing 57.6 percent of the composite. By contrast, the Canadian dollar has a weight of just 9.1 percent of the index value. When the DXY was created in 1973 it was set at a baseline of 100. Since 1973 the index has risen and fallen (the high being in 1985 at 164.72) and by Election Day in the United States, November 6, 2012, it stood at 80.64. The USD has experienced periods of strength and weakness. From 1980 to 1985, for example, the USD rose significantly in value (even though the US was experiencing an increasing deficit in trade) causing leaders from the Group of Five (Germany, Great Britain, France, Japan, and the US) to hold an emergency meeting in New York to discuss the matter. The result of this meeting (held at the Plaza Hotel) led to the "Plaza Accord" whereby the countries would sell dollars in order to bring down the value of the USD. The agreement worked and the USD decreased in value to a point where the process was stopped and the dollar eventually allowed to once again rise.

In recent years the USD has seen a weakening, with the exception of the financial crisis in which investors flocked to the dollar as a safe harbor. A number of factors can explain the weakening, from government spending in the US to the strengthening of some economies due to global demand for their natural resources. The weakness in the dollar could be attributed to the efforts of quantitative easing (QE) in which the Federal Reserve through a series of rounds injected money into the economic system, in essence, printing money. The rising supply of a currency, all other things being equal, will reduce its value relative to other currencies. However, Japan and other developed countries have also had quantitative easing programs. In the case of Japan especially, the program was not effective in curbing the rising value of the Japanese yen.

According to an article in *The Economist*, many countries no longer see a strong currency as a positive and necessary aspect of economic development. Especially after the financial crisis which began in 2008 countries sought to have weak currencies in order to increase exports and create jobs. When in the past a strong or at least stable currency was seen as desirable, that view is not shared by all today. When a country's currency declines in value it makes its exports cheaper in the global market.

Perhaps increasing the trend towards a weak currency is the ability of countries to manipulate their currency values. In terms of manipulating a currency it is easier to devalue than revalue one. To revalue or increase the value of a currency, that currency must be purchased using foreign reserves, which for many countries is increasingly more difficult. To

CASE 5
cont'd

devalue a currency all that is needed is to increase the supply of the currency, essentially printing more. In recent years that process has not always proved to be as effective as in the past.

Interest rates also play a part in determining currency values. According to the International Fisher Effect a country's currency value is inversely related to nominal interest rates. In other words, if nominal interest rates are rising in Country A relative to Country B, Country A's currency will be decreasing in value relative to Country B. Interest rates are driven, in part, by inflation. Again, that relationship does not seem to be, at least in the short-term, as predictable as in the past. As interest rates in much of the developed world have fallen and inflation fears replaced by the fear of deflation, increasing interest rates can attract more capital from abroad, thus increasing demand for the currency.

A weakening dollar has a number of effects for Americans, both positive and negative. On the negative side, a weakening dollar makes imported goods more expensive for consumers. In addition, imported component parts and commodities used in producing goods in the United States rise in price. The price of oil and its derivatives such as gasoline also rise. While oil is for the most part priced globally in dollars, it is assumed that oil producers attempt to manipulate the price in order to make up for their declining revenue from a weakening dollar. In addition to imported goods, international travel for Americans becomes more expensive, both for leisure as well as for business purposes.

A weak dollar does have a number of advantages as well. As previously mentioned, a weak currency can help a country increase exports as those goods become less expensive to foreigners. Increased exports can then produce more jobs as export demand rises. However, in the case of the United States at least, the theory of a devalued currency promoting export growth has not been very robust. Even if export growth is not as strong as predicted by devaluation, American firms report higher profits from foreign operations as their foreign earnings are translated into more dollars. In addition, when the dollar weakens foreign investors may see greater opportunities in the US as these investments too become more financially attractive.

To resolve the question of which is better for the United States, a strong or weak dollar, some have proposed that one only needs to look at modern history for an answer. For example, Charles Kadlec, writing in *Forbes* says, if one compares the dollar policies of the last six presidents, a clear pattern emerges. Under Presidents Reagan and Clinton a strong dollar policy was followed resulting in strong economic growth. Under Presidents Carter, Bush 41, Bush 43, and Obama, a weak dollar policy was followed resulting in less stable economic growth. The validity of this means of making an assessment could be challenged as overly simplistic. Factors driving economic growth are complex, and even factors driving the strength of the dollar are complex, however, a decision on policy which favors a strong or weak dollar is important to the United States and the rest of the world.

CASE 5 cont'd	CASE DISCUSSION POINTS:

CASE DISCUSSION POINTS:

1   What is the effect of a strong or weak dollar for the rest of the world?
2   Some countries, many being developing countries, peg their currency to the US dollar. What effect does a rapid appreciation or devaluation of the dollar have on those countries?
3   If you were an exporter from an emerging country to the United States would you prefer a strong or weak dollar? Explain.

Source: *The Economist*, 2012, "The weak shall inherit the earth," October 6; C. Kadlec, 2012, "Mitt Romney's glaring economic Achilles heel," *Forbes*, January 2; E. Klein, 2011, "Renaming the 'strong' and 'weak' dollar," *The Washington Post*, May 19; B. McTeer, 2011, "Is the dollar weak or strong?" *Forbes*, December 30.

Case prepared by Charles A. Rarick

Notes

1   R. K. Rajhans and A. Jain, 2015, "Volatility spillover in foreign exchange markets," *Paradigm, 19*(2), pp. 137–151.
2   Robert J. Carbaugh, 2012, *International Economics*, Mason, OH: South-Western.
3   www.currencysystem.com/kb/3-138.html
4   *The Economist*, 2016, "Lights out," May 7, pp. 31–32.
5   Joseph P. Daniels and David D. VanHoose, 2005, *International Monetary and Financial Economics*, Mason, OH: South-Western.
6   D. R. Adhikari and K. K. Guru-Gharana, 2015, "Why China wants to peg its currency? An empirical investigation," *Journal of International Business Research, 14*(1), pp. 117–126.
7   D. Pilbeam, 2015, "Currency interventions: Effective policy tool or shortsighted gamble?" *Intereconomics, 2*, pp. 64–81.
8   L. G. Mengesha and M. J. Holmes, 2015, "Does dollarization reduce or produce inflation?" *Journal of Economic Studies, 42*(3), pp. 358–376.
9   L. G. Mengesha and M. J. Holmes, 2015, "Does dollarization reduce or produce inflation?" *Journal of Economic Studies, 42*(3), pp. 358–376.
10 A. Krupkina and A. Ponomarenko, 2015, "Deposit dollarization in emerging markets," *Bank of Finland Discussion Papers, 32*, pp. 3–20.
11 A. C. Arize, J. Malindretos and D. Ghosh, 2015, "Purchasing power parity-symmetry and proportionality: Evidence from 116 countries," *International Review of Economics and Finance, 37*, pp. 69–85.
12 M. Bahmani-Oskooee and A. B. M. Nasir, 2015, "Purchasing power parity and the law of one price: Evidence from commodity prices in Asian countries," *Global Economy Journal, 15*(2), pp. 231–240.
13 A. C. Arize, J. Malindretos and D. Ghosh, 2015, "Purchasing power parity-symmetry and proportionality: Evidence from 116 countries," *International Review of Economics and Finance, 37*, pp. 69–85.
14 J. Kim and J. Kim, 2015, "Financial regulation, exchange rate exposure and hedging activities: Evidence from Korean firms," *Emerging Markets Finance and Trade, 51*, pp. S152–S173.
15 H. Maniar, 2016, "Hedging practices used by Indian companies in managing foreign exchange risks," *IUP Journal of Financial Risk Management, 8*(2), pp. 41–62.

CHAPTER 6

Global Capital Markets

After reading this chapter you should be able to:

- Understand the nature of capital markets with a special focus on emerging markets.

- Know the terminology and basic structure of a bond issue.

- Understand stocks and stock markets from a domestic and international perspective.

- Know the basics of how banks make money and the effects of regulations.

- Be familiar with the motivations to seek capital outside of one's home country.

- Understand the implications of regulations for the choice of country of stock market listings.

- Be prepared for the changing nature of international stock markets and understand the challenges and opportunities in an emerging market context.

International Business   *Preview IB Emerging Market Strategic Insight*

Raising Capital in Global Markets

As trade globalizes and capital markets become increasingly connected, more companies are now seeking to raise equity capital outside of their market. This is occurring in both emerging markets and other markets. Consider that in 2010, 41 small-cap Chinese firms raised a total of $4.1 billion on the US stock exchange. Furthermore, in 2005, the Chinese search giant baidu.com successfully raised $109 million when it went public on NASDAQ. Recent statistics show that the London market is a popular market for initial public offerings (IPOs) with nearly half of the IPO proceeds coming from Russian firms.

Additionally, it is not just emerging market multinationals raising money in global capital markets. US companies have also been very successful in raising money in other countries. Consider the cases of Enova Systems, Zambeef Products, and Armor designs, which all decided to go public on London's Alternative Investment Market (AIM) exchange. Furthermore, in 2015, Verseon, the California biotechnology company went public and successfully raised $100 million.

To give you further insights on the degree to which multinationals are increasingly looking to international markets to raise capital, Exhibit 6.1 below shows some of the top initial public offerings (IPOs) between 2010–2011. As you can see, many of these IPOs came from the BRIC emerging markets.

Why are we seeing more multinationals raising capital in foreign markets? Experts argue that many market exchanges have seen fewer regulatory barriers related to trading and this has made trade much easier. Furthermore, many new forms of financial instruments are now available to investors worldwide. Finally, many state-owned and other local multinationals have decided to forego local capital markets in favor of international markets.

Source: Based on R. Bell and A. A. Rasheed, 2016, "Seeking capital abroad: Motivations, process and suggestions for success," *Journal of Applied Corporate Finance*, 28(1), pp. 104–113.

Amount Raised (US billion)

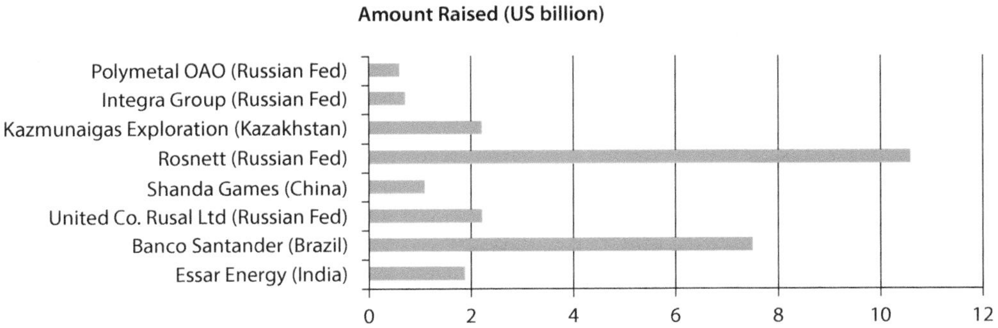

Exhibit 6.1 Top Cross-border Initial Public Offerings, 2010–2011
Source: Based on R. Bell and A. A. Rasheed 2016, "Seeking capital abroad: Motivations, process and suggestions for success," *Journal of Applied Corporate Finance*, 28(1), pp. 104–113.

The Preview IB Emerging Market Strategic Insight shows you how global companies can get money needed for expansion and growth outside of their own country. It shows one of many options companies use to get needed funds. In this chapter, you will find some basic background on the array of sources that all companies use to get needed funds. However, more importantly, you will learn how these sources of funds are becoming more globalized. You will also learn that emerging markets pose additional challenges because the capital markets are still maturing. Such challenges provide additional difficulties operating in these markets.

There is an old saying that "it takes money to make money." So, if companies want to buy the raw materials needed for production, expand into new markets, develop new products or services, or build or remodel their factories, it takes money. Of course, very profitable companies might take all of their profits and reinvest them to accomplish such goals. However, this is somewhat like saying to individuals who want to buy a new house or a new car that they should save the money from their earnings until they have sufficient money to buy the car or house. Not many people can do this, so instead, if for example an individual wants to buy a new house and does not have the $120,000 plus in savings that almost any house will cost, he or she will usually go to a bank or credit union and get a loan for 80–90 percent of the value of the house. With a fixed interest rate, they pay back the loan over 15 to 30 years with one constant payment per month. At the end of 15 to 30 years, they own the house but have also paid the bank a lot of money in interest. For example, imagine that your friend Juan takes a $100,000 25-year mortgage at 6 percent interest. Juan will pay $639.81 per month for 25 years. At the end, he will have paid off that $100,000 by making a total of $191,943 in payments.

Like most individuals, companies at some time also need cash beyond what their profits and savings can generate. Companies can go to commercial banks for similar loans to home loans, but they usually do not do this as companies use banks mostly for short-term cash needs. Instead, for large cash needs over longer terms, companies get money from other sources. These other sources for cash are known as **capital markets**, and in the next section you will learn about the options companies use to get needed money.

capital markets
markets where individuals, governments, and businesses that do not have an immediate use for their money transfer that money to individuals, governments, and businesses that do have a need and a use for that money

What are Capital Markets?

In simple terms, a capital market is a market where individuals, governments, and businesses that do not have an immediate use for their money transfer that money to individuals, governments, and businesses that do have a need and a use for that money.

Businesses have short-term needs for money, for example if they need to buy raw material to produce their products or are waiting to be paid by customers but still must pay their employees. Most often, they meet these short-term cash needs by short-term loans from commercial banks.

Commercial banks are banks that specialize in making loans to companies rather than to individuals as customers. However, as the banking industry has been deregulated, many commercial banks offer bank services to consumers as well. The major commercial banks in the US are Citigroup, Bank of America Corp., J.P. Morgan Chase & Company, and Wells Fargo. Since companies most often use bank loans for short-term financing, many have lines of credit, similar to a credit card, so they can cover cash needs quickly.

When companies need money for longer-term investments such as opening a new factory, they usually turn to the major capital markets. These markets are the bond market and the stock market. When we think of markets we often think of people buying and trading commodities such as wheat or livestock or gold and silver. However, in financial markets people and organizations can buy and trade financial instruments that represent either debts owned by companies (bonds) or partial ownership of companies (stocks).

As you can see from above, capital markets are critical aspects of any company's attempt to raise capital. However, these markets are still maturing in many emerging markets. Consider the following BRIC Insight.

The Chinese Stock Exchange

A properly functioning capital market plays a critical role in any economy. For instance, through stock exchanges, capital markets provide the ability for companies to fund themselves through equities by selling shares rather than just taking on debt. As you will see later, another aspect of a capital market is a bond market that also provides an alternative source of funding to companies and local governments. Additionally, a transparent capital market also provides investors with the necessary information to help them price capital.

Although a properly functioning capital market is critical for companies to access the required capital they need to grow, a recent review of many emerging markets suggest that their capital markets are still at an early stage of development. Consider the case of China's capital market and its volatile nature. For instance, in June of 2015, the Shanghai composite index fell by 32 percent while the more technology-oriented Shenzhen composite index fell by 40 percent. Despite quick intervention, the government was unable to stem the outward flow of capital. This seems to suggest a stock bubble that the government hopes does not result in panic selling.

The bond market in China has also seen rapid growth. Experts believe that such growth is because investors do not see Chinese bonds as having high risk. Local investors perceive that bonds are backed by the government and less likely to default. However, experts believe that such perception is dangerous as the government may not be able to back bonds indefinitely as the Chinese economy slows down.

Despite the above challenges, many also believe that there are improvements currently occurring. Although the Chinese stock market is dominated by 'small-time' investors, there is now a new breed of professional and knowledgeable investors. The bond markets are also attracting seasoned players. Such changes coupled with reforms will likely lead to the necessary changes to make the Chinese capital market more mature in the long-term.

Source: Based on *The Economist*, 2016, "Special report: Finance in China," May 7, pp. 9–11; K. Kehler, 2015, "Why China's stock market meltdown could hurt us all," Time.com, July 13, 2015.

The above shows some of the challenges of operating in emerging markets. Now let us consider how each of these financial markets works.

The Bond Market

The **bond market** is where companies can take on debt using a financial instrument called a bond. Companies have used bonds for a long time.

Bonds are a form of debt, somewhat like a loan from a bank but with a slightly different relationship to investors. Although bonds are loans, the terminology is different from what we usually hear regarding loans that an individual might take to buy a car or a new house. The **bond issuer** is the borrower, the **bondholder** is the lender, and the **coupon** is the interest rate. Unlike getting a loan from a single bank, issuing bonds allows bondholders to come from a large group of potential investors. Pension funds and banks often purchase corporate bonds, but individuals can do so as well. Thus, when a company has a bond issue it is usually not dependent on one lender but can have many lenders. Issuing bonds allows companies to finance long-term investments using external funds.

Bondholders receive interest payments from the company until the redemption date, which is the end of the loan period. At the redemption date, the company agrees to pay the bondholder the value of the bond. For example, following the illustration in Exhibit 6.2, assume a company issues $20,000 bonds with a ten-year maturity and a 7 percent coupon or interest rate. If you

bond market
a market where companies can take on debt using a financial instrument called a bond

bonds
a form of debt like a loan from a bank but with a slightly different relationship to investors

bond issuer
the company borrowing money

bondholder
the individuals or institutions lending money to a company

coupon
the interest rate for a bond

Exhibit 6.2 Illustration of a Bond Payment

buy or hold one of these bonds, you will receive $1,400 (7 percent of $20,000) each year for ten years. Most bonds are paid in semiannual installments (in this case it would be $700 twice a year) for each bond held by an investor, but some are paid at other periods. At the end of ten years, you would get back the face value of your bond ($20,000). Like stocks, bonds can be traded or sold to other investors.

The Stock Market

Like individuals, who can only make payments on a limited number of credit cards, auto loans, and home loans, there is a limited amount of debt that companies can tolerate. For example, mortgage payments on a house can often be as high as 30 percent of a family's take-home earnings. Similarly, for a company, both bank loans and bonds require paying back interest, which can sap a company's cash.

In place of taking on debt and having to pay back the amount of the loan or bond with interest, a company can get needed funds in a stock market by selling shares of ownership to the general public or private investors. A **stock market** is a financial institution where companies can sell shares of ownership and investors also can trade these shares to other investors. That is, for example, a company can sell shares of its ownership to get needed cash. Once purchased, these shares of ownership can be sold to other investors.

The stock market is a critical aspect of any country's economic development. Consider the following IB Emerging Market Strategic Insight.

> **stock market**
> a market where companies sell shares of ownership and investors trade shares of ownership to other investors

Stock Market in Ukraine

IB EMERGING MARKET
STRATEGIC INSIGHT

Experts agree that an effective and efficient stock market is critical to economic development. This is even more critical for newly emerging markets such as Ukraine. Having an effective stock market will allow better integration into global financial markets. This will not only allow local investors and companies to seek capital globally, it will also facilitate much needed capital investment from foreign investors in the local economy.

Recent statistics show that the Ukrainian stock exchange keeps growing. Exhibit 6.3 below shows that the trading volume on the Ukrainian stock exchange increased from 131.29 billion hryvnia (or US5.25 billion) in 2010 to 629.43 billion hryvnias (or US$25.18 billion) in 2014.

Despite this increase in trading, experts identify several barriers that have limited the growth of the stock exchange. These include the lack of political stability and other unattractive aspects of the economic environment. However, others also lament that there is a shortage of qualified professionals to bring some credibility to the market. Additionally, the Ukrainian stock exchange lacks the transparency and other qualities to ensure that trades can occur with the highest level of integrity.

Nevertheless, experts also agree that a number of steps can be implemented so that the Ukrainian stock market can be more easily integrated into the global capital markets. Implementation of regulatory steps to protect investors as well as increasing the transparency of the market will go a long way to help the Ukrainian stock exchange prosper.

Source: O. Dovhal, 2015, "Stock market of Ukraine: Current situation and perspectives of development," *Socio-Economic Problems and the State*, *13*(2), pp. 76–81.

Trading Volume (billions of Ukrainian Hryvnias)

Exhibit 6.3 Trading Volume on Ukrainian Stock Exchange (in billions of Hryvnias)
Source: Based on O. Dovhal, 2015, "Stock market of Ukraine: Current situation and perspectives of development," *Socio-Economic Problems and the State*, *13*(2) pp. 76–81.

Stocks are known as equities because the stock owners have an equity or ownership position in the company. The first stock offering by a company is called the IPO, or initial public offering. Companies can later issue more stocks or buy back stocks from investors. The first known stock issue was by the Dutch East India Company in 1602.

In the US, stocks used to be traded mainly on the New York Stock Exchange (NYSE). However, to promote competition, the Securities and Exchange Commission (SEC) passed regulations to encourage more exchanges. Today, investors can trade on around a dozen of exchanges. The two main share-trading markets now are NYSE and NASDAQ and they each have around 1/5 of the market.[1]

When investors buy shares or equity ownership in a company, as partial owners of the company they are entitled to share in the profits of the company. To share the profits most companies pay **dividends**. That is, a certain percent of the profits of a company is paid out to the owners (stockholders) in the form of dividends. The more shares owned, the greater the

dividends
the proportion of a company's profits paid to the owners (stockholders)

ownership of the company, and the greater the share of the profits in dividends. Once stocks are issued they are often traded among investors in a secondary market such as the New York Stock Exchange. If the stock price rises, investors can sell them to other investors at a profit or, if the price falls, selling would be at a loss. Companies usually like to see the price of their stock going up, because if they issue more stock they can get more money more easily.

Global Financial Markets

Most companies look first to home country banks and capital markets for loans or to issue bonds or stock. However, as you saw in the Preview IB Emerging Market Strategic Insight, companies are increasingly attracted to the benefits of capital markets outside of their own countries. Why would companies leave the comfort of doing business at home? As it turns out, there are many benefits to getting needed funds outside of your own country.

The major benefit of seeking needed capital (i.e. money) outside of your own country, be it from banks, bond markets, or stock markets, is that there is often a lower cost of capital for the borrower. What this means is that if you can shop for loans or issue stock in many different countries, you are likely to find more investors, lower interest rates, or perhaps less costly regulations. As such, companies can often borrow needed funds at a lower cost than available to them domestically.

When there are more investors, there is more competition among lenders, and it is likely that you can find a lower interest rate for your loans or bonds. When issuing stocks in many countries not only are there more potential investors, there are also chances of being in markets that are performing better than a home country's stock market. Also, and perhaps more importantly, international capital markets often have minimal regulations, which helps to lower the cost of capital that lenders must charge to make a profit.

Global Banking

How do government regulations influence bank loan rates? The story goes back to the collapse of banks in the 1929 depression. But first let us consider how banks operate as businesses.

Banks make money by first holding money deposited by savers and paying them interest. They then lend some of the money received from the savers to borrowers. To make a profit, banks charge borrowers a higher interest than they pay the savers. Of course, if banks are lending the money you deposit to other people, they never have all of your money available at any time. This works fine as long as not everyone tries to withdraw his or her money at one time. When too many people try to withdraw all their money at once, as happened in 1929, banks cannot meet the depositors' demands and banks fail. To make sure this does not happen, bank regulators want to ensure that at least the banks in their own country have enough money on hand should a large number of people want to withdraw their money at one time.

As such, most countries closely regulate the lending of their own currencies. They do this by limiting the amount of money a bank can lend relative to the amount it receives in deposits. That is, a bank cannot lend 100 percent of the money people deposit. Although banks must keep some money on hand in case people want to withdraw their money, they also must place a certain percentage of the money they do not lend out in national banks such as the Federal Reserve in the US and the Bank of England in the UK.

The US government's requirement for deposits to the Federal Reserve can be as high as 10 percent, depending on the value of the deposit.[2] In contrast, most countries do not place the same restrictions on the lending of currencies from other countries, so banks can lend more of the foreign money they receive, making the cost of doing business cheaper for the bank. In turn, that reduced cost is passed onto the borrower in lower interest rates. Later you will see an example of just how this works.

The market for getting loans in a currency that is different from the lending bank's home currency is called the **Eurocurrency market**. When companies borrow money in a country using a currency other than the local currency, they are borrowing a Eurocurrency. Any currency held by banks outside of its country of origin is a Eurocurrency.

The most common currency banked outside of its country of origin is the US dollar, known as **Eurodollars**.[3] For example, US dollars held by a Japanese bank are a Eurocurrency deposit or, more specifically, a Eurodollar deposit. If a US company borrows these dollars from the Japanese bank, it is borrowing Eurodollars. Because the Japanese bank is lending Eurodollars and not yen it does not have to follow Japanese or US regulations regarding loans.

The concept of Eurocurrency can be a bit confusing since the European Union adopted the euro as its currency, but they are not related. Eurocurrency has existed since the early 1950s, long before the euro, which went into effect in 1999. The "Euro" in Eurocurrency comes from its European origin. During the Cold War, the Soviet Union and other Eastern bloc countries withdrew much of the dollar deposits that they had made in US banks. They had used this money to finance trade with the US. However, they did not want to keep their dollars in US banks, fearing loss of the money to the US government for political reasons. During the communist era, many US citizens lost money when communist governments took over US-owned assets (companies, land, etc.) without adequate payments. Leaders from these communist bloc countries feared that any money they left deposited in the US might be confiscated to pay back US citizens for their losses or for other political reasons. To safeguard their money, the strategy was to deposit their dollars outside of the US, with most of these US dollars banked in London. London bankers were willing partners, seeing this as an opportunity to dominate financial markets.[4]

Currently, countries such as China and Japan, which have large reserves of US dollars, provide much of the supply of Eurodollars available to MNCs to finance their operations.

Eurocurrencies generally have the following characteristics:[5]

- *Little or no disclosure requirements* In contrast, the Securities and Exchange Commission in the US requires that firms disclose financial information and financial reports that meet US accounting standards.
- *No reserve requirements* Deposits made in Eurocurrencies do not have to have a certain percentage held back from being loaned to others.
- *Avoiding interest rate regulations* There are no caps or other regulations on interest rates.
- *No deposit insurance requirements* In the US, deposits in commercial banks are insured up to $100,000.

Why do these characteristics of Eurocurrencies lead to a separate market from deposits and borrowing in domestic currencies? As you learned before, banks make money by taking deposits, for which they pay interest to the depositors, and then lend the money to others, for which they charge a higher interest rate than they pay to depositors. Imagine that a bank takes deposits for which it pays 3 percent interest to the depositors. It then loans this money to businesses for 5 percent. The 2 percent difference is called the **spread**. In the Eurocurrency market, however, banks offer higher deposit interest and lower loan interest. Because of efficiencies in dealing with Eurocurrencies, in particular the lack of reserve requirements, banks can accept a smaller spread and still make money.

You can see how this works by looking at Exhibit 6.4. On a $100,000 deposit, when compared to a US bank loaning dollars the bank dealing in Eurocurrency pays its depositors a quarter of a percent higher interest and charges its borrowers a quarter of a percent less interest and still makes the same gross profit because it has more money to lend.

Eurocurrency market
the market for getting loans in a currency that is different from the lending bank's home currency

Eurodollars
US dollars banked outside the US for loans to companies without the restrictions of borrowing within the US

spread
the difference between the interest a bank pays its depositors and the interest it charges borrowers

	Deposit	Reserve	Interest Rate for Depositors	Interest Paid to Depositors	Available to Loan	Interest for Borrowers	Interest Received from Borrowers	Gross Profit
US bank	$100,000.00	$10,000.00	3.0%	$3,000.00	$90,000.00	5.0%	$4,500.00	$1,500.00
Eurocurrency bank	$100,000.00	$0.00	3.25%	$3,250.00	$100,000.00	4.75%	$4,750.00	$1,500.00

Exhibit 6.4 How a Eurocurrency Deposit Can Pay Higher Interest to Depositors and Result in Cheaper Loans for Borrowers

London Interbank Bid Rate (LIBID)
the interest rates the London banks pay other banks to make deposits in Eurocurrencies

London Interbank Offer Rate (LIBOR)
the interest rates the London banks charge other banks for loans in Eurocurrencies

The rates for Eurocurrency deposits and loans are often quoted based on rates offered by London banks, since about 50 percent of the Eurocurrency transactions take place in London. The **London Interbank Bid Rate (LIBID)** is the interest rate the London banks are willing to pay other banks to make deposits in Eurocurrencies and the **London Interbank Offer Rate (LIBOR)** is the interest rates the London banks are willing to charge other banks for loans in Eurocurrencies. The rates that companies receive when they borrow Eurocurrency are higher than the LIBOR charged to other banks. Usually companies must pay an additional 0.15 to 0.25 percentage points above the interbank rate, depending on the credit rating of the company. To check the current LIBOR rates, go to www.theice.com/iba.

However, multinationals do not always rely on local banks or the Eurocurrency market. Some emerging markets see the emergence of an informal banking sector known as shadow banking. Consider the following Emerging Market Brief.

As has been described, multinationals have other sources of funding rather than traditional banks. Nevertheless, the lack of regulation of such shadow banks makes for potential financial disasters. Now that we have considered how MNCs can get loans based on foreign currencies, we can look at how bonds and stocks are traded internationally.

The International Bond Market

foreign bonds
bonds issued by a foreign company in a local currency (i.e. the country in which they are doing business)

Eurobonds
bonds issued in a currency other than the local currency

global bonds
similar to Eurobonds but issued in several currencies at once

As with the domestic bond market, for longer-term debt companies can issue bonds outside of their own country. Recall that the bond issuer is the borrower and the bondholder is the lender. Just as in their own country, issuing bonds outside the home country allows companies to finance long-term investments using external funds rather than cash or profits. There are several types of international bonds issued by MNCs. These include: foreign bonds, Eurobonds, and global bonds.[6]

When a foreign company issues bonds in the local currency (i.e. the country in which they are doing business), these bonds are **foreign bonds**. For example, if a US company issues bonds in Japan in Japanese yen, this is a foreign bond. Foreign bonds often have nicknames to show the country of origin. Samurai or sushi bonds are issued in Japan by foreign companies, and Yankee bonds are issued in the US by foreign companies. **Eurobonds** are like Eurodollars. That means that any bond issued in a currency other than the local currency is a Eurobond. For example, an MNC might issue bonds denominated in yen in Great Britain and these would be Eurobonds. The most common Eurobonds are issued in US dollars, Japanese yen, British pounds, and the euro. **Global bonds** are similar to Eurobonds but are issued in several currencies at once, which can include the currency of the country in which they are issued.

Shadow Banking

The above discusses sources of funding from the traditional banking sector regulated by the government. However, emerging markets often see the emergence of unregulated forms of financing. **Shadow banking** is represented by the entities that provide loans to those borrowers and industries that are shunned by traditional banks. These entities are often not regulated by governments. They act like traditional banks by being the intermediary between borrowers and lenders. However, unlike traditional banks, the deposits made by the lenders are not guaranteed by the government. Unfortunately, this often leads to financial disasters as some shadow banks fail.

Consider the case of shadow banking in China. While traditional banks accounted for all loans in the early 2000s, this share has fallen to around three fifths of new loans. The rest is now accounted for by shadow banking. Financial institutions involved in shadow banking will often provide loans at higher interest rates. However, these institutions will also need to do a better job managing the risks involved in giving loans. Unfortunately, because of the lack of government oversight, some shadow banking institutions tend to be reckless and this often results in financial disaster for those lending the money. A good example is Fanya Metals Exchange which borrowed money from individual lenders and then lent the money to buyers of rare industrial metals. It originally promised a return rate of 13 percent on investments. Many Chinese investors were disillusioned with the low rate of return of traditional banks. These investors also did not want to put their savings in the volatile Chinese stock market. Many pensioners and others ended up investing most of their savings in Fanya. Unfortunately, because of the decline of the value of its stock of metals, it was unable to keep paying the high returns. It therefore suspended all withdrawals resulting in serious losses for most of its investors.

Although Fanya took advantage of these investors, the Chinese government did not intervene. The government argued that investors should have done their due diligence before investing in an entity that is considered illegal. Many investors have therefore lost all of their savings.

Source: Based on *The Economist*, 2016, "Shadow banks: Dark and stormy," May 7–13, pp. 7–9.

shadow banking
the unregulated entities providing loans to those shunned by traditional banks

The incentives to issue Eurobonds and global bonds are similar to the incentives for borrowing Eurodollars. That is, companies can shop for the best deals in interest rates and they can avoid local regulations that increase the costs of them getting needed cash. Most often, MNCs use Euro or global bonds to avoid paying higher taxes. This is often a very complex decision as the tax laws in the country of issue and the home country can be complex and subject to change.

Because of the differences in tax laws and other restrictions on bond issues and loans, multinational managers must always consider carefully the legal and ethical consequences of their actions. Below in the Emerging Market Ethical Challenge you can see how companies operating in Islamic nations get needed financing while remaining true to Islamic law, which prohibits the charging of interest.

How Can You Issue Bonds When Interest is Forbidden?

As countries in the Middle East and Northern African regions continue to grow economically, they are becoming critical markets in the financial industry area. Western and emerging market multinationals are increasingly looking to these markets for expansion. Furthermore, recent estimates suggest that Islamic financial services are growing at an astonishingly high rate. The market grew around 21 percent from 2009 to 2010.

Because many countries in the above regions are primarily Islamic, the local financial services have to follow Islamic principles governing financial services. In fact, under the Shari'ah or Islamic law, charging or paying interest, or *riba*, is forbidden. It is not allowed to make money from just money alone. Thus, issuing or buying bonds, where the seller pays interest and the purchaser makes money only from interest, is not allowed. Credit cards are also not permitted. Yet, to compete in increasingly globalized markets, companies that wish to adhere to Shari'ah need access to money. The financial certificate that provides the Shari'ah-compliant function of a bond is called the Sukuk.

The prohibition on interest raises the question of why one would buy a Sukuk when there is not payment in interest. However, the Sukuk does provide a potential return to the investor. To be acceptable under Islamic law, the Sukuk must be linked to some tangible asset, such as a factory. The investors are then paid back the loan based on the performance of that asset. If it makes money, the investors get a return; if not, the investors may lose money. This is something like the risk one takes by owning stock in a company—you may make or lose money—but without the ownership position in the company.

One country that has become a leader in the provision of Shari'ah-compliant products is Malaysia. It offered such Shari'ah-compliant products first in 2011 and this has grown considerably since then. Today, it has become a leader in the provision of Sukuk. Furthermore, while Sukuks have been linked to traditional assets such as factories, Malaysia's Sukuk offerings have also been based on other innovative bases such as transportation rights. Holders of Sukuk certificates are allowed to receive revenue from transportation-related aspects such as sales of vehicles etc.

Source: Adapted from R. Berger, A. Silbiger, R. Herstein and B. R. Barnes, 2015, "Analyzing business-to-business relationships in an Arab context," *Journal of World Business, 50*, pp. 454–464; *The Economist*, 2006, "Finance and economics: Call the faithful: Islamic finance," December 9, p. 86; A. Lee, 2015, "Malaysia sukuk drives Islamic finance diversification," International Law Review, May 25, p. 1; W. Mansour, K. J. Jedidia and J. Majdoub, 2015, "How ethical is Islamic banking in the light of the objectives of Islamic law?" *Journal of Religious Ethics, 43*(1), pp. 51–77.

Global Stock (Equity) Market

Just as with bonds, MNCs in need of capital can issue stock or equity (ownership) in their company, not only in their own countries but also in foreign countries. The top 10 major stock markets of the world are listed in Exhibit 6.5. The exchanges are ranked by market capitalization, which means the market value of the stocks traded on the exchange during a year.

As you can see, the New York Stock Exchange is the leading stock market in the world. However, the list also includes emerging markets such as the Shanghai Stock Exchange and the Brazilian BM&F Bovespa exchange market.

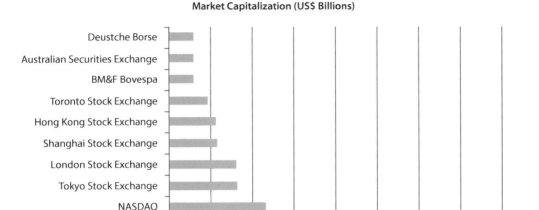

Market Capitalization (US$ Billions)

Exhibit 6.5 The World's Largest Stock Exchanges by Market Capitalization
Source: Adapted from www.world-stock-exchanges.net/top10.html

Again, like bonds, most companies issue stock or sell equity shares in their companies in the stock exchanges located within their countries. This is convenient and managers often feel most comfortable dealing with markets in their own country and culture.

However, the world is seeing more companies issuing stock outside of their home countries. Why is this becoming more popular? There are several reasons why companies choose to list stock in foreign markets. Companies can list in large efficient markets such as the New York Stock Exchange or the London Stock Exchange and have access to a large pool of investors. More investors often means that the company has a greater potential to get a higher value for its stock. Some companies may try to anticipate which markets are performing best (highest stock prices) and list in those markets.

Multinationals also seek to participate in global capital markets for a variety of other reasons. In some cases, a multinational can acquire another firm by buying existing shares from owners. Foreign exchange markets therefore offer foreign multinationals the ability to acquire another firm without the need to buy the firm using cash.

In addition to the above factors, more multinationals are interested in the reputational and ethical advantages of being listed on a more developed stock exchange market.[7] Being listed abroad has reputational and valuation benefits. However, by being listed on a foreign exchange, multinationals also signal their desire to be more ethical by abiding to stricter governance requirements. Additionally, other research suggests that companies also want to be listed in those countries where they are selling their products as a marketing and public relations mechanism.

Exhibit 6.6 summarizes the main reasons why multinationals may decide to participate in global markets.

• Access to better valuation because of larger number of investors
• Access to greater liquidity because of the reputation and maturity of leading markets such as the London Stock Exchange and New York Stock Exchange
• Provides ability to make foreign acquisitions by purchasing shares of these foreign companies rather than infusing cash
• Signals reputation and valuation to investors as firms get listed on more reputable markets
• Potential marketing and public relations benefits as multinationals are listed in home markets where they sell products
• Signals better governance as multinationals commit to much stricter standards of reputable exchange markets
• Shows that the multinational is more serious about addressing business ethics issues as being listed on reputable international markets invites scrutiny

Exhibit 6.6 Reasons Why Multinationals Participate in Global Markets
Source: Based on R. Bell and A. A. Rasheed, 2016, "Seeking capital abroad: Motivations, process and suggestions for success," *Journal of Applied Corporate Finance*, 28(1), pp. 104–113.

Another reason to list in a different market is to avoid regulations that may be costly. You will learn more about how regulations can increase costs after we consider alternative ways of listing on an exchange.

An Alternative Way to List on a Foreign Exchange   There is an alternative way for companies to list on foreign exchanges and sell equity in their companies without actually selling stock directly. This way of raising capital indirectly from the stock market is called a depository receipt. A depository receipt is a certificate issued by a bank called the depository bank. The depository bank actually holds the stocks and then allows certificates (i.e. the depository receipts) to be sold or traded in a stock market. The most popular depository receipt is the **American Depository Receipt (ADR)**, which allows foreign companies to sell their stocks indirectly and raise capital in the US.[8] The ADR is the way most foreign companies trade their stock in the US.

For example, say a Polish company wishes to raise capital in the US without directly listing on the New York Stock Exchange. To use ADRs, the Polish company would sell its shares to a broker—brokers are agents who help people conduct transactions, such as a real-estate broker who helps sell a house. The broker would then deposit the shares in a branch bank of a US bank located in Poland, usually the Bank of New York. Once the Bank of New York certifies that it now owns shares of the Polish company, it begins trading the shares in the US as ADRs. Investors who purchase ADRs have the right to the original stocks if they wish. ADRs make it easier for US Americans to invest in foreign companies because they do not have to buy stock directly in another currency. ADRs make it easier for the foreign company to get investors from the US because the company does not have to register with and meet the regulations of the US Securities and Exchange Commission regarding accounting practices. Individual shares of a foreign company represented by an ADR are called **American Depository Shares (ADS)**.[9] Sometimes an ADR can be made up from shares from several companies/places. You can see ADR listings at www.adrbny.com/.

Other depository receipts include **Global Depository Receipt (GDR)**. GDRs are like ADRs, except that they are traded in several countries at once. For example, the Polish company described above might use GDRs in Europe and the US at the same time.[10] When depository receipts are priced in Euros, they are often called European Depository Receipts. Recently,

American Depository Receipt (ADR)
allows foreign companies to sell their stocks indirectly and raise capital in the US

American Depository Shares (ADS)
individual shares of a foreign company represented by an ADR

Global Depository Receipt (GDR)
like ADRs, but traded in several countries at once

companies in China are using Chinese Depository Receipts (CDRs) to raise capital for Chinese companies by making it easier for foreigners to buy stock indirectly using the CDR rather than directly buying the Chinese stock.

Although ADRs traditionally dominated the depository receipt market, GDRs are gradually taking over the market. Why is this happening? Much of the shift away from the US stock market, both for direct listings and ADRs, stems from controls put into place after Enron and other companies' failures led to great losses among investors. Listing in the US requires following provisions in the **Sarbanes–Oxley Act**. Even emerging market nationals are required to follow these rules if they decide to list in the US.

To give you further insights into the requirements of the Sarbanes–Oxley Act (SOX), the following IB Emerging Market Strategic Insight below describes some of the provisions and consequences of this legislation.

Sarbanes–Oxley Act law passed by the US Congress that requires increased disclosure of financial practices designed to protect stockholders from the unethical practices in financial reporting

Managing in Stock Issues in the Regulated US Market: The Sarbanes–Oxley Act

IB EMERGING MARKET
STRATEGIC INSIGHT

In response to several scandals involving companies such Enron, Tyco International, and WorldCom, the US Congress determined that publicly traded companies and their accounting firms needed stricter oversight. Sponsored by Senator Paul Sarbanes and Representative Michael G. Oxley, the legislation became known as the Sarbanes–Oxley Act. The objective of the Act was to make sure that stockholders are protected from those unethical practices that had resulted in many people losing money by investing in the suspect corporations. The legislation established new or enhanced standards for all US public companies and, importantly, also applies to those foreign companies selling stocks in the US. The Act's 11 sections identify important responsibilities and reporting procedures for corporate boards, executives, and accounting firms. The Act also specifies penalties for failing to follow these procedures.

Some of the major provisions of the Sarbanes–Oxley Act include:

- It specifies an obligation that public companies evaluate the effectiveness of their financial reporting. Independent auditors must confirm the effectiveness of these procedures.
- It requires chief executive officers and chief financial officers to certify financial reports.
- It regulates the type of work accounting firms can do for their company clients if the firm also acts as the auditor. Some accounting firms were acting as both auditors and consultants, resulting in potential conflicts of interest. This helps ensure independence.
- It creates a new government agency called the Public Company Accounting Oversight Board (PCAOB) to monitor the accounting firms.
- It requires fully independent audit committees for companies that wish to list stock exchanges.
- It increases the criminal and civil penalties for violations related to managing stock transactions.
- It increases the maximum jail sentences and the fines for corporate executives found guilty of knowingly and willfully falsifying the financial statements of their company.

Source: Adapted from US Congress House Resolution 3763.

The most recent research estimates that compliance with the SOX Act is very costly and has been increasing over the years. On average, 58 percent of large companies (companies with revenues of $10 billion or more) spent an average of $1 million or more to comply with the SOX Act. Ninety-five percent of small companies (companies with revenues of less than $100 million) reported that they spent less than $500,000. This suggests that the larger the company, the more money is spent on SOX Act compliance. Additionally, the report also mentions that more companies are spending significant resources on automation of IT processes and controls.[11] The direst and most negative predictions come from the consulting firm McKinsey. McKinsey anticipates that the law will eventually cost New York its spot as the world's financial capital. Consider that, at its peak, NASDAQ had 57 percent of the world's IPOs in 1999. Just a couple of years after the passage of Sarbanes–Oxley, NASDAQ had only 18 percent.[12]

Not all predictions are so pessimistic. Professor Sharad Asthana, an expert on the law's impact, notes, "Despite the increased costs, it's [the law] improved public perceptions about the markets. Investors see requiring the signing off by the CEO and CFO as being positive and that they can feel more secure in the quality of earnings."[13] In addition, the tightening up of rules in the US has caused other countries to follow suit. Australia, Brazil, Canada, the EU, Germany, and the UK are introducing laws that make the audit committees on boards of directors more accountable for monitoring the financial practices of companies listed on their exchanges. Listing outside the US may not always offer companies havens from oversight and regulations.

Of course, as with many international business activities, local country regulations may become less important. In the next section, you will see how stock markets are consolidating into multinational operations, making local regulations less important.

A Changing Future for the World's Stock Markets

Like many companies in today's global economy, stock markets are also becoming more globally connected and concentrated. For instance, both the US financial crisis in 2008 and the Brexit decision in 2016 resulted in almost immediate drops in the prices of US stocks, and this was followed within hours by stock markets around the world. In addition, beyond financial linkages, organizational links are expanding as well. For example, in 2007, the New York Stock Exchange acquired the Paris-based exchange Euronext NV. In the same year, the New York Stock Exchange also acquired a 20 percent stake in India's largest exchange, the National Stock Exchange. In 2015, NASDAQ agreed to buy Chi-X Canada and in 2016, it emerged that the London Stock Exchange was in talks with Germany's Deutsche Börse for a merger.[14]

Cross-border consolidation among stock markets will make stock markets MNCs in their own right. With a presence in many countries, the former national stock exchanges will attract investors from more nations. Local economic conditions will have less impact in attracting investors because multinational exchanges, like MNCs, can locate in the most favorable conditions.

What this means for companies is that they will have increased access to the global capital markets without ever leaving their home countries. Also, managers will not have to learn the operation of foreign exchanges as they can do one-stop global financing at one exchange. A listing on a multinational exchange will attract investors from everywhere in the world as well. Like companies that seek the advantage of raising capital without concern for local economic conditions, investors will be able to shop for stocks in the best companies in the world without concern for a company's nationality.

As you have also seen after reading the previous discussion, emerging markets will continue presenting significant opportunities for companies as markets for sources of capital. Both small investors as well as larger companies will find that they can look to emerging markets for new

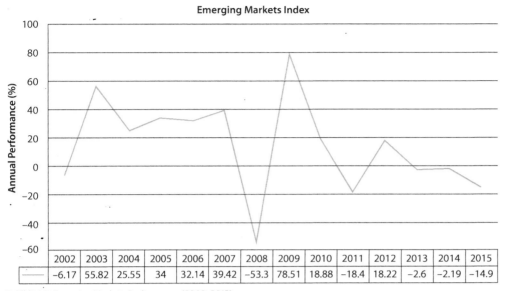

Exhibit 6.7 Emerging Markets Performance (2002–2015)
Source: Based on MSCI Emerging Markets Index, www.msci.com/emerging-markets

sources of capital as well as investments. However, these markets carry some risks that may be different from more established markets. In fact, a recent look at the performance of emerging markets shows declining fortunes.

Exhibit 6.7 shows the performance of the emerging markets index between 2002 and 2015. The index is made up of 23 of the world's major emerging markets and reflects the performance of the markets in these countries.

As Exhibit 6.7 shows, emerging markets are reflective of the economic conditions of these countries. The years 2002–2007 illustrate the general exuberance around these emerging markets and the performance during those years were spectacular with a return of 55.85 percent in 2003 and 78.51 percent in 2009. The dip in 2008 shows the effects of the financial meltdown.

Data for the most recent years (2013–2015) reflect the general economic slowdown in these regions. This slowdown has also resulted in a number of other risks. Furthermore, an important part of these risks stem from the fact that these markets are not as developed as more established markets. Such risks and economic conditions raise a number of challenges including:

- **Lack of government oversight**—experts argue that some emerging markets present challenges because of the lack of government oversight. The major markets of China and India present such challenges. For instance, a recent article discussed the lack of appropriate government regulation in the banking sector in India.[15] Many of India's biggest banks have made loans to companies that cannot pay the loans back. Such risks may destabilize the financial sector thereby potentially affecting multinationals.
- **Too much government oversight**—while emerging market governments have been reluctant to implement regulatory policies to correct challenges inherent in the system, such governments have been willing to intervene in ways that interfere with the free market. For instance, the Chinese government's decision to intervene during the June 2015 stock prices collapse or the Chinese government's backing of bonds have removed elements of risk from the market.[16] This suggests that investors could potentially assume that the government will

always intervene. Additionally, the government has also been reluctant opening the financial market to foreign companies. This also suggests that foreign multinationals will have to be cautious. Furthermore, as discussed earlier, another issue that is challenging for multinationals is capital controls whereby governments implement measures to control the flow of currency outside of the country. This can adversely affect the ability of a multinational to extract dividends from its emerging market investments.[17]

• **Poor economic conditions, high corporate debt, and declining commodity prices**—many emerging markets seem to be suffering from an economic slowdown. This slowdown has been precipitated in Brazil, Russia, and China by the plunging commodity prices. Additionally, many emerging nations are also seeing massive corporate debt fueled by bad loans. For example, China has seen bad loans total $1.3 trillion yuan [18] Such indicators suggest that multinationals and investors need to be careful as they assess the emerging markets.

• **Lack of transparency**—although not all emerging markets suffer from this risk, many markets are characterized by a lack of transparency. This means that investors can often suffer losses that may not be necessarily due to market forces. Additionally, there is research that suggests that higher market integrity is linked to high market efficiency.[19]

All this suggests that multinationals and investors alike need to be cautious when operating in emerging markets. However, not all experts are pessimistic about these markets. Some argue that fundamentals in emerging markets such as China, India, and Mexico are strong enough that there should be no concerns in the long-term.[20] While performance may suffer in the short-term, such markets are likely to rebound and display stronger performance in the future. Additionally, many emerging markets are very interested in attracting foreign investment. As such, many of the emerging markets such as China, Taiwan, and India have implemented major regulatory changes that are not only making these markets more accessible but are also protecting investor rights.[21] It is therefore likely that these markets will recover quickly and provide the same protection that investors enjoy in more developed markets.

Chapter Review

This chapter has provided you with an overview of how capital markets work in today's global economy with an enhanced focus on emerging markets. In simple terms, a capital market is a market where investors that do not have an immediate use for their money transfer that money to individuals, governments, and businesses that have a need and a use for that money. The two major capital markets for long-term financing are the bond market and the stock market. For the shorter term, financial companies often use loans from commercial banks.

In the bond market, companies issue bonds to borrow money from bondholders. This is a loan and is known as debt financing. In the stock market, companies sell shares of ownership to investors and these investors have equity in the company.

In today's global economy, companies are no longer constrained to borrow money or sell stocks in their company within their country of origin. Often, companies can get cheaper loans in the Eurocurrency market: that is, the market for getting loans in a currency that is different from the lending bank's home currency. Similarly, companies can issue bonds in countries where they do business (foreign bonds) or in other currencies (Eurobonds, global bonds).

In this chapter, you also learned that the world of global finance is changing. Concerns over the unethical practices of some US corporations, which led to great losses by investors, led the US government to pass the Sarbanes–Oxley Act. The law forces companies to reveal more of their financial operations and holds managers responsible for these disclosures. While this has caused some flight of stock listings from the US to other countries, similar regulations are spreading around the world. Stock markets are also consolidating across borders, making them MNCs in their own right. This will also result in a convergence of global standards of stock market operations and further the increase of money flowing across borders. Companies will find it easier to seek capital worldwide and investors will find it easier to buy stock from any company regardless of nationality.

The chapter concluded with the observation that emerging markets will continue posing significant challenges. Many factors such as weak economic growth, low commodity prices, high corporate debt etc. will amplify the risks of seeking capital in such markets. However, some experts are more optimistic arguing for stronger performance in the long term.

Discussion Questions

1   What is a capital market?

2   Why do companies use capital markets to finance growth, new products, R&D, etc.? Would it be better just to keep profits and reinvest them in the company?

3   Discuss the basics of how the bond market works. How does this differ in structure and terminology from the types of loans people get to buy their homes?

4   Discuss the basics of how a stock market works. What are the advantages and disadvantages of listing on a foreign exchange?

5   Discuss the advantages and disadvantages of dealing with Eurocurrencies.

6   Discuss the competing perspectives regarding increased regulations, especially regarding financial reporting, for companies. What are the effects of country differences, and what do you anticipate will result as stock markets converge across borders?

7   What are some of the challenges of capital markets in emerging markets?

International Business Skill Builder

Understanding how Stock Markets Work

For this exercise, you will play the game called "The Stock Market Bakery." You will assume the roles of companies by producing "chocolate-chip cookies." The companies will sell stock to raise money for new equipment and research. The companies then make the "cookies" and use some of their earnings to pay dividends to stockholders. Students also take the roles of savers who invest in the stock market.

Chapter Internet Activity

In this project, you will explore how several companies use the Eurobond market to raise capital.

1   Google search "raising capital with Eurobonds."

2   Search within these results for companies from three different countries (e.g. Russia, Japan, and China).

3   Prepare a paragraph for each company describing how it used the Eurobond market.

Key Concepts

- American Depository Receipt (ADR)
- American Depository Shares (ADS)
- bondholder
- bond issuer
- bond market
- bonds
- capital markets
- coupon
- dividends
- Eurobonds
- Eurocurrency market

- Eurodollars
- foreign bonds
- global bonds
- Global Depository Receipt (GDR)
- London Interbank Bid Rate (LIBID)
- London Interbank Offer Rate (LIBOR)
- Sarbanes–Oxley Act
- shadow banking
- spread
- stock market

CASE 6

Islamic Finance
A Growing Niche in the
Global Financial Market

It is estimated that over $500 billion in assets are managed around the world in accordance with Islamic principles. With an estimated 1.3 billion followers of Islam, many in areas of the world where excess funds have been recently accumulating, increased interest has been generated in Islamic finance. Islamic banking centers have been developed in places such as Dubai, London, Kuala Lumpur, Singapore, and Bahrain. According to Standard and Poor's, Islamic banking has been growing by about 10 percent per year for the past decade. A number of the world's largest banks and financial institutions have begun to offer Islamic financial services, including Citigroup and HSBC. Dow Jones has even created the Dow Jones Islamic Market Index, signifying the importance of this growing financial niche.

According to *The Economist* magazine, about 20 percent of the world's population is Muslim, but Islamic finance represents only 1 percent of the world's financial instruments. This gap is seen as an opportunity for growth. Islamic finance based on *Shari'ah*, or Islamic law, prohibits the payment of interest, or usury. Also prohibited are investments in certain industries such as those tied to alcohol, pornography, pork production, tobacco, and gambling. Bonds based on *Shari'ah*, called *sukuk*, do not pay interest, but rather pay the investor based on the profit generated from the asset that underlies the bond. Islamic finance mandates a degree of risk sharing not found in traditional finance.

After the terrorists' attack in the United States on September 11, 2001, the US government froze bank accounts of certain wealthy Muslims. This caused capital flight by others fearful of having their assets confiscated. Much of this money ended up in places like Malaysia where the assets were deemed safer. Rising oil prices increased the cash position of a number of Muslim countries, and a rising middle class in many Muslim countries created the need for an alternative financial system. A financial system consistent with Islamic principles became more necessary, and lucrative. Even business schools have taken note of the trend and have begun offering courses and seminars in Islamic finance.

Not charging interest on loans is a central element of Islamic finance. According to Sheikh Nizam Yaquby, a noted advisor to Western investment firms: "There is no sin the Koran, not even drinking, not even fornicating, not even homosexuality, which could be as abhorrent and serious as dealing in riba (interest)." The prohibition of charging interest is not just linked to Islam. Early Christians prohibited usury, however,

CASE 6
cont'd

over time the definition changed to allow interest to be charged for loans, but not at an excessive rate. Not being able to charge interest on loans has forced Islamic bankers to be more creative in their business. Loans are typically made by adding a profit to the balance, and then dividing the sum by equal payments. Variable rate interest loans are generally not permitted under Islamic finance. Since interest cannot be charged to borrowers, other arrangements can be made such as when a house is financed by a bank, the bank may buy the house and value it at its expected appreciated price when the loan has ended. The inflated price is then divided into equal payments over the life of the loan. No interest is paid by the borrower. Shared risk is an important part of Islamic finance. Some business loans are made on the basis of *mudharaba*. A *mudharaba* is a partnership between the lender and the borrower. In this case, no interest is charged the person, or business, needing the loan. Instead, the borrower shares in the profit generated by the loaned funds. The borrower and lender become partners, sharing in the profit or loss of the enterprise.

Islamic finance prohibits the selling of something that one does not own. Short-selling, for example is not allowed under Islamic finance, as well as a number of other more risky Western investment practices such as derivatives. Some have proposed that the financial crisis that began in 2008 would have been avoided if the world's financial institutions had followed *sharia*. As a result of the requirement of an underlying asset base, however, Islamic finance is more concentrated in property assets and subject to the market fluctuations of those assets.

Oversight of Islamic finance, and the determination of the appropriateness of investments, is of some concern. Some Islamic banks operate in countries with few regulations, such as in North Africa, and only a handful of people determine what is a proper investment under Islamic law. The availability of religious scholars who also have training in finance, and a good command of the English language, is limited. The shortage of such individuals means that the price of investment advice is quite high, reported to be in the six figure range for each fatwa, or investment decision. With the limited number of skilled Islamic advisors, many of the advisors work for competing firms, creating the perception of a conflict of interest in the minds of some. In the world's largest Muslim country, Indonesia, Islamic finance makes up a small percentage of total financial transactions. The limitation of qualified personnel, perception of a lower return, and a lack of understanding of Islamic finance have slowed growth potential in some markets.

Even with the limited number of qualified advisors, and other concerns, Islamic finance is, nevertheless, expected to continue to grow in the years ahead. Islamic finance may appeal to non-Muslims as well, in that some socially responsible investors may like the idea of avoiding investing in "sinful" industries, and feel that their investments are safer in an Islamic style investment arrangement.

CASE 6 cont'd	CASE DISCUSSION POINTS:

CASE DISCUSSION POINTS:

1 Do you feel that Islamic finance is a safer alternative to Western finance? Explain.

2 Some critics feel that Islamic finance is only a disguise for traditional finance and the process "rent-a-sheikh" allows for possible manipulation of financial decisions. What is your opinion?

3 Do you feel that Islamic finance can grow beyond its current small niche in the financial market and be beneficial to emerging markets? Explain.

Source: J. Black, 2008, "An unhealthy interest?" *The Middle East*, July; B. Bremner and S. Assif, 2007, "The ties that bind the Middle East and Asia," *BusinessWeek Online*, May 21; F. DiMeglio, 2007, "A fresh take on Islamic finance," *BusinessWeek Online*, March 27; E. Eaves, 2008, "Good and mammon," *Forbes*, April 21; *The Economist*, 2008, "Savings and souls," September 6; V. Modi, 2007, "Writing the rules: The need for standardized regulation of Islamic finance," *Harvard International Review*, Spring; C. Power, 2009, "Faith in the market," *Foreign Policy*, January–February; B. Quinn, 2008, "London warms to Islamic finance," *Christian Science Monitor*, November 11; V. Ram, 2008, "The enforcers," *Forbes*, April 21; P. Swastika, 2016, "Why market share of Islamic banks is so small in Indonesia," *The Jakarta Post*, July 15.

Case prepared by Charles A. Rarick

Notes

1 *The Economist*, 2016, "Complicate, then prevaricate," February 27, pp. 59–60.

2 www.federalreserve.gov/monetarypolicy/reservereq.htm# fn3

3 Kirt Butler, 2012, *Multinational Finance* (5th edn), Hoboken, NJ: Wiley.

4 Kirt Butler, 2012, *Multinational Finance* (5th edn), Hoboken, NJ: Wiley.

5 Kirt Butler, 2012, *Multinational Finance* (5th edn), Hoboken, NJ: Wiley.

6 www.investopedia.com/university/advancedbond/advanced bond1.asp

7 R. Bell and A. A. Rasheed, 2016, "Seeking capital abroad: Motivations, process and suggestions for success," *Journal of Applied Corporate Finance*, 28(1), pp. 104–113.

8 Securities and Exchange Commission, 2016, "Investor Bulletin: American depositary receipts," www.investor.gov

9 http://en.wikipedia.org/wiki/American_Depository_Receipt

10 Depository Receipt Division, Bank of New York, 2003, "The case for investing in depositary receipts." In *The Global Equity Investment Guide*, New York: Bank of New York; Anthony Moro, 2006, "Role of depository receipts." In *A Guide for European Companies to Listing on the US Securities Markets*, New York: Bank of New York.

11 http://en.wikipedia.org/wiki/American_Depository_Receipt

12 Deepak Gopinath, 2007, "Strict IPO rules raise anxiety on Wall Street marketplace by Bloomberg," *International Herald Tribune*, February 21, p. 18.

13 Aissatou Sidime, 2007, "The good and bad of Sarbanes–Oxley," *Knight Ridder Tribune News*, February 16, p. 1.

14 *The Economist*, 2016, "Stocks exchanged," February 27, p. 27.

15 *The Economist*, 2016, "Bureaucrats at the till," June 24, pp. 69–70.

16 K. Kehler, 2015, "Why China's stock market meltdown could hurt us all," Time.com, July 13.

17 V. Ryan, 2016, "The most serious emerging-market risk," *CFO*, June, pp. 16–18.

18 *The Economist*, 2016, "Special report: Finance in China: Breaking bad," May 7, pp. 5–7.

19 M. J. Aitken, F. H. Harris and S. Ji, 2015, "A worldwide examination of exchange market quality: Great integrity increases market efficiency," *Journal of Business Ethics*, 132, pp. 147–170.

20 A. K. Smith, 2016, "More pain for emerging markets," *Kiplinger's Personal Finance*, April, p. 59.

21 V. Ryan, 2016, "The most serious emerging-market risk," *CFO*, June, pp. 16–18.

THE INSTITUTIONAL AND CULTURAL CONTEXT OF
MULTINATIONAL COMPETITIVE STRATEGY

CHAPTER 7

Culture and International Business in Emerging Markets

After reading this chapter you should be able to:

- Understand the importance of culture and the need to appreciate cultural differences in emerging markets.

- Know two of the most popular cultural frameworks (Hofstede and GLOBE) and how they explain differences between countries.

- Appreciate these cultural differences and implications for international business and specifically the business culture in emerging markets.

- Be aware of cultural paradoxes and some of the dangers of making broad generalizations based on culture.

- Learn about how multinational managers can prepare for cultural differences with a special emphasis on emerging markets.

International Business   *Preview IB Emerging Market Strategic Insight*

International Cultural Blunders

As emerging markets growth stalls, they still remain critical markets. In fact, growth in markets in China and Africa, etc. will continue to be a source of growth for multinationals worldwide. The potential for cultural blunders in these markets remains strong. Consider the example where you are sent to Malaysia to close an important contract. In a flashy ceremony, you are introduced to an important potential customer you thought was named Roger. You spend the negotiations calling that person Roger and even Rog. You find that your hosts are insulted and you realize later that the potential client was actually a rajah, a noble title. You also find out that many states in Malaysia are actually headed by rajahs.

In another case, you arrive in Beijing hoping to have an important real-estate transaction signed. You meet with your potential customers and spend the evening socializing. After a few days, you start losing interest as you find that the negotiations are not progressing as smoothly as you wished. At the end of the third day, you produce a detailed contract hoping to get the contract signed. Your hosts decide to abruptly end the negotiations and you are unable to get them back to the negotiation table.

In yet another example, you are asked to investigate why the same business approach to selling wireless services is not equally successful worldwide. You find that customer satisfaction is less important in predicting loyalty in emerging markets compared to value in such markets. You also find that in developed markets, the quality of the service is much more important than the value provided by the service. To adapt to such differences, you find that you need to focus your marketing message in emerging markets on prices more than in other markets.

Source: Adapted from *The Economist*, 2016, "The yuan and the markets," January 16, p. 11; F. V. Morgeson, P. N. Sharma and R. Hult, 2015, "Cross-national differences in customer satisfaction: Mobile services in emerging and developed markets," *Journal of International Marketing*, 23(2), pp. 1–24; *Real Estate Issues*, 2006, "The impact of cultural mistakes on international real estate negotiations," Fall.

The Preview IB Emerging Market Strategic Insight describes several situations where cultural mishaps occurred. Such mistakes can be costly to MNCs as potentially important contracts are lost. Furthermore, the third situation describes circumstances where differences were not adapted to. However, the most important point about these situations is that you can easily avoid them. This chapter provides you with a basic understanding of national cultures and how to prepare for cultural differences in international business activities. Emerging markets are especially difficult to break in and by properly preparing for cultural differences, an international manager can be more successful by behaving in ways consistent with local expectations.

This chapter contains four major sections. In the first section, you are introduced to some of the major reasons why cultural differences need to be understood. In the second section, you are exposed to two of the most important frameworks that have been developed to understand culture. In the third section, you look at some of the ways national cultures affect business through a special emphasis on business cultures. Finally, you will examine some ways MNCs and their employees can prepare for cultural differences.

After reading this chapter you should understand how cultural differences impact behaviors and attitudes of people in a country. You will look at how national culture relates to and influences the business environment and business culture for any MNC. You will also be made aware of some of the dangers of making broad generalizations based on the cultural differences we discuss. Finally, you should be able to recognize what can be done to prepare for such challenges.

National Culture

National culture is the pervasive and shared values, beliefs, and norms that guide life in any society.[1] It tells people who they are, what behaviors are appropriate, and what behaviors are not acceptable in any society. It adds predictability and ensures behaviors of people are not random. For instance, you regularly hear about the American dream or about rags-to-riches stories. They reflect the cultural belief that anyone has the potential to become very successful if he or she works very hard in the United States. This represents a cultural aspect of US society.

National Culture Components

A country's national culture is reflected in many different ways. For instance, as just discussed, culture can be manifested in **cultural beliefs,** which represent people's perception of what is true. Culture can also be shown in terms of cultural norms. For example, while it is acceptable to jump line in countries such as India or China, people are expected to respect lines in other countries such as Germany. This is an example of a **cultural norm**, a shared understanding of what people can do and what they cannot do. Culture can also manifest itself in **cultural symbols, stories, and rituals,** which represent physical manifestations of culture. Symbols may take the form of monuments or buildings, such as the Great Wall of China as a reflection of China's past. Stories are passed on from generation to generation to reinforce the culture. Finally, rituals are activities such as baptisms that are used to reinforce cultural messages. Culture can also manifest itself through customs. **Customs** are behaviors or habits that are passed on from different generations and are appropriate in different situations. For example, in many Islamic countries, women are expected to wear the *burka* or veil as a reflection of the custom. Furthermore, some Islamic states also have customs preventing women from being in the same room with men.

Culture can therefore manifest itself in various ways. But why should you be concerned with culture? As you saw in Chapter 1, no one is immune to the forces of globalization. A good understanding of culture is necessary for anyone to navigate the workplace. Most countries are seeing an influx of workers from other countries, and understanding culture can be helpful in understanding diversity in the workplace. A basic understanding of culture can be helpful in navigating the very diverse local workplace environment.

How important is cultural understanding for the multinational? Consider the following BRIC Insight.

As the following BRIC Insight shows, MNCs need to be able to adopt the ability to manage cultural differences if they want to succeed globally. Furthermore, many now realize that the key to success is the ability to hire the best individuals regardless of background. Consider that many of the best ideas for new product innovations are now coming from employees located around various parts of the world.[2] However, having employees of diverse backgrounds collaborate can sometimes result in conflict and cultural misunderstanding. Understanding culture can help the MNC build a work environment where cultural differences are respected and diversity is used as the means to contribute to profitability.

Many human resource management experts also agree that having cultural and international experience will be an important asset in the future. Because of global expansion, many companies are looking for employees with international experience to deal with diverse cultural backgrounds. Understanding the local culture can therefore be a source of competitive advantage for promotion opportunities in the future.

national culture
pervasive and shared values, beliefs, and norms that guide life in a society

cultural beliefs
people's perception of what is true

cultural norms
shared understanding of what people can and cannot do

cultural symbols, stories, and rituals
manifestations of culture through monuments, stories, or other practices

customs
behaviors or habits that are passed from generation to generation

Brazilian Multinationals and Global Expansion

A recent study of Brazilian multinationals provides some insights into the importance of understanding cultural differences when expanding worldwide. In that study, the researchers examined a large number of Brazilian multinationals and their subsidiaries. Senior managers in these companies were surveyed on their global mindedness. Global mindedness refers to the degree to which the manager has a global orientation (making efforts to understand global markets), global knowledge (ability of the manager to understand foreign cultures), and global skills (the availability of cultural sensitivity and ability to work with foreign individuals). Senior managers with stronger global mindedness tend to be better at managing and adapting to cultural differences.

Results of the study showed that those Brazilian multinationals with senior managers who had stronger global mindedness were more likely to have subsidiaries that had stronger competencies. Global mindedness resulted in the subsidiaries having stronger competences in many of the aspects critical to successful performance. Such competencies included stronger development of products, marketing, and sales as well as better planning and financial management.

The study also showed that those multinationals that had senior managers with the strongest Brazilian cultural attributes consistent with Brazilian management (high power distance and uncertainty avoidance) had less of the competencies. Such results suggest that Brazilian multinationals have to constantly balance local cultural attributes with the need to adopt global mindsets.

Source: Adapted from G. G. Reis, M. T. L. Fleury, A. C. C. Fleury and F. Zambaldi, 2015, "Brazilian multinationals' competences: Impacts of a 'tug of war' between cultural legacies and global mindedness," *Brazilian Business Review*, *12*(1), pp. 55–79.

Experts also argue that the competitive landscape is changing dramatically and that the future will see global companies with headquarters located in emerging markets.[3] Consider India's Tata Motors, Brazil's Embraer, or Mexico's Cemex, all major global multinationals that are competing with the traditional multinationals from Western countries. To be able to compete successfully with these new challengers, a strong cultural understanding of the various consumers around the world is needed. Additionally, as the earlier example showed, many emerging market multinationals are also expanding substantially in other markets. Understanding cultural differences will therefore be key if multinationals want to understand how to compete for customers.

Moreover, you will find that most companies you choose to work for will have some form of international operations. Even if your company is not involved in international markets, it will still have to compete with MNCs operating within your local country. As such, it is important to understand a country's culture as it will give you a better appreciation of what people value in other countries. This appreciation can be very useful as it allows you to avoid some of the cultural blunders we discussed earlier. Furthermore, an appropriate understanding of culture can help you avoid conflict with workers from other countries and also put you in a better position to understand the local market. Consider the following IB Emerging Market Strategic Insight and how McDonald's became successful in India.

McDonald's and Doing the Right Thing in India

In 1996 McDonald's opened its first restaurant in India. In 2007 it had over 56 restaurants and in 2016 it has over 380 restaurants. How did McDonald's manage such a feat? It carefully examined cultural differences and found ways to address these cultural challenges. For instance, recognizing the more vegetarian nature of Indian society, McDonald's developed many vegetarian menu items while also integrating local foods. It also recognized the very diverse nature of Indian society and has the appropriate regional foods offered in different regions. McDonald's understood the family- and child-centric nature of Indian society. It strives to target children with many programs such as birthdays, children's parades, free polio vaccinations, and even low-height children-friendly counters in some locations. McDonald's also understood India's colonized past and the need to counter potential conflict. McDonald's has made a large effort to hire only local managers while also playing an important role in the community: for instance, it donates to local environmental causes. McDonald's has worked hard to develop relationships with local suppliers, going so far as helping local suppliers improve their processes. Finally, McDonald's is very aware of pricing issues in India and provides products that target a wide range of incomes.

McDonald's continues to face the competition head-on. Since it opened, it has seen competition coming from many other well-known companies such as KFC, Dunkin Donuts, Carl's Jr, and Starbucks. It is also facing competition from local start-ups such as Johnny Rockets and Burger Singh. However, it recently decided to modify its two-decade-old recipe for its Maharaja, its best selling chicken burger. To respond to current needs, it is now using a thicker patty and offers jalapeno sauces. Additionally, to respond to cultural needs, it also launched a meatless Big Mac.

Source: Adapted from G. Das, 2015, "Burger wars," *Business Today*, December 20, pp. 50–60; "McDonald's in India," www.mcdonaldsindia.com/aboutus/index.html, 2016; P. Rana, 2016, "McDonald's, Pizza Hut cook up new plans for India," *Wall Street Journal* (online), March 23.

The IB Emerging Market Strategic Insight shows how McDonald's took great pains to understand the local Indian culture and to adapt its operations to fit cultural dispositions. Such actions are surely more likely to increase the chance of success. How can you understand which aspects of culture to pay attention to, though? In the next section, we look at some of the most important ways societies differ in terms of culture. National culture affects many aspects of international business. However, one of the most important influences of culture is on human behavior. You will notice that many of the examples discussed pertain to discussion of the influence of culture on individual behaviors.

National Culture: Hofstede and the Global Organizational Behavior and Leadership Studies

To understand how countries differ on culture, we will consider two of the most popular cultural frameworks. There are many cultural models that have been proposed over time (e.g. Trompenaars' cultural framework or Ronen and Shenkar's framework). However, we focus on the Hofstede framework and the GLOBE framework. We consider the Hofstede model as it is by far the most popular cross-cultural model and has generated important understanding of cross-cultural management.[4] In fact, recent reviews of 30 years of research on Hofstede's model shows that the dimensions we discuss below are still very relevant.[5]

However, Hofstede's cultural framework was conducted in the 1970s and is sometimes seen as outdated. We therefore also consider the GLOBE studies as one of the most up-to-date cultural frameworks.[6] The GLOBE studies complement Hofstede's study and suggest that there are several other cultural dimensions that explain how societies differ. In the next few pages, we consider these cultural dimensions and implications for various aspects of international business.

Hofstede's Model of National Culture

Hofstede,[7] a Dutch social scientist, developed the **Hofstede model of national culture** by surveying over 88,000 employees in IBM subsidiaries from 72 countries.[8] However, he reduced the number of countries to 40 based on responses and later added ten more countries and three regions to his findings. He developed his cultural model primarily on the basis of differences in values and beliefs regarding work goals. Thus, it has easily identifiable implications for international business by providing a clear link between national and business cultures. You will see later in the text numerous examples of Hofstede's ideas providing the background to understanding differences in international business practices.

The first cultural dimension proposed by Hofstede is power distance. **Power distance** refers to the degree to which societies accept power differences and authority in society. In societies with high power distance, people are more likely to accept that inequality is good and acceptable. In such societies, people are also more likely to accept that there are some people who are in charge and that these powerful people are entitled to privileges.[9] Exhibit 7.1 shows selected countries and their ranking on Hofstede's power distance function. It should be noted that the Hofstede scores range from 100 (high) to 0 (low).

As Exhibit 7.1 shows, many emerging markets in Latin American, Latin European, and Asian countries have high power distance. In these countries, the concern for hierarchy and inequality in organizations is rooted in early socialization in the family and school. In high power distance cultures, children are expected to obey their parents and elders. In schools, teachers assume the role of dominance and are often seen as father figures. Children must not challenge a teacher's authority. Later in life, organizations assume many of the roles of parents and teachers. In contrast, countries such as the US, UK, and Germany have lower power distance. There are no expectations that hierarchy and power differences are appropriate.

Power distance has important implications for many aspects of international business. For instance, MNCs operating in high power distance societies will often have to hire managers who can show their leadership qualities. Employees are more deferential to their supervisors and will expect more explicit directions about what needs to get done. Managers are therefore expected to show their position in the company. Consider the experience of a US vice president, who was meeting with vice presidents from the Indian affiliate of the company.[10] When the US vice president entered the room, she saw a room in disarray. She asked for help from one of the Indian executives to arrange the chairs but was ignored. Later the Indian told her that he couldn't believe that she was moving chairs when she could have delegated this task to the office staff. The Indian executive couldn't believe that she was engaging in a task that was perceived as below her skills. Because of the Indian culture's high power distance, those at the executive level of the organization are expected to behave accordingly.

MNCs also often find that they need to send older employees when negotiating with their counterparts in high power distance societies. Age tends to be equated with wisdom and experience. Consider Exxon Mobil's experience when they sent some of their employees from Angola and Russia for cross-cultural training in Canada.[11] Both Angolans and Russians equated

Hofstede model of national culture
cultural dimensions based on surveys of IBM employees from over 50 countries

power distance
degree to which people accept power and authority differences in society

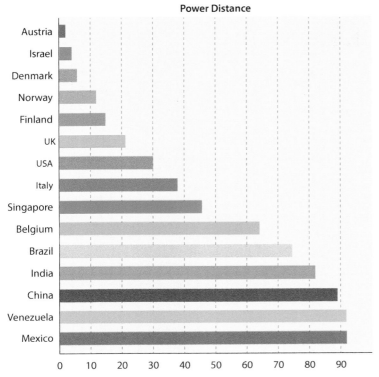

Exhibit 7.1 Power Distance for Selected Countries
Source: Based on G. Hofstede, 2001, *Culture's Consequences: Comparing Values, Behaviors, Institutions, and Organizations Across Nations* (2nd edn), Thousand Oaks, CA: Sage.

age with authority, a characteristic of high power distance societies. Exxon Mobil had to train these workers to accept that younger employees may sometimes have authority.

However, power distance does not always operate in isolation. Power distance can have an impact based on combination with other factors. Consider the following Emerging Market Brief.

The second cultural dimension proposed by Hofstede is uncertainty avoidance. **Uncertainty avoidance** refers to the degree to which people in a society are comfortable with uncertainty and unpredictable situations. A higher uncertainty avoidance culture seeks to structure social systems (politics, education, and business) where order and predictability are crucial. In such countries, rules and regulations dominate. In high uncertainty avoidance societies, risky situations create stress and upset people. Exhibit 7.2 shows selected countries and their scores on uncertainty avoidance.

> **uncertainty avoidance**
> degree to which people are comfortable with uncertainty and unpredictable situations

As you can see, many of the Nordic (e.g. Sweden, Denmark) and Anglo (e.g. the USA, Australia) countries have low uncertainty avoidance. In such societies, people are comfortable with change and ambiguity. In contrast, high uncertainty societies can be found in many of the emerging markets in Latin America and also include many of the Latin European societies (e.g. France, Spain). In these countries, people generally react with stress and anxiety when rules of behavior are not clear. They prefer order and structures to cover situations in daily life.

Power Distance and Creativity

EMERGING MARKET BRIEF

As the above discussion shows, power distance can have an important impact on many aspects of multinational operations. A recent study comparing creativity of Americans versus Chinese individuals provide some insights on how power distance can also combine with other factors to affect employees within multinationals. In high power distance societies, employees tend to accept that supervisors have more authority and will defer to supervisors' views and directions. The authors therefore argue that in high power distance societies, employees are less likely to be creative if they are asked to generate ideas in front of their supervisors. In such societies, the employee will be more likely to defer to the norms and not bring up ideas that may deviate from the supervisors' viewpoints or the norms. In an interesting experiment comparing Chinese and American individuals, the authors do find support for their hunch. They find that Chinese employees' creativity was lower in the presence of a supervisor and much higher when working alone. This study provides important insights on the effects of power distance working with the social context.

Source: Adapted from R. Nouri, M. Erez, C. Lee, J. Liang, B. D. Bannister and W. Chiu, 2015, "Social context: Key to understanding culture's effects on creativity," *Journal of Organizational Behavior, 36*, pp. 899–918.

For international business, uncertainty avoidance suggests that the MNC is well advised to provide structure and order if they operate in societies with high uncertainty avoidance. Managers should give clear and explicit directions to subordinates. Such clear instructions make subordinates less anxious, since subordinates know exactly what is expected of them. This reduces ambiguity regarding job expectations. The boss tells workers exactly what to do. Similarly, organizations in these cultures have many written rules and procedures. Like the situation produced by the task-directed leader, extensive rules and procedures tell employees exactly what the organization expects of them. Consequently, employees believe that these rules should not be broken.

A third important cultural dimension proposed by Hofstede is the individualism dimension. **Individualism** refers to the degree to which society focuses on the relationship of the individual to the group. In more individualistic societies, people are viewed as unique and are valued for their achievements. In contrast, in societies that are low on individualism, the individual is seen as being part of a wider group such as the family, social class, or even team. In more collectivistic societies, rewards and recognition go to groups rather than any single individual. Exhibit 7.3 shows selected countries and their rankings on the individualism dimension.

As you can see from Exhibit 7.3, the US has the highest individualism scores. In fact, many of the Anglo cultures, such as the UK and Australia, also have very high individualism scores. In these countries, people are rewarded and recognized for their achievements. In contrast, many of the emerging markets in Asian and Latin American societies have low individualism scores. In these countries, social groups such as the family and the organization are emphasized over each individual. These societies tend to be seen as more collective in nature.

individualism
refers to the degree to which society focuses on the relationship of the individual to the group

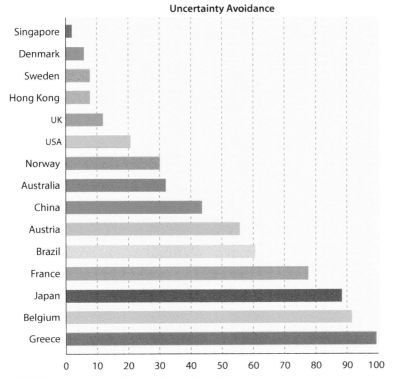

Exhibit 7.2 Uncertainty Avoidance for Selected Countries

Source: Based on G. Hofstede, 2001, *Culture's Consequences: Comparing Values, Behaviors, Institutions, and Organizations Across Nations* (2nd edn), Thousand Oaks, CA: Sage.

Individualism has important implications for international business. In countries with low individualism, MNCs will find that employees are hired and promoted mostly on the basis of association with a larger group such as a university or high school. In such societies, emphasis is placed on loyalty, seniority, and age. As mentioned earlier, MNCs operating in more collectivistic societies need to appreciate the importance of the larger social group. Consider Procter & Gamble's Canada subsidiary and their effort to understand diversity in their workforce. Because of the emphasis on the group and group harmony, they realized that in more collectivist cultures it is necessary to reward groups rather than individuals in some cases.[12] If they were to reward individuals within a team, they would potentially create conflict among the team members.

How is business impacted for multinationals operating in low individualistic societies? Consider how the following BRIC Insight provides some understanding of the implications of low individualism for relationship management.

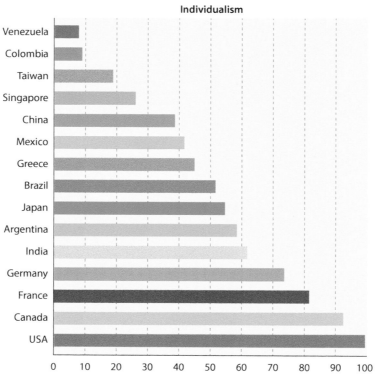

Exhibit 7.3 Individualism for Selected Countries

Source: Based on G. Hofstede, 2001, *Culture's Consequences: Comparing Values, Behaviors, Institutions, and Organizations Across Nations* (2nd edn), Thousand Oaks, CA: Sage.

Building Relationships in China   BRIC INSIGHT

As Exhibit 7.3 shows, China has relatively low levels of individualism and is thus seen as a collective society. As such, Chinese companies often occur through complex relationships. Chinese businesspeople are often members of complex networks that are difficult for outsiders to understand. These networks, known as *guanxi*, need to be developed and cultivated if outside multinationals want to succeed.

Guanxi, reflective of Chinese low individualism, evolved to provide Chinese businesses as a way to reduce uncertainty while also respecting the collective need for harmony and satisfaction of obligations. Today, most Chinese businesses are respectful of *guanxi* and need to go through these channels to be successful.

How can foreign multinationals cultivate *guanxi*? A recent in-depth survey of local Chinese managers and how they manage channels of distribution provides some insights. Local companies tend to hire individuals with *guanxi* connections. This thus provides ready access to connections within critical networks. However, companies also need to develop *guanxi* internally. In such cases, many multinationals offer training programs that allow employees to connect with each other. Many foreign multinationals often call such training programs as colleges and hold them at universities or resorts. Additionally, many multinationals also have formal processes in place to document *guanxi* connections. For example, in some multinationals, salespeople are encouraged to work with teams. In other local Chinese companies, salespeople are encouraged to socialize with customers. Such connections are then documented in case the salesperson decides to leave the organization.

Source: Based on J. Y. Murray and F. Q. Fu, 2016, "Strategic guanxi orientation: How to manage distribution channels in China?" *Journal of International Management, 22*, pp. 1–16.

The BRIC Insight clearly shows that for the collective culture, it is important for the MNC to respect local network connections. Establishing *guanxi* is therefore a key factor leading to success in China.

The fourth cultural dimension proposed by Hofstede is masculinity. **Masculinity** refers to the degree to which a society emphasizes masculine cultural characteristics such as emphasis on advancement and earnings. In societies with a high degree of masculinity, work tends to be very important and central to people's lives. Furthermore, these societies tend to see occupations clearly categorized by gender. In contrast, less masculine societies tend to value quality of life over a job and earnings. Work tends to be less central and important in people's lives. Exhibit 7.4 shows selected countries and their respective scores on masculinity.

Exhibit 7.4 depicts that many of the Anglo countries such as the US and the UK have high levels of masculinity. This suggests that MNCs operating in these countries will encounter employees who see work as very important in their lives. In these societies, people tend to work

masculinity
degree to which society emphasizes masculine cultural characteristics such as emphasis on advancement and earning

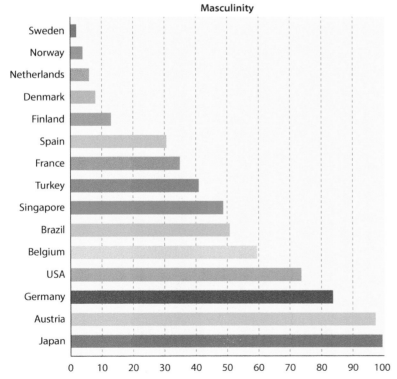

Exhibit 7.4 Masculinity for Selected Countries
Source: Based on G. Hofstede, 2001, *Culture's Consequences: Comparing Values, Behaviors, Institutions, and Organizations Across Nations* (2nd edn), Thousand Oaks, CA: Sage.

very long hours and recognition on the job is seen as an important motivator. The Exhibit also shows that many of the Nordic societies such as Sweden, Denmark, and Norway have low levels of masculinity. In these societies, people tend to work less and take longer vacations. MNCs operating in these countries should expect a workforce that is less dedicated to work and more focused on quality of life. Consider France, for instance, where employees typically get around 40 days off compared to only 15 in the US.[13] Many French employers actually offer company-owned ski cabins or beach houses as benefits to motivate employees. Such practices are consistent with the emphasis on quality of life in France because of the low levels of masculinity.

High levels of masculinity have also been implied to mean more inequality between genders regarding occupations. In more masculine societies, jobs are clearly defined by gender and some jobs are automatically reserved for males. However, in less masculine societies, occupations tend to be less gender-based. High levels of masculinity are also perceived to be associated with a worse work environment for women. Is this accurate? Consider the following Emerging Market Ethical Challenge.

India and Gender Equality

India has a moderately high score on the masculinity dimension. It is therefore not surprising to see that promotion of equality in Indian workplaces has been difficult. An important barrier that has held Indian women from workplaces is the cultural mindset that women have the responsibility for child-bearing and child raising. However, another important barrier is that even those women who hold jobs often have the double burden of employment and also caring for the family. Such barriers have made it difficult for Indian women to advance despite considerable progress in recent years. Exhibit 7.5 below shows some of the most common barriers identified by a recent survey of business leaders in Asia.

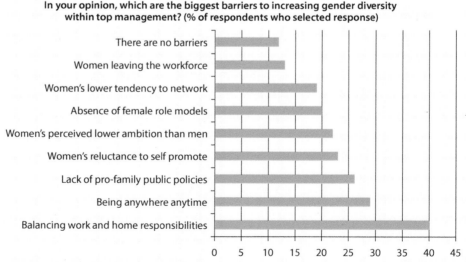

Exhibit 7.5 Barriers Preventing Gender Equality

Source: Based on McKinsey Report, 2012, "Women matter: An Asian perspective," file:///D:/User%20Account/Downloads/Women_Matter_An_Asian_perspective.pdf

Given these challenges, what can multinationals do to encourage gender equality? In India, McDonald's is working hard to hire women and to work closely with them to ensure that they have a career. For example, it has moved some of its female employees from full-time positions to consultants on specific projects so that these employees have the flexibility to manage both work and family life. McDonald's is also implementing a number of best practices such as support of diversity from the highest level and training programs to help women develop the skills to network as well as understand core aspects of the company culture. McDonald's hopes to be able to have gender equality in the future.

Source: Adapted from S. C. Saha, 2016, "Breaking boundaries at work," November, www.humancapitalonline.com

However, despite the important understanding the Hofstede model has generated, it has also received some criticisms.[14] First, some have argued that Hofstede's model is too simplistic and that cultures cannot be reduced to a few dimensions. As you will see later, understanding a country's culture is indeed very difficult and takes long periods of training. Second, Hofstede's data were from IBM managers. There is some concern over whether IBM managers in a country are sufficiently similar to the average person in that country to make conclusions about the country's culture. Third, Hofstede's model is also seen as static as it cannot detect how culture changes over time. For instance, many countries in Eastern Europe have experienced dramatic changes in the last decades. Hofstede's cultural dimensions may not necessarily be able to reflect such changes. The final critical aspect of Hofstede's model is that the data were collected in the 1970s and that the model is outdated.

Despite the above criticisms, Hofstede's study has been very useful in helping multinational managers navigate cultural differences. Hofstede's dimensions have been shown to influence many key aspects of multinational strategic management. Furthermore, a recent review of three decades of Hofstede's work has shown that these dimensions are still relevant today.[15] Because of the many criticisms against Hofstede's model, a large team of researchers conducted the GLOBE studies. We will consider that model next.

The Global Leadership and Organizational Behavior Studies Model of Culture

The Hofstede model discussed earlier provides a good understanding of many of the critical ways countries differ on culture. However, while the Hofstede data were collected more than three decades ago, a more recent study by the Global Leadership and Organizational Behavior Studies researchers (GLOBE) provides additional insight into understanding culture.[16] The GLOBE project involves 170 researchers who collected data on 17,000 managers from 62 countries around the world. Many of the cultural dimensions studied by the GLOBE researchers are similar to the ones studied by Hofstede. Specifically, the GLOBE researchers found evidence of nine cultural dimensions such as power distance, uncertainty avoidance, societal and institutional collectivism (similar to Hofstede's individualism and collectivism dimensions), assertiveness (similar to Hofstede's masculinity), and gender egalitarianism (similar to Hofstede's femininity). Given the similarity with Hofstede's dimensions, many of the implications discussed earlier for Hofstede's cultural dimensions would also apply for the similar GLOBE dimensions.

However, three of the dimensions the GLOBE researchers studied are fairly unique. Below we consider these three dimensions; namely future orientation, humane orientation, and performance orientation.

future orientation
degree to which people believe that their current behavior will impact their future

Future orientation deals with the degree to which individuals believe that their current behavior will impact their future. This dimension was developed to reflect how people use time to organize their experiences and events. It is actually similar to another of Hofstede's dimensions known as the Confucian dynamism or more long-term orientation. However, we focus on GLOBE's future orientation measure as it is most recent and covers a wider range of societies than Hofstede.

Cultures that are low on the future orientation scale (present orientation) tend to be more spontaneous and prefer enjoying the current moment. In contrast, societies that have high future orientation tend to think more of the future and engage in planning and strategies in order to achieve future goals. Exhibit 7.6 shows selected countries and their scores on future orientation. The GLOBE scale runs from a 1 (low) to 7 (high).

As you can see from the chart, many of the former communist emerging market societies such as Poland, Russia, and Hungary have relatively low future orientation scores. It is possible that decades of communism have resulted in individuals preferring instant gratification rather than planning ahead. Given the relative deprivation that people in many of these societies had to endure, they probably prefer the present rather than planning for an uncertain future. It is also interesting to note that many of the Nordic societies score relatively high on this dimension. It seems possible that the relative periods of wealth they have enjoyed make it possible to plan for the future.

Future orientation has important implications for international business. MNCs should expect less preference for strategic planning and more inflexible management systems in societies with low future orientation. Furthermore, people may also be more interested in what the MNC

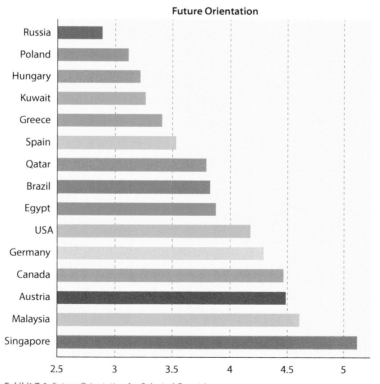

Future Orientation

Exhibit 7.6 Future Orientation for Selected Countries
Source: Based on R. J. House, P. J. Hanges, M. Javidan, P. W. Dorfman and V. Gupta (eds), 2004, *Culture, Leadership and Organizations: The GLOBE Study of 62 Societies,* Thousand Oaks, CA: Sage.

has to offer in the immediacy (job security) rather than future prospects. However, in higher future orientation societies, there tends to be more of a future-looking perspective.

Performance orientation refers to the degree to which the society encourages societal members to innovate, to improve their performance, and to strive for excellence. This dimension is similar to Weber's Protestant work ethic and reflects the desire for achievement in a society. Countries such as the United States and Singapore have high scores on performance orientation, while countries such as Russia and Greece have low scores on the dimension.

An important reflection of the performance orientation cultural dimension is how status is conferred in society. High performance societies tend to be more similar to achievement societies where people are evaluated on the basis of their accomplishments. In contrast, low performance societies are ascription societies where status is given to people based on characteristics such as age, family connections, gender, and education.

Exhibit 7.7 shows selected countries and their scores on performance orientation.

Countries that have high performance orientation scores tend to favor training and development, while in countries low on performance orientation, family and background are more important.[17] In societies with high performance orientation, people are encouraged to take initiative and are rewarded for performing with the belief that one can succeed by trying hard. In contrast, low performance orientation societies reward harmony with the environment, emphasizing loyalty and integrity while regarding assertiveness as unacceptable.

How much impact do these cultural dimensions have? The following IB Emerging Market Strategic Insight examines the impact of these dimensions on bilateral trade and provide some responses.

performance orientation degree to which the society encourages societal members to innovate, to improve their performance, and to strive for excellence

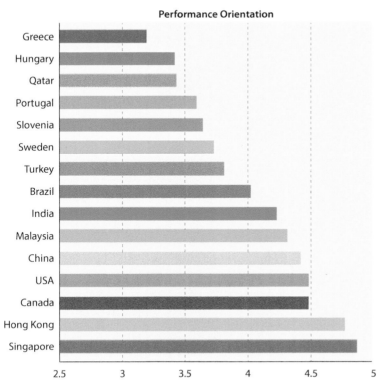

Exhibit 7.7 Performance Orientation for Selected Countries

Source: Based on R. J. House, P. J. Hanges, M. Javidan, P. W. Dorfman and V. Gupta (eds), 2004, *Culture, Leadership and Organizations: The GLOBE Study of 62 Societies*, Thousand Oaks, CA: Sage.

Impact of Culture on Competitiveness

A recent study provides some insights on the importance impact of culture on competitiveness. In that study, the researchers examined how the GLOBE cultural dimensions have an influence on competitiveness in terms of bilateral trade performance. The bilateral trade performance indicates the amount of goods that can be imported from a trading partner based on exports sent to the partner. The measure applies to all industries and is typically a good measure of competitiveness countries have relative to others.

Results of the study show that countries that have high performance orientation, high future orientation, and high gender egalitarianism (similar to Hofstede's femininity) all lead to high competitiveness. When examined in the light of emerging markets, such results are not surprising as emerging markets such as China, India, Malaysia, and Brazil all have fairly high levels of both performance and future orientation.

Source: Based on D. Mornah and R. MacDermott, 2016, "Culture as a determinant of competitive advantage in trade," *International Journal of Business and Economic Sciences Applied Research, 9*, pp. 69–76.

---

humane orientation
degree to which people are expected to be friendly, generous, and caring

As the above IB Emerging Market Strategic Insight shows, the GLOBE cultural dimensions are also critical aspects to understand. The final cultural dimension we discuss is humane orientation. **Humane orientation** refers to the degree to which people within a society are expected to be friendly, generous, and caring. In societies with high humane orientation, people see others as very important and value kindness, benevolence, generosity, and love. In contrast, low humane orientation societies tend to place emphasis on self-interest and value material possessions. Exhibit 7.8 shows selected societies and their scores on the humane orientation dimension.

As the chart shows, many of the emerging Asian societies score highly on humane orientation. It is surprising to see Zambia has the highest score on the dimension. However, high humane societies are characterized by the expectation that members of the society will help each other and provide material and financial help. This is typical of many Asian and African societies where the individual can rely on the extended family for support. The US has a fairly moderate level of humane orientation, while many of the Latin European countries and Germany have lower levels of humane orientation.

Humane orientation affects international business in that MNCs should expect to provide an environment that is based on relationships in more humane oriented societies. Such societies tend to be characterized by more informal relationships among people. From a human resources perspective, MNCs in such societies will tend to be more trusted. In contrast, low humane orientation societies tend to be more formal, and MNCs should expect more control from the state and unions.

country clusters
group of countries with similar cultural patterns

Although the GLOBE data provide many insights into a large number of countries, further analysis has shown that the cultural dimensions' implications can be simplified when applied to country clusters. **Country clusters** are groups of countries, such as Anglo, Latin American, and Latin European, with roughly similar cultural patterns. Ten clusters were found in the GLOBE project and include the Anglo cluster, the Confucian Asia cluster, the Eastern Europe cluster, the Germanic Europe cluster, the Latin America cluster, Latin Europe cluster, the Middle East cluster, the Nordic Europe cluster, the Southern Asia cluster, and the sub-Saharan cluster. Exhibit 7.9 shows the various clusters and corresponding countries in the cluster.

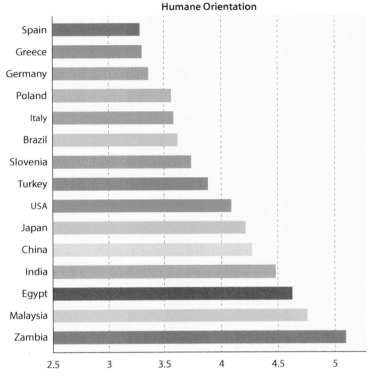

Exhibit 7.8 Humane Orientation for Selected Countries

Source: Based on R. J. House, P. J. Hanges, M. Javidan, P. W. Dorfman and V. Gupta (eds), 2004, *Culture, Leadership and Organizations: The GLOBE Study of 62 Societies*, Thousand Oaks, CA: Sage.

Country clusters share many similarities with regards to cultural patterns. Exhibit 7.10 shows the various clusters and where these clusters stand on selected GLOBE cultural dimensions.

Why should you be concerned with country clusters? Although cultures differ within these broad classifications, such summaries are useful for condensing cultural information. They are useful to predict likely cultural traits when specific information is not available on a national culture. Clusters are important as they provide important information to multinationals regarding similarity of cultures. Multinationals may find it less risky to enter other countries with cultures that are similar to their own, and clusters provide readily available information.

The information discussed in this section shows the importance of understanding national culture in international business. Nevertheless, it should be noted that the GLOBE model has also been criticized for many of the same points as the Hofstede model. As you will see later, cultures are extremely complex, and some argue that research based on questionnaires can never accurately assess a country's cultural profile. However, using the Hofstede and GLOBE cultural models is a good starting point and provides crucial information about how countries differ on critical cultural dimensions. National culture affects how individuals behave and think, and an appropriate understanding of culture reduces the chance of making cultural blunders. Furthermore, national culture has an undeniable influence on the business culture and etiquette within any society. In the next section, we consider some of the linkages between national culture and business culture.

Anglo	Latin Europe	Eastern Europe	Latin America	Confucian Asia
Australia	Israel	Albania	Argentina	China
Canada	Italy	Georgia	Bolivia	Hong Kong
Ireland	Portugal	Greece	Brazil	Japan
New Zealand	Spain	Hungary	Colombia	Singapore
South Africa (White)	France	Kazakhstan	Costa Rica	South Korea
United Kingdom	Switzerland (French)	Poland	El Salvador	Taiwan
USA		Russia	Guatemala	
		Slovenia	Mexico	
			Venezuela	

Nordic Europe	Germanic Europe	Sub-Saharan Africa	Middle East	Southern Asia
Denmark	Austria	Namibia	Qatar	India
Finland	Switzerland	Nigeria	Morocco	Indonesia
Sweden	Netherlands	South Africa (Black)	Turkey	Philippines
	Germany (former East)	Zambia	Egypt	Malaysia
	Germany (former West)	Zimbabwe	Kuwait	Thailand
				Iran

Exhibit 7.9 GLOBE Country Clusters

Source: Based on Vipin Gupta, Paul J. Hanges and Peter Dorfman, 2002, "Cultural clusters: Methodology and findings," *Journal of World Business, 37,* pp. 11–15.

Cluster	Performance Orientation	Assertiveness	Future Orientation	Humane Orientation	Institutional Collectivism	In-group Collectivism	Gender Egalitarianism	Power Distance	Uncertainty Avoidance
Comparison with Hofstede	Unique	Masculinity	Long-term orientation	Unique	Collectivism	Collectivism	Femininity	Power Distance	Uncertainty Avoidance
Anglo	High	Medium	Medium	Medium	Medium	Low	Medium	Medium	Medium
Confucian Asia	High	Medium	Medium	Medium	High	High	Medium	Medium	Medium
Eastern Europe	Low	High	Low	Medium	Medium	High	High	Medium	Low
Germanic Europe	High	High	High	Low	Low	Low	Medium	Medium	High
Latin America	Low	Medium	Low	Medium	Low	High	Medium	Medium	Low
Latin Europe	Medium	Medium	Medium	Low	Low	Medium	Medium	Medium	Medium
Middle East	Medium	Medium	Low	Medium	Medium	High	Low	Medium	Low
Nordic Europe	Medium	Low	High	Medium	High	Low	High	Low	High
Southern Asia	Medium	Medium	Medium	High	Medium	High	Medium	Medium	Medium
Sub-Saharan Africa	Medium	Medium	Medium	High	Medium	Medium	Medium	Medium	Medium

Exhibit 7.10 GLOBE Country Clusters and Cultural Dimensions

Source: Based on Mansour Javidan, Peter W. Dorfman, Mary Sully de Luque and Robert J. House, 2006, "In the eye of the beholder: Cross-cultural lessons in leadership for project GLOBE," *The Academy of Management Perspectives,* February, 20(1), pp. 67–90.

How important are country clusters? Consider the following IB Emerging Market Strategic Insight.

Country Clusters and the GLOBE Project

IB EMERGING MARKET STRATEGIC INSIGHT

	Latin America	Confucian Asia	Anglo	Sub-Saharan Africa	Germanic Europe	Middle East
Charisma	High	Medium	High	Medium	High	Low
Team-oriented	High	Medium/High	Medium	Medium	Medium/Low	Low
Participative	Medium	Low	High	Medium	High	Low
Autonomous	Low	Medium	Medium	Low	High	Medium

Exhibit 7.11 GLOBE Country Clusters and Preferred Leadership Attributes
Source: Based on Mansour Javidan, Peter W. Dorfman, Mary Sully de Luque and Robert J. House, 2006, "In the eye of the beholder: Cross-cultural lessons in leadership for project GLOBE," *The Academy of Management Perspectives*, February, *20*(1), pp. 67–90.

Country clusters represent a simple but powerful way to summarize information about countries with similar cultural profiles. Javidan et al.[18] provide some evidence of the usefulness of country clusters. They examined the cultural backgrounds of the ten country clusters and whether people in specific clusters preferred leaders with specific profiles. They considered such leadership profiles such as charisma (ability to inspire and motivate others), team-oriented (ability to motivate employees to work as a team), participative (degree to which the leader involves others), and autonomous (degree to which the leader behaves in individualistic manner), and found definite preference for specific leadership traits among clusters.

Consider their findings for the Latin American cluster. This cluster contains many of the emerging markets found in Latin America. This cluster has countries where people frown on individualism. Furthermore, Latin American countries have high power distance and high levels of uncertainty avoidance. As such, those leaders who do well are typically those who make decisions collectively, those who treat their subordinates with formality, and those who display charisma. It is therefore not surprising to see that the preferred leader in the Latin American cluster displays a high level of charisma, is team-oriented and has moderate levels of the participative profile. Multinationals need to make note of such preferences when operating in such markets.

In contrast, consider the emerging markets in the Middle East cluster where countries tend to score low on uncertainty avoidance and high on collectivism, while medium on power distance. Because of the low levels of uncertainty avoidance, subordinates are often reluctant to make decisions that involve risk. As such, preferred leaders are those who display low levels of the participative dimension. Furthermore, the good leader in this cluster behaves in a collectivistic manner and tries to maintain harmony because of the high levels of collectivism.

As you can see from the above, country clusters are crucial tools to understand cultures of emerging markets. Exhibit 7.11 shows selected leadership profiles and appropriateness in different clusters.

Source: Based on Mansour Javidan, Peter W. Dorfman, Mary Sully de Luque and Robert J. House, 2006, "In the eye of the beholder: Cross-cultural lessons in leadership from project GLOBE," *Academy of Management Perspectives*, February, *20*(1), pp. 67–90.

National Culture and Business Culture

business culture
values, beliefs, and norms regarding how to conduct business in a society

business etiquette
range of acceptable and unacceptable behaviors when doing business

A society's **business culture** reflects the values, beliefs, and norms regarding how business is conducted in any society. It reflects the appropriate and inappropriate behaviors when conducting business in any society. Understanding business culture is extremely critical as, similar to national culture, it provides insights regarding appropriate aspects of doing business in a culture. Obviously, a country's business culture is heavily influenced by its national culture. Such aspects of the business culture tend to be manifested in **business etiquette**, the range of expected acceptable and unacceptable behaviors when doing business. In this section, we consider a few key aspects of business etiquette and how they are affected by national culture.

One of the most important aspects of business etiquette is whether to use a person's formal title and last name when meeting that person. In the US, the business culture tends to be more informal and managers seldom use last names and titles to refer to each other. However, in other societies such as the emerging markets of China and India, it is expected that titles and formality are respected when addressing someone. One of the important cultural differences that explains the degree of formality is power distance. Because of the emphasis on hierarchy and privileged position of the powerful in countries with a high degree of power distance, there is an expectation that this hierarchy will be respected through the appropriate use of titles.

High power distance tends to be associated with formality in many other aspects of the business environment. For instance, in a high power distance society, business people are expected to dress more conservatively, to be punctual for appointments, to make more formal presentations, and to value the use of a business card. Additionally, when negotiating with individuals in high power distance societies, it is very likely that those with the highest seniority are the decision makers. It therefore makes sense to know the seniority and rank of those involved in negotiations.

Another important aspect that pertains to the business environment in a society is the nature of relationships between business partners. In some societies such as China, it is expected that business partners will be patient and consider any partnership through a long-term perspective. However, in the US business negotiators may not necessarily view a business partnership as long-term. The cultural dimension of collectivism provides some explanation for these differences. In more collectivistic societies, personal relationships are extremely important. It is therefore expected that US companies negotiating with Chinese companies will want to develop relationships first. Unlike the US preference for completing negotiations in as timely a fashion as possible, Chinese negotiators often prefer to socialize and to cultivate the relationship before getting to business matters. This also suggests the importance of being properly connected to undertake business operations. To give you further insight on how business etiquette works, consider the following BRIC Insight on small businesses attempting to establish contacts in China.

As the BRIC Insight shows, the cultural dimension of collectivism has a strong influence on the business culture in China. The implications for business etiquette are that people should expect to engage in non-business conversations with individuals from more collectivistic societies. During meetings, more time can be spent talking about non-business issues so that the partners get to know each other.

Business Culture in China

Despite the recent slowdown, China continues to present tremendous opportunities for businesses. In fact, many smaller companies rely on Chinese companies for manufacturing and prototyping purposes. As such, it is critical for companies negotiating with the Chinese keep in mind the appropriate business etiquette. Chinese experts suggest that small-business employees keep in mind the many aspects of Chinese business culture:

- Schedule appointment meetings at least one week ahead of time. Provide the Chinese with a list of those who will be meeting with details on their titles, positions etc.
- Handle business cards with two hands and delicately. Chinese business people tend to view handling of business cards as a sign of respect. It is also polite to have business cards with Chinese lettering on the other side.
- It is customary for Chinese partners to have large banquets. Try to eat a little bit of everything. Always leave a little food on the plate.
- Dress conservatively. Avoid suits with bright colors.
- Show up on time for meetings. Punctuality is extremely critical in the Chinese business environment.
- Cultivate personal relationships.
- Try to get consensus on decisions rather than create conflict.
- Be patient but persistent with negotiations.
- Don't use slang with your hosts. Use a confident tone and do not speak too fast.

Source: Adapted from *The Economist*, 2016, "The yuan and the markets," January 16, p. 11; Dave Archer, 2006, "Doing business in China," *Journal of Commerce*, October 30, p. 1; Dave Hannon, 2006, "The dos and don'ts of doing business in China," *Purchasing*, May 18, pp. 52–54; Executive Planet—China—2016 www.executiveplanet.com/china-2/

Furthermore, care must be taken to give opportunities for collectivistic individuals to avoid loss of face. For instance, it is important to understand that a "yes" in Japan may not have the same connotation as a "yes" in the US. In the US, if someone says "yes," that person is indicating agreement with your statement. Disagreement is simply indicated with a "no." However, the Japanese negotiator may be reluctant to say "no." In fact, the Japanese negotiator may say "yes" when, in reality, the "yes" means "possibly" or even "no." As such, it is important not to place collective individuals in such precarious positions. Consider, for instance, that ITT China was facing high employee turnover in its Shanghai sales office.[19] Local managers soon found out that the performance ratings were influencing turnover. Employees who were rated a 3 on a 1–5 performance scale were more likely to quit shortly thereafter. These employees could not face their peers as they were losing face when receiving such low ratings. For them, it made more sense to quit. ITT decided to drop such performance ratings altogether in most of the collective countries where it was operating.

Because of the focus on the collective, it is also important to know that teams are very important in collectivistic societies. In teams, people strive to reach consensus and generally avoid conflicts. Teams would rather show consensus than disagreement in front of their hosts. As a reflection of the business culture, it is important for individuals from more individualistic societies to realize that they may have to deal with teams rather than individuals.

It is important to understand the impact of the masculinity dimension on business etiquette. Because work is a big aspect of an individual's life in more masculine societies, you can expect a strong work ethic and discussion of work-related matters long into the night. However, for the more feminine societies, such as the Danes, meetings are expected to end in the afternoon. Danes prefer to work intensely on the job and end work early so that they can spend time with their families.

A final critical aspect of the business culture of a country is the use of language in the communication context. The anthropologist Edward T. Hall identified an important distinction among the world's languages based on whether communication is explicit or implicit. Hall focused on how different cultures use the context or the situation in which communication takes place to understand what people are saying. Languages in which people state things directly and explicitly are called **low-context languages**. The words provide most of the meaning. You do not have to understand the situation in which the words are used. Languages in which people state things indirectly and implicitly are called **high-context languages**. In the high-context language, communications have multiple meanings that one can interpret only by reading the situation in which the communication occurs.

low-context languages
people say things directly and explicitly

high-context languages
people state things indirectly and implicitly

Most northern European languages, including German, English, and the Scandinavian languages, are low context. People use explicit words to communicate direct meaning. Thus, for example, if a German manager says "yes," she means "yes." In addition, most Western cultures attach a positive value to clear and direct communication. This is particularly apparent in negotiations, where low-context languages allow clear statements concerning what a negotiator wants out of the relationship. In contrast, many of the Asian and Arabic languages used in emerging markets are among the most high-context languages in the world. In Asian languages, often what is left unsaid is just as important as what is said. Silent periods and the use of incomplete sentences require a person to interpret what the communicator does not say by reading the situation. Arabic introduces interpretation into the language with an opposite tack. Extensive imprecise verbal and nonverbal communication produces an interaction where reading the situation is necessary for understanding. This suggests that multinationals have to be very careful when interacting with others from such emerging markets.

National Culture: Some Cautions and Caveats

The preceding paragraphs discuss some of the ways countries are different based on culture and how the national culture affects business culture. However, you need to keep in mind that these are broad generalizations that provide the basis to understand how people are different across countries, and that not all individuals within a society will fit the cultural profile for that country. Furthermore, most countries have **subcultures**, which represent the ways of life of groups of people within a culture. For example, considering India as a homogeneous culture can be damaging for any multinational. There are significant differences among regions and among castes. McDonald's adjusted its menu significantly to address such regional subcultures. It tailored its menu to address regional variations in terms of preference of meat and vegetarian menus as well as preference for local fares. In this section, we therefore discuss some of the dangers of making broad generalizations and how to better prepare to understand such differences.

subcultures
groups of people with similar culture within a culture

Cultures do not determine exactly how each individual behaves, thinks, acts, and feels. Assuming that all people within one culture behave, believe, feel, and act the same is known as **stereotyping**. Using a cultural stereotype to understand another culture is not necessarily wrong, if it is used carefully. Broad generalization about a culture can serve as a starting point for understanding the complexities of cultural differences. Another important danger related to understanding culture is **ethnocentricity**. Ethnocentricity is the belief that one's own culture is superior to others. Many international business projects fail because multinational managers are ethnocentric and they ignore the benefits of other cultures.

stereotyping
assuming that all people within a particular group behave, believe, feel, and act the same

ethnocentricity
belief that one's own culture is superior

Even when an effort is made to understand culture, experts often find that there are a lot of exceptions to the generalizations we discussed earlier.[20] For instance, consider that although the US is one of the most individualistic societies, it has one of the highest percentages of charitable giving in the world. Similarly, although Japan is very high on uncertainty avoidance, business partners often find that Japanese contracts tend to incorporate significant ambiguity clauses compared to specific and direct US contracts. Such **cultural paradoxes**, where observations often contradict cultural expectations, suggest that you need to be very careful when you are trying to understand culture in any society.

The cultural differences we outlined earlier are very useful tools for understanding how countries differ on culture. However, they can be limited in understanding the wide variations in cultural patterns within a country. It is therefore imperative for you to be very attentive to situations or contexts that may make an individual behave contrary to cultural expectations. In other words, you cannot assume that all business people in the US prefer participative management styles because of low power distance. In fact, although the US generally prefers a more egalitarian culture, CEOs are often allowed to be authoritarian and people accept an unequal degree of power. As you can see, this reflects a cultural paradox where US Americans accept inequality and power characteristic of higher power distance societies. How can multinational managers face such challenges? Consider the following IB Emerging Market Strategic Insight.

cultural paradoxes refers to situations that contradict cultural expectations

Country Culture or Generations

IB EMERGING MARKET
STRATEGIC INSIGHT

International business research has traditionally assumed that cultures reside exclusively within countries. However, from the earlier examples it is clearly shown that there are significant variations in culture within countries. Assuming that cultures and countries are equivalent can therefore be erroneous. In fact, recent research supports this incorrect assumption finding that only 80 percent of cultural variation is within countries. An examination of other factors suggests that it may be more beneficial to understand cultures in the context of other aspects such as professions or socio-economic classes. In other words, significant differences may be more likely to exist between professions or whether the citizens of the countries are poor or rich.

An examination of generations in Africa provides some insights into this perspective. Africa has one of the world's youngest populations with around 200 million people between the ages of 15 and 24. This number is predicted to double by 2045. Researchers find that despite cultural differences among African countries, African residents between the ages of 15 and 24 tend to think and behave similarly. Members of this generation (Generation Y) tend to have much more disposable income than their older peers; tend to be more likely to multitask—i.e. they can tackle multiple screens at once; and, additionally, may be more likely to pay attention to their friends' perception of a product rather than to professional reviews. Marketers therefore need to understand this African youth culture if they want to succeed in Africa.

Companies such as Red Bull have been extremely successful marketing to this youth culture by means of marketing efforts through multiple channels targeting the young. For example, they have a recording branch that signs music groups that target young people and they also have a sports division that sponsors major teams worldwide.

Source: Based on J. Pienaar, 2015, "Tapping into Africa's youth market," finweek, November 5, pp. 38–40; V. Taras, P. Steel and B. L. Kirkman, 2016, "Does country equate with culture? Beyond geography in the search for cultural boundaries," *Management International Review, 56*, pp. 455–487.

As you can see above, understanding youth culture may be more critical for marketers if they want to market to African youth rather than understanding cross-national cultural differences. Furthermore, culture can also be very subtle and difficult to understand. How can you prepare for the subtleties of understanding culture? Culture experts suggest using the cultural dimensions we discussed earlier as basic tools. Beyond that, you need to understand that cultures are incredibly complex and cannot be reduced to simple dos and don'ts. For instance, appropriate understanding of a country's history and a country's logic can be very helpful. Through cultural mentors, culture students can also get a more in-depth understanding of cultural nuances. Finally, you should always remain open-minded and try to understand the reasoning behind cultural paradoxes

Fully understanding the local cultural context is important. Consider some of the examples of cultural paradoxes mentioned earlier. Why would the US have the highest levels of charitable giving when this is clearly a behavior that contradicts the high levels of individualism? US history shows that the US prospered based on a communal tradition of religions and cultural values. It is therefore not surprising to see such high levels of charitable giving.[21] Similarly, the more ambiguous clauses contained in Japanese contracts reflect the more collectivistic nature of Japanese culture. The Japanese believe that they can rely on and trust others, and such aspects take precedence over any uncertainty about the contract. Therefore, they do not need to specify all aspects of a contract as they leave some flexibility to deal with contingencies. Both examples suggest that a more in-depth appreciation of the cultural context can bring better cultural understanding.

National Culture: Cross-cultural Training

It is obvious from this chapter that understanding cultural differences is crucial to today's global manager. It is not expected that you may be asked to take an international assignment when you start your career. For the company sending personnel into the international arena, there are significant costs involved. Consider that an expatriate may often require a salary premium of 10 to 25 percent above his or her salary on international assignments. Furthermore, extra expenses are incurred through the provision of housing, a company vehicle, cost-of-living adjustments, medical and other benefits (private school, spousal support) to support the family.[22] With such high costs, it is imperative that the MNC ensures that the expatriate has a chance to succeed. A big factor contributing to success is cultural training.

cultural intelligence
cultural competencies
and abilities that allow
managers to deal with
the complexities of
cultural differences

There is enough evidence that cross-cultural training is extremely valuable for multinationals.[23] To be able to succeed internationally, multinational managers will need to have high cultural intelligence.[24] **Cultural intelligence** simply refers to cultural competencies and abilities that allow managers to deal with the complexities of cultural differences. Research has shown that managers who have high cultural intelligence are more likely to make better cross-cultural decisions while also achieving stronger cross-cultural performance.

How important is cultural intelligence? The Emerging Market Brief below provides some evidence of cultural intelligence for international performance.

Cultural Intelligence and Export Performance of Thai Companies

EMERGING MARKET BRIEF

How important is cultural intelligence to small and medium firms? A recent interesting study of small and medium enterprises in Thailand provides some insights. In that study, researchers examined the export performance of 129 Thai firms. The author surveyed the cultural intelligence of employees of these firms and used a detailed measure of how well these companies did in terms of exports. Results of the study showed that those companies with higher cultural intelligence had stronger export performance. Specifically, companies that had higher cultural intelligence had stronger ability to acquire international knowledge. The latter simply reflects the level of knowledge a firm has about its international markets. With such higher international knowledge, it is not surprising to see that such firms had stronger ability to do well in the export markets.

Source: Based on P. Charoensukmongkol, 2016, "Cultural intelligence and export performance of small and medium enterprises in Thailand: Mediating roles of organizational capabilities," *International Small Business Journal*, 34(1), pp. 105–122.

The above clearly shows the importance of cultural intelligence and the consequent need for cross-cultural training. Cross-cultural training provides the recipient with better skills to adjust to the new culture. Such adjustment enhances the likelihood that the person will do well at the job. Furthermore, appropriate training also reduces the likelihood that an expatriate will leave the job. Cross-cultural training also increases self-confidence and well-being in the new culture.

In the final section, we therefore examine some of the ways MNCs can prepare their employees to understand new cultures.

Culture Training Methods

The aim of most culture training courses is to increase the cultural intelligence of employees.[25] To give you further insights into cultural intelligence, Exhibit 7.12 below shows you the various questions that can be used to assess cultural intelligence.

Questions Asked to Determine Cultural Intelligence (assessed on a 7-point scale from strongly disagree to strongly agree)
• I am conscious of the cultural knowledge I apply to cross-cultural interactions
• I know the rules for expressing nonverbal behaviors in other cultures
• I enjoy interacting with people from other cultures
• I change my verbal behavior when cross-cultural interactions require it
• I know the cultural values and beliefs of other cultures
• I check the accuracy of my cultural knowledge as I interact with people from different cultures

Exhibit 7.12 Assessing Cultural Intelligence
Source: Based on P. Charoensukmongkol, 2016, "Cultural intelligence and export performance of small and medium enterprises in Thailand: Mediating roles of organizational capabilities," *International Small Business Journal*, 34(1), pp. 105–122; M. Li, W. H. Mobley and A. Kelly, 2013, "When do global leaders learn best to develop cultural intelligence? An investigation of the moderating role of experiential learning style," *Academy of Management Learning and Education*, 12(1), pp. 32–50.

low-rigor cultural training programs
cultural training that necessitates minimal effort and mental involvement

higher-rigor cultural training progams
cultural training that is more involved

simulations
training programs that offer participants the chance to experience a foreign culture through role-playing and other forms of instruction

How can employees be trained to develop cultural intelligence? There is a range of training techniques available for cross-cultural training.[26] The selection of the technique used depends on the nature of the assignment. For short-term assignments, **low-rigor cultural training programs**, where more limited mental involvement and effort is extended to complete the program, may be adequate. However, for long-term expatriate assignments, **higher-rigor cultural training programs** may be more appropriate. Below we discuss the forms of training and corresponding levels of rigor.

There are two basic forms of cultural training available: simulations and field experiences.[27] **Simulations** tend be of lower rigor, where participants are offered the opportunity to experience the foreign culture through role-playing and other programmed instruction. One of the most basic forms of simulation cultural training can be of the instructional type. In this form of training, employees are exposed to various forms of instructional material such as lectures, tutorials, and reading assignments about the new culture. Participants can also engage in role-playing as well as participating in case studies. In some cases, MNCs provide some form of cultural awareness training. The basic assumption behind cultural awareness methods is that someone can better appreciate cultural differences if the person is aware of his or her own culture. Finally, this method may also involve some form of language training whereby participants are taught the basic aspects of the language so that they have a rudimentary knowledge of the language.

Although low-rigor training may seem the most primitive of cross-cultural training technique, recent research suggests that it can be effective in increasing students' cultural intelligence.[28] In that study, the authors examined the impact of traditional cross-cultural management classes on students' cultural intelligence. Using data from two large group of students, the researchers find that academic cross-cultural management classes had a significant impact and increased the students' cultural intelligence after students took the classes. These results therefore confirm that low-rigor training can also be effective.

The major advantage of these low-rigor methods typical of the simulations discussed above is that they tend to be very cost-effective and typically involve minimal work disruption. Companies can bring cross-cultural experts to the employees' workplace to provide convenient training. Furthermore, these methods are also amenable to delivery via the Internet and can thus involve minimal work disturbances. Such methods can also be effective in a classroom setting.

The major drawbacks include the fact that instructors have to be very experienced or participants may not take the exercise very seriously. For instance, for case studies and experiential forms of learning, instructors need to have the skills and experiences to provide lessons that are as realistic as possible. Also, because most of the instructions can be offered in a classroom, participants also suffer from the "classroom" syndrome. They may not believe that the exercises are very realistic and may thus doubt the effectiveness of the approach. In some cases, they may just be recipients of static information without having the chance to engage in experiential activities to digest the information.

field experiences
cultural training programs that offer participants the opportunity to learn by experiencing the new culture

The **field experiences** techniques are usually of higher rigor and participants are given the opportunity to learn through experience. Employees can participate in field trips, where they visit and experience the host culture first hand for a significant period of time. Some MNCs also offer on-the-job training where the employee is coached and trained on the job. This method allows the trainee to see not only the new culture but also how that culture interacts with the work environment. In other cases, employees get interaction training whereby they learn from the expatriate they will be replacing. This allows the new employee to get firsthand training on the appropriate business behaviors in the country as well as giving the person the chance to meet the key people in the new workplace and to learn how to interact with the new community. This method eases expectations regarding daily operation in the new culture.

Most cultural training experts suggest that field experiences are the most effective means of training.[29] Participants get a direct and strong appreciation of the new culture by experiencing the culture firsthand. Furthermore, with on-the-job coaching they experience not only the culture but also the workplace environment, meeting key individuals and getting to know the organizational culture. This learning and experience is valuable in giving the recipient an experience as close as possible to reality, thereby increasing the likelihood of success.

The major disadvantage associated with field experiences is that they tend to be both time-consuming and costly. For instance, sending someone on a field trip may involve significant costs. In many cases, it may also be necessary to send the whole family, costing thousands of dollars more. Additionally, on-the-job training can be very disruptive for the trainer. Expatriates tend to be very busy individuals, and unless they are provided with the additional time and resources they may feel overburdened if they have to train a new person.

Which training method should be used? Researchers argue that the types of training should be based on three main factors: the degree to which the employee's national culture is different from the one she or he will be experiencing; the degree to which the employee will need to interact with locals; and the length of the cultural assignment. If assignments are short term, for instance when a person is sent to negotiate in a different culture for a short period of time, low-rigor simulations may work well. However, if a manager is sent for a long period of time, for instance, as an expatriate, higher-rigor types of training may be necessary.

What else should the multinational keep in mind when developing training programs? The following IB Emerging Market Strategic Insight suggests that the learning style of the employee will also affect the effectiveness of the training.

Culture Training: Best Practices

In this final section, we examine some of the best practices regarding cross-cultural training based on a review by Littrell and Salas and others.[30] They argue that any cross-cultural training has many aspects that need to be tailored according to the training needs. Specifically, the three crucial aspects of cross-cultural training include the design, delivery, and evaluation. With regard to design, many of the issues discussed earlier apply here. For instance, the nature of the assignment should play a role in determining the length of the training. More complex international assignments obviously require more rigorous training. Additionally, cross-cultural training works best if it is also offered to the accompanying family. The ability of a manager to succeed on a foreign assignment also depends on the family's level of adaptation to the new culture. Furthermore, as we saw earlier, adapting to the learner's learning style and personality is also critical. The multinational should ensure that the right individuals are selected for the experience. Finally, a properly designed program should involve the human resource (HR) management department. The HR department can play a critical role in selecting the best individual and also tailoring the program based on the individual's personality.

With regards to delivery, many methods such as simulations and field experiences are available. Best practices suggest that a combination of the various methods may work best. For instance, employees can be exposed to instructional material about the new culture and also participate in field trips. Traditional academic courses in cross-cultural management can also be effective.[31] However, a combination of methods is likely to enhance learning. Many experts also suggest the use of online facilities and programs to deliver training. For instance, important cultural information can be made available online for viewing at the employee's discretion. It is also advisable to provide training both before and after the employee is on the assignment. Such approaches maximize learning and adaptation to the culture.

International Experience and Learning Styles

IB EMERGING MARKET
STRATEGIC INSIGHT

Experts agree that the best approach to train employees to become more culturally intelligent is to send them on actual international assignments. In this scenario, the best predictor of cultural intelligence is the number of years of work experience someone has worked abroad. Spending years abroad gives the employee the ability to learn from such experiences and to become a better cross-cultural manager. However, research also suggests that employees do not equally benefit from such experiences. Some employees learn more from international experience than others. Why do some employees learn more than others from the same international experience?

A recent study of international executives in China and Ireland provides some insights into this question. The researchers surveyed the learning styles of these executives and found that learning styles did indeed have an impact on how much these executives learned from the international assignment. The researchers found that those executives who had a divergent learning style were more likely to benefit and learn from international experiences compared to executives with other learning styles. A divergent learning style suggests that the learner is able to reflect and attach feelings to their experiences. In other words, they can look at a situation and understand assumptions and make changes as needed to adapt to the situation. In contrast, executives with other learning styles such as the assimilative learning style tend to be less focused on people in situations and more focused on abstract understanding of the situation. Such learning styles tend to be less effective for executives.

For the multinational, the implication is that they must work to train their executives to adapt the best learning style to gain maximally from international experiences. Multinationals should select those employees that display the highest propensity to learn through the divergent learning style. Others must also be encouraged to pay more attention to their feelings and to reflect when experiencing cross-cultural situations. Such experiences will help the executive get the most from the learning.

Source: Based on M. Li, W. H. Mobley and A. Kelly, 2013, "When do global leaders learn best to develop cultural intelligence? An investigation of the moderating role of experiential learning style," *Academy of Management Learning and Education*, *12*(1), pp. 32–50.

Finally, no training program can be complete without adequate evaluation. Experts suggest that programs be evaluated regularly. It is also advisable to use multiple measures of both success and failure. Best practices suggest that successful companies incorporate failure factors such as delayed productivity, lost opportunities, etc. Additionally, employees receiving training should be surveyed to determine their level of satisfaction and improved performance resulting from the training. Finally, human resource management departments of multinationals need to assess whether the cross-cultural training is being applied to the actual work setting.

Chapter Review

In this chapter, we discussed how crucial it is to understand cultures and cross-cultural differences. Understanding of culture is becoming more important as the world becomes more global and emerging markets become increasingly important to international expansion. Not only do companies get a better understanding of their markets and consumers if they have a better understanding of cultures, but their employees also perform better when sent on international assignments. Given the growth of international trade and cross-border operations, no company is immune to these forces, and you will benefit from understanding culture.

To understand how countries differ culturally, we looked at two of the most popular cultural frameworks. The Hofstede framework is certainly the one that has received the most attention and proposes that countries differ mostly on four cultural dimensions. However, we also integrated more recent research by considering the Global Leadership and Organizational Behavior (GLOBE) studies and two additional dimensions. We discussed many international business implications of these cultural differences.

One of the most important ways that national culture affects international business operations is through the business culture. We considered some of the most important cultural differences and implications for business culture. We also emphasized business etiquette as one of the important manifestations of a country's business culture.

We examined some of the dangers of making broad generalizations using these cultural dimensions. The best cultural students stay open-minded and are very careful about their interpretations. Finally, we examined some of the popular types of cross-cultural training and some of the best practices regarding design, delivery, and evaluation of such programs.

Discussion Questions

1   Discuss some of the major reasons why it is important to understand national culture.

2   Discuss three of Hofstede's national culture dimensions. What are some of the implications of these dimensions for international business?

3   What is future orientation? What can an MNC expect when it decides to invest in a country with high future orientation?

4   What is business culture? Does national culture affect business culture? Discuss some implications of national culture for business culture.

5   Discuss how national culture affects the business culture and the business etiquette in a country.

6   What are cultural paradoxes? How can one prepare against making wrong assessments of culture?

7   How can multinationals prepare their employees to understand cross-cultural differences?

International Business Skill Builder

Designing a Cross-cultural Training Program

Step 1: You have been approached by a large MNC with no operations yet in China or India. Research the selected countries in the popular press and make a list of cultural differences compared to the US.

Step 2: For each cultural difference, discuss some of the implications for someone who will conduct negotiations in that country.

Step 3: For each country, design a training program that will allow a negotiator to prepare him or herself for cross-cultural differences.

Step 4: Discuss how the training program will be different if you are asked to develop a program for expatriates.

Chapter Internet Activity

Visit the Executive Planet website by going to **www.executiveplanet.com**. Explore the business etiquette of the countries listed.

Key Concepts

- business culture
- business etiquette
- country clusters
- cultural beliefs
- cultural intelligence
- cultural norms
- cultural paradoxes
- cultural symbols, stories, and rituals
- customs
- ethnocentricity
- field experiences
- future orientation
- higher-rigor cultural training progams
- high-context languages

- Hofstede model of national culture
- humane orientation
- individualism
- low-rigor cultural training programs
- low-context languages
- masculinity
- national culture
- performance orientation
- power distance
- simulations
- stereotyping
- subcultures
- uncertainty avoidance

CASE 7

BUSINESS > INTERNATIONAL

A Clash of Cultures

Ted Dorman was looking forward to his new assignment as plant manager at a newly formed American-Mexican joint venture in Guadalajara, Mexico. The American company, Sterling Metal, produced hardware and decorative fixtures for furniture manufacturers in the United States and Mexico. The new joint venture was an attempt to lower labor costs by operating in Mexico.

Ted had worked at Sterling Metal since graduating from college with a degree in accounting. He had worked his way up in the company through accounting, and eventually shifted his career focus to production. Ted found the challenges of managing the production function very interesting, and he was successful in this area. His position at the new company, SterMexicana, would be a promotion for him, and he looked forward to the opportunity of building a new company.

Although Ted had not worked outside the United States before, he felt confident that his managerial abilities would transfer "south of the border." He and his wife enjoyed vacationing in Cancun and they both liked Mexican food, so the idea of spending a few years building a new company in Mexico appealed to him. Ted's wife, Kim was not as excited about the move, since she and their two small children would have to leave family and friends. Kim would also probably not be working in Mexico, as she had done in the United States.

Before the move, both Ted and Kim read travel books on Mexico and visited Guadalajara to select suitable housing. While Kim had reservations about the move, she felt that it would be a good opportunity for Ted and that she and the children would learn to adapt to their new surroundings. After all, she reasoned, they were only planning on living in Mexico for two years; just long enough for Ted to get the plant up and running and profitable. None of the Dorman's spoke Spanish fluently; however, Kim thought that she could get by, since she had taken three years of Spanish in high school. She had heard that Guadalajara was home to a large expatriate community, and that she could isolate herself and the children from Mexican culture if she felt the need. Ted would be working with English speakers mostly, and many people at the plant could do translating for him. A number of SterMexicana managers had been to the United States and were familiar with its culture. Ted and Kim concluded that cultural adaptation would not be difficult, and no matter how hard the assignment, its short duration was manageable.

When the family arrived in Guadalajara, Manuel Angel Menendez Mata met them at the airport. Manuel would be Ted's Mexican counterpart, acting in the official capacity of assistant plant manager, and unofficially as a cultural mentor. Ted and Kim were surprised by the warmth and friendliness of Manuel and his wife Adriana, and they felt very welcomed by their new Mexican friends. Over the next few days

CASE 7
cont'd

Manuel and Adriana helped the new expatriates get settled in and familiar with their new home. Ted appreciated the personal attention Manuel was giving him and his family; however, Ted was anxious to begin discussing the needs of the new business. It sometimes seemed to Ted that Manuel didn't care to discuss the business or that he was very excited about the new opportunity. Manuel seemed more interested in showing Ted and his family the city and discussing its history, politics, and culture.

Once the Dorman family had settled in, Ted was able to turn his attention toward the business. He had many matters to attend to, including a review of the preliminary work Manuel had done in securing the facility, hiring a workforce, and establishing an organizational structure. Manuel explained what he had done and how it would work well. He predicted that the new plant would be fully functional in less than two weeks. Ted was very impressed with Manuel's work and looked forward to the opening of the plant.

During their many conversations, Ted felt that Manuel was very friendly and polite, but that he was a bit too formal and not very relaxed. Manuel wore a suit and tie, even when Ted told him that a more casual form of dress would be appropriate. Ted stated that he had no intention of ever wearing a tie the whole time he would be in Mexico. Manuel sometimes referred to Ted as "Mr. Dorman," even though Ted had instructed him to call him by his first name. During their meetings with outside business associates, Ted noticed that Manuel was even more formal. Manuel, who had visited the United States many times and spoke English very well, understood that Americans were more relaxed when it came to such matters, but he was not happy when Ted began to call him "Manny." Manuel was also unhappy with Ted's refusal to recognize his title, "Licenciado" (licensed one), and that he sometimes referred to him as Senor Mata.

Although things seemed to be progressing toward the opening of the plant, Ted began to worry that Manuel's estimate of when the plant would be functional was too optimistic. Manuel insisted that everything was on schedule and that there would be no problems. It did, however, become obvious as the days went by that the plant was not going to be ready, as Manuel had promised. Ted felt that he had been misled by Manny and that he would have to explain to his superiors back in the US why the plant was not going to open on schedule. Manuel finally admitted that some problems had developed with work permits, but he assured Ted that the plant would be operational in an additional week's time. The plant finally opened, five weeks past the scheduled date.

This delay had caused tension between Manuel and Ted, and Ted felt that he could not trust Manuel. Manuel felt that Ted was too impatient, and that he was not sensitive enough to the problems sometimes found in conducting business in Mexico. Manuel complained to a friend that Ted was trying to do business in Mexico, "gringo style." He offered as an example the failed attempt Ted had made to establish a business relationship with a new supplier. Manuel had arranged for a business

CASE 7
cont'd

lunch between Ted, himself, and representatives from a well-respected metals supplier. Manuel explained how Ted offended the Mexican businessmen by attempting to get down to business quickly. The supplier's representatives felt that Ted was too concerned about business matters, especially price, and that he was rushing to close a deal. They were also offended when Manuel offered to take the visiting businessmen on a tour of the city and show then some important cultural sites and Ted refused to come along. Ted later told Manuel that he felt that the suppliers were not really serious about getting SterMexicana's business, and that, if they wanted to do business with the company, they would have to send only one representative to his office with samples and a price list. Ted told Manuel that he would no longer spend hours discussing politics, sports, and history without any consideration given to the actual business deal.

The plant had been functioning for about six months without any serious problems when Ted received word from corporate headquarters that the plant needed to improve its efficiency. The quality of the product was considered acceptable; however, the American managers were disappointed with the productivity of the plant. Sterling's main incentive for investing in Mexico was the desire to reduce its labor costs and improve its overall operational efficiency. Ted worried that his career mobility was in serious jeopardy if he did not make major improvements. With this in mind, Ted began to look more carefully at Manuel's work.

From the beginning Ted had turned over to Manuel the day-to-day responsibility for running the plant, but he now felt that he would have to intervene and make some significant changes. After analyzing the situation Ted concluded that three major changes should be made. He proposed to Manuel that an incentive pay system be introduced, that a more participative approach to decision making be implemented, and that a number of workers be fired.

The productivity level of the plant was considered low by American standards, and Ted felt that there was simply no incentive for workers to do more than the minimum level of work. He proposed a pay-for-performance plan in which workers would essentially be paid on a piece-rate basis. The workers would also be given more responsibility for planning and organizing their work, and, in some cases, even planning their own schedules. Ted felt that a more flexible scheduling system would eliminate the excessive time off requested by many workers to handle family matters. Ted also created a list of the lowest-performing workers and instructed Manuel to fire all of them immediately. Since the unemployment rate was much higher in Mexico than in the United States, Ted reasoned that he would have no problem replacing the workers.

Manuel was stunned by what he was hearing from Ted. Manuel was upset, first, that Ted had chosen to invade his areas of responsibility, and he was further upset by Ted's recommendations. Manuel felt that Ted was being too aggressive and insensitive in labor relations matters, and that his recommendations would not be successful in Mexico. He told Ted that there would be problems with these proposed changes; however, Ted did not seem to want to listen.

CASE 7
cont'd

Although Manuel did not agree with the recommendations, he did as Ted had instructed and began by firing some of the employees Ted had targeted as low performers. He then implemented the pay-for-performance plan and attempted to explain how it would work. Most workers felt confused by the complex, flexible working-hours plan, which involved basic quotas, a two-tiered pay system, and a time borrowing option, which could be used for personal time off, such as doctor's appointments. Manuel simplified the plan so that workers could go home when they had met their quota, or they could continue to work for additional compensation at a slightly lower per-unit rate. Ted felt that workers would be willing to work longer hours even at a reduced rate if their total compensation would rise. After all, he reasoned, "Mexico is a dirt-poor country and people really need money." Finally, Manuel told the plant supervisors about the plan to empower factory workers and allow them some of the decision-making authority that the supervisors had exercised in the past.

Ted had high hopes that his recommendations for change would produce significant improvements at SterMexicana. He was aware that Mexican culture was different from his; however, he felt that business activities were for the most part universal and that efficiency was not a cultural issue. Ted felt that the proposed changes would result in an immediate improvement in overall operating efficiency.

Slowly, however, Ted began to realize that problems were developing with his recommendations. The first problem he confronted was notification that severance pay would have to be paid to the employees he had recently fired. Ted was unaware, and Manuel did not mention, that Mexican law does not operate the same way as US law, in which workers are considered to be hired at will and subject to at-will termination. Ted was also surprised to learn that not all the employees he had targeted for termination had, in fact, been fired. After investigating the situation further, he discovered that five of the employees whom he had instructed to be fired were still working for the company. Ted was shocked to learn that the five employees were close relatives of Manuel. When confronted with this fact, Manuel just shrugged his shoulders and told Ted that he could not bring himself to fire them.

Although Ted was upset with Manuel's insubordination, he was far more concerned with the lack of any productivity gains at the plant. He was told that most workers did complete their tasks more quickly under the incentive plan; however, they elected to go home rather than work additional hours for more money. Ted was confused by this behavior so he asked some of the supervisors to explain it. They didn't provide satisfactory answers so Ted decided that he should conduct interviews with the employees themselves. Working through an interpreter, Ted asked workers about their jobs and what he could do to make them more productive. He was frustrated by the lack of responses he was getting from the employees. When Ted probed more deeply he discovered that the supervisors had not implemented the participative management practices he had ordered.

CASE 7
cont'd

Faced with poor operating results during the first year of operation, Ted wondered if the decision to take the job in Mexico had been a mistake. To make matters worse, Ted's family was very unhappy about living in Mexico. Ted had been working long hours at the plant and had basically discounted the complaints he had heard from his wife and children. At this point he began to feel that perhaps they were right in their frequent criticisms of Mexican culture. With over a year left in his assignment in Mexico Ted felt frustrated and wondered what he should do next.

CASE DISCUSSION POINTS:

1 What mistakes did Ted make in his management of SterMexicana?
2 What role did culture play in the events of the case?
3 What should Ted do now to correct the situation?

Case prepared by Charles A. Rarick

Notes

1 G. Hofstede, 2001, *Culture's Consequences: Comparing Values, Behaviors, Institutions, and Organizations Across Nations* (2nd edn), Thousand Oaks, CA: Sage.
2 Cynthia Waller Vallario, 2006, "Creating an environment for global diversity," *Financial Executive*, 22(3), pp. 50–52.
3 *The Economist*, 2008, "The challengers," January 12, pp. 62–64.
4 Bradley L. Kirkman, Kevin B. Lowe and Cristina B. Gibson, 2006, "A quarter century of culture's consequences: A review of empirical research incorporating Hofstede's cultural values framework," *Journal of International Business Studies*, 37, pp. 285–320; V. Taras, P. Steel and B. L. Kirkman, 2011, "Three decades of research on national culture in the workplace: Do the differences still make a difference?" *Organizational Dynamics*, 40, 189–198.
5 V. Taras, P. Steel and B. L. Kirkman, 2011, "Three decades of research on national culture in the workplace: Do the differences still make a difference?" *Organizational Dynamics*, 40, 189–198.
6 R. J. House, P. J. Hanges, M. Javidan, P. W. Dorfman and V. Gupta (eds), 2004, *Culture, Leadership and Organizations: The GLOBE Study of 62 Societies*, Thousand Oaks, CA: Sage.
7 G. Hofstede, 2001, *Culture's Consequences: Comparing Values, Behaviors, Institutions, and Organizations Across Nations* (2nd edn), Thousand Oaks, CA: Sage.
8 Bradley L. Kirkman, Kevin B. Lowe and Cristina B. Gibson, 2006, "A quarter century of culture's consequences: A review of empirical research incorporating Hofstede's cultural values framework," *Journal of International Business Studies*, 37, pp. 285–320.
9 V. Taras, B. L. Kirkman and P. Steel, 2010, "Examining the impact of culture's consequences: A three-decade, multilevel, meta-analytic review of Hofstede's cultural value dimensions," *Journal of Applied Psychology*, 95(3), pp. 405–439.
10 Wirefeed, 2007, "Bridging Indian–US business cultures: Will the twain meet?" *The Hindustan Times*, January 21.
11 Shannon Klie, 2006, "Cultural training a 'two-way street'," *Canadian HR Reporter*, 19(16), p. 9.
12 Rhonda Singer, 2006, "Watch for cultural biases in assessing employees," *Canadian HR Reporter*, 19(12), pp. 15.
13 Jena McGregor, 2008, "The right perks," *BusinessWeek*, January 28, pp. 42–43.

14 Bradley L. Kirkman, Kevin B. Lowe and Cristina B. Gibson, 2006, "A quarter century of culture's consequences: A review of empirical research incorporating Hofstede's cultural values framework," *Journal of International Business Studies*, 37, pp. 285–320.

15 V. Taras, P. Steel and B. L. Kirkman, 2011, "Three decades of research on national culture in the workplace: Do the differences still make a difference?" *Organizational Dynamics*, 40, 189–198.

16 R. J. House, P. J. Hanges, M. Javidan, P. W. Dorfman and V. Gupta (eds), 2004, *Culture, Leadership and Organizations: The GLOBE Study of 62 Societies*, Thousand Oaks, CA: Sage.

17 R. J. House, P. J. Hanges, M. Javidan, P. W. Dorfman and V. Gupta (eds), 2004, *Culture, Leadership and Organizations: The GLOBE Study of 62 Societies*, Thousand Oaks, CA: Sage.

18 Mansour Javidan, Peter W. Dorfman, Mary Sully de Luque and Robert J. House, 2006, "In the eye of the beholder: Cross-cultural lessons in leadership from project GLOBE," *The Academy of Management Perspectives*, February, pp. 67–90.

19 Jena McGregor, 2008, "To adapt, ITT lets go of unpopular ratings," *BusinessWeek*, January 28, p. 46.

20 Joyce S. Osland, Allan Bird, June Delano and Matthew Jacob, 2000, "Beyond sophisticated stereotyping: Cultural sensemaking in context," *The Academy of Management Executive*, 14(1), pp. 65–79.

21 Joyce S. Osland, Allan Bird, June Delano and Matthew Jacob, 2000, "Beyond sophisticated stereotyping: Cultural sensemaking in context," *The Academy of Management Executive*, 14(1), pp. 65–79.

22 William Maurice Baker and F. Douglas Roberts, 2006, "Managing the costs of expatriation," *Strategic Finance*, 87(11), pp. 35–41.

23 Lisa N. Littrell, Eduardo Salas, Kathleen P. Hess, Michael Paley and Sharon Riedel, 2006, "Expatriate preparation: A critical analysis of 25 years of cross-cultural training research," *Human Resource Development Review*, 5(3), pp. 355–388.

24 P. Charoensukmongkol, 2016, "Cultural intelligence and export performance of small and medium enterprises in Thailand: Mediating roles of organizational capabilities," *International Small Business Journal*, 34(1), pp. 105–122.

25 J. Eisenberg, H. Lee, F. Bruck, B. Brenner, M. Claes, J. Mironski and R. Bell, 2013, "Can business schools make students culturally competent? Effects of cross-cultural management courses on cultural intelligence," *Academy of Management Learning and Education*, 12(4), pp. 603–621.

26 Lisa N. Littrell and Eduardo Salas, 2005, "A review of cross-cultural training: Best practices, guidelines, and research needs," *Human Resource Development Review*, 4(3), pp. 305–334.

27 Leandra Celaya and Jonathan Swift, 2006, "Pre-departure cultural training: US managers in Mexico," *Cross Cultural Management: An International Journal*, 13(3), pp. 230–243.

28 J. Eisenberg, H. Lee, F. Bruck, B. Brenner, M. Claes, J. Mironski and R. Bell, 2013, "Can business schools make students culturally competent? Effects of cross-cultural management courses on cultural intelligence," *Academy of Management Learning and Education*, 12(4), pp. 603–621.

29 Leandra Celaya and Jonathan Swift, 2006, "Pre-departure cultural training: US managers in Mexico," *Cross Cultural Management: An International Journal*, 13(3), pp. 230–243.

30 M. Li, W. H. Mobley and A. Kelly, 2013, "When do global leaders learn best to develop cultural intelligence? An investigation of the moderating role of experiential learning style," *Academy of Management Learning and Education*, 12(1), pp. 32–50. Lisa N. Littrell and Eduardo Salas, 2005, "A review of cross-cultural training: Best practices, guidelines, and research needs," *Human Resource Development Review*, 4(3), pp. 305–334.

31 J. Eisenberg, H. Lee, F. Bruck, B. Brenner, M. Claes, J. Mironski and R. Bell, 2013, "Can business schools make students culturally competent? Effects of cross-cultural management courses on cultural intelligence," *Academy of Management Learning and Education*, 12(4), pp. 603–621.

CHAPTER 8

The Strategic Implications of Economic, Legal, and Religious Institutions for International Business

After reading this chapter you should be able to:

- Understand the meaning of institutional voids within the context of emerging markets.

- Understand the consequent importance of institutions and their impact on both individuals and MNCs.

- Know the basic political and economic systems and implications for international business operations in emerging markets.

- Appreciate the various legal systems around the world.

- Understand political risk and ways companies can prepare for political risk.

- Learn about the world's key religions and implications for multinational operations.

- Know how MNCs can prepare for institutional voids in emerging markets.

institutional voids
absence of typical
mechanisms that exist in
more developed markets
to regulate market
activities

International Business   *Preview IB Emerging Market Strategic Insight*

Institutional Voids

Emerging markets are characterized by institutional voids. **Institutional voids** refer to the "absence of specialized intermediaries, regulatory systems and contract enforcing mechanisms" that companies can typically count on in more developed markets. These voids suggest that entities or other institutions that are present to support markets are often weak or non-existent in emerging markets. For example, entrepreneurs in emerging markets may not always be able to pursue their entrepreneurial interests because institutional voids create an environment where these entrepreneurs may not have access to financial resources. Institutional voids mean that those lending money may not always be able to recover the money they lent.

Another important contributor to institutional voids is that local governments are weak at formulating or enforcing regulations. Such an environment can result in existing laws not being respected. In fact, authorities in countries such as India, China, and Russia have been willing to let multinationals violate existing regulations to encourage foreign direct investment. Such poor formulation and lax enforcement have resulted in environmental pollution, violation of labor regulations, and even poor consumer regulations.

As others have also pointed out, institutional voids can also result in a business environment where bribery is expected to conduct business. Recent surveys suggest that employees in multinationals operating in emerging markets tend to observe more instances of bribery relative to other markets. Such data also suggest that institutional voids can have damaging effects on the global business environment.

Source: Based on S. Chakrabarty and E. Bass 2013, "Encouraging entrepreneurship: Microfinance, knowledge support, and the costs of operating in institutional voids," *Thunderbird International Business Review, 55*(5), pp. 545–562; D. Currell and D. Bradley, 2012, "Greased palms, giant headaches," *Harvard Business Review*, September, pp. 21–23; T. Khanna and K. Palepu, 1997, "Why focused strategies may be wrong for emerging markets," *Harvard Business Review, 75*(4), pp. 41–51; M. Zhao, J. Tan and S. H. Park, 2014, "From voids to sophistication: Institutional environment and MNC CSR crisis in emerging markets," *Journal of Business Ethics, 122*, pp. 655–674.

The Preview IB Emerging Market Strategic Insight portrays the environment facing anyone interested in doing business in emerging markets. An understanding of international business is not complete without an adequate understanding of the environment facing any business. Specifically, important elements of the institutional environment such as the political and legal environment are crucial. The Preview IB Emerging Market Strategic Insight shows that both the lack of properly functioning institutions and poor enforcement of such institutions are playing important roles in shaping the business environment facing those doing business in emerging markets. It therefore becomes critical for the international business manager to understand these institutions and how such voids can be addressed.

This chapter therefore focuses on typical institutions and how their absences or weaknesses create voids. Although there are many institutions, three seem to be of most relevance to understanding emerging markets; namely, the economic system, the legal system, and religion. This chapter therefore contains several major sections. In the first section, you are introduced to a basic definition of institutions and the effects they have on both organizations and individuals. In the second section, you will be exposed to critical elements of the political environment with a focus on emerging markets. In the third section we will look at some of the key aspects of the legal system and the different types of legal systems around the world. We will also examine the legal system in the light of emerging markets. In the fourth section, we will examine some of the world's most important religions, another key institution that affects international business. We discuss key international business implications of each institution. Finally, we will also discuss ways that MNCs can operate to deal with challenges inherent in institutional voids.

After reading this chapter you should understand some of the key institutions affecting international business in emerging markets. You will be able to comprehend some of the key elements of a country's political environment through an understanding of the various types of economic systems. You should be able to recognize some of the ways legal systems are different around the world. You should also be able to understand some of the basic religions practiced by people around the world. You should understand the implications of these various aspects of the environment for international business. Finally, you should be able to understand the various aspects of these institutions in emerging markets and how the voids they create can be dealt with.

Social Institutions

A **social institution** is "a complex of positions, roles, norms, and values lodged in particular types of social structures and organizing relatively stable patterns of human resources with respect to fundamental problems in … sustaining viable societal structures within a given environment".[1] In other words, similar to national culture, social institutions provide boundaries and norms that guide both companies and individuals regarding appropriate behavior.

Why should you be concerned about social institutions? Chapter 7 discussed the many cultural differences impacting international business. However, an understanding of a country's business environment is not complete without an appropriate understanding of social institutions such as the economic system and the legal and religious environment. Each of these social institutions has an important impact on how business is conducted in the country. Without an understanding of these social institutions, it is difficult to have a complete understanding of the environment facing the multinational.

Furthermore, as we discussed in Chapter 7, understanding a country only through culture has some drawbacks. Many of Hofstede's cultural dimensions are outdated, while the GLOBE project also provides a static view of culture. However, changes in many countries today suggest that institutions are gradually changing the way things are done in a country. Such changes suggest that, in addition to an appropriate understanding of culture, we also need to get a solid understanding of institutions in order to better appreciate a country's environment.

Developed economies tend to have institutions that are typically stable and supportive of market operations. However, as mentioned earlier, such institutions tend to be weak or nonexistent in emerging markets. As such, MNCs have to contend with an environment that may not always be as supportive of efficient market operations. Such challenges also need to be understood to achieve strong international business. Consider the IB Emerging Market Strategic Insight regarding business in an Arab context.

As the IB Emerging Market Strategic Insight shows, because of institutional voids and the absence of functioning market intermediaries, Arab societies have developed a system that favors building of relationships. *Wasta*, heavily influenced by Islamic values of social solidarity and loyalty to the tribe, suggests that MNCs need to strive to build relationships if they want to succeed in Arab markets. In fact, recent research also argues that MNCs can be successful getting access to important government contracts in the region only if they have access to appropriate *Wasta*.[2] Losing *Wasta* is extremely disastrous for any international company.

Given the above, it is important for the multinational manager to understand how critical relevant institutions function. In the next section, we consider one of the most critical institutions, namely the economic system.

social institutions complex of positions, roles, norms, and values lodged in particular types of social structures

"Wasta" in the Context of Arab Business-to-Business Relationships

IB EMERGING MARKET
STRATEGIC INSIGHT

Business models in the Western world typically tend to be based on more individualistic tendencies. In the presence of institutions supportive of exchanges, negotiations tend be more impersonal. What is being exchanged tends to be much more important than who are making these exchanges. It is therefore not surprising to see that decision-making styles in Western-based multinationals are often more decentralized and flexible. People making the decisions are not as important as the nature of the decisions themselves.

Although the Arab world has much to offer in terms of business opportunities and market size, it has been generally ignored by business researchers. However, Arab societies are characterized by significant differences in terms of business system compared to Western societies. Adapting to these differences is critical if the MNC wants to succeed in Arab societies. For example, Arab cultures tend to be much more collective, placing significant emphasis on group orientations and family connections. Arab societies tend to also be low trust societies whereby there is reluctance to rely on non-family members for important business decisions. As a result, in contrast to the Western world, Arab business models center around building relationships. In such cases, who makes the exchanges tends to be much more important than what is exchanged.

An important mechanism that Arab societies have developed to deal with the preference for relationships is *Wasta*. *Wasta*, which means in the middle, is a form of dispute resolution that originated from the tribal origins of most Arab societies in the Middle East and North Africa regions. These societies were based on tribal structures as a result of living in desert conditions that required collective efforts to combat the inherent challenges of such an environment. Individuals in such societies have therefore developed strong loyalty for those who are in their tribe or family. Such loyalty to the tribe has also been heavily influenced by the critical emphasis Islam places on the importance of the family and reciprocal support.

Wasta has a strong impact on business systems in the Arab world today. Arab businesses will tend to prefer others from similar tribes to do business. Additionally, *Wasta*'s modern evolution has also meant that an individual can gain key benefits by having another person intervene on his or her behalf with a third party. Such actions often mean that a business may get a contract not based on merit but based on who is intervening on their behalf. Western MNCs are finding that it is not always easy to operate in such an environment.

Source: Based on R. Berger, A. Silbiger, R. Herstein and B. R. Barnes, 2015, "Analyzing business-to-business relationships in an Arab context," *Journal of World Business*, 50, pp. 454–464; M. Kilani, R. A. Junidi and R. A. Riziq, 2015, "The role that nepotism (Wasta) plays in conflict and conflict management within groups in private organizations in Jordan and MENA region," *Middle East Journal of Business*, 10(3), pp. 59–69.

Economic Systems

economic system
structures and processes that guide conduct of business

The **economic system** refers to the structures and processes that guide the conduct of business activities that lead to the production of goods and services consumed by the members of a society. The economic system can be characterized according to the degree to which the government or private individuals are allowed to make economic decisions guiding production. At one extreme, the government owns and controls all production resources, thereby resulting in a centrally planned economy. At the other extreme, private individuals are allowed to make the majority of economic decisions, thus describing a capitalist society. Because of the differences in terms of who makes economic and production decisions, multinationals need to be aware of these issues when engaged in international business.

Types of Economic Systems

The **capitalist or market economy** refers to an economic system where production activities are "decentralized to private-property-rights holders (or their agents) who carry out these activities for the purpose of making profits in a competitive market".[3] In other words, in capitalist societies private individuals make most economic and production decisions and the government does not interfere in such matters. Examples of capitalist economies include the United Kingdom, Canada, Hong Kong, and the USA. When applied to the case of the multinational, the capitalist multinational exists to produce value for shareholders.[4]

In contrast, the **socialist or command economy** is one where production resources are owned by the state and production decisions are centrally coordinated.[5] In such societies, the government owns and controls all resources. The government decides what will be produced, in what quantities, and the price at which the products will be sold. Instead of allowing the invisible forces of the market to dictate production, as is the case in a market economy, the government's hand plays a very visible role in all production matters. In its most extreme form, the command economy is found in communist societies. There remain few command economies today and examples include Cuba and North Korea.

Capitalism and socialism are the extremes of the economic system spectrum. In reality, many countries fall in between these two extremes. Such economies are known as the **mixed economy**, which combines aspects of the capitalist and socialist economic systems. In such economies, the state determines that some sectors of the economy cannot be run by private interests and thus intervenes and takes control of such sectors (e.g. health care and education). The state makes resource allocation and production decisions. Countries such as Sweden, France, Denmark, Italy, and India are examples of mixed economies.

When looking at multinationals, the corporatist model is the best representation of the mixed economy.[6] In such cases, shareholder value does not drive the corporation. Instead, the government acts as a partner to achieve goals that are mutually compatible. Rather than allow markets to be the basis for economic decisions, firm goals are guided by negotiations between the government and these firms.

Mixed economies ideally combine advantages of the market-based and centrally planned economies. Thus, while private decisions about production are allowed, the government controls those sectors that it sees as critical to national stability and security. However, many countries have found that government control of specific sectors has led to waste, economic inefficiencies, and lack of accountability and responsibility regarding cost control. The more recent evidence thus suggests that more countries are moving more towards market-based economies.

International Business Implications of Economic Systems

As discussed above, while there are three major types of economic markets, the evidence suggests that most emerging markets tend to be more of the mixed economy type. In such cases, the government will often intervene in the marketplace to influence various aspects of the market. However, such intervention may not always be expected or consistent with expectations MNCs have in developed markets. Consider the following examples:

capitalist or market economy
economic system where private individuals make economic and production decisions

socialist or command economy
economic system where the government owns production resources and makes production decisions

mixed economy
economic system that combines elements of the capitalist and socialist economies

- Recent development suggests that the Chinese economy may be slowing down as a result of slowing demand and rising debts. Such indicators coupled with other negative macroeconomic indicators have resulted in massive sell-offs on the Shanghai stockmarket. However, the Chinese government has intervened in several ways to contain the sellout. They suspended transactions after 90 minutes. Additionally, because of the rapid selling of shares, there has been a massive outflow of capital. The Chinese government has also intervened to buy yuan in a bid to slow down the devaluation of the currency.[7]
- In India, Facebook has worked with local mobile-telecoms operators to provide Free Basics, a program that allows users in India to get free access to Facebook and a number of other online services. However, this service has met with many critics. Some believe that the service is a way for Facebook to grab the large number of Indians who are now online. Others feel like Facebook will be able to get access to too much intelligence data. As a consequence, the government branch that regulates mobile operators (the Telecom Regulatory Authority of India, TRAI) has asked Facebook to suspend the program. TRAI is still gathering data and will decide whether the service can continue.[8]
- In Nigeria, the South African mobile-telecom company MTN faced a massive fine. The Nigerian government had suggested that the company had broken important rules when registering SIM cards. The government imposed a fine of $1,000 per incorrectly registered account thereby amounting to a $5.2 billion fine. Other companies have also faced volatile regulations in Nigeria.[9] Although Nigeria presents MNCs with tremendous potential, there are also significant risks.

The evidence presented above suggests that MNCs operating in many emerging markets should be prepared for governmental intervention. However, such intervention and influence may not be consistent. It therefore becomes critical for MNC managers to properly assess the country's economic environment and the likelihood that governmental intervention may occur. In that context, experts make several suggestions. Consider the following Emerging Market Ethical Challenge.

As the Emerging Market Ethical Challenge shows, MNCs operating in emerging economies have to be aware of some of the intervention in free markets. As you will see later, such intervention also creates some voids that MNCs must prepare against.

Another critical international business implication pertaining to economic systems applies to transition economies. **Transition economies** are those societies that are moving from socialism to a more market-based system. The post 1980s saw a large number of countries in Russia, Eastern Europe, and Asia (i.e. China and Vietnam) undergo governmental efforts to promote capitalism. Many of these economies are also emerging markets. For most MNCs, such open-market policies have presented incredible opportunities as they provide these companies with new markets and access to skilled but relatively cheap labor. However, such opportunities have also come with significant challenges.

An important challenge for most MNCs in transition economies has been to understand the lingering effects of communism and its effects on workers and companies. Under socialism, most enterprises were factories with no need for cost control, lacking strategic planning, accounting, or marketing departments. The government often guaranteed the survival and inefficiencies of these firms by setting up prices that were not accurate reflections of costs. Banks also were managed according to the needs of central planners, where loans were often made to enterprises on the basis of connections and personal relationships rather than credit-worthiness.

transition economies economies that are transitioning from socialism to capitalism

Assessing Potential for Governmental Intervention

In Nigeria, several South African multinationals have failed despite significant investment in the country. Why such failures? A big part is that these multinationals were not necessarily aware of the particular influence the government has on the business landscape. Many of these multinationals found that if they didn't have the right contacts at the ports, products would not move. For example, Woolworths has had to leave Nigeria because it took months before products it had imported would leave the port. How can companies anticipate such challenges? Experts suggest that MNC managers carefully consider the wider environment that businesses operate in. To understand the potential for governmental intervention, they suggest asking several questions:

- To whom are politicians accountable?
- Does the government go beyond business regulation and interfere with the running of businesses?
- How strong do local laws protect property rights?
- Are businesses dominated by family ties?
- Are foreign direct investments welcome in the country? What has been the experience of other multinationals?
- Is the media fairly independent? Can they report freely on issues?
- Are companies restricted in terms of where they can set up business in the country? How easy is it to set up a business?

Source: Based on *The Economist*, 2016, "Is it worth it," April 16, Special Report: Business in Africa, pp. 11–13; T. Khanna and K. G. Palepu, 2010, *Winning in Emerging Markets*, Boston, MA: Harvard Business Press.

These traditional approaches to doing business have resulted in significant hurdles for many of the transition economies. For example, workers may not necessarily trust MNCs as they no longer have the same job security as in the past. Furthermore, significant effort has to be devoted to encourage workers to trust each other to function effectively in teams. Multinationals also have to deal with inefficient financial systems and corrupt individuals. Furthermore, transition economies also still experience significant governmental interference. Consider the following BRIC Insight.

As the BRIC Insight shows, transition markets also present significant challenges that result in institutional voids. MNCs need to be astute scanners of the business environment and address these voids. At the end of this chapter, you will learn about some of the things MNCs can do to address such voids.

Doing Business in Russia   BRIC INSIGHT

Russia remains one of the most difficult places to do business. A survey of multinationals in over 50 cities placed Moscow as the worst place in the world to do business. As in many transition economies, setting up a business requires significant paperwork and many businesses consider such efforts as wasted time. Furthermore, because of the lack of clear rules and guidelines, government officials and bureaucrats will often make decisions based on their whims and personal relationships. Such lack of clear guidance is often a major deterrent for multinationals interested in investing in Russia.

The 2016 survey of the World Bank's "Doing Business" report also suggests that there are some specific areas where it is difficult even for local businesses to do business in Russia. The "Doing Business" project looks at the regulatory environment with respect to various aspects of running a business in 189 economies. The report suggests that Russia ranks 170 in terms of "trading across borders." This means that it is very burdensome for companies to try to import and export products. However, this ranking is not too surprising given that Russia has imposed many trade restrictions recently. For instance, it imposed a trade embargo on farm products from the European Union as retaliation against sanctions imposed by Western countries. As a result, local enterprises are trying to produce cheese to satisfy the local markets.

Two other problematic aspects of doing business in Russia are "dealing with construction permits" (time and cost to complete the formalities to build a warehouse—ranked 119) and "protecting minority shareholders" (degree to which minority shareholders' rights and interests are protected—ranked 66).

However, despite these challenges, Russia does have some bright spots. For example, it ranks fifth worldwide with respect to "enforcing contracts" (time and cost needed to resolve a commercial dispute) and ranks eighth along the "registering property" aspect (time and cost to transfer property).

Source: Based on *The Economist*, 2016, "Russia's dairy embargo: War and cheese," April 9, pp. 54–55; Alan M. Field, 2007, "Russia in the fast lane," *Journal of Commerce*, September 3, p. 1; www.doingbusiness.org (accessed April 2016).

---

index of economic freedom
index reflecting the ease of doing business in any given country

Economic systems thus have many important implications for international business. Different economic systems present different environments regarding decision making for resources and production. However, one other important component of the economic system is the degree of governmental interference in the conduct of business. In that context, MNCs may consider the **index of economic freedom**, which refers to "the absence of government coercion or constraint on the production, distribution, or consumption of goods and services beyond the extent necessary for citizens to protect and maintain liberty itself."[10] Since 1995, the Heritage Foundation, a US-based research foundation, has been constructing the index. The index includes ten indicators, ranging from trade policy (i.e. the degree to which the government hinders free trade through tariffs), taxation policies, and the level of governmental intervention in the economy to property rights (freedom to accumulate private property) and regulation (i.e. ease of obtaining a business license).

Free	Mostly Free	Moderately Free	Mostly Unfree	Repressed
Hong Kong	Ireland	Poland	Sri Lanka	Angola
Singapore	Canada	Peru	Egypt	Ecuador
Australia	Chile	Thailand	Indonesia	Argentina
Switzerland	Mauritius	France	Tanzania	Venezuela
New Zealand	Japan	Ghana	Vietnam	Burma
	Colombia	Mexico	China	Turkmenistan
	Taiwan	South Africa	Russia	Ukraine
	Czech Republic	Slovenia	Brazil	Cuba
	Norway	Armenia	Algeria	North Korea
	Finland	Jamaica	Nigeria	Bolivia
	Austria	Panama	Tunisia	Iran
	UAE		Kenya	Zimbabwe

Exhibit 8.1 Index of Economic Freedom

Source: Based on Heritage Foundation Index of Economic Freedom, www.heritage.org

Exhibit 8.1 shows selected countries and where they stand on the index of economic freedom. Representative countries are listed for each of the five categories of economic freedom, namely those nations that are (1) free, (2) mostly free, (3) moderately free, (4) mostly "unfree," and (5) repressed. MNCs can use the index to determine their presence in different countries. Obviously, they can expect higher levels of difficulty as they move into countries with less economic freedom.

As Exhibit 8.1 shows, many of the largest emerging markets such as China, India, South Africa, Indonesia, Nigeria, and Brazil are in the "mostly unfree" category. Such results are consistent with earlier discussions that such countries suffer from institutional voids that make the business environment less ideal. MNCs can therefore use this index to discuss how to adapt to the market as well as which area they need to target.

In this section, you were exposed to critical aspects of the economic system and how they influence business operations. In the next section, we consider another critical institution, namely the legal system.

Legal Systems

The **legal system** refers to the unique systems of regulations, laws, and rules that affect the choices made by individuals in any society and that govern the ways these individuals are responsible for their decisions and actions. For the MNC, of more importance is the international business law system representing the law and rules of any nation that affect the types of business decisions made in that country.[11] Consider the following IB Emerging Market Strategic Insight.

legal system
represents the unique systems of regulations, rules, and laws of a country

Market Regulation of the Coffee Industry in Kenya

IB EMERGING MARKET STRATEGIC INSIGHT

Although Kenyan Arabica coffee grown around Mount Kenya has a strong reputation worldwide, recent production of the coffee has hit a low of 45,000 tons. This is in sharp contrast to the record 127,000 tons that was harvested in the 1987-1988 harvest.

What led to such decline while the neighboring country of Uganda has seen a doubling of production? Experts attribute this decline partly to the ending of coffee quota by the global coffee cartel. However, many believe that the onerous regulation governing coffee sale in Kenya is also to blame. Instead of a market where buyers and sellers can compete to buy the coffee and sell directly to exporters, Kenyan regulations require that farmers deal with a number of intermediaries that ultimately reduces the price they are given. Most small local farmers belong to cooperatives that process the coffee beans for sale. Once the coffee beans are bagged, they are sold by one of the eight marketing agents to around 60 domestic and international coffee dealers. These transactions occur as auctions at the Nairobi Coffee Exchange.

Because of regulations requiring so many intermediaries, local farmers tend to receive lower prices. In fact, these farmers complain regularly that the coffee dealers tend to have agreements to keep prices low. The auctions are often hushed events where traders press buttons to signal their intention to buy. Additionally, many of the dealers and marketing agents tend to belong to the same sister companies. They can also collude to keep prices low.

Source: Based on *The Economist*, 2016, "Kenya coffee: A bitter harvest," March 26, pp. 80-81.

The IB Emerging Market Strategic Insight shows how important it is to understand the laws and regulations in any society if one wants to be able to compete internationally. Consider, for example, that in India, it is extremely hard to fire workers. Similarly, consider that an entrepreneur needs to go through 12 procedures that may take up to 97 days if they want to start a business in Indonesia.[12] Finally, consider that MNCs are facing increased regulations and have to contend with activists and local populations when considering mining operations in Latin America.[13] Ignoring aspects of the legal environment can be very costly and may doom the business from the start. In this section, you will be exposed to some of the most popular legal systems around the world, namely common law, civil law, and Islamic law. We then look at some international business implications of these legal systems.

Types of Legal Systems

common law
legal system based on the concept of legal precedence

civil law
legal system based on detailed set of rules and regulations that form part of the legal code

Common law originated in England and is practiced by many of the former British colonies, including the US. **Common law** is based on the concept of precedent, whereby the law is applied after an examination of past cases.[14] In common law, the judge tends to be very neutral and will allow lawyers for parties to demonstrate their cases. The lawyers will examine prior cases and make their arguments to convince a jury of their position. In common law, the choice of lawyers plays a critical role in successfully defending a case.[15]

Civil law, which can be traced back to the Romans, is based on a very detailed set of rules and regulations that forms part of a country's legal code. Cases are decided based on the legal code and there is usually no interpretation of laws according to previous cases. In contrast to common law, where the judge is more neutral, in civil law the judge is a key element in cases, taking on the role of lawyer in deciding what information is to be presented in deciding a case. The judge typically determines the extent of guilt. The jury is not used in civil law countries. Because of the use of established codes, civil law often tends to ignore specific circumstances of cases.

Another legal tradition practiced in many nations today is known as Islamic law. **Islamic law** is based on the Shari'ah, the Law taken from the Qur'an, Islam's sacred text. Islamic countries believe that all humans must live according to the structures prescribed in the Qur'an. The Qur'an expresses Islamic ethic and the ethical duties in life. However, as you will see later, it also contains rules that apply to conduct of business, such as general guidance regarding the need to honor contracts and appropriate behaviors in commercial transactions. We will discuss Islamic law and implications for international business in greater depth later when we examine religions.

Islamic law
legal tradition based on the Qur'an, Islam's sacred text

Exhibit 8.2 shows selected countries and their respective legal system.

Although one should be aware of the limits of generalizing legal system differences around the world, it is important to recognize the implications of a country's particular legal system on international business. For instance, it is usual for business contracts in common law countries to be very lengthy. The latter is necessary to ensure that all contingencies are covered. It is therefore important for MNCs to devote significant resources to understand a common law country's legal system through legal advice. Because of the need to interpret laws based on precedent, multinationals typically employ legal teams to navigate the legal environment.

In civil law countries, the legal system is less confrontational compared to common law countries. Instead of lawyers colliding to interpret the law, there is more reliance on written rules and regulations. As a consequence, fewer resources tend to be devoted to understanding the law. For instance, multinationals tend to be more concerned about precise wording in contracts to ensure consistency with the relevant codified laws. Consider the following BRIC Insight.

Common Law	Civil Law
Australia	Armenia
Bahamas	Azerbaijan
Cyprus	Belarus
Fiji	Belgium
Hong Kong	Cameroon
India	Denmark
Ireland	France
Japan	Luxembourg
Mexico	Montenegro
New Zealand	Panama
Tonga	Portugal
United Kingdom	Russia
USA	Serbia
Zambia	Taiwan

Exhibit 8.2 Legal Systems Around the World
Source: Based on CIA World Factbook, http://cia.gov/cia/publications/factbook

Legal Environment in China

China's legal environment has been very challenging for MNCs. As China has been transitioning to a more market-based economy where economic decisions are governed by demand and supply, MNCs are facing significant hurdles. For instance, consider that it is very difficult for Chinese financial firms to be sued in the US even when they operate there. Chinese authorities argue that abiding by US laws would violate China's state and banking secrecy laws. Similarly, MNCs have found it very difficult to sue Chinese companies for intellectual property copyrights violation. Chinese intellectual property regulations require that MNCs prove that trade secrets were stolen and such evidence is not easy to provide. Additionally, technology firms such as Google and Facebook are finding that they need to abide by local regulations whereby they are required to provide technical help and user data on matters that are related to terrorist activities.

However, while some have complained about the value of the Chinese legal system and the ability of the courts to enforce contracts, recent evidence suggests that MNCs can strategically structure contracts that are enforceable in Chinese courts. In 2016 China ranked 7th in the world in terms of the "enforcing contract" criteria of the World Bank. As such, if MNCs are cautious in devising properly crafted contracts, the chances of getting the Chinese courts to enforce such contracts are very successful. In fact, recent evidence suggests that well written contracts signal to Chinese partners the MNCs' care as well as intention. Well-written contracts also allow the Chinese partner to know what is expected of them.

How should contracts in China be structured? Experts suggest the following:

- Structure the contract in formal written form. Some MNCs tend to rely on emails and other communication and those may not be as effective in case of contract infringement.
- The written contract should be in Chinese. MNCs should work with lawyers fluent in Mandarin to translate the contracts. Additionally, rather than use the obscure language typical of US contracts, it is highly advisable that the language be kept as simple as possible. Furthermore, because China follows civil law, there is a preference for shorter and simpler contracts that do not repeat codes in the law. This is more typical in more common law countries such as the US and UK where contracts are much longer and more legalistic.
- Contracts should be specific about which laws and courts the MNCs will use if there is contract violation. This is important because MNCs will be more successful getting the contract enforced if they specify which laws could be broken. It is also more advisable to specify which Chinese courts will take the case. MNCs are also advised to deal with such cases in Chinese courts. As mentioned earlier, China is less likely to enforce a court award coming from some other country.
- Specify what the Chinese company needs to do to satisfy the contract in great detail. Do also specify damages in case the Chinese company violates the contract.

■ Finally, ensure that the contract is signed by a legal representative of the Chinese partner. In the US, contracts are based on the concept of "apparent authority." As long as someone is seen as having the authority to sign a contract, the company is liable for the terms of the contract. However, the legal representative of the Chinese partner must be the one signing the contract. Another alternative is for the Chinese company to stamp with their "chops." The chop is a unique seal assigned to each Chinese company.

Source: Based on *BusinessWeek*, 2016, "China—the government demands more data and boosts local companies," January 25–31, pp. 29–30; C. Carr and D. Harris, 2015, "Strategic contracting in China for foreign firms," *Thunderbird International Business Review*, *57*(3), May/June, pp. 241–254; D. C. K. Chow, 2014, "Navigating the minefield of trade secrets protection in China," *Vanderbilt Journal of Transnational Law*, *47*, pp. 1007–1048; J. Evie, 2015, "The great firewall of China," *ABA Journal*, *101*(11), p. 17.

Other Aspects of the Legal Environment: The "Doing Business" Project

While it is difficult to provide a comprehensive treatment of differences in the legal systems around the world, the World Bank, through its **"Doing Business" project**, provides valuable insight into the key issues that need to be taken into consideration when doing business in any nation. Earlier you saw some aspects of the Doing Business project in the context of doing business in Russia. In that context, the World Bank collects data worldwide and provides objective measures of the various aspects of the legal infrastructure in a society. Specifically, the World Bank considers various aspects of the regulative environment of any society. Here, you are exposed to four key aspects pertaining to international business; namely, starting a business, employing workers, getting credit, and enforcing contracts.

Any form of involvement in a new country requires an understanding of the various legal and bureaucratic requirements that need to be fulfilled. The "Starting a Business" measure provides an objective view of the various issues an entrepreneur or multinational needs to consider when starting a commercial or industrial business with over 50 employees. It includes the number of procedures that are needed to register a firm, the time spent for each procedure, the expenses associated with each procedure, and the minimum capital required as a percentage of income. This gives a good indication of what you may face when you decide to open a business in any selected country. Exhibit 8.3 below shows the rankings of selected countries on the "Starting a Business" dimension.

How can you use these rankings? Consider the following IB Emerging Market Strategic Insight.

A second crucial aspect of the legal environment is the enforcing of contracts. The World Bank's "Enforcing Contract" measure provides an indication of the time and cost involved in resolving commercial disputes. The index also considers the quality of the court system in the country. Why should MNCs be concerned by efficient contract enforcement? Many MNCs use strategic alliances or other forms of agreement to enter a new country. Most of these agreements are based on contracts, and a multinational's ability to have contracts respected is dependent on the degree to which a country enforces these contracts.

From an economic development, research suggests that efficient contract enforcement reflects basic respect of the law and protection of basic rights. Such characteristics tend to have positive effect on economic growth as well as a stronger business climate and innovation.[16]

Exhibit 8.4 and Exhibit 8.5 show various indices of "Enforcing Contract." Exhibit 8.4 shows the number of days it takes to resolve the commercial dispute by region.

"Doing Business" project
project undertaken by the World Bank providing important information about the ease of conducting business in various nations

Where to Start a Business

You have developed a product prototype that you believe will do very well. You also believe that you can manufacture and sell the product anywhere in the world. Where do you start your business and set up a plant? Consider Exhibit 8.3.

Country	Starting Business Rank
New Zealand	1
Canada	3
Australia	11
UK	17
South Korea	23
Russia	41
USA	49
Chile	62
Mexico	65
Peru	97
Tunisia	103
South Africa	120
China	136
Nigeria	139
Kenya	151
Haiti	188

Exhibit 8.3 "Starting a Business" Index
Source: Based on World Bank's "Doing Business" project, http://doingbusiness.org

As you can see, starting businesses in countries in many of the emerging markets tends to be more difficult. For instance, starting a business in the Latin American/Caribbean region can take an average of around ten procedures, with each procedure lasting over 70 days.

Similarly, both Latin America and the Middle East/North Africa region have the highest costs associated with starting a business. Many of the emerging markets ranked low on this index. In contrast, the members of the Organization for Economic Co-operation and Development (OECD), including most industrialized nations such as Canada, the UK, Germany, Italy, and the US, among others, have environments that are very conducive to setting up new businesses.

Source: Based on Doing Business website, www.doingbusiness.org

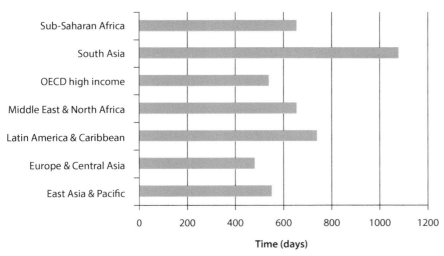

Exhibit 8.4 "Number of Days Taken to Resolve Contract Disputes" Index
Source: Based on World Bank's "Doing Business" project, http://doingbusiness.org

Exhibit 8.5 shows the attorney, enforcement, and court cost of as a percentage of the total claim. This also gives an idea of the costs of attorney fees as well as other court fees in resolving the disputes.

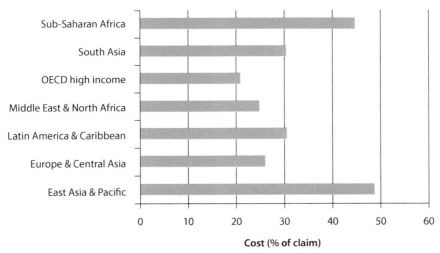

Exhibit 8.5 "Cost as a Percentage of Claim" Index
Source: Based on World Bank's "Doing Business" project, http://doingbusiness.org

Both Exhibits 8.4 and 8.5 show that contract enforcement is much more difficult in the South Asian, sub-Saharan African, and Latin America/Caribbean regions. Often these regions have less developed legal systems to deal with business matters. In contrast, the OECD countries, as well as Europe and the US, have a more developed infrastructure to enforce contracts.

Hence, as has been shown, adequate understanding of the legal context in any society is extremely important for any multinational operating in that country. The "Doing Business" project provides important insights in these areas. Next, we consider political risk.

Political Risk

Earlier in this chapter, you read about the various economic and legal systems. One aspect of the combined effects of the economic and legal system in a society is political risk. As such, in this section we look at political risk, some elements of political risk and what companies can do to minimize political risk.

political risk
threat of a country's social, political, or economic factors affecting a company's profitability

Political risk refers to the "threat that social, political or economic factors in a foreign country may affect the feasibility and profitability of an organization's global operations."[17] Political risk can take many forms. It can take the form of political interference by elected or unelected politicians.[18] It can also take the form of unilateral cancellation of contracts. In fact, many emerging markets have seen cancellations of airport management contracts (Hungary, Philippines, etc.) as a result of political risk. Airport management contracts tend to be more prone to political risk as they are public utilities that require large amounts of investment and are also very regulated.[19]

As more multinationals engage in foreign investments, they are being increasingly confronted with political risk. MNCs run the risk of destruction of their foreign plants or even the ability to repatriate currency. Nevertheless, many countries with high levels of political risk often offer the best opportunities. The challenge for the multinational is to accurately predict and manage such risks.

Political risk can impact a multinational negatively on many levels. For instance, political risk can influence the degree to which currency can be freely converted to other currency for use. Host governments may restrict the transfer of local currency into a freely usable currency, thereby limiting the multinational's access to its own capital. Furthermore, host governments can also place conditions on an MNC's ability to control its own plant, thus leading to governmental interference. Additionally, countries with high levels of political risk may also have higher levels of political violence and more contracts breached. Political risk may also influence the degree to which the government has the power or desire to enforce the legal and bureaucratic system to support business operations. Finally, in countries with high political risk, governments may sometimes confiscate a multinational's assets by nationalizing the industry. Host governments may also force multinationals to sell their operations, thus resulting in expropriation.

Political risk can also affect local businesses. Consider the following BRIC Insight.

As the BRIC Insight shows, even local companies can be subject to political risk. This therefore makes it even more critical for the MNCs to accurately understand political risk. How can a multinational assess the level of political risk? Various issues contribute to the political risk of any country.[20] For instance, you can examine the degree of political stability, the ease of transitioning to new governments, the freedom of non-governmental institutions such as trade unions, the degree of social unrest, and the level of political violence. Other factors contributing to the level of political risk include issues such as the resilience of the political system, the level of social inequality and unemployment, the level of corruption, the threat of terrorism and other threats to security, and even infrastructure risk.

While some companies such as Royal Dutch Shell or AIG have departments dedicated to understanding political risk, other MNCs rely on services provided by assessment firms such as the Economist Intelligence Unit (www.eiu.com) or the Political Risk Services Group (www.prsgroup.com) to determine the level of political risk in a nation. Such information can be very useful as the MNC contemplates expansion in new regions. Furthermore, the index of economic freedom discussed earlier can also provide an idea of the degree to which governmental interference can be expected.

Political Risk and Microfinance in India

Although political risk is often thought as mostly impacting MNCs, political risk can also influence individuals setting up local businesses. Consider the case of Vikram Atula in India and his efforts to set up a microfinance business. He wanted to create the business to provide loans to the poor. Microcredit usually takes the form of small loans to individuals without requiring collateral. However, Mr. Atula found that his company was a threat to existing businesses. As a result, the Indian state of Andhra Pradesh passed regulations that closed most microfinance businesses in the state.

Such political risk in the microfinance industry occurs regularly in emerging markets. Reviews of events in countries such as Bolivia, Pakistan, Nicaragua, and India show patterns of political risk that have interfered with the microfinance industry. In fact, in these countries, political risk has taken many forms. In some cases, governments can impose political risks by directly influencing borrowers by asking them not to pay loans back. In other cases, government can interfere through laws and regulations by setting interest rate caps.

Political risk in the microfinance industry can also take indirect forms. For example, governments can decide to set up their own microfinance institutions to compete with private microfinance organizations. Governments can have the luxury of offering subsidized interest rates that may not be sustainable for private enterprises. Additionally, governments can also forgive loans thereby pressuring private microfinance institutions to also offer such benefits. As such, there is always danger that political risk is manifested through political interference that is often masked as prudent regulation.

Source: Based on A. Dowla, 2015, "Political interference in microfinance," *Enterprise Development and Microfinance, 26*(4), pp. 358–373.

To give you more insights into political risk, Exhibit 8.6 shows the average political risk for selected regions such as East Asia, North America, etc. The index ranges from 0 to 100 where low numbers indicate high political risk.

Although accurately assessing a country's political risk can be very tricky, MNCs can be proactive and take some steps to minimize the potential disruption of political risk. Consider the BRIC Insight below, which discusses some of the steps a company can take to minimize political risk in China (and any other country).

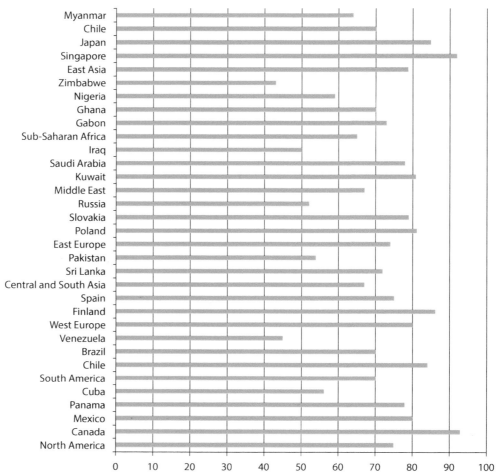

Exhibit 8.6 Political Risk Index

Source: Based on PRS Group www.prsgroup.com/category/risk-index

Political Risk in China and Other Countries

BRIC INSIGHT

China and many of the emerging markets present tremendous opportunities for multinationals. However, these countries also present significant political risk in the form of dislocation of large populations, widening incomes, and potential for large industrial accidents that can result in social unrest. How can an MNC or entrepreneur operating in any country protect its business from political risk? While accurately predicting political risk is difficult, there are various things MNCs can do. These include:

- Accurately assessing the likelihood of political risk. There are various institutions that provide data on political risk. MNCs can consult with these companies to accurately assess political risk. These include the Organization for Economic Co-operation and Development (www.oecd.org), the Economist Intelligence Unit (www.eiu.com), and the Office National du Ducroire (www.ducroire.lu/en).

- Conducting due-diligence with respect to risk assessment. It is undeniable that MNCs can only protect themselves against the risk they identify. As such, experts suggest the use of local law firms, financial advisers, and auditing firms that can conduct due diligence covering the political risk in the country.

Once the appropriate political risk has been identified, there are some possible actions that MNCs can take to hedge against such risks. These include:

- Obtaining political risk insurance. Private companies offer insurance against various risks, such as political violence, foreign currency inconvertibility risks, expropriation risks, and other interference with business operations. The US governmental agency Overseas Private Investment Corporation (OPIC) (www.opic.gov) also provides such insurance.
- Creating emergency plans. Any business can anticipate potential disruption by planning for such circumstances. By having emergency plans in place, an MNC is in a better position to respond to problems associated with political risk.
- Diversifying political risk. Any multinational is strongly advised to have different business activities in different countries. Concentrating all activities in one region may make the business more vulnerable.
- Being socially responsible. Companies that are socially responsible and contribute to local charities tend to build stronger relations with local communities. Such efforts may mitigate effects of political risk.
- Having an exit strategy. MNCs must have emergency plans for the eventuality of their needing to leave any country. For example, although China's economy presents opportunities, there are potential long-term difficulties and having a plan to leave rapidly is useful.

Source: Based on I. Bremmer and F. Zakaria, 2006, "Hedging political risk in China," *Harvard Business Review*, November, pp. 22–25; C. E. Sottilotta, 2015, "Political risk assessment and the Arab Spring: What can we learn?," *Thunderbird International Business Review*, 57(5), pp. 379–390; D. F. R. Stiller, 2016, "Political risks: How to effectively mitigate political risks, deal structure, financing and political risk insurance," *Airport Management*, 9(2), pp. 133–143.

The BRIC Insight provides some critical ways in which a multinational may try to prevent political risk. As we saw earlier, properly crafted contracts can be enforced in China. Additionally, most countries abide by international laws that prohibit expropriation or unfair compensation. These multinationals can thus resort to international laws to receive adequate compensation for their lost investments.

In the next section, we look at religion and its implications for international business.

Religion

Religion, the shared set of beliefs, activities, and institutions based on faith in supernatural forces,[21] remains a critical force in most countries. Although religion has a significant influence on culture, most experts see it as an institution that needs to be examined on its own merit. Most countries are now seeing a strong growth in popularity of religions. For instance, the rise of Islam in many parts of the world, the tremendous growth of Protestantism in Latin America, the sustained influence of Buddhism in Asia, and the continued role of Hinduism in Indian society all suggest that religion has significant influences on how most societies and individuals within them operate.[22] Furthermore, even countries such as Russia and China, where religion

religion
set of beliefs, activities, and institutions based on faith in supernatural forces

was banned, are now seeing dramatic increases in the popularity of religions. And as you saw earlier, religion can also have major influences on the business environment. For example, the development of *Wasta* in the Middle East region was strongly influenced by religion.[23] It is therefore critical to understand religion and its impact on international business.

How does religion impact international business? At a fundamental level, religions provide guides regarding the appropriate way to deal with societal expectations. Religions provide individuals with a set of principles to live by. However, through its effects on people, religion also affects both MNCs and their operations through its influence on business procedures. As an example, consider that any MNC needs to be acutely aware of religious holidays in the many countries where they operate. For instance, many Islamic countries, such as Saudi Arabia and Pakistan, have lower levels of productivity during the months of the Ramadan fast. Similarly, Asian countries slow down considerably during celebrations for the Chinese New Year, while the pace of work in many European nations will slow down during the Easter holidays. As you can see, an appropriate understanding of religion is extremely important if an MNC wants to function efficiently.

Religions can also impact how emerging market companies approach business. For instance, a recent study of 4,159 companies in China showed that family firms that were founded by religious entrepreneurs were less risk takers than other firms.[24] This was especially true of owners who are adherents of Western religions in comparison to Asian religions. A multinational negotiating with such family businesses needs to be aware of how religions impact the owner's perspective of risk. This also provides evidence of the indirect ways religion can impact the business environment.

To further understand the impact of religion on international business, the next few paragraphs consider some of the most popular religions around the world. Specifically, you will be exposed to the four major religious traditions; namely, Buddhism, Christianity, Hinduism, and Islam. Judaism and Confucianism will also be considered briefly because they also have impact on international business. You will also see how each religion affects the business environment. Exhibit 8.7 shows the various religions and the percentage of people who practice these religions.

Buddhism

Buddhism
religious tradition based
on the teachings of the
Buddha

Buddhism refers to a religious tradition that focuses primarily on the reality of worldly suffering and on the ways one can be freed from such suffering.[25] Gautama Buddha, born as a prince around the sixth-century BC in India, founded Buddhism. The basic teaching of Buddhism argues that there is no "self" or "I." Every person and everything in the world is assumed to be interconnected and the impact of one's actions affects others. Today Buddhism is very popular in Europe and the US, although most of its followers are found in countries such as Cambodia, China, Japan, Korea, Laos, Sri Lanka, and Thailand.

MNCs operating in Buddhist societies will find that Buddhism has strong influences on the work environment. Buddhism is based on the philosophy that all beings are interconnected and interdependent. Such beliefs have important bearings with regards to how people treat each other. Buddhists see boundless compassion and love as important goals in life. Moreover, Buddhism provides actual practical guidance to living according to such high ethical standards and selflessness. Multinationals operating in Buddhist environments should be aware of the consequences of their actions and ensure that decisions are made within such ethical boundaries. Although Buddhism does not necessarily condemn wealth creation and profit, multinationals nevertheless need to understand that a company exists for the betterment of society and other beings.

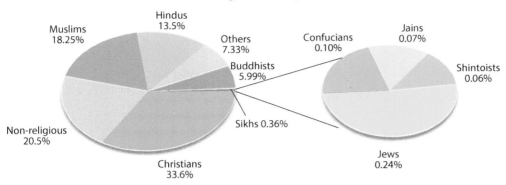

Percentage of World Population

Exhibit 8.7 Religions Around the World

Source: Adapted from Mary P. Fisher, 2010, *Living Religions* (8th edn), Upper Saddle River, NJ: Prentice-Hall.

Additionally, Nanayakkara's interpretations of the Buddha's teachings suggest that the Buddha saw poverty as the major reason for the decline of ethical behavior in society.[26] Buddhism therefore prescribed a strong work ethic that encouraged workers to engage in their best efforts, while laziness is seen as a very negative quality and heavily discouraged. Multinationals should expect workers to have a generally positive view of work. It is also important for multinationals to be aware that Buddhism emphasizes teamwork and ethical means to achieve success at work. MNCs need to provide the environment where workers can flourish.

Christianity

"**Christianity** is a faith based on the life, teachings, death and resurrection of Jesus"[27] and is clearly the most practiced religion around the world. Christians all share the same belief that Jesus is the incarnation of God who was sent to clean the sinfulness of humanity. Jesus is often associated with love and the possibility of humans to connect with God through penance, confessions of one's sins, self-discipline, and purification.

The impact on the development of capitalism of Protestantism, a branch of Christianity developed by Martin Luther, a German monk, is seen as major evidence of the link between religion and the economic structuring of societies. Protestantism emphasized wealth and hard work for the glory of God and allowed the focus on goals attached to economic development and wealth accumulation. This explained the sustained development of capitalism in the Western Protestant societies.

Multinationals are very likely to have access to environments that encourage the conduct of business in most Christian countries. In general, Christians generally support the freedom to accumulate wealth and possessions. However, human greed and selfishness is nevertheless viewed with contempt and attempts are made to ensure that there is equality of opportunity and fairness for the less fortunate.

However, despite the general support of international business and profits, MNCs should respect Christian beliefs and values when operating in Christian countries. For instance, consider that the church authorities in many countries are blaming global companies for enticing people to consume more than they need through ad campaigns. Similarly, any use of Christian religious imagery in ad campaigns tends to be considered offensive. Consider Ryanair's experience when it used someone resembling the pope in one of its ad campaigns. The Church accused Ryanair of serious blasphemy in portraying the Pope.

Christianity
faith based on the teachings of Jesus

Hinduism

Hinduism is a broad and inclusive term referring to those individuals who mostly respect and accept the ancient traditions of India, "especially the Vedic scriptures and the social class structure with its special respect for Brahmans (the priestly class)."[28] The quest for Brahman, the ultimate reality and truth and the "sacred power that pervades and maintains all things" is the ultimate quest for many Hindus. There are currently around 760 million Hindus residing in India, Malaysia, Nepal, Surinam, and Sri Lanka. Many of the Hindus outside of India share ancestors from India.

One aspect of Hinduism that is most likely to have international business implications is the caste system, which refers to the ordering of Indian society based on four occupational groups. The highest caste includes the priests, followed by the kings and warriors, and merchants and farmers. The fourth caste includes the manual laborers and artisans. Unfortunately, the lower castes have been seriously discriminated against and many people of the lower caste still live in poverty. A recent survey by the Indian government suggests that around 70 percent of the Indian population is from the lower castes.

Multinationals operating in India thus have to be aware of the caste system. These MNCs will need to be aware of caste conflicts when hiring employees. As an example, having a lower-caste member supervise higher-caste individuals can be a major source of conflicts. Furthermore, when meetings are held, it is important to consider how the various castes interact. Such considerations are necessary if a multinational wants smooth operations in India.

Despite these challenges, multinationals can nevertheless play a critical role in facilitating change by hiring Indians from lower castes. Consider, for example, Infosys, India's leading software giant, and its training program geared towards lower castes. Infosys started a special seven-month program to train low-caste engineers who had failed to get jobs. When the program started, the trainers had to give lessons in basic self-presentation and table manners. However, with time, the trainees gained confidence and started scoring as well as other higher castes. At the end of the program, only four of the 89 low-caste trainees did not have jobs.[29] Such programs suggest that multinationals can play an important role in helping change the caste system in India.

MNCs should also respect traditional Hindu beliefs when operating in India. While the Indian middle class is growing and has significant purchasing power, companies need to be careful when treading in the Indian environment. For instance, Hindus generally consider cows as sacred animals and do not consume beef. Furthermore, some regions of India have predominantly vegetarian populations and investing companies are well advised to take such issues into consideration. In fact, recent events suggest that Hindu nationalism is on the rise.[30] Many Indian states are actually considering banning of beef sales. This suggests that MNCs will have to be very careful about such issues. Consider the following Emerging Market Ethical Challenge.

**McDonald's and Food
Controversies in India**

EMERGING MARKET
ETHICAL CHALLENGE

McDonald's has been very successful in understanding and adapting to the Indian market. In a country where 200 million people are strictly vegetarian while around 500 million seldom eat meat, McDonald's serves mostly vegetarian meals. Furthermore, because India's Hindus don't eat beef while the Indian Muslims don't consume pork, McDonald's does not serve beef or bacon products. However, to get to this point, McDonald's was involved in an ethical controversy that severely damaged its reputation.

The case began in the US in 2007 when three vegetarians (two of them Hindus) sued McDonald's for concealing the use of beef in their French fries. Although McDonald's claimed that their French fries are cooked in 100 percent vegetable oil, they were in reality using beef flavoring. Given that devout Hindus don't eat beef, they felt that McDonald's had fraudulently induced them to eat something that was clearly not vegetarian. When this controversy was revealed in India, it resulted in strong demonstrations where windows were smashed at many franchises. Many Hindu fundamentalists even called for the government to close all 27 McDonald's outlets in India. In the face of such controversy, McDonald's eventually settled the suit and agreed to pay $10 million to charitable groups supporting vegetarianism. It also issued a public apology and appointed a committee to look into vegetarian needs.

However, despite these controversies and the rise of Hindu nationalism, recent evidence suggests that McDonald's and others have adapted well to the market. For instance, the equivalent of the Big Mac in India, the Chicken Maharaja Mac, is made with chicken patties. In 2016, the company tweaked with its recipe making the chicken patty thicker while also adding jalapeno and habanero sauce. It changed its recipe based on its surveys of Indian consumers. McDonald's has also several vegetarian burger patties made with potatoes and other vegetarian ingredients. Similarly, other companies such as Pizza Hut and Domino's have introduced pizzas with vegetarian ingredients.

Source: Based on U. Butalia, 2015, "Captive to their own myths," *New Internationalist*, June, pp. 20–23; Laurie Goering, 2007, "Young carnivores in a veggie nation," *Knight Ridder Tribune News Service*, March 21, p. 1; H. D. S. Greenway, 2001, "Arches not so golden to some in India," *Boston Globe*, June 4, p. A11; P. Rana, 2016, "5 dishes U.S. fast-food chains invented for Indian customers," *Wall Street Journal*, March 23, p. A1; Ameet Sachdev, 2002, "McDonald's nears settling vegetarians' lawsuits," *Knight Ridder Tribune News Service*, March 6, p. 1.

Islam

The essence of **Islam** as described in the Qur'an is the submission to the will of Allah (God). Islam is currently the second largest of the world's religions and has adherents in countries in Africa, the Middle East, China, Malaysia, and the Far East. It continues to grow rapidly in many countries, especially in Europe.

Islam
religious traditions based on the submission to the will of Allah, or God

Today, the Muslim lives in a society that is heavily influenced by Islamic standards and norms. Islam provides encompassing guidance in all spheres of life, both social and economic. An important aspect of living in an Islamic society is the presence of Islamic law. Islamic law is based on the Qur'an, Islam's holy book. The Qur'an is not necessarily a code of law. Rather, it expresses the Islamic work ethic and the rules that should guide Muslims as they encounter situations in their daily lives.

Islam has implications for MNCs on many levels. For instance, Islam has clear rules for commercial transactions. The *riba* strictly forbids receiving or giving interest. The major reason behind such prohibition is that interest represents profits gained without incurring risks.[31] Such practices of forbidding interest are not just ideals but are actually respected in many countries, including Pakistan. In such countries, governments have instituted financial laws that see interest as illegal. For an MNC operating in a Muslim country, the prohibition of interest presents a serious challenge. However, many Muslim societies have been working in profit-sharing plans to avoid the payment or receipt of interest.

As such, although Islam provides specific prescriptions governing conduct of business, some companies are findings ways to work around some of these principles. Consider the following:

Islam and the Tobacco Industry

In addition to principles governing conduct of business, Islam has a long history of opposition to smoking. The Qur'an, Islam's holy book, provides spiritual guidance to adherents regarding smoking. As early as 1600, a religious decree of fatwa was made against smoking. This ban was not taken too seriously as it was not believed that smoking was dangerous to one's health. However, this changed in the mid-20th century as evidence mounted as to the negative effects of smoking on one's health. As such, the spiritual status of smoking became prohibited as the Qur'an prohibits substances that can cause self-harm.

As the rate of smoking in developed markets declines, multinationals such as British American tobacco are looking to new markets. Such tobacco multinationals are expanding in heavily Muslim emerging markets such as Egypt and Algeria (both countries have more than 90 percent of Muslim population), Bangladesh, Pakistan, and Indonesia. These markets have a young population with rapidly rising living standards. Most importantly, many of these countries are also experiencing changes that make smoking more acceptable.

Given the general ban of smoking by Islam, tobacco multinationals have resorted to several tactics to decrease resistance to smoking. A recent report suggests that the tobacco companies have tied Islamic objections to smoking to Islamic fundamentalism. The industry has also hired Islamic consultants to monitor general feelings among Islamic scholars about smoking. The industry has also sought to reinterpret the Qur'an to suit its needs.

Source: Based on M. Petticrew, K. Lee, H. Ali and R. Nakkash, 2015, "Fighting a hurricane: Tobacco industry efforts to counter the perceived threat of Islam," *Government, Law and Public Health Practice*, *105*(6), pp. 1086–1093.

As the above shows, some industries have found ways to adapt to the principles of Islam. However, in addition to the rule regarding interest and other Islamic principles, multinationals need to be aware of other aspects of the religion. Muslims can live the pious life according to the Shari'ah based on five pillars; namely, confession, prayer, alms-giving, fasting, and the pilgrimage to Mecca.[32] These pillars have important implications for international business. For instance, if an MNC is operating in a Muslim country, it has to accommodate the Muslim's need to pray five times a day. Muslims need to pray in the early morning, noon, mid-afternoon, sunset, and evening.[33] Furthermore, during Ramadan, the month of fasting, multinationals will face some decline in productivity. During that month, Muslims are not allowed to eat, drink, smoke, and even take medicines from dawn till dusk. As such, multinationals are advised to take the necessary steps to ensure that business activities are not disrupted.

The alms-giving pillar also has critical implications for multinational strategic management and how Islam views business. In general, the Qur'an is supportive of entrepreneurship and earning of profits through legitimate business activities while also allowing accumulation and protection of wealth. However, Muslims are naturally concerned with issues of social justice and fairness. As such, Muslims are likely to condemn the pursuit of profits through exploitation of others. Multinationals thus have to ensure that their business activities are conducted in a socially just manner.

Judaism
religious traditions
associated with Jewish
people

Judaism

Judaism, which has no single founder or leader, represents the family of religious traditions associated with Jewish people. It represents an evolution of religious tradition starting with the Tanakh—called the Old Testament by Christians—culminating in a compilation of Jewish law and lore in the Talmud. Although it is difficult to discuss central tenets of the Jewish faith, several common themes can be extracted from the Torah (the first five books of Moses), namely the concept of one God and love for God, the sacredness of human life, and appreciation of suffering.[34]

Like the other religions we have discussed, Judaism also has important implications for international business. For instance, Judaism has clear laws regarding many aspects of business. Multinationals are well advised to respect such rules and laws when operating in predominantly Jewish countries. Human resource managers need to be aware of the Sabbath where work schedules have to be adjusted. Practicing Jews do not work or travel during the Sabbath, which lasts from sundown on Friday until sundown on Saturday. Retailers should also be aware of banned foods. For instance, devout Jews don't consume pork. Finally, it is also important to note that Judaism has a very positive view of work. Most Jews view a hard work ethic as associated with living the pious life.

Confucianism

Confucianism refers to the school of thought developed by Chinese philosopher K'ung Fu-tzu (or Confucius), based on ancient Chinese beliefs. From these traditional Chinese roots, Confucius developed a religion that emphasizes moral virtues and the importance of political involvement to make changes in the world.[35] It is crucial to understand Confucianism as it is the dominant religion in many of the economically advanced Asian nations such as Japan, South Korea, and China. Confucianism is also important in countries with a significant ethnic Chinese population, such as Singapore.

Confucianism has important implications for international business. For instance, because of its emphasis on hierarchy, piety, and order, management systems based on loyalty, relationships, and placing the interest of the group over the individual have developed. Some even argue that such qualities have led to the economic transformation of countries such as Japan, South Korea, and Singapore. Another important aspect of Confucianism in China is *guanxi*, a network of relationships linking individuals with families and clans.[36] Similar networks can also be found in South Korea (*chaebol*) or Japan (*keiretsu*). Because of the Confucian emphasis on loyalty and relationships, business deals tend to be typically arranged among businesses that have already developed a relationship with each other. *Guanxi* thus represents these networks of relationships where businesses trust each other, support each other, and even reciprocate on past favors. As such, it is crucial for MNCs interested in doing business in China to have access to such *guanxi*.

In this section, you learned about the world's major religions and implications for international business in emerging markets. In the final part of the chapter, you will learn some of the ways multinationals can deal with institutional voids.

Confucianism
school of thought developed by Confucius and based on ancient Chinese beliefs

Dealing With Institutional Voids

This chapter has exposed you to the many critical aspects of institutions that are relevant for multinationals operating in emerging markets. As was mentioned at the start of this chapter, an important challenge for multinationals is to operate in environments characterized by institutional voids. Here we discuss some of the ways companies can prepare for institutional voids.

- Experts suggest that an important aspect of dealing with institutional voids is to ask the appropriate questions to determine which types of institutional voids exist. The chapter covered many areas such as the type of political system, religion, and the legal environment. Multinational managers can examine each of these areas and try to consult with locals to better understand the environment. Earlier you saw some questions to ask to determine if there is potential for governmental intervention. Exhibit 8.8 below shows some examples of other key questions.

- Once institutional voids have been identified, multinationals can determine ways to best deal with such voids. One of the important ways to adapt to voids is to partner with a local company to get access to local knowledge that may not always be apparent to foreign multinationals. There is strong evidence that having access to insider insights can be very beneficial. For example, a study of Indian firms showed that being part of a business group (i.e.., network of independent firms operating in different industries with a common owner) gave the firms the ability to see business opportunities that are hidden by institutional voids.[37] Having access to a variety of knowledge and perspectives provides the necessary ability to see such opportunities. Another study showed that having political connections was more useful for companies to use courts to resolve disputes in China.[38] Although one would suspect that politically connected firms would be more likely to rely on informal methods to resolve disputes, they were actually more likely to be successful using the formal courts to resolve such disputes. This also provides evidence of the need for multinationals to engage in partnerships to deal with voids. The guidelines discussed in Chapter 9 about partner selection and joint ventures should be applied here.

Type of Institution	Possible Questions
Legal	• Is employee mobility from company to company easy? • What are the laws governing recruitment of employees? • Does the local culture look favorably on foreign managers? • Are the rights of workers protected? • Can multinationals get access to capital? • Are there strong governance mechanisms in place? • Are courts equipped to deal with fraud? • Do courts enforce contracts? • Do laws protect property rights?
Religion	• What are the dominant religions? • What are the expectations from multinationals regarding religious principles? • Are there many religions? • Do people with different religions co-exist peacefully?
Other	• Can multinationals get access to reliable data on consumers? • Is it easy for multinationals to get access to raw materials? • How strong are family ties in business? • What is the infrastructure like? Is it easy to distribute products? • What are the dominant retail channels? • Are there large retailers in the country? • Do consumers use credit cards?

Exhibit 8.8 Identifying Institutional Voids

Source: Based on T. Khanna and K. G. Palepu, 2010, Winning in Emerging Markets, Boston, MA: Harvard Business Press.

contextual intelligence
ability to question the assumptions and limitations of accepted knowledge and to adapt such knowledge to new situations

- Finally, recent evidence suggests that multinationals need to be able to develop contextual intelligence when operating in emerging markets. **Contextual intelligence** refers to the ability to question the assumptions and limitations of accepted knowledge and to adapt such knowledge to new situations.[39] Consider, for instance, the case of the cement industry. It is well accepted that the technology is an extremely critical factor determining success in most markets. However, in the case of emerging markets, success also hinges on the ability of the multinational to ensure that they receive supplies that live up to the necessary standards of that industry. Additionally, such multinationals may also have to work with local trade unions which may impede normal plant operation. As such, although most multinationals can count on technology as the most critical success factor, the case of emerging markets requires understanding of local contextual knowledge. Multinationals will therefore have to rely on more localized insights to succeed.

Chapter Review

Chapter 7 discussed some of the important aspects of the cultural environment of a country. However, the business environment of a country is not complete without an understanding of social institutions. In this chapter, social institutions were defined and you saw some of the potential effects of institutional voids and the challenges such voids represent.

The first social institution examined in this chapter was the economic system. You were exposed to the various types of economic system (market-based, command, and mixed economies) and their implications for international business in emerging markets. That section also discussed the unique challenges facing countries that are transitioning from a socialist economic system to a more capitalist market system.

You also looked at the world's dominant legal systems. Specifically, international business implications of common law and civil law were examined. Crucial elements of the World Bank "Doing Business" project were also discussed. Finally, because political risk combines elements of the economic and legal system, we discussed some key elements of political risk. You were also exposed to some of the ways MNCs can minimize political risk.

The final social institution discussed was the world's major religions. Specifically, Buddhism, Christianity, Hinduism, and Islam were covered and international business implications detailed. Finally, we also looked at two other important religions, Judaism and Confucianism. This section should give you a good background on the international business implications of the world's major religions.

The final section discussed how multinationals can spot institutional voids and what they can do about such voids. Potential responses discussed include identification of voids, potential strategies of joint ventures to deal with such voids, and the importance of developing contextual intelligence.

Altogether, this chapter provides you with some crucial information pertaining to the business environment facing any MNC operating in an emerging market. An appreciation of these factors is very important if any organization wants to maximize its chance of success. The chapter also discusses some of the important ways multinationals can prepare for and adapt to these institutions.

Discussion Questions

1   What are institutional voids? What effects do institutional voids have on how business is conducted in societies?

2   What are social institutions? What effects do social institutions have on people?

3   Discuss the three most important influences of social institutions. Give some examples of each of the three forms of influence.

4   Discuss the main types of economic systems. How do they affect the conduct of international business?

5   Discuss the main types of economic system prevalent in emerging markets. How do they affect the conduct of international business in such markets?

6   What can multinationals do to tackle governmental intervention?

7   Discuss some of the major legal systems that exist around the world. What are some of the most important differences between common and civil law?

8   Discuss some of the key elements of the World Bank's "Doing Business" project.

9   What is political risk? What are the important elements of political risk? How can companies prepare for political risk?

10 Discuss three of the world's major religions. What are some implications of these religions for international business?

11 Discuss some of the main ways to deal with institutional voids.

International Business Skill Builder

Where to Start a Business?

Step 1: Find a local business interested in expanding internationally.

Step 2: Interview the company executives to find out what products they make and where they want to sell their products.

Step 3: If you cannot find a real business, create a hypothetical company with a hypothetical product.

Step 4: Using the many resources provided in the text, recommend to the company which countries make most sense for them to enter. Focus your recommendations on the institutions discussed in the text.

Chapter Internet Activity

Go to the World Bank "Doing Business" project website at **www.doingbusiness. org** and the Heritage Foundation website at **www.heritage.org**. Locate the various measures related to ease of doing business. Explore the many components of both websites. Select ten emerging market countries and compare measures from both websites. Are they similar? Why or why not?

Key Concepts

- Buddhism
- capitalist or market economy
- Christianity
- civil law
- common law
- Confucianism
- contextual intelligence
- "Doing Business" project
- economic system
- Hinduism
- index of economic freedom

- institutional voids
- Islam
- Islamic law
- Judaism
- legal system
- mixed economy
- political risk
- religion
- social institutions
- socialist or command economy
- transition economies

CASE 8

BUSINESS > INTERNATIONAL

IKEA Trying to Build a Future in Uncertain Markets

As firms seek business opportunities in more developing countries throughout the world they run the greater risk of asset loss due to instability of governments and social structure. Political risk can be found in all countries, including the United States but the risk is generally greater in developing countries. Political risk is present in all countries as it involves changes in government policies that affect business operations. The level and type of political risk varies tremendously across the globe, with some countries having very small risk while others can be fraught with danger. Political risk can be defined as the risk that comes from changes in governmental action that can adversely affect profitability and/or asset value. While examples of major political risk, such as the Cuban revolution in 1959, or the fall of the Shah of Iran in 1979, are not too common, lesser and more recent changes can be seen in the events of the Arab Spring and the policy changes and future uncertainties found in Venezuela.

Political risk more frequently involves less dramatic events than revolutions and regime change. It can include changes in governmental policy that alter taxation, repatriation of profits, changes in import/export rules, changes in laws governing employees, currency convertibility restrictions, corrupt government officials, and many other possible perils. Changes that affect the inability to enforce contracts in foreign countries represent one of the more common examples of political risk. According to the Multilateral Investment Guarantee

CASE 8
cont'd

Agency (MIGA) of the World Bank Group, breach of contracts represents the most common example of recent political risk in emerging countries. Changes in regulation and policy changes concerning asset transfer and convertibility are also significant risks. Less common risks are war (internal and external) and acts of terrorism.

There are ways of reducing political risk when operating abroad which include ways of managing the business and its stakeholders (nonfinancial), in addition to insuring against political risk (financial). Foreign firms operating abroad can reduce the adverse impact of political changes by integrating with the host country or reducing their assets at-risk. Political risk can be reduced by establishing foreign subsidiaries as joint ventures and sharing the risk with a local partner. Not only are fewer assets at risk, but the local partner can reduce some of the "foreign" image of the business. Also, being a good corporate citizen and integrating with the community can help protect against political risk. By integrating with the host country, the firm can be viewed as a local business and less vulnerable to adverse governmental action. This integration sometimes involves supporting charities, sponsoring youth sports teams, and even building needed social facilities such as clinics and schools. Another strategy is to reduce the assets in place in foreign countries. Leasing facilities and even equipment instead of owning reduces the assets at-risk in the event of confiscation or political/social violence. In addition, political risk insurance (PRI) can be purchased by various private insurers such as Chubb, AIG, Zurich North America, and others. Political risk insurance can be acquired by MIGA—the insurance arm of the World Bank Group. Having the assets underwritten by the World Bank with its political clout can provide some additional protection over private insurers. American firms can seek PRI from the Overseas Private Investment Corporation (OPIC), a self-funding governmental agency. While OPIC has shifted its focus in recent years away from PRI and more towards investments of interest to US foreign policy, PRI can be purchased from OPIC that protects not only assets, but loss of income from foreign investment as well. Combining the nonfinancial and the financial approaches to risk reduction is the most risk adverse and expensive approach to political risk management.

As a child, Ingvar Kamprad was making deals in his small Swedish town. He traded whatever he could find and sell at a profit. In the 1940s the talented entrepreneur started the innovative and successful furniture and home goods store called IKEA. His entrepreneurial talents, global expansion ambitions, and fascination with Russia would cause him to send Lennart Dahlgren, an IKEA employee, to Russia in 1998 to begin scouting business opportunities. Kamprad had high hopes for establishing IKEA stores and megamalls in the former communist country, stating that it was his "last big hobby." However, by 2009 IKEA announced that it was suspending all further investment in Russia, fired two Swedish IKEA executives operating in Russia, and also

CASE 8
cont'd

accused the Russian utility companies of stealing millions of dollars from IKEA. It is reported that Mr. Kamprad wept when told of the corruption problems IKEA was experiencing in Russia. The problems IKEA faced in Russia were something the company had not experienced before in its successful history.

The company that started in a small village in Sweden has evolved into a global retail chain with about 300 stores in 39 countries, and made its founder one of the world's wealthiest men. The name IKEA is derived from the initials of its founder (Ingvar Kamprad), and the names of his farm (Elmtaryd) and village (Agunnaryd) in Sweden. IKEA operates stores in 26 European countries (including Russia), in 8 Asian countries, 4 in Middle East countries, and stores throughout North America.

The company prides itself on innovative design, low prices, and ethical business practices. While the company officially has a Dutch corporate domain, its Swedish roots run deep in the management of the firm. According to Transparency International, Sweden is one the least corrupt countries in the world, ranking very close to the top (4 out of 182) of the corruption-free index.

As earlier states, IKEA's entry into the Russian market began in 1998, just as the Russian economy was experiencing a financial crisis. The Russian ruble lost much of its value and the standard of living of Russian citizens was falling. It was at this time that IKEA sent Dahlgren to scout out possible store locations. He bought property rights to a location outside Moscow to build the first IKEA store in Russia, and with the help of the local mayor the store was quickly completed and opened in 2000. The store was an instant success with Russian consumers who were longing for Western products, especially those that were of high quality, innovative, and low-priced. With the success of its first store, IKEA then developed a plan to build a shopping mall with the IKEA store as an anchor to the property. Things progressed well until the local mayor was replaced with an ex-military official who made increasing demands on IKEA. The company would experience many more obstacles in its expansion in Russia from many more government officials.

With the fall of the Soviet Union in 1991, Russia quickly converted its economy to capitalism. While many foreign companies dreamed of the riches that could be made in the former communist country, few have been successful (outside of extraction firms in natural resources). Compared to the clean practices of Sweden, Russia ranks 143rd out of the 182 countries surveyed by Transparency International. This indicates very serious corruption problems in the Russian Federation. Russia, one of the BRIC countries (Brazil, Russia, India, and China), or important emerging market countries popularized by Goldman Sachs has fallen out of favor with investors. Private equity firms, either general partnerships (GPs) or limited partnerships (LPs), consider Russia to be the least attractive of the BRIC countries and even lower in attractiveness

CASE 8
cont'd

than Middle East and North African countries. In particular, Russia is considered an unattractive market for retail, ranking 26 out of 30 emerging markets according to AT Kearney. Giant French retailer, Carrefour pulled out of Russia in 2009 and Walmart closed its exploratory office in Russia as well.

In Russia the political system has been less than stable, with the president wielding much power relative to the legislative branch of government, and on occasion, providing unfavorable treatment to those that oppose the office. In March 2012 Vladimir Putin was elected president for a third time in an election that was not perceived as "fair and free" and resulted in mass protests in Russia. Putin had served twice as Russia's president, and when unable to serve a third consecutive term became prime minister under what was generally regarded as a puppet presidency. Dmitry Medvedev served as president but it was generally assumed that Putin was still very much in charge of the country. The political system has been descried as a political oligarchy with very little tolerance for opposition. Putin instituted increased restrictions and penalties for opposition protests and has found ways of silencing his opposition.

Russian laws have been described as confusing, contradictory, and ever-changing. Judges are often not impartial and hand down unreliable rulings. Political risk is the major reason that Russia is considered a less attractive investment market. Russia is considered to be a higher political risk than even Sub-Saharan Africa, a part of the world where all too frequently civil war and revolution occur.

While economic conditions have improved significantly for many Russians since 1998, the country suffers from a declining population due to a very low birth rate. Life expectancy is relatively low, especially for males, who can expect to live only 59 years. Poor medical care, excessive alcohol consumption, and violence contribute to the short life expectancy. Russia does have a large population of 141 million, and its economy has benefited from its vast natural resources, especially oil. Per capita income in Russia has been rising significantly due to the rising value of its natural resources. With increased disposable income, increased opportunity for marketers should result, although in Russia that opportunity has not been easy for multinational firms.

IKEA's operations in Russia have been hampered by numerous difficulties with government officials, and its unwillingness to pay bribes. An opening ceremony for a new IKEA mall was halted at the last moment by a government official who proclaimed the parking lot dangerous because it was too close to an underground gas pipeline. In another case, a store in the Russian city of Samara was not allowed to open because a government building inspector insisted that the building be able to withstand hurricane-force winds. Such wind speeds have never been recorded in Samara. A suggestion was made for the store to be fixed by "friendly" local contractors though. In yet another case, during a period of negotiations over other obstacles, IKEA was not

CASE 8
cont'd

allowed to advertise the opening of a store because a Russian official felt that advertising may cause "unstable psyches to act in a dangerous manner." Building inspectors, tax officials, customs officials, and others can intervene and cause difficulties for firms operating in the Russian Federation. At the same time, the mountains of necessary paperwork can be eliminated with a payment to the right government official.

While some companies feel that paying bribes to government officials is part of doing business in Russia, IKEA is not such a company. The man who succeeded Dahlgren in Russia, along with another Swede, was fired for their involvement in a bribery incident in which an illegal payment was made to connect a St. Petersburg IKEA mall to the local power grid. Former Russian President, Dmitry Medvedev declared a war on corruption; however, the results seem to be less than impressive. While convictions have increased, most penalties involve a small fine and are often assessed on the one paying the bribe, and not the one receiving the bribe. With $4B already invested in Russia IKEA is finding its founder's "last big hobby" very challenging, but the company in 2012 affirmed its commitment to remain in Russia.

In addition to differences in corruption between Russia and Sweden, the two countries possess major culture dimensional differences as well. In terms of the Hofstede cultural classification model the two countries are almost opposites. Where Sweden is feminine, Russia is masculine. Russian culture is more collectivist, higher in power distance, and has a much lower tolerance for uncertainty.

Undeterred by its problems in Russia and cultural differences, and seeking even more growth, in 2012 IKEA begun to move into India. The company has asked the Indian government for permission to open 25 stores in the country with a potential investment of almost $2 billion. India represents a huge potential market with its population of over 1 billion, but it is hampered by rules and regulations concerning retail operations. Only recently did India allow for 100 percent foreign ownership of some retail operations and the country still has a requirement that at least 30 percent of a store's inventory be sourced from India. India is not perceived as corrupt as Russia, ranking 95 out of 182 in the Transparency International index, however, corruption is still prevalent and poses a problem for some firms. India has a bloated government bureaucracy and sometimes confusing regulatory structure. Even with the restrictions, India will have more IKEA stores than in Russia, if all goes as planned.

Political problems in India are not insignificant. The world's largest democracy has more than its share of political infighting, and the current administration of Prime Minister Singh has been hit by corruption scandals. While India has experienced impressive economic growth since the early 1990s, the current level of growth is at its slowest pace in nearly a decade. Rising fuel and food prices are causing some social unrest, and tensions between the Hindu majority and Muslim minority are ever-present.

CASE 8
cont'd

In addition to its push into India, IKEA was planning on investing billions more in developing countries including China. India and China represent very large consumer markets for IKEA with their combined populations of over 2.4 billion. In addition to the large populations, both India and China have robust economic growth compared to the United States and Europe. IKEA is attempting to capture the growing markets in developing countries and to reduce its exposure, especially in Europe. With the European Union and its member states experiencing economic difficulties, IKEA is seeking growth markets outside that region. In particular, the economies of Western Europe (long the source of income for IKEA) are not viewed as favorable now and the company is looking to the East. IKEA has recently experienced its strongest growth in sales in the developing markets of China, Russia, and Poland. Sometimes the developing markets present unique issues besides political risk. In China for example, IKEA stores have become hangouts for seniors and others who use the stores and their comfortable furniture to sit, drink free coffee, and socialize. While issues such as these present small problems in developing countries, the larger, more important concerns lie in the stability of the political environment. With increased opportunity comes increased risk, and as IKEA and other multinational firms continue their move into developing markets they must find ways to mitigate those increased risks.

CASE DISCUSSION POINTS:

1   Should IKEA have used the non-financial approaches to managing political risk to avoid the problems it faced in Russia, in your opinion? Would they have been successful? Explain.

2   If you were advising IKEA, what would you suggest concerning their Russian operations?

3   Is the move into India and other emerging markets a good one for IKEA? Explain your answer.

Source: *The Economist*, 2007, "Of coups and coverage: Political turmoil is costly. Unless you are fully insured," April 4; M. Anthonova, 2010, "Ex-IKEA boss bares Russia's 'chaotic reality'," *The Moscow Times*, March 25; K. Braun, 2012, "The political risk of doing business overseas," *Risk Management*, June; L. Burkett, 2011, "In China, IKEA is a Swede place for senior romance, relaxation," *The Wall Street Journal*, December 1; J. Bush, 2009, "IKEA turns sour on Russia," *Spiegel Online*, June 25; J. Bush, 2009, "Why IKEA is fed up with Russia," *Bloomberg BusinessWeek*, July 2; J. Heath, 2010, "IKEA in Russia: Now 'everything is possible' … for a price," *Open Democracy*, February 22; P. Jarvis, 2012, "Ikea to invest $3.9B in stores, factories," *Bloomberg*, June 20; A. Kramer, 2009, "IKEA plans to halt investment in Russia," *The New York Times*, June 24; A. Osipovich, 2010, "Bed, bath, and bribes," *Foreign Policy*, September–October; A. Pasricha, 2012, "Indian PM urges revival plan for slowing economy," *VOA*, June 29; K. Rapoza, 2012, "Protestors powerful, but Putin even more so," *Forbes*, June 12; V. Ryan, 2011, "A world of risk: In emerging

markets, the clash between politics and profits poses multiple risks," *CFO Magazine*, June 1; A. Sharma, 2012, "IKEA applies to invest about $2 billion in India," *The Wall Street Journal*, June 24; C. Weaver, 2012, "Russia retail: Losing appeal," *Financial Times*, June 18; www.geert-hofstede.com/russia, accessed on February 8, 2012; www.geert-hofstede.com/sweden, accessed on February 8, 2012; www.ikea.com, accessed on September 5, 2010 and on February 8, 2012; www.state.gov, Background Note: Russia, accessed on September 14, 2010; www.statinfo.biz, accessed on June 20, 2012; www.transparency.org, accessed on June 28, 2016; www.ikea.com, accessed on June 29, 2016.

Case prepared by Charles A. Rarick

Notes

1   J. H. Turner, 1997, *The Institutional Order*, New York: Addison-Wesley Educational Publishers, p. 6.

2   Haradimos Tsoukas, 1994, "Socio-economic systems and organizational management: An institutional perspective on the socialist firm," *Organization Studies*, 15, pp. 21–45, p. 24.

3   Haradimos Tsoukas, 1994, "Socio-economic systems and organizational management: An institutional perspective on the socialist firm," *Organization Studies*, 15, pp. 21–45, p. 24.

4   D. Detomasi, 2015, "The multinational corporation as a political actor: Varieties of capitalism revisited," *Journal of Business Ethics*, 128(3), pp. 685–700.

5   Haradimos Tsoukas, 1994, "Socio-economic systems and organizational management: An institutional perspective on the socialist firm," *Organization Studies*, 15, pp. 21–45.

6   D. Detomasi, 2015, "The multinational corporation as a political actor: Varieties of capitalism revisited," *Journal of Business Ethics*, 128(3), pp. 685–700.

7   *The Economist*, 2016, "The yuan and the markets." "A crisis of faith," January 16, p. 11; pp. 23–26.

8   *The Economist*, 2016, "Can't give it away," January 9, p. 55.

9   *The Economist*, 2016, "Is it worth it?" April 16, Special Report: Business in Africa, pp. 11–13.

10 http://www.heritage.org

11 John H. Willes and John A. Willes, 2005, *International Business Law*, New York: McGraw-Hill–Irwin.

12 www.doingbusiness.org

13 *The Economist*, 2016, "Mining in Latin America. From conflict to co-operation," February 6, pp. 31–33. www.doingbusiness.org

14 Richard Schaffer, Beverly Earle and Filberto Augusti, 2005, *International Law and its Environment* (6th edn), Mason, OH: Thomson South-Western.

15 John H. Willes and John A. Willes, 2005, *International Business Law*, New York: McGraw-Hill–Irwin.

16 www.doingbusiness.org/~/media/GIAWB/Doing%20Business/Documents/Annual-Reports/English/DB16-Full-Report.pdf, accessed April 2016.

17 Jared Wade, 2005, "Political risk in Eastern Europe," *Risk Management*, 52(3), pp. 24–29, p. 24.

18 A. Dowla, 2015, "Political interference in microfinance," *Enterprise Development and Microfinance*, 26(4), pp. 358–373.

19 D. F. R. Stiller, 2016, "Political risks: How to effectively mitigate political risks, deal structure, financing and political risk insurance," *Airport Management*, 9(2), 133–143.

20 Jared Wade, 2005, "Political risk in Eastern Europe," *Risk Management*, 52(3), pp. 24–29, p. 24.

21 Rodney Stark and William S. Bainbridge, 1985, *The Future of Religion*, Berkeley, CA: University of California Press.

22 Laurence R. Iannaconne, 1998, "Introduction to the economics of religion," *Journal of Economic Literature*, 36, pp. 1465–1496.

23 R. Berger, A. Silbiger, R. Herstein and B. R. Barnes, 2015, "Analyzing business-to-business relationships in an Arab context," *Journal of World Business*, 50, pp. 454–464

24 F. Jiang, Z. Jiang, K. A. Kim and M. Zhang, "Family-firm risk-taking: Does religion matter?" *Journal of Corporate Finance*, 33, pp. 260–278.

25 Mary Pat Fisher, 2013, *Living Religions* (9th edn), Upper Saddle River, NJ: Prentice Hall.

26 S. Nanayakkara, 1992, "Ethics of material progress: The Buddhist attitude," Colombo: The World Fellowship of Buddhist Activities Committee.

27 Mary Pat Fisher, 2013, *Living Religions* (9th edn), Upper Saddle River, NJ: Prentice Hall, p. 273.

28 Theodore M. Ludwig, 2001, *The Sacred Paths* (3rd edn), Upper Saddle River, NJ: Prentice Hall, p. 64.

29 *The Economist*, 2007, "With reservations: Business and caste in India," October 6, p. 93.

30 U. Butalia, 2015, "Captive to their own myths," *New Internationalist*, June, pp. 20–23; Theodore M. Ludwig, 2001, *The Sacred Paths* (3rd edn), Upper Saddle River, NJ: Prentice Hall, p. 64.

31 W. Mansour, K. B. Jedidia and J. Majdoub, 2015, "How ethical is Islamic banking in the light of Islamic law?" *Journal of Religious Ethics*, 43(1), pp. 51–77.

32 Theodore M. Ludwig, 2001, *The Sacred Paths* (3rd edn), Upper Saddle River, NJ: Prentice Hall.

33 Theodore M. Ludwig, 2001, *The Sacred Paths* (3rd edn), Upper Saddle River, NJ: Prentice Hall.

34 Mary Pat Fisher, 2013, *Living Religions* (9th edn), Upper Saddle River, NJ: Prentice Hall.

35 Mary Pat Fisher, 2013, *Living Religions* (9th edn), Upper Saddle River, NJ: Prentice Hall.

36 Loong Wong, 2005, "Chinese management as discourse: 'Chinese' as a technology of self and control?" *Asian Business and Management*, 4, pp. 431–453.

37 K. S. Manikandan, and J. Ramachandran, 2015, "Beyond institutional voids: Business groups, incomplete markets, and organizational form," *Strategic Management Journal*, 36, pp. 598–607.

38 Y. Y. Ang and N. Jia, 2014, "Perverse complementarity: Political connections and the use of courts among private firms in China," *Journal of Politics*, 76(2), pp. 318–322.

39 T. Khanna, 2015, "A case for contextual intelligence," *Management International Review*, 55, pp. 181–190.

MULTINATIONAL OPERATIONAL AND FUNCTIONAL STRATEGIES

CHAPTER 9

Entry Strategies for MNCs

After reading this chapter you should be able to:

- Understand an MNC's options for exporting to and from emerging markets.

- Know how MNCs use licensing and franchising to enter foreign markets.

- Understand when and how companies use international strategic alliances in emerging markets.

- Know the differences between equity joint ventures and cooperative alliances.

- Appreciate the benefits and potential risks of FDI as an entry strategy.

- Choose an appropriate entry strategy based on the strengths and weaknesses of each approach and the needs of the MNC.

- Understand the relationship between multinational strategies and entry strategies.

International Business   *Preview IB Emerging Market Strategic Insight*

Marcopolo and Expansion in China

Marcopolo is a Brazilian multinational that specializes in bodies for bus chassis. It is a market leader in Brazil with a market share of around 47 percent of the Brazilian bus body market. However, it is also a major multinational exporting to over 80 countries in all continents. It has manufacturing facilities in countries such as Portugal, Argentina, Mexico, South Africa, and licensing agreements in China.

A look at its history provides important insights into how Marcopolo expanded internationally. It began international operations by exporting to a bus company located in Uruguay. This helped the company realize that it had tremendous opportunities in the Latin American market and it created an export department to compete with European firms. Because of lower freight costs, Marcopolo did extremely well in the Latin American market and it soon started establishing exclusive representatives in these markets. In 1995, it started exporting to Africa after realizing that its own buses were much more compatible with local road conditions than European buses. South Africa became an incredibly critical market.

The company continued its international growth through acquisition of standards and knowledge from other countries. For instance, it visited several Japanese factories to learn Japanese manufacturing techniques. It then applied such knowledge to the various markets it was operating in.

The final phase of global expansion was through foreign direct investment. The company would partner with local manufacturers and build factories to manufacture bus bodies locally. For instance, in 2005, it was at a crossroads with regards to the Chinese market. It had determined that although the Chinese market is perceived as difficult, it would need to establish a strong presence in that market. Executives at the company believed that the Chinese market represents tremendous potential as it contains a significant percent of the world's population and a significant proportion of the population uses buses.

To enter the Chinese market, it first established a licensing agreement in 2000 with IVECO, an Italian group. The latter had a joint venture agreement with the Changzhou Bus Company. The licensing agreement required that Marcopolo provides a package of technology and technical know-how and a factory to produce bus bodies. However, over time, it decided that it would need to invest more directly in the Chinese market. The best option for such direct investment would be through a strategic alliance with local manufacturers.

Source: Adapted from B. B. de Góes and A. da Rocha, 2015, "International expansion of Marcopolo (A): Adventures in China," *Journal of Business Research*, 68, pp. 225–240.

To carry out their multinational strategies, whether it be multidomestic, transnational, international, or regional, international managers must choose exactly how they will enter each country in which they wish to do business. The Preview IB Emerging Market Strategic Insight describes how Marcopolo, a well-known Brazilian bus body manufacturer used various options to expand internationally. At first, the company was somewhat tentative and only relied on exports. However, over time, it started becoming more involved in international markets through licensing agreements, joint ventures, and foreign direct investments.

In this chapter, you will therefore see that multinational companies have many options, including exporting strategy, regarding how to sell or do other business functions outside of their own country. The strategies that deal with the choices regarding how to enter foreign markets and countries are called **entry strategies**. For example, international managers must decide: Will we export only? Will we have our products or services manufactured or provided by foreign companies? Will we use licensing or franchising so that foreign companies that use our business models or technologies pay us a fee? Or, will we build our own manufacturing plant in another country? This section reviews several entry strategies popular with multinational companies, including exporting, licensing, strategic alliances, and foreign direct investment.

entry strategies
options MNCs have to
enter foreign markets
and countries

MNC Entry Strategies

As you remember from Chapter 2, MNCs can locate any of their value-chain activities anywhere in the world. This means, for example, that a company might do R&D in one country, manufacture in another country, sales in a third country, and after-market service in a fourth country. The basic function of entry strategies is to provide mechanisms to conduct the various value-chain activities in other locations.

For example, let us look at how Apple Computer Company uses entry strategies in its European operations.

Apple originally entered Ireland in the early 1980s to manufacture the Mac for the European market. At that time, Apple managers decided it was most efficient to build their own plant close to the European market rather than ship from the US or other locations. Today, due in part to the high-quality labor force in Ireland, that plant has evolved into the European headquarters, providing not only manufacturing and regional management but also other value-chain activities such as research and development and after-market service.

From the sales perspective, Apple Ireland is primarily an exporter to the rest of Europe. From the manufacturing, research and development, and service perspectives, Apple, as a US company, is a foreign investor in Ireland. This example shows how one company can use a variety of entry strategies for sales and other activities in different countries. The placement of these activities, based on location advantages, allows Apple to use aspects of a transnational strategy in the intensely competitive world of PCs and other electronic devices.

In the following sections, we will explore in more depth the nature of entry strategies and consider the conditions that suggest the use of each. First, you will see how companies use exporting for international sales.

Exporting

Exporting is the easiest way to sell a product to customers in another country. Often companies begin as **passive exporters,** where the effort can be as little as treating and filling overseas orders like domestic orders. A company gets an order over its website or while showing its goods at a trade fair and just treats the foreign customer the same as any other customer. Many small businesses start out as passive exporters and then progress to more involved programs. However, even some larger businesses such as REI, the sporting goods retailer, is a passive exporter. REI fills international orders from its catalogue and website sales but makes no particular effort to target any international market.

Alternatively, an MNC can put more resources into exporting using, for example, a dedicated export department or division or an international sales force. In the United States, most export sales in dollars go to large companies. The aircraft manufacturer Boeing, for example, sells very expensive products (e.g. a 747) and makes over half of its revenues from exports. However, in terms of number of MNCs, most US exporters are small companies.

How critical is exporting? Consider the following BRIC Insight.

passive exporters
companies that treat and fill overseas orders like domestic orders

India and Fresh Vegetables

According to experts, India is the second largest vegetable producer in the world. However, although it has an advantage exporting vegetables such as tomatoes, potatoes, eggplant, cauliflower, and cabbage, India only accounted for 2 percent of all agricultural exports worldwide. This therefore suggests that India has not been able to achieve high export competitiveness in vegetables.

What are the reasons for this lack of competitiveness? A recent examination of factors suggests that around a quarter of all fresh vegetables are lost after harvest. Furthermore, Indian vegetable farmers do not have access to adequate infrastructure to be able to transport, store, and ship the products. It is also very likely that these farmers do not have adequate knowledge of export rules and regulations to be able to export their fresh produce.

Despite these challenges, the recent study suggests that India has huge potential to export vegetables to several markets. Analysis of available fresh vegetable data suggests that Bangladesh would be a strong and stable market for the export of tomatoes. The markets of the Maldives, Nepal, and Mauritius should be targeted for potato exports. Finally, both the United Arab Emirates and Bangladesh would represent stable markets for onion exports.

To reach such potential, Indian farmers should be trained in terms of furthering their export knowledge. Additionally, providing the necessary infrastructure and improved post-harvest technology should minimize loss and help increase export trade and market share.

Source: Adapted from S. M. Vanitha, G. Kumari and R. Singh, 2015, "Export competitiveness of fresh vegetables in India," *International Journal of Vegetable Science*, 20, pp. 227–234.

As you can see from the above BRIC Insight, exporting can be extremely critical to help Indian farmers achieve their maximum potential. The chapter therefore discusses the many export options.

Active Export Strategies

Once a company moves beyond passive exporting, there are two general export strategies for the MNC: indirect and direct exporting.

Indirect exporters use go-between companies to provide them with the knowledge and contacts necessary to export into different countries. Smaller companies and beginning exporters that are looking for an export option without the complexities of doing it alone often favor this approach.

The **export management company (EMC)** and the **export trading company (ETC)** are the most common intermediaries or go-between companies.[1]

When a company uses an EMC, it is outsourcing the functions that the company otherwise does internally with an export unit or international sales force. That is, instead of the exporting company, the EMC promotes the company's products to international buyers and distributors. An EMC can conduct business in the name of the producer it represents or in its own name for a commission, salary, or retainer plus commission. EMCs usually specialize in selling particular types of products or understanding the cultures and markets of particular countries or regions. Some have both product and country specializations. Thus, they provide a beginning export company with ready-made access to particular international markets.

For example, an EMC might specialize in fruit products for the Asian market, and an apple producer who wished to export to Japan would seek an EMC with that specialization. Good

indirect exporter
uses intermediaries or go-between firms to provide the knowledge and services necessary to sell overseas

export management company (EMC)
intermediary specializing in particular types of products or particular countries or regions

export trading company (ETC)
intermediary similar to EMC, but it usually takes title to the product before exporting

EMCs know their products and countries very well and have strong links to networks of foreign distributors.

Typical EMC functions include:

- attending trade shows to promote their client's products;
- providing market research to locate new markets;
- adapting packaging for local tastes;
- local advertising and translations;
- finding the overseas representatives, distributors, and suppliers;
- managing export documentation, customs forms, logistics, regulation compliance, and payment.

Export Trading Companies provide many of the same services as EMCs. They differ, however, in that the ETC usually takes title to the product before exporting. Taking title means that the ETC buys the goods from the exporter, and then resells them in another country. ETCs most often act as independent distributors that link domestic producers and foreign buyers. Rather than representing a manufacturer in a foreign market, the ETC identifies what products or services are in demand in a foreign market. It then seeks out domestic companies that can provide what the foreign market desires.

The most important advantage for an exporting company using an EMC or an ETC is that the company enters a foreign market quickly, but at a low cost in management and financial resources.

Contrasting with indirect exporting, **direct exporting** is the more active exporting entry strategy. Direct exporters take on the duties of the intermediaries, the ETCs and EMCs, performing them within the company. That is, the exporters make direct contact with customers located in foreign countries. To get their products to end users in foreign markets, direct exporters often start out by using local sales representatives, distributors, or retailers. Direct exporters that wish to sell direct to end users may set up their own branch offices in foreign countries.

Local sales representatives work in the target foreign markets by using the company's promotional literature and samples to sell the company's products to local buyers. Sales representatives are not usually employed by the direct exporters but, rather, have a contract relationship with the exporter. Such contracts define the sales representatives' commissions, assigned territories, length of agreements, and other details. They may work for several exporters at once. Foreign distributors differ from foreign sales representatives in that they buy products from exporting sellers at a discount and then resell the products in a foreign market to make a profit.

Direct exporters can sell directly to foreign retailers. For example, some Korean and Japanese companies such as Samsung and Sony sell electronics products directly to large retailers, such as Walmart. Depending on their resources and local laws, direct exporters can also sell directly to foreign end-user customers. However, this direct sales approach is more common for companies selling industrial products to other companies than for an exporter trying to sell consumer products like toothpaste or shampoos to individual consumers. An industrial sales example is Schweitzer Engineering Laboratories from Pullman, Washington. They sell special circuit breakers that allow utility companies to identify the location of breaks in underground cables. Their customers are utility companies from all over the world. One technique that does work to sell to individual customers through exporting is using catalog sales or website catalogs. Examples of successfully marketing internationally using this approach include Austad (golfing equipment), Dell Computer (PCs), and L.L. Bean (outdoor clothing).

Clearly, exporting is one of the easiest ways to go international. But does it provide any additional benefits? Consider the following IB Emerging Market Strategic Insight.

direct exporting more aggressive exporting strategy, where exporters take on the duties of intermediaries and make direct contact with customers in the foreign market

Benefits of Exporting

Firms that are involved in exporting tend to be more productive, larger, and tend to have higher wages than non-exporting firms. In other words, exporting firms tend to be much more successful and tend to acquire many new critical capabilities as a result of exporting. Experts argue that firms often face challenges as they enter the export market. For example, emerging market firms may encounter critical challenges as they face more sophisticated customers in more developed markets. Or they may find that they are operating in markets that are much larger or more competitive. Additionally, they may also face other technical or managerial challenges.

To rise to such challenges, companies need to implement many new systems. For example, emerging market multinationals may need to retrain their workers to deal with more sophisticated customers. They may need to upgrade production processes and improve quality control and inventory management systems. As such, in the process of tackling such challenges, employees learn new skills that help them improve the company's productivity and performance.

A recent study of emerging market Colombian manufacturers shows that firms do indeed benefit from exports. The study found that those firms that had begun exporting the year before had higher productivity than other firms. Conversely, those firms that had stopped exporting the previous year saw a drop in productivity. The researchers note, however, that there are some diminishing returns to export experience. Specifically, the learning-by-exporting benefits are lowest for the more experienced exporters.

Source: Adapted from A. M. Fernandes and A. E. Isgut, 2015, "Learning-by-exporting effects: Are they for real?" *Emerging Markets Finance & Trade, 51*, pp. 65–89.

The above clearly shows that firms can experience significant learning because of exporting. Next we consider the best way for multinationals to export.

Which Way to Go—Passive or Direct?

Although exporting is the easiest and cheapest entry strategy, it may not always be as profitable as other entry strategies. However, export is often the first step to internationalize a company or, for more established MNCs, the way to minimize risk or to test new markets. Consequently, most MNCs continue exporting, often used in combination with more sophisticated entry strategies. However, every MNC that wants to export must answer the question of which form of exporting it should choose.

As with most business decisions, both types of export strategies have some advantages and some disadvantages. Basically, the international manager must consider whether the greater potential profits of direct exporting can offset the greater financial risk and commitment of resources associated with this strategy.[2] In addition, international managers must consider whether the needs and capabilities of their company warrant the bigger investment in direct exporting. International managers can use the following diagnostic questions to help select the export strategy that best fits their company:[3]

- *How important is the control of foreign sales, customer credit, and the eventual sale of the product and customer?*

The more important the control of these activities, the more likely the international manager should choose direct exporting. In direct exporting, the company does not pass off these functions to EMCs or ETCs as in indirect exporting.

- *Does the company have the resources, both financial and human, to design and run an effective export department to manage its export operations?*

Indirect exporting often makes more sense for smaller companies that do not have people with international expertise in their employment. Even for a larger company, creating a new unit can involve substantial costs that may not be offset until exporting becomes a larger share of the business. In the short term, EMCs or ETCs allow the company to outsource export functions (for a price) and avoid the investment of its own resources.

- *Does the company have the resources, both financial and human, to design and execute international marketing activities (for example, create foreign-language advertisements, deal directly with foreign customers, etc.)?*

Managers must ask whether they have anyone in their company that can write ads in foreign languages and can travel to trade shows and successfully promote their materials in foreign languages. If they do not have such skills, or resources to hire people with such skills, companies usually rely on the expertise of intermediaries and choose indirect exporting.

- *Does the company have the resources, financial and human, to support extensive international travel for sales or an expatriate sales force located in the foreign market, and the time and expertise to develop its own overseas contacts and networks?*

Extensive travel takes managers away from company activities and may require hiring additional managers for the home office. Expatriates may cost three times their home country salaries. Yet, if the exporting business is substantial, companies may still find it more profitable to do these functions themselves and avoid the commissions and discounts required by intermediaries.

The next option we will consider of how to enter a foreign market is licensing and franchising.[4]

Licensing and Franchising

International **licensing** is a contractual agreement between a licensor in one country and a licensee in another country. A licensor has some valuable asset that it will allow the licensee to use for a price. This asset might include a valuable patent, trademark, technological know-how, or company name that the licensor provides to the licensee in return for a payment. For example, consider the case of Himalaya Herbal brand, an Indian multinational specializing in herbal supplements and remedies.[5] Given the tremendous growth of the herbal industry, Himalaya Herbal has decided to use franchising as a form of licensing to expand internationally. This has allowed the company to expand their brands worldwide and in the US.

Like exporting, licensing provides one of the easier, lower-cost, and least risky mechanisms for going international. As such, it is often an attractive option for small companies or for companies with limited capital. However, when the conditions are right, even very large MNCs use licensing as an entry strategy.

licensing
contractual agreement between a domestic licensor and a foreign licensee (licensor usually has a valuable patent, technological know-how, trademark, or company name that it provides to the foreign licensee)

The licensing agreement or contract specifies the legal nature of the relationship between the licensee and the licensor. Exhibit 9.1 shows some of the contents that you will find in a typical licensing agreement. As you can see in the Exhibit, these contracts can be complex. Because of these complexities, most MNCs will hire specialized attorneys from both countries to prepare an agreement that is valid in the legal systems of both countries.

What you get to use	How can you use it?	How do the licensors get paid?	Other issues to consider
• Trademarks: Brand names such as Hilton	• Who: Which companies have the right to use the licensed asset?	• Currency: In what currency are payments made to the licensor?	• Law: In what country will the contract law apply?
• Designs: The right to use the same design or production processes of the licensor	• Where: Identifies the nations in which the licensee is allowed or prohibited from operating	• Method: Types of payments, which can be lump sum, installments, royalties as a percentage of profits	• Language: What is the official language of the contract?
• Patents: The right to use otherwise legally protected processes or inventions such as a cancer drug	• Performance: What exactly is required of the licensee?	• Minimum payments: Agreements stating the minimum payment	• Disputes: What type of dispute-resolution mechanism will be used?
• Copyrights: The use of intellectual property such as computer software or written material	• Improvements: What happens if the licensee or licensor makes improvements in licensed property?	• Other: Fees for product improvements, technical assistance, training, etc.	• Reports: What and when must the licensee report?
• Products and Processes: The use of standardized process such as real estate selection and products that have instant name recognition	• Conflicts: Franchisors and franchisees can often have conflict stemming from a number of issues. Agreements need to be in place to deal with such conflicts.	• Other: Fees for product use and training, etc.	• Training: Who should be trained? What types of training should be provided? What standard processes should be implemented to deal with all managerial aspects?
• Knowledge: Access to special knowledge or technology such as a reservations system in a hotel group	• Duration: How long does the license contract last?	• Schedule: When payments to the licensor are due	• Penalties: What penalties are in place if either party fails to live up to the agreement?
	• Confidentiality: Specific provisions in the agreement that require the licensee to protect trade secrets or designs from others		• Inspections and audits: What are the rights of the licensor to monitor the licensee?
			• Termination: How to end the agreement

Exhibit 9.1 What is in a Licensing Agreement?

Source: Adapted from Paul Beamish, 2003, *International Management: Text and Cases*, Boston, MA: McGraw-Hill; S. Singh, 2014, "Franchising—A viable option in the Indian retail sector," *International Journal of Franchising Law*, *12*(4), pp. 41–48; Franklin Root, 1994, *Entry Strategies for International Markets*, New York: Lexington, pp. 129–130.

International Franchising: A Special Licensing Agreement

International franchising is a comprehensive licensing agreement between a franchisor (licensor) and a franchisee (licensee). The international franchisor licenses to the franchisee the use of a whole business model. The business models usually include trademarks, business organization structures, technologies and know-how, and training. Franchisors, such as McDonald's, may even provide company-owned stores.

Most multinational franchise operations require the franchisee to follow strict rules and procedures. This provides a standardized product or service. In return for a known business model, the franchisor receives compensation, typically based on the franchisee's revenues. Dominant players in the use of franchising as an international entry strategy include companies such as Holiday Inn, Kentucky Fried Chicken, McDonald's, and 7-Eleven.[6]

India presents tremendous potential for franchising. Consider the following BRIC Insight.

international franchising
comprehensive licensing agreement where the franchisor grants to the franchisee the use of a whole business operation

Franchising in India   BRIC INSIGHT

As the Indian markets continue growing, it presents tremendous potential for franchising relationships. More consumers now have access to disposable income and experts agree that franchising represents one of the most desirable ways to enter the Indian market. For instance, although the Indian retail segment is worth $24 billion, only 2.5 percent of this amount is represented by franchising. However, while there are no specific laws applicable to franchising, various other laws and regulations in India suggest that it is one of the most viable ways to enter the Indian market.

The recent example of Burger King provides some insights into the potential that the Indian markets offer. Burger King only opened its first store in India in November 2014. However, it started pre-selling its burgers on ebay and sold 1,200 Whoppers online ahead of the opening. Five thousand individuals waited in line for the store opening in New Delhi. Despite the fact that McDonald's has over two decades of experience in India, Burger King has already been very successful.

To expand in the Indian market, the multinational fast food chain chose Everstone as the master franchise in India. Everstone is one of the biggest mall developers in India and expects to make Burger King very successful. Everstone took great pains to understand the Indian market to ensure a successful launch. It prepared a menu customized to Indian taste by travelling India to understand food preferences of middle-class Indians. It also tested the menu prior to launch with around 5,000 consumers across India. While challenges are ahead, Burger King expects to do well in a market that presents serious potential.

Source: Adapted from N. Karmali, 2016, "Burger King helping hands in India," *Forbes*, January 28 (online edition); S. Singh, 2014, "Franchising—A viable option in the Indian retail sector," *International Journal of Franchising Law*, 12(4), pp. 41–48.

When to Choose a Licensing Entry Strategy

When considering international licensing, international managers often look at three factors: the characteristics of their product, the characteristics of the target country in which the product will be licensed, and the nature of their company.

The Product   Companies that license older technologies avoid giving potential competitors their innovations, while using the license to continue to profit from earlier investments. As such, the MNC should consider licensing if it has products that are older or are using a soon-to-be-replaced technology.

Another consideration in the licensing decision is if the company has a product that no longer has domestic sales potential, perhaps because of the domestic market saturation or domestic buyers anticipating new technologies. However, older technologies may remain attractive in different countries. Potential countries as licensing candidates include those where there are no competitors with recent technology, which may lead to strong demand still existing for a licensed product. In other countries, particularly in developing nations, foreign licensees may not have production facilities capable of producing the latest technology and may welcome the opportunity to learn production methods or other information from a licensor's older technology.[7]

Finally, it is important to note that some products may be appropriate for franchising because of the nature of the mission and the business model.[8] Consider the following Emerging Market Ethical Challenge.

Aflatoun and Franchising

EMERGING MARKET
ETHICAL CHALLENGE

Aflatoun is an Indian social enterprise that originated in the streets of Mumbai. Its creators believed in the principle that if children are trained to become self-confident, socially responsible, and financially competent, they will be able to better their own situation while also improving societal lives. The company started in India in 2005. It now operates around 21,000 sites worldwide in 103 countries.

How did the company grow so quickly? A big reason is the franchising strategy they adopted. Similar to commercial franchises, the central organization created an operating model that reduced most risks. It then recruited other organizations that quickly adopted the model and led to Aflatoun's quick growth and expansion.

The nature of the product also helped with the expansion. Aflatoun's mission is to help children become financially independent. Over time, Aflatoun found that there were many more organizations believing in such missions. It successfully recruited many governments and other charitable organizations to sponsor programs in many countries. Furthermore, unlike commercial franchising, the role of social franchises is to contribute to society rather than make money. Aflatoun has therefore been able to get major sponsors for all of their programs worldwide and children in these educational programs are not charged. Many studies have shown that Aflatoun is very successful achieving its goals. Children who attend their program tend to be much more financially independent (more children in the program start saving after they spend time in the program) and were more socially adjusted.

Source: Adapted from S. Amar and S. Munk, 2014, "Franchising a 'fireball'," *Stanford Social Innovation Review*, Summer, pp. 23–25.

Characteristics of the Target Country   Characteristics of a local market that add costs to a product often make licensing more attractive than exporting or other entry strategies. For example, if a country has trade barriers such as tariffs or quotas, these add costs to finished goods. These costs increase the price of your goods, reduce demand, and can often make exporting them to a high-tariff country unprofitable. In this situation, rather than transferring a physical product, an MNC can transfer the intangible know-how through a license. For example, a brewing company that exports beer may face complex bottling and labeling regulations as well as high import tariffs. This might make exporting unprofitable. However, if the brewer licenses the brewing process to a local brewer—licensing know-how—regulations and tariffs are avoided and the licensee can still make some money from the royalties.

Another issue that can make licensing a consideration is the distance between two countries. Exporting long distances, especially with products that are heavy or perishable, can add significantly to costs and make the produce unattractive locally. For example, the international managers working in the brewery from the example above realize that their product is about 90 percent water—making it quite heavy to transport. Beer also has a limited shelf life. In considering a target market some distance from their home country, these managers also realize that overseas shipping will be bulky, heavy, and probably too expensive. In such cases, when transportation costs can make a product prohibitively expensive in a target country market, international managers often decide to license the technology to local producers. Another factor that makes licensing a good entry choice includes government requirements. For example, for sensitive military and high-technology products, local governments require local production to avoid dependence on production facilities located in other countries. In other situations, licensing minimizes risk associated with a country. Political instability in the target country can make the lower risks of licensing attractive. In an unstable political environment, since licensing does not require the MNC to contribute equity or transfer products to the host country, the only risk is losing the licensing income. Furthermore, in countries such as India, multinationals have found that it is easier to use a licensing strategy to benefit from the knowledge of local companies while also respecting local governmental requirements. Such strategies have made it easier for many companies in the fast food industry to become successful in India.[9] Finally, for some target countries, the market is small and does not warrant any investment other than licensing.[10]

The Nature of the Company   If your company lacks adequate financial, technical, or managerial resources to export or to invest directly in foreign operations, licensing can be an attractive entry strategy. With licensing, the company does not have to invest much to manage international operations. There is no need to hire EMCs or ETCs. There is no need to spend the money to create an export department, manage a foreign sales force, or build or buy an overseas unit. The company's managers need only limited expertise regarding operations in the target market or how to adapt their product to local needs. As such, with a license the licensor transfers to the licensee the costs and risks associated with these tasks and responsibilities. Thus, because licensing is a low-cost option, demanding little from the licensing company, small MNCs often find it the most attractive.[11]

MNCs with several products may find it advantageous to license when some of its products are more peripheral or sideline products. Since such products are not their key or most important products, their use in licensing does not give outsiders access to the core of the company. This prevents licensees, who are often potential competitors as well, from copying core technologies. However, it still allows the licensing MNC to get additional profits from licensing some less important products.

When to Choose Franchising

Why do individuals decide to buy franchises? An interesting recent study provides some insights into why Indian owners decided to go through the franchising route. The study of 45 domestic franchise owners in several industries such as food and beverage and clothing and education are shown below in Exhibit 9.2.

Exhibit 9.2 Reasons to Start a Franchise

Source: Based on B. K. Soni and J. Trivedi, 2016, "Franchising in India: A study of the relationship between the franchisor and franchisee," *International Journal of Asian School of Business Management, 1*, pp. 57–69.

As Exhibit 9.2 shows, the most important reason why Indian individuals decide to become franchisees is because they want to become entrepreneurs. This is sensible given that franchising provides immediate access to a business with most processes already structured. However, because of the tremendous opportunities presented by the Indian markets, many see franchising as a sure way to become successful in a business as franchises tend to have established brand names and business models. Owners don't have to try to build a business model or build a new brand.

Although not all types of businesses can be franchised, many are good candidates for both domestic and international franchising. Candidates for international franchising include companies with the following attributes:[12]

- Newer or unique business models must meet customer needs in many markets. The product or service must catch the eye of potential franchisees because it is different or new.
- A high degree of control over the products or services must be possible. Franchises succeed when they produce consistent output to their customers.
- Brands that are easily identifiable and travel well cross-culturally, such as the Subway brand, succeed in international franchising.
- Systems must be easily copied and able to be replicated many times.
- Systematic operating systems and procedures must be well developed and easy to train cross-culturally.
- There must be predictable high profitability potential for each unit so that the franchisor can attract franchisees. Franchisees that follow the system should be able to achieve high returns on their investment. They must be able to pay the royalties to the franchisor and still have a reasonable profit.
- The franchises must be affordable in the countries of operation. Franchises under $100,000 are popular in the US because many people can afford investments of that size.

Some Disadvantages of Licensing and Franchising
Although these entry strategies are low cost and low risk, certain disadvantages are possible for MNCs that use them.

First and most important, granting a license may create *a new competitor*. A licensee may use the knowledge about your product or service to compete against you, not only in the licensee's country but also in other countries. As you saw earlier, one of the main reasons why some individuals decide to franchise is to become an entrepreneur.[13] Through franchising, an individual experiences significant learning that can be used in other businesses. Furthermore, even when a licensing contract prohibits future use of the licensed asset, local laws may not support this restriction or may not be enforced. In addition, even with the protection of local laws, foreign litigation to compel the licensee to give up copying your product or service may prove too costly. Similarly, franchisees may copy the business model and open their own stores with only slight modifications if local laws are not strong regarding brand protection. As Tony Chen from Tricon Greater China (parent company of KFC, Pizza Hut, and Taco Bell) notes, "We get copycat restaurants all the time. There is a Taiwanese restaurant chain in China with very similar branding—the look is the same down to the old gentleman, he just doesn't have the Colonel's beard."[14]

Second, licensing or franchising can give up or weaken *control*. Once a licensing or franchise agreement is signed and the asset (e.g. trademark, technology, know-how, or business model) is transferred, controlling the behavior of the licensee/franchisee can be problematic, short of revoking the agreement. For example, a licensee may not price a product appropriately or correctly, or the franchisee may not follow the quality requirements. Much depends on local laws regarding licensing and franchising regarding how the contracts can be enforced, so caution is advised.

Third, licensing or franchising may result in *lower profits* for the licensee or franchisor. If licensees have their own products besides those that are licensed, they are less motivated to sell a licensed product with its shared profits than to sell their own, homegrown products. To attract good franchisors, franchising fees need to be low enough so the franchisees can make a sufficient profit. The fees can be lower than the profit a company might make in its own store.

Fourth, licensing or franchising have *opportunity costs*. That is, the typical agreement gives licensees or franchisees the exclusive legal right to use business models, trademarks, or technologies in their countries. This excludes even the licensor or franchisor. The result is that the licensor or franchiser cannot enter the country of the licensee or franchisee through potentially more profitable entry strategies, such as foreign direct investment—a least for a specified period. This is a potential lost opportunity for making more money than provided by licensing should the country prove profitable.

In the next section you will see how MNCs develop closer relationships with foreign partners by using strategic alliances.

International Strategic Alliances

When two or more companies from different countries agree to engage jointly in business activities, we call this an international strategic alliance. These cooperative ventures may include any value-chain activity, from joint R&D, to joint manufacturing, to joint sales and service. The international business manager has two basic options for an international strategic alliance: the equity international joint venture, typically called an IJV, and non-equity-based alliances, typically called international cooperative alliances.

To form an equity **international joint venture (IJV)** two or more firms from different countries must have an equity (or ownership) position in a new, separate company. Although 50/50 ownership between two companies is the most common form, some IJVs have several participants and any individual company may have a majority, minority, or equal ownership in the IJV. To form a non-equity-based **international cooperative alliance (ICA)**, all that is

international strategic alliance
agreement between two or more firms from different countries to cooperate in any value-chain activity from R&D to sales

international joint venture (IJV)
an agreement where two or more firms from different countries have an equity (or ownership) position in a new, separate company

international cooperative alliance (ICA)
an agreement for cooperation between two or more companies from different nations that does not set up a legally separate company

necessary is that two or more firms from different countries agree to cooperate in any value-chain activity. Unlike the IJV, an ICA does not require the participating companies to set up a separate company. Instead, the participants usually sign a contract agreeing to cooperate in some venture. For example, the French company Renault and the US company Ford jointly design, produce, and sell utility vans in Europe for the commercial market. Although quite profitable on per unit sales, the market for commercial vans is not big enough to warrant single companies investing in design and production and then competing with each other.

During the last decade, international strategic alliances have become one of the more popular entry strategies for MNCs. Even those largest MNCs that have the financial resources and international expertise to operate directly in foreign countries have turned increasingly to using international strategic alliances as entry strategies.[15] Consider the following BRIC Insight.

Strategic Alliances and China   BRIC INSIGHT

Despite China's economic slowdown, a recent survey of around 300 senior executives from a variety of companies and countries reveals that China remains an important destination for strategic alliances. Seventy-six percent of foreign respondents revealed that they were planning to enter into business partnerships in China. Furthermore, 70 percent of Chinese respondents also mentioned that they had plans to enter into local strategic alliances. Additionally, a large majority of the respondents saw the prospects of a partnership as very positive and attractive.

Why do Chinese companies remain attractive strategic alliance partners despite the obvious difficulties of the market? First, the Chinese market now has increasingly world class consumers who have significant disposable income. In the past, companies had partnerships in China to manufacture products. However, now they want access to the market. However, operating in such markets is not easy. Alliances provide foreign multinationals with the opportunity to learn about the market and to do well. Having access to local companies' resources and expertise can benefit foreign multinationals as they try to attract Chinese consumers.

The recent strategic alliance between the candy maker giant Mars and the Alibaba group provides further evidence of the potential that the Chinese market offers. Popular products such as Snickers, Dove, and M&M's will now all be available because of a partnership with China's leading online e-commerce site, Alibaba. Through this partnership, Mars will be able to offer all of its products to younger Chinese consumers. The younger generation tends to prefer online channels for purchases and prefers more trusted e-commerce sites such as those owned by Alibaba.

Source: Adapted from C. Lindell, 2016, "Mars, Alibaba Group partner to sell all Mars' brands online in China," *Candy Industry*, August, pp. 12–14; PWC, 2015, "Courting China Inc: Expectations, pitfalls, and success factors of Sino-foreign business partnerships in China," www.pwccn.com/webmedia/doc/6357057019633 46674_china_joint_venture.pdf

When to Choose Strategic Alliances

MNCs use strategic alliances for several reasons. Most reasons derive from the logic that when two or more companies have different capabilities their combined efforts can lead to competitive advantages. Some of the reasons for forming alliances follow.

The Local Partner's Knowledge of their Market   MNCs, especially the smaller ones, often use alliances when they are newly arrived in a country and want to tap a local partner's knowledge of the local market.[16] This works particularly well when an MNC can find a local partner with similar products or services. Naturally, such a partner would have more insights regarding needs of local customers and the local mechanisms, such as government regulations, necessary to get a product or service to market. Often such partnerships begin only as sales and marketing agreements. For example, Jochen Zeitz, former CEO and chairman of the German athletic shoe and sporting goods company PUMA AG, notes:

> Swire Pacific [their joint venture partner in Hong Kong] possesses very valuable market know-how that, combined with our knowledge, will allow us to further accelerate our rapid expansion in this highly important area. Our goal is to at least quadruple sales in the next five years and to firmly establish PUMA in the top three of the industry's global brands in China.[17]

Alliances may later progress to joint manufacturing and sourcing of raw material when the foreign partner is confident that its products or services will succeed in the local market.[18]

Local Government Regulations and Requirements   Especially in developing countries, local governments often want to ensure that their nationals have an ownership position in any foreign venture. Local governments may even require MNCs to use joint ventures as a condition of entry into the country. For example, the United Arab Emirates requires that 51 percent of the ownership be local. In countries such as China and in many of the former Eastern bloc countries, the government itself is often a joint venture partner. Some countries do not require joint ventures but, instead, make it more attractive by giving favorable treatment in areas such as lower taxes.

Local government regulations can also be difficult for a foreign firm to understand and manage. Just as local partners can bring knowledge of the local market, they can also bring a good knowledge of how to deal with local government bureaucracies. When equity positions are not required by the government, non-equity-based alliances may also provide necessary contacts and information regarding the local government. This is also especially true of requirements of the Chinese market.[19]

Sharing Risks among Partners   Sometimes, a potential venture is too risky for one company to take on by itself. An alliance allows partners to share not only the potential profits of the venture but also the risks. Factors that might increase risk include, for example, projects using a new or untested technology or when the start-up costs of the project require a heavy investment. Some projects are so expensive relative to the size of the firm that a failure would doom a single firm to bankruptcy. For example, in the commercial airline industry, no one European company was willing to take on the US giant Boeing—one failed project would doom the company. Instead, several European companies formed a joint venture, which became the Airbus consortium. Spreading the risks over more than one company allowed each participant in the alliance to take on a project that would otherwise have been too risky.

Sharing Technology   Not all companies have the same technological strengths. As a result, many MNCs use alliances with companies from other countries that have complementary technological strengths. In combination, two or more companies often can bring a new product to market more quickly and with higher quality. One example is Sony Ericsson. This is a 50/50 joint venture between the Swedish telecommunications company Ericsson and the Japanese consumer electronics company Sony Corporation. After forming the joint venture, both companies stopped making their own cell phones. The logic is to let the joint venture company use Sony's knowledge in consumer electronics and Ericsson's expertise in cellular technology. The joint venture's management is located in London. Sony Ericsson has R&D sites in Sweden, Japan, China, the United States, and the United Kingdom. Another example is Mars in the earlier feature. Mars is partnering with Alibaba in China to get access to the company's expertise in e-commerce.[20]

Economies of Scale   Strategic alliances can often provide the most efficient size to conduct a particular business. For example, Ford uses Nissan's design for a front-wheel-drive minivan. Nissan and Ford then share the production costs at Ford's Avon Lake, Ohio, truck-assembly plant. Ford gets the design faster and cheaper and can produce a product that otherwise might not have been cost-effective. Small businesses may team up to compete successfully with larger global firms.[21]

To give you further insights as to why multinationals choose strategic alliances, Exhibit 9.3 shows some of the main reasons why both foreign multinationals and local Chinese companies decide to enter joint ventures/strategic alliances. The findings are based on a survey of 300 senior executives based in China.

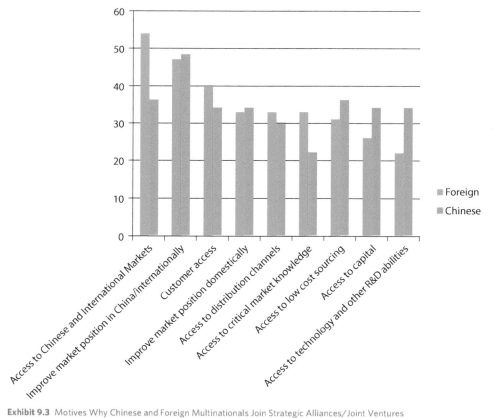

Exhibit 9.3 Motives Why Chinese and Foreign Multinationals Join Strategic Alliances/Joint Ventures
Source: Adapted from PWC, 2015, "Courting China Inc: Expectations, pitfalls, and success factors of Sino-foreign business partnerships in China,"www.pwccn.com/webmedia/doc/635705701963346674_china_joint_venture.pdf

As Exhibit 9.3 shows, both foreign and Chinese multinationals share many similar reasons for entering joint ventures. It is also important to note that getting access to markets and customers tends to be among the most important reasons why these multinationals decide to enter into joint ventures.

Despite the popularity of joint ventures/strategic alliances, success rate tends to be very low with a recent survey suggesting that almost half of the respondents reporting the alliance as a failure.[22] As such, it is very important for multinationals to be careful about their partner. Multinationals need to make sure that they have similar goals as the partner and that both sides are committed to the project. Additionally, it is important to ensure that the partner has resources and capabilities that complement the multinational's own resource base. Finally, it is critical that there is some form of culture fit.

Although IJVs involve ownership of foreign assets, MNCs often choose to go it alone and set up their own operations in a foreign country. The next section explores the nature of such decisions regarding foreign direct investment.

Foreign Direct Investment

Foreign direct investment (FDI) is the highest stage of internationalization. FDI means that the MNC owns, in part or in whole, a business unit in another country. Although IJVs also involve ownership, the IJV is a separate organization from the parent companies while FDI usually means that the foreign unit is an internal part of the MNC.

MNCs use FDI to set up any kind of subsidiary along the value chain. This might include units for R&D, sales, manufacturing, etc., located in a country other than the headquarters country. When a multinational sets up a company from scratch, this is called a **greenfield investment**. The term is meant to convey the image of a company building a brand new factory on a previously green field. Of course, in reality, most companies buy land or buildings for their factories or offices just as local companies, and the lots need not be green. FDI also occurs when MNCs buy existing companies in another country, called an **acquisition**, or merge with existing companies in another country.

According to the latest United Nations' *World Investment Report*,[23] FDI recovery in 2015 showed the most significant improvement since the 2008–2009 economic crisis. Global foreign direct investment jumped by 38 percent to $1.76 trillion. Additionally, most of the increases were in the manufacturing sector. Because of the serious decline in basic commodity prices, FDI in the primary sectors fell. Furthermore, the most recent data also reflect the continued importance of emerging markets. Consider the following IB Emerging Market Strategic Insight.

foreign direct investment (FDI) multinational firm's ownership, in part or in whole, of an operation in another country

greenfield investment starting foreign operations from scratch

acquisition buying or merging with existing companies in another country

FDI and Emerging Markets

Despite the economic slowdowns in the BRICS and many emerging economies, FDI in emerging markets remained strong. This was especially significant in developing Asian markets that became the largest recipient of FDI in 2015. Exhibit 9.4 below shows some of the trends in FDI inflows by region over 2013–2015.

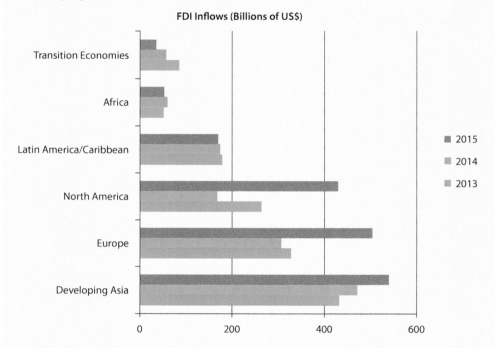

Exhibit 9.4 Trends in FDI by Region
Source: Based on United Nations Conference on Trade and Development, 2015, *World Investment Report*, http://unctad.org/en/PublicationsLibrary/wir2015_en.pdf

As Exhibit 9.4 shows, the FDI growth in developing Asia was dramatic. This large increase in FDI in Asian economies largely offsets drops in other emerging markets such as Africa and the transition economies, hence resulting in FDI increases in emerging economies. This significant increase was due to strong Asian economies and favorable conditions emphasizing investment liberalization.

African economies saw an FDI drop in 2015. This drop in FDI in these societies was mostly due to a drop in commodity prices thereby discouraging investment in these sectors. However, trends suggest that Africa will see increases in FDI inflows in the future. Many African nations will continue investment liberalization efforts and some state-owned enterprises will become private.

The latest data reflect the importance of emerging nations in more nuanced fashion. While Russia's FDI in other countries decreased because of their reduced access to international markets as a result of economic sanctions, many emerging markets saw drastic increases in their outward FDI. China remained the third largest investor in the world and saw increases of outward FDI to $128 billion. Other emerging markets such as Kuwait, Thailand, and Latin American economies also saw increases in outward flows of FDI.

Source: Based on UNCTAD, 2016, *World Investment Report, 2016*, http://unctad.org/en/pages/PublicationWebflyer.aspx?publicationid=1555

As the IB Emerging Market Strategic Insight shows, emerging markets will remain critical emphases of FDI. However, experts agree that while FDI in emerging markets will continue growing, overall FDI may see a decline in the near future. To give you more insights into the factors that may enable increases or decreases of FDI in the future, Exhibit 9.5 shows the results of a recent survey of executives and the percentage who thought the factors would lead to either an increase or decrease in future FDI.

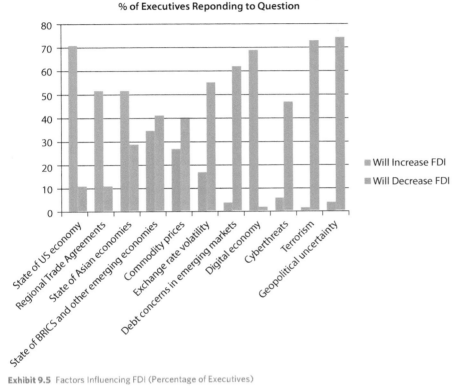

Exhibit 9.5 Factors Influencing FDI (Percentage of Executives)
Source: Adapted from UNCTAD, 2016, *World Investment Report, 2016,* http://unctad.org/en/pages/PublicationWebflyer.
aspx?publicationid=1555

As Exhibit 9.5 shows, it is not too surprising to many people that the state of the growing economies of the world such as the state of the US and Asian economies will likely encourage increases in FDI. However, the survey also reveals some interesting insights as to the potential factors leading to decreases in FDI. Issues such as cyber security, terrorism, and the debt concerns in emerging markets are all very likely to result in less FDI.

FDI can occur anywhere in the value chain. For example, some MNCs use foreign operations only to extract raw materials that may not exist in their home countries. Later in the value chain, they use these raw materials to support production at home. This type of FDI is common in what are known as the extraction industries, where raw materials such as iron and oil are refined to produce steel and gasoline. Other MNCs use their foreign operations for production using low-cost or high-quality labor or because of proximity to suppliers. Products or components produced in the manufacturing country can then be shipped to the home country or to other markets anywhere in the world. Ford, for example, assembles some automobiles in Mexico that are returned to the US, and some in Thailand primarily for export to other Asian markets.

Although there are many uses in the value chain for FDI, the most important is developing a foreign market for direct sales in that country or region. That is, the major motivation to invest abroad is a base for production or sales in their target countries.[24]

The scale of FDI often changes as firms gain greater returns from their investments or perceive less risk in running their foreign operations. For example, a multinational manufacturing firm may begin with only a sales office, later add a warehouse, and still later add a plant or acquire a local company with the capacity only to assemble or package its product. Ultimately, at the highest scale of investment, the MNC builds or acquires its own full-scale production facility.[25]

Deciding in which country to invest and the choice of local partners are often part of the FDI and alliance decisions. However, deciding on which types of FDI (greenfield or acquisition) to pursue is also critical. Consider the following Emerging Market Brief.

Greenfield or Acquisition: A Study of Polish Multinationals

EMERGING MARKET BRIEF

In making FDI decisions, one of the critical choices facing multinationals is whether they want to acquire another company in another country or build a plant from scratch (greenfield FDI). Unfortunately, there is not much research regarding the factors that determine this choice in emerging markets. Nevertheless, a recent study of Polish multinationals provides some insights into this choice for these multinationals.

To explore the main determinants of FDI mode choice, the researchers examined a number of factors such as the political stability of the markets, previous exposure to the host country, as well as host country market attractiveness.

Findings from the study show that multinationals that have prior exposure to the host country and find such markets attractive tend to favor greenfield investments. Such findings are not surprising given that greenfield investments tend to be the most involved type of investment and require that the multinational is sure of the host country and is familiar with the country. In contrast, lack of exposure resulted in the choice of acquisitions as the FDI mode. Acquisitions enable a multinational to readily become involved in a country and indeed help with prior lack of exposure. Furthermore, political stability also resulted in more greenfield investments.

Source: Adapted from M. Gorynia, I. Nowak, P. Trapczynski and R. Wolniak, 2015, "Establishment mode choices of emerging multinationals: Evidence from Poland," *Managing Global Transitions, 13*(2), pp. 101–124.

FDI Advantages and Disadvantages

Usually, but not always, MNCs try exporting, licensing, or alliances prior to FDI. Experience with these other entry strategies helps prepare the MNC and its managers for the complexities of FDI and helps minimize the risks associated with failure. As such, all but the most experienced MNCs usually try other forms of entry strategies before they select direct investment. Regardless of a company's international experience, however, the advantages and disadvantages of FDI should be considered prior to making an entry decision.

Exhibit 9.6 summarizes the advantages and disadvantages of FDI that the international managers should consider.

Advantages	Disadvantages
• Usually more profitable—especially in emerging markets such as China and India	• Increased costs of capital investment
• Easier to adapt products to the local markets	• Can require expensive expatriate managers to staff FDI or to train local management
• More control of marketing and local strategy	• Higher cost to coordinate units located in different countries
• Improved local image of the product or service	• Increased exposure to local political risks
• Easier to provide after-market service	• Increased exposure to financial risks
• Reduces costs of selling locally in host countries or regions	
• Avoids tariffs or import quotas on finished products or supplies	
• Diversification of markets	

Exhibit 9.6 FDI: Advantages and Disadvantages

Source: Adapted from K. G. Kulkarni, P. Tapas and R. Dangre, 2016, "FDI Compare Statistics: China and India," *Journal of Indian Management*, March, pp. 50–56; Franklin R. Root, 1994, *Entry Strategies for International Markets*, New York: Lexington Books.

Selecting the Entry Strategy: Some General Strategic Considerations

Before finalizing the choice of an entry strategy, international managers must consider several broader strategic issues as part of formulating such a strategy. In particular, international managers must consider: (1) their company's strategic intent regarding short- and long-term goals such as profits versus learning; (2) the international capabilities of their company to conduct business in the target country markets; (3) local government regulations relevant to their company's products or services in the target countries; (4) the cultural and institutional characteristics of the target product and market; (5) geographic and cultural distance between the home country and target country or region; and (6) and (7) the trade-off between risk and control. (This section relies heavily on Root[26] and others.)

Strategic Intent

If the strategic goal is immediate profit, then multinational managers often look at the best immediate return on their investment. As you will see in Chapter 11 in this text, managers can project the estimated revenues for projects using particular entry strategies (for example, licensing versus exporting). Using the forecast revenues and costs associated with the investment options yields a forecast profit for each entry strategy. If the immediate goal is a profitable return on the international investment (and other considerations are similar), the international managers usually choose the most profitable entry strategy.

Certainly, profit must be the major goal of all companies if they are to survive. However, other goals such as learning a new technology or management approach or beating a competitor into a new market encourage companies to internationalize their operations. For example, many MNCs have entered China and India with the realization that profits may not materialize immediately.[27] Instead, the long-term potential in these markets is so attractive that the MNCs focus on learning about the local market and developing the business contacts necessary to take advantage of potential opportunities. In such cases, joint ventures are often a mechanism for learning because of the direct association with a local partner.

Company Capabilities

The first question that governs almost every entry choice is: What can the MNC afford? For many and especially smaller companies, exporting is the only financially possible option for internationalization. However, recent research also suggests that small firms from emerging markets may use strategic alliances as a way to counter their own resource limitations. Entering into a strategic alliance allows the smaller emerging firms the opportunity to enter new markets without the need to build their brands.[28] A second issue considered by international managers concerns the human resource capabilities of the company. For example, a company might consider whether it has or can recruit managers with the necessary skills to transfer to a joint venture, to run a wholly owned subsidiary in a different nation, or even to supervise a local export department. A third consideration for international managers, beyond financial and human resource capabilities, concerns whether their company has the home country production capabilities to produce the types of products in demand in foreign markets. Or, perhaps the international managers should consider finding a partner company or an FDI investment to meet to build these capabilities.

Local Government Regulations

A company that decides to go international confronts a whole new set of regulations in the target market countries. Many issues must be decided. Consider the examples we note below. What kinds of import or export tariffs, duties, or restrictions exist? Excessive import tariffs, for example, may inflate the price of components for products produced in a foreign country or home country products exported into the foreign country. Laws might restrict foreign ownership or entry in local firms. For example, in some countries, majority ownership by foreign companies is not possible under local laws. Other legal and regulatory issues that demand careful consideration in the entry strategy decision might include, depending on the company, product, and industry, patent laws, consumer-protection laws, labor laws, tax laws, and local-content laws (how much of the product or raw material must be produced or supplied locally).

Target Market and Product Characteristics

Factors related to the targeted international market affect the entry decision in several ways. Consider just a few examples. One major concern is how and where the product is sold. This means that international managers must figure how to get the product or service to its customers. For example, a small wine-maker in Argentina might need to figure out how to get the wine on to the shelves of stores or into restaurants in Tokyo. Can they use local channels of distribution, such as having local distributors sell their wine to the sales points? If not, our wine company example might consider using a joint venture to let a local alcohol company navigate the often complex steps from producer to end user.

Characteristics of products are equally important. For example, a product such as beer that is mostly water and difficult to transport might not be a strong candidate for exporting. Perhaps this is why Heineken exports only its formula and yeast and uses local water for production. Depending on customer needs, some products may need extensive adaptations in packaging, labeling, coloring, taste, etc. In such cases an MNC may lean toward using a joint venture or FDI to get closer to the customer and to be better able to understand local needs.

Cultural and Geographic Distance

Large distances between two countries, in either geography or culture, affect the entry decision.

Cultural distance is the degree that two national cultures differ on fundamental beliefs, attitudes, and values. For example, the US and Saudi Arabia have greater cultural distance than do the US and Australia. A large cultural distance usually encourages the foreign MNC to avoid direct investment, at least initially. In such situations, joint ventures are often attractive entry strategies because the local partner can deal with many local cultural issues. McDonald's, for example, uses joint ventures in the Middle East because McDonald's management feels that local cultures are so different from that of the US that it is safer to allow a joint venture partner to operate its local franchises. Licensing and exporting are entry strategies that also remove the foreign MNC even further from the necessity of dealing directly with the local culture.

Physical distance also raises entry strategy considerations for the international manager. For example, a long distance between producing and consuming countries may discourage an exporting strategy because of excessive transportation costs. Even with direct investment for production, it is sometimes necessary to ship components or raw material from another country to the producing country. Distance also has a psychological component for the MNC's managers. Even in today's electronic world, a lack of proximity making it more difficult for face-to-face communication may cause local managers to feel "out of the loop" in corporate decision making and limit the quality of their interactions with headquarters.

Political and Financial Risks of the Investment

Not all potential or otherwise attractive international markets have stable political systems. Governments change, and policies toward foreign companies can change just as quickly. Usually, foreign companies hold off on equity investments (that is, direct investments or joint ventures) until governments show some degree of stability. However, MNCs that take risks in unstable political environments can sometimes gain first-mover advantage in new international markets.

Like political systems, economic systems can be unstable and risky for MNCs. Take, for instance, international trade, and thus exporting, which is more complex and difficult when currencies fluctuate widely in value. In Chapter 12 you will learn some techniques available for international managers to manage such situations. Another consideration for the entry strategy focuses on the general economic situation regarding inflation or recession. Rapidly rising local prices or decreases in spending can affect the profitability of local investments making an FDI or joint venture entry more risky and less attractive. This is why most MNCs stick to licensing or exporting in risky economic environments unless a joint venture or direct investment has a potential for extremely high profits.

Need for Control

When an MNC selects an entry strategy, its managers must determine how important it is that their company controls operations directly in the international operation. Potentially important areas for control include product quality and price, advertising and promotional activities, where and how the product is sold, and after-market service. Franchising companies such as McDonald's, Subway, and some hotel chains that use their uniform product quality as a competitive advantage over local competition necessarily have high needs for control. Franchisees must follow very specific regulations to maintain their franchise membership. In countries with well-developed contractual laws, such as most of Europe, the franchise contract provides adequate control. In other countries, even these companies that predominately franchise may use FDI and build company-owned stores as they usually provide the most control.

The above list shows some of the factors that most multinationals use to decide on what entry strategies they want to use depending on various factors. Ultimately, such factors tend to be much more external in nature. However, the business environment is also characterized by many state-owned enterprises that also go international. What factors do they base their decisions on? Consider the following BRIC Insight.

Petrobas and Internationalization Efforts

The business environment also includes many influential state-owned enterprises (SOEs), entities that are legally independent companies that are directly owned by the country they are in. A majority of these SOEs are often from emerging markets. Furthermore, an examination of the largest SOEs in the world reveals that most of them are from petroleum and related industries. Many of these multinationals have significant international operations.

A recent case study of Petrobas, the Brazilian SOE involved in the petroleum industry, shows that SOEs may not always follow the same path as private enterprises when considering internationalization. While many multinationals will consider internationalization because of external pressures such as the need to be more internationally competitive or the need to access new markets, Petrobas' decision to enter the international arena was guided by internal considerations.

Petrobas engaged in FDI in three different phases because of different reasons. During the oil crisis in the 1970s, Petrobas engaged in FDI to help minimize Brazil's dependence on foreign oil resources. It invested in politically risky countries that had friendly relationships with Brazil. During this phase, Petrobas was more interested in securing resources. As such, rather than the typical reasons to access new markets for new customers, Petrobas was more interested in securing more oil and related technologies.

In later phases of Petrobas' internationalization efforts, its decisions were guided more by the governmental decisions to liberalize the market. Such liberalization meant that Petrobas was no longer a monopoly in Brazil. Exposure to foreign competition meant that Petrobas had to be more competitive. In this phase of internationalization, Petrobas' objectives in FDI became more strategic. Latter FDI efforts were devoted more to a defensive strategy dedicated to acquisition of foreign assets.

The final stage of Petrobas' FDI efforts was influenced by the deregulation of the oil sector in Brazil. FDI efforts become more strategic in nature and involved acquisitions of energy multinationals in geographically close countries. This was done to ensure that Petrobas would be able to benefit from synergies across close markets in Latin America and benefit from synergistic efforts in marketing and distributions in these markets. In the last phase, Petrobas' efforts were mostly emphasizing the need to be a stronger strategic player in the industry.

Source: Adapted from F. R. Cahen, 2015, "Internationalization of state-owned enterprises through foreign direct investment," *Revista de Administracao de Empresas*, *55*(6), pp. 645–659.

Exhibit 9.7 summarizes the preferred entry strategies for companies facing different conditions for the issues just discussed. Ultimately, and perhaps most importantly, entry strategies must align with the multinational strategy. Next, we address this final issue in the section on formulating an entry strategy.

| Participation Strategies | MNC's Situation | | | | | Local Government | Geography | Culture | | |
| | Strategic Intent | Need for Control | Company Resources | Product | | | | | | |
	Immediate Profit	Learn the Market	High	International Expertise	Strong Financial Position	Easy to Adapt	Difficult to Transport	Favorable Regulatory Environment	Long Distance Between Markets	Large Cultural Distance
Indirect Export	✓✓✓						✓✓			✓✓
Direct Export	✓✓✓			✓		✓✓		✓		✓
Licensing	✓✓	✓				✓✓	✓✓	✓	✓✓	✓✓
IJVs/Alliances	✓	✓✓	✓✓	✓✓✓	✓✓	✓	✓✓	✓✓	✓✓	✓✓✓
FDI	✓	✓✓✓	✓✓✓	✓✓✓	✓✓✓	✓✓	✓✓	✓✓✓	✓✓	✓

Exhibit 9.7 A Guide for Formulating Entry Strategies

Key:

✓	=	Good situations for entry strategy
✓✓	=	Better situations for entry strategy
✓✓✓	=	Best situations for entry strategy

Source: Adapted in part from Franklin R. Root, 1994, *Entry Strategies for International Markets*, New York: Lexington, pp. 36–38; John B. Cullen and K. Praveen Parboteeah, 2016, *Multinational Management*, Mason, OH: CENGAGE Learning.

Entry Strategies and Multinational Strategies

Most MNCs do not use a single entry strategy for all markets or for all products. Rather, they use combinations of entry strategies that reflect the best strategic choices for local conditions that best support the more general multinational strategy of their company.

The first question most international managers ask is, "Why do we want to be in this country?" Potential answers might include getting raw materials, manufacturing products or selling products, or perhaps any combination of these. More importantly, however, the answer to the question why a company is in a specific country follows from the understanding of how the country provides the right platform to carry out the multinational strategy. In this sense, entry strategies represent the "nuts and bolts" (e.g. sales, production, etc.) regarding how and why an MNC uses specific country locations to carry out its more general multinational strategies.

Because transnational strategists seek location advantages more than other strategists do, they use any entry strategy for any value-chain activity that can minimize costs or increase quality. Because multidomestic and regional strategists seek more local adaptation, the issue becomes whether the multinational uses modified home-country exports or uses FDI that locates the entire value chain in each country or region. Thus, the basic diagnostic question for the international manager is what entry strategy best serves the company's strategic objectives for being in a given country or region.

Exhibit 9.8 gives a summary of how companies with the various multinational strategies might use the different entry options.

Multinational	Strategies		Entry Strategies	
	Exporting	Licensing	IJVs/Cooperative Alliances	Foreign Direct Investment
Multidomestic	Export unique products/services to each country	License local companies allowing flexibility to adapt to a country's unique conditions	Employ when partner's knowledge of country's conditions such as adaptation for product or service is necessary	Own full value-chain activities in each country, from raw materials to service
Regional	Export similar products to each region served	License regional companies allowing flexibility to adapt to the region's unique conditions	Employ when partner's knowledge of regional conditions such as adaptation for product or service is necessary	Own full value-chain activities in regions, distribute activities within regions for location advantages
International	Export worldwide global products produced in the home country	License as a substitute strategy if local requirements or import barriers rule out exports from home country	Employ IJVs or alliances for upstream value-chain activities to complement or supplement own resources (e.g. shared investment costs); employ downstream under same conditions as licensing	Employ for downstream value-chain activities such as sales and after-market service activities
Transnational	Export global products/services worldwide from most advantageous cost or quality locations	License under similar conditions to the international strategy if other conditions prevent imports from optimal production locations or if local risk factors or other barriers counter-indicate FDI	Employ IJVs or alliances for upstream value-chain activities to complement or supplement own resources (e.g. shared R&D knowledge); use downstream under same conditions as licensing	Employ FDI for any value-chain activity anywhere in the world where location advantages are possible

Exhibit 9.8 Choosing Entry Strategies to Support Multinational Strategies

Source: Adapted from John B. Cullen and K. Praveen Parboteeah, 2014, *Multinational Management: A Strategic Approach*, Mason, OH: CENGAGE Learning, p. 239.

Chapter Review

Companies of all sizes have the option to go international and must choose the appropriate mechanisms to do so. With the growth of global competition, more and more companies seek international locations for R&D, raw materials, manufacturing, and sales. This chapter reviewed entry choices that companies can use to operate in the international marketplace. It also addressed major issues that an international manager must consider in selecting an entry strategy.

The selection of an entry strategy depends on a complex array of factors, including, but not limited to, the company's multinational strategy, its strategic intent, and its need for control of its products. Most MNCs will choose a mixture of entry strategies to fit different products or different businesses.

For the MNC, entry into the international market may occur anywhere in the value chain from R&D to after-market service. The majority of MNCs go beyond sourcing on the international market and thus must choose entry strategies that focus on the downstream value-chain activities of selling their products or services. Sales can take place using all entry strategies, from exporting to FDI. Although it can provide other strategic benefits such as learning about the market, exporting focuses primarily on sales. In addition to sales, the other entry strategies, including licensing, strategic alliances, and FDI, can serve other value-chain activities. For example, an MNC might use FDI for R&D and manufacturing in one country and use a joint venture for sales in a third country.

The complexities of choosing an entry strategy that complements the company's multinational strategy or strategies represent significant challenges to international managers. To name only a few issues, you saw that the nature of the product, the financial and political risks of the operation, the nature of the governmental regulations where the company locates, and the needs of the international managers to control operations must be considered when formulating entry choices for the MNC. To illustrate these complexities in the real world, the IB Emerging Market Strategic Insight showed you how practicing international managers react to the challenges of formulating successful entry strategies.

Discussion Questions

1   Discuss some of the major issues to consider when choosing between an active or passive exporting strategy.

2   You work for a small company that has an innovative low-cost production method for high-capacity jump drives. A Japanese firm approaches your CEO to license the technology for use in Japan. Assume that your CEO has just asked you to write a report detailing the risks and potential benefits of this deal.

3   You work for a company with no international experience that has an efficient production method for small engines. A Vietnamese company approaches your CEO with a proposal to form a joint venture with your company in Vietnam. Assume that your CEO asks you to write a report detailing the risks and potential benefits of this deal.

4   Discuss some advantages and disadvantages to consider when considering FDI in a developing nation.

5   Identify a business that is not already franchising but has potential for international franchise success. Support your position.

6   As you saw in the chapter, China is attracting an increasing level of FDI for the R&D of MNCs. What are the drivers of this attraction and what are the major risks?

7   Look in your local business press and identify some local businesses that may have potential for international operations. What entry strategies would you advise and why?

International Business Skill Builder

Identifying the Value-chain Activities and Entry Strategies

Step 1: Choose a global industry such as the automobile industry or the cellphone industry and identify two major competitors in the industry.

Step 2: Research the selected companies in the popular business press and make a list of their major value-chain activities.

Step 3: For each company, identify value-chain activities located outside of the home country.

Step 4: For each company, write an analysis showing the entry strategies used in each location.

Chapter Internet Activity

1   Explore the following websites: **www.franchise.org/; www.franchise opportunities.com/; www.franchisegator. com**

2   Compare and contrast international franchising opportunities in different industries.

Key Concepts

- ☐ acquisition
- ☐ direct exporting
- ☐ entry strategies
- ☐ export management company (EMC)
- ☐ export trading company (ETC)
- ☐ foreign direct investment (FDI)
- ☐ greenfield investment

- ☐ indirect exporter
- ☐ international cooperative alliance (ICA)
- ☐ international franchising
- ☐ international joint venture (IJV)
- ☐ international strategic alliance
- ☐ licensing
- ☐ passive exporters

CASE 9   BUSINESS > INTERNATIONAL

A Bold Franchise Move

When considering moving a franchise overseas most firms first think of markets which are geographically and culturally close to home. For most American franchisors, for example, Canada is considered a good and safe bet. According to *Entrepreneur* magazine, the most popular franchise expansion locations for American companies are (in order): 1) Canada, 2) Western Europe, 3) Mexico, 4) Asia, Australia, New Zealand, and 5) South America. Increasingly major franchise opportunities are seen in emerging markets. One interesting case is that of Moran Family of Brands in Midlothian, Illinois. This Chicago area company franchises three types of automotive services and has sold their first international that will operate in Nigeria.

Moran Family of Brands consists of the following franchises: Mr. Transmission, Milex Complete Auto Care, and Alta Mere. Mr. Transmission is a transmission repair and replacement service, Milex is a general automotive service center, and Alta Mere is a franchise providing automobile window tinting and alarms. Investors can choose to co-brand and include two or three units in their operations.

Franchise information on the three options can be seen below:

Mr. Transmission

Total Franchise Investment	= $173,000–247,000
Franchise Fee	= $30,000
Royalty Fee	= 7%
Ad Royalty Fee	= 1%
Total Franchisees	= 100 approximately (down 11 units in the last three years)

Milex Complete Auto Care

Total Franchise Investment	= $168,000–251,000
Franchise Fee	= $30,000
Royalty Fee	= 7%
Ad Royalty Fee	= 1%
Total Franchisees	= 35 approximately (down 4 units in the last three years)

Alta Mere

Total Franchise Investment	= $115,000–196,000
Franchise Fee	= $30,000–35,000
Royalty Fee	= 7%
Ad Royalty Fee	= 1%
Total Franchisees	= 12 approximately (down 2 units in the last three years)

**CASE 9
cont'd**

Moran Family of Brands began construction on their first foreign facility in March, 2016 in Nigeria. The co-branded franchise of Mr. Transmission/ Milex was sold to a couple who will also attempt to develop the Moran franchise in Nigeria. Moran Family of Brands began its existence in 1958 when Dennis Moran began an automotive business. The company changed its name to Moran Industries in 1990 when it acquired Mr. Transmission, and further expansion led to the current name (Moran Family of Brands) in 2012. Moran Family of Brands has a management philosophy which states: *We value initiative, creativity and an independent mind. We want team members that will question the wisdom of something they consider to be bad decisions.* Some might challenge the choice of Nigeria as the first international location for the company.

Nigeria, with a population of 158 million is Africa's largest country. This oil-rich country in West Africa has a democratic form of government, however, the country has a long history of ethnic and religious conflict. Nigeria has gained the unwanted reputation of being a source of international fraud activity, and Transparency International ranks the country 136 out of 168 in terms of the most corrupt countries surveyed. GlobalEDGE gives Nigeria a grade of D (the lowest grade given) in terms of business climate stating: *the business environment is very difficult; and the legal system makes debt collection very unpredictable.* Nigeria receives a grade of C (second lowest) in terms of country risk with globalEDGE stating that Nigeria has: a *very uncertain political and economic outlook.* Undeterred, current president of Moran Family of Brands, Pete Baldine feels confident that Nigeria is the right choice for initial international expansion. Mr. Baldine thinks the franchisees are ideal choices for a franchise in Africa and he is looking for further expansion in other African countries, especially Liberia. Auto repair is not well developed in many African countries and he hopes to bring a degree of efficiency and superior service to these neglected markets. With declining franchisees in the US, Morgan Family of Brands hopes to find growth in emerging and frontier markets.

CASE DISCUSSION POINTS:

1   What problems may Moran Family of Brands experience by franchising in Nigeria?
2   Is franchising in general the best mode of entry into the Nigerian market? Explain.
3   In addition to Nigeria and Liberia, what other African countries might be good for Moran Family of Brands to explore? Are other areas of the world better choices for expansion?

Source: *Entrepreneur*, 2016, "Africa Calling: An automotive repair franchise takes a leap," July, www.entrepreneur.com, accessed on July 21, 2016; www.globaledge. msu.edu/nigeria, accessed on July 23, 2016; www.moranfamilyofbrands.com, accessed on July 20, 2016; *CIA World Fact Book 2016*; Transparency International, www.transparency.org, accessed on July 25, 2016.

Case written by Charles A. Rarick

Notes

1 www.unzco.com/basicguide/c6.html
2 Jack S. Wolf, 1992, *Export Profits: A Guide for Small Business*, Dover, NH: Upstart Publishing.
3 Jack S. Wolf, 1992, *Export Profits: A Guide for Small Business*, Dover, NH: Upstart Publishing.
4 Franklin R. Root, 1998, *Entry Strategies for International Markets*, New York: Lexington Books; John B. Cullen and K. Praveen Parboteeah, 2016, *Multinational Management*, Mason, OH: CENGAGE Publishing.
5 R. Srivastava, 2016, "How Indian pharmaceuticals companies are building global brands: The case of the Himalaya Herbal brand," *Thunderbird International Business Review*, 58(5), pp. 399–410.
6 Franklin R. Root, 1998, *Entry Strategies for International Markets*, New York: Lexington Books.
7 Franklin R. Root, 1998, *Entry Strategies for International Markets*, New York: Lexington Books; Paul J. Beamish, Allen J. Morrison, Andrew Inkpen and Philip M. Rosenzweig, 2003, *International Management*, New York: McGraw-Hill.
8 S. Amar and S. Munk, 2014, "Franchising a 'fireball'," *Stanford Social Innovation Review*, Summer, pp. 23–25.
9 N. Karmali, 2016, "Burger King helping hands in India," *Forbes*, January 28 (online edition); S. Singh, 2014, "Franchising—A viable option in the Indian retail sector," *International Journal of Franchising Law*, 12(4), pp. 41–48.
10 Paul J. Beamish, Allen J. Morrison, Andrew Inkpen and Philip M. Rosenzweig, 2003, *International Management*, New York: McGraw-Hill.
11 Franklin R. Root, 1998, *Entry Strategies for International Markets*, New York: Lexington Books.
12 Mark Henricks, 2005, "Franchise your business," www.entrepreneur.com, December 1; B. K. Soni and J. Trivedi, 2016, "Franchising in India: A study of the relationship between the franchisor and franchisee," *International Journal of Asian School of Business Management*, 1, pp. 57–69.
13 B. K. Soni and J. Trivedi, 2016, "Franchising in India: A study of the relationship between the franchisor and franchisee," *International Journal of Asian School of Business Management*, 1, pp. 57–69.
14 Ed Young, "Franchising in China: A dead duck," www.Brandchannel.com
15 Paul J. Beamish, Allen J. Morrison, Andrew Inkpen and Philip M. Rosenzweig, 2003, *International Management*, New York: McGraw-Hill.
16 PWC, 2015, "Courting China Inc: Expectations, pitfalls, and success factors of Sino-foreign business partnerships in China," www.pwccn.com/webmedia/doc/635705701963346674_china_joint_venture. pdf
17 http://about.puma.com/news.jsp?year=05&id=33&lang=eng
18 Paul J. Beamish, Allen J. Morrison, Andrew Inkpen and Philip M. Rosenzweig, 2003, *International Management*, New York: McGraw-Hill.
19 PWC, 2015, "Courting China Inc: Expectations, pitfalls, and success factors of Sino-foreign business partnerships in China," www.pwccn.com/webmedia/doc/635705701963346674_china_joint_venture. pdf
20 C. Lindell, 2016, "Mars, Alibaba Group partner to sell all Mars' brands online in China," *Candy Industry*, August, pp. 12–14
21 Paul J. Beamish, Allen J. Morrison, Andrew Inkpen and Philip M. Rosenzweig, 2003, *International Management*, New York: McGraw-Hill.
22 CMO Council, 2014, A report on the strategic value of business alliances and compatible partner matching, www.cmocouncil.org/authority-leadership/reports/285
23 UNCTAD, 2016, *World Investment Report, 2016*, http://unctad.org/en/pages/PublicationWebflyer. aspx?publicationid=1555; *World Investment Report: Transnational Corporations and the Internationalization of R&D*, New York: United Nations.
24 Franklin R. Root, 1998, *Entry Strategies for International Markets*, New York: Lexington Books.
25 Paul J. Beamish, Allen J. Morrison, Andrew Inkpen and Philip M. Rosenzweig, 2003, *International Management*, New York: McGraw-Hill.
26 Franklin R. Root, 1998, *Entry Strategies for International Markets*, New York: Lexington Books.

27 K. G. Kulkarni, P. Tapas and R. Dangre, 2016, "FDI compare statistics: China and India", *Journal of Indian Management*, March, pp. 50–56.
28 S. K. Tiwari, S. Sen and R. Shaik, 2016, "Internationalization: A study of small firms from emerging markets," *Journal of Developing Areas*, 50(6), pp. 355–364.

CHAPTER 10

International Marketing and Supply-chain Management for MNCs

After reading this chapter you should be able to:

- Understand how complex global markets can be and the need for relevant information on foreign markets.

- Understand market responses in terms of the global–local dilemma.

- Understand how the marketing mix can vary in global markets.

- Understand the implications of the global–local dilemma in the marketing mix.

- Understand the implications of global supply chains and outsourcing.

- Understand the unique challenges for international marketing in emerging markets.

International Business *Preview IB Emerging Market Strategic Insight*

Zeno and the Global Market for Acne Treatment

Tyrell, Inc. a Houston, Texas, based company, is pioneering an exciting new product category of home-based medical devices. The first of these groundbreaking products is the acne treatment device, Zeno™. Zeno is a hand-held portable electronic device for clearing mild to moderate individual inflammatory acne pimples. Zeno works through a precisely controlled application of heat to the acne pimple. When applied for a specific amount of time the heat causes acne bacteria to self-destruct and the pimple disappears. The product has met with significant success in the US, but should Tyrell consider taking Zeno global?

The global appeal of such a product depends on many factors. The first is cultural values. Some national cultures, for example Turkey, see acne as a natural course of life, and unless it is chronic, would not be responsive to aggressive and expensive acne treatment for a normal teenage case. Other cultures, such as the US, see people as more in control of nature and the environment and would respond well to a product that controls acne. In the US, people tend to feel that they can and should be able to control many aspects of nature such as normal teenage acne and the effects of aging.

The second factor affecting the success of Zeno in global markets is demand and spending power. This involves not only the population of a potential foreign market in terms of the number of people who would be interested in purchasing such a product but also how the income is distributed across the population. Countries with large middle classes, where a large part of the population makes enough money to spend something on products that are not essential to live, are highly attractive markets in general. The presence of a sizable middle class with middle-class and upper middle-class incomes would mean that there is sufficient market potential for Zeno. This need might be a challenge for products such as Zeno to succeed in emerging markets. Beyond this, of course the specific market segments still must be researched and understood.

The third major influence in taking a product like Zeno global is infrastructure. Zeno sells for US$200, and in the US it is sold through dermatologists, dermatology clinics, medical spas, and trained aestheticians. One version is only sold by MDs. In other words, people buy this product because a trained professional, a doctor, nurse, or medical technician, specializing in skin disorders, recommends it. And quite often the customer sees the product promoted in the doctor's office or skin treatment center. While Zeno does not require a prescription, because of its cost it benefits from being "sold" through the medical community. If Zeno is to be successful in foreign markets, the company will need the right medical clinics, the right medical specialists, and treatment centers through which Zeno can be recommended and distributed. The Korean (Brazilian, Chinese, etc.) consumer interested in acne treatments must have access to information about the existence of the product, how it works, and its effectiveness through medical establishments. A country without the medical infrastructure to provide this would not be viable for Zeno.

So Tyrell must understand consumer preferences and address the segment of consumers that would appreciate and value acne treatments. It must research its potential markets and make sure the economy is developed to the level that there are enough people with enough money to buy Zeno. Tyrell must further research its potential markets to make sure that the medical infrastructure is advanced enough to support the marketing of Zeno. In addition, it must research all medical and import regulations in each market that will affect Zeno. All of this is a daunting and complex task. Yet the potential success of a product like Zeno makes the idea quite attractive.

Source: *Houston Business Journal*, 2008, "Acne attack attracts Zeno investors," July 20; chungyu-tech, 2015, "Amazing devices—Zeno acne clearing device," December 20, www.chuangyu-tech.com/amazing-devices-zeno-acne-clearing-device/; *Bloomberg*, 2016, Company overview of LumaTherm, Inc., www.bloomberg.com/research/stocks/private/snapshot.asp?privcapId=12107014

What makes products successful in foreign markets? Why do some products succeed and others fail? How does the international manager know what makes a product valued in one culture compared to another? How does the international manager communicate with potential customers in various cultures? What makes a product's packaging appealing? Do customers in a foreign market prefer to buy products in large modern department stores or in small family-owned corner stores? What sorts of services do they want when they buy a product? As the Preview IB Emerging Market Strategic Insight shows, these questions involve everything the international manager does to connect, communicate, and deliver products to customers—this is

marketing mix
the combination of an MNC's product offering, distribution, pricing, and all marketing communication components

global–local dilemma
choice between a local responsiveness or global approach to a multinational's strategies

marketing. We can understand the way marketing works in terms of the **marketing mix,** which is (1) the product offering, (2) distribution, (3) pricing, and (4) all the components of marketing communications.

Of all the areas where the **global–local dilemma** affects international business, marketing may be the one where it is the biggest factor. All the cost and management advantages of a global integration strategy where the marketing mix is standardized across every country are still great. Yet, the greatest pressure for a local-responsiveness strategy comes from important differences in what customers want and how customers respond from country to country. One of the key factors in helping the international manager figure out the balance of where and when to respond locally and where and when to standardize is knowledge about the markets in question.

Market Research—The Knowledge Advantage

When you were deciding on the college you wanted to attend, where did you start? Rather than simply tossing a coin, you most likely started by systematically gathering information on various colleges to consider. Gathering this information gave you a knowledge advantage as it helped you understand many of the factors involved in making the best decision for your future. International managers approach decisions associated with marketing in foreign countries in much the same way. **International marketing research** is the systematic gathering of objective information in and about foreign markets that will help the international manager understand customer wants and needs. This research provides a knowledge advantage because it provides a critically important guide to the international manager in balancing the global–local dilemma, developing the appropriate marketing mix, and, as we discuss below, segmentation, targeting, and market growth decisions.

international marketing research
the systematic collection of objective information in and about foreign markets that helps international managers understand customer wants and needs

One of the first issues in building the knowledge advantage is to understand what kind of marketing information is needed. This comes directly from the questions that the international manager needs answered. Some questions about foreign markets can be answered with secondary data. **Secondary data** are data that already exist and were gathered for some previous purposes, sometimes by governments, the UN, the World Bank, or various agencies and trade associations. For example, an MNC considering marketing an acne treatment device in Asian countries might look at income levels from government data and the sales of pharmaceuticals of certain types available from the UN. This would provide the international manager with information about whether people can afford to buy such a device and whether such products are acceptable in a culture.

secondary data
data that already exist and were gathered for some previous purpose, sometimes by governments, the UN, the World Bank, or other agencies and trade associations

Exhibit 10.1 provides an assessment of the market potential using Global Edge's Market Potential Index (MPI) for 25 emerging market countries with the most potential. This index is derived from secondary data as identified in the table.

If the international manager cannot answer his or her questions regarding a foreign market with secondary data, primary data may be needed. **Primary data** are gathered specifically to provide the information needed by the international manager; they did not previously exist. Primary data most often involve surveys asking customers, for example: how satisfied they are with the product; what types of services are most important; what they believe is a reasonable price for the coffee; and how much they would be willing to spend for a movie. Another form of primary data involves customer panels, where the same set of customers are surveyed to measure changes over time, for example in product awareness or product knowledge, or in responses to advertising messages.

primary data
data that did not previously exist and were specifically collected to provide the information needed by a manager, and often involving surveys of customers or customer panels

Overall Score MPI	Country	Market Size	Market Growth Rate	Market Intensity	Market Consumption Capacity	Commercial Infra-structure	Economic Freedom	Market Receptivity	Country Risk
100	China	100	95	1	92	62	22	7	78
48	India	37	78	32	66	28	45	7	67
38	South Korea	9	61	48	81	52	63	20	85
29	Brazil	17	59	48	47	40	49	5	56
29	Poland	3	53	53	67	51	66	14	77
28	Czech Republic	2	43	38	72	53	70	25	77
28	Malaysia	3	68	41	54	47	52	23	77
28	Turkey	6	71	63	61	40	48	10	50
26	Indonesia	11	69	32	58	30	46	8	61
26	Mexico	9	54	58	41	27	53	24	67
26	Russia	18	51	42	58	49	24	8	39
24	Peru	2	81	45	45	23	57	9	72
24	Vietnam	4	83	39	51	32	24	25	50
23	Chile	2	53	58	39	38	75	16	68
23	Philippines	4	65	58	46	27	49	10	72
21	Bulgaria	1	39	50	60	40	59	19	62
20	Argentina	4	58	74	60	38	38	6	17
20	Bangladesh	4	74	53	56	17	36	7	39
20	Hungary	1	32	36	67	44	59	26	56
20	Thailand	4	61	30	47	38	37	20	56
16	Colombia	3	66	43	25	25	56	8	61
16	Guatemala	1	63	80	26	21	45	11	51
14	Honduras	1	58	69	31	21	40	21	34
14	Ukraine	4	29	56	68	46	35	15	1
11	South Africa	5	46	43	1	47	55	10	56
9	Venezuela	3	46	55	54	30	13	10	1

Dimensions and Measures of MPI

Dimension	Measures	Secondary Data Sources
Market Size	• Electricity Consumption (2012) • Urban Population (2014)	• World Bank, *World Development Indicators*
Market Intensity	• GNI per Capita Estimates Using PPP (2014) • Private Consumption as a percentage of GDP (2014)	• World Bank, *World Development Indicators*
Market Growth Rate	• Compound Annual Growth Rate (CAGR) of Primary Energy Use (2008–2013) • Compound Annual Growth Rate (CAGR) of GDP (constant 2005 US$) (2009–2014)	• US Energy Information Administration, *International Energy Annual* • World Bank, *World Development Indicators*
Market Consumption Capacity	• Consumer Expenditure (2014) • Income Share of Middle-class (2013) • Household Annual Disposable Income of Middle-class (2014)	• Euromonitor International, *Global Market Information Database* • World Bank, *World Development Indicators*

Exhibit 10.1 Top 25 Emerging Market Countries Based on the Market Potential Index (MPI) Estimated From Secondary Data

Dimension	Measures	Secondary Data Sources
Commercial Infrastructure	• Cellular Mobile Subscribers (2014) • Households with Internet Access (2014) • International Internet Bandwidth (2013) • Number of PCs (2014) • Paved Road Density (2014) • Population per Retail Outlet (2015) • Available Airline Seats (2015) • Logistics Performance Index (LPI) (2014)	• International Telecommunication Union, *ICT Indicators* • World Bank, *World Development Indicators* • Euromonitor International, *Global Market Information Database* • World Economic Forum, *Global Competitiveness Report* • World Bank, *Logistics Performance Index*
Market Receptivity	• Per Capita Imports from US (2015) • Trade as a Percentage of GDP (2014)	• US Census Bureau Foreign Trade Division, *Country Trade Data* • World Bank, *World Development Indicators*
Economic Freedom	• Economic Freedom Index (2015) • Political Freedom Index (2015)	• Heritage Foundation, *The Index of Economic Freedom* • Freedom House, *Survey of Freedom in the World*
Country Risk	• Business Risk Rating (2015) • Country Risk Rating (2015) • Political Risk Rating (2015)	• Swiss Export Risk Insurance, *Country Risk Survey* • Coface, *Country Risk Survey* • Credimundi, *Country Risk Survey*

Exhibit 10.1 Top 25 Emerging Market Countries Based on the Market Potential Index (MPI) Estimated From Secondary Data
Source: Adapted from http://globaledge.msu.edu/mpi

back translation
the repeated translation, back and forth, between two languages until a common meaning is consistent between both languages

Primary data can be gathered in person by trained interviewers, by mail, by e-mail, or by websites. Regardless of how the data are collected, there are a number of complications in international marketing research, most of which involve language and cultural differences. Developing questionnaires in a different language requires more than simple translation. To avoid serious mistakes in interpretation, back translation can be used. **Back translation** is when the questionnaire is repeatedly translated back and forth between the two languages until all of it agrees and is consistent between both languages.

Other problems in international marketing research can come from cultural biases. In some cultures, there can be a bias to respond in a certain way regardless of how you really feel. For example, the Japanese find it extremely difficult to say "no" directly or to disagree, so the agree–disagree statements often used in market research must be avoided in Japan. Besides Japan, there is a cultural bias against saying "no" or disagreeing in a number of other countries. Likewise, many cultures have a courtesy bias. That is, the person responding will strive to be polite and give you the answer that they believe you want, which may be totally unrelated to how they really feel about the product. In other cultures, getting customers to respond and participate in market research at all can be problematic. There can be strong biases against revealing any information about feelings and opinions. There may also be gender issues. For example, in the Middle East, it is often difficult to get the opinions of female consumers.

focus group
a small group of actual or potential customers specifically brought together to discuss and talk about a particular topic or idea that a manager needs to understand

Another important marketing research tool is focus groups. A **focus group** is a small group of actual or potential customers that are gathered specially to discuss and talk about the topic or idea that the international manager needs to understand. For example, an MNC attempting to market an acne treatment device in Korea might gather a group of six to eight teenagers to discuss the whole notion of acne and acne treatment. The **moderator**, the trained professional who runs the focus group, might show the teenagers the actual device and ask them to discuss various features or aspects of the actual product. Again, some of the same biases are a problem for focus groups: a cultural norm of always agreeing or of seeing different opinions as discourteous, or of getting consumers to participate and provide information at all.

moderator
a trained professional who leads and facilitates a focus group

The IB Emerging Market Strategic Insight below shows an example of how the use of a focus group provides the wine industry insights into the Chinese market for wines.

In sum, to build a knowledge advantage, it is critical to adapt research procedures to local conditions so that valid and useful information results. Because cultural sensitivity is so important in market research, sometimes hiring a local market research company is the best alternative. Local market research companies have the specialized understanding and experience with local conditions that are necessary in certain countries such as China and the Arab states. The international manager must carefully screen local research agencies to ensure that they provide high-quality information.

While international market research is typically much more expensive than domestic research, the quality of information should be the focus and must not be compromised because of cost. Another issue is the ability to integrate the new market research information with the MNC's programs. International market research provides important information to develop global plans and strategies and to help decide the extent of local adaptation that is necessary.

Focus Groups on Wine in China

IB EMERGING MARKET
STRATEGIC INSIGHT

The enjoyment of drinking wine is growing in popularity and thus presents a huge market opportunity in many countries. Research is being done to understand what the preferences are in these various countries and what drives consumer response.

One of the fastest growing wine markets is China, yet there remains much to understand about that market in terms of mainstream customer response to wine labels. As such, to gain some knowledge about market preferences so that companies can develop this quite large and potentially rich wine market, marketing researchers have begun using focus groups.

Of particular concern when entering a new market is trade dress. Trade dress refers to the physical appearance of the product and suggests what marketers can do to make it more appealing. In wine, this is the color and shape of the bottle, and of particular concern is the label. Wine labels have become much more colorful, artistic, and sometimes even whimsical, with cartoon-like images and various depictions of animals (this trend is called "critter" labeling).

Recent focus groups in China suggest that wine labels should be bold according to a new report from Wine Intelligence. Wine Intelligence tested eight styles of labels in focus groups with 1,000 "urban upper middle class drinkers" of imported wine, from Beijing, Shanghai, Guangzhou, Shenzhen, Hangzhou, Chongqing, Shenyang, and Wuhan. Key findings from the study show that more contemporary, bold, and idiosyncratic designs work well.

In another study, researchers assembled groups of 20-something Chinese men and women. Several key challenges immediately emerged. The first involved the gender mix of groups. In mixed groups, the interactions and levels of participation were imbalanced. Often, regardless of how the moderator tried to direct interaction, one gender, typically the men, dominated the discussion, while the other gender was quiet. To gain reliable information, the focus groups had to be split by gender.

Suggestions for focus group use in China include:

- It takes longer than in the West for people to get comfortable sharing opinions. The focus group leader needs patience to convince participants to reveal their feelings about a brand.
- The ideal focus group leader is similar to the focus group members in demographics, which facilitates more discussion

■ Focus groups in China work better when divided by age and gender. It is difficult for younger people to express differences from older people and for women to express different opinions than men.

Source: Adapted from Mark Graham, 2005, "China's wine revolution," *The Wine Spectator*, November, pp. 60–74; Gentlemen Marketing Agency, "Daxue consulting is the leader for Focus Groups in China," 2014, marketingtochina.com/daxue-consulting-leader-focus-group-research-china/; Lucy Britner, 2015, "Chinese wine drinkers prefer contemporary labels—research," June, www.just-drinks.com/news/chinese-wine-drinkers-prefer-contemporary-labels-research_id117229.aspx

The knowledge advantage is very important in the first basic decision that the international manager makes—is the foreign market large enough so that the MNC can make profits by offering its products or services there? This question involves estimating the market potential and forecasting demand in the local market. Before deciding to enter the market, the MNC needs an understanding of whether or not local consumers would buy the product and how much of the product they would buy. Some large international research companies, such as Nielsen, can provide estimates of market demand, but such information is expensive. Various methods that rely on secondary data published by local governments, the World Bank, or the UN can also be useful. Here again, local market research companies can be very helpful.

Understanding Global Demand—Segmentation

segmentation
the process of grouping consumers according to any characteristics that influence their buying and consumption behavior, allowing MNCs to tailor marketing programs and products to satisfying the particular needs of distinct consumer groups

Segmentation drives our understanding of market demand. **Segmentation**, the process of grouping consumers according to their preferences and needs, allows the MNC to tailor marketing programs and products that focus on filling those particular needs. Segmentation is based on any characteristic that associates with how a consumer decides to spend his or her money. For example, incomes and spending power, gender, profession, or the presence of children all associate with the types of products needed in various segments.

Sometimes market research uncovers segments that are global. Global segments are made up of customers with similar needs regardless of their country. For example, consumers throughout the world have a need and preference for reliable, convenient, and accessible communication. Advances in communications technology have made it possible for cell-phone companies such as Apple to tap into these global segments. Cell-phone manufacturers can offer their products in Europe, Africa, the Middle East, Asia Pacific, Greater China, and North, South, and Latin America.[1]

Market research can also reveal regional segments where customer needs and preferences are similar within regions that cross several countries. This can be seen in certain regions such as Central America or Southern Europe. Also as an example, Afia, the Saudi Arabian food company, has capitalized on consistent preferences for its products across Persian regions and recently expanded to over 30 national markets.[2]

On occasion, market research reveals that segments are unique by country: that is, customer preferences are so diverse that cross-border grouping is not possible. How consumers' preferences cluster and group together across and within countries is a key consideration in solving the global–local dilemma. When segments are global or regional, it is possible to take advantage of standardized marketing programs. However, when segments are unique within a country, offerings must be adapted specifically for those unique local needs. As you will see below, this is related directly to how to solve the global–local dilemma introduced in Chapter 2.

Products and Brands—Global or Local?

For the marketer, a **product** provides a set of benefits that satisfy needs for the consumer. It consists of all the physical or tangible components, such as color, as well as all intangible components, such as service, reputation, prestige, and other elements that the customer cannot feel and see. All these components and characteristics, whether they are tangible or intangible, can bring value to the consumer, and taken as a whole are the product. In international business, the MNC can extend its products, adapt its products, or it can develop new products to take to foreign markets. Of course, this relates back to the research that shows you whether or not and how consumer needs and preferences group across foreign markets.

When the MNC's product meets the needs of customers in foreign markets with little or no change, marketers say it can be extended directly. **Direct extension** may involve only language changes on the label or instructions, as with soft drinks or bicycles, for example. However, sometimes even that is not necessary and a completely standardized product can be offered. The most famous example of direct extension is Coke. In many markets, it is not even necessary for Coke to change the language in product labeling. **Standardization** means that the product is uniform and consistent from country to country. Sometimes standardized products can be extended directly to only one or a few countries when there are regional segments. Direct extension works when consumers have highly common needs and common conditions of use and purchase in many countries. In such cases, the MNC's existing product can fill needs with little or no change. For example, the French luxury bag marketer Louis Vuitton directly extends its product offering with no modifications to consumers throughout the world. You can buy the same bag in New York, Paris, or Tokyo.

While there are many cost advantages to standardized products, much of the time, entering foreign markets means that some product changes are necessary. In some markets, these can be substantial. When consumer wants and needs differ from country to country, or when the conditions when or how the consumer uses the product differ, an **adaptation strategy** is appropriate. Adaptation means that the MNC customizes and adapts its products to local wants, needs, and conditions. Adaptation is rarely a question of "yes" or "no," but instead it involves questions of what features to customize, how much, and in which ways to customize them for which countries. Too much customization is costly and may not necessarily better serve consumer needs. Too little customization may ignore important differences in needs from country to country, and cost the MNC sales and market share.

When entering foreign markets, the MNC may decide to develop a new product from scratch. In the case of new product development for multiple foreign markets, the decisions of standardization or adaptation are not eliminated. There are still concerns over where and how much local adaptation is appropriate from market to market. Also, there are still decisions about the extent and scope of advantages to be gained from standardization. However, because the new product begins with a global scope, the global–local dilemma is managed from the very beginning. For example, when the product is "born global," from the very beginning there is a strong focus on tapping the commonalities across various foreign markets. Likewise, from the beginning, the new product formulation can be designed so that adaptation to local situations and local market preferences is accomplished more easily. Certain components and features are easily changed out or added in for various markets.

Experts often refer to the 70/30 rule here, meaning that at least 70 percent of a global product must remain consistent while 30 percent can remain flexible for response to local conditions.[3] For example, BMW's models are configured slightly differently between European and US markets. If you own a laptop computer, you can see that the only local physical

product
a set of benefits that satisfies needs for the consumer, including all physical or tangible components as well as all intangible components, such as service, reputation, prestige, and other elements that the customer cannot feel and see

direct extension
marketing the same product to customers across foreign markets with only minor modifications like language changes on the label or instructions, or no changes at all

standardization
maintaining a product's uniformity and consistency from country to country

adaptation strategy
customizing or adapting an MNC's products to the local wants, needs, and conditions of different foreign markets

adaptation necessary is to change the cord that plugs into the power converter to adapt to differences in electricity receptacles. Operating systems do require different languages.

Global and Local Branding

The **brand** is the identity of a product. It includes the name, logo, symbols, terms, song, colors, special packaging characteristics, product appearance, words, or anything else used to establish our association with the product and identify the product. For example, the Nike brand is based on the "swoosh" symbol, the "Just do it" slogan, as well as an array of other things that establish the image of Nike products and our positive association with them. Below, you can see an example of how dolls from Japan can have different brand images in different cultures.

brand
the identity of a product embodied in the name, logo, symbols, terms, song, colors, special packaging characteristics, product appearance, words, or anything else used to establish our association with the product and identify the product

Hello Kitty—What Do Brands Mean Across Cultures?

IB EMERGING MARKET
STRATEGIC INSIGHT

Since its creation in 1974 by Japan's Sanrio Company, Hello Kitty has grown by leaps and bounds. Generating over $5 billion a year, Hello Kitty ranks as the third most recognized Asian brand and is recognized in more than 40 countries across the world. Kitty's creator purposely did not develop many details about Kitty or her life, except her place of birth as London. With her oversized moon-shaped face, button nose, six whiskers, and dot eyes, she was simply cute. In Japanese this is known as *kawaii* style where something is infantile, delicate, and pretty. This style allowed her beholders, initially mostly young girls, to make Kitty whatever they needed her to be.

This turned out to be a very smart move, as across the globe the little cat seems to convey a message. Exactly what this message is likely varies from culture to culture. Some experts believe that in collectivist cultures such as China and Japan, where groups such as family, co-workers, and peer groups have great influence on behavior, people react to a brand such as Hello Kitty only because it is what everyone else does. According to these experts, consumers in collectivist cultures are more interested in the concrete product features and do not respond to abstract personality traits and characteristics portrayed in brands. While initially a product for schoolgirls the *kawaii* Hello Kitty is now a national brand in Japan and most of Asia.

In individualistic cultures like the US where people tend to "do their own thing," brands such as Hello Kitty have wide appeal precisely because she can mean a variety of things to different people. In individualistic cultures people respond to unique brand personalities and like brand portrayals that are friendly, according to experts.

However, some experts also suggest that these notions of collectivism versus individualism do not necessarily apply across all aspects of a person's life. In their public lives, the Japanese have an aversion to standing out, or challenging authority and social norms. Yet in their private lives, the Japanese highly value ideals of self-expression, freedom, and uniqueness—notions they would and could never express at work or in the educational system. So it could be that brand portrayals based on certain personalities and characteristics do appeal across cultures. The challenge in global branding is tapping into these customer responses that cross cultural and national boundaries. The lesson from Hello Kitty is that simplicity may be key.

One early detriment for Hello Kitty entering emerging markets was protection of its brand from copies. Perhaps an indicator of the future of Hello Kitty in emerging markets is its new store in Cambodia. Sanrio Co Ltd, the Japanese maker of Hello Kitty, opened its first shop in Phnom Penh's Aeon Mall in 2015. Betting on a growing market for the brand and increasing confidence in the Cambodian protection of intellectual property against knock-offs, the company plans to open more stores and even a Hello Kitty coffee shop.

Source: Adapted from Randall Frost, 2006, "Cultures split over brand personality," www.brandchannel.com, April 19; Esther Walker, 2008, "Top cat: How 'Hello Kitty' conquered the world," *The Independent*, May 20; Elad Granot, Thomas B. Alejandro and La Toya M. Russell, 2014, "A socio-marketing analysis of the concept of cute and it consumer culture implications," *Journal of Consumer Culture*, *14*(1); Igor Kossov, 2015, "Hello Kitty sees opportunity in Cambodia," *Khmer Times*, July 29.

In branding strategies and decisions, the MNC again faces the global–local dilemma. Whether extending an existing product or developing a new product for foreign markets, the MNC must decide whether to use one brand across all markets or a separate brand for regional markets or even a separate brand for each country market. When a product has a global identity, when there is a single brand for the product throughout the world, it is called a **global brand**. A global brand has a consistent identity with customers in all markets. A global brand has the same product benefits and characteristics, the same brand name, logos, and slogans, all with the same meaning for consumers throughout the world.

There are very few truly global brands. Exhibit 10.2 shows the top 25 brands in the world. Each year, Interbrand, a consulting company, tracks the performance of top global brands. As we can see, these global brands can be extremely valuable for the MNC. A major part of the advantage of global brands comes from economies of scale. The development and marketing costs for a global brand can be spread over large sales volumes in many markets. Global brands are much more visible than local brands because of their consistent identity. When customers travel around, they see the product in other countries as well as their own. In addition, global brands gain from media overlap. Potential customers in the US can view many Canadian TV channels and listen to many Canadian radio stations. With the advanced communications technology making satellite TV and radio more and more common, this media overlap will become commonplace and even more beneficial to global brands.

In spite of the powerful advantages of global brands, global branding strategies are not always possible and not always the most desirable approach. Local branding strategies may be necessary because the brand name may have some undesirable associations or offensive meanings in the local culture. Likewise, certain terms may have a specific meaning that is not consistent across cultures. For example, product brand names do not contain the term "diet" in association with caloric content in France because diet is a specific medical term requiring sale in a pharmacy. Brands like Diet Coke must be sold as Coke Light. In Japan, the diet is the national legislature. There are many examples of brand names that have restricted global use. For example, the "nova" in the Chevy Nova brand translates into "no go" in Spanish.

Local brands can be a great asset. Local branding can signal that the company is sensitive to cultural differences and committed to serving the local market. Customers may feel resentment toward a certain country or toward big MNCs in general. In such cases, local brands are preferable. Local brands can sometimes enjoy more support from local retailers when they advise customers on product choices. Local brands may also have wider distribution with more local retailers. This means that after-sales services, such as product repair and maintenance, are more available and easier for customers. Finally, even though it may not always be true, buyers

global brand
a single brand used for a product throughout the world. A global brand has a consistent identity with customers in all markets, using the same product benefits and characteristics, the same brand name, logos, and slogans, with the same meaning for consumers in all countries and markets

2008 Rank	2015 Rank	Brand	Sector	Country of Origin	2015 Brand Value ($m)	Change in Brand Value (2014–2015)
24	1	Apple	Computer Hardware	United States	170,276	43%
10	2	Google	Internet Services	United States	120,314	12%
1	3	Coca-Cola	Beverages	United States	78,423	–4%
3	4	Microsoft	Computer Software	United States	67,670	11%
2	5	IBM	Computer Services	United States	65,095	–10%
6	6	Toyota	Automotive	Japan	49,048	16%
21	7	Samsung	Consumer Electronics	Republic of Korea	45,297	0%
4	8	GE	Diversified	United States	42,267	–7%
8	9	McDonald's	Restaurants	United States	39,809	–6%
58	10	Amazon	Consumer Discretionary	United States	37,948	29%
13	11	BMW	Automotive	Germany	37,212	9%
11	12	Mercedes-Benz	Automotive	Germany	36,711	7%
9	13	Disney	Media	United States	36,514	13%
7	14	intel	Computer Hardware	United States	35,415	4%
17	15	Cisco	Computer Services	United States	29,854	–3%
23	16	Oracle	Computer Software	United States	27,283	5%
29	17	Nike	Apparel	United States	23,070	16%
12	18	HP	Computer Hardware	United States	23,056	–3%
20	19	Honda	Automotive	Japan	22,975	6%
16	20	Louis Vuitton	Luxury	France	22,250	–1%
22	21	H&M	Apparel	Sweden	22,222	5%
14	22	Gillette	Personal Care	United States	22,218	–3%
	23	Facebook	Communications	United States	22,029	54%
26	24	Pepsi	Beverages	United States	19,622	3%
15	25	American Express	Financial Services	United States	18,922	–3%

Exhibit 10.2 The 25 Top Global Brands
Source: Interbrand, "Best global brands," www.interbrand.com/best_global_brands.aspx

may believe that global or regional brands offered by well-known MNCs are more expensive than local offerings. Customers in local markets may see local brands as better value for their money. For example, in Turkey consumers see appliances produced by the Turkish company Arcelik as providing better value for their money than the better-known, more prestigious brands from Western MNCs.

When an MNC decides to take its products to foreign markets a big issue is the **country of origin (COO) effect**. This means that consumers can take strong messages based on the location where the product is made and marketed. The COO influence can be positive if the country is viewed positively, or negative if the country is viewed negatively. Sometimes the COO signals quality, as with French wines. Sometimes it signals less desirable cues such as the unfair competitive practices associated with China or substandard quality. The COO effect often comes from the "made in" label, but it can also come from the customer's perceptions about where the product originates. The following IB Emerging Market Strategic Insight examines the COO of the "made in China" label.

country of origin (COO) effect
the meanings and messages consumers derive from where a product is made and marketed. The influence can be positive if the country is viewed positively and negative if the country is viewed negatively

Country of Origin Effects of "Made in China"

IB EMERGING MARKET STRATEGIC INSIGHT

What does the "made in China" tag mean in the marketplace? A recent survey of marketing executives showed that country of origin (COO) effects are strong for Chinese products. Importantly, a majority of these marketing experts believe that the strong effect of the "made in China" label is negative and harmful in the marketplace. Similarly, a recent overseas' consumer survey reported only 32 percent had faith in products "made in China." They reported that Chinese products are seen as cheap, poor value, poor quality, unreliable, and unsophisticated (i.e. very basic). Importantly, this is not a perception confined to the US but also from Europe, Latin America, and even the Asia/Pacific regions. Also, it is not an impression limited to specific product categories because it includes cars, furniture, food, appliances, clothing, toys, and computers, among others.

Interestingly, many Chinese companies mass-produce unbranded and unidentified parts and components designed and developed by MNCs as ingredients in their own global brands. In this domain China already has over 100 world-class companies producing products for other manufacturers with known global brands.

Believe it or not, this situation is very similar to the one for the "Made in Japan" tag in the 1960s and 1970s. The Japanese undertook an aggressive strategy to upgrade their low-quality image and successfully transformed it to the extent that beginning in the 1980s and continuing through today. The Korean automobile manufacturers followed a very similar strategy entering the US. Originally perceived as just cheap, more quickly than the Japanese Korean vehicles and other manufacturing and electronics products are now seen as premium. Led by Toyota and Samsung, the labels "made in Japan" or "made in Korea" now stand for extremely high-quality and highly innovative products.

The Chinese see this as a road that they intend to follow and have embarked on a carefully orchestrated and coordinated strategy. First, Chinese companies have acquired a number of brands that are well established with strong brand equity such as the Haier Group's acquisition of GE's appliance division and Lenovo's acquisition of the IBM PC division. Second, with each acquisition they are absorbing the expertise in brand development and management that comes with the acquired brand and then incorporating it throughout their companies. These Chinese companies are gaining not only the equity and credibility of established brands but also the knowledge and talent to apply to their own homegrown brands. Chinese-owned brands are already benefiting from this strategy and are expected to climb in status and equity in the next five years.

While current perceptions of Chinese brands are clearly hurting the image of their products, the Japanese and Koreans demonstrated that such perceptions can indeed be overcome. At this time, there is only one Chinese brand, the information technology company Huawei ranked at 88, in the top 100 worldwide brands. However, given the newly acquired expertise coupled with the established brand names and the ingrained low-cost production capacity, powerful Chinese brands may come sooner than we think.

Source: Jeff Systun, Fred Burt and Annie Ly, 2005, "The strategy of Chinese brands," Interbrand White Paper; Doreen Wang, 2015, "What will it take for Chinese brands to be accepted by global consumers?" www.forbes. com, March 20; Sharon Kahn, 2016, "3 ways emerging markets can build breakout brands," *Columbia Business School Chazen Global Insights*, February 18.

Although COO effects can be quite strong, they can change over time. Products from Japan and Korea were once thought to be of poor quality but are now seen as among the highest-quality products in the world. In formerly communist countries such as the Czech Republic, US brands such as Nike and Reebok are associated with freedom. Interestingly, COO effects remain intact even when they do not actually apply to the product. With the increased economic connections between countries and the increasingly globalized supply chains we describe below, products may actually come from several countries. A consumer may buy a Dodge Ram pickup truck thinking that it is an American product. Edmunds lists its manufacturing locations as:[4]

Percent US/Canadian Content: 61
Final Assembly Country: US, Mexico
Engine Source: US, Italy
Transmission Source: US, Germany.

This is not much different than the Japanese Toyota Tacoma built for the US market:

Percent US/Canadian Content: 60
Final Assembly Country: US, Mexico
Engine Source: Japan
Transmission Source: Japan, US

Delivering Products Across the Globe—Distribution and Supply Chains

distribution channel
the set of intermediaries, mostly wholesalers and retailers, that help get products to end users but do not manufacture the products

direct distribution
MNCs selling products directly to consumers with no wholesale or retail intermediaries

Have you ever thought about how products in the supermarket—say, for example, Tillamook cheese—find their way to you? All the companies that help get the cheese from the dairy farmer to you make up the distribution channel for cheese. A **distribution channel** consists of intermediaries, mostly wholesalers and retailers, that do all the work to get products to you, the end user. In addition to traditional retail stores, more and more these days the company's products reach the consumer through e-tailers, stores that sell products through websites on the Internet. In rare cases, the company may act as its own distribution channel. This is called **direct distribution** because the company sells its products directly to the consumer. When this happens, it is most often through the Internet. A majority of the time, however, it is just too expensive for the company to sell product items one at a time to customers when intermediaries (wholesalers and retailers) can do it at a much lower cost. In taking its products to foreign markets, a company may use multiple distribution channels as shown in Exhibit 10.3.

Retailing in Global Markets

Retailers are intermediaries who are closest to the customer and serve the customer directly. Because of this, retailing is most often a localized activity. There are vast differences in retailing from country to country. People in the US are used to seeing mostly large stores with a vast array of products, such as Walmart superstores. In some countries, more retail stores are small mom-and-pop stores, sometimes carrying only a very limited line of items. This is the case for Italy, Algeria, and many parts of France, for example. In some countries, much retailing activity still happens through temporary open-air markets or bazaars. The merchants rent a spot and set up their temporary shop, sell their products for the afternoon, day, or evening, then pack up and repeat the same routine the next week or next evening.

In any case, although retailers always interact directly with customers, there is variance from country to country in the services provided to consumers. In many stores in the US, customers do not get any attention from salespeople, who are there only to complete transactions at the cash register. In Japan, certain components of retail service are legendary and contrast decidedly with the US. For example, at the checkout, the clerk typically wraps the product, boxes it, artistically wraps the box again, and then puts the package in an attractive shopping bag. In France, it is not unusual for the customers to bring their own shopping bags.

Though retailing varies greatly from country to country, overall it is rapidly changing worldwide. These changes involve three major trends: increasing retailer size, increases in

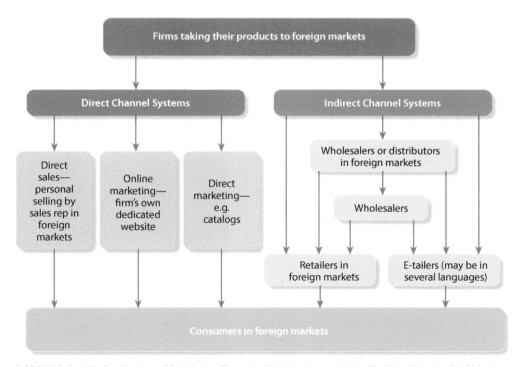

Exhibit 10.3 Possible Combinations of Distribution Channels with Various Intermediaries That May Be Involved in Global Distribution

e-tailing, and the growing importance of global retailers. First, although there are still many countries where small, specialty shops, or mom-and-pop stores predominate, there is a strong trend of larger retail stores developing a stronger presence worldwide. In China, for example, consumers can shop in large supermarkets and department stores more than ever before.

Exhibit 10.4 shows how retail establishment size has increased recently in China. Even in France, where traditional small merchants have been preferred historically, large *supermarchés* and department stores are seen more and more frequently—and their parking lots are jammed!

As mentioned earlier, MNCs can use their websites as a promotional tool. Increasingly, the Internet also is used in all types of buying and selling and various business transactions. This is generally known as **e-commerce**. The MNC can sell its products through its own website; however, for efficiency reasons, more often Internet distribution intermediaries, virtual retail stores, are used. These intermediaries are called **e-tailers**. Probably the most famous example of an e-tailer is Amazon.com. Importantly, MNCs can benefit from the spillover as communications technologies, e.g. the Internet, have freed up the access to foreign products. Consumers from all over the world can log on to Amazon.com to view and purchase products. MNCs taking their products to foreign markets have an increased chance to serve those markets through the Internet and various e-tailers. To ensure success in foreign markets, websites should be designed with cultural sensitivity in mind, just as print or television ads are, and even developing websites in other languages. Later, in Chapter 15, you will learn more about e-tailing in international business.

e-commerce
buying and selling transactions conducted through the Internet

e-tailers
Internet distribution intermediaries (virtual retail stores)

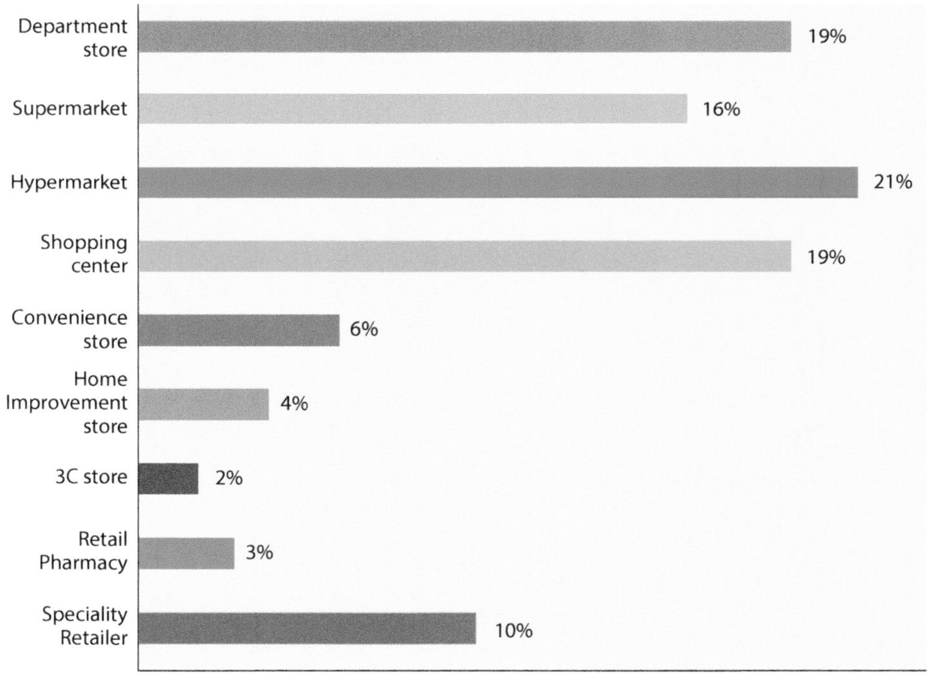

Exhibit 10.4 Retailing in China

Notes:

Hypermarket—usually defined as being 2,500 square meters or bigger; similar to the Super Walmart in the US.

3C store—a semi-specialty type of store carrying communication products, information technology products, and digital products.

Source: Adapted from *China Business Review*, 2010, "Understanding the Chinese market," www.chinabusinessreview.com/understanding-chinas-retail-market/

The third important trend in international distribution is the growth and increasing importance of global retailers. **Global retailers** are large-scale retailing MNCs. Not only are these individual retail establishments larger, they are located throughout various regions of the world and some of them are truly global. For example, Walmart has stores in China, Europe, Latin America, the Caribbean, Canada, Japan, and Korea. IKEA, the Scandinavian home furnishing retailer, has stores in Europe, Asia, and the United States. Carrefour, the French *hypermarché*, has opened stores in Latin America, China, and other parts of Asia. The number and influence of these mega-retailers continues to increase in the global market.

<aside>
global retailers
large-scale retailing MNCs that have locations throughout various regions of the world
</aside>

Wholesaling in Global Markets

Often, especially in international markets, the MNC's products do not go directly to a retailer. The MNC first sells its products to a wholesaler or distributor located in that country or at least in that region. These wholesalers or distributors are companies that transfer products from the manufacturer down the distribution channel so that they eventually get to a retailer and then to you, the consumer. The distributor in the local market sells the foreign product to the local retailers in the local markets. Several wholesalers may be involved in the distribution of a product before it gets to the retailer. For example, in Japan, products pass through three or sometimes even more wholesalers. Countries differ in the services provided by wholesalers to retailers. In Japan, retailers expect to be able to return all unsold goods to the wholesaler.[5] Oftentimes, local conditions make it necessary for MNCs to use wholesalers in foreign markets. These challenges can involve getting products through regulation in the foreign market or negotiating the complexities of local infrastructures such as transportation and warehousing.

Global Supply-chain Management

Distribution channels closely relate to supply-chain management. **Supply chains** involve all the tasks and services that connect everything that happens to a product from raw material to the consumer. Distribution channels are the later part of the supply chain that delivers the product to the end user. However, the sourcing of subcomponents and subassembly components and raw materials used to make the products also are part of the supply chain.

<aside>
supply chains
all the tasks and services that connect everything that happens to a product from raw material to the consumer. Distribution channels are the later part of the supply chain that delivers the product to the end user
</aside>

Supply chains involve all the linkages between the origination of raw materials, to the various processing points of raw materials, to the production facilities, and then to the distribution channels described above. Supply chains involve transporting of goods and materials, inventory management and flows, order processing, materials handling, and warehousing. Many parts and subcomponents used in products, as well as raw materials, are sourced from other countries. Thus, in many ways it is hard to find a business where the supply chains are not in fact global supply chains. For example, the Ford Crown Victoria is assembled in Canada; 75 percent of the Toyota Avalon assembly is done in the US; and the PT Cruiser is a product of Chrysler that is assembled in Mexico. Exhibit 10.5 shows a simplified example of Nikon's global supply chain. Note the reliance on emerging market countries for locations. Many of these global networks between MNCs are much more complex.

An increasingly important issue for MNCs includes the complexities of managing an ethical supply chain. Consumers are increasingly aware that an MNC's brand image rests not only on the ethical management of their own company but also on how their suppliers deal with issues such as child labor, fair pay, working conditions, and environmental impact. The Emerging Market Ethical Challenge box below shows not only how a UK company takes care in sourcing sustainable wood products for its home improvement business but, also, how emerging markets present potential ethical challenges for both local businesses and MNCs.

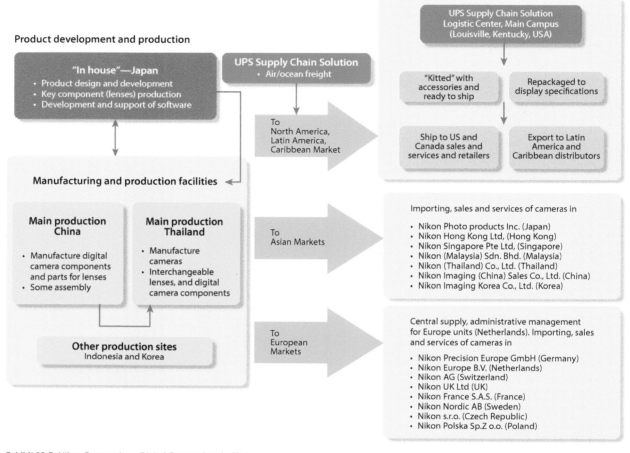

Exhibit 10.5 Nikon Corporation—Digital Camera Supply Chain

outsourcing
MNCs buying subcomponents and subassemblies needed in their own finished products from other companies

Rather than just buying raw materials such as steel or plastic and producing a product entirely on their own, many MNCs now buy completed subcomponents and subassemblies needed in their own finished products from other companies. This is called **outsourcing** in the supply chain. GM, the automaker, provides an example of outsourcing when it buys electronically controlled car seats from Johnson Controls rather than making the seats itself.

There are several reasons for the growth of global outsourcing. The first is cost savings. As you might imagine, a share of this comes directly from cheaper overseas labor costs. However, because outsourcing allows for the concentration of specialized skills, specialized companies that provide outsourced production to many companies gain economies of scale, often saving even more. Also, this concentration of specialized skills increases the quality and reliability of outsourced goods. For example, companies in India have made massive investments in the most advanced communication technologies and in language training that ensures that customers can hear no traces of Indian accents. This has facilitated extensive and high-quality outsourcing of customer service functions by a vast range of companies from American Express to Delta Airlines.[6] As an additional but very important benefit, because outsourcing allows the MNC to minimize investments in its own plants, equipment, training, and manufacturing facilities, and thus limit its fixed costs and overheads, the MNC that outsources can be more flexible in important strategic areas. This increased flexibility allows the MNC to be adaptable and deal with changing conditions so that it can remain competitive.

Stewarding Sustainable Forestry in Bolivia and Other Emerging Markets

EMERGING MARKET
ETHICAL CHALLENGE

Almost half (47 percent) of Latin America is covered by natural forest. However, the forest is shrinking dramatically as unsustainable and often illegal logging takes an estimated 58 million hectares of forest every year. Counter to this trend, Bolivia has become a leader in providing sustainable wood products to world markets.

Bolivia has over five million acres, more than a quarter of the country's forest coverage, certified under Forest Stewardship Council (FSC) rules. Sixteen of the major forest harvest operations in Bolivia are certified according to the FSC's rules. FSC rules not only cover protection of water and other natural resources, but also require respect for the rights of indigenous people and protection of the economic well being of local communities and forest workers.

Bolivia is now Latin America's leading sustainable timber producer. Notes Daniel Arancibia, Latin American representative of the Forest Stewardship Council, "One of the key successes of Bolivia was the willingness of the government, private sector and non-profit groups to work together to establish a system-wide arrangement that would in turn create the preconditions for sustainable forest management."

The "Bolivia certified" label now has an impact in the overseas markets for Bolivian wood products, mostly tropical hardwoods sold as doors, furniture, floorboards, chairs, and sawn timber in the EU and the US. Exports now exceed $20 million a year.

Typical of the Bolivia certified wood importers is the UK retailer B&Q, a home-improvement store. B&Q is one of the main importers of Bolivia certified forest products and yearly sources over 1,700 cubic meters of round wood, mostly used in its garden furniture. B&Q has a commitment to ensuring all its wood and paper products come from sustainable forests or recycled material.

Like Bolivia, many other emerging countries have extensive forests and the use of those forests for timber production has yielded considerable income. For some, increasing trade in forest products has supported economic growth and a reduction of poverty. However, the model has not worked for all and resulted in misconduct in some countries. Experts argue, if not managed sustainably, there can be severe economic, environmental, and social costs while forest clearance generates a one-time cash windfall from the timber sold, it ultimately reduces the prospects for long term forest-based livelihoods. In developing local regulations, such as those in Bolivia, countries, such as Brazil, Gabon, Guyana, Malaysia, and Peru have made progress while Cambodia, Democratic Republic of Congo, Nigeria, and Papua New Guinea still have major challenges. The Food and Agricultural Organization of the United Nations argues that, "Safeguards must be firmly put in place to ensure that trade is based on legal and sustainable forest use, fair labour conditions and equitable sharing of benefits. Good governance is essential in setting the rules for sustainable production and trade."

Source: Adapted from *The Ethical Corporation*, 2006, www.ethicalcorp.com/content.asp?ContentID=4174, March 28; Karen Ellis, 2015, "WWF makes the economic and business case for sustainable timber," *GreenBiz*, April 24; Food and Agricultural Organization of The United Nations, 2016, "Forest products trade and marketing," www.fao.org/forestry/trade/en/, July 4.

To gain all of the advantages of a global supply-chain network, the MNC must understand the many complexities involved. First, outsourcing increases the importance of the purchasing and acquisition function in the company. When the MNC is purchasing important subcomponents from outside manufacturers, the international purchasing managers buying those subcomponents are making decisions that are much more important than if they were simply reordering paper for the copy machine. The management of key sourcing decisions has made purchasing a core strategic function. Second, the supply chain must be viewed and managed as a system with full understanding of how all the linkages affect one another. The MNC can no longer focus only on vendors with whom it deals directly, but must also consider its suppliers' suppliers and its customers' customers. Third, because of the complex interconnections between all the MNCs in the supply chain, data and tracking information have become much more important. In managing global supply chains, MNCs are tending to rely more and more on software platforms such as those dedicated specifically to supply-chain management, but also on others such as CRM (customer relationship management) and EMS (enterprise management systems). These specialized management information systems accumulate the data necessary to track the flows of goods and products through the global supply chains. They help ensure that the goods and products arrive on time at the right locations, many of which are often dispersed throughout the world.

Perhaps one of the most sophisticated global supply chains is that used by Dell Computer. In the IB Emerging Market Strategic Insight you can see how this system works for the competitive advantage of Dell.

Dell's Emerging Market-dominated Global Supply Chain

IB EMERGING MARKET
STRATEGIC INSIGHT

So when Dell produces a laptop from where do the parts originate? Keep in mind that there are 30 or so major components in the computer. The Intel microprocessor comes from a plant in the Philippines, Costa Rica, Malaysia, or China. The memory comes from Korea, Taiwan, Germany, or Japan. The graphics card, motherboard, and modem come from China. The cooling fan comes from Taiwan. The displays come from South Korea, Japan, or Taiwan. The wireless card comes from China, Malaysia, or Taiwan. The battery comes from Mexico, Malaysia, China, or South Korea. The disk drives come from Singapore, Thailand, Indonesia, China, Taiwan, or the Philippines. The power adapter comes from Thailand, Taiwan, or China. The power cord comes from Malaysia or India. The removable memory stick comes from Israel or Malaysia. And finally, the carrying bag comes from China. The list above indicates where the supplier's manufacturing plants are located so this is where the parts actually originate. Importantly, while some of these manufacturing facilities are owned by companies located in the same country, a number are also owned by companies in England, Ireland, the US, Japan, Korea, and Germany, expanding the global scope of this supply-chain symphony even more.

Keep in mind that the 30 components above are only the main part of the picture. There are a number of smaller components as well. In fact, the total supply chain for the computer involves about 400 companies from start to finish. Likewise, keep in mind that Dell uses multiple suppliers for each part. That way, if one supplier breaks down or cannot meet Dell's needs, others can step in. This keeps the flow going continuously.

In Exhibit 10.6 you can see the list of Dell's suppliers and it shows Dell's heavy reliance on emerging market companies:

Supplier	Location	Supplier	Location
AMD	Dongguan (China)	Lihua Shin Shin	Shanghai (China)
Amphenol	Xiamen (China)	Lishen	Tianjin (China)
AUO	Suzhou, Shanghai (China); Longtan, Taichung (Taiwan)	Liteon	Hsinchu (Taiwan)
Boardtek	Taiwan	LiteOn / Silitek	Dongguan (China)
BOE B3	Hefei (China)	Luxshare	Dongguan, Jiangxi (China)
BTI	Guangzhou (China)	Micron	Muar (Malaysia); Singapore; Xi'an (China)
Buruize	Xiamen (China)	MingJi	Dongguan (China)
C2G	Kunshan, Shenzhen (China)	Mitac	Shunde (China)
Catcher	Suqian (China)	Molex	Dongguan (China)
CEC Panda	Nanjing (China)	MSI	Shenzhen (China)
Celestica	Suzhou (China)	Multek	Zhuhai (China)
ChangYun	Kunshan (China)	Panasonic	Suzhou, Wuxi (China)
Chicony	Dongguan (China)	Pegatron	Suzhou (China); Taiwan
Compal	Jundiai (Brazil); Chengdu, Kunshan (China); Taiwan	Plastoform	Shenzhen (China)
Coretronic	Kunshan (China)	PLDS	Beihai (China)
Costlight	Zhuhai (China)	Power Star	Fujian (China)
CPM	Jurong (China)	Primax	Chongqing (China)
Dazhi	Suzhou (China)	Qisda	Suzhou (China); Taiwan
ECS	Shenzhen (China)	QM	Shanghai (China)
Ergotron	Dongguan (China)	Quanta	Shanghai (China)
Fagerdala	Chengdu, Xiamen (China)	RiTeng(Casetek)	Shanghai (China)
Finisar	Wuxi (China); Malaysia	RRD	Chengdu (China)
Flextronics	Sorocaba (Brazil); Penang (Malaysia); Zhuhai (China)	Samsung	Suzhou (China)
Founder	Chongqing, Zhuhai (China)	Sandisk	Shanghai (China); Penang (Malaysia)
Foxconn	Jundiai (Brazil); Kunshan, Yantai, Chongquing, Tianjin, Wuhan (China); Juarez (Mexico)	SDI	Suining, Tianjin (China); Seremban (Malaysia)
FSC	Xiamen (China)	Sharp	Wuxi (China)
GBM	Shenzhen (China)	Simplo	Chongqing, Changshu (China)
GCE	Changshu, Suzhou (China); Taiwan	SinHer	Kunshan, Chongqing (China)
GN Netcom	Shenzhen (China)	SK Hynix	Wuxi (China)

Exhibit 10.6 A List of Dell's Suppliers Showing its Reliance on Emerging Market Companies

Supplier	Location	Supplier	Location
Guangkuotiandi	Chengdu (China)	Speed Wireless	Huizhou (China)
Hannstar	Jiangyin, Nanjing (China); Tainan (Taiwan)	SZS	Suzhou (China), Taiwan
HengHao	Kunshan (China)	Taiyi	Kunshan (China)
Hexing	Xiamen (China)	Tasun	Chongqing, Suzhou (China)
Higgstec	Yilan (China)	TE(Tyco)	Shunde (China)
Hitachi	Prachinburi (Thailand)	Torgusa	Xiamen (China)
HLDS	Bangi (Malaysia)	Toshiba	Shanghai (China); Philippines
Hyna	Xiamen (China)	TPK	Xiamen (China)
IBM	China, Mexico	TPT	Wuxi (China)
Icon Trans	Penang (Malaysia)	TPV	Fujian, Fuqing (China)
Innolux	Foshan, Ningbo (China); Tainan (Taiwan)	Tripod	Wuxi (China)
Intel	Vietnam	TSST	Sephil (Philippines)
Interplex(Amtek)	Huizhou, Shanghai, Shenzhen (China)	Veritiv	Lodz (Poland); Chengdu, Suzhou (China)
Inventec	Shanghai (China)	VGT	Huizhou (China)
Iretex	Xiamen (China)	VIA Optronics	Suzhou (China)
Jarlly	Dongguan, Fuqing (China)	Viasystems	Guangzhou (china)
Jingda	Kunshan (China)	Weili	Taizhou (China)
Job Square	Pulau Pinang (Malaysia)	Western Digital	Brazil
Kensington	China, Taiwan	Wistron	Chengdu, Zhongshan (China); Juarez (Mexico)
Kerry	Beijing (China)	Worldmark	Chongging (China)
Kingslide	Taiwan	Wuzhu	Dongguan (China)
Kingston	Shanghai (China)	XIP	Shenzhen (China)
Korrun	Dongguan (China)	YCT	Wujiang (China)
Laibao	Chongqing (China)	YFY	Kunshan (China)
Leoho	Suzhou (China)	Younglighting	Guangzhou, Shanghai (China)
Lexmark	Dongguan (China); Mexico	Yuandeng	Taiwan
LGC / LG Chem	Chongqing, Nanjing (China)	Zhuchang	Shanghai (China)
LGD / LG Display	Dongguan, Guanzhou, Nanjing (China); Gumi (South Korea)	Ziyan	Shanghai (China)
Lianhong	Suzhou (China)	Zylux	Shenzhen (China)
Lianyi	Zhongshan (China)		

Exhibit 10.6 A List of Dell's Suppliers Showing its Reliance on Emerging Market Companies

Source: Adapted from Tomas L. Friedman, 2005, *The World is Flat: A Brief History of the 21st Century*, New York: Farrar, Straus and Giroux; www.dell.com/learn/us/en/uscorp1/cr-social-responsibility

Pricing—Global or Local?

Pricing in foreign markets is a critically important element of the marketing program because its effects on the MNC are very direct in terms of revenues and profits. While, of course, the price must cover product costs, beyond that the international manager must understand how the consumer in a foreign market values the MNC's product: that is, what the customer is willing to pay. These two factors set the lower and upper boundaries of the price, as Exhibit 10.7 shows. Other factors in foreign markets, such as competitors, distribution channels, and government policies, make the pricing decision quite complex.

For several reasons, competitors play a big part in an MNC's pricing decisions. First, the number of competitors can vary greatly from country to country. In some countries there are only a few competing products, while in other foreign markets there may be many others competing for the same customers. Second, the form or type of competitors can be quite different in various local and regional markets. Some competitors may be small, others may be state-owned, and still others may be large MNCs. Third, the support competitors enjoy can differ greatly across the various foreign markets. Even if competitors are not state-owned, they may enjoy preferential treatment from the local governments. They may get cheap loans, subsidies, and better access to land and materials needed, for example.

Distribution channels in the foreign market are another important factor in pricing decisions. The margins demanded by wholesalers, distributors, or retailers are often higher in foreign markets than in the home country market. Yet, if the MNC wants to compete, it must pay the margins and pass as much of the costs as possible on to the consumer in the price. Complex distribution channels with more layers can also increase costs. For example, as noted above, in Japan, products must pass through several wholesalers before they finally reach the retailer, where the customer may purchase them. The retailer in turn must offer more services than would a similar store in the US. The result is that similar goods sold in the US and Japan are often more expensive in Japan, even when they are Japanese goods. For example, the most expensive Toyota Camry would cost over $50,000 before taxes in Japan but only approximately mid $30,000s in the US.[7]

Finally, government regulations and policies influence pricing. Some governments, even those that are seemingly friendly, find ways to keep foreign products off the shelves, and they often do this through pricing. Some countries are openly protectionist, with steep taxes on foreign

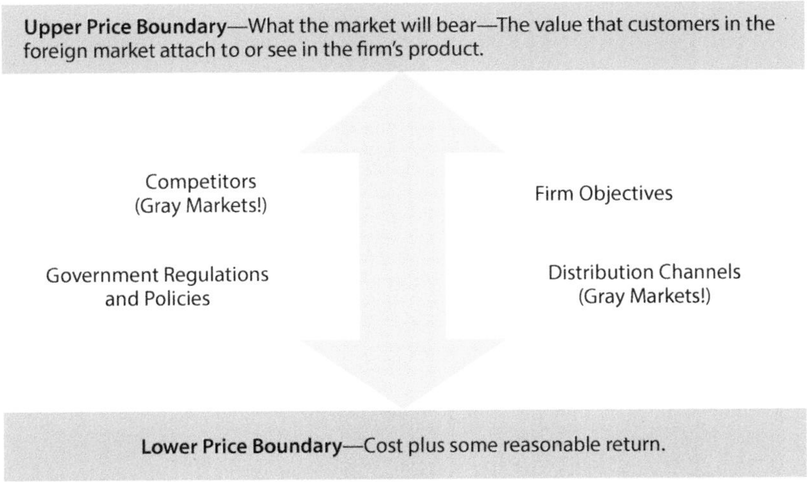

Upper Price Boundary—What the market will bear—The value that customers in the foreign market attach to or see in the firm's product.

Competitors
(Gray Markets!)

Firm Objectives

Government Regulations
and Policies

Distribution Channels
(Gray Markets!)

Lower Price Boundary—Cost plus some reasonable return.

Exhibit 10.7 Pressures and Factors Influencing Global Pricing

products and heavy red tape and bureaucracy meant to bog down and limit market access to foreign products. For example, because China is trying to develop its own wine industry, foreign wines there are heavily taxed and heavily burdened with forms and bureaucratic red tape. This greatly inhibits the ability to market wines in China. Some countries directly regulate the price of foreign products through price controls. Sometimes these controls can force foreign companies to price their products so low that they cannot make a reasonable return. Some governments are even quite tolerant of knock-off or counterfeit products that can be priced to undercut foreign products.

If the marketer misjudges the upper price boundary and sets the product price too high in a foreign market, customers will avoid the product and the MNC will lose sales. Alternatively, competitors may see a high price as an opportunity to introduce cheaper knock-off versions of the company's product. This can undercut the foreign product's chances to make gains in the market.

However, setting the price too low can sometimes be an even bigger problem. Local governments can see low prices as an attempt at dumping. **Dumping** occurs when a foreign competitor sells products in a local market at prices that are below local product costs. Because dumping puts local companies at a serious disadvantage, local governments will step in and cause problems for the foreign company. Alternatively, low prices can attract the attention of governments and encourage them to tax or regulate MNCs to protect their domestic companies. Foreign customers may also associate a low price with low quality and stay away from the product.

Another possible harmful outcome of setting the price too low is gray markets. A **gray market** is created when a low-priced product in one market is bought up by unauthorized distributors at the lower price and resold in another market at a higher price. Low prices in one market lead unauthorized dealers to make money by selling the MNC's product in another market at a higher price.

All of these factors make pricing decisions in foreign markets very complex. In terms of the global–local dilemma, these factors among others we discussed in earlier chapters, such as currency movements and transfer pricing, make coordination and standardization of pricing extremely difficult. Of all the elements in marketing, pricing may be the one that is most driven by local considerations.

dumping
foreign competitors selling products in a local market at abnormally low prices that are below product costs

gray market
unauthorized distributors buying a low-priced product in one market and reselling the product in another market at a higher price

Talking to Customers Across the Globe—Marketing Communications

communication mix
anything that an MNC uses to inform customers about its products, promote its products, and persuade customers to buy and use its products. Communication mix includes advertising (print, radio, the Internet, or TV); promotions such as coupons, point-of-purchase displays, event sponsorship, or contests; and personal selling

How do you hear about products? What gets you interested in trying a different product? Sometimes you hear about products from your friends or family, but most often you hear about products through the MNC's communication mix. Advertising in the mass media, whether it is print, radio, the Internet, or TV; promotions such as coupons, point-of-purchase displays (in-store displays or signs), event sponsorship, or contests; and personal selling by someone in the store or someone who calls on you in your home—all are part of the MNC's **communication mix**. As the term indicates, the communication mix is anything that the MNC uses to inform customers about its products, promote its products, and persuade customers to buy and use its products. When products are being taken to foreign markets, the communication mix brings a number of unique and special challenges for the MNC. Again, the global–local dilemma heavily influences communication strategies and programs.

Advertising in the mass media may be the most visible component of the MNC's communication mix. The MNC's biggest problems often happen with language. It is more than a matter of simple translation. For example, marketing experts note that there are five different Spanish words for "tire."[8] Often, words, phrases, or terms have subtle meanings that are unique to the culture. For example, in Quebecois French, *ma blonde* means "girlfriend," not "my blond," as it would in the US, and *ma chum* means "boyfriend," not "buddy." It is wise to remember that words do not always translate directly and can have meanings that the MNC never intended. Also, animal sounds vary by culture. In the US a pig says oink. In Japan a pig says ruff-ruff.

In advertising, there are strong cultural taboos that must be avoided, especially when dealing with religion and gender issues. The use of images and drawings of religious deities is strictly forbidden in Islam, for example. Appeals to women and girls are greatly restricted in Arab countries. In Turkey, L'Oréal once used naked female body images in ads for its cellulite treatment products. The conservative Turkish government banned the ads and imposed heavy penalties on the company. Likewise, despite the huge influence of Western culture in China and India, these societies remain extremely conservative regarding gender-related issues. Any messages that include even the slightest sexual connotation or image meet with a negative reception in these countries. In France, it is highly desirable for advertising to have a strong artistic component, with more music, drama, and flourish in the product presentation in ads. The French see US advertising as stark and clinical.

In addition to language and cultural differences, advertising regulations and access to advertising media, such as TV, radio, newspapers, and magazines, differ widely from country to country. In some countries, media are not available because they do not exist, while in others they are less developed. For example, the postal system in China is highly limited when compared to the US, so the international manager must allow for this in any advertising that depends on postal delivery. Even when media for advertising are abundant, some countries limit the use and access. In Germany, for example, TV advertisements can appear only at certain times. The content of advertisements is highly controlled in certain countries such as Malaysia. Exhibit 10.8 shows global media spending on the major forms of advertising. Exhibit 10.9 shows the recent growth trends in advertising by county.

Regardless of all these differences in the existence and use of mass media for advertising, advancements in communication technologies are bringing great changes. Satellite TV and radio are blurring national boundaries at an astounding rate. These technologies have resulted in worldwide spillover of advertising messages. A message designed and intended for a local or even regional audience can be viewed all over the world. Another great equalizing force in the communication mix is the Internet. Earlier, we discussed the impact of the Internet in retailing, but it also serves as a powerful device for promoting the MNC's products. MNCs can use banner advertisements placed on popular sites to attract and inform potential customers. These potential customers can then seek additional product information from the MNC's dedicated websites. While the difficulties with the global–local dilemma will always be with us in advertising, it seems that communication technologies are making global strategies more and more viable.

Promotions, devices such as coupons, contests, or point-of-purchase displays, are generally growing in popularity in markets. Point-of-purchase displays are displays or signs that are set up in the retail store, often at the end of the aisle. The use of point-of-purchase displays has greatly increased in China as the size of retail establishments has grown. In other countries, where many stores are still smaller, e.g. Japan and France, point-of-purchase displays are not appropriate.

promotions
devices such as coupons, contests, or point-of-purchase displays

The use of coupons, probably the most common promotional device in the US, varies greatly from country to country. Some countries, such as Germany and Austria, currently have laws forbidding the use of coupons. In France, Sweden, and Great Britain, for example, any promotional devices that involve or hint at games of chance, such as lotteries, sweepstakes, or contests, are greatly restricted or forbidden.[9] In addition to the laws, infrastructures and cultural acceptance of promotions vary. For example, as mentioned earlier, though it is rapidly improving the postal service in China is still not well developed, making the delivery of coupons by mail impractical. In addition, Chinese consumers are somewhat embarrassed to use coupons.

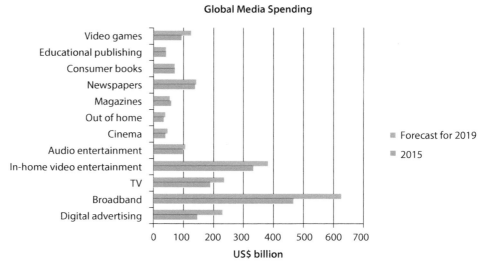

Exhibit 10.8 Global Media Spending
Source: Adapted from Moinak Bagchi, Sonja Murdoch and Jay Scanlan, 2015, "The state of global media spending," McKinsey & Company, December.

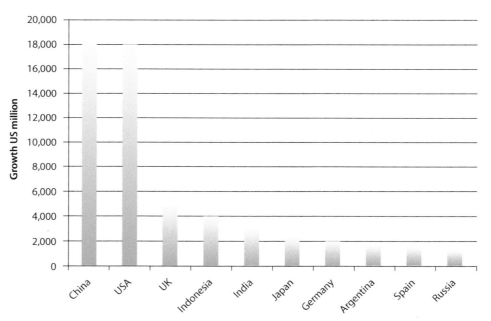

Exhibit 10.9 Leading Countries in Growth and Advertising Spending, 2015–2018
Source: Adapted from ZenithOptimedia, 2016, "Executive summary: Advertising expenditure forecasts," March.

In terms of the global–local dilemma, promotions are much more effective when managed locally. Given the vast differences in laws and regulations, as well as cultural acceptance of various promotions, there are few opportunities for global programs. Sponsorship of high-profile world sporting events may be the most compelling exception. For example, sponsorship of the Olympic Games offers such an opportunity. Look at Exhibit 10.10 for the sponsors of recent summer and winter Olympic Games. Check out the follow websites for more information: www.sponsorship.com/Latest-Thinking/Rio-2016-Olympic-Sponsorship-Insights. aspx; www.sponsorship.com/Sponsorship-Consulting/Sochi-2014-Olympic-Sponsorship-Insights.aspx show the sponsors of some recent Games. It is probably no accident that several of these sponsors are found on our list of top global brands. Local top brands also appear. Such sponsorship, while highly effective in building the MNCs' brands and communicating the MNCs' products, is extremely costly.

Because marketing communications practices and local country laws vary so greatly, it is especially important to have local guidance and information, and this often comes in the form of an advertising agency. Advertising agencies design print, television, and radio advertisements and buy spots in media so that the ads are aired on television and radio programs and placed in magazines and newspapers. In many countries, local advertising agencies are quite rare. This may explain why, in the last decade or so, global or world advertising agencies such as Dentsu or J. Walter Thompson Co. have become increasingly important. These MNCs establish local operations, with local personnel and in-depth understanding of local conditions from country to country. While they can be expensive, they may be worth the cost if they can prevent costly mistakes. Importantly, because of their global perspective these agencies can help develop and coordinate standardized communications programs where possible and appropriate.

Personal selling, where the MNC's representative interacts one-on-one with customers to sell the MNC's product, is an expensive but powerful communication tool for the MNC. It is often used for selling large and complex products such as airplanes or steel plants. When, for example, Boeing signed the contract for $6 billion in airplanes to six Chinese airlines, no doubt a lion's share of the work in that deal involved various elements of personal selling.

For the most part, personal selling efforts for MNCs take place within countries. The MNC hires local sales representatives because they are invaluable in bridging cultural differences. In working with Korean companies, for example, the sales directors of a US semiconductor design company noted how important it is to "have someone on the ground" so that the company has

personal selling
an MNC's representative interacts one-on-one with customers to sell the company's product

Sponsors of the Rio 2016 Summer Olympic Games			
Coca-Cola	Atos Origin	Bridgestone	Dow
McDonald's	P&G	Omega	Panasonic
Samsung	Visa	Bradesco	Bradesco Seguros
Correios	Embratel	Claro	Nissan
Aliansce	ApexBrasil	Cisco	Estacio
EY	Globo	Sadia	Qualy
Skql	Latam	361	

Sponsors of the Sochi 2014 Winter Olympic Games			
Coca-Cola	Altos	GE	Bridgestone
Samsung	Dow	P&G	McDonald's
Omega	Panasonic	Visa	EF
Avaya	Baltika	Ottobock	Jet Set
Kommepcaht	Adecco	Arcelor Mittal	Cadbury
Cisco	Deloitte	Thomas Cook	UPS

Exhibit 10.10 Olympic Sponsors

Source: www.rio2016.com/en/sponsors; www.datalounge.com/thread/13145547-official-list-of-sochi-winter-olympics-sponsors-and-suppliers

a full understanding of the customer, their needs, and the local situation. This extends beyond language differences into understanding laws, regulations, local infrastructure, and cultural traditions.

Cross-cultural negotiation is one of the biggest challenges in global selling. Even with a strong local representative, managers from local buying companies and foreign selling companies often must get together to negotiate agreements. Successful negotiations depend on how well the international managers adjust and accommodate cultural differences. Exhibit 10.11 shows the stages in the cross-cultural negotiation process; they include preparation, building the relationship, exchanging information and the first offer, persuasion, concessions, agreement, and post-agreement. Preparation involves gathering information on the issues and objectives, the people involved as negotiators, the company, and the setting. Relationship building begins when the people from the two companies actually meet. The focus is on simply getting to know one another and developing a sense of trust.

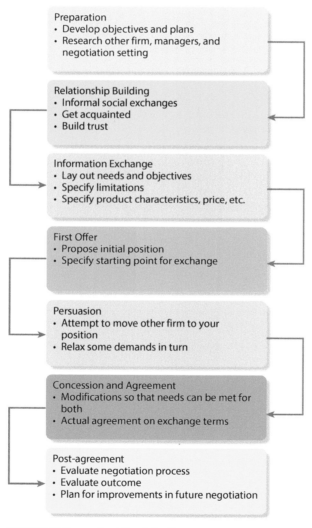

Exhibit 10.11 Cross-cultural Negotiation Process

The real work in cross-cultural negotiation begins with information exchange and the first offer. This stage is where each company reveals its needs and objectives. In this stage, the negotiators lay out the technical limitations and standards for the product features, characteristics, price, and quality. Here both sides present their first offer, which is the first proposal of what they would like to get in the agreement.

The next step, persuasion, is the heart of the negotiation process and where each side attempts to get the other side to see its own position and agree with it. Concessions and agreement is where the final agreement is reached after some modification of demands. Usually both sides must relax some of their demands to satisfy each other's needs. Post-agreement is where the process is re-evaluated so that the negotiators can see what worked and understand what did not work so that better negotiation can result the next time.

These steps are all important, but it is even more important to remember that there is great variance from culture to culture in the role of each stage and when and how they occur. For example, in the US the early informal stages are short and less important, while in Japan the social non-business parts of the process are critical in setting the stage for any success later on. This is the most important stage and cannot be rushed because it builds the personal context on which the whole negotiation process relies. In China, the later parts of the process are key because important agreements and concessions do not take place until very late in the process. The international manager must be highly flexible in terms of ending times when negotiating with the Chinese. Some cultures, such as Japanese, are quite comfortable with silence in the negotiation process while others, such as the Brazilians and Americans, tend to speak constantly. No matter what the culture, doing your homework is key. Gathering as much information and understanding of the other company, the national culture, and even the individual managers from the other company is necessary.

Chapter Review

The global–local dilemma may play out in the biggest way in marketing. To succeed in global markets, the MNC manager must understand when and how to be sensitive to the differences in global markets. At the same time, international managers can gain key cost and competitive advantages if they understand how and when to capitalize on the similarities across markets, both regionally and globally. The first step in developing marketing programs that effectively respond to these differences and similarities involves gathering information and gaining a knowledge advantage with regard to foreign markets. International market research including primary and secondary data can answer important marketing questions about demand, market segmentation, and consumer preferences to help international managers develop effective programs.

Effective global marketing programs rely on the marketing mix that consists of the product, distribution, pricing, and marketing communication to reach customers in foreign markets. Decisions about the extent to which the product offering and product brand development are standardized or adapted are among the first decisions that need to be made by the MNC manager when going global. At times, MNCs may extend a product and brand directly to other markets with little or no change. However, most of the time there must be at least some minimal adaptation— some changes made to the product and branding in response to local conditions in various markets. Rather than a question of "yes" or "no," adaptation and standardization in products and brands is a matter of the right amount in the right places. For example, sometimes products and brands can be standardized across regions but not throughout the world. Global brands are products where the offering and branding are pretty much standardized across the world. In reality, these are quite rare as some level of cultural sensitivity and adaptation to local conditions is usually necessary.

Distribution and supply chains comprise an important element of global marketing. The international manager must develop a system for delivering the product in local markets so that it is readily available to the customer. There are times when direct distribution, most likely through the Internet, works well. However, usually indirect distribution through retailers and wholesalers in the foreign market is needed to get the product to the customer. The Internet is increasingly important in providing customers with access to products from MNCs across the globe. This e-commerce is sometimes done through e-tailers, which are Internet retailers. In addition to e-tailing, other trends are affecting retailing throughout the world. For example, global retailers, large-scale retailers with stores throughout the world, are becoming more important and retail establishments are getting much larger generally.

Global supply chains are an important aspect of global distribution and of global business in general. Supply chains have become more important because companies now outsource much more than in the past. Technology, cost savings, and flexibility have made global outsourcing very attractive. All the components and parts in a Dell computer can come from companies in dozens of countries, for example.

Global pricing is influenced by a number of factors in foreign markets, for example the type and extent of local competition, margins demanded in distribution channels, and government regulations. If the price is set too low in foreign markets, the MNC can be seen as dumping or gray markets can be created. If the price is set too high, customers in the foreign market will turn to local products or products of competing MNCs.

The marketing communication mix consists of advertising, promotions, and personal selling, everything that the MNC uses to talk to its customers. If personal selling is needed, having local sales personnel in place in the foreign market is critical. However, advertising may become more standardized because of spillover in all the communication technologies. The Internet and satellite television and radio allow customers from all over the world to access whatever information they want. Nonetheless, cultural norms, laws, and regulations regarding promotions and advertising vary greatly from culture to culture.

Discussion Questions

1   What are the major strategic differences between marketing domestically and marketing internationally?

2   What are the major challenges of marketing in emerging markets?

3   Discuss the importance of marketing research for international marketing. What challenges face marketing researchers when they enter other countries?

4   Describe the choices in the marketing mix in relationship to the global–local dilemma.

5   Explain how and why the marketing mix can vary in global markets.

6   Explain why consumer products often require more adaptation than industrial products sold in business-to-business markets.

7   Discuss the incentives for MNCs to develop global supply chains such as that described in the chapter for Dell. What are the major management challenges for managing such global supply chains?

International Business Skill Builder

Test Your Cross-cultural Advertisements

Step 1: Pick three popular television advertisements that you think are a reflection of popular culture and record them.

Step 2: Find three students who have arrived in your school this last year from a foreign country—try to pick someone from Asian countries, from Arab countries, the Americas, or from Europe, as appropriate.

Step 3: Play the ads for the students and interview them to get their impressions about the advertisements. First, ask each student to directly interpret the advertisements in their own language and then back-translate it.

Step 4: Apart from the direct interpretation, ask each student what the commercials would mean, what the message would be, to a typical person from their country.

Step 5: Ask each student if there would be anything offensive to their culture or to subgroups (e.g. genders) in their cultures.

Chapter Internet Activity

1   Look at the websites for Kia, Tata Motors, Toyota, GM, and BMW in different countries.

2   Translate if necessary using **http://babelfish.altavista.com/**.

3   Analyze the differences in how these famous brands are presented to local customers.

4   How does the marketing communication differ by country and for emerging market companies?

Key Concepts

- adaptation strategy
- back translation
- brand
- communication mix
- country of origin (COO) effect
- direct distribution
- direct extension
- distribution channel
- dumping
- e-commerce
- e-tailers
- focus group
- global brand
- global–local dilemma
- global retailers
- gray market
- international marketing research
- marketing mix
- moderator
- outsourcing
- personal selling
- primary data
- product
- promotions
- secondary data
- segmentation
- standardization
- supply chain

BUSINESS > INTERNATIONAL

Frito-Lay with
Chinese Characters

In the 1930s, two men in different parts of the United States began businesses that would eventually come to dominate the global snack food market. In 1932, Elmer Doolin, an ice cream salesman, stopped for lunch at a local San Antonio café. He noticed a package of corn chips at the café and purchased it for five cents. This small purchase would come to change his career and his life. The chips Doolin purchased were made from corn dough used for centuries by Mexicans to bake bread. Impressed with the product, Doolin sold his ice cream business and purchased the corn chip producer's business for one hundred dollars. The brand, Frito, was created in the kitchen of his mother, along with the early production of the corn chips. Doolin would bake the chips at night and sell them during the day. Early sales were in the range of $8–10 a day. As business expanded, the company was moved from San Antonio to Dallas. Frito became a major chip producer in the Southwestern United States.

Around the same time, an entrepreneur in Tennessee named Herman W. Lay was selling potato chips produced by an Atlanta company. Lay sold the chips from his personal automobile until 1938 when the chip manufacturer fell on hard times. Lay managed to buy the business and changed its name to H.W. Lay and Company. The company's products became popular with consumers due to their good taste and convenience making Lay the dominant producer of snack foods in the Southeastern United States.

After World War II, the two companies began to cooperate in the area of product distribution. At this time they were still limited to their respective geographic markets, with Frito in the Southwest and Lay in the Southeast. In 1961, the two companies merged to form Frito-Lay, Inc., and in 1965 the company was merged again, this time with the Pepsi-Cola Company. The Pepsi-Cola Company became PepsiCo and consisted of the Pepsi-Cola Company, the Frito-Lay Company, and Tropicana Products. The company now also markets the popular brands Quaker Oats and Gatorade.

Although the US market is the largest market in the world for snack foods, due to its saturation, Frito-Lay has expanded significantly into international markets. The company tries to capitalize on its economies of scale and global brand image to compete with local brands. The typical entry strategy is to first learn which company is the leading snack company in the foreign market, and then attempt to purchase that company. If that fails, Frito-Lay aggressively competes against that local company. Frito-Lay's international operations add $9 billion to PepsiCo's $25 billion revenue. International markets have in many cases been more profitable for PepsiCo than the domestic market of the United States.

CASE 10
cont'd

Pepsi entered China in 1981 to sell soft drinks, and since that time has invested more than $1 billion. In 1994 Frito-Lay entered the Chinese market with its popular Cheetos brand snack. Potato chips were not introduced into the Chinese market until 1997, due to the Chinese ban on potato imports. Frito-Lay had to establish its own farms in order to grow potatoes acceptable to company standards. Early adaptation to local markets required Frito-Lay to make significant changes. For example, Frito-Lay's Cheetos sold in China do not contain any cheese due to the propensity of the Chinese to be lactose intolerant. Instead of cheese flavoring, Cheetos is offered with barbecue or seafood flavoring. In addition, the packaging was made smaller so that the price would be more acceptable. Other international adaptations had previously been made in other markets by Frito-Lay, including the popular Thai product, Nori Seaweed Chips.

Frito-Lay found that the Chinese market was not a single entity. Regional tastes and preferences had to be considered and products altered accordingly. Chinese living in Shanghai, for example, prefer sweeter foods, and Chinese living in the Northern region prefer a meaty taste. Frito-Lay also has found that having a good understanding of culture helps sell products. The Chinese belief in the Great Unity, or yin and yang, have marketing and product development implications. Yin and yang are the opposing forces in the universe and seek balance. The Chinese also seek balance, including balance in their foods. Fried food is seen as hot and not appropriate in the summer months so Frito-Lay developed a new product, cool limon potato chips. This product consists of chips dotted with lime specks and mint and packaged with cool climate images to connote winter months.

Promotion in China has required other adaptations, including advertisements showing the peeling of potatoes to indicate the product's basic ingredient. Promotion in China has successfully related collectivist tendencies of the Chinese people and the desire of the Chinese to try new products outdoors, in a conspicuous fashion. Early adopters in China want others to see their consumption of Western products. As with many Western products, young consumers are the first to try the product, and in the case of Frito-Lay, the focus has been on young women. As Jackson Chiu, sales director for Frito-Lay states: "We market to girls and the boys follow." Frito-Lay has been very creative in its promotion efforts in China, however, one advertisement resulted in a small problem. Using the picture of Mao Zedong's cook in its promotion resulted in the company being ordered to offer an apology and to pay the cook 10,000 yuan (1,200USD) for violating a Chinese law that requires getting permission before using someone's picture.

Frito-Lay's entry into the Chinese market has also caused some controversy. Some critics charge that companies like Frito-Lay have caused the Chinese diet to become unhealthy. Many Chinese can remember when food was rationed, long food lines existed, and consumers were offered little choice. Today the Chinese have a large

CASE 10
cont'd

variety of food options, and snack foods are a popular choice. As a result of their dietary changes, the Chinese have become more overweight. In the past ten years, the percentage of the Chinese population considered overweight has risen from almost none to a little under one third of the population. A common way of greeting someone in Chinese is the English equivalent of "Have you eaten yet." The Chinese are now able to answer yes more often to that question, and many are selecting foods that are considered by some to be unhealthy.

Concerned with the health effects of its products, not only in China, but also in health-conscious markets such as the United States, PepsiCo has begun to change its product offerings. Based on medical advice, PepsiCo has divided its products into three groups: 1) "Good for you" foods such as Gatorade and oatmeal; 2) "Better for you" foods such as Nacho Cheesier Baked Doritos; 3) "Fun for you" foods such as Pepsi Cola. The good for you foods are naturally healthy or engineered to be healthy. The better for you foods contain more wholesome ingredients or have reduced fat and sugar. The fun food isn't considered to be especially healthy. PepsiCo is moving product development towards the "good for you" and "better for you" groups. According to nutrition expert, Professor Marion Nestle of New York University, "Frito-Lay products are still high in calories, salt, and rapidly absorbed carbohydrates." For now the Chinese do not seem too concerned and Frito-Lay continues to develop this rapidly expanding market. Recently the company opened its sixth manufacturing plant in China and plans to expand its brand and product offerings into Central and Western China, ever mindful of differing regional tastes and preferences. While Frito-Lay has been successful in China, its parent company, PepsiCo still only accounts for 3.5 percent of the savory food market in China. However, Frito-Lay is planning to introduce newly developed flavored chips from abroad into the US market including Szechuan Chicken to increase the variety of domestic offerings.

CASE DISCUSSION POINTS:

1   Evaluate the approach Frito-Lay used as it entered the Chinese market.
2   What lessons can be learned by examining the experiences of Frito-Lay in China?
3   Are there any things MNCs can learn from their experiences that can be used in the domestic market? Explain.

Source: *The Economic Times*, 2004, "Frito-Lay sees crunchy business for chips here," June 3; China Economic Net, 2004, "Chairman Mao's cook wins lawsuit vs Pepsi," July 23; R. Flannery, 2004, "China is a big prize," *Forbes*, May 10; E. Kurtenbach, 2004, "Urban Chinese struggle with battle of the bulge," LaTimes. Com, July 18; T. Parker-Pope, 1996, "Custom-made: The most successful companies have to realize a simple truth—all consumers aren't alike," *Wall Street Journal*, September 26; P. Sellers, 2004, "The brand king challenge," *Fortune*,

CASE 10 cont'd

March 21; www.abcnews.com, *Using Potato Chips to Spread the Spirit of Free Enterprise*, September 9, 2004; www.fritolay.com, accessed on July 12, 2004; www.pepsico.com, accessed on July 12, 2004; F. Culliney, 2012, "PepsiCo Lay's must tantalize Chinese taste-buds further," Food Navigator, July 17; *PRNewsWire*, 2016, "Grab your passport ... Lay's potato chips debuts four timely global flavors to store shelves nationwide," www.prnewswire.com/news-releases/grab-your-passport-lays-potato-chips-debuts-four-timely-global-flavors-to-store-shelves-nationwide-300299223.html, July 18.

Case written by Charles A. Rarick

Notes

1 Roger Fingas, 2016, "How the iPhone SE will help drive Apple's sales internationally," *appleinsider*, March 28.

2 "The 1005 DS100: Consumer brands of the top 100 companies in the Muslim world," 2006, www.brandchannel.com, April 19; www.expectad.com/white_paper/Muslim_Brands_Expect_Advertising_Inc.pdf

3 "Going global: Risks and rewards," 2006, www.brandchannel.com, April 19.

4 www.edmunds.com/car-reviews/top-10/top-10-most-american-trucks-for-2015.html

5 Jean L. Johnson, Tomoaki Sakano, Joseph A. Cote and Naoto Onzo, 1993, "The exercise of intercompany power and its repercussions in US–Japanese channel relationship," *Journal of Marketing*, *57*(2), pp. 1–10.

6 Thomas L. Friedman, 2005, *The World is Flat*, New York: Farrar, Straus, and Giroux.

7 http://blogs.wsj.com/japanrealtime/2011/09/05/is-one-japanese-camry-worth-2-5-made-in-the-u-s/

8 Masaaki Kotabe and Kristiaan Helsen, 2014, *Global Marketing Management* (6th edn), Hoboken, NJ: Wiley.

9 Masaaki Kotabe and Kristiaan Helsen, 2014, *Global Marketing Management* (6th edn), Hoboken, NJ: Wiley.

CHAPTER 11

Financial Management for MNCs

After reading this chapter you should be able to:

- Understand the nature of country risk with a special focus on emerging markets.

- Understand how country risk relates to international investments.

- Know how to estimate the cost of capital and the future value of an international investment and understand the additional challenges in an emerging markets situation.

- Understand how international managers decide on the mix of debt and equity for the capital structure of an MNC's subsidiary.

- Know the basic methods of payment in international trade.

- Be familiar with export financing options.

International Business *Preview IB Emerging Market Strategic Insight*

Weighing the Risks of Major International Investment in Markets

As you have seen throughout the text, investments in new markets carry risks that are difficult to predict. Whether a firm decides to invest in an emerging market or established markets, such decisions need to be made carefully. Consider investments in the emerging markets in Africa. As MTN, a South African telecommunications company found, its operations in Nigeria were heavily disrupted in October 2015. The local cash-strapped government argued that MTN had violated the law when registering SIM cards. The Nigerian government therefore decided to fine MTN $1,000 per improperly registered account. The total fine amounts to $5.2 billion and represents more than three times MTN's profits in Nigeria.

But emerging market multinationals are not only concerned about risks in emerging markets. Investments in more established markets also carry significant risks. Consider the case of Europe and the anti-immigration sentiments that seem to prevail there. Additionally, the Brexit phenomenon has caught many business experts by surprise. This has also meant that multinationals are having a hard time predicting the future business environment in Europe and the UK.

Consider the situation as more Chinese multinationals go on binge acquisitions worldwide. A good example of such a multinational is ChemChina, a state-owned company that has recently acquired a number of companies worldwide. Exhibit 11.1 below shows the various companies ChemChina has acquired and their nationality.

Company	Industry	Country
ADAMA Agricultural Solutions	Agrichemicals	Israel
Adisseo	Animal-feed ingredients	France
Elkem	Silicon	Norway
KraussMaffei	Industrial machinery	Germany
Mercuria	Oil trader	Switzerland
Pirelli	Tires	Italy
Parts of Rhodia	Organic silicon	France
Qenos	Plastics	Australia

Exhibit 11.1 ChemChina and Recent or Ongoing Acquisitions
Source: The Economist, 2016, "Better than barbarians," January 16, pp. 70–71.

As the Exhibit 11.1 shows, Chinese multinationals are making acquisitions in many different new industries or countries. While such acquisitions are providing the necessary technologies and talent the Chinese multinationals are looking for, they are also facing potential future challenges. Anti-immigration sentiments mean that emerging market multinationals may run into potential future opposition from locals and local politicians. Furthermore, the acquisition of local iconic brands such as ChemChina's acquisition of Pirelli, the Italian tire manufacturer, may also mean that emerging market multinationals may face nationalist backlashes. Such emerging market multinationals must also contend with risks and uncertainties associated with operating in a foreign market.

Source: Adapted from *The Economist,* 2016, "Better than barbarians," January 16, pp. 70–71; *The Economist,* 2016, "Special report on doing business in Africa: Is it worth it?" April 16, pp. 11–13.

As you can see in the Preview IB Emerging Market Strategic Insight, multinationals worldwide are taking major risks by expanding operations in markets unknown to them. For instance, South African telecommunications company MTN invested in Nigeria hoping that the strategy would pay off. While its initial operations went very well and it took advantage of the Nigerian opportunities, the more recent governmental intervention spells disaster for the company. As mentioned earlier, the fine that is being arbitrarily imposed by the Nigerian government represents more than three times the multinational's profits in Nigeria. It therefore runs the risk of needing to cease operations in Nigeria thereby losing all of its investments.

As such, whether a person starts a new business, an MNC opens a factory in another country, an individual buys stock in an existing company, or a company manufactures a new product, there is a chance that the company or project will not produce enough money to meet financial obligations. If a company or project does not produce sufficient cash, then the business may go bankrupt or the project may be abandoned and the investors may lose money. Moreover, even if the project does make money, investors may make less money than they would have from other investments.

International investments often have more and different kinds of risk than domestic investments. As part of the strategic and financial decision to enter a country, the international manager must know how the unique characteristics of a country make it more or less of a risky environment in which to do business. Broadly speaking this type of risk is often called country risk. **Country risk** pertains to how a country's business environment might influence the MNC's profits or the value of its assets (e.g. factories, inventory) within the specific country. Many factors affect the risk of doing business in different countries for the MNC. How do international managers assess the risk in various countries? The first starting point is often to use one of several companies that specialize in developing risk ratings for different countries.

Although there are many companies preparing country risk information, one popular risk rating service is the International Country Risk Guide (ICRG).[1] The ICRG's ratings focus on three types of risk. **Economic risk** considers a country's economic strengths and weaknesses and how these might affect investments. **Financial risk** considers the ability of the country to finance its trade debt and commercial obligations. As you recall from Chapter 9, **political risk** assesses political stability in areas such as civil unrest, war, terrorism, and changing regulations. *The Economist*[2] and Aon Global[3] produce similar risk ratings.

While you learned about political risk in depth in Chapter 8, both economic and financial risks are extremely critical factors when evaluating the financial crises a multinational can face in any country. In that respect, the Organization for Economic Co-operation and Development (OECD) computes country risk data based on such risks in that country.[4] The OECD computes the data based on transfer and convertibility risk (the threat that a multinational will have to deal with government foreign-exchange controls that places limits on profits repatriation and use of foreign currency) and other potential for major disasters such as war, civil disturbances, etc. Exhibit 11.2 shows the country risk for selected countries. The index is classified into 8 categories ranging from 0 (extremely low country risk) to 7 (high country risk).

As Exhibit 11.2 shows, the country risk of some emerging markets such as Argentina and Kenya reflects the somewhat volatile situations in these countries. In contrast, other emerging markets such as China and India have more moderate country risks Finally, nations such as Singapore and Taiwan both have very low risks.

In addition to the above risks, an increasingly important but nontraditional risk category is **sustainability risk**. Sustainability risk refers to factors that may increase the cost of capital or reduce profits due to changing environmental conditions or changing regulatory environments. When considering either domestic or foreign investments, the next-generation international manager will likely factor sustainability risk into any investment decisions. Exhibit 11.3 highlights some of the sustainability risk areas and their potential impacts on capital performance.

Estimating sustainability risks are also extremely critical today in emerging markets. Consider the following Emerging Market Ethical Challenge.

country risk
how a country's business environment might influence the MNC's profits or the value of its assets (e.g. factories, inventory) within the specific country

economic risk
considers a country's economic strengths and weaknesses and how these might affect investments

financial risk
considers the ability of the country to finance its trade debt and commercial obligations

political risk
the political stability of a country in areas such as civil unrest, war, terrorism, and changing regulations

sustainability risk
the factors that may increase the cost of capital or reduce profits through changing environmental conditions or changing regulatory environments

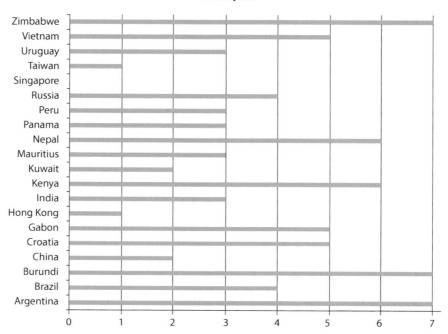

Country Risk

Exhibit 11.2 Country Risk for Selected Countries
Source: www.oecd.org/tad/xcred/crc.htm

The Case for Building Sustainability Risk into the Capital Investment Decision

EMERGING MARKET
ETHICAL CHALLENGE

Multinationals are very aware of the sustainability risks in their operations today. In fact, companies such as IKEA, Ford, Staples, and GM have all had issues related to their suppliers and are dedicating resources to monitoring and collaborating with them. In such cases, problematic sustainability incidents arose thus casting a negative light on the companies involved. Recent research suggests that dealing with an adverse sustainability issue has been linked to a 12 percent decline in market capitalization. Sustainability risks are therefore critical aspects of operations in any country.

Major multinationals are taking sustainability risks very seriously. Consider the ecological risks associated with packaging. While packaging has traditionally been done to ensure that the product gets to the consumer in original condition and can be stored easily, the more recent concerns have centered around the packaging costs to the environment. Packaging is associated with carbon emissions and these vary by industry. However, many companies have implemented measures to reduce the amount of packaging being used while also increasing the use of biodegradable packaging material. Companies such as Walmart, UPS, and Unilever have all implemented new packaging processes (introduction of packing scorecard for suppliers, establishment of eco-responsible packaging programs, etc.) to counter sustainability risks.

Source: Adapted from S. Dharmadhikari, 2012, "Eco-friendly packaging in supply chain," *The IUP Journal of Supply Chain Management*, *2*, pp. 7–18; S. Hajmohammad and S. Vachon, 2016, "Mitigation, avoidance, or acceptance? Managing supplier sustainability risk," *Journal of Supply Chain Management*, *52*(2), pp. 48–65.

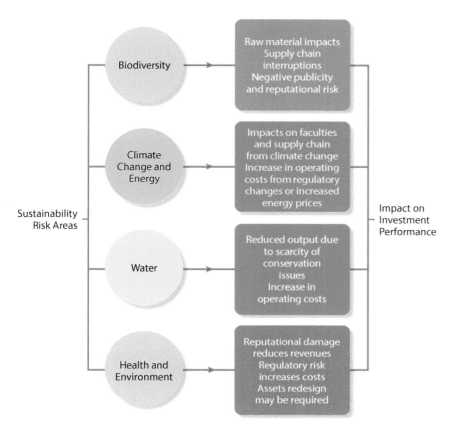

Exhibit 11.3 Sustainability Risk Areas and the Potential Impact on Investment Performance
Source: Adapted from EXCEL Partnership and The Delphi Group, 2016, http://delphi.ca/environmental-leadership-excel-partnership/

As you can see from above, properly appreciating sustainability risks and all other risks is extremely critical for the multinational. In later sections of this chapter you will see more detail on how risk must be factored into the MNC's international investment decisions. First, however, you will learn some basic techniques that companies use to estimate the financial returns from investments.

The Cost of Capital and Project Valuation

As you saw in Chapter 6 regarding capital markets, MNCs can finance their operations using both debt (usually in the form of bonds) and equity (issuing stock or using retained earnings from their profits). However, the decision making is more complex than simply getting the required money and going forward with the project.[5]

The process of determining whether a project should be financed based on its expected financial returns is called the **capital budgeting decision**. Financial managers use several methods to predict the viability of an investment decision. We will review one popular method called **net present value, or NPV**.

The NPV approach gives managers a way of estimating whether and when an initial capital investment will lead to future cash flows that exceed the cost of the capital. Later in the chapter you will learn more about the cost of capital. However, for this section, just consider it as the

capital budgeting decision

the process of determining whether a project should be financed based on its expected financial returns

net present value, or NPV

a technique used to estimate whether and when an initial capital investment will lead to future cash flows that exceed the cost of the capital

cost a company must pay to get money now, like the interest you must pay on a credit card if you want to buy something right away but do not have the available cash.

NPV is usually estimated by the following formula:

$$\text{Net Present Value} = \sum_{t-1}^{n} \frac{CF^t}{(1+k)^t} - IO$$

Where

CF^t = the predicted cash flows in year t,
k = the required rate of return for the investment,
n = lifetime of the project in periods (years, months, weeks, etc.),
IO = the initial investment for the project.

To understand how NPV works, we can look at an example of a hypothetical US MNC called Sportif that is considering opening a subsidiary in the EU. Look at Exhibit 11.4. It contains two scenarios for NPV that multinational managers might consider in deciding whether to go forward with the project. In each scenario you will see when a project pays off based on different circumstances. You will also see how financial information enters into the formula.

In both scenarios, the assumption is that all profits will be returned to the parent company and that the parent company's initial investment (IO) will be $10,000,000. In the examples, we are looking at four years for the lifetime of the project (n), although we could do the calculations for any length of time.

In Scenario 1, managers have decided that they need a return of 15 percent on the investment. This means that, in order to make this project worthwhile from a purely financial point of view, the managers have to decide how best to invest any money they have from retained earnings, stock issues, or bond issues. If, for example, other possible projects can return up to 14 percent, then this project may need a return of 15 percent to become the investment of choice.

Risk also is a factor. Less risky projects may make sense with lower rates of return because there is more certainty that the company will make money. Conversely, more risky projects require projecting higher rates of return to compensate for the gamble of the investment.

All capital budgeting decisions begin with an estimate of how much money the project will generate over several periods. Sales forecasts for the product or service at various price levels help the financial managers estimate future revenues. You can see the project revenues projected for Sportif's subsidiary in line 1 in the example. Of course, all operations have expenses and have to pay local taxes, so what is remaining after these expenses is the cash flow to the subsidiary (line 4). For simplicity, we assume that all of the subsidiary's earnings after taxes and expenses are returned to Sportif's headquarters back in the US (line 7).

To understand the concept of NPV, one has to also understand that the future cash flows shown on line 7 must be valued for their worth today given a specified rate of return. Because there are alternative investments with potential returns, the future value of money is always lower than its face value. This is called the present value of the cash flow (PV) and is shown on line 9. In Scenario 1, this means that the $5,000,000 Sportif received from its subsidiary in year 1 is discounted or reduced based on a chosen rate of return (line 8) that Sportif's managers judged necessary to make this investment versus others.

For each year, line 9 shows the present value of the cash generated by the subsidiary for that year. Again, because of the need to discount or reduce the value of the cash in the future, each dollar has less value as each year passes. To compute the cumulative NPV, these discounted cash flows are subtracted from the initial $10,000,000 investment that Sportif uses to fund its subsidiary in the EU. Thus, in Scenario 1, it is not until the third year that Sportif would be expected to cover its initial investment.

The general rule of thumb is that the investment should be made if the cash flows are positive assuming that no better investment exists, say for example, in this case, investment in a subsidiary in another location. If the cash flows are negative, the investment should not be made. It is a strategic choice based in part on the financial strength of the company regarding the time international managers are willing to wait for positive cash flows.

Capital budgeting analyses are not unique to MNCs. However, a variety of issues can make the decision more complex for the multinational. Scenarios 1 and 2 give an example of how an MNC might come to a different decision, even though the projected revenue for the subsidiary is the same. In Scenario 1, the assumption was made that the $/€ exchange rate would remain at $1.25/€1.00. It was also assumed that a 15 percent rate of return was sufficient to choose this project. In Scenario 2, the exchange rate was set at $0.75/€1.00.

As you can see comparing lines 6, the exchange-rate differences significantly reduce the cash returned to Sportif from $5,000,000 to $3,000,000. In addition, the multinational managers in Scenario 2 increased the required rate of return to 20 percent, perhaps because of different

Scenario 1	Year 0	Year 1	Year 2	Year 3	Year 4
1 Subsidiary revenue		€21,000,000	€21,000,000	€36,000,000	€38,000,000
2 Expenses		€16,000,000	€16,000,000	€29,000,000	€30,000,000
3 Host government tax (20%)		€1,000,000	€1,000,000	€1,400,000	€1,600,000
4 Cash flow to subsidiary		€4,000,000	€4,000,000	€5,600,000	€6,400,000
5 After earnings remitted to parent		€4,000,000	€4,000,000	€5,600,000	€6,400,000
6 Exchange rate of the $		$1.25	$1.25	$1.25	$1.25
7 Cash flow to parent		$5,000,000	$5,000,000	$7,000,000	$8,000,000
8 Required rate of return (discount rate)	15%				
9 *PV* of parent cash flows		$4,347,826	$3,780,718	$4,602,614	$4,574,026
10 Initial investment by parent	−$10,000,000				
11 Cumulative *NPV*		−$5,652,174	−$1,871,456	$2,731,158	$7,305,184
Scenario 2	Year 0	Year 1	Year 2	Year 3	Year 4
1 Subsidiary revenue		€21,000,000	€21,000,000	€36,000,000	€38,000,000
2 Expenses		€16,000,000	€16,000,000	€29,000,000	€30,000,000
3 Host government tax (20%)		€1,000,000	€1,000,000	€1,400,000	€1,600,000
4 Cash flow to subsidiary		€4,000,000	€4,000,000	€5,600,000	€6,400,000
5 After earnings remitted to parent		€4,000,000	€4,000,000	€5,600,000	€6,400,000
6 Exchange rate of the $		$0.75	$0.75	$0.75	$0.75
7 Cash flow to parent		$3,000,000	$3,000,000	$4,200,000	$4,800,000
8 Required rate of return (discount rate)	20%				
9 *PV* of parent cash flows		$2,500,000	$2,083,333	$2,430,556	$2,744,416
10 Initial investment by parent	−$10,000,000				
11 Cumulative *NPV*		−$7,500,000	−$5,416,667	−$2,986,111	−$241,696

Exhibit 11.4 Capital Budget Analysis for Sportif Shoes

alternative investment opportunities or greater risk in the country of location for the subsidiary. The result is that with these different assumptions, Sportif will not recover its initial investment by year 4. Other things being equal, multinational managers would be more likely to go forward with building the subsidiary under the conditions in Scenario 1 than Scenario 2. Of course, this is only a simple example, as other factors such as local government tax rates or local government regulations regarding taking money from the country can affect the multinational manager's decisions. For example, if Sportif negotiated a more favorable local tax rate of 10 percent rather than the 20 percent shown in the Exhibit, the NPV in year 4 would be positive.

Appropriately assessing the future cash flows is very critical to success but not always easy. Consider the following IB Emerging Market Strategic Insight.

Tesco Global Expansion and Failures: Assessing Cash Flows

IB EMERGING MARKET STRATEGIC INSIGHT

Third in the world behind Walmart and Carrefour, the UK retailer Tesco has expanded rapidly over the last few years. However, many of its international expansion plans failed. For example, because of a late entry into the Chinese market and poor marketing, it was forced to abandon its expansion plans and sell part of its stake to a local competitor. It also suffered from a fall in sales in markets in South Korea, Thailand, and Malaysia. Limits on opening hours in South Korea and political instability in Thailand all led to major losses. Many incorrect assumptions and miscalculations resulted in failure.

Tesco's plans to open Fresh & Easy local groceries in the US in 2007 shows the dangers of not conducting a realistic capital budgeting process. Although it carried out extensive market research and found support for the concept of a grocery store selling only fresh food, it had to abandon the project in 2013. Where did Tesco go wrong? A look at the events leading to the abandonment of the project shows many instances of incorrect assumptions when examining the viability of the project.

First, Tesco grossly underestimated the original investment needed to get the project going. Although Tesco initially planned on investing 250 million pounds and believing that would work, it found out that it needed to invest much more. For instance, it found that getting easy access to suppliers was problematic in the US. It therefore decided to build its own food preparation center in California and that facility alone cost $100 million. As it kept adding new aspects to the project, the initial investment ended up closer to 1 billion British pounds.

A second problem was that the model was only going to work if the project was done on a large scale and sales per square feet were high. Tesco therefore continued expanding the number of stores. Furthermore, Tesco decided to open new stores rather than acquire existing businesses. This added even more cost to the project and ended up in major losses. It is estimated that Tesco lost about 850 million British pounds during the early parts of the expansion.

Third, related problems doomed the project. First, many of the stores were located in larger edge-of-town areas and those got hit by the rise of internet shopping. Second, individuals were also becoming more socially conscious of the needs to buy local and were more likely to shun larger grocery stores. Finally, the expansion also coincided with the economic recession. These factors also contributed to Tesco grossly overestimating demand for its store format and led to even more losses as the predicted revenues did not match the actual revenues.

Source: Based on A. Felsted, 2015, "Tesco set to close door on American dream," *Financial Times*, April 12, financialtimes.com; M. Simms, 2014, "Tesco: why did it all go so wrong?" *The Guardian*, September 22, www. guardian.com.

As the above box shows, it is not always easy to predict aspects of the capital budgeting process. Inaccurate assumptions or incorrect estimates can make multinational managers overestimate the chances of the project's chance of success. In Tesco's case, while market research showed that the project had promise, many local factors led to major problems and the project's failure.

Once international managers determine that an investment is worthwhile financially, the next issue they must consider is how to get the needed cash to make the investment. As you learned in Chapter 6, companies get money from issuing debt, selling stocks, or by keeping some of their profits as retained earnings. The next section of this chapter considers how MNCs decide the best mix of financing options.

MNC Capital Structure

A major decision for the chief financial officer of an MNC is assessing the best mixture of debt and equity for his or her company. This mixture of debt and equity is called the **capital structure**.

The main objective of managing the capital structure is to reduce the cost of capital. As you learned in Chapter 6, there is a cost to getting money from others, and there are costs to the owners (stockholders) of using retained earnings since this reduces their dividends. All these factors are called the **cost of capital**. Bondholders expect to receive interest payments and stockholders expect dividends. Since more retained earnings reduce dividends, the cost of retained earnings comes from the lost opportunities of the owners to invest their money elsewhere.

More than 50 years ago, Nobel prizewinners Franco Modigliani and Merton Miller published research showing that it does not matter whether a company finances its activities with equity or debt or some combination. However, they noted that there is often an advantage to using debt because most countries allow tax deductions for interest payments.[6] That is, interest payments can be deducted from revenues, thus lowering a company's taxes. However, when a company takes on debt it has to make the interest payments, and these payments, just like the payments a college student who has large credit card balances must make each month, can drain available cash. Moreover, companies that have more debt relative to their equity are considered more risky to outside investors resulting in higher interest payments and lower stock prices.

Generally, the cost of capital in terms of debt is estimated by the interest that must be paid, adjusting that value by the tax savings from interest deductions. For example, a company issues bonds to buy a new machine and pays €10,000 in interest payments to bondholders in a year. The company then takes a €10,000 tax deduction, reducing its reported profits by that amount. If the corporate tax rate is 30 percent, the company reduces its taxes by €3,000, which makes the cost of the capital in terms of debt equal to €7,000.

Calculating the cost of equity is a little more complex. To put a value on the cost of equity, financial managers use the logic that stockholders give up the opportunity to invest their money in other ventures. Therefore, the cost is what shareholders might have earned had they invested the funds themselves. One way of estimating the cost of new equity (issuing stocks) is known as the **constant dividend growth model**. As you can see below, the formula uses the current stock price and current and future dividends to estimate the opportunity costs (i.e. the money that could be earned from other investments) for investors. The cost of capital new equity is always more expensive than using retained earnings because of flotation costs. Flotation costs are the additional costs related to the expenses of selling new stock in the company. The formula for the constant dividend growth model is:

$$Cost\ of\ Equity = \frac{Dividends\ per\ Share}{(Current\ Market\ Value\ of\ Stock - Flotation\ Costs)} + Growth\ Rate\ of\ Dividends$$

capital structure
a company's mixture of debt and equity

cost of capital
the cost of getting money for projects either from owners' (stockholders') retained earnings, from issuing new stocks, or by borrowing

constant dividend growth model
a technique to estimate the cost of new equity (issuing stocks)

Cost of Capital for the MNC

The cost of capital for an MNC is often different from domestic-only companies. There are several factors and risks associated with being multinational that can make the cost of capital different from that of domestic companies. Most of these differences relate to how MNCs deal with cash flow. **Cash flow** means the availability of cash to pay bills. Its relevance to the cost of capital is the MNC's ability to have enough cash to pay interest owed to bondholders and dividends to stockholders. Next, you will see a series of issues that MNCs encounter when considering the cost of capital. Exhibit 11.5 summarizes the factors that cause the cost of capital to be different for the MNC than for domestic firms.[7]

Access to International Capital Markets   Unlike a purely domestic company, the MNC is more likely to take advantage of issuing bonds or selling stock in different capital markets. The regulations in different countries make the mixture of debt and equity financing complex for the MNC, but taking advantage of these regulations can reduce its cost of capital and thus make the company more valuable. For example, local subsidizers of the MNC may have access to local capital markets, where the subsidiary is often treated like a domestic company and gains advantages similar to local companies, such as lower interest rates or fewer regulations to list on local stock exchanges. However, capital markets in different countries can differ fundamentally, letting the MNC seek the best deal in any country.

Why are there country differences in the cost of debt and the cost of equity? Differences in the cost of debt are determined by two components of interest rates, the risk-free rate and the risk premium.

The **risk-free interest rate** is the cost of borrowing money determined by the supply and demand for funds. Like all supply–demand relationships, if there are more funds available for a level of demand the price will be lower. Similarly, if the demand for funds increases at a fixed level of supply, the price will rise. For example, the demand for borrowing might be greater in

cash flow
the availability of cash to pay bills

risk-free interest rate
the cost of borrowing money determined by the supply of and demand for funds

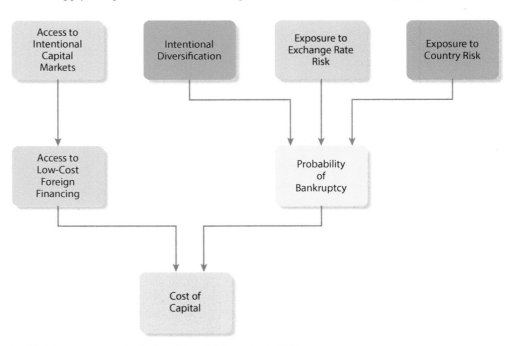

Exhibit 11.5 Factors that Make the Cost of Capital Different for the MNC
Source: Adapted from Jeff Madura, 2014, *International Financial Management*, Mason, OH: Cengage Learning.

one country because tax laws allow companies to make deductions on interest paid. On the supply side, countries with older populations or cultural traditions of high savings provide more money for financial institutions to lend to companies, thus reducing interest rates. Central banks also control the supply of money, which can lower or increase interest rates. Economic conditions, such as those faced in many emerging economies with high rates of inflation, require higher interest rates to compensate investors for the potential decline in the value of currencies.

The **risk premium** is the additional interest creditors must charge borrowers to offset any characteristics of the company or their situation that may increase the likelihood of a default. Just as you have a credit rating, which can affect the interest rate a credit card company charges you, a company's bond rating is based on its financial strength and affects the interest charged. However, oftentimes more important for the MNC is that country risk also affects the risk premium. For example, if the probability of a recession is high in a particular country, borrowers face a greater chance of defaulting so creditors add to the risk premium.

Assessing the risk premium for emerging markets is not always easy. Consider the following Emerging Market Ethical Challenge.

risk premium
the additional interest creditors must charge borrowers to offset any characteristics of the company or their situation that may increase the likelihood of a default

Assessing Risk Premium in Emerging Markets

EMERGING MARKET
ETHICAL CHALLENGE

Assessing the risk premium in emerging markets can be very challenging. Consider the case of the Arab Spring, the political unrest that affected the Middle East and North African (MENA) region. Many experts did not predict this massive and significant wave of social unrest that had a dramatic influence on the business climate in the countries involved. In fact, a recent report suggests that most of the country political risk assessment done by major organizations such as the Organization for Economic Co-operation and Development and Political Risk Services tends to be flawed. None of the five major institutions had any of the MENA countries on the list of the top risk countries. The Arab Spring therefore took the business world by surprise and has resulted in major losses for many multinationals because of the disruption of the business climate.

The Arab Spring was not the only event that was difficult for political risk assessment companies to predict. Events in other countries such as the geopolitical situation in China with the South China sea and anti-Western sentiments in Russia have all made political risk assessment unpredictable. Accurately assessing the risk premium is therefore very critical for any multinational. It is not surprising to see the growth of smaller boutique type and global consulting organizations providing such services. For example, understanding the risk in Brazil has been very unpredictable lately given the many incidents such as the president's impeachment and several bribery scandals. While multinationals are still keeping the generic forecasts provided by larger institutions such as those mentioned earlier, local firms such as Brazil's Prospectiva, are providing more specific company-specific risks. In fact, most multinationals have shrunk in-house risk assessment departments in favor of external advice. These new companies are providing less generic and more in-depth, industry specific risk for stronger risk premium assessment.

Source: Based on *The Economist*, 2016, "Risk premiums," May 21, p. 61; C. E. Sottilotta, 2015, "Political risk assessment and the Arab Spring: What can we learn?" *Thunderbird International Review*, *57*(5), pp. 379–390.

In some countries, such as Japan and Germany, financial institutions have a greater tolerance for debt carried by their borrowers. That is, even though the chance of default increases when a company has more debt (as it does for an individual), financial institutions in some countries may not increase the risk premium as much as in other countries. In contrast to Japan and Germany, similar companies in the US would pay a much higher interest rate because US financial institutions have a more risk-averse approach, due in part to a decreased likelihood of the government coming to the rescue of failing companies. Thus, the cost of debt for an MNC relates not only to its own bond or credit rating but also to the local risk-free interest rate and local country factors that affect the risk premium charged by lenders.

Fundamentally, the cost of capital derives from the opportunity costs of investors who could have invested their money elsewhere. For example, if investors took the money they have in the value of their stocks and invested in, say, a bank with guaranteed interest rates, then the baseline for the cost of equity is the level of potential returns from this other possible investment. This is the same risk-free interest rate considered in the cost of debt. Likewise, because the risk-free interest rates vary across countries, so does the cost of equity. Again, because companies and countries also have different degrees of risk to the stockholder, just as they do to those who lend them money, a risk premium must be added to the cost of equity.[8]

Another factor that affects the cost of equity in a country is the extent of other opportunities for investing. More opportunities in a country mean that, since investors have more choice in purchasing stocks, it is likely expected returns will be greater and this will increase the cost of equity.

International Diversification   One of the advantages of being an MNC is that your profits and cash flows are not dependent on the economic conditions in a single country. To the extent that economies are independent, it is likely that the MNC located in many countries has a more stable cash flow to meet its debt needs, since good and bad economic conditions tend to cancel each other out. This is attractive to investors because they have more certainty that an MNC can take funds from high-profit units and transfer them to struggling units, giving even the struggling units the ability to cover interest payments. For example, if your European subsidiary is having a profitable year but your Japanese subsidiary is losing money, as long as the net cash flow is positive for the MNC, it can cover it debts and pay dividends in both countries. Thus, the cost of capital can be lower for the MNC.[9]

Exchange-rate Risk Exposure   As you learned in an earlier chapter, MNCs must manage their operations in two or more currencies. While setting up operations in several countries can make cash flows more stable, it also has the potential of being more volatile if a company does business in a foreign country with an unstable exchange rate with the parent company's country. For example, if a US company sets up operations in several emerging markets that have unstable currencies, the company could find that the earnings from these subsidiaries decrease if the US dollar gets stronger against these currencies. Thus, from the perspective of the cost of capital, costs are higher when a company faces more exchange-rate risk exposure.

Country Risk   Unstable political systems, weak enforcement of laws and contracts, changing tax systems, local wars, environmental or health disasters, and government policies regarding MNCs are, as you saw above, just a few of the factors that make up country risk. When MNCs enter countries with greater risk, MNC finance officers realize that investors will require a greater return on their investments to offset the greater likelihood that the company could lose money or fail because of the local country situation. Thus, when country risk increases, investors require higher returns, and the cost of capital is greater.[10]

How MNCs Decide on the Mixture of Debt and Equity in their Capital Structure

The capital structure is a company's choice of how much debt or equity to use to finance its operations. For the MNC this is more complex because the capital structure may differ for subsidiaries located in other countries. The characteristics of the company and the characteristics of the country influence the choice of more debt or equity.[11]

Company Factors

- *Cash flows.* Of course, just like for individuals where richer people can take on more debt, companies with more cash can handle more debt. However, the stability of the cash flows is also important. Interest payments on bonds and bank loans must be made periodically over the year. Therefore, in order for a company to have sufficient cash to pay these debts when they are due, company managers must be confident that cash will be coming into the company when needed. From a personal point of view, consider that your credit card company wants payments every month and is not willing to wait until the payer gets a summer job in a few months.

- *Credit risk.* You probably see the many advertisements today telling people to check their credit scores. Credit scores are based on your history of paying your debts and the amount of debt you have. If you have a lot of debt or you do not have a good record of paying on time, then you have a lower score and you are a higher credit risk. Credit risk is the estimate of the probability that you will not be able to pay off a loan. Similarly, companies have degrees of credit risk. When they use bonds to finance debt, their credit rating score is the bond rating. In any case, the logic is similar for individuals and companies. The higher the credit risk, the higher the interest a lender will charge, or possibly the loan may even be denied. As such, companies with a lower credit risk have more access to debt financing at lower interest rates and therefore are more likely to use more debt in their capital structure.

- *Availability of retained earnings.* If a company is profitable, the managers have a choice. They can pay all the profits to the owners in terms of dividends or they can keep some of the profits to use to fund company activities as retained earnings. Thus, profitable companies can use this type of equity financing—remember, it is still equity because it is the owners' money. The use of retained earnings is often adequate to fund smaller projects, but when companies want to grow rapidly or make major investments in plants and equipment, they usually have to look to debt or issuing new stock.

- *Parent company guarantees.* Subsidiaries of MNCs can often get lower interest rates on loans when their parent company agrees to back the debt. This means that the parent company will pay the debt should the subsidiary default. This reduces the risks for the lenders and increases the lenders' willingness to give more favorable terms. This same thing sometimes happens to people when they do not have the financial resources to get a loan to buy a car or a house. For example, parents might back the loan for a young couple so that they can buy their first house. However, this is a two-sided coin. When an MNC backs a subsidiary, the parent company may see its credit risk increase because it is now liable for more debt.

What determines the debt–equity mix in emerging markets? The following Emerging Market Brief gives some insight of the debt–equity mix in the emerging nation of Poland.

Debt–Equity Choice in Poland

EMERGING
MARKET BRIEF

While the previous paragraphs discussed the factors that determine the debt–equity mix for multinationals involved in businesses across borders, how do local multinationals decide between the debt–equity mix? An interesting study of Polish non-financial firms listed on the Warsaw stock exchange provides some insights. The study showed that those companies that were larger, had higher growth rate and profitability were less likely to have debt. In other words, in the study, the larger the Polish companies are, the less likely they were to hold debt. The authors suggest that the smaller a company is, the easier it is for them to issue equity. Additionally, the higher the growth rate of the company, the more likely these companies are to issue equity as there is a preference for the companies to have shareholders bear the risks of the expansion. Finally, the higher the profitability, the more money a company has to reinvest thereby reducing the need for debt.

The study also showed that a different set of principles applied to the Polish companies studied. Earlier you read about Modigliani and Miller's trade-off theory suggesting that the there is really no preference for a company to choose between debt or equity except for the consideration of the costs and benefits of debt. The Polish study's results provide support for another theory, namely the pecking order theory. The **pecking order theory** argues that a company will always prefer internal sources of funding such as equity over external sources of funding such as debt. The examination of the Polish companies studied here shows that many of the firm characteristics show a small relationship with debt.

Source: Adapted from B. Kazmierska-Jozwiak, J. Marszałek and P. Sekuła, 2015, "Determinants of debt-equity choice—Evidence from Poland," *Emerging Markets Journal, 5*(2), pp. 1–8.

pecking order theory
theory that argues that a company will always prefer internal sources of funding such as equity over external sources of funding such as debt

The above shows some of the more local factors that affect Polish companies' decisions to choose between equity and debt. Next, we consider some of the country level factors.

Country Factors   Except for the ability of the parent company to back the debt of a subsidiary, the company factors that influence the capital structure of an MNC are similar to those of a domestic company. However, unlike a domestic company that must respond only to one country's context, the MNC must consider country conditions everywhere it operates. Some country factors to consider include the following:

- *Stock market regulations* Types of financial reporting required by local stock markets (see the chapter on accounting), restrictions on foreign companies, and reluctance of local investors to invest in foreign companies can sometimes make it difficult to raise capital through equity in some countries. Alternatively, if a country's laws restrict investments in other countries or otherwise create barriers such as unfavorable tax rules for investing in foreign markets, local investors may have fewer opportunities to buy stocks. This restricted supply of local investment opportunities makes the prices of stocks higher and makes it more attractive for an MNC to use equity rather than debt financing in such locations.

- *Strength or weakness of local currencies* If the currencies in a host country are weak relative to the currency of the parent company's country, there is an incentive to use local debt financing rather than borrowing from the parent company's retained earnings. The reason that this makes sense is that, from the perspective of the parent company, paying interest in a weaker currency means that the MNC gets cheaper loans That is, interest paid in a weaker currency provides cheaper loans than with a stronger currency. Alternatively, if the financial officers of the MNC believe that the host country's currency will appreciate relative to the home country's, there is an incentive to invest more of the parent company's retained earnings in the subsidiary as those investments will grow in value based on the home country currency. Similarly, there is also an incentive to have the subsidiary retain more of its earnings so that investment will grow in value based on the home country currency.

- *Host country risk* High degrees of country risk encourage multinational managers to find ways to increase local investors' commitment to the success of the company. The common tactic is to use more local debt financing. In this case, should a local government do anything that hurts the performance of the MNC's subsidiary, it puts local investors at risk. Since local citizens rather than foreigners are at risk, there is more pressure on the government to look out for the welfare of the local subsidiary.

- *Local tax laws* Countries often require MNC subsidiaries to pay taxes on earnings that they return to their parent company. Most countries also give tax reductions for interest payments on loans from local financial institutions. This situation encourages local debt financing because it reduces the taxes on money returned to the parent company. It is particularly attractive in high tax rate countries because the deductions for interest payments reduce taxes even more.[12] Exhibit 11.6 summarizes the effects of country conditions on debt financing.

Host Country Conditions	Financing with Local Subsidiary Debt	Financing with Parent Company Debt
Higher risk	Higher	Lower
Higher interest rates	Lower	Higher
Lower interest rates	Higher	Lower
Currency expected to weaken	Higher	Lower
Currency expected to strengthen	Lower	Higher
Higher local taxes	Higher	Lower

Exhibit 11.6 The Impact of Host Country Conditions on MNC Subsidiary Financing

How do these factors apply in emerging markets? Consider the following Emerging Market Brief.

Country Level Factors Affecting Capital Structure in Emerging Markets

EMERGING MARKET BRIEF

Many of the country level factors affecting the capital structure have not been very encouraging in emerging markets. For instance, China's stock market has been plagued with many dysfunctional aspects that have limited its growth. The Shanghai Stock Exchange has experienced insider trading, corruption, and even governmental intervention. Multinationals are therefore very reluctant to rely on such stock markets for financing.

Another important country level factor affecting the capital structure is the exchange rate changes over the last few years. Consider many of the emerging markets in Latin America. Many of these emerging market multinationals hold debt in US dollars. However, the last few years has seen the US dollar appreciate considerably relative to emerging market currencies. This therefore means that more emerging market multinationals run the risk of default as they cannot meet their obligations in US$.

A final country level factor that is uncertain for emerging markets is currency flows. As you saw in Chapter 5, countries such as Venezuela are now strictly regulating the flow of foreign currency. The revenues for the Venezuelan government have fallen dramatically because of the fall in oil prices. However, social programs such as subsidies for electricity and imported foods are still in place despite these heavy losses. To save US$ to import food and other items, the government is resorting to more drastic foreign currency control. This also means that multinationals operating in such emerging nations will have difficulties repatriating revenues and this will affect the capital structure of the company.

Source: Adapted from *The Economist*, 2016, "Lights out," May 7, pp. 31–32; *The Economist*, 2016, "Special report—finance in China: Risky returns," May 7, pp. 9–11; J. Gallup and M. Fitzgerald, 2016, "Time bombs in emerging market debt," *International Financial Law Review*, April 4, p. 5.

As you learned in the chapter on international strategies, MNCs not only have investment opportunities in other countries but also often engage in exporting or importing. In the next section, you will learn some of the procedures used in the financial transactions of this international trade.

Financing International Trade

As you saw from the statistics reported in Chapter 1, international trade continues to grow and is often a part of an MNC's international business transactions. In this section, we review some of the major points regarding financial transaction in international trade.

Methods of Payment in International Trade

For companies to engage in international trade, the importer, the exporter, or financial institutions must provide credit in the sense that there is a lag between when payments are made and when goods or services are delivered. While multinationals use a variety of payments in emerging markets or other markets, there are four basic methods of payment to settle an international trade transaction, each with different levels of risk for the importer or exporter. The type of payments used in specific transactions depends on how well the participants trust each other, the countries involved, and the competition that may require giving one side or the other more favorable terms to make the sale.

The most common terms of purchase are as follows:

1. Cash-in-advance (pre-payment)
2. Letters of credit
3. Documentary collections
4. Open account.

Exhibit 11.7 gives an overview of each payment method and Exhibit 11.8 shows the balance of risks for each side in the exchange. We discuss each method in more detail below.

Cash-in-advance   Under the **cash-in-advance** or pre-payment method, the exporter does not ship the goods until payment is received. Thus, the exporter avoids credit risk or the risk of not being paid. Bank wire transfers provide a common and secure cash-in-advance option for exporters. However, foreign buyers must then take the risk that the goods may not be sent after they have made their payment in advance. Exporters who demand such terms may lose customers to competitors who offer more favorable payment terms and do not insist on pre-payment. Experts suggest this type of payment is best for high-risk trade relationships.

Letters of Credit   A **letter of credit** (LC) is a commitment by a bank on behalf of the importer to pay the exporter when all required shipping documents are presented. Banks deal only in documents and not the actual goods shipped. The importer makes no payment until the bank receives documents showing that the goods were shipped or otherwise delivered as promised. Because documents are the key to the transaction, an LC is also called a documentary credit.

cash-in-advance
a payment method when the exporter does not ship the goods until payment is received

letter of credit
a commitment by a bank on behalf of the importer to pay the exporter when all required shipping documents are presented

Method	Time of Payment	Goods Available to Importer	Risk to Exporter	Risk to Importer
Cash-in-advance (pre-payment)	Before shipment	After payment	None	Completely dependent on exporter to ship goods as ordered
Letters of credit	When shipment is made	After payment	Little or none	Shipment is assured but dependent on exporter to ship goods as noted in documents
Documentary collections	When the importer receives documents that shipment has been made	After payment	If the importer does not pay, exporter must do something with the shipped goods	Same as above except that the importer can inspect the goods prior to payment
Open account	As agreed	Before payment	Completely dependent on importer to pay as agreed	None

Exhibit 11.7 Payment Methods in International Trade
Source: Adapted from Jeff Madura, 2014, *International Financial Management,* Mason, OH: Cengage Learning (12th edn).

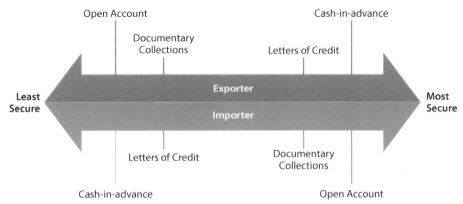

Exhibit 11.8 Balance of Risks for Importers and Exporters
Source: US Department of Commerce, 2016, *Trade Finance Guide,* trade.gov/media

draft
a document that states that one party will pay the other party immediately or at some future date

commercial invoice
a document that identifies the parties involved, the terms of payment, price, shipping information, and quantity, weight, packaging, etc., associated with the product

bill of lading
the receipt showing that the merchandise has been shipped; it is usually required that the importer present this receipt to get the merchandise

documentary collections
when the exporter's bank (called the remitting bank) collects the payments for the exporter

open account transaction
means that the exporter ships the goods before payment is due

Typical documents include a draft, a commercial invoice, and a bill of lading. A **draft** states that one party will pay the other party immediately or at some future date. A **commercial invoice** is a document that identifies the parties involved, the terms of payment, price, shipping information, and quantity, weight, packaging, etc., associated with the product. The **bill of lading** is the receipt issued to the exporter by the transportation carrier showing that the merchandise has been shipped. A bill of lading serves three purposes: as a receipt that the carrier has taken the merchandise listed; as a contract between the exporter and the carrier to provide transportation services of the merchandise for an agreed fee and deliver to the importer; and as a document of title, so that the exporter can obtain payment (or written promise of payment) before the merchandise is released to the importer.

In the transaction, the bank in the importer's country, called the issuing bank, authorizes a bank in the exporter's country, called the advising bank, to make payment to the exporter when they receive the agreed-upon documents. Two major types of LCs include an irrevocable letter of credit and a confirmed letter of credit. An irrevocable LC means that it may not be changed or cancelled without the agreement of both the buyer and the seller. A confirmed letter of credit means that the exporter's advising bank guarantees to pay the exporter if the foreign bank fails to do so. This type of LC makes sense when the exporter is worried about the credit risk of the foreign bank or the political risk of the importing country. It is a type of insurance for the exporter.

Documentary Collections In **documentary collections** (DCs), the exporter's bank (called the remitting bank) collects the payments for the exporter. After shipping goods to the importer, the exporter receives documents from the importer and provides them to its bank. The exporter's remitting bank then sends these documents to the importer's bank (called the collecting bank) along with instructions for payment. Upon receipt of the payment, the collecting bank releases the documents to the importer. The collecting bank then sends the money paid by the importer to the exporter's remitting bank, and this bank credits the exporter's account when the money is received. To receive the shipped goods, the importer goes to the shipping carrier and presents the documents.

Open Account Just the opposite of a pre-payment, an **open account transaction** means that the exporter ships the goods before payment is due. Usually, the importer agrees to pay within 30 to 90 days. This is the highest-risk option for an exporter. Ideally, to accept an open account, the exporter should be confident that the importer will pay at an agreed-upon time, and that the importing country is a low-risk political, economic, and commercial environment. However, in competitive export markets, foreign buyers often demand open accounts if they can get open accounts from the exporter's competitors.

Export Financing

Like a company that needs capital to finance building a plant in another country, exporters also need access to funds to finance their operations. Remember, it is often a long time between when the exporter begins building a product and when the exporting company finally receives its payments from the importers. This is especially critical for smaller and medium enterprises as they consider going international. Consider the following IB Emerging Market Strategic Insight.

Small and medium-sized enterprises (SMEs) play critical roles in most societies. SMEs tend to employ a sizable proportion of societal members and also create a significant number of new jobs. Understanding how SMEs finance their operations is therefore very critical. This issue is even more relevant in emerging markets where economic and political conditions tend to be unstable. As SMEs look to expand to international markets, credit availability is critical. What conditions do SMEs face as they raise capital?

A recent study of more than 90,000 firms in 119 emerging markets reveals some insights. The study found that SMEs are more likely than large firms to have difficulties in raising capital. This is evidenced by the findings that smaller and younger firms are more likely to rely on internal financing. However, this lack of financing to SMEs suggests that these firms may not be able to expand internationally because of the lack of financing.

Why are SMEs in emerging markets more likely to face financing difficulties? First, as has been mentioned several times throughout the book, emerging markets face more institutional voids thereby limiting financing options for SMEs. Second, SMEs tend to also be more opaque than larger firms. It is often easier for banks to get credit information about large firms than smaller firms. Finally, banks are also more likely to lend to larger firms just because of their size.

Given the difficulties emerging market SMEs face to get financing, it is important often for governments to intervene to facilitate financing. For instance, the US based Export–Import Bank (EXIM) can help SMEs get working capital loans (see below) by acting as a guarantee to private banks. The EXIM also provides Export Credit Insurance where the SMEs are protected if they sell on credit to a foreign buyer and the latter defaults.

Source: Adapted from Y. Dong and C. Me, 2014, "SME financing in emerging markets: Firms characteristics, banking structure and institutions," *Emerging Markets Finance & Trade*, *50*(1), pp. 120–149; Export–Import Bank, 2016, www.exim.gov/

The above shows the difficulties for SMEs to secure financing in emerging markets. Next we discuss the types of financing available to exporters.

Working Capital Financing

When an exporter needs to cover the entire cash cycle from purchase of raw materials through the ultimate collection of the payments, one option is the use of **export working capital**. Commercial banks usually provide export working capital facilities so that the exporter can buy the raw materials and build the products to ship to importers in foreign countries. The bank can provide this money in the form of a loan or revolving line of credit. A revolving line of credit is like a credit card that allows companies to borrow money up to some preset limit over a period of time.

While products in Western markets seem to always be coming from emerging markets, there are situations where the flow of products is from Western markets to emerging markets. The BRIC Insight below shows how one small business from Alabama succeed in the export business to China by getting working capital export financing.

export working capital
money loaned to an exporter so that the exporter can buy the raw materials and build the products to ship to importers in foreign countries

An Alabama Small to Medium-sized Enterprise (SME) Finds Financing to Propel its Exporting Success to China

BRIC INSIGHT

Weichai Power Co. Ltd, Weifang City, Shandong, China, put out a call for bids for a contract to engineer and build a cupola-melt facility and emission control system for a diesel engine manufacturing plant. A cupola is a vertical furnace used to melt iron. After several companies contacted Weichai Power about the project, the Chinese company came directly to Gregory R. Bray, president and CEO of Electric Controls and Systems Inc. (EC&S) of Birmingham, Alabama, asking for a bid on the project. Weichai Power recognized that EC&S has an excellent reputation for engineering and producing machinery for heavy industrial processing plants. Bray agreed to bid, offering a price of $11.8 million and getting the contract over a German competitor.

However, noted Bray, "One of our challenges was financing, but with the assistance of First Commercial Bank and the Alabama International Trade Center, we were able to obtain a working capital guarantee from the Export–Import Bank of the US for the issuance of a performance bond required for the project." Weichai Power's cupola is now running and there are other possible projects in China for EC&S. EC&S is now involved in many other projects such as foundries, steel mills, etc.

Source: Adapted from Alabama International Trade Center, University of Alabama, www.aitc.ua.edu/success. html

Export Factoring

export factoring
occurs when an exporter transfers title or ownership of its short-term foreign accounts receivables to a factor for cash but less the face value of the account receivables

Another option that exporters can use to get needed funds is called **export factoring**. As you remember from your accounting class, accounts receivables are payments due the company from customers who have been billed but who have not yet paid. Export factoring focuses on short-term receivables (payments due in up to 180 days). In this system, the exporter transfers title or ownership of its short-term foreign accounts receivables to a factor, which is a bank or a specialized financial firm that purchases account receivables. The factor then gives the exporter cash but less the face value of the account receivables. The amount it falls below the face value of the receivables is called the discount and this is like the interest on a loan. Thus, the exporter gets less money than the face value of the account receivables, but the company gets the money right away and does not have to wait for payments from customers. It is like a loan but with the additional benefit that the factor handles the collections and risks of nonpayment.

Export factoring has grown tremendously over the years. In fact, one of the main networks of factoring companies and banks is Factors Chain International (FCI), https://fci.nl/en/home. Exhibit 11.9 below shows the growth of two factor volume (export and import factoring) as reported by the members of the FCI.

Forfaiting

forfaiting
occurs when an exporter transfers title or ownership of its medium-term foreign accounts receivables, typically for larger projects, to a factor for cash but less the face value of the account receivables

Forfaiting is similar to factoring except that it focuses on the sale of medium-term receivables (180 days to seven years). However, unlike factors, forfaiters typically work with exporters on larger projects, typically over $100,000. As such, mostly larger established companies use forfaiting. More recently small and medium-sized companies are using forfaiting when they deal with importers from countries considered high risk. You can find forfaiters by going to the website of the International Forfaiting Association (IFA), https://ifta.org.

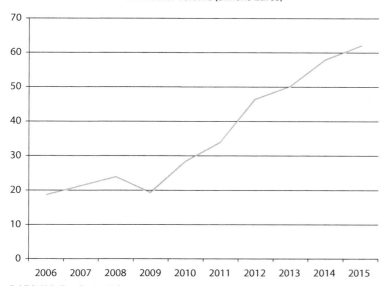

Two Factor Volume (Billions Euros)

Exhibit 11.9 Two Factor Volume
Source: Adapted from https://fci.nl/en/home

Chapter Review

This chapter began with a discussion of risk. You saw that country risk related to how a country's business environment might influence an MNC's profits or the value of its assets in that country. You learned that many emerging markets have more risks. Before MNCs enter a country, the international managers must consider how risk might affect their investments. Tesco's managers, for example, decided that entering the US market with many stores all at once was risky but worth the potential financial loss because the potential pay-off is high. Thus, risk plays an essential role in considering any financial investment, and as the example shows, assessment of risk is very complex when investment crosses borders.

Although there are many strategic reasons to consider a major project such as entering a new country, ultimately companies need to make money and the investment needs to return more than the cost. This process is called the capital budgeting decision, and one popular technique to estimate when an investment will pay off is called net present value or NPV. Importantly for the international manger, NPV calculations allow considerations of how much return is necessary to match the risk and how issues such as changing exchange rates and local tax rates influence the expected outcomes. Additionally, you saw how it is not always easy to make accurate estimates when considering investments in some emerging markets.

Of course, once international managers decide that an investment makes sense strategically and financially, they must decide the best way to get the money to fund the venture. As you remember from previous chapters, they can do this with debt or equity. The challenging decision is to decide the capital structure, which is the mixture of debt and equity. The basic criterion is based on which will cost the company more, the interest paid on debt or the dividends lost to the stockholders. However, many factors come into play when international managers determine the capital structure of their foreign subsidiaries. One important factor is the degree to which the local tax structure and laws allow deductions of interest payments on bonds and thus reduce taxes. However, numerous other issues such as available cash flows and local country risk are also considered.

The MNC faces financing issues not only when considering foreign investments but also in import and export transactions. For MNCs involved in international trade, financial institutions, importers, or exporters must provide credit to cover the lag between when goods are delivered and when payments are made.

There are various methods of payments in international trade. In this chapter, you learned about cash-in-advance or pre-payments, letters of credit, documentary collections, and open accounts. Each of these has varying degrees of risk for the exporter, importer, or participating financial institutions, depending on which party receives the payments or goods first.

The chapter concluded with a discussion of the types of financing that exporters often use to cover cash flow needs between the time when the exporter begins production of goods and when the company finally receives payments from an importer. Working capital financing from commercial banks allows companies to borrow up to certain amounts, often with revolving credit similar to a credit card. Other forms of financing, export factoring and forfaiting, allow export companies to sell their accounts receivables at a discount in order to receive the money prior to the payments from the exporters.

Chief financial officers, or CFOs, in MNCs have very complex jobs to manage financial operations often in many countries, each with its own unique financial environment. It is the duty of the CFO to work with other top international managers to provide the technical expertise to help determine the best financial options in implementing international strategies. Such challenges become even more difficult in the context of the emerging markets.

Discussion Questions

1 Identify political factors that might affect the risk to do business in a country.

2 Identify financial factors that might affect the risk to do business in a country.

3 Discuss the statement: Any level of risk can be OK if the potential returns are sufficiently high.

4 SEL in Washington State plans to establish a European subsidiary. SEL's financial managers expect that the euro will appreciate over the next few years. How might this affect SEL's decision regarding the use of headquarters' retained earnings or its subsidiary's retained earnings as sources of capital?

5 Discuss factors that must be considered for capital budgeting for an MNC's foreign subsidiary that might not be considered for a domestic investment.

6 Consider investments in Brazil, Hungary, and Germany and discuss the factor of risk in making a capital budgeting decision regarding investments in these countries.

7 Discuss reasons why the capital structure of an MNC's subsidiary might differ from the parent company.

8 Why might the capital structures of companies from different countries differ?

9 What is the role of commercial banks in international trade transactions?

10 Discuss situations where an MNC might prefer a debt-intensive capital structure or an equity-intensive capital structure.

11 Discuss the risks or benefits to the exporter that uses factoring for accounts receivables.

12 Discuss the role of the factor for the exporter. How does the factor help an exporter?

13 Contrast the options of forfaiting and factoring.

14 Identify and discuss the basic documents used in international trade transactions.

International Business Skill Builder

Making NPV Decisions

Practice making NPV decisions for investments under different exchange rates and required rates of return. Go to http://spreadsheets.google.com/ccc?key= pfiFjc0K9uyyj1FpTTU29Kg or to your text's website support, where you can download the Excel spreadsheet for Exhibit 11.4, which shows two different scenarios for NPV for a hypothetical company. In the example, the host government's tax rate is 20 percent; the exchange rate of the dollar is 1.25 (shown in line 6); the discount rate is shown as 15 percent in line 8; and the initial investment is shown as $10,000,000 (entered as a negative) in line 10. You can change any of these values or other values in the colored cells and experiment with what happens to NPV.

Chapter Internet Activity

Search the web for export factoring companies. Identify at least three companies. You can have a mixture of domestic companies or factor companies in other countries. Compare and contrast their services. Pick one that you would use as a small to medium-sized business and provide a rationale for your choice.

Key Concepts

- bill of lading
- capital budgeting decision
- capital structure
- cash flow
- cash-in-advance
- commercial invoice
- constant dividend growth model
- cost of capital
- country risk
- documentary collections
- draft
- economic risk

- export factoring
- export working capital
- financial risk
- forfaiting
- letter of credit
- net present value, or NPV
- open account transaction
- pecking order theory
- political risk
- risk-free interest rate
- risk premium
- sustainability risk

CASE 11   BUSINESS > INTERNATIONAL

Williamson International: International Capital Budgeting

Williamson International is a chain of over 100 luxury hotels found mostly in developed countries. George Wilson, a former Chicago sales representative who frequently traveled internationally, started the company. As an international business traveler, Wilson found that hotel quality varied from country to country. He quit his very successful sales job and started a hotel in Dublin, Ireland, a country known for its extensive bed-and-breakfast industry. Wilson felt that business travelers needed a greater selection of hotels in Dublin, particularly in the higher-priced market. The Williamson of Dublin was an immediate success with business travelers and, with the help of a venture capitalist George was able to expand his hotel concept to 20 countries.

CASE 11
cont'd

Wilson has always sought hotel opportunities in more developed countries in Europe and Asia. George and his associates felt that the problems found in less-developed countries presented too much risk for his company; thus, they avoided most countries of the world. Because the countries in which Wilson operates are considered politically stable and present little political risk, the investment decisions are normally made on the basis of revenue projections using a net present value approach. The firm's cost of capital is used as a means of discounting expected cash flow. If the net present value (NPV) of the investment is above zero, the hotel is constructed. This approach has worked well for the company over the years.

With the possibility of market saturation beginning to rise, George is considering an opportunity to expand into other markets. He has been approached by a trade representative of St. Charles, a small and moderately industrialized island in the Caribbean, who proposes that Williamson International build a small boutique business hotel in the capital, Dominic. The trade rep has assured George that an additional hotel is needed in the capital due to the country's expanding industrialization. St. Charles has always enjoyed a brisk tourist trade, and now the country is diversifying its economy into light manufacturing.

Multinationals from the United States and Europe have established customer service operations on the island, and a number of garment manufacturers have begun operations there as well. The trade representative tells George that managers from these companies frequently visit the island, and they need a more luxurious hotel in which to stay. The hotel would certainly be profitable, reasons the trade rep.

Financial analysts for the company have created a report indicating that, using the present financial model, a small hotel would be a good investment. Data included in the model can be seen below.

Williamson International—St. Charles Operation
Preliminary Financial Analysis

Yearly Expected Cash Flow from Operations:	$750,000US
Expected Life of the Investment	25 years
Williamson International Cost of Capital	12%
Investment	$5,000,000US

Basic Financial Model: (12% PVF of 7.84314)
(Present Value of Cash Flows – Investment) = NPV (5,882,355 – 5,000,000) = $882,355

Some Williamson analysts argue, however, that a higher discounting factor than cost of capital should be used. It is proposed by some that a more appropriate discounting factor would be 15% (with a PVF of 6.46415), due to the higher risks associated with the investment environment.

George is uncertain about the proposed investment. While he sees the need for the company to find new markets, he is also troubled by reports he has read about increasing social unrest on the island. Although George and his associates do not consider St. Charles to be a high-risk country, they are concerned about recent increases in petty street crime and social unrest. It

CASE 11 cont'd

has been reported that citizens have resorted to violent street protest to express their displeasure with the increasing prices of some consumer goods. The currency of St. Charles, the Caribbean dollar, has been devalued against most hard currencies of the world and, as a result, imported goods have increased in price. On the other hand, St. Charles has no currency or foreign direct investment restrictions, and allows for full repatriation of company profits. In recent years, the government has been attempting to promote the island as an attractive location for foreign investment.

With declining opportunities in more stable environments, George must consider the feasibility of this opportunity, and the necessary change of strategic direction it would mean for Williamson International.

CASE DISCUSSION POINTS:

1   What additional information might be useful to consider before making this investment decision?
2   Would you recommend that Williamson International build a hotel on St. Charles? Are there any alternatives to consider other than building the hotel or staying out of the country? Explain.
3   Do emerging markets present any unique problems when conducting a financial analysis? Explain.

Case prepared by Charles A. Rarick

Notes

1   www.prsgroup.com/ICRG.aspx
2   http://country.eiu.com/AllCountries.aspx?view=all
3   www.aon.com/2016politicalriskmap
4   www.oecd.org/tad/xcred/crc.htm
5   This section relies heavily on Jeff Madura, 2014, *International Financial Management*, Mason, OH: Cengage Learning (12th edn).
6   Franco T. Modigliani and Merton Miller, 1958, "The cost of capital, corporate finance, and the theory of investment," *American Economic Review*, 48, pp. 655–669; Franco T. Modigliani and Merton Miller, 1961, "Corporate income taxes and the cost of capital: A revision," *American Economic Review*, 53, pp. 433–442.
7   This section relies heavily on Jeff Madura, 2014, *International Financial Management*, Mason, OH: Cengage Learning (12th edn).
8   Claude Erb, Campbell Harvey and Tadas Viskanta, 1995, "Country risk and global equity selection," *Journal of Portfolio Management*, 21, pp. 74–83; *The Economist*, 2016, "Risk premiums," May 21, p. 61.
9   Susan Chaplinsky and Latha Ramechand, 2000, "The impact of global equity offerings," *Journal of Finance*, 55, pp. 2767–2789.
10 Claude Erb, Campbell Harvey and Tadas Viskanta, 1996, "Political risk, financial risk and economic risk," *Financial Analysts' Journal*, 52, pp. 28–46.
11 This section relies heavily on Jeff Madura, 2014, *International Financial Management*, Mason, OH: Cengage Learning (12th edn). See also Raghuram G. Rajan and Luigi Zingales, 1995, "What do we know about capital structure? Some evidence from international data," *Journal of Finance*, 50, pp. 1421–1460.
12 Mihir A. Desal, C. Fritz Foley and James R. Hines Jr, 2004, "A multinational perspective on capital structure choice and internal capital markets," *Journal of Finance*, LIX, pp. 2451–2487.

CHAPTER 12

Accounting for Multinational Operations

After reading this chapter you should be able to:

- Understand the purpose of accounting and the differences between managerial accounting and financial accounting.

- Understand why nations originally adopted different accounting systems and the types of systems in use around the world.

- Understand the complexities and challenges for an MNC's accounting practices in emerging markets.

- Identify the pressures that lead to the harmonization and standardization of accounting procedures.

- Understand the basics of International Accounting Standards.

- Know how MNCs account for exchange-rate differences and translate foreign currencies for financial reporting.

- Appreciate the complexities of accounting for transfer pricing between units of MNCs taking into account the new OECD rules on country-by-country reporting of financial information.

- Be able to apply basic tax planning strategies.

International Business   *Preview IB Emerging Market Strategic Insight*

A Cultural Revolution in Accounting

In its former planned state economy, accounting in China focused on providing the numbers that state planners needed—mostly production quota numbers. Capitalist information such as costs, debt, and especially profit was ignored. In the 1990s, as China gradually moved to a capitalist economy, the role of accounting changed. To manage and value companies where profit is necessary for survival, accounting numbers had to make sense to investors and managers.

In 2007, the Ministry of Finance directed the 1,200 companies listed on the Shanghai and Shenzhen stock markets to adopt accounting standards and practices similar to International Financial Reporting Standards (IFRS). These or similar standards have replaced local accounting and financial reporting standards in many countries including the EU. The benefits of using IFRS are that investors and managers will be able to tell how well a company is performing. That is, revenues, costs, debts, and profits will be transparent and comparable to other companies. This will not only have local consequences but will allow Chinese companies to attract foreign capital and help Chinese companies wishing to invest in other countries.

The reality, however, is that this change is difficult. There are approximately 300,000 certified public accountants in China for a population of over 1.3 billion as compared to the UK with over 300,000 for a population of 64 million. Detailing the financial status of companies that have extensive overlapping ownership, common in China, is extremely difficult and time consuming. Estimates are that China needs at least five million more qualified accountants to raise corporate governance standards to world class levels.

Currently, Chinese companies that trade on US stock exchanges are allowed to use IFRS. Domestic Chinese companies must use Chinese Accounting Standards for Business Enterprises (ASBEs). Chinese companies whose securities trade on the Hong Kong stock exchange can chooses among IFRS, Hong Kong Financial Reporting Standards, or Chinese standards.

Source: Adapted from IFRS, 2016, IFRS application around the world jurisdictional profile: People's Republic of China, June 16; *The Economist*, 2007, "Cultural revolution," www.economist.com, January 11; *The Economist*, 2007, "Trust from facts," www.economist.com, January 11; *Reuters*, 2015, "China needs millions more accountants to raise standards," May 15.

The purpose of accounting is to provide standardized information that helps stakeholders in an organization (e.g. managers, investors) make sound economic and business decisions. As you can see from the Preview IB Emerging Market Strategic Insight, accounting practices can differ widely in their design and implementation in different countries. In this chapter we will explore how these differences influence the activities of MNCs. First, however, let us consider some of the basic types of accounting.

managerial accounting
accounting information
reported for internal use
by a company's
managers; generally does
not have to follow any
universal standards

financial accounting
provides information to
external stakeholders
regarding the company's
performance

Managerial accounting focuses on the information gathered for internal use by a company's managers and generally does not have to follow any universal standards. In contrast, **financial accounting** provides information to external stakeholders regarding the company's performance. Stockowners, bondholders, and other investors (e.g. banks) need relevant, valid, and reliable (consistently applied to all organizations) information about the financial state of a company. For example, think of yourself as an investor. Before you loan your money to a company or use your money to buy stock, you would want to be certain that the financial reports issued by the company are correct. Like investors, governments are also interested in the quality of financial reports. Since corporations pay taxes based on their profits, governments need to have an accurate assessment of the financial performances of companies in their countries. Unlike managerial accounting, financial accounting follows rules created by standard-setting bodies. In the US, the standard-setting body is called the Financial Accounting Standards Board (FASB) and its rules are called the US GAAP or Generally Accepted Accounting Principles. Many countries have their own GAAP standards that reflect the financial accounting rules in use in their country. However, the trend worldwide is to use IFRS or international financial reporting standards or standards that are close to IFRS. Such uniform standards make it easier for companies to list on foreign stock markets since investors can assess the companies using a common standard.

Since accounting provides information to make business and economic decisions, the differences in accounting systems used in different nations becomes an important consideration for international business people. Thus, international business managers must be aware of how differences in accounting systems in the countries in which they do business affect issues such as measure of financial performance, cash flows, and taxation. To deal with these issues, the field of international accounting is becoming increasingly important in our globalizing world. International accounting focuses on the differences among countries in accounting principles and reporting practices, the state of international and regional harmonization of accounting principles and reporting practices, foreign currency translation in financial reporting, accounting reporting for taxation, and the financial performance assessments of foreign subsidiaries and companies.[1]

In the remainder of this chapter we will answer several important questions related to international accounting. If we are in a world of increasingly global trade and investment, why have accounting standards historically differed by region and nation? What are the efforts that are making standards similar around the world? In spite of the move to similar accounting and financial reporting standards, some differences remain. Thus, what are the implications of having different accounting principles and standards used by different country units for the MNC?

How Did Nations Evolve Different Accounting Systems?

As you have seen for many business practices discussed in this book, the national context of social institutions and national culture provide two drivers of why accounting systems differ.[2] Exhibit 12.1 summarizes the forces that led to different accounting systems. First ,we will consider cultural issues, and then the institutional context.

National Culture

The classic view of accounting practices and culture links country practices with the Hofstede cultural dimensions that you studied earlier in the book.[3] Some of these accounting values also derive from dimensions of national culture identified by Trompenaars.

There are four major accounting values that studies show are related to national culture.[4] These are:

- *Professionalism versus statutory control* In individualistic, low-power distance cultures and those with low uncertainty avoidance, there is a preference for accountants using individual professional judgment rather than following strict legal requirements.
- *Conservatism versus optimism* In cultures with high power distance, high uncertainty avoidance, and strong affective norms (see Chapter 7), there exists a preference for accountants to take a cautious approach to financial measurement in contrast to being more laissez-faire.
- *Secrecy versus transparency* In high power distance and particularistic cultures, there is a preference for accountants to behave with strict confidentiality, only disclosing financial information about a business to managers and those who provide financing. This contrasts with accounting systems that encourage more transparency and publicly available information regarding companies.
- *Uniformity versus flexibility* In high uncertainty avoidance and universalistic cultures there is a preference for accountants to adopt uniform accounting practices applied similarly to all companies at all times. This contrasts with a flexible and particularistic approach to using accounting data that favor flexibility in accordance with the unique circumstances of individual companies.

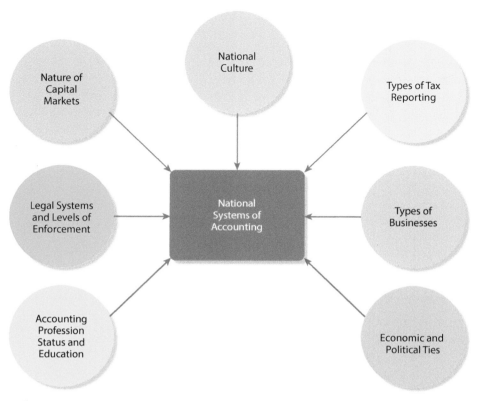

Exhibit 12.1 Why National Accounting Systems Differ

Social Institutions

In addition to national culture, the institutional context also influences how accounting systems develop and how they are used. In this section, we consider the nature of capital markets, type of tax reporting, the legal system and levels of enforcement of regulations, the types of businesses, the status of the accounting profession and accounting education, and economic and political ties with other nations.[5]

The Nature of Capital Markets   As you learned in Chapter 6, companies get needed finances by using debt (bank loans and bond) or equity (stocks). In countries such as Canada and the US, larger companies issue stock to get needed financing. In contrast, in Japan and Germany, it is more common to use bank financing. In equity market countries, there is more pressure to use accounting reports to present the company in the most favorable light. This is more likely to attract more stockholders and keep the price of stocks high. To protect investors there is also pressure from government regulators that requires companies to use more sophisticated accounting methods. For example, as we have seen earlier, the Sarbanes–Oxley Act in the US requires more disclosure of financial information to protect potential investors from the dubious acts of companies like Enron.

The Type of Tax Reporting   Countries can be separated on the degree to which there are separate rules for tax reporting and financial reporting. In the US and UK, for example, the rules are mostly independent. Companies file corporate tax returns like individuals and they issue annual reports to their stockholders to show the performance of their companies. In this case, the incentive is to be optimistic to the stockholders and report the lowest earnings possible to the tax collectors. In countries with a single reporting system, within the boundaries of the law, companies will tend to report lower earnings.

The Legal System and Levels of Enforcement of Regulations   There are three basic types of legal systems, common law, code or civil law, and theocratic law. The code law system, used in countries such as France, attempts to predefine rules for acceptable behavior in all situations. For the code to evolve, the governing body must change it. In a common law system, such as that used in the US and the UK, law evolves based on the interpretations of the law by judges and courts. In a theocratic law system, such as that used in Iran, civilian laws must be consistent with religious principles such as those in the Qur'an and religion supersedes civil law. In sum, common law is based on tradition, precedent, and custom; code law is based on codes; theocratic law is based on religious beliefs.

In code law countries, accounting practices also tend to be legislated and are very detailed and procedural. The objective is to protect those who lend money to the company. In common law countries, accounting practices evolve in response to evolving financial systems with the emphasis on presenting a fair and accurate portrayal of the company to shareholders. Theocratic law generally has more broad-based influences on the whole financial system rather than accounting practices.

Regardless of the type of legal system in use, countries differ in willingness and ability to enforce rules and laws regarding accounting practices. The Asian economic crises, some argue, occurred because personal ties between banks and companies kept the financial positions of many companies hidden until they reached crisis proportions. Even in the US, accounting scandals such as Enron and WorldCom have demonstrated that it takes considerable governmental resources to correct such situations. Importantly, the move to similar accounting and financial reporting standards does not offset differences in countries' willingness and ability to enforce such regulations.

We can get insights into the likelihood of enforcing rules and laws by looking at the World Bank Governance Indicators. Exhibit 12.2 shows how the World Bank ranks BRIC and other emerging economies and selected countries on regulatory quality; that is, the ability of the government to formulate and implement sound policies and regulations that permit and promote private economic development. The data show percentile ranks based on worldwide data. Note that the BRIC countries rank below the mean while some transition economies are near the top.

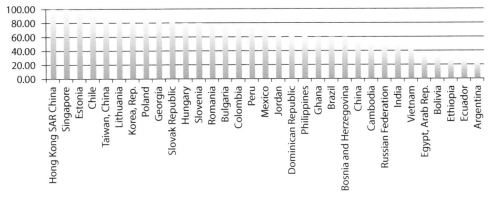

Exhibit 12.2 Percentile Rank Regulatory Quality: BRIC and Other Selected Economies
Source: http://info.worldbank.org/governance/wgi/index.aspx#home

The Types of Businesses   The financial reporting practices that evolve in different countries reflect the need of the types of companies that exist in the country. In the developed countries of the world, which spawn the large and highly complex MNCs, accounting practices evolve with the complexities of these businesses. In contrast, in much of the developing world there are few large and complex companies. Simple financial reporting is often all that is needed to provide valid and reliable information concerning these companies.

The Status of the Accounting Profession and Accounting Education   The prestige and influence of different occupational groups is not the same in all countries. For example, the role of the physician in Russia does not carry the status and prestige that it does in the US. The accounting profession is no different. In countries where the accounting profession is viewed as largely a book-keeping occupation, its influence is diminished and audit reports have less respect in the business community. In contrast, where accountants are viewed as independent professionals who follow independent professional norms, there is often more trust in what the accountants report. It is also assumed that the companies that are clients of accountants have less influence on the content of the financial reports certified by accountants. For accounting to evolve into a professional status, there must be established educational systems to train accountants. The degrees awarded must be considered legitimate certifications of accounting knowledge by the organizations and the investors in the country. Similarly, there are often licensing or certification requirements from the government or from a professional association that assure the professional competency of the accountants.

Economic and Political Ties with Other Nations   Cross-border trade and investment and membership in trade groups such as the EU and the ASEAN expose different nations to each other's accounting practices. Within trade groups, for example, there is pressure to adopt similar standards to make cross-border transactions simpler and more efficient. For the emerging market countries, there is also pressure to mimic the practices of the developed countries to facilitate trade and investment.

These drivers of national accounting systems result in many different types of systems. In the next section, we consider some basic classifications of systems.

Types of National Accounting Systems

In an attempt to simplify our understanding of differences among national accounting systems, several accounting scholars have developed classification systems that group different nations into similar types. Before we consider these systems, you should realize that national accounting systems change in response to local and global pressures. As such, these are general overviews to help you see the most basic differences. They also give us insights into the historical uses of accounting systems and how such systems developed in different countries.

The traditional way to view differences among accounting systems divides them into two groups: the microeconomic and the macroeconomic.[6] The micro and macro roughly follow the differences in legal systems discussed earlier. The micro systems occur mostly in common law countries and the macro systems occur mostly in codified or rule-based legal systems.

In the macroeconomic approach, accounting practices are developed largely to serve national economic planning and taxing functions. Accounting has a macro function because it most serves macro or nation-level interests. Examples include Italy, France, and Sweden. In the microeconomic approach, accounting serves the need of businesses, hence it is micro or at an organizational level. Examples include the US, Australia, and Canada.

Exhibit 12.3 shows the basic groups of accounting systems based on this classification and more specific historical influences.

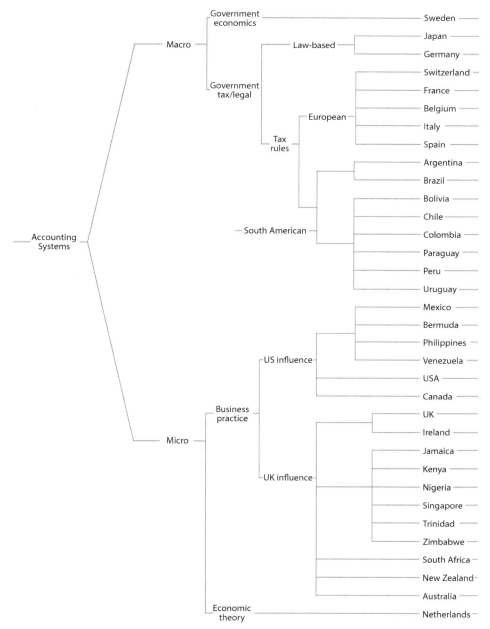

Exhibit 12.3 Classification of Historical Types and Uses of Accounting Systems

Source: Jan Berry, 1987, "The need to classify worldwide accountancy practices", *Accountancy*, October, pp. 90–91; T. S. Doupnik and S. B. Salter, 1993, "An empirical test of a judgmental international classification of financial reporting practices," *Journal of International Business Studies*, 24, pp. 41–60.

However, as noted above, accounting practices are not fixed. Many of the pressures of globalization are forcing countries to modify their accounting practices to fit into an interrelated global economy. It is not uncommon now for countries to use both local and international practices simultaneously. The general pressure for accounting practices to become more similar worldwide is called **harmonization** and is the topic of the next section.

harmonization means that differences among national accounting practices should be minimized to make it easy to translate accounting numbers from one system into another

Harmonization

Harmonization should not be confused with standardization, which means that all companies and countries use the same accounting practices. Harmonization is more flexible, meaning that differences among national accounting practices should be minimized to make it easy to translate accounting numbers from one system into another.

The pressures for harmonization come from many sources. One driver is that investors are able to understand a company's accounting numbers and invest in the best companies anywhere in the world. That is, potential stockholders are less likely to invest in companies in countries where it is difficult to understand the financial position of a company.

A second reason for harmonization is that MNCs have units located in many countries and must expend considerable resources to develop separate financial statements that meet local needs and then reconcile these statements to the practices of their home country. A third driver for harmonization is the needs of tax and investment regulators in different countries. While it might be most simple to make any foreign company conform to local accounting practices, such an approach has the undesirable effect of driving away foreign investors. For example, if a Germany company was considering opening a plant in the US or Canada to serve the North American market, one consideration in the location decision would be how costly and difficult it might be to reconcile EU accounting practices with those in the US.

The fourth major driver for harmonization is the stock exchanges. As you saw in Chapter 6, stock exchanges want foreign companies to list on their exchanges. Stock exchanges are also merging into multination entities that operate in more than one country. Since listing on a stock exchange in a country usually requires the foreign company to adopt international or local accounting reporting practices, exchanges see advantages in international or more harmonized systems.

Setting International Accounting Standards   While many see the benefits of harmonized accounting standards, the process of developing such standards started with the formation of the International Accounting Standards Committee (IASC) in 1973. Set up by professional accounting organizations from ten countries—Australia, Canada, France, Germany, Ireland, Japan, Mexico, Netherlands, the United Kingdom, and the United States—this body became the major standard-setter for over 30 years.

In March 2001, the IASC was reorganized into two units. Incorporated in the State of Delaware, the Accounting Standards Committee Foundation (IASCF, now the IFRS Foundation) is the parent organization of the **International Accounting Standards Board (IASB)**. The IASB is an independent accounting standard-setter located in London, UK, which assumed the accounting standard-setting duties from the IASC on April 1, 2001.

The mission of the IASC Foundation is:

International Accounting Standards Board (IASB) an independent accounting standard-setter located in London, UK

(a) to develop, in the public interest, a single set of high-quality, understandable and enforceable global accounting standards that require high-quality, transparent and comparable information in financial statements and other financial reporting to help participants in the world's capital markets and other users make economic decisions;

(b) to promote the use and rigorous application of those standards;

(c) in fulfilling the objectives associated with (a) and (b), to take account of, as appropriate, the special needs of small and medium-sized entities and emerging economies; and

(d) to bring about convergence of national accounting standards and International Accounting Standards and International Financial Reporting Standards to high-quality solutions.[7]

You can see the structure of the IASC Foundation and board in Exhibit 12.4.

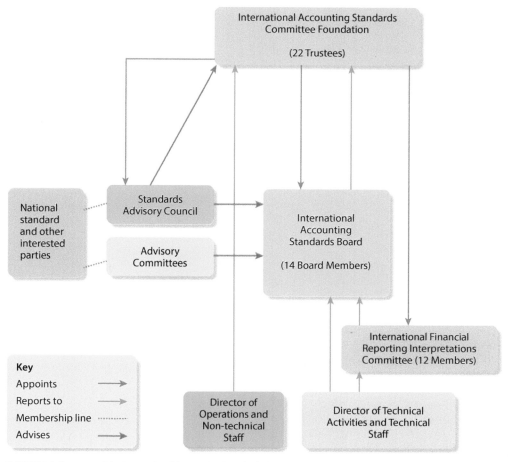

Exhibit 12.4 Structure of the International Accounting Standards Committee Foundation

The IASC Foundation has produced two sets of standards. One is for accounting practices, known as International Accounting Standards (IAS), and the other is for financial reporting, known as IFSR or International Financial Reporting Standards. A detailed description of these standards is beyond the scope of an introductory text. However, you can see from Exhibit 12.5 the array of issues considered in financial reporting. Students with more advanced backgrounds in accounting can read the technical summaries available on the IASB's website, www.iasb.org/IFRS%20Summaries/Technical%20Summaries%20of%20International%20Financial%20Reporting%20Standards.htm. Full details of the standards are also available for professional accountants.

International Financial Reporting Standards
• IFRS 1 First-time Adoption of International Financial Reporting Standards
• IFRS 2 Share-based Payment
• IFRS 3 Business Combinations
• IFRS 4 Insurance Contracts
• IFRS 5 Non-current Assets Held for Sale and Discontinued Operations
• IFRS 6 Exploration for and Evaluation of Mineral Resources
• IFRS 7 Financial Instruments: Disclosures
• IFRS 8 Operating Segments

International Accounting Standards
• IAS 1 Presentation of Financial Statements
• IAS 2 Inventories
• IAS 7 Cash Flow Statements
• IAS 8 Accounting Policies, Changes in Accounting Estimates and Errors
• IAS 10 Events after the Balance Sheet Date
• IAS 11 Construction Contracts
• IAS 12 Income Taxes
• IAS 16 Property, Plant and Equipment
• IAS 17 Leases
• IAS 18 Revenue
• IAS 19 Employee Benefits
• IAS 20 Accounting for Government Grants and Disclosure of Government Assistance
• IAS 21 The Effects of Changes in Foreign Exchange Rates
• IAS 23 Borrowing Costs
• IAS 24 Related Party Disclosures
• IAS 26 Accounting and Reporting by Retirement Benefit Plans
• IAS 27 Consolidated and Separate Financial Statements
• IAS 28 Investments in Associates and Joint Ventures
• IAS 29 Financial Reporting in Hyperinflationary Economies
• IAS 31 Interests in Joint Ventures
• IAS 32 Financial Instruments: Presentation
• IAS 33 Earnings per Share
• IAS 34 Interim Financial Reporting
• IAS 36 Impairment of Assets
• IAS 37 Provisions, Contingent Liabilities and Contingent Assets
• IAS 38 Intangible Assets
• IAS 39 Financial Instruments: Recognition and Measurement
• IAS 40 Investment Property
• IAS 41 Agriculture

Exhibit 12.5 Overview of International Financial Reporting Standards (IFRS) and International Accounting Standards (IAS)
Source: www.iasb.org/IFRSs/IFRS.htm

Why are the International Accounting and Financial Reporting Standards Important for International Business? The major reason that you, as a potential international business person, should be concerned with international accounting and reporting standards is they are rapidly becoming the world's standard. Consider Exhibit 12.6, which shows areas of the world that have adopted IFRS standards. The data show information for 143 countries that make up over 50 percent of the world's capital markets. For these countries, over 80 percent allow or require IFRS for larger companies. Adoption is less for small to medium sized enterprises as only 80 of the 143 jurisdictions require or permit the IFRS for SMEs.

The European Union led the movement to adopt international accounting and financial reporting standards. While there remains some variation by country and not all standards are accepted in exact IASB form, the EU actions represented a significant step in the move toward standardization. As the vice chairman of the IASC foundation noted to the European parliament:

The European Union with the support of the European Parliament took a visionary step when it decided not to choose a uniquely European approach to financial reporting. The result is an effort aimed at establishing an international system relevant for the evolving marketplace. Other countries agreed. It is significant that the major economies of the world are increasingly adopting IFRSs, rather than national accounting standards. As someone who believes strongly in European integration and at the same time the benefits of IFRSs, it is my hope that [the] European Union and, in particular, the European Parliament will remain the standard-bearer in promoting consistent application of IFRS.[8]

In another important development, the US has agreed with the EU to allow companies to use either US GAAP or IFRS in either jurisdiction without a requirement for reconciliation. However, the US, the largest capital market in the world, remains a holdout for complete adoption of IFRS, with no plan to change. The remaining major capital market without an IFRS mandate, Japan, has voluntary adoption but no mandatory transition date has been set. India plans to retain its own accounting for several years as they significantly converge with IFRS. China plans to adopt IFRS standards but has set no future date.[9]

More detail on the status of accounting standards for BRIC countries is noted below in the BRIC Insight.

IFRS Use in BRIC Countries

BRIC INSIGHT

IFRS has been mandatory, with some minor modifications, in Brazil since 2010 for companies that trade debt or equity securities. Small and medium-sized companies use Brazilian Generally Accepted Accounting Practices.

IFRS Standards became mandatory for the Russian Federation in 2012. Companies must also prepare separate financial statements using Russian GAAP.

India has not yet adopted IFRS Standards. Indian companies are required to use Indian Accounting Standards. However, these are quite similar to IFRS Standards with some changes in terminology and modifications of principles for recognizing income, expenses, assets, and liabilities.

Similar to India, China uses national accounting standards that are substantially similar to IFRS Standards. The IFRS Foundation and the Chinese Ministry of Finance now have a joint working group to advance the use of IFRS Standards in China, particularly for Chinese companies involved in international business.

In sum, the BRIC countries show substantial progress in the move to both harmonize and standardize accounting standards.

Source: Adapted from IFRS, 2016, IFRS application around the world jurisdictional profile: Brazil, June 16; IFRS, 2016, IFRS application around the world jurisdictional profile: Russia, June 16; IFRS, 2016, IFRS application around the world jurisdictional profile: India, June 16; IFRS, 2016, IFRS application around the world jurisdictional profile: People's Republic of China, June 16.

Stages of IFSR Adoption for 140 Countries			
Afghanistan	Denmark	Latvia	Rwanda
Albania	Dominica	Lesotho	Saint Lucia
Angola	Dominican Republic	Liechtenstein	Saudi Arabia
Anguilla	Ecuador	Lithuania	Serbia
Antigua and Barbuda	Egypt	Luxembourg	Sierra Leone
Argentina	El Salvador	Macao	Singapore
Armenia	Estonia	Macedonia	Slovakia
Australia	European Union	Madagascar	Slovenia
Austria	Fiji	Malaysia	South Africa
Azerbaijan	Finland	Maldives	Spain
Bahamas	France	Malta	Sri Lanka
Bahrain	Georgia	Mauritius	St Kitts and Nevis
Bangladesh	Germany	Mexico	St Vincent and the Grenadines
Barbados	Ghana	Moldova	Suriname
Belarus	Greece	Mongolia	Swaziland
Belgium	Grenada	Montserrat	Sweden
Belize	Guatemala	Myanmar	Switzerland
Bermuda	Guinea-Bissau	Nepal	Syria
Bhutan	Guyana	Netherlands	Taiwan
Bolivia	Honduras	New Zealand	Tanzania
Bosnia and Herzegovina	Hong Kong	Nicaragua	Thailand
Botswana	Hungary	Niger	Trinidad & Tobago
Brazil	Iceland	Nigeria	Turkey
Brunei Darussalam	India	Norway	Uganda
Bulgaria	Indonesia	Oman	Ukraine
Cambodia	Iraq	Pakistan	United Arab Emirates
Canada	Ireland	Palestine	United Kingdom
Cayman Islands	Israel	Panama	United States
Chile	Italy	Paraguay	Uruguay
China	Jamaica	Peru	Uzbekistan
Colombia	Japan	Philippines	Venezuela
Costa Rica	Jordan	Poland	Vietnam
Croatia	Kenya	Portugal	Yemen
Cyprus	Korea (South)	Romania	Zambia
Czech Republic	Kosovo	Russia	Zimbabwe

Exhibit 12.6 The Use of International Financial Reporting Standards around the World

Notes

• The 116 countries in black require IFRS for all or most domestic publicly accountable entities.

• Countries colored blue permit or require IFRS for at least some domestic publicly accountable entities.

• Countries colored red do not require or permit IFRS for any domestic publicly accountable entities.

Source: Adapted from Paul Pacter, The global reach of IFRS is expanding. IFRS Foundation and the IASB, September 2, 2015, www.ifrs.org/Features/Pages/Global-reach-of-IFRS-is-expanding.aspx

Even if all companies and countries used the same accounting practices and financial reporting, MNCs would still face accounting challenges based to a large degree on the use of different currencies and different national tax laws. In the next sections, you will see how international accountants handle some of these issues.

Accounting for Exchange Rates

As you read in the previous chapters, doing business in different countries requires international managers to deal with different currencies and the changing values of these currencies relative to each other, namely exchange rates. There are two major areas of concern in accounting regarding how to report the effects of exchange rates on financial reports. The first is called **foreign currency transaction** and the second is called **foreign currency translation**. For readers without any background in accounting, the Appendix to this chapter provides an overview of the basic financial reports.

foreign currency transaction refers to the procedures for reporting financial transactions based in a foreign currency, including the possibility of gains or losses due to changing exchange rates

Foreign Currency Transactions

Any time an MNC has a transaction based in a foreign currency, it faces a possibility of gains or losses due to changing exchange rates. For example, say a US hard disk manufacturer agrees to sell drives to a Japanese PC manufacturer for ¥1,000,000,000 when the exchange rate was ¥115 = $1. The US manufacturer anticipates receiving $8,695,652 in payment when the drives arrive in Japan a month later. However, when the bill comes due, the exchange rate is now ¥120 = $1, meaning that when the Japanese company pays its bill in yen, the US company will now only receive $8,333,333, which is $362,319 less than anticipated.

foreign currency translation refers to the procedures for restating financial statements from a foreign subsidiary into the currency of the country of the parent company

The accounting issue is how to enter data on this sale into a balance sheet. Should it be based on the transaction date, when the agreement is made, or the settlement date, when the payment is made? The US system requires that the accountant enter the information as two transactions:

On the transaction date:

Accounts receivable	8,695,652
Sales	8,695,652

On the settlement date:

Cash	8,333,333
Loss on foreign exchange	362,319
Accounts receivable	362,319

Foreign Currency Translation

Foreign currency translation refers to the procedures for restating financial statements from a foreign subsidiary into the currency of the country of the parent company. For example, BMW has subsidiaries in many parts of the world including the US. However, being a German company, BMW presents its financial statements in euros. As such, for example, the financial statements from its US subsidiary that uses dollars must be translated into euros. Having all financial statements presented in one currency also gives investors a consistent picture of the performance of the company. This is called a **consolidated financial statement**, which means the financial reports treat the MNC as one entity in spite of having locations in different parts of the world that use different currencies. Unlike foreign currency transactions, in which actual money changes hands, no money changes hands in translation.

consolidated financial statement a financial report that treats the MNC as one entity in spite of having locations in different parts of the world that use different currencies

Of course, if exchange rates among currencies never changed, translation would be easy. However, as you learned in the previous chapter, exchange rates for most currencies vary continuously and this makes the issue of foreign currency translation more complex. To deal with this complexity, accountants have devised four common methods to prepare consolidated financial statements for MNCs, namely the current rate method, the current–noncurrent method, the monetary–nonmonetary method, and the temporal method.[10]

current rate method
a currency translation in which all assets and liabilities are translated into the base currency on the date of the balance sheet

In the **current rate method**, which is the simplest, all assets and liabilities are translated into the base currency on the date of the balance sheet. Dividends are translated based on the exchange rate on the day they are declared. Revenue and expense items on the balance sheet use a weighted average of exchange rates over the period covered. No adjustments are made for differences in accounting principles in different locations. This keeps financial performance ratios (e.g. return on investment; money gained/money invested) the same in the foreign currency and in the parent company currency. The current rate translation method is the most popular method.

current–noncurrent method
a currency translation in which balance sheet items are divided into current and noncurrent types

In the **current–noncurrent method**, balance sheet items are divided into current and noncurrent types. Current assets include items such as cash, accounts receivable, and inventory that can be converted to cash within one year. Current liabilities are payments that must be made within one year, money owed for interest, accounts payable, short-term loans, and any other debts that must be paid within the year. Any other asset or liability is considered noncurrent. With the current–noncurrent method, translation of current assets and liabilities uses exchange rates on the balance sheet date. Exchange-rate translations for noncurrent assets and liabilities use the exchange rates in existence when the asset was acquired or the liability incurred.

monetary–nonmonetary method
a currency translation that divides the balance sheet into monetary and nonmonetary items

Also using balance sheet classifications, the **monetary–nonmonetary method** divides the balance sheet into monetary and nonmonetary items. Any balance sheet item shown in fixed currency—as, for example, cash and receivables—is considered monetary. Other items such as prepaid insurance are considered nonmonetary. Monetary items are translated based on the exchange rate on the balance sheet date, and historical rates are used for nonmonetary items. Many accounting scholars consider both the current–noncurrent and monetary–nonmonetary methods suspect because they do not believe the classifications are relevant to translations.

temporal translation method
a currency translation that uses exchange rates at the date of measurement

The **temporal translation method** translates foreign currency into the parent company financial statement's currency using exchange rates at the date of measurement. This results in cash, receivables, and payables translated on the balance sheet date. The historical exchange rate in place is used for other items such as fixed assets and inventories.

Exhibit 12.7 presents a summary of the different types of translation methods and their applications to balance sheets and income statements.

Foreign Currency Translation Rules for US Firms and for International Accounting Standards   The *Statement of Financial Accounting Standards No. 52* is the regulation that US companies must follow to translate financial statements from their international subsidiaries.[11] This standard allows US companies to translate financial statements using either the temporal or the current rate method. The choice of the method depends on the functional currency of the subsidiary. **Functional currency** is based on selecting the primary economic environment in which the subsidiary or other unit, including divisions, branches, and joint ventures, operates. To use a functional currency other than the dollar, the unit must conduct most of its operations (sales, financing, investing, production, etc.) locally. Making the choice of a functional currency is not always an unambiguous decision. For example, even in the same industry, Texaco uses the US dollar as its functional currency while Exxon Mobil uses foreign currencies, even though both companies have subsidiaries in the same countries.[12]

functional currency
the primary economic environment in which the subsidiary or other unit operates

	Exchange Rate for Translation Method			
	Current Rate	Current–Noncurrent	Monetary–Nonmonetary	Temporal
Cash	C	C	C	C
Current receivables	C	C	C	C
Inventory—cost basis	C	C	H	H
Long-term receivables	C	H	C	C
Long-term investments—cost basis	C	H	H	H
Long-term investments—market basis	C	H	H	C
Property, plant, equipment	C	H	H	H
Intangible assets	C	H	H	H
Current liabilities	C	C	C	C
Long-term debt	C	H	C	C
Common stock	H	H	H	H
Retained earnings	B	B	B	B
Revenues	A	A	A	A
Cost of goods sold	A	A	H	H
Depreciation expense	A	H	H	H
Amortization expense	A	H	H	H

Exhibit 12.7 Translation Method Exchange Rates for Selected Balance Sheet and Income Statement Items

Notes

A = Weighted average exchange rate for the current period

B = Balancing or adjustment factor

C = Current exchange rate at the balance sheet date

H = Historical exchange rate

Source: M. Zafar Iqbal, 2002, *International Accounting: A Global Perspective*, Mason, OH: South-Western, p. 48; www.cengage.com/resource_uploads/downloads/0324381980_74247.pdf; http://www.fasb.org/summary/stsum52.shtml

Exhibit 12.8 shows the decision rule for choosing a translation method based on functional currency. As you can see, the choice of a translation method depends directly on the choice of a functional currency.

The translation method required under international accounting standards is simpler than that required in the US. Assets and liabilities are translated from the subsidiary's functional currency to the currency of the unit's country on the date of the balance sheet. Income and expenses are translated based on the exchange rate existing on the date of transaction.

In the IB Emerging Market Strategic Insight overleaf, you can see how a major MNC such as BMW handles the issues of translation.

Up to this point in the chapter, we have considered primarily issues related to international financial accounting. Now we are going to consider some managerial accounting issues related to international operations. As you have seen, financial accounting information deals with providing useful information to investors and others from outside of the company. Managerial accounting, in contrast, is concerned with providing accounting information inside the company to managers for making better managerial decisions.

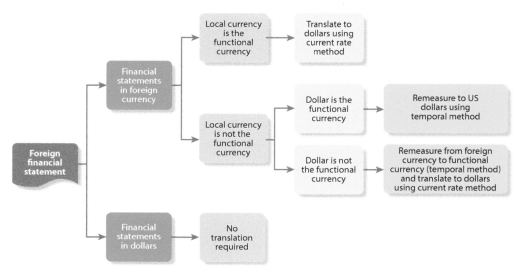

Exhibit 12.8 Decision Rule for US Companies Choosing a Translation Method

Foreign Currency Translation at BMW: Emerging Market Countries are Now Significant in the BMW Mix of Currencies

IB EMERGING MARKET
STRATEGIC INSIGHT

With its headquarters located in Germany and thus subject to the EU's adoption of International Accounting Standards, BMW Group reports its translation procedures as follows:

> The financial statements of consolidated companies which are drawn up in a foreign currency are translated using the functional currency concept (IAS 21 The Effects of Changes in Foreign Exchange Rates) and the modified closing rate method. The functional currency of a subsidiary is determined as a general rule on the basis of the primary economic environment in which it operates and corresponds therefore usually to the relevant local currency. Income and expenses of foreign subsidiaries are translated in the Group Financial Statements at the average exchange rate for the year, and assets and liabilities are translated at the closing rate. Exchange differences arising from the translation of shareholders' equity are recognized directly in accumulated other equity. Exchange differences arising from the use of different exchange rates to translate the income counted for as a general rule using the equity method when significant influence can be exercised (IAS 28 Investments in Associates and Joint Ventures). As a general rule, there is a rebuttable assumption that the Group has significant influence if it holds between 20 percent and 50 percent of the associated company's or joint venture's voting power. Statements are also recognized directly in accumulated other equity. Foreign currency receivables and payables in the single entity accounts of BMWAG and subsidiaries are recorded, at the date of the transaction, at cost. At the end of the reporting period, foreign currency receivables and payables are translated at the closing exchange rate. The resulting unrealized gains and losses as well as the subsequent realized gains and losses arising on settlement are recognized in the income statement in accordance with the underlying substance of the relevant transactions. The exchange rates of those currencies which have a material impact on the Group Financial Statements are shown in Exhibit 12.9 below:

	Closing Rate 31.12. 2015	31.12. 2014	Average Rate 2015	2014
US dollar	1.09	1.21	1.11	1.33
British pound	0.74	0.78	0.73	0.81
Chinese Renminbi	7.07	7.53	6.97	8.19
Japanese yen	130.74	144.95	134.28	140.38
Russian Rouble	79.91	70.98	68.01	51.03
Korean Won	1,278.92	1,255.38	1,324.84	1,397.80

Exhibit 12.9 Exchange Rates Used in BMW Financial Reporting

Note that the emerging countries of China, Russia, and Korea have "material impact" on BMW's bottom line. Ten years ago, these countries were not mentioned.

Source: *BMW Group 2015 Annual Report*, www.bmwgroup.com/content/dam/bmw-group-websites/ bmwgroup_com/ir/downloads/en/2016/Annual_Report_2015.pdf, p. 101.

Major International Managerial Accounting Issues: Transfer Pricing and International Taxation

The two major international managerial accounting issues we will examine in this chapter are transfer pricing and international taxation. **Transfer pricing** represents the prices for goods and services that units within a company charge each other. For example, a watch factory in Italy may charge its US parent company €50/watch. The parent company "buys" the watches from its own factory rather than from another manufacturer. **International taxation** refers to the need to appreciate the diversity and complexity of tax systems in different nations and their implications for multinational operations.

transfer pricing represents the prices for goods and services that units within a company charge each other

international taxation refers to the need to appreciate the diversity and complexity of tax systems in different nations and their implications for multinational operations

Transfer Pricing

As you saw in the chapter on international strategy, MNCs are increasingly more likely to set up units or platforms in any corner of the world, including to a greater degree emerging market countries. These units exchange services (e.g. call centers), manufactured components, finished goods, and even the results of R&D with each other. One job of the accountant then is how to establish a measurable price for these intra-company exchanges.

Why Have Transfer Pricing?   The first question that often comes to mind regarding transfer pricing is why not just exchange goods and services among all units of a company for free? It is the same company, after all. One reason for transfer pricing, for both domestic and MNCs, is to provide a system of management control and evaluation. That is, if a unit of a company pays for its components and services secured internal to the company and external to the company and sells its output either externally or internally to other company units, the unit and thus the managers have profits or losses. However, for an MNC a variety of other factors come into play.

Factors Affecting Transfer Pricing   One very important issue for the MNC is the effects of transfer pricing on taxes. Consider, for example, a US MNC that faces a higher tax rate in the US than its subsidiary faces in Thailand. If the Thai subsidiary charges the parent company a higher transfer price for its goods sold to the parent, it will make more profit in Thailand. Alternatively, since it is paying a high price for its goods, the US parent will make less profit.

Although it is likely that most companies comply with local tax regulations, examples exist of MNCs stretching the interpretation of "arm's length" transactions among subsidiaries around the world.

For example:

Overpriced imports from MNC units in low tax rate countries into other MNC units in high tax rate countries are used to create losses or lower profits, for the exporting unit thus lowering the MNC's tax payments in the high tax rate country. This works when the tax paid in the lower tax rate country is less than the tax that would have been charged for a market arm's length price in the high tax rate country. Some examples include:

- From the Czech Republic, $972.98 for plastic buckets
- From Canada, $1,853 for fence posts
- From China, $4,121.81 for a kilo of toilet paper
- From Israel, $2,052 for apple juice
- From Trinidad, $8,500 for ballpoint pens
- From Japan, $4,896 for tweezers.

From the opposite perspective, underpriced exports that lower profits or create losses for MNC subsidiaries in high tax rate countries reduce their taxes. Some examples include:

- To Hong Kong, $1.75 for toilet bowl and tank
- To Trinidad, $1.20 for prefabricated buildings
- To Venezuela, $387.83 for bulldozers
- To Israel, $52.03 for missile and rocket launchers.

Consider a similar strategy by Microsoft. Microsoft has shifted intellectual property (IP) rights and earnings for software developed in the US to divisions in lower-tax Puerto Rico, Ireland, and Singapore. After doing this, these units had an average effective tax rate of just 4 percent. With just 1,1914 employees, they booked $15.4 billion of pre-tax profit, which at the time was 55 percent of Microsoft's worldwide total. These employees were responsible for $8m of profit each, which was quite striking given the $312,000 each for the remaining 88,000 employees in Microsoft. One critic, Professor Stephen Shay of Harvard Law School notes that the claim by Microsoft that this was fair transfer pricing is "just not credible given the bottom-line outcome." In Microsoft's defense, however, tax avoidance, when following the rules in the US and foreign locations is not illegal.

Source: Adapted from Prem Sikka, 2003, "Comment: Plastic bucket: $972.98," *The Guardian*, June 30; *The Economist*, 2012, "Corporate tax avoidance: The price isn't right," September 21.

Of course, no country wants its tax base to shrink and lose revenue because of transfer pricing. As such, most adopt tax rules that attempt to have each country get its fair share of the taxes. Many nations, including the US, follow the international guidelines of the Organization for Economic Co-operation and Development (OECD) that are based on the **arm's length principle**. As of July 2016, 85 nations have agreed to follow OECD policies and more are expected to join. Essentially the OECD policies regarding the arm's length principle means any transfer pricing between units of an MNC should be set as if the units were making the exchange in the open market with other companies.

OECD calls this project the Base Erosion and Profit Shifting projects or BEPS. The idea is to have a worldwide system so "that profits will be reported where the economic activities that generate them are carried out and where value is created."[13] The three objectives of these policies are (1) to insure that taxpayers give appropriate considerations to transfer pricing among units; (2) to provide administrations with information to monitor such transactions; and; (3) to provide administrations with information to audit transfer pricing activities when deemed necessary. Beginning in 2017 companies in participating countries will be required to provide what the OECD calls "country-by-country" reporting of local financial activities. Exhibit 12.10 shows the OECD template for that report.

In spite of the agreements among countries and local tax codes, there remains a temptation for some MNCs to take advantage of reduced taxes by manipulating transfer pricing. The Emerging Market Ethical Challenge above, gives some of the potentially more egregious examples.

In addition to taxes, other factors also come into play when an MNC determines the best transfer pricing strategy between the parent and a subsidiary. For example, import or export tariffs and duties may encourage companies to raise or lower transfer prices to adjust for these costs. Similarly, differences in inflation rates may, for example, cause a parent to change a higher transfer price to a subsidiary in a high inflation country to offset the lowering value of local currency. Exhibit 12.11 provides a summary of conditions that encourage under- and overpricing transfers from a parent to a foreign subsidiary.

arm's length principle means that any transfer pricing between units of an MNC should be set as if the units were making the exchange in the open market with other companies

Name of the MNE group:
Fiscal year concerned:
Currency used:

Tax Jurisdiction	Revenues			Profit (Loss) before Income Tax	Income Tax Paid (on Cash Basis)	Income Tax Accrued – Current Year	Stated Capital	Accumulated Earnings	Number of Employees	Tangible Assets other than Cash and Cash Equivalents
	Unrelated Party	Related Party	Total							

Exhibit 12.10 OECD Country-by-Country Reporting Template

Source: OECD, 2015, *Transfer Pricing Documentation and Country-by-Country Reporting, Action 13—2015 Final Report*, OECD Publishing, Paris. DOI: http://dx.doi.org/10.1787/9789264241480-en

Overpricing Condition	Underpricing Condition
Higher local tax rates	Lower local tax rates
Lower tariffs on imports	Higher tariffs on imports
High inflation rate	Low inflation rate
Local government restrictions on profits	Local loans based on financial appearance of subsidiary

Exhibit 12.11 Local Conditions for Over or Under Transfer Pricing from a Parent to a Foreign Subsidiary

The relationship of taxes to transfer pricing is only one area of taxation of concern to MNCs. However, as you can see in Exhibit 12.12, it is considered among the most important.

In the next section, you will see other relevant aspects of taxation for the MNC.

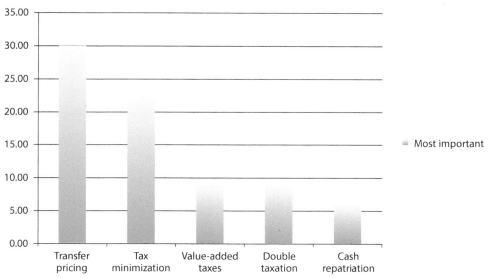

Exhibit 12.12 Most Important Tax Issues for MNC Tax Directors
Source: Ernst & Young, 2010 *Global Transfer Pricing Surveys*, New York: Ernst & Young.

International Taxation

Next to dealing with different currencies, managing the complex and different national tax systems is one of the more challenging areas for managerial accountants. While there is general agreement that MNCs should be taxed similarly to domestic companies for domestic income, there is less agreement on how to tax foreign income.[14]

There are two basic types of national tax systems encountered by international managers. The **territorial tax system** taxes only income earned within a country's borders. That is, income earned by the MNC for subsidiaries in other countries is not taxed. An alternative approach is the **worldwide tax system**. In a pure worldwide tax system, MNCs are taxed on their worldwide income, regardless of the country or countries from which the income is derived. To avoid double taxation of foreign income, most countries taking a worldwide approach allow a foreign tax credit. For example, if a US company pays taxes on profits earned in the UK, it does not have to pay these taxes again in the US. In reality, no country has a pure territorial or worldwide system, with all countries having some tax laws that lean to one system or the other. The US, for example, favors a more worldwide system while most European countries favor a more territorial system.

territorial tax system
taxes only income earned within a country's borders

worldwide tax system
taxes all profits earned by an MNC, regardless of location

To avoid double taxation of their companies in other countries, many countries negotiate tax treaties. These are agreements among governments as to how to tax companies from each other's countries. A listing of US tax treaties is located at www.treasury.gov/resource-center/tax-policy/treaties/Pages/default.aspx.

Tax Planning Strategies for the MNC   Of course, all companies want to make as much profit as possible, and one certain way to do this is to reduce expenses. Paying less tax is one strategy that companies and individuals use to have more money. Tax planning should not be confused with illegal activities to avoid taxes. Rather, companies must examine the nature of the operations and the tax codes of the countries in which they operate and use legal strategies to pay the lowest taxes possible. In this chapter, we consider two strategies: thin capitalization and the business model approach.[15]

thin capitalization
occurs when an MNC
finances a subsidiary in a
foreign country by
borrowing money rather
than issuing stock

Thin capitalization occurs when an MNC finances a subsidiary in a foreign country by borrowing money rather than issuing stock. As you remember from your readings on capital markets, companies finance new operations not only from profits that they reinvest in the company but also from money they borrow (usually by issuing bonds) or by selling stock. The advantage of borrowing money locally is that most countries give tax deductions for interest paid on borrowed money. This is similar to what happens to individuals who buy a home in the United States. When you borrow money to pay for the home, the interest you pay each year is deducted from your gross income. So, for example, if you make $50,000/year and you buy a new house and pay $4,000 in interest to a bank, your gross income is now $46,000 and you will not pay as much in taxes to the US government.

Increasingly, this thin capitalization strategy is becoming more difficult for companies to implement. Fearing loss of tax revenues, countries are passing laws that make tax deductions more difficult. Exhibit 12.13 shows some of these laws in effect in Europe and the BRIC countries. As you can see, most of these laws restrict the amount of debt a company can take on and thus reduce the amount of interest that can be used as a tax deduction. The restrictions in the EU countries are slightly more than in the BRIC countries but no longer appreciably different.

**business model
approach**
seeks location costs
advantages by locating in
countries with lower
taxes

As you learned earlier, MNCs can adopt transnational strategies to locate activities anywhere in the world where they can be done cheapest and best. International managers can also extend this general strategic approach to tax planning and strategies. As with labor costs, different countries provide potential tax savings if an MNC locates its operations in a lower tax country. Accountants call this the **business model approach** for tax planning and strategy. Of course, greater tax savings result if the business grows in the lower tax country. Otherwise, the cost savings from lower taxes may be offset by other losses of doing business in a stagnant or declining market.

Country	Summary of selected thin capitalization rules
Germany	• Limited to a 1.5:1 debt-to-equity ratio, which is also applicable to holding companies. • *De minimis* rule that allows the deductibility of intercompany interest that is less than €250,000 ($333,892). • Disallows interest on intercompany or guaranteed loans where loans arose in connection with the acquisition of share from a related party.
France	• Limited to a 1.5:1 debt-to-equity ratio and disallowance of interest in excess of 25 percent of relevant profits. • Non-deductible interest to be carried forward, reduced by 10 percent, and deducted in subsequent accounting period (subject to 25 percent relevant profit restriction). • The Charasse amendment re disallowance of interest remains in existence.
Italy	• Limits deductibility of interest when debt is used to finance holdings that benefit from the participation exemption. • Limited to a 4:1 debt-to-equity ratio and complex rules that determine the quantum of the equity element of the computation.
Netherlands	• Limited to a 3:1 debt-to-equity ratio. • Disallows related party interest when funds are used to purchase shares of a company intragroup, fund capital contributions and dividend payments. • Allows deductions for interest where the interest receipt is subject to "reasonable" taxation in the hands of the lender. • No offset of intragroup interest expense against the operating income of the fiscal unity for eight years after acquisition.
Brazil	• The Brazilian thin capitalization rules establish that interest paid or credited by interest may only be deducted for income tax purposes if the interest expense is viewed as necessary for the activities of the local entity. • Limited to a 2:1 debt-equity ratio in the amount of debt granted by a foreign related party does not exceed relative to the net equity of the Brazilian entity. • If the 2:1 ratio is exceeded, the portion of interest related to the excess debt amount is not deductible for Brazilian income tax purposes.
Russia	• Under the Russian Tax Code, interest on loans received from foreign shareholders owning more than 20 percent of capital is deductible with restrictions. • Limited to a 3:1 debt-equity ratio for most enterprises. • Limited to a 12.5:1 debt-equity ratio for banks and leasing companies. • For loans exceeding debt-equity ratios, excess interest on such loans is reclassified as dividends paid to foreign shareholders and subject to a tax of 15 percent.
India	• No prescribed thin capitalization rules regarding debt-to-equity ratios exist under Indian taxation law. • Tax officers have the options to disallow tax deductions for interest paid to foreign related parties at rates or on terms that are deemed unreasonably high.
China	• Chinese thin capitalization rules disallow interest expenses arising from excessive related party loans. • A 5:1 debt-equity ratio is required for enterprises in the financial industry. • For enterprises in other industries the required debt ratio limit is 2:1. • If ratios are exceeded but tax officials judge that sufficient evidence shows that the financing arrangements were at arm's length, interest payments may still be fully deductible.

Exhibit 12.13 Restrictions on Thin Capitalization in Europe and BRIC Countries

Source: Price, Waterhouse, Coopers, Worldwide Tax Summaries: Corporate Taxes 2015/16, www.pwc.com/taxsummaries; Nick Woodford and Christopher Schreiber, "Debt financing loses appeal as tax planning strategy," *International Tax Review*, April 2005.

Social Responsibility Reporting and Accounting

With an increasing awareness of the importance of corporate social responsibility, there is also an increasing concern over how to report social performance. That is, evolving beyond the traditional financial reporting of profits and losses, assets and liabilities, there is a growing concern over how to report information on environmental and social performance.

A recent survey by KPMG found

- CR reporting is over 90 percent for the Fortune Global 250 companies
- The Asia Pacific region leads the globe in CR reporting
- The highest CR reporting rates in the world are in four emerging economies: India, Indonesia, Malaysia, and South Africa
- Three out of five companies now insert CR data into annual financial reports
- Two thirds of the G 250 companies provide third party independent assurance of CR information, usually by major accountancy organizations

The most common reporting format comes from the Global Reporting Initiative (GRI) (www. globalreporting.org/AboutGRI/WhatWeDo/). The GRI reporting framework provides a consistent method used by over 20,000 companies worldwide to report on their social performance to all stakeholders. The GRI's mission is to make social reporting as common as financial reporting. To address the issue of assurance (i.e. making sure that the reports are accurate and truthful), the International Auditing and Assurance Standards Board (IAASB) has a group to consider the development of specialized accounting standards on the emerging issues of social reporting.[16]

Chapter Review

This chapter provided you with a basic understanding of the accounting function in MNCs. The chapter began with an overview of the purpose of accounting and explained the differences between managerial accounting and financial accounting. For students who have yet to study any accounting, the chapter also has an Appendix that provides an overview of the basics of accounting terminology and financial reports.

National culture and a nation's social institutions influence many business functions and the accounting function is no exception. As such, the chapter provided an explanation of the forces that lead different countries to adopt different accounting practices. However, again as with many business functions, globalization and the increasing importance of doing business anywhere in the world pressures national accounting systems to become more similar. Harmonization and standardization of accounting practices resulted in response to this pressure. There is now strong pressure on nations and MNCs to adopt accounting practices that are standardized throughout the world. The International Accounting Standards Board promotes two sets of standards for accounting. One is for accounting practices, known as International Accounting Standards (IAS), and the other is for financial reporting, known as IFRS or International Financial Reporting Standards. Importantly, the EU led the way and adopted these standards and practices leading to increased pressure on other nations to follow suit.

One major problem for MNCs is how to report accounting numbers from units located in different nations that have different currencies. Earlier in the book you learned how exchange rates among currencies are in constant flux. MNCs that buy, sell, and earn profits or losses in other countries deal continuously with the issue of how to value business transactions in their home currency. In this chapter you learned that MNCs use a variety of techniques to account for exchange-rate differences and to translate foreign currencies for financial reporting to their stockholders and managers.

Business units provide each other with goods and services. A common way to account for the value of these transfers is transfer pricing. That is, units buy and sell goods and services as if they are in a market. In this chapter, you learned that the management of transfer pricing becomes much more complex when units are located in different countries with different currencies and different tax laws. Although there is pressure to buy and sell among units so that more profits are earned in lower tax countries (e.g. low transfer pricing to low tax country units reduces costs and increases profits), most local laws require that prices reflect market values—the price the company would pay if it bought the good or service outside the company. Additionally, the Organization for Economic Co-operation and Development (OECD) has developed reporting procedures that makes transparent intercompany transactions across country level units making it more difficult for companies to take advantage of gaps in tax rules.

The issue of transfer prices makes it clear that if your company has operations in different countries then differences in tax laws can affect your bottom line. In this chapter, you learned that nations tend to favor worldwide income taxing (tax profits from every location) or territorial taxing (tax only local profits, although no system is pure).

To learn how MNCs deal with taxation, the chapter reviewed two strategies for dealing with international taxation. One is thin capitalization, where companies set up operations by borrowing money rather than issuing stock so that they can get tax deductions based on interest payments on their loans. The other focuses on the business model, which means one of the reasons an MNC chooses a location is favorable local tax law.

An emerging challenge for the accounting profession is how to develop international standards and assurances for social responsibility reporting. Corporate social responsibility is an increasing concern for investors and other stakeholders. As such, these reports may become as important as financial reports, the traditional province of accountants. In this chapter you learned some of the worldwide trends regarding how the world's largest companies are building social responsibility reporting as a supplement to financial reporting.

As future international business people, you will rely on professional accountants to produce the accurate and reliable financial reports that will help you manage international operations in a financially complex world. Also, investors in your company and local regulatory bodies will rely on your international accountants to report on the state of your company. This brief introduction to the international accounting function should help you better understand the role of accounting professionals in your companies.

Discussion Questions

1   Discuss several reasons regarding the importance of international accounting.

2   Compare and contrast managerial accounting with financial accounting.

3   Identify differences in the economic role of accounting in different countries. Discuss factors that lead to differences in the use of accounting in these countries.

4   Select two emerging nations and discuss how enforcement of accounting rules might affect the nature of financial reporting in these countries.

5   Consider the professionalization of accounting in your discussion.

6   Discuss the pressures that led to harmonization/standardization of financial reporting. What are the benefits and what are the drawbacks?

7   Discuss the implications of the growing move to accept most of the IASB standards. How does this affect Japanese and US companies, which lag behind?

8   Identify the accounting issues related to gains or losses from foreign currency transactions.

9   Compare and contrast the different foreign currency translation methods.

10 Identify what is unique for transfer pricing for MNCs as opposed to domestic-only companies.

11 Compare and contrast the types of tax systems used in different emerging countries.

12 Discuss the nature and strategic advantages of thin capitalization.

International Business Skill Builder

Exploring Accounting Standards

Step 1: Select four major MNCs, two from the US or from the EU and two from the emerging market countries. Make sure the companies are in the same industry.

Step 2: Download their most recent annual reports.

Step 3: Search the annual reports for information on the type or types of accounting standards used in the reports, the impact of foreign currency exchanges on the company, foreign currency translation methods, and foreign taxation.

Step 4: Based on what you have learned in this chapter, prepare a report examining how international accounting information might influence managerial decisions and investor decisions regarding these companies.

Chapter Internet Activity

Explore the use of Deloitte's website on global corporate taxes at **www2.deloitte.com/global/en/pages/tax/articles/global-tax-rates.html**.

Use this site to look at tax rates and tax treaties. Consider the tax implications of a company from your home country doing business in at least three different countries around the world.

Take the IFRS Quiz to see how much you know about these standards: www.proprofs.com/quiz-school/story.php?title=NzQ1OTAwYE3I

Key Concepts

- arm's length principle
- business model approach
- consolidated financial statement
- current rate method
- current–noncurrent method
- financial accounting
- foreign currency transaction
- foreign currency translation
- functional currency
- harmonization

- International Accounting Standards Board (IASB)
- international taxation
- managerial accounting
- monetary–nonmonetary method
- temporal translation method
- territorial tax system
- thin capitalization
- transfer pricing
- worldwide tax system

Chinese Accounting: From Abacus To Advanced System?

China has been experiencing record-breaking economic growth and has captured the attention of the world. In less than 40 years China has gone from being a closed country with extreme poverty to a more open country with the world's most dynamic economy. While it appears that a "China play" is an obvious choice for foreign investors, problems with corruption, transparency, a shortage of qualified accountants in China, and accounting irregularities have caused some to use caution in Chinese investing. Of particular concern is the validity of the Chinese accounting system. With differing accounting standards and a system historically based on a lack of openness, overall confidence in financial reporting from Chinese companies is not high. While China has moved towards the adoption of International Financial Reporting Standards (IFRS), serious concerns remain as the world's second largest economy and largest socialist state makes the transition to modern accounting principles and practices.

China has a long history of accounting for transactions, dating back to the beginning of the country's unification in 221 BCE, however, more modern accounting practice did not begin in China until the early 1900s. Shortly after the overthrow of the imperial system in 1911, China adopted the Accounting Laws of the Republic of China. The first accounting regulations were essentially the adoption of the Japanese accounting system. Further regulations were adopted in 1932 with the Unification Government Accounting System. When the Communists came to power in 1949, the socialist state adopted a Soviet style system of accounting, one suited for a non-market based economy. Chinese accounting, like many aspects of Chinese business suffered during the Cultural Revolution. From 1966–1976, accountants not being part of the working class were considered enemies of the state. China survived the Cultural Revolution but it devastated the accounting profession. After the death of Mao, China moved forward, especially in terms of its economic development.

With the economic reforms begun by Deng Xiaoping and the movement towards a market economy, the need for accounting reform became obvious. The legitimatizing of the concept of profit made the previous system of accounting less useful. In 1985 China enacted the Accounting Law of the People's Republic of China, and in 1993 amended the law in a move towards modernization. In 2006 the Chinese government enacted Accounting System for Business Enterprises and announced its intention to move towards adoption of the International Financial Reporting Standards (IFRS). China would be joining the growing list of countries using, or planning on using, the international system. While China has enacted many reforms in many parts of its economy, through the Ministry of Finance there is strong government control over accounting standards and the accounting profession.

**CASE 12
cont'd**

While China has its own accounting system, and has proclaimed moving towards the adoption of IFRS, in practice Chinese companies do not always follow a unified accounting system. This makes the evaluation of financial performance difficult. Accounting statements can be prepared according to existing Chinese standards, the IFRS, or in cases where the firm seeks a listing on an American exchange, Generally Accepted Accounting Principles (GAAP). In addition, Chinese law requires that accounting firms be locally owned, reducing the participation of large international firms. While international accounting firms, including the Big Four, do operate in China, they must affiliate with local firms, which in some cases may reduce their independence.

The preparation of accounting statements can be influenced by culture. Issues such as face saving, relationships, the value of transparency, and corruption can influence the reporting of financial results. In 2016 China ranked 79 out of 175 countries surveyed by Transparency International, placing the country in the mid-range of perceived corruption. Being in the mid-range on corruption is troubling for the world's second largest economy, and one that is increasingly seeking capital outside its own country.

Chinese companies have increasingly been listing shares on American exchanges. In many cases share prices have increased dramatically. Firms like Youku (similar to YouTube, which is banned in China) and Baidu (similar to Google, which is also banned in China) experienced a very warm welcome by American investors. The prospects of tapping into China's large and increasingly prosperous market, coupled with solid financials make many Chinese firms seem like good investment decisions. Not all investors, however, agree. Respected hedge fund manager, James Chanos, for example has alleged that accounting fraud is widespread in China. Whether almost all financial reporting in China is suspect, as Chanos would suggest, is subject to debate; however, there have been many cases of accounting irregularities and fraud reported.

Some accounting irregularities have come to light with the increasingly popular practice of reverse mergers. While reverse mergers are not limited to Chinese companies, the practice has grown as Chinese firms seek a quick method of becoming publicly traded companies. Listing requirements on the Shanghai Stock Exchange are difficult and time consuming. Similarly, becoming a publicly traded company in the United States is difficult, and may be impossible for many smaller Chinese companies. With the reverse merger in the case of Chinese companies, the Chinese firm finds an American publicly traded firm that is near bankruptcy or has little or no assets. Its only value is being publicly traded. It acquires, or is acquired by this firm. The Chinese firm changes the name of the company and replaces its board. It then is a publicly traded firm which did not need to go through the lengthy and detailed process of an Initial Public Offering (IPO). The Chinese company can now raise capital by issuing new stock. One such case of accounting irregularities involved RINO International, a Chinese environmental

**CASE 12
cont'd**

engineering firm. RINO used a reverse merger to become listed on NASDAQ, but has since been delisted due to unreliable financial statements, along with allegations of other fraudulent practices. RINO reported $11M of revenue to its Chinese regulators in 2009 but in the same year reported revenues of $195M in reports filed with the Securities and Exchange Commission (SEC) in the United States. A number of other Chinese companies have also run afoul of the SEC for accounting practices.

Another area of concern is the auditing of Chinese financial statements. Questions of independence and inappropriate relationships have been raised. With a shortage of qualified accountants in China and changing accounting standards, the legitimacy of auditing work is sometimes of concern. This problem can manifest itself again with Chinese firms listed on American exchanges. The question of auditor independence arose in a well-publicized case involving a Chinese firm called American Dairy (another reverse merger firm). The infant formula and milk powder company was investigated by the SEC when its American accounting firm hired a Chinese auditor who was a principal in a firm that provided services to American Dairy. The Chinese business practices of establishing strong business relationships and networking can run contrary to auditing independence.

China has come a long way in a very short period of time. It has experienced economic growth envied by developed countries, and increased its political clout and public standing in the world. With this growth comes many difficulties, including playing catch-up with its accounting system. Whether China adopts the IFRS, or simply adapts its current system to be similar to IFRS is still in question. Given China's growing economic power and influence it may be positioned to develop its own standards developed for its own conditions. China now has the world's fastest train, the world's fastest supercomputer, and the world's fastest growing economy of size. With a hybrid economic system (mix of capitalism and socialism) China may seek to shape international accounting, or simply develop its own standards and force the world to accept its independence. What is known for certain is that China has come a long way in a short period of time in terms of not only its economic development, but also the development of its accounting system. The future of Chinese accounting may not be so certain.

CASE DISCUSSION POINTS:

1 Would you invest in a Chinese firm with its shares traded on an American exchange? Explain your answer.
2 What would you suggest be done in order for China to create an accounting system which matches its position in the global economy?
3 What are the international implications if China decides to adapt the IFRS to its own needs?

CASE 12
cont'd

Source: C. Coulson 2010, "Panic over Chinese stocks just a matter of accounting," *China Daily*, November 2; B. Einhorn and F. Balfour, 2007, "Going public, Chinese style," *BusinessWeek*, March 5; R. Flannery, 2010, "Are U.S. investors in China's stocks playing pin the tail on the donkey?" *Forbes*, December 7; T. Kaplan, 2010, "Chinese I.P.O. frenzy raises talk of a bubble," *The New York Times*, December 13; R. Lawson, 2009, "How accurate are Chinese costing practices?" *Strategic Finance*, May, pp. 41–46; L. Norton, 2008, "Who's minding the minders of Chinese accounting?" *Barron's*, February 18; D. Lampert and M. Sullivan, 2008, "Chinese accounting lagging but improving," *Forbes*, November 20; W. Lu, J. Xu-dong and M. Aikens, 2009, "Governmental influences in the development of Chinese accounting during the modern era," *Accounting, Business & Financial History*, 19(3), pp. 305–326; www.ifrs.org, accessed on December 17, 2010; www. transparency.org, accessed on December 18, 2015.

Case was written by Charles A. Rarick

Appendix

A Primer on Accounting Statements[17]

There are four main financial statements. They are: (1) balance sheets; (2) income statements; (3) cash flow statements; and (4) statements of shareholders' equity. Balance sheets show what a company owns and what it owes at a fixed point in time. Income statements show how much money a company made and spent over a period of time. Cash flow statements show the exchange of money between a company and the outside world also over a period of time. The fourth financial statement, called a "statement of shareholders' equity," shows changes in the interests of the company's shareholders over time.

Let us look at each of the first three financial statements in more detail.

Balance Sheets

A balance sheet provides detailed information about a company's assets, liabilities, and shareholders' equity.

Assets Are things that a company owns that have value. This typically means they can either be sold or used by the company to make products or provide services that can be sold. Assets include physical property, such as plants, trucks, equipment, and inventory. They also include things that cannot be touched but nevertheless exist and have value, such as trademarks and patents. In addition, cash itself is an asset. So are investments a company makes.

Liabilities Are amounts of money that a company owes to others. This can include all kinds of obligations, like money borrowed from a bank to launch a new product, rent for use of a building, money owed to suppliers for materials, payroll a company owes to its employees, environmental clean-up costs, or taxes owed to the government. Liabilities also include obligations to provide goods or services to customers in the future.

Shareholders' equity is sometimes called capital or net worth. It is the money that would be left if a company sold all of its assets and paid off all of its liabilities. This leftover money belongs to the shareholders, or the owners, of the company.

The following formula summarizes what a balance sheet shows:

ASSETS = LIABILITIES + SHAREHOLDERS' EQUITY

A company's assets have to equal, or "balance," the sum of its liabilities and shareholders' equity.

A company's balance sheet is set up like the basic accounting equation shown above. On the left side of the balance sheet, companies list their assets. On the right side, they list their liabilities and shareholders' equity. Sometimes balance sheets show assets at the top, followed by liabilities, with shareholders' equity at the bottom.

Assets are generally listed based on how quickly they will be converted into cash. *Current* assets are things a company expects to convert to cash within one year. A good example is inventory. Most companies expect to sell their inventory for cash within one year.

Noncurrent assets are things a company does not expect to convert to cash within one year or that would take longer than one year to sell. Noncurrent assets include *fixed* assets. Fixed assets are those assets used to operate the business but that are not available for sale, such as trucks, office furniture, and other property.

Liabilities are generally listed based on their due dates. Liabilities are said to be either *current* or *long-term*. Current liabilities are obligations a company expects to pay off within the year. Long-term liabilities are obligations due more than one year away.

Shareholders' equity is the amount owners invested in the company's stock plus or minus the company's earnings or losses since inception. Sometimes companies distribute earnings, instead of retaining them. These distributions are called dividends.

A balance sheet shows a snapshot of a company's assets, liabilities, and shareholders' equity at the end of the reporting period. It does not show the flows into and out of the accounts during the period.

Income Statements

An income statement is a report that shows how much revenue a company earned over a specific time period (usually for a year or some portion of a year). An income statement also shows the costs and expenses associated with earning that revenue. The literal "bottom line" of the statement usually shows the company's net earnings or losses. This tells you how much the company earned or lost over the period.

Income statements also report earnings per share (or EPS). This calculation tells you how much money shareholders would receive if the company decided to distribute all of the net earnings for the period. (Companies almost never distribute all of their earnings. Usually they reinvest them in the business.)

To understand how income statements are set up, think of them as a set of stairs. You start at the top with the total amount of sales made during the accounting period. Then you go down, one step at a time. At each step, you make a deduction for certain costs or other operating expenses associated with earning the revenue. At the bottom of the stairs, after deducting all of the expenses, you learn how much the company actually earned or lost during the accounting period. People often call this "the bottom line."

At the top of the income statement is the total amount of money brought in from sales of products or services. This top line is often referred to as gross revenues or sales. It is called "gross" because expenses have not been deducted from it yet.

The next line is money the company does not expect to collect on certain sales. This could be due, for example, to sales discounts or merchandise returns.

When you subtract the returns and allowances from the gross revenues, you arrive at the company's net revenues. It is called "net" because, if you can imagine a net, these revenues are left in the net after the deductions for returns and allowances have come out.

Moving down the stairs from the net revenue line, there are several lines that represent various kinds of operating expenses. Although these lines can be reported in various orders, the next line after net revenues typically shows the costs of sales. This number tells you the amount of money the company spent to produce the goods or services it sold during the accounting period.

The next line subtracts the costs of sales from the net revenues to arrive at a subtotal called "gross profit" or sometimes "gross margin." It is considered "gross" because there are certain expenses that have not been deducted from it yet.

The next section deals with operating expenses. These are expenses that go toward supporting a company's operations for a given period—for example, salaries of administrative personnel and costs of researching new products. Marketing expenses are another example. Operating expenses are different from "costs of sales," which were deducted above, because operating expenses cannot be linked directly to the production of the products or services being sold.

Depreciation is also deducted from gross profit. Depreciation takes into account the wear and tear on some assets, such as machinery, tools, and furniture, which are used over the long term. Companies spread the cost of these assets over the periods they are used. This process of spreading these costs is called depreciation or amortization. The "charge" for using these assets during the period is a fraction of the original cost of the assets.

After all operating expenses are deducted from gross profit, you arrive at operating profit before interest and income tax expenses. This is often called "income from operations."

Next, companies must account for interest income and interest expense. Interest income is the money companies make from keeping their cash in interest-bearing savings accounts, money-market funds, and the like. On the other hand, interest expense is the money companies pay in interest for money they borrow. Some income statements show interest income and interest expense separately. Some income statements combine the two numbers. The interest income and expense are then added or subtracted from the operating profits to arrive at operating profit *before* income tax.

Finally, income tax is deducted and you arrive at the bottom line: net profit or net losses. (Net profit is also called net income or net earnings.) This tells you how much the company actually earned or lost during the accounting period. Did the company make a profit or did it lose money?

Earnings Per Share or EPS   Most income statements include a calculation of earnings per share or EPS. This calculation tells you how much money shareholders would receive for each share of stock they own if the company distributed all of its net income for the period.

To calculate EPS, you take the total net income and divide it by the number of outstanding shares of the company.

Cash Flow Statements

Cash flow statements report a company's inflows and outflows of cash. This is important because a company needs to have enough cash on hand to pay its expenses and purchase assets. While an *income statement* can tell you whether a company made a profit, a cash flow statement can tell you whether the company generated cash.

A cash flow statement shows changes over time rather than absolute dollar amounts at a point in time. It uses and reorders the information from a company's balance sheet and income statement.

The bottom line of the cash flow statement shows the net increase or decrease in cash for the period. Generally, cash flow statements are divided into three main parts. Each part reviews the cash flow from one of three types of activities: (1) operating activities; (2) investing activities; and (3) financing activities.

Operating Activities   The first part of a cash flow statement analyzes a company's cash flow from net income or losses. For most companies, this section of the cash flow statement reconciles the net income (as shown on the income statement) to the actual cash the company received from or used in its operating activities. To do this, it adjusts net income for any non-cash items (such as adding back depreciation expenses) and adjusts for any cash that was used or provided by other operating assets and liabilities.

Investing Activities   The second part of a cash flow statement shows the cash flow from all investing activities, which generally include purchases or sales of long-term assets, such as property, plant and equipment, as well as investment securities. If a company buys a piece of machinery, the cash flow statement will reflect this activity as a cash outflow from investing activities because it used cash. If the company decided to sell off some investments from an investment portfolio, the proceeds from the sales would show up as a cash inflow from investing activities because it provided cash.

Financing Activities   The third part of a cash flow statement shows the cash flow from all financing activities. Typical sources of cash flow include cash raised by selling stocks and bonds or borrowing from banks. Likewise, paying back a bank loan would show up as a use of cash flow.

Notes

1   Hervé Stolowy, 1997, "The definition of international accounting through textbook contents," paper presented at the 8th World Congress of the International Association for Accounting Education and Research (IAAER), Paris, France, October 23–25.
2   This section draws heavily on the work of Shahrokh M. Saudagaran, 2004, *International Accounting: A User Perspective*, Mason, OH: South-Western.
3   S. J. Gray, 1988, "Towards a theory of cultural influence on the development of accounting systems internationally," *Abacus*, 24, pp. 1–15; Y. Yuan Ding, Thomas Jean and Hervé Stolowy, 2005, "Why do national GAAP differ from IAS? The role of culture," *International Journal of Accounting*, 40, pp. 325–350.
4   H. Fechner and A. Kilgore, 1994, "The influence of cultural factors on accounting practice," *International Journal of Accounting*, 29, pp. 265–277; Chris Robinson and George Venieris, 1996, "Economics, culture, and accounting standards: A case study of Greece and Canada," *Revue Canadienne des Sciences de l'Administration*, June.
5   This section draws heavily on the work of Shahrokh M. Saudagaran, 2004, *International Accounting: A User Perspective*, Mason, OH: South-Western.
6   T. S. Doupnik and S. B. Salter, 1993, "An empirical test of a judgmental international classification of financial reporting practices," *Journal of International Business Studies*, 24(1), pp. 41–60; G. G. Mueller, 1968, "Accounting principles generally accepted in the United States versus those generally accepted elsewhere," *International Journal of Accounting*, 3, pp. 91–103; C. W. Nobes, 1983, "A judgmental international classification of financial reporting practices," *Journal of Business Finance and Accounting*, Spring, pp. 1–19.
7   Quoted from www.iasb.org/About+Us/About+the+ Foundation/Constitution.htm
8   www.iasb.org/News/Announcements+and+Speeches/ Vice+Chairman+of+the+IASC+Foundation+addresses+ European+Parliament.htm, July 10, 2007.
9   www.pwc.com/us/en/cfodirect/issues/ifrs-adoption-convergence.html
10 M. Zafar Iqbal, 2002, *International Accounting: A Global Perspective*, Mason, OH: South-Western; Shahrokh M. Saudagaran, 2004, *International Accounting: A User Perspective*, Mason, OH: South-Western.

11 Financial Accounting Standards Board, 1981, *Statement of Financial Accounting Standards No. 52, Foreign Currency Translation*, Stamford, CN: FASB, December.

12 M. Saudagaran, 2004, *International Accounting: A User Perspective*, Mason, OH: South-Western.

13 OECD, 2015, *Transfer Pricing Documentation and Country-by-Country Reporting, Action 13—2015 Final Report*, OECD Publishing, Paris. DOI: http://dx.doi.org/10.1787/9789264241480-en, p. 3.

14 M. Zafar Iqbal, 2002, *International Accounting: A Global Perspective*, Mason, OH: South-Western.

15 Nick Woodford and Christopher Schreiber, 2005, "Debt financing loses appeal as tax planning strategy," *International Tax Review*, April.

16 KPMG International, 2015, *KPMG Currents of Change: International Survey of Corporate Responsibility Reporting 2015*, New York: KPMG; OECD, 2015, *Transfer Pricing Documentation and Country-by-Country Reporting, Action 13—2015 Final Report*, OECD Publishing, Paris. DOI: http://dx.doi.org/10.1787/9789264241480-en

17 Reproduced from www.sec.gov/investor/pubs/begfinstmt guide.htm

CHAPTER 13

Organizational Structures for MNCs

After reading this chapter you should be able to:

- Understand the basic components of organizational design.

- Learn about the key organizational designs used by multinationals, namely the export department, international division, worldwide product and geographic structure, matrix and transnational structures with special emphasis on emerging markets.

- Appreciate some of the key approaches to coordinating units within a multinational.

- Learn about global and virtual teams.

- Appreciate the importance of knowledge management to multinationals.

International Business   *Preview IB Emerging Market Strategic Insight*

Organizational Structure in Emerging Markets

As many emerging markets including China and India continue to grow in stature in international business and globalization continues its inexorable growth path, multinationals are finding that it is becoming increasingly complicated to maintain old ways of organizing their businesses. Global multinationals have often centralized activities that are similar across locations/regions while providing customized responses to country differences. However, the recent growth of emerging markets means that such multinationals built on regional layers are no longer useful. Emerging markets are often geographically far from each other but may share many similarities. Having a multinational organized along regional divisions does not work with these new markets. Furthermore, while it made sense previously to have corporate headquarters gather information and distil such information geographically for strategic reasons, the developments in information technology means that companies can now quickly gather data and analyze and synthesize such information. As a result, it is becoming more realistic for multinationals to organize along other issues such as strategic goals rather than region.

Consider the bedrock of the way multinationals have been traditionally organized—the corporate headquarters in charge of strategizing the long-term direction of the multinational. Most developed world multinational headquarters are located in their home countries. However, many multinationals are finding that having a headquarters at home means being located far from where most of the action is occurring. As a result, many multinationals are now creating second or lighter headquarters to be closer to major customers. For instance, the Dutch giant ABB has moved its robotics business head office from Detroit to Shanghai. Most of the demand for robots is coming from Asia and the company decided that it would be better served having a robotics R&D in Shanghai. Additionally, the oil and gas company Halliburton has also created a second headquarters in Dubai to be closer to its customers.

Source: Based on *The Economist*, 2016, "The yuan and the markets," January 16, p. 11; T. Gibbs, S. Heywood, L. Weiss and G. Jost, 2012, "Organizing for an emerging world," *McKinsey Quarterly*, 3, pp. 81–91.

As the Preview IB Emerging Market Strategic Insight shows, MNCs are facing increasing complexities as they strive to become better global competitors. Many of what are considered traditional principles of how multinationals should be structured are being questioned. Emerging markets are presenting new challenges that cannot be addressed through traditional organization principles. Most multinationals are facing such challenges today, and this chapter will discuss some of these important issues.

This chapter first discusses the organizational design options available to implement the various multinational strategies. **Organizational design** represents how organizations structure subunits and coordinate and control mechanisms to achieve their goals. As the Preview IB Emerging Market Insight shows, many multinationals have traditionally been structured along regional divisions. Through such a design, a multinational can respond to different country needs by organizing similar activities along geographic areas. However, current needs are requiring important changes. Consider, for instance, that IBM decided that having each country in Asia run its own businesses resulted in duplication of effort. Many of the countries shared similarities.[1] As such, IBM Asia reorganized along functions such as supply-chain, marketing, etc. This has allowed them to respond better to the needs of its Asian customers.

As you can see from above, there are many complex and varied choices regarding how to set up an organization. Each organizational design has costs and benefits regarding the appropriate way to deliver a product or service to the customer. This chapter will therefore discuss the many options available to design the organization and will also show how having the right organizational design is crucial for MNCs to achieve their multinational strategic goals.

This chapter first discusses the organizational structures used by MNCs with a special emphasis on emerging markets. However, because organizational structure effectively breaks down the organization in terms of logical subunits, it is also necessary to implement various

organizational design represents how organizations structure subunits and coordination and control mechanisms to achieve their strategic goals

mechanisms to help integrate these entities. The chapter will look at some of the most popular ways that multinationals use to coordinate their various subunits. It will also discuss teams in depth, as many companies are now relying on both virtual and real teams to coordinate their subunits.

Finally, in this chapter, you will also read about knowledge management. As the competitive environment changes and multinationals are being forced to combine knowledge from around the world to innovate, they are feeling increased pressure to adequately manage information and knowledge. Organizational design and coordination aspects are very closely related to an organization's ability to manage information and knowledge. The final aspect of the chapter will therefore discuss some of the key knowledge management issues.

Organizational Design: Challenges, Forms, and Basic Designs

Experts see organizational design as the key to success in the future.[2] Many changes are occurring favoring organizational designs that require companies to be more flexible and quick to respond. As mentioned earlier, many of the traditional boundaries characterizing competition in the past are slowly disappearing. Globalization is erasing national boundaries while strategic alliances are slowly erasing traditional barriers between companies. Furthermore, the increased popularity of e-commerce is also minimizing traditional market boundaries while allowing rapid access to information.[3] Finally, responding to the needs of emerging markets is also introducing complex challenges that multinationals have to attend to.[4] All of these changes are requiring that companies design systems that can maximize coordination among their subunits while making rapid use of mass amounts of information.

In the next few paragraphs, you will learn about the function of organizational design approaches. In the subsequent sections, you will read about the traditional approaches multinationals use as they enter the global market.

The Functions of Organizational Design

Organizational design addresses two basic questions for an organization: (1) How shall the work among the organization's subunits be divided? and, (2) How shall the efforts of the units created be coordinated and controlled?[5] In very small organizations, most employees have to be involved in all aspects of running the company and organizational design is not necessary. Consider, for example, the hypothetical situation where you decide to open a restaurant. When the restaurant is relatively small, there is little reason to divide the work. For instance, you can act as the cook and waiter, and even perform accounting and finance functions. However, as the restaurant grows you find that you need to hire more cooks, waiters, managers, and even someone to answer the phone. You also decide to open restaurants in other locations and you find that you need to begin dividing the work. As such, you may start dividing work first into specialized jobs. Different people perform different tasks. Later, if one restaurant becomes big enough, with enough people doing the same tasks, a supervisor is required, and managers divide their organizations into specialized subunits. As such, in smaller organizations, the subunits are usually called departments. In larger organizations, divisions or subsidiaries become the major subunits.

Once an organization has specialized subunits, managers must develop mechanisms that coordinate and control the efforts of each subunit.[6] For the restaurant example, the human resource department must work closely with the operations to determine the personnel needs of the company. As another example, a manufacturing company must make sure that the production department produces the goods to be available at the time the marketing department promised the customers. Similarly, an MNC must ensure that its foreign operations support the parent company's strategic goals. Some companies monitor their subunits very closely.

Organizational Designs for Multinationals

To understand how multinationals choose the various options available, it is necessary to understand the process that companies experience as they go international. As such, for a company selling domestically only, the **functional structure**, where departments perform separate business functions such as marketing or manufacturing, is appropriate. The functional structure is the simplest structure for an organization. However, although it is the simplest structure, that doesn't mean it is not useful. Consider the following IB Emerging Market Strategic Insight.

Although the IB Emerging Market Strategic Insight below shows that use of functional structure can be helpful for some major multinationals, the major reason to choose a functional structure for a subunit is efficiency through economies of scale in each function, as there are cost savings when a large number of people do the same job in the same place. The downside is that, because functional subunits are separated from each other and serve functional goals, coordination among the units can be difficult. Exhibit 13.1 shows a functional structure.

functional structure departments perform separate business functions such as marketing, finance, or manufacturing

New Organizational Structure at IBM Asia

IB EMERGING MARKET STRATEGIC INSIGHT

IBM Asia used to be organized along countries. Each country in Asia would have its own set of business services to support the needs of the various countries. As Asian emerging markets gained traction and importance, IBM found that this structure was not properly serving its customers. It found that similar services were being duplicated across countries thereby resulting in unnecessary complexity in each country. To resolve the situation, IBM leaders in each country examined the services that were similar and found that these could actually be categorized along a functional structure. IBM therefore decided to change its structure to a simpler functional structure to better serve the different Asian markets. This has resulted in a cultural transformation and as one executive puts it "instead of taking people to where the work is, you take the work to where the people are."

The new functional structure is organized along the typical functions such as supply chain, legal, communications, marketing, HR, and finance. Each function has been assigned a global leader and that leader is responsible for coordinating and refining operations to support the function in the different countries. These leaders then eliminated redundant activities across countries.

In practice, the new structure has meant that IBM has different markets served by functional specialists in different countries. For instance, its growth market operations are now served by accounts receivables specialists in Shanghai, accounting in Kuala Lumpur, HR functions done in Manila, and customer service desk in Brisbane. This new functional area is requiring that IBM undergoes a cultural transformation.

Source: Based on *The Economist*, 2016, "The yuan and the markets," January 16, p. 11; T. Gibbs, S. Heywood, L. Weiss. and G. Jost, 2012, "Organizing for an emerging world," *McKinsey Quarterly, 3*, pp. 81–91.

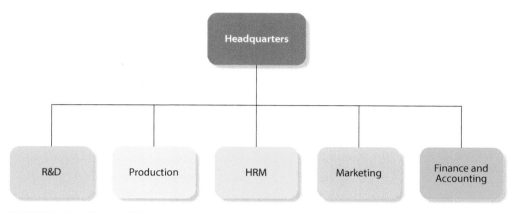

Exhibit 13.1 A Basic Functional Structure

When a company goes international, it seldom changes its basic organizational structure. Most companies in such cases are interested in exploiting the international market on a very limited basis. Such organizations tend to act first as passive exporters. Passive exporters simply fill orders using the same structures, procedures, and people used in domestic sales. Furthermore, such companies tend to be relatively small by multinational standards.

However, when international sales become more central to a firm's success, more sophisticated multinational and participation strategies usually become a significant part of a company's overall business strategy. As a result, companies must then build appropriate organizational structures to manage their multinational operations and implement their multinational strategies. The following sections focus on the structural options for MNCs.

The Export Department

Although passive exporting can be a good way to internationalize operations, certain changes may occur forcing any company to adopt new structures. For instance, exporting over time may result in increased competition from both domestic and international firms. These pressures thus result in a greater threat to the company's market share. As such, when exports become a significant percentage of company sales and a company wishes to have greater control over its export operations, managers often create a separate **export department**. A separate department shows that top management believes that the investment of human and financial resources in exporting is necessary to sustain and build international sales. Exhibit 13.2 shows a hypothetical organization with a functional structure and an export department.

How important is an export department to companies and what can be done to encourage exports? Consider the following IB Emerging Market Strategic Insight.

export department
separate organizational unit to deal exclusively with exports when the latter becomes a significant percentage of sales

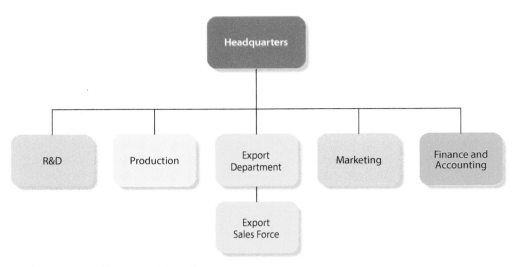

Exhibit 13.2 Functional Structure with Export Department

Small Firms and Export Departments

How important is an export department? Many small US firms find that exporting can be the key to expanding their business opportunities. In fact, the e-government portal http://export.gov suggests that around 95 percent of the world's consumers live outside of the US. As any small company faces the limits of the domestic market, they can benefit tremendously by exporting and eventually creating an export department.

A few other key points regarding exporting worth remembering are:

- The vast majority of new exporters are small and medium firms.
- Small and medium-sized businesses account for over 97 percent of all exporters of US goods.
- Export helps small businesses grow and become more competitive in their various markets.
- Most small firms export only to one country, suggesting tremendous potential to expand to other countries.

Experts agree that exports are also critical in emerging markets where small and medium-sized enterprises have contributed significantly to the economies through exports. Exports are so critical that researchers often try to identify why some firms export more than others. In doing so, governments can implement policies to encourage exports.

A recent study of 147 Chilean small and medium-sized firms provides some insights as to the factors encouraging and inhibiting export intensity in the emerging market of Chile. Export intensity simply represents the share of exports as a proportion of total sales of a company. Researchers found that the degree to which management is committed to exports results in higher export intensity. Additionally, firms where managers perceived they had higher firm resources and abilities that would help the firm export (e.g., skills in languages, export training, etc.) also had higher export intensity. However, not surprisingly, Chilean small and medium-sized firms that had managers with little international management experience and skills had lower export intensity.

The above reveals some insights into some of the factors that can encourage small and medium-sized firms to export. It is therefore not surprising to see that the USA and many emerging market governments have implemented programs to help firms export.

Source: Based on http://export.gov; C. Bianchi and R. Wickramasekera, 2016, "Antecedents of SME export intensity in a Latin American market," *Journal of Business Research*, *69*, pp. 4308–4376.

As the above IB Emerging Market Strategic Insight shows, export departments are critical to firms in all markets. The export department thus deals with all international customers for all products. Managers in the export department often control the pricing and promotion of products for the international market. People within the department may have particular country or product expertise. Export department managers have the responsibility to deal with export management companies, with foreign distributors, and with foreign customers. When the company uses a direct exporting strategy, sales representatives located in other countries may also report to the export department management.

The International Division

As companies become more international in terms of sales force and set up manufacturing in other countries, the export department often grows into an international division.[7] The **international division** differs from the export department in that it is usually larger and has greater responsibilities. Furthermore, all international activities tend to be grouped in a subunit and a senior executive from local headquarters is assigned to the new division.

Besides managing exporting and an international sales force, the international division oversees foreign subsidiaries that perform a variety of functions such as, most often, the sales units. However, other units that provide raw material and produce the company's products in other countries are also common. The international division also has more extensive staff with international expertise. Top management expects these people to perform functions such as negotiating licensing and joint-venture agreements, translating promotional material, or providing expertise on different national cultures and social institutions. Exhibit 13.3 shows a domestic product structure with an international division.

international division
a separate department that groups all international activities and headed by a senior executive from headquarters

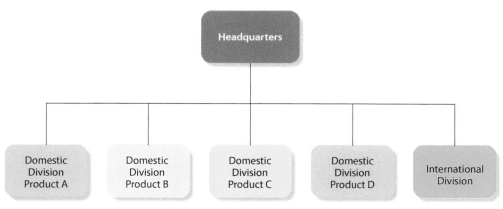

Exhibit 13.3 International Division with a Product Structure

When are international divisions appropriate? International divisions work when a company is still at the early stages of internationalizing its markets. In such cases, international sales tend to be comparatively small compared to domestic sales. Furthermore, an international division works well when the company has a limited number of products or a limited number of geographic areas it is serving.

The international division structure has become less popular and for multiproduct companies operating in many countries it is not considered an effective multinational structure.[8] The major challenge is that worldwide strategic planning tends to shift to the corporate headquarters. However, such thinking means that multinationals often miss out on strategizing to take advantage of opportunities in emerging markets. Consider the following Emerging Market Brief.

Decline of Divisional Structure

EMERGING
MARKET BRIEF

As mentioned earlier, multinationals have traditionally approached international markets using the divisional structure. In such structures, the multinational has vice presidents of different regions while concentrating all strategic functional planning and decisions at home. However, this structure presents many challenges for the multinationals. Companies no longer seek to do business in emerging markets only for suppliers and raw materials. Most multinationals are looking at emerging markets as sources of customers. Additionally, many multinationals are looking to emerging markets as sources of innovative products. Consider GE's recently developed portable electrocardiography products that were developed using local Indian engineers who better understand the needs of the Indian market. A traditional divisional structure where all major product decisions are concentrated at the corporate headquarters level would have made such a product impossible.

Multinationals realize the importance of such changes. For example, given China's growing clout in terms of customers, Starwood Hotels found that China became its second largest market with a large number of properties there. Although its headquarters remain in White Plains, New York, Starwood Hotels now shifts their headquarters one month a year to major emerging markets. In 2011, its eight-member top management team did business in Shanghai. It has held this monthly meeting in other major emerging markets such as Brazil, Dubai, and India. This could signal an eventual move of the headquarters to an emerging market.

Source: Based on W. Aghina, A. De Smet and S. Heywood, 2014, "The past and future of global organizations," *McKinsey Quarterly*, www.mckinsey.com/quarterly/overview; *The Economist*, 2016, "The yuan and the markets," January 16, p. 11; N. Kumar and P. Puranam, 2011, "Have you restructured for global success?" *Harvard Business Review*, October 11.

As the above Emerging Market Brief shows, the divisional structure has many disadvantages. First and most importantly, as we see in the example, the creation of a separate international division means that international operations become isolated and are not necessarily integrated within other operations in the multinational. Additionally, too many products can overwhelm the capacities of the international division. In sales, for example, it is difficult for people in the international division to know the whole product line and sell it worldwide. Second, when the number of locations in different countries grows, it is difficult for the international division to manage these various locations. How can a remote headquarters division know local needs and adapt products and strategies accordingly? Finally, some companies start seeing conflict between domestic and international managers as they compete for resources.

For companies of moderate size with a limited number of products or country locations, the international division remains a popular and potentially effective organization. However, to deal with the shortcomings of the international division structure, MNCs have several options, such as the worldwide geographic structure, the worldwide product structure, the matrix structure, and the transnational network structure. We discuss these various options next.

Worldwide Geographic Structure

For domestic-only companies, using **geographic structure** enables the company to serve customer needs that vary by region. Rather than one large functional organization that serves all customers, the smaller, regional organization focuses all functional activities (e.g. marketing, finance, human resources) on serving the unique needs of the regional customer. However, for the multinational, in the **worldwide geographic structure**, regions or large-market countries become the geographical divisions of the MNC. The main reason to choose a worldwide geographic structure is the existence of important differences in an area's product or service needs or in channels of distribution. Because of the significant differences in the product or service, the multinational needs to differentiate its products or services by country or region. Exhibit 13.4 shows PepsiCo's worldwide geographic structure.

The geographic structure differs from the international division in that markets are no longer viewed as domestic and international. Instead, the managers in a worldwide geographic structure view all markets as important and the domestic market simply becomes another market. As such, executives for each region become responsible for developing operations in their own region. Furthermore, executives from each region or area typically work together to develop a coherent plan for the overall multinational.

geographic structure
focus of all functional activities on serving unique needs of regional customer

worldwide geographic structure
where regions or large countries become the geographical divisions of the MNC

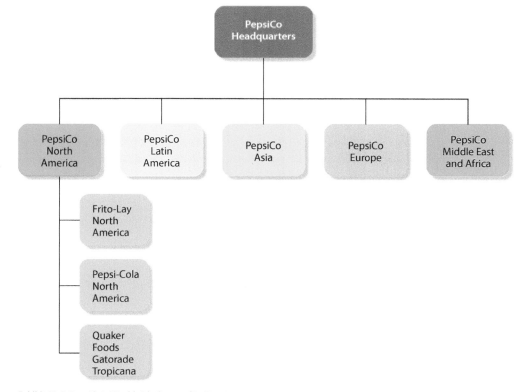

Exhibit 13.4 PepsiCo's Worldwide Geographic Structure

For all purposes, the geographic structure is appropriate when a country's market size is sufficiently large or important to support a separate organization. Separate divisions often make sense for larger market countries such as the United States, France, Germany, or Japan. Regional divisions combine smaller, similar countries such as a Southern European division for Italy, Spain, and Portugal. Furthermore, as mentioned earlier, PepsiCo also has a worldwide geographic structure (e.g. PepsiCo Asia, PepsiCo Europe, PepsiCo Middle East and Africa, etc.; see www.pepsico.com).

As you may have realized, there are no best organizational structures and the worldwide geographic structure also suffers from a number of drawbacks. Most importantly, the duplication of functions across countries means that the overall cost structure is much higher. However, because of the emphasis on geographic region, the MNC may also find it hard to coordinate the various functions around the world. For instance, if one geographic area develops some specific competencies that reduce costs, this may not always be transferred to other countries. As such, there are significant coordination difficulties in other activities such as research and development, product planning, and so on.

The major drawback of the global geographic structure is that the focus on geographic areas detracts from major developments in the product. To solve such problems, multinationals can adopt a global product structure, which you will read about next.

Worldwide Product Structure

product structure
subdivision of company along product lines

worldwide product structure
subdivision of multinational along product lines where all product divisions are responsible for selling their products around the world

For the domestic company, in the **product structure** the organization is subdivided along product lines. The product structure must still perform the functional tasks of a business (e.g. marketing and accounting), which are duplicated for each product department. Such product divisions also form the basic units of **worldwide product structures** for MNCs. Each product division is responsible for producing and selling its products or services throughout the world.

Managers of a worldwide product division are typically in charge of all the functional activities (marketing, finance, human resources) associated with a product or specific product groups. Each product group is also responsible for coordinating and managing both domestic and international operations within that group. However, the corporate headquarters provide the overall strategy to coordinate the various product groups. Exhibit 13.5 shows a worldwide product structure.

Product structures work well when a multinational has a large number of products. Furthermore, as you may realize, a worldwide product structure will fulfill some of the functions that a worldwide geographic structure cannot provide. For instance, if there is a strong need to coordinate and integrate the various functional areas related to a product, the product structure works well. Furthermore, a product structure is appropriate in cases where little adaptation is needed for the various international markets in which the multinational operates. Additionally, many emerging market multinationals are organized along the product structure. Consider the following IB Emerging Market Strategic Insight.

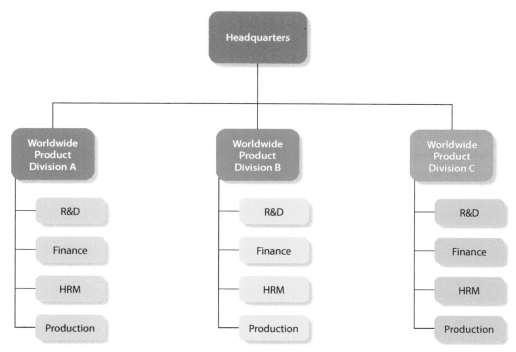

Exhibit 13.5 Worldwide Product Structure

Organizational Structure in Emerging Markets

IB EMERGING MARKET
STRATEGIC INSIGHT

As many emerging markets including China and India continue to grow in stature in international business, a close scrutiny of large multinationals in such emerging markets shows that they are very different than those in developed markets. While large conglomerates with many diversified businesses are shunned in many of the developed countries, emerging markets tend to prefer such larger conglomerates. These businesses, called *chaebol* in South Korea or *grupos economicos* in Latin America, are often very profitable and outperform other ways of organizing.

Consider the case of the Indian multinational Tata Group. Tata is organized along business groups represented mostly by products along a very large number of sectors. These include industries such as automotive, chemicals, communications, consumer products, financial services etc. While the Western multinationals have generally avoided being in many unrelated sectors, emerging market multinationals do very well in many unrelated industries. Furthermore, these many distinct businesses are owned by one large owner.

Such success is very intriguing and offers some lessons for developed country multinationals. In fact, these companies' single ownership often means that the owners are aware of the assets and resource base of each business group. They are therefore better able to exploit these knowledge bases to develop new products and to achieve synergies relative to traditional multinationals. Furthermore, many of such conglomerates have group centers that gather the owners and various top managers to explore potential ideas and opportunities. However, these multinationals are also working hard to integrate the various departments through formal channels of communication such as assigning integrating roles and shared decision making. Later you will read about the various forms of integration and coordination.

Source: Based on K. S. Ramchandran, K. S. Manikandan and A. Pant, 2013, "Why conglomerates thrive," *Harvard Business Review*, December, pp. 111–119.

As you can see from the above, for emerging market multinationals, structuring along a loose form of product structure works. But the global product structure nevertheless suffers from a number of drawbacks. Most importantly, the global product structure requires duplication of functional areas and the associated human resource needs. Such duplication obviously makes the product structure more costly. Also, the focus on products means that managers are more likely to pursue product opportunities at the expense of other characteristics. For instance, a manager may focus more on the domestic aspect of the business if a product is doing well there, and ignore international markets.

Both the worldwide product structure and the worldwide geographic structure have advantages and disadvantages for multinational strategy implementation. As you read earlier, the product structure best supports strategies that emphasize global products and rationalization (worldwide products using worldwide, low-cost sources of raw materials, and worldwide marketing strategies). The geographic structure best supports strategies that emphasize local adaptation (managers are often local nationals and are sensitive to local needs). Most MNCs, however, adopt strategies that include concerns for local adaptation as well as for the economic and product-development benefits of globalization. Consequently, most large multinationals have structures that are hybrids, or mixtures of product and area units. You will read about these hybrid structures next.

The Matrix and the Transnational Network Structure

matrix structure
mixture of traditional hierarchical structures, such as product and geographic, where both divisions have equal line of authority

To balance the benefits produced by geographic and product structures and to coordinate a mixture of product and geographic subunits, some multinationals create a worldwide matrix structure. Unlike hybrid organizations, the worldwide **matrix structure**, shown in Exhibit 13.6, is a symmetrical organization: it has equal lines of authority for product groups and for geographic divisions. Ideally, the matrix provides the structure for a firm to pursue both local and more global strategies at the same time. Geographical divisions focus on national responsiveness, and product divisions focus on finding global efficiencies. The matrix structure works well only when there are nearly equal demands from the environment for local adaptation and for product standardization with its associated economies of scale. Without these near-equal demands, the organization tends to evolve into a product or geographic structure, based on whichever side is more important for competitive advantage.

On paper, the matrix structure produces quality decisions because two or more managers reach consensus on how to balance local and worldwide needs. It typically allows the multinational to explore new opportunities as the focus is usually on both product and geography. Managers who hold positions at the intersection of product and geographic divisions are called "two-boss managers," as they have a boss from the product side of the organization and a boss from the geographic side of the organization. Product bosses tend to emphasize goals such as efficiency, while geographic bosses tend to emphasize local or regional adaptation. As such, for managers at all levels, the matrix gives the multinational the opportunity to explore both product needs and geographical needs. Furthermore, the matrix structure enables better communication and movement of information.

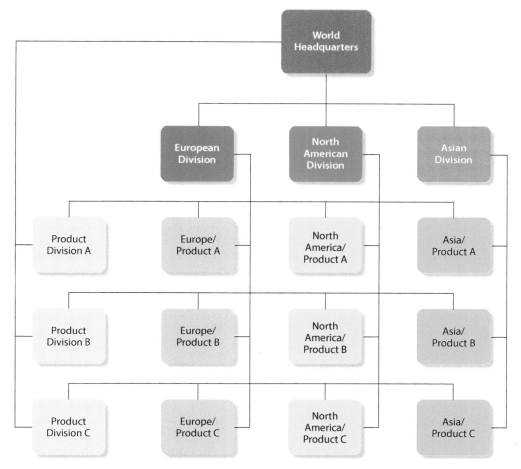

Exhibit 13.6 Matrix Structure

The major drawback associated with a matrix structure is that it is extremely difficult to manage.[9] For instance, to succeed at balancing the inherent struggles between global and local concerns, the matrix requires extensive resources for communication among the managers. Middle- and upper-level managers must have good human relations skills to deal with inevitable personal conflicts originating from the competing interests of product and geography. The middle-level managers must also learn to deal with two bosses, who often have competing interests. Furthermore, upper-level managers, in turn, must be prepared to resolve conflicts between geographic and product managers. Finally, while decisions that are made may be better, they typically take much longer to reach. Although the matrix structure can be complicated, experts agree that special steps can be taken to make the matrix work.[10] Having a strong corporate culture is helpful so that organizational members are aware of accountability both in terms of financial results and behavior. Additionally, having the right individuals in the right place to ensure that individuals with the right mindsets are where they should be is critical. The right individuals should have the experience, maturity, and self-confidence to both negotiate and compromise. Inflexible individuals will likely fail. Frequent and quality communications are critical. This will ensure that all employees are on the same page.

The **transnational network structure** represents another solution to the complex demands of being locally responsive while also taking advantage of global economies of scale and seeking

transnational network structure
network of subsidiaries and divisions that link the company throughout the world

location advantages such as global sources of knowledge. It combines functional, product, and geographic subunits. However, unlike the symmetrical matrix structure, the transnational has no basic form. It has no symmetry or balance between the geographic and product sides of the organization. Instead, the transnational is a network that links different types of transnational subsidiaries throughout the world. Exhibit 13.7 shows the transnational network at Philips, the Dutch multinational.

The transnational organization is different from the other forms of organization in a number of important ways. First, while other forms tend to focus on only one aspect (i.e. on the product in the product structure, etc.), the transnational structure tends to provide legitimacy to the various internal perspectives.[11] Furthermore, while the company's physical and human assets are spread globally, there is a very high level of interdependence among these elements. In contrast

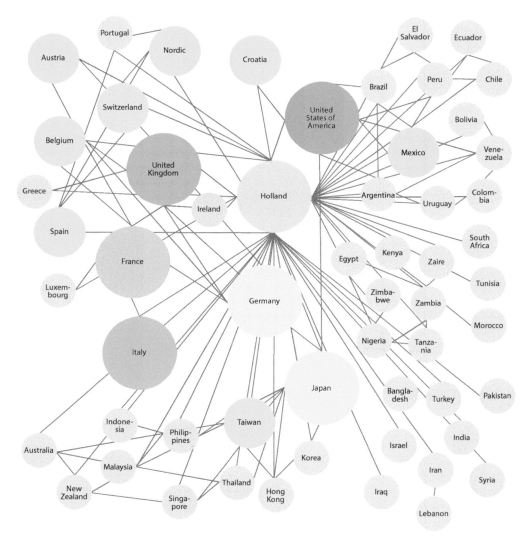

Exhibit 13.7 Philips Transnational Structure

Source: Sumantra Goshal and Christopher A. Bartlett, 1990, "The multinational corporation as an interorganizational network," *Academy of Management Review, 15*, pp. 603–625. Republished with permission of the Academy of Management; permission conveyed through Copyright Clearance Center, Inc.

to other forms where power is concentrated, the transnational structure works by decentralizing authority to the various national units. The local managers are given entrepreneurial freedom to develop new solutions to problems but are also expected to contribute such knowledge to the global operations. As such, managers are expected not only to be creative but also to have the necessary skills to contribute their knowledge for the good of the transnational.

Hence, nodes, the units at the center of the network, coordinate product, functional, and geographic information. Different product-group units and geographical-area units have different structures, and often no two subunits are alike. Rather, transnational units evolve to take advantage of resources, talent, and market opportunities wherever they exist in the world. Resources, people, and ideas flow in all directions.

A transnational structure works well when industries become very complex and volatile. In such situations, a typical hierarchy may not work. For instance, companies such as Asea Brown Boveri or Philips Electronics operate in extremely complex industries where companies' traditional boundaries have disappeared and where global operations and local operations need to be integrated to build competitive advantage. However, similar to the matrix organization, a transnational structure is extremely complicated to manage. Unlike other structures, there is no set form that a transnational structure can take.

Although multinationals have traditionally made choices along the lines suggested earlier, recent research on emerging markets suggest that multinationals may need to adopt a new way of organizing. Consider the following IB Emerging Market Strategic Insight.

T-Shaped Country Structures?

IB EMERGING MARKET
STRATEGIC INSIGHT

As you have seen, any specific organizational structures seem appropriate in some situations but not others. However, recent research suggests that many of the options discussed above may not necessarily work for multinationals seeking to succeed in emerging markets. Such organizations are facing challenges as emerging markets are no longer only sources of cheap products but attractive destinations for customers. Furthermore, emerging markets are also becoming sources of new product ideas that may lead to highly innovative products. Current structures seem insufficient to address such challenges. Structures such as the matrix or the transnational structure all work well in order to make some aspects such as products or regions or customers the focus of the organization. But current trends suggest that the challenges facing multinationals in emerging markets require new thinking.

Current multinationals face a number of pressures. First, they need to become much more nimble responding to local customer needs. Front end operations need to become highly localized to give local markets the attention they need because of increased competitiveness. Second, however, the back end of the value chain needs to be broken up and integrated across countries to achieve the necessary level of innovation. For example, multinationals can no longer centralize specific innovative activities such as R&D and product development in specific countries. Rather, they should be able to break up these operations across countries to take advantage of the knowledge in these countries and integrate them across the world.

Experts therefore agree that the T-shaped country structure will likely be preferred in the future. The T-shaped structure is organized horizontally along the lines of loose integration of activities across countries. However, the vertical links in the T-shaped structures would represent the level of depth in functions needed across countries. As an example, the global R&D centers in

India for companies such as Intel and GE will not only be responsible for developing new and innovative products for the Indian market but will also contribute to work in global product development.

Other experts also agree that the ability to be both flexible and have standardized processes along the many aspects of the value chain will be critical. For instance, the Dutch giant Philips has now reorganized its operations along processes such as idea to market, market to order, and order to cash rather than the traditional product structure.

Source: Based on W. Aghina, A. De Smet and S. Heywood, 2014, "The past and future of global organizations," *McKinsey Quarterly*, www.mckinsey.com/quarterly/overview; N. Kumar and P. Puranam, 2011, "Have you restructured for global success?" *Harvard Business Review*, October 11, http://hbr.org

As the above shows, the future will likely see many new forms of organizational structure. In the next and final section, you will read about which structure a multinational should use.

Choosing the Appropriate Structure: Strategy and Structure

An important point to remember is that there is no one best organizational design. The choice of an organizational design depends mostly on the choice of strategy.[12] That is, some design options are more effective for implementing different strategies. As you read earlier, most small companies act first as passive exporters. They simply fill orders using the same structures, procedures, and people used in domestic sales. Even with greater involvement in exporting, companies often avoid fundamental organizational changes. Instead, they use other companies to provide them with international expertise and to run their export operations. Furthermore, even with licensing, companies do not need complicated structures to collect royalties. However, as we discussed earlier, as exports become more important, an export department works well.

For the multinational extensively involved with international operations, the appropriateness of a structure depends on the basic multinational strategies discussed in Chapter 2. A multinational can pursue each of four main strategies: namely, multidomestic, transnational, international, and regional. Each of these strategies requires a different approach to organizational structure. Below, we discuss each strategy briefly (for more detail, please refer to Chapter 2) and the appropriate organizational structure.

A multidomestic structure focuses on local responsiveness where the multinational customizes products for the needs of the local markets. Furthermore, as you may recall from Chapter 2, a regional strategy is also an approach where products are customized for local market needs. The most appropriate structure to implement a multidomestic or regional strategy is a worldwide geographic structure. Since a company with a multidomestic or regional strategy needs to differentiate its products or services by country or region, it needs an organizational design with maximum geographical flexibility. The semi-autonomous regional or country-based subunits of the worldwide geographic structure provide that flexibility to tailor or develop products that meet the particular needs of local or regional markets.

A company pursuing an international strategy attempts to gain economies of scale by selling worldwide products with most upstream activities based at home. Adaptation to local customs and culture, if any, is limited to minor adjustments in product offerings and marketing strategies. Often, the international strategist decides to concentrate its R&D and manufacturing strengths at home, hoping it brings greater economies of scale and quality than the dispersed activities of the transnational. For multinationals pursuing an international strategy, worldwide product structures are appropriate. Worldwide product structures support international strategies because they provide an efficient way to organize and centralize the production and sales of similar products for the world market. The worldwide product structure sacrifices regional or local adaptation strengths derived from a geographic structure to gain product development and manufacturing economies of scale.

Finally, for the company pursuing a transnational strategy, the transnational structure is obviously the most appropriate structure. The transnational strategy gives two goals top priority: seeking location advantages and gaining economic efficiencies from operating worldwide.[13] "Location advantages" means that the transnational company disperses or locates its value-chain activities (e.g. manufacturing, R&D, and sales) anywhere in the world where the company can "do it best or cheapest," as the situation requires. The transnational structure provides the necessary flexibility to achieve transnational strategies.

Next, we examine multinational coordination strategies.

Coordination Mechanisms

As you read earlier, the task of selecting the appropriate organizational design emphasizes breaking down the multinational into subunits to perform specialized tasks and responsibilities. However, top managers must also design organizational systems to coordinate the activities of their subunits. This is a very difficult task. Foreign subsidiaries differ widely by geographical location, local markets, cultures, and legal systems, as well as by the talents and resources available to the subsidiary.[14] Even subunits within a multinational may have different goals and operate differently. **Coordination mechanisms** become critical for any multinational to coordinate its various subunits. This section therefore reviews coordination systems used by MNCs to coordinate their dispersed activities.

What's the nature of such coordination? Consider the Emerging Market Ethical Challenge below.

coordination mechanisms
ways to coordinate the various subunits in a multinational

Tata and the Swach

EMERGING MARKET
ETHICAL CHALLENGE

Multinationals in the future will need to explore many ways to coordinate and integrate their activities. Although these companies will be expected to distribute specialized functions across countries, they will be also expected to find ways to make sure that the various activities are integrated to achieve the necessary synergies to succeed. If such multinationals are able to find the right level of coordination, they also have the potential to discover new and innovative products.

For instance, consider the development of Tata's cheap water purifier, the Swach. The water purifier was developed by Tata to address the inability of poor people to access drinking water at a reasonable rate. The product was developed through the collaboration of three unrelated business groups from the Tata enterprise. The product was initially created by Tata's Research, Design and Development Center. However, the Swach was then shelved because the group did not see the potential. When several senior executives visited the center, they saw the potential of the product and integrated Tata Chemical to improve on the product. Because of their expertise in nanotechnology, Tata Chemical was able to add nano particles of silver to enhance the ability of the purifier by increasing the efficiency of the antibacterial water treatment. A third group, the Titan company, joined the project and added their precision engineering expertise.

In the end, through the integration of three business groups, Tata has developed a product that is making water available to the world's poorest individuals. The product now sells at a much lower price than competitors' Swach has significant potential. Although there are 220 million households in India, only around 10 million use water purifiers. Tata is poised to serve this growing segment while also fulfilling its mission of being in "business with a humanitarian face."

Source: Based on J. Baker, 2010, "A thirst for innovation," *ICIS Chemical Business*, October 11, p. 32; N. Kumar and P. Puranam, 2011, "Have you restructured for global success?" *Harvard Business Review*, October 11, http://hbr.org; K. S. Ramchandran, K. S. Manikandan and A. Pant, 2013, "Why conglomerates thrive," *Harvard Business Review*, December, pp. 111–119.

As the Emerging Market Ethical Challenge illustrates, finding ways to integrate and coordinate various departments in a multinational is critical. Tata's efforts at integrating various business groups have resulted in a product that saves lives. The organizational design aspects discussed earlier usually set up the formal nature of the organization. However, the informal aspects of the organization can also be very important in achieving the goals of the multinational. A multinational may need to coordinate various subunits with entities such as cross-functional teams or virtual teams. Furthermore, as argued by Chen and Cannice,[15] appropriate coordination and integration allows a multinational to minimize duplication, thus saving costs. Global integration also allows a multinational to enjoy global economies of scale, thus becoming more globally efficient. Next, you will read about the various coordination mechanisms.

Coordination and Integration

Coordinating and integrating a multinational's subunits is crucial. However, implementing systems to make such coordination and communication happen is not easy. One of the most important barriers to coordination is that different subunits may develop different goals and may thus have their own agendas. For instance, in a functional structure, the various functional areas may develop orientations favoring their own perspectives. Building coordination requires dedicated efforts from multinationals.

According to Jones,[16] there are seven coordination and integration mechanisms. The first and simplest integrating device is the **hierarchy of authority**, depicting who has authority and who reports to whom. Consider, for instance, the worldwide geographic structure discussed earlier. In its simplest arrangement (see Exhibit 13.4), each of the managers from the various functions reports to the area manager. This establishes a hierarchy of authority and responsibility but also coordinates the various geographic areas. However, if a multinational feels that the different geographic areas are too isolated and that several geographic areas may need to coordinate, the hierarchy of authority may be changed whereby a manager is assigned to coordinate the work of two geographic areas and report to higher-level managers.

Another important coordination mechanism is **direct contact**, where managers or workers interact face to face. For MNCs, direct contact often requires sophisticated video-conferencing and knowledge of a common language. Direct contact can be an important way to eliminate barriers among subunits. By establishing personal relationships, a multinational can build the necessary collaborative efforts needed to counter subunit orientations.

Liaison roles are fulfilled by individuals in one department whose specific responsibility is to communicate with people in another department. For example, in an MNC, one manager in each country subsidiary might be given the responsibility of coordinating marketing efforts

hierarchy of authority
integrating device depicting authority and accountability

direct contact
face-to-face interaction

liaison roles
specific responsibilities of a person from one department to communicate with people from other departments

within a region of the world. However, some multinationals can also create **full-time integrating roles**. Full-time integrators are similar to liaison roles but have coordination as their sole job responsibility. Product managers are often full-time integrators. In the MNC, they often serve as a link between the production units and local-country operations. Furthermore, some organizations can go as far as creating **integrating departments**. In such cases, rather than have one manager coordinate the work of different subunits, teams of managers are assigned such roles.

Task forces are temporary teams created to solve a particular organizational problem such as entering a new market. They usually link more than one department. A good example stems from Gerstner's efforts at IBM.[17] He launched a diversity task-force initiative and created eight focused teams representing various minority groups at IBM (women, Asians, etc.). These groups were created primarily to help IBM get a better understanding of the market. This initiative has paid off. For instance, the women's task force found that there is a lack of female experts in the technology industry. The task force recommended the creation of technology camps for middle-school girls to encourage interest in math and sciences and to show how these areas can translate into successful careers.

The final coordination mechanism available to multinationals is teams. Because of the importance of teams to most multinationals, you will read about teams in the next section.

Teams

Teams are the strongest coordination mechanisms, and unlike task forces, which have a short-term life span, teams are permanent units of the organization. Teams come from several organizational subunits to specialize in particular problems. For example, a team doing new-product development might include a scientist from R&D and managers from production and marketing.

Why are teams so crucial to multinationals? In today's hypercompetitive environment, multinationals often need to develop and launch new products that need to meet local and global needs while at the same time taking advantage of knowledge and expertise located around the world. Teams of individuals located around the world are often used to develop and launch such new products. Teams allow multinationals to bring together important expertise representing both local and global customer needs while also taking advantage of knowledge around the world. Consider the IB Emerging Market Strategic Insight below.

full-time integrating roles
similar to liaison roles but with full-time coordination responsibilities

integrating departments
departments responsible for coordination

task forces
temporary teams created to solve organizational concerns or problems

teams
permanent groups of people specialized to deal with particular problems

Multinationals and Global Teams

IB EMERGING MARKET STRATEGIC INSIGHT

How important are global teams to multinationals today? Many large multinationals such as Dow Chemical, Nokia, and Accenture make extensive use of global teams as they strive to navigate the hypercompetitive environment. They are finding that global teams give them the ability to coordinate activities of globally dispersed workers with special skills and expertise.

As an example, consider the case of Accenture. The company makes sure that all of its consultants and service workers take collaboration courses. In addition, Accenture also picks the most promising managers and puts them through a special leadership course emphasizing collaboration and teamwork. Such efforts are very important as Accenture assigns international teams to work on most of its projects.

Infosys, the Indian software giant, also uses teams in many different situations. For instance, it has a team of elite coders responsible for solving the most difficult complex software challenges. For example, if a client faces a difficult challenge and finds a software glitch ahead of a product launch, Infosys will put together the best team of software coders to solve such problems. This has proved extremely useful for Infosys as it helps solve some of the most difficult problems. These teams are put together with the specific purpose of solving those challenges. Similarly, Accenture also relies on teams of expert coders to solve complex problems.

Source: Based on FRPT Software Snapshot, 2015, "Infosys putting together crack team of coders: Will help solve complex software challenges for the clients," pp. 23–24; Pete Engardio, 2007, "A guide for multinationals. One of the greatest challenges for a multinational is learning how to build a productive global team," *BusinessWeek*, August 20, 4047, p. 48.

Recent research by Barczak and McDonough also shows that global teams are crucial for multinationals for a variety of other reasons.[18] Teams are often useful in helping multinationals identify common product platforms that can help develop global products. Global products are often desirable because they are cheaper to produce and market. Teams also allow multinationals to bring together key dispersed resources and expertise. By bringing together expertise located around the world (e.g. manufacturing expertise in one country, R&D in another country, etc.), a team is more likely to capitalize on the various strengths and expertise. In fact, the earlier example of Tata's Swach water purifier product also reflects such teams. Furthermore, as you will read later, teams can now exist at the virtual level, thus bringing minimal disruption to the team members' lives and also minimizing costs.

Despite the key advantages, a recent survey of around 300 teams in over 230 companies found that global teams face a number of key challenges.[19] First and foremost, global team members are located in different countries around the world. Important differences exist in terms of cultural backgrounds, languages used, and even the local subsidiary's culture. Additionally, a multinational can have different business units with different terminologies or technologies.[20] Such differences can often result in misunderstanding or create other barriers to communication if not addressed properly. However, beyond such differences, global team members have to often deal with logistic and other practical challenges. For instance, a simple video-conferencing with a colleague in South Korea may turn out to be challenging because of the significant time difference. Furthermore, as Kumar discusses, traveling can soon become very tiresome and become very disruptive in terms of both work and family.[21]

A more recent study of 13,616 interactions among 2090 members of 289 teams of a large multinational provides further insights.[22] In that study, the authors examine both position-based differences such as geographic and structural differences as well as person-based differences such as nationality and demographic differences. The results of the study show that position-based differences created greater barriers to knowledge seeking than person-based differences. Such results are not surprising as geographic differences means that there are more difficulties because of the greater costs of communication. Time differences etc. mean that it is harder to find mutually acceptable times to communicate. Also, even when contact is established, there are difficulties in communicating effectively. The study also showed that familiarity with individuals from a previous team reduced barriers in communication.

Given the above, what can multinationals do to deal with such challenges? For cultural background differences, it is important to encourage team members to be more culturally aware. Many of the training and other awareness methods discussed in Chapter 7 on national culture can be applied here. However, for the language differences, a team leader can implement various steps to ensure smooth communication.[23] It is important to distribute critical documents ahead of time to allow all team members to comprehend and respond to shared information. It is also advisable for team members to provide a written description of meetings to ensure that everyone is on the same page. Furthermore, it is also critical to make sure that team members are trained regarding potential misunderstandings using a common language. Additionally, because of the challenges of operating in different countries and different time zones, it is important for the team leader to establish clear project goals and to assign appropriate responsibilities. If possible, such goals and responsibilities should be assigned collectively to ensure buy-in and commitment from all team members.

A final but important measure to ensure that global teams function effectively is regular communication. Global team members should be encouraged to communicate regularly through e-mail, telephone, and other available technology. However, it is also crucial to have regular face-to-face meetings to build trust and relationships. To get things done, a global team needs to rely on the expertise of its members and their propensity to trust each other to collaborate. Face-to-face meetings can be a good step towards building relationships and trust. In fact, Mastercard, the global financial services company, requires that its teams meet once a year in a specific location.[24] Additionally, weekly conference calls are held to ensure that team members are all on the same page while also respecting holidays, time zones, and even prayer times. As well as this, the company uses technology to mimic actual face-to-face meetings through monthly teleconferences.

Global Virtual Teams

The new global workplace is also seeing an increased use of **global virtual teams**. Global virtual teams are groups of people who work together from different parts of the world by using information and communication technologies such as intranets, web meetings, WIKIs, e-mails, and instant messaging.[25] Global virtual teams are also becoming increasingly important for multinationals. Consider the case of IBM and its goal to make its 360,000 employees work together as a global virtual team.[26] IBM has implemented a global web system where any employee with a new product idea can use online chat boxes to create a team and have access to market intelligence. Employees around the world can collaborate immediately on new product ideas, and develop and test prototypes. Similarly, Cisco has created a virtual platform to help its 15,000 global managers to transition from a hardware company to a customer-focused digital solutions driven organization.[27] The platform hosts formal and informal training through a learning management system. The system also includes social networking tools as well as career-related blogs and other tools to allow employees to collaborate worldwide.

Given the importance of global virtual teams to multinationals, it is important to understand some of the key challenges and opportunities facing such teams. According to Brake,[28] virtual teams suffer from many major drawbacks. First, virtual teams suffer from the lack of information richness that is typically afforded by a face-to-face environment. When teams function face to face, team members can pay attention to social and other cues to react or attend to. Such cues are missing in virtual teams. Second, such lack of cues can also result in misunderstanding and confusion. However, Gerke also argues that the virtual team leader faces some challenges such as the difficulty of getting to know team members in a virtual world while also communicating effectively.[29] Other challenges for the virtual team leader include the ability to recognize problems before such problems occur, and also the ability to assign responsibilities and duties and monitor such issues in an environment where team members never actually meet. In addition to the above challenges, virtual global teams also face many of the same challenges that traditional global teams face. For instance, both cultural and language differences may potentially result in misunderstanding and low productivity.

global virtual teams groups of people around the world collaborating using information and communication technologies

Although virtual teams suffer from a number of potential drawbacks, most experts agree that the most critical step to ensure that a global virtual team works well is to build a social community to ensure that team members don't feel isolated.[30] As such, if possible, team members may want to meet face to face at least once to build relationships. However, if face-to-face meetings are not possible, the team leader should schedule regular conference calls as well as one-to-one phone calls to build trust and collaboration. Furthermore, it is important for virtual team members to discuss other issues than work to build camaraderie. Inquiries about family and other social aspects are more likely to give a chance for virtual team members to get to know each other.

Another key issue pertaining to virtual global teams is staying focused on the task at hand. It is imperative for the team leader to take steps to assign and clarify responsibilities judiciously as well as assigning goals and deadlines. Frequent feedback and updates on the team progress may also be useful. Finally, the team leader should be prepared to modify responsibilities and goals as required.

Recent research also provides evidence of the need to consider leadership when designing virtual teams.[31] Specifically, empowering leadership refers to the ability of the team leader to empower other members to take initiatives, to voice their opinions, and even to find solutions to problems. The research showed that virtual teams that had leaders who empowered members were more likely to see stronger virtual team collaboration and team performance. Furthermore, such results were stronger for teams that were more geographically dispersed. This provides support for the importance of empowered leadership. To give you more insights into empowered leadership, Exhibit 13.8 shows some of the associated empowering leadership factors and expected behaviors.

This section completes consideration of organizational design by showing how managers can coordinate the various types of subunits that multinational organizations employ. In the final section, we look at knowledge management, a design issue that is becoming increasingly crucial for most multinationals.

Factor	Behaviors
Leading by example	Sets high standards through his/her own behavior
	Leads by example
	Works as hard as anyone in the group
Coaching	Suggest ways to improve team performance
	Encourage team members to solve problems together
	Helps group see areas where more training is needed
Participative decision making	Encourages group members to express ideas
	Gives all group members chance to voice opinions
	Considers group ideas when he/she disagrees with them
Showing concern	Cares about group members' personal problems
	Shows concerns for group members' well being
	Stays in touch with work group

Exhibit 13.8 Empowering Leadership Factors and Behaviors

Source: J. Arnod, S. Arad, J. A. Rhoades and F. Drasgow, 2000, "The empowering leadership questionnaire: the construction and validation of a new scale for measuring leader behaviors," *Journal of Organizational Behavior, 21*, pp. 249–269; S. N. Hill and K. M. Bartol, 2016, "Empowering leadership and effective collaboration in geographically dispersed teams," *Personnel Psychology, 69*, pp. 159–198.

Knowledge Management

In this chapter, you read about not only how multinationals can break down the organization into subunits, but also how they coordinate these subunits. An increasingly related and important area is knowledge management. As you will read below, the way a multinational organizes its information through its various structures and coordination mechanisms can be very important as it strives to survive in today's global environment.

Knowledge management refers to the systems, mechanisms, and other design elements of any organization to ensure that the right form of knowledge is available to the right individual at the right time.[32] Knowledge management is focused on the processes related to the creation, acquisition, and dissemination of critical knowledge and information to enhance learning and performance in the organization. Many well-known multinationals such as HP, British Petroleum, Xerox, Chevron, Ford, Siemens etc., have all implemented knowledge management systems.[33]

Why is knowledge management so critical? Many experts agree that knowledge management is critical to successful product innovation and creation of competitive advantage. For example, knowledge management systems allow companies to create and combine critical knowledge that can lead to knowledge creation for new products. Recent research also suggests that knowledge management results in stronger innovation performance when the environment is fast changing.[34] This also underscores the importance of a knowledge management system during turbulent times. Furthermore, many multinationals now have to face forces for both global integration and local differentiation while achieving global innovation. Multinationals need to be able to implement systems that are capable of combining worldwide knowledge from local sources to create and transfer innovation to new products for international markets. Appropriately managing knowledge can give multinationals the means to create the global flexibility they will need to survive.[35]

Knowledge management systems are even more critical for emerging markets and emerging market multinationals. Consider the following Emerging Market Brief.

According to experts, an effective knowledge management is composed of many important tools or mechanisms.[36] In its ideal form, an effective knowledge management system is one where employees are encouraged to share what they know with others while also being able to seek critical knowledge and expertise when needed. One of the important facets of any knowledge management system is the presence of the appropriate technical environment to facilitate storage and sharing of information. In fact, Holsapple argues that a modern knowledge management cannot be separated from computer-based and information technology and any knowledge management system needs the appropriate technology to collect, store, and access critical knowledge as needed while also disseminating such information to those who need it.[37] For instance, consider how IBM's intranet portal including global messaging, local information, employee and other human resource-related information has helped IBM become more global and integrated.[38] The portal has provided an environment where IBM employees can chat, collaborate, and contribute knowledge while also allowing them to communicate with critical external groups such as suppliers and other partners. As you will read later in Chapter 15 on e-commerce, a multinational has access to many information technology tools that can help enhance a knowledge management system. Such tools can also be used to enhance a company's sustainability efforts.

knowledge management
systems and mechanisms in place to collect and disseminate knowledge in the multinational

Emerging Markets and Knowledge Management

Although there is strong evidence that knowledge management systems are critical for emerging market multinationals, several recent studies suggest that knowledge management systems are not always properly implemented in such multinationals. For example, a recent survey of top management from 76 Russian firms showed that none of the knowledge management practices had an impact on organizational outcomes such as customer value creation. Such results are likely given the Russian business culture and the environment in which these companies operate. However, it is also possible that the companies did not properly implement their knowledge management systems.

Another study of Chinese car companies shows some of the challenges these multinationals are facing. Although these Chinese multinationals are interested in expanding internationally, the knowledge and innovation flow is often limited to the international joint venture partners they are engaged in. Most of their knowledge is limited to their joint venture partners from developed world multinationals and such constraints place limits on the innovation that these companies can engage in. Emerging market multinationals therefore often face knowledge constraints and many are now recruiting new research and development staff and also cooperating with new research institutions such as universities.

Source: Based on R. Lynch and Z. Jin, 2016, "Knowledge and innovation in emerging market multinationals," *Journal of Business Research, 69*, pp. 1593–1597; T. Andreeva, T. Garanina, Y. Bezginova and A. Sergeeva, 2014, "Customer value creation process in Russian companies: Role of intellectual capital and knowledge management practices," *Proceedings of the International Conference on Intellectual Capital, Knowledge Management & Organizational Learning*, pp. 9–19.

Beyond an effective IT system, multinationals can establish knowledge management systems by enhancing knowledge flows between headquarters and R&D subsidiaries. Multinationals will often establish systems to ensure that knowledge flows adequately to R&D centers to ensure innovative performance. However, recent research suggests that for advanced economy firms, the knowledge management system is often designed so that information flows from headquarters to international R&D subsidiaries.[39] In contrast, for emerging market multinationals, information flows often occur from foreign R&D subsidiaries to headquarters. Foreign R&D subsidiaries often provide key knowledge to help emerging market multinationals catch up with industry leaders.

A properly designed knowledge management system cannot function without the human element. Employees must not only be willing and motivated to contribute and share information, but must also be willing to seek information when needed. As such, it is critical for a multinational to first identify and eliminate human barriers. Riege discusses the many human barriers, such as lack of time to share knowledge, fear of sharing information, differences in experience level, lack of understanding of the critical nature of sharing information, etc.[40] By identifying and eliminating such barriers, a multinational can start building an effective knowledge management system. To eliminate such barriers, it is important for any multinational to show the value created by knowledge management systems. Success stories and importance of the knowledge management system should be constantly communicated to the employees.[41]

In addition to removal of potential barriers, employees must also be motivated to participate in a knowledge management system. Employees should not only be made aware of the importance of knowledge management systems but should also be given appropriate incentives and rewards to participate in such networks. Case studies of successful knowledge systems show that identification and support of knowledge "activists" is a key success factor.[42] Such activists will take the initiative of convincing others of the importance of knowledge management systems while also ensuring that the process flows smoothly. Such actions are more likely to motivate others to fully contribute to the new knowledge management system. To give you further understanding of the process, consider the IB Emerging Market Strategic Insight below.

Building a Knowledge Management System at Siemens

IB EMERGING MARKET
STRATEGIC INSIGHT

Siemens, the German-based multinational, is one of the largest companies with respect to many information and communication products and services in a large number of industries such as transportation, energy, windpower and renewables, and healthcare. It has more than 348,000 employees based in more than 200 countries. Siemens has presence in all of the major emerging markets such as Brazil, India etc.,

To take full advantage of its vast capabilities in global knowledge, it launched several knowledge management systems to connect its employees. For instance, the Siemens ShareNet knowledge management system was created to connect over 17,000 of its sales and marketing employees around the world. Additionally, its Global Application Management system was initially developed in India and rolled out worldwide to bring together employees in the IT industry.

Siemens' ShareNet is composed of a web-based knowledge library where employees can contribute their experiences from present and past projects based on predefined categories. The system also includes an urgent request forum, where employees can post urgent questions and other users can provide answers to such questions. Finally, the system also includes a forum where knowledge can be shared. Although some knowledge can easily be communicated to others, other forms of knowledge can be of a tacit nature and Siemens' system has in-built processes to ensure that such tacit knowledge can be communicated to others.

In contrast, Siemen's Global Application Management system was developed specifically for its IT solutions and services arm. The knowledge management system was developed to ensure that employees could have easy access to the knowledge base of the company with regards to IT solutions. Additionally, the company wanted the system to allow employees to collaborate worldwide without reinventing the wheel. Finally, Siemens hoped that the new system would limit brain drain with outgoing employees while also facilitating learning for new employees.

Source: Based on M. Saxena, 2016, "An integrated management model for global application management," www.siemens.com/press/pool/de/materials/sis/2011-04-sis/whitepaper_integrated_knowledge_management_en_2010.pdf; Sven C. Voelpel and Zheng Han, 2005, "Managing knowledge sharing in China: The case of Siemens ShareNet," *Journal of Knowledge Management*, *9*(3), pp. 51–63.

As the IB Emerging Market Strategic Insight shows, building an effective knowledge management system is very complex and time consuming. Many knowledge management systems can also suffer from the same challenges facing global and virtual teams, such as cultural and background differences, language barriers, etc. Any multinational must also be willing to address such challenges. However, if done properly, a knowledge management system can be an extremely important survival tool in today's global environment.

Chapter Review

In this chapter, you read about important multinational issues as they relate to organization design and coordination. As the competitive environment gets more complicated for multinationals and as they are pressured to become more innovative while at the same time integrating global and local expertise, organization design and coordination issues will become even more crucial in the future. As the many IB Emerging Market Strategic Insight showed, many multinationals are changing their structure or making more effective use of coordination mechanisms to better face the competition. The growth of emerging markets and the constant challenges of operating in such markets are increasing the need for multinationals to experiment with various structures.

In the first section, you learned about the many important functions that organizational design plays. Additionally, you read about the various design structures available to multinationals. These include traditional structures such as the export department, international division, worldwide geographic and product structures. However, you also read about mixtures of the more traditional structures including the matrix and transnational structures. You read about the T-shaped structure and how it may help multinationals deal with the challenges of emerging markets. You also learned about the appropriateness of each structure based on the multinational's strategy.

While organizational structures show how the multinational can separate subunits, there is also a strong need to coordinate these subunits. The second section of the chapter discussed the many options available to multinationals, including the hierarchy of authority, direct contact, liaison roles, and task forces. Because teams are becoming so widely used, you also read about the many challenges facing multinationals as they use both global and virtual teams. Finally, you learned about some of the things multinationals can do to tackle such challenges.

In the final section of this chapter, you read about knowledge management. Because most multinationals are now under pressure to properly manage their information and knowledge to face the hypercompetitive world, you learned about the key roles played by a properly designed knowledge management system. You read about the key aspects of a knowledge management system. Finally, you also learned about the best way to properly design the many aspects of a knowledge management system.

Discussion Questions

1   What is organizational design? Why is organizational design so important to any multinational?

2   What is an export department? How is an export department different from an international division?

3   Discuss the worldwide geographic structure. When is a worldwide geographic structure appropriate? What are some of the most important drawbacks of a worldwide geographic structure?

4   Compare and contrast a worldwide geographic structure with a worldwide product structure. When is a worldwide product structure more appropriate than a worldwide geographic structure?

5   What is a matrix structure? What are some of the benefits of using a matrix structure? What are some of the drawbacks?

6   What is a transnational structure? When is a transnational structure appropriate?

7   Discuss four coordination mechanisms.

8   What are global teams? What are some of the challenges of using global teams? What can multinationals do to prepare their employees for global teams?

9   What is knowledge management? Discuss some of the most important aspects of a knowledge management system.

10 What is a T-shaped structure? When is a T-shaped structure appropriate?

International Business Skill Builder

Building a Knowledge Management System

Step 1: A local company, exporting cheese and other dairy products to many locations around the world, has approached you to create a knowledge management system. Advise them on the important aspects of the knowledge management system.

Step 2: Discuss some of the knowledge you believe the company should be collecting.

Step 3: Advise the company on how the collected information can be used to enter new markets or to stay competitive.

Step 4: Advise the company on some ways to motivate employees to contribute knowledge and information to the system.

Chapter Internet Activity
Identify four well-known multinationals. Go to their websites and find information about the organizational structure they use. Discuss why such structures are appropriate for these multinationals' strategies.

Key Concepts

- coordination mechanisms
- direct contact
- export department
- full-time integrating roles
- functional structure
- geographic structure
- global virtual teams
- hierarchy of authority
- integrating departments
- international division
- knowledge management
- liaison roles
- matrix structure
- organizational design
- product structure
- task forces
- teams
- transnational network structure
- worldwide geographic structure
- worldwide product structure

CASE 13

BUSINESS > INTERNATIONAL

San Miguel Corporation From Beer to Planes, Trains, and Roads

San Miguel Corporation has grown into one of the largest and most diversified companies in Southeast Asia. One of the most popular and well-known brands of beer in the Philippines and throughout Southeast Asia, San Miguel, has been brewing beer for well over one hundred years. The company's brewing business produces such well-known and popular brands as San Miguel Pale and Red Horse. The company also owns Ginebra San Miguel distillers, San Miguel Pure Foods, and San Miguel Packaging. The company has a vertically integrated structure in the food and agriculture industry, ranging from breeding, to canning, to retail branding. Recently the company has moved aggressively into many unrelated industries. The company has become an extremely diversified firm with holdings in many unrelated businesses. Questions have arisen as to whether this form of diversification is a wise strategic move for the company.

San Miguel Corporation began as La Fabrica de Cerveza de San Miguel in 1890, operating in Manila under a royal charter from Spain. The company incorporated in 1913, and in the 1960s changed its name to San Miguel Corporation (SMC). Early in the company's existence it began a process of backwards vertical integration in which it acquired barley fields, and later expanded into other agricultural products. The company eventually expanded into soft drinks, spirits, and packaging operations. San Miguel has the distinction of being the first foreign bottler of Coca-

Cola, acquiring the franchise in 1927. Today the company is the largest food and beverage business in the Philippines, as well as all of Southeast Asia. The company operates over 100 facilities in the Philippines, Southeast Asia, China, and Australia.

San Miguel controls approximately 90 percent of the beer market in the Philippines, and significant shares of the processed meat and poultry markets. San Miguel is attempting to leverage its management and business skills into high growth industries. Domestic beer sales are not expected to increase significantly and the company wants to diversify into any industry that provides high growth potential. As company chairman, Eduardo Cojuangco stated, "We want to be in industries that have scale and will grow, and we are determined to build leadership positions in key areas where important trends are driving future growth, not just for San Miguel but for the Philippines too." San Miguel has moved into areas that are important to the economic growth of the Philippines such as power generation. The demand for electricity in the Philippines is expected to continue to grow, and forecasts show that current supply will soon be insufficient to meet public demand. San Miguel feels that the company can capitalize on the privatization of electrical services in the Philippines. Many of the power generating facilities in the Philippines are twenty five years or older, and supply isn't always dependable. Some feel that the government owned service is poorly managed, and traditionally has operated as a drain on the Filipino government budget. As such, San Miguel has purchased three power generating units and expanded into mining operations.

In addition to being in the electricity business, San Miguel has purchased ownership of Petron, an oil refinery and marketing business. The company has begun to build toll roads to reduce the traffic congestion found in major parts of the Philippines, and has even purchased an airport and a 49 percent stake in the flagship carrier, Philippines Airlines. In addition San Miguel has become a housing developer and is creating new communities in certain parts of the country. With a rapidly growing population and rising incomes in the Philippines there is an increased need for more and better housing. San Miguel has also bought into public rail transportation, owns a bank and insurance brokerage company, and several telecommunication companies.

In 1982 Tom Peters and Robert Waterman published the now classic book titled, *In Search of Excellence*, in which they advised firms to "stick to the knitting." The strategy of focusing on your core competencies was also the message of Michael Porter's research and publications. Porter found that diversification can lead to lower returns as a firm moves into unrelated businesses. He proposed that the competitive advantage of a firm is difficult to leverage across unrelated businesses. The acquisitions and diversification have raised the revenue of San Miguel. In 2011 the company reported sales of $12.2B and by 2015 sales were $14.3B. Net income, however, decreased from $399M in 2011 to $264M in 2015. Diluted EPS decreased during the same time period from $.11 to $.05. It appears that San Miguel is attempting to diversify into industries that are helpful to the

CASE 13 cont'd

growth of the Philippines and fulfill its social mission core value. The wisdom long-term of such excessive diversification is yet to be determined.

CASE DISCUSSION POINTS:

1 What challenges does San Miguel face as the company diversifies into unrelated industries?
2 Is it possible that the strategic issue of diversification is different between developed and developing countries?
3 Is organizational structure influenced by the culture, the level of economic development, or other factors found in the country? Explain.

Source: AsiaMoney, 2007, "Energy—Powering up for privatization," June; H. Bulos, 2005, "San Miguel's buying binge," *BusinessWeek*, April 25; L. Cuevas-Miel, 2007, "SEC clears spin-off of San Miguel beer unit," *Knight Ridder Tribune Business News*, July, 30; L. Cuevas-Miel, 2007, "San Miguel profit almost doubles in first six months," *Knight Ridder Tribune Business News*, August 10; R. Dumaual, 2007, "San Miguel earmarks $8M to double Vietnam plant capacity," *Business World*, August 24; R. Landingin, 2007, "San Miguel investors agree to beer spin-off," *Financial Times*, July 25; T. Lopez, 2006, "SMC the biggest corporation," *Manila Times*, November 20; V. Marsh, 2007, "San Miguel switches its growth focus," *Financial Times*, October 9; J. Pedrasa, 2006, "Big power consumers seek to purchase electricity directly from Napocor," *Business World*, May 23; P. Sevilla, 2007, "San Miguel share prices being watched," *Business World*, September 28; www.hoovers.com, accessed on October 10, 2007; www.sanmiguel.com.ph, accessed on July 11, 2016; financial information on San Miguel is from Hoovers, accessed on July 21, 2016.

Case prepared by Charles A. Rarick

Notes

1 T. Gibbs, S. Heywood, L. Weiss and G. Jost, 2012, "Organizing for an emerging world," *McKinsey Quarterly*, 3, pp. 81–91.
2 G. Bruce Friesen, 2005, "Organization design for the 21st century," *Consulting to Management*, 16(3), pp. 32–51.
3 G. Bruce Friesen, 2005, "Organization design for the 21st century," *Consulting to Management*, 16(3), pp. 32–51.
4 T. Gibbs, S. Heywood, L. Weiss and G. Jost, 2012, "Organizing for an emerging world," *McKinsey Quarterly*, 3, pp. 81–91.
5 Gareth R. Jones, 2012, *Organizational Theory, Design and Change*, Upper Saddle River, NJ: Pearson Prentice Hall.
6 Gareth R. Jones, 2012, *Organizational Theory, Design and Change*, Upper Saddle River, NJ: Pearson Prentice Hall.
7 Gareth R. Jones, 2012, *Organizational Theory, Design and Change*, Upper Saddle River, NJ: Pearson Prentice Hall.
8 J. M. Stopford and L. T. Wells, Jr, 1972, *Managing the Multinational Enterprise*, New York: Basic Books.
9 N. Schreiber and M. Rosenberg, 2015, "How to make the matrix work," *IESE Insight*, Third Quarter, pp. 46–53.

10 N. Schreiber and M. Rosenberg, 2015, "How to make the matrix work," *IESE Insight*, Third Quarter, pp. 46–53.

11 Christopher Bartlett, Sumantra Ghoshal and Paul Beamish, 2008, *Transnational Management* (5th edn), New York: McGraw-Hill.

12 Craig T. Williams and Juliet Rains, 2007, "Linking strategy to structure: The power of systematic organization design," *Organization Development Journal*, 25(2), pp. 163–170.

13 Christopher A. Bartlett and Sumantra Ghoshal, 1989, *Managing Across Borders: The Transnational Solution*, Boston, MA: Harvard University Press.

14 David Cray, 1984, "Control and coordination in multinational corporations," *Journal of International Business Studies*, Fall, pp. 85–98.

15 Roger Chen, and Mark V. Cannice, 2006, "Global integration and the performance of multinationals' subsidiaries in emerging markets," *Ivey Business Journal*, January/February, pp. 1–9.

16 Gareth R. Jones, 2007, *Organizational Theory, Design and Change*, Upper Saddle River, NJ: Pearson Prentice Hall.

17 *Strategic Direction*, 2005, "The strategic message from IBM: Diversify or die," April, *21*(4), pp. 13–15.

18 Gloria Barczak and Edward F. McDonough, 2003, "Leading global product development teams," *Research Technology Management*, November/December, *46*(6), pp. 14–18.

19 Gloria Barczak, Edward F. McDonough and Nicholas Athanassiou, 2006, "So you want to be a global project leader?" *Research Technology Management*, May/June, *49*(3), pp. 28–35.

20 S. Vollmer, 2015, "How to promote knowledge flows within multinationals," *CGMA Magazine*, November 10, http://cgma.org

21 Janaki Mythily Kumar, 2006, "Working as a designer in a global team," *Interactions*, March/April, pp. 25–27.

22 M. R. Haas and J. N. Cummings, 2015, "Barriers to knowledge seeking within MNC teams: Which differences matter most?" *Journal of International Business Studies*, 46, pp. 36–62.

23 Gloria Barczak, Edward F. McDonough and Nicholas Athanassiou, 2006, "So you want to be a global project leader?" *Research Technology Management*, May/June, *49*(3), pp. 28–35.

24 S. Vollmer, 2015, "How to promote knowledge flows within multinationals," *CGMA Magazine*, November 10, http://cgma.org

25 Terence Brake, 2006, "Leading global virtual teams," *Industrial and Commercial Training*, 38(3), pp. 116–121.

26 Pete Engardio, 2007, "A guide for multinationals. One of the greatest challenges for a multinational is learning how to build a productive global team," *BusinessWeek*, August 20, 4047, p. 48.

27 S. F. Gale, 2015, "Cisco reinvents social learning," Chief Learning Officer, September, pp. 40–41, 49.

28 Terence Brake, 2006, "Leading global virtual teams," *Industrial and Commercial Training*, 38(3), pp. 116–121.

29   Susan K. Gerke, 2006, "If I cannot see them, how can I lead them?" *Industrial and Commercial Training*, 38(2), pp. 102–105.

30 Terence Brake, 2006, "Leading global virtual teams," *Industrial and Commercial Training*, 38(3), pp. 116–121; Susan K. Gerke, 2006, "If I cannot see them, how can I lead them?" *Industrial and Commercial Training*, 38(2), pp. 102–105.

31 S. N. Hill and K. M. Bartol, 2016, "Empowering leadership and effective collaboration in geographically dispersed teams," *Personnel Psychology*, 69, pp. 159–198.

32 Junxia Wang, Hans Peter Peters and Jiancheng Guan, 2006, "Factors influencing knowledge productivity in German research groups: Lessons for developing countries," *Journal of Knowledge Management*, 10(4), pp. 113–126.

33 Sven C. Voelpel and Zheng Han, 2005, "Managing knowledge sharing in China: The case of Siemens ShareNet," *Journal of Knowledge Management*, 9(3), pp. 51–63.

34 R. Kamasak, M. Yavuz and G. Altuntas, 2016, "Is the relationship between innovation performance and knowledge management contingent on environmental dynamism and learning capability? Evidence from a turbulent market," *Business Research*, 9, pp. 229–253.

35 J. G. Davis, E. Subramanian and A. W. Westerberg, 2005, "The 'global' and 'local' in knowledge management," *Journal of Knowledge Management*, 9(1), pp. 101–112.

36 Stewart Johnston, and Angela Paladino, "Knowledge management and involvement in innovations in MNC subsidiaries," *Management International Review*, 47(2), pp. 281–302; C. Rivinus, 2007, "Demonstrating value at Parsons Brinckerhoff," *Knowledge Management Review*, January/February, 9(6), pp. 24–27.

37 Clyde W. Holsapple, 2005, "The inseparability of modern knowledge management and computer-based technology," *Journal of Knowledge Management*, 9(1), pp. 42–52.

38 Philip Weiss, 2007, "Looking through the portal," *Communication World*, May/June, 24(3), pp. 20–23.

39 S. Awate, M. Larsen and R. Mudambi, 2015, "Accessing vs sourcing knowledge: A comparative study of R&D internationalization between emerging and advanced economy firms," *Journal of International Business Studies*, 46, pp. 63–86.

40 Andreas Riege, 2005, "Three dozen knowledge-sharing barriers managers must consider," *Journal of Knowledge Management*, 9(3), pp. 18–35.

41 Jane McKenzie, 2005, "How to share knowledge between companies," *Knowledge Management Review*, November/December, 8(5), pp. 16–19.

42 Mikael Schönström, 2005, "Creating knowledge networks: Lessons from practice," *Journal of Knowledge Management*, 9(6), pp. 17–29.

CHAPTER 14

International Human Resource Management

After reading this chapter you should be able to:

- Understand what international human resource management is.

- Know the basic human resource management functions, such as recruitment, selection, training and development, performance appraisal and compensation, and how they apply to international workers with a specific focus on emerging markets.

- Appreciate the various labor and union relations in emerging markets.

- Understand expatriates and how international human resource management applies to expatriates.

- Understand the growth of non-traditional and women expatriates in the future.

International Business   *Preview IB Emerging Market Strategic Insight*

Labor in Emerging Markets

As the pace of growth accelerates in some emerging markets while it slows down in others, the challenges facing companies in such markets with respect to human resource management (HRM) practices are daunting. In India, for instance, multinationals are facing increased competition for talented workers. Such competition has created a focus on what Indian employers can do to retain and engage their employees. As another example, many African nations have seen an increased investment from Chinese companies. This investment has meant that more Chinese companies have been sending expatriates to these nations. Furthermore, this increased investment has also meant competition for local employees from other multinationals such as those from India as well as those locally based.

The challenges mentioned above are not too surprising. Consider that most global companies were entering emerging markets as a way to sell mature products while also looking for ways to reduce costs and to increase supply chain efficiency. As a consequence of such activities, having appropriate human resource management strategies was not a big priority. However, things are rapidly changing. As the emerging markets are becoming the focus of the new world economy, multinationals are paying stronger attention to the human resource management functions. Many more multinationals are realizing that having an appropriate HRM strategy can lead to competitive advantage. However, having the appropriate HRM strategy means to first confront key challenges such as:

- Competition for talent is very fierce in most emerging markets. As a result, multinationals are finding that they need to implement innovative ways to attract and keep talented workers.
- Employees are also finding that they are increasingly being courted by employers. Rather than simply accepting employment, employees are also becoming increasingly more selective in whom they want to work for. This new perspective also means that both local companies and multinationals need to find more effective ways to attract the attention of potential new employees.
- Companies have also seen a drop in employee loyalty. While the decision of an employee to leave could easily be addressed with salary increases, many companies are finding that simply increasing salaries may no longer be sufficient. They are resorting to other approaches such as providing high-quality food in cafeterias, gym memberships, etc., as a means to retain talented employees.

Source: Based on A. Bailey, 2016, "Emerging markets—has HR got it right?" Chapman CG Newsletters; F. L. Cooke, G. Wood and F. Horwitz, 2015, "Multinational firms from emerging economies in Africa: Implications for research and practice in human resource management," *International Human Resource Management Journal, 26*(1), pp. 2653–2675; J. P. Morrison, S. Kounkel, J. Pearce, M. Szuhaj and I. Gantcheva, 2013, "Emerging markets talent strategies," March 19, Westlake, TX: Deloitte University Press.

The Preview IB Emerging Market Strategic Insight portrays the environment facing any company with international operations. As the MNC hires workers in the different countries in which it operates, it faces significant challenges regarding human resource management practices. This is especially difficult in emerging markets. However, the human resource management function is an extremely critical aspect of a multinational's ability to successfully implement its strategy. Properly designed human resource management systems provide the company with the critical human resources to enable the company to create the necessary ability to compete successfully.

Why is cross-cultural human resource management so challenging? Countries have widely different human resources environments because of cultural and social institutional differences. To succeed in their operations, MNCs need to be able to understand these differences and the way they affect the human resource management practice. However, beyond differences, the international workforce environment is rapidly changing. Many multinationals are finding that it is difficult to attract and retain talented individuals. Whether a multinational is hiring a middle manager in China or an assembly-line worker in Central Europe or a software engineer in India, many companies are facing significant difficulties in finding such workers.[1] Even if they can hire such individuals, they find it very difficult to keep these workers for a long time. Human resource management is thus becoming an increasingly important aspect of a multinational's ability to succeed, and this chapter will inform you of the key issues for MNCs as they face these human resource management challenges in emerging markets.

This chapter contains several major sections. In the first section, we define international human resource management. You are then exposed to the many human resource management functions, namely recruitment, selection, training and development, compensation, and performance appraisal. These various human resource functions are discussed in the context of MNCs hiring workers in foreign locales. Labor relations and trade unions are also discussed as an important aspect of international human resource management. Throughout the chapter, you will be first exposed to a discussion of HRM functions within the US context. You will then read about contrasts with emerging markets. Implications of such differences will be discussed.

In a subsequent section, you are exposed to issues pertaining to expatriates. Most MNCs approach human resource management for expatriates differently compared to domestic workers. In this section, you will be presented with the unique human resource management challenges facing multinationals as they hire expatriates in many emerging markets.

After reading this chapter you should understand some of the key issues of human resource management as they are applied internationally with a focus on emerging markets. You should be able to understand the important human resource management functions and how they apply to workers for multinationals with foreign operations. You should also be able to appreciate the unique challenges facing companies when they hire expatriates. Finally, you should understand the future of expatriates in terms of growth of numbers of female expatriates.

International Human Resource Management: The International Setting

An MNC cannot function without people or the human assets. From a strategy perspective, human resources are extremely critical as they provide the multinational with the necessary skills and capabilities to outsmart rivals. Managing and developing the human assets are thus the major goals of human resource management. Human resource management (HRM) deals with the entire relationship of the employee with the organization. When applied to the international setting, the HRM functions become **international human resource management (IHRM)**. What do HR managers do? Consider the following IB Emerging Market Strategic Insight.

international human resource management (IHRM) application of the various human resource management functions in an international setting

Role of HR Managers

IB EMERGING MARKET
STRATEGIC INSIGHT

What roles do HR managers play? Traditional roles have been more short-term and operational in nature including being employee champions whereby the HR manager is engaged in the more typical HR activities geared towards hiring of employees and other people processes in the organization. Traditional roles have also included being administrative experts whereby the HR manager is in charge of operational activities such as the maintaining of employee programs and updates on personnel files.

The changes in the last few decades have demanded increasingly important roles of HR managers. The changing global business environment characterized by factors such as increased global competition, increased role of emerging markets, changing values of the workplace, etc. have meant that HR managers are being expected to play more important roles in companies. As such, these changes have resulted in more long-term/strategic roles such as being a strategic partner where HR strategies are aligned with business strategy. Another important new role has included the participation of HR managers in being a change agent managing people within organizations.

Are there differences between emerging markets and Western markets with regards to HR roles? An interesting study of HR professionals of companies in five countries (Australia, Canada, and USA, and emerging markets of Malaysia and the Philippines) provides some insights. As Exhibit 14.1 shows, all five countries had moderate to high scores on the more traditional roles of HR managers. On the five-point scale, all HR managers in these countries saw the employee champion and administrative expert roles as fairly critical. However, some differences emerged for the more long-term roles. In this case, Malaysia's HR managers did not see the strategic partnership and change agent roles as critical as in Canada and the USA. Furthermore, the Philippines also showed similar importance attached to the long-term roles. Surprisingly, Australia had lower scores than all other four countries for the other roles.

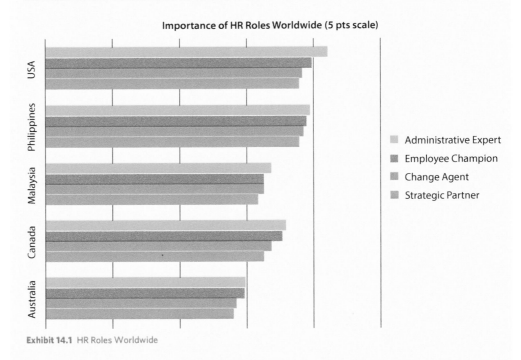

Importance of HR Roles Worldwide (5 pts scale)

Administrative Expert
Employee Champion
Change Agent
Strategic Partner

Exhibit 14.1 HR Roles Worldwide

Source: Based on M. C. Galang and I. Osman,, 2016, "HR managers in five countries: what do they do and why does it matter?" *International Journal of Human Resource Management, 27*(13), pp. 1341–1372.

What can we learn from the IB Emerging Market Strategic Insight? Although the study did not show systematic differences between Western and emerging markets, the researchers also examined the impact of the four roles on organizational performance. Results showed that the basic role of employee champion had an impact on organizational performance in all four countries. The study also showed the importance of the role of being a strategic partner in several areas.

Taken together, it shows that as companies continue to encounter new challenges, there will be expectations for companies to allow HR managers to play critical roles. Also, when a company enters the international arena, the human resource management function takes on added complexity due to cultural and institutional differences. It therefore becomes necessary for multinational managers to decide if or how to adapt the company's HRM policies to the national cultures, business cultures, and social institutions where the company is doing business. Furthermore, companies will also be challenged to have the HR managers play increasingly long-term/strategic roles. This chapter will provide the necessary background to examine these challenges and implement practices to address such challenges.

In the next few sections, we examine the basic HRM functions, including recruitment and selection, training and development, performance appraisal, compensation, and labor relations.

Recruitment and Selection

Recruitment refers to the process of identifying and attracting qualified people to apply for vacant positions in an organization. The recruitment stage usually begins with a company's assessment of its needs in terms of human resources. The company then decides how it will make potential applicants aware of the job vacancies. There are wide variations in preference for recruitment around the world. To appreciate these differences, you are first exposed to the various forms of recruitment.

For all types of positions, companies use a variety of methods to recruit. These include, among others, applications and advertisements placed in newspapers or on the Internet, internal job postings where companies post a list of vacancies on their websites or internally, use of private or public agencies, and use of recommendations from current employees. In fact, companies used to rely on newspaper advertising as a primary means to connect with potential new employees.[2] Prior research shows that US managers see newspaper advertising as one of the most effective recruitment channels, while university recruitment was judged among the most effective only for professional and technical jobs.[3] In contrast, other forms such as employee referral and use of personal contacts for recruitment purposes are not seen as very effective. Such methods can potentially run into legal issues and may not necessarily fulfill the typical US company's goal of finding the best person for the job.

Companies are also increasingly relying on social media for recruitment purposes. In the US, many companies rely on social media sites such as Facebook and Twitter for recruitment purposes.[4] An important factor behind the increased use of such sites is because potential employees are already sharing lots of personal information on social media. Use of such means of recruitment allows the employer to easily verify whether the information being provided is accurate. Additionally, use of social media tends to be very easily accessible to many without high costs.

While the above shows some of the preferred means of recruitment in the US, other parts of the world don't always prefer open forms of recruitment such as open advertisement in newspapers. Consider, for instance, that for many of the collectivist societies such as Japan, South Korea, and Taiwan, referrals from friends or family tend to be much more important. In South Korea, many blue-collar jobs are filled through referrals from friends and family. Such practices are not surprising as collectivist societies place emphasis on harmony and loyalty. By only recruiting from friends and family or other important social groups (e.g. high schools, universities, clubs), an MNC can maximize the chances of finding someone who can fit the organization's culture. Furthermore, friends and family referrals suggest that these individuals can vouch for the potential employees' work ethic and ability to fit.

To get additional insights on recruitment practices around the world, consider Exhibit 14.2.

For the Exhibit, data collected through the International Social Survey Program was analyzed.[5] Respondents who were looking for jobs were asked whether they asked their friends or relatives for jobs. As the Exhibit shows, countries such as the US, Denmark, and New Zealand tend to have more open recruitment and do not show preference for such methods. In contrast, many emerging markets (and former socialist countries) such as Poland, Bulgaria, and Russia show high scores, as the former communist system emphasized personal relationships

recruitment
refers to the process of identifying and attracting qualified people to apply for vacant positions in an organization

Asked Friends or Relatives

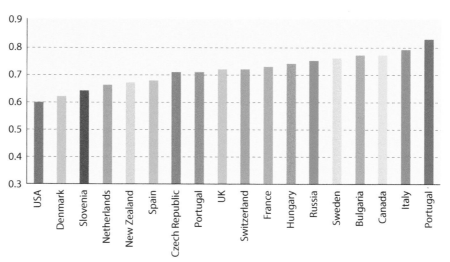

Exhibit 14.2 Recruitment Methods

Source: Based on International Social Survey Program, 1999/2000, International Social Survey Program: Work Orientations II, 1997, Ann Arbor: Inter-university Consortium for Political and Social Science Research.

and more closed forms of recruitment. People were more likely to get jobs based on contacts rather than openly competing for such jobs.

As multinationals continue to expand in such emerging markets, they will need to carefully assess local preferences for recruitment methods and implement the appropriate HRM strategies. To give you more insights into an important emerging market, consider the following BRIC Insight.

Recruitment Practices in Indian IT Companies

BRIC INSIGHT

A recent study was conducted among leading Indian IT companies to determine the preferred recruitment methods of these companies. As the IT sector has grown in India, competition for rare IT talent has intensified. Large multinationals from many other nations are also competing with these local companies. Understanding the modes of recruitment is therefore very critical.

To assess the preferred recruitment methods, HR managers in the leading IT companies in India (e.g., WIPRO, Infosys, etc.) were surveyed. They were asked about the use of seven critical recruitment channels. These include: (1) employee referral whereby existing employees recommend potential candidates for positions; (2) campus recruitment where the employer approaches universities to attract the attention of potential employees; (3) advertising referring to the more traditional forms of recruitment with postings in newspapers; (4) recruitment agencies involving some external agency conducting the recruitment service for the company; (5) job sites and portals representing websites and other online portals dedicated exclusively for recruitment purposes; (6) company websites—the company's own website portal available for recruitment purposes; and (7) social media use including Facebook, Twitter, LinkedIn, etc.

Exhibit 14.3 shows the percentages used by the leading IT companies. Not surprisingly, the traditional forms of recruitment such as newspaper advertisement and recruitment agencies are not as popular. Instead, results show the popularity of the new forms of recruitment such as job sites as well as social media. Furthermore, these results also show the importance of campus recruitment. The latter reflects the preference for local IT companies to work closely with universities and other educational institutions to identify and encourage talented individuals to apply for jobs. Global multinationals are also encouraged to adapt their recruitment practices to reflect such local Indian preferences in this sector.

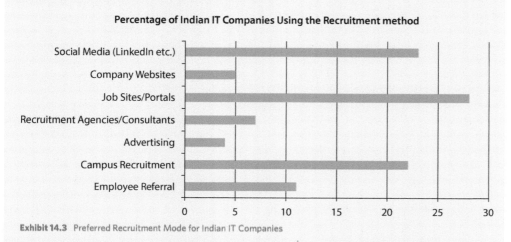

Percentage of Indian IT Companies Using the Recruitment method

Exhibit 14.3 Preferred Recruitment Mode for Indian IT Companies

Source: Based on V. Sinha and P. Thaly, 2013, "A review of changing trends of recruitment practice to enhance the quality of hiring in global organizations," *Management, 18*, pp. 141–156.

After an MNC has developed a list of potential candidates for a job, it has to select a person for the job. The process by which a company chooses a person to fill a vacant position is known as **selection**. Similar to recruitment, selection criteria vary widely around the world. Let's first look at selection in the context of US companies.

In the US, the aim of selection practices is to gather credible information on a candidate's job qualifications. Previous work experience, performance on tests, and perceptions of qualifications from interviews help inform human resource managers about the applicant's qualifications. The US individualistic culture promotes a focus on individual achievements (e.g. education, natural ability, experience) and not on group affiliations such as the family. The ideal selection then results in a match between the specific skills of the job applicant with the specific job requirements.

Similar to recruitment, selection is also affected by cultural practices. One of the most critical differences pertains to more collectivist countries. As Hofstede (1991) notes,

> the hiring process in a collectivist society always takes the in-group into account. Usually preference is given to hiring relatives, first of the employer, but also of other persons already employed by the company. Hiring persons from a family one already knows reduces risks. Also relatives will be concerned about the reputation of the family and help correct misbehavior of a family member.[6]

selection
the process by which a company chooses people to fill a vacant position

In selecting employees, collectivist cultural norms value trustworthiness, reliability, and loyalty over performance-related background characteristics. Personal traits such as loyalty to the company, loyalty to the boss, and trustworthiness are the traits that family members can provide. As such, in smaller companies, preference is given to family members.

However, larger and technically oriented companies may need professional managers and technicians with skills not available within the family. In these cases, the selection process still prioritizes personal characteristics over technical characteristics. If one cannot have a family member, then the priority is to find employees who have the personality characteristics and background necessary to fit into the corporate culture.

What can a multinational do to ensure smooth recruitment and selection on a worldwide basis? At a basic level, an MNC needs to understand and adapt to local practices. Thus, for example, foreign multinationals in the United States probably have most success using the typical US recruitment practices—advertising in newspapers and going to college campuses. In emerging markets, the multinational manager will also need to discover and use local recruitment and selection practices. As we saw earlier, the preference for Indian IT multinationals is to use social media.[7] However, adaptation to local recruitment and selection practices is difficult. In societies where backdoor or personal contacts are acceptable recruitment strategies, foreign multinationals may not have access to the appropriate recruitment channels. Furthermore, such recruitment methods may violate ethical codes that require competitive access to all open jobs. However, when a company does not follow local norms in recruitment and selection, it may offend local cultural norms or break host country laws. Thus, multinational managers must always assess the trade-off between following home practices that get what they believe are the "right" people for the job against the costs and benefits of following local traditions.

After the MNC has selected individuals for the job, it needs to train these employees. In the next section, we look at training and development.

Training and Development

training and development
refer to the efforts of the MNC to provide education and other programs to better equip their employees to do their job

Training and development refer to the efforts of the MNC to provide education and other programs to better equip its employees to do their job. Such training at work may involve formal training, informal training, learning embedded in the workplace, and other forms of learning.[8] With globalization, many countries are seeing an increased emphasis on training as their people are required to learn more than ever before to adapt to the new work environment. However, many multinationals are finding that appropriate training and development can be an asset as they try to retain workers. Furthermore, the ability to identify and train leadership talent is also becoming critical as multinationals face a shortage of talented executives. This is also becoming especially critical in emerging markets.[9] Consider the following IB Emerging Market Strategic Insight.

Role of Training in Emerging Markets

How critical is training in emerging markets? Two studies in different sectors in Ethiopia and Jordan reveal the importance of training. In the first study, researchers surveyed 333 employees of three public banks in Ethiopia and examined whether the HRM functions have effects on the employees' job satisfaction. The study included data on recruitment and selection, training and development as well as performance appraisal and compensation (discussed later). The results of the study showed that training and development, performance appraisal, and compensation have some of the strongest effects on employee satisfaction. However, most importantly, all HRM functions had positive effects on employee satisfaction.

A second study shifted the focus from employees to the firm-level. Researchers looked at the HRM practices of all 104 firms in the financial sector (banking, insurance, real estate, brokerage, and others) in Jordan. Jordan is an important emerging market and plays a critical role in the Middle East. The study examined whether the typical HRM practices such as recruitment and selection, training, performance appraisals, and internal career opportunity had any impact on firm performance. Unlike the previous study, results showed that only training had a positive effect on organizational performance. In fact, the researchers conducted a survey on perceived financial performance (respondents were asked to rate their performance relative to their rivals on selected indicators such as profitability, market share, etc.) and also collected data on actual performance indicators such as return on assets and return on equity. Results showed that training had a positive effect on both performance measures.

Source: Based on A. W. Ijigu, 2015, "The effect of selected human resource management practices on employees' job satisfaction in Ethiopian public banks," *Emerging Markets Journal*, 5(1), pp. 1–16; T. K. Darwish, S. Singh and G. Wood, 2015, "The impact of human resource practices on actual and perceived organizational performance in a middle eastern market," *Human Resource Management*, 55(2), pp. 261–281.

As you can see from the above IB Emerging Market Strategic Insight, training will become critically important in emerging markets. To do well, multinationals will need to first understand what is the preferred training mode in each country. In fact, similar to the other human resource management functions you read about, training and development also vary by country. You will first be exposed to the training and development programs in the US. In the late 90s, US companies with over 100 employees invested more than $60 billion in training costs per year.[10] However, a more recent study reveals that $164.2 billion was spent on learning and development by US companies.[11] Of that, around 11 percent of the expenditures went to tuition reimbursement as companies supported their employees getting external university or other training. Furthermore, around 61 percent went to internal expenses dedicated to training. The typical employee spent an average of 30.3 hours a year on training. The most popular training content was in managerial and supervisory training. Other forms of popular training included mandatory and other compliance training as well as process and procedures training. Additionally, the per employee amount spent on training has gone up steadily over the years in US companies. Exhibit 14.4 shows the progression of per-employee training over the years.

As you can see, expenditure on training has increased steadily over the years. However, similar to other HRM functions, training also depends on the country. How is training different around the world? An interesting study provides some insights on the matter.[12] The authors categorize countries on the types of institutional environments based somewhat on the institutions we discussed in Chapter 8. They argue that the emphasis on training is dependent

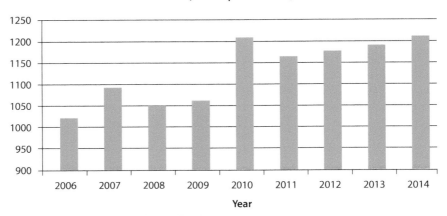

Exhibit 14.4 Per Employee Expenditure on Training
Source: Based on L. Miller, 2014, "2014 State of the Industry Report," *TD*, November, pp. 3–35.

on the institutional environment. In some environments, such as those found in Italy or Germany or Japan, companies find it difficult to hire or fire workers. Consequently, they have no choice but to focus on cultivating the existing workforce. As such, companies in these countries place a heavy emphasis on employee training.

In contrast, in countries such as the UK and the USA, there is emphasis on the short term and on efficiency. There is adversarial competition with employees and a focus on an efficient external labor market. It is therefore not surprising to see that such countries place relatively low emphasis on training and development. Finally, in other emerging markets found in Central and Eastern Europe, there is a focus on the need to control costs. Such cost control is often achieved by reducing the number of employees in companies that historically had too many employees. These countries also do not place much emphasis on training.

The above clearly shows that there are wide variations in terms of the importance of training around the world. However, the nature of training can also be different. For instance, consider the dual system, which is probably the most important component of vocational training in Germany. The dual system combines in-house apprenticeship training with part-time vocational-school training leading to a skilled-worker certificate. This training can be followed by the *Fachschule*, a college giving advanced vocational training. The training and certificate qualifications are standardized throughout the country. This produces a well-trained national labor force with skills that are not company-specific.

What are the implications for MNCs? The extent of training will depend on what the MNC expects of its workers. If employers want to keep local workers out of headquarters' managerial ranks, there is more emphasis on respecting local training norms. However, if the MNC wants to source local talent for its worldwide operations, training practices should follow the corporate culture. The extent of localization of the training practices also depends on the nature of the industry. A large number of companies realize the importance of training in many of the emerging countries around the world. In fact, as we mentioned earlier, there is tremendous competition for talented workers. Training is seen as one way that multinationals can attract and retain employees. Consider the following BRIC Insight below.

Training in China and India

Multinationals operating in China and India have slowly realized that training is an essential component of their ability to do well. Why is training so important? Training is important to impart the necessary skills to develop the employees. However, many multinationals are finding that training is crucial if they want to be able to attract and retain talent. Consider that the demand for top talent in China and Hong Kong is extremely high. It is not surprising for employees to receive phone calls from new employers with offers of double and even triple their current salary. However, companies in China also find that Chinese employees do not always place emphasis on compensation packages. Chinese nationals place very high value on training opportunities and those multinationals that provide such training to their employees are more likely to retain the talent. Such training needs will remain despite the economic slowdown.

India is also having similar experiences. Both local market multinationals and foreign multinationals are finding that training can be an important asset to organizational performance. Various practitioners have called for increased training in industries such as insurance and others. Some have also commented on the need of training at a national level. For instance, given that micro, small, and medium enterprises contribute to a significant percentage of Indias GDP, training for micro-entrepreneurs has been suggested. These entrepreneurs often lack basic management, knowledge, and entrepreneurial skills. Training in these areas would be very beneficial.

Source: Based on D. Breitenstein, 2005, "Developing skills for success in an MNC," *China Staff*, 11(10), pp. 10–11; J. Liapidova, 2015, "Growing talent in Hong Kong," *TD*, November, p. 16; D. Nag and N. Das, 2015, "Development of various training methods for enhancing the effectiveness and skill development among micro-enterprises in India," *Journal of Entrepreneurship Education*, 18(1), pp. 1–18; S. Singh, 2015, "The key to right selling," *Human Capital*, April, pp. 28–30.

It should also be noted that the training elements will depend on who is being trained. For instance, in the case of expatriates and other managerial-level workers, important culture training may need to be offered. Such issues are discussed in depth in Chapter 7 on culture. Furthermore, for a multinational to deploy a training program successfully, it needs to make sure that the training is consistent with local workplace customs and traditions. Consider Grace and Co.'s cultural gaffe when it was training employees in China. The Maryland-based specialty chemicals company had developed an "Eraser Man" concept to train its employees worldwide. The "Eraser Man" was used to emphasize the need to eradicate or "erase" costs.[13] However, Grace's trainers were surprised to see the Chinese trainees perplexed and even frustrated. After further investigation, they found that erasers in Chinese connote "invisible" rather than "erase." The Chinese trainees were not impressed with what was perceived as an "invisible" program. Also, Grace's "Eraser Man" was pink and the Chinese did not want to be associated with what is perceived to be a feminine color. Grace and Co. had to adapt its training program to fit Chinese local customs. Multinationals should generally strive to make such adjustments.

Training can also be provided for more social reasons. Consider the recent study of women bank managers in India.[14] In that study, the researchers examined the barriers to career advancement for women managers in state banks of India. Arguing that India remains a male-dominated society, the researchers suggest that Indian companies will benefit greatly by increasing leadership opportunities for women. They find that two of the greatest barriers to career advancement for women is lack of skills as well as performance in challenging assignments. Multinationals are therefore encouraged to increase training for women to increase their leadership potential while also addressing some of the career advancement barriers.

After the company has trained its employees, it also needs to assess its employees' performance. We discuss performance appraisal next.

Performance Appraisal

performance appraisal the process by which companies appraise their employees

The process by which companies appraise their employees is known as **performance appraisal**. All companies must assess their employees' performance to identify people to reward, promote, demote, develop and improve, retain, or fire. Not everyone can move up the ladder of the organizational pyramid and the performance appraisal function serves as an important assessment tool.

The US performance appraisal system is highly rational, logical, and legally oriented. It represents cultural values that include individual rights, duties, and rewards, and respect of the legal system, thereby promoting equal opportunity. Ideally, US appraisal systems provide management with objective, honest, and fair data on employee performance. Consequently, human resource decisions, such as pay or promotion, can be based on these performance appraisal data. Although issues regarding seniority, experience, and security are not ignored, the US ideal is a meritocracy, where good performers get more rewards.

Similar to the other human resource management functions, performance appraisal is also dependent on the culture. One of the dimensions that seems to impact performance appraisal is the collectivist cultural dimension. Recall that in collectivist societies, the group takes precedence over individuals and harmonious relationships are emphasized. As such, in more collectivistic cultures, both employer and employee accept as correct and fair that human resource decisions should take into account personal background characteristics more than achievement. In such cases, the usefulness of a US-style performance appraisal system is less clear because who you are and how old you are may count more than how you perform. Furthermore, according to Hofstede, managers in collectivist societies often avoid direct performance appraisal feedback.[15] An open discussion of performance may clash with the society's norm of harmony, which takes precedence over other values. For example, during the first eight to ten years of their careers, Japanese managers may never encounter the appraisal system. All beginning managers get the same salary and promotions, based on age and seniority.

In other collectivist societies, such as South Korea, there is preference for seniority-based promotions, rather than appraisal-based promotion.[16] This follows from the Confucian tradition that strives to preserve harmony (since it is unseemly for younger employees to supervise older ones). While job performance is important and most companies do have appraisal systems, seniority is most important for advancement. Because of the long-term orientation of Korean culture, Korean performance appraisal systems focus on sincerity, loyalty, and attitude on an equal footing with job performance.

As you can see, international performance appraisals can be very complex. Consider also that while the major objective of performance appraisal is to provide feedback, some societies may not engage in such practices. In emerging nations such as China and India, feedback is generally not given to save face.[17] To preserve harmony, appraisals may be done through group meetings rather than the more typical individual appraisals carried out in individualistic societies.

Despite the above concerns, performance appraisal is expected to play a more critical role in emerging markets in the future. Consider the following Emerging Market Ethical Challenge.

Performance Appraisal in Ghana

Performance appraisal plays a critical role in ensuring appropriate human resource management. Performance appraisal enables the multinational to determine how well the employee is doing to implement appropriate strategies to keep employees performing. However, despite the best intentions, performance appraisal systems may not work because systems are not implemented correctly. Furthermore, in some emerging markets, multinationals may avoid performance appraisals to prevent employees from losing face.

A recent study of performance appraisal in the Ghanaian civil service sector provides some insights into the challenges facing that sector. Despite the introduction of the system in the early 1990s, the study finds that the performance appraisal system has not resulted in increased employee performance. The authors identify a number of factors that have severely constrained the performance appraisal system's effectiveness. These include:

- Lack of expectations from the system—the effectiveness of any performance appraisal system is clear communications of the intent of the system. Unfortunately, this is not communicated to Ghanaian public sector employees. In fact, the process is used mostly for promotion rather than ongoing individual development. Employees therefore do not take the process seriously.
- Lack of objectivity—another critical challenge noted by those interviewed suggests that the performance appraisal is not conducted objectively. Most appraisees get positive reviews and almost everyone expects good ratings. This thus limits the usefulness of the system.
- Lack of incentives in the appraisal system—performance appraisal can have motivating effects on employees if it includes appropriate incentives. Unfortunately, the performance appraisal system in the Ghanaian civil service has no clear links between strong performance appraisal and desirable outcomes. If one gets an excellent appraisal, there are no rewards associated with strong ratings.
- Self-ratings—most performance appraisals were completed by the individual rather than by his/her supervisor. They were therefore more likely to be lenient in their ratings. This, coupled with the fact that most employees get high ratings, means that the information garnered from the performance appraisal is severely limited.
- Lack of managerial interest in the process—a performance appraisal system is effective if the supervisors and other raters have positive attitudes about the system. In Ghana, most supervisors did not put much faith in the process. This also therefore severely limited the ability of the process to help individuals develop.

Source: Based on F. K. Ohemeng, H. B. Zakari and A. Adusha-Karikari, 2015, "Performance appraisal and its use for individual and organisational improvement in the civil service of Ghana: The case of much ado about nothing?" *Public Administration and Development*, 35, pp. 179–191.

Although the above pertains to the civil service in the emerging market of Ghana, multinationals need to still ensure the many factors that contributed to the downfall of the system do not occur. For example, the aims of the performance appraisal system need to be clearly communicated to employees and ratings done objectively. Employees also need to see the connection between high ratings and some form of rewards. Finally, supervisors also need to see the value of what they are doing.

In addition to the above recommendations, a recent study of Indian banks reveals characteristics of performance appraisal systems that are seen as effective in another emerging market. The study examined the perception of the fairness of the performance appraisal system on job satisfaction.[18] The researchers found that if employees perceived the performance appraisal system to be fair, they were more likely to be satisfied with their jobs. This underscores the need for multinational managers to design fair performance appraisal systems. The expectations and feedback of the performance appraisal system need to be clearly communicated to employees. Employees should also be made aware of the decision process behind the appraisal process. Finally, it is also strongly recommended that employees have a chance to appeal appraisal decisions. Such measures are likely to result in a system that is perceived as being fair.

Additionally, as you saw with recruitment and selection, an MNC must often match its performance appraisal system to fit the local culture. Failure to do so may result in unnecessary conflict with local workers. Next, let's consider compensation.

Compensation

compensation
efforts of the multinational to distribute wages and salaries, incentives such as bonuses, and benefits such as retirement contributions

Compensation includes the efforts of the multinational to distribute wages and salaries, incentives such as bonuses, and benefits such as retirement contributions. Compensation is also a critical aspect of the types of HRM policies companies use to motivate their employees. This is even more pronounced in emerging markets. Consider the following IB Emerging Market Strategic Insight.

Compensation in Emerging Markets

IB EMERGING MARKET STRATEGIC INSIGHT

Despite economic slowdown for many emerging markets, demand for talented individuals stays high. As multinationals increasingly look to emerging markets as sources of product innovation and development rather than mere cost control, competition for high level jobs is heating up. As a consequence, both emerging market multinationals and foreign multinationals are finding ways to attract and retain talented employees.

Compensation plays a big role in attracting such talented individuals. In fact, recent studies suggest that while Western Europe and US economies have seen some of the world's lowest salary increases averaging 3 percent, emerging markets have seen averages double those of Western Europe. Compensation is therefore a critical aspect of any effective HRM system.

In addition to compensation represented by pay and salaries, multinationals are also grappling with an increased focus on other benefits and perks. In China, for instance, benefits represented by work–life balance as well as timing of paycheck disbursement are important. In Mexico, employees prefer getting paid through direct-deposit debit card accounts. In other emerging markets, having access to high quality food and the latest technologies such as mobile phones and computers is proving to be effective. The challenge for the multinational is to therefore find the right benefits to attract and retain talent.

Source: Based on A. Bailey, 2016, "Emerging markets—has HR got it right?" Chapman CG Newsletters, http://chapmancg.com/news/thought-leadership/2015/03/emerging-markets-has-hr-got-it-right; J. P. Morrison, S. Kounkel, J. Pearce, M. Szuhaj and I. Gantcheva, 2013, "Emerging markets talent strategies," March 19, Westlake, TX: Deloitte University Press.

Hence, as can be seen, compensation is an especially critical HR function given the intense competition facing multinationals in emerging markets. Understanding how to properly compensate is important. Furthermore, there are wide variations both among countries and among organizations within countries concerning how to compensate workers. Some differences stem from whether compensation should be based on achievement or performance. Other important differences include whether everyone in a team should be paid the same or whether compensation should be based on individual performance. Below we consider the US compensation practices and consider compensation around the world.

The highly mobile US labor market requires that US companies design compensation systems that focus on external equity (i.e. Do we pay at or above market level?). The individualistic US culture views careers as private and personal, and mobility, advancement, and higher wages often require leaving a company. As such, most US companies develop formal and systematic policies to determine wages and salaries taking into consideration external and internal factors. External factors include local and national wage rates, government legislation, and collective bargaining. Internal factors include the importance of the job to the organization, the affluence of the organization or its ability to pay, and the employee's relative worth to the business (merit).

Most US companies also develop procedures to establish that people receive equitable pay for the types of jobs they perform. A variety of methods help establish a grading of jobs based on the worth to the company. Issues such as responsibility, skill requirements, and the importance of the job's tasks to the organization contribute to the worth of a particular job. Those who occupy the higher-ranked jobs are paid higher. Furthermore, although the worth of a job to the company largely determines the base pay assigned to a certain position, raises in pay are determined mostly by merit.

Compensation practices clearly vary around the world. Previous studies report that the cultural dimensions reported in the earlier chapter on culture can help MNCs design appropriate compensation systems. For instance, recall that uncertainty avoidance refers to the level of tolerance individuals living in a society have for uncertainty. It is therefore sensible to minimize uncertainty in high uncertainty avoidance countries by minimizing variable pay. As such, emerging markets in Latin American and Germanic countries (i.e. Austria, Germany) are more likely to favor fixed pay plans because multinationals want to minimize uncertainty.[19]

Another important cultural dimension that impacts compensation is the individualism–collectivism cultural dimension. Recall in the chapter on culture that in individualistic societies like the US, individuals are only loosely connected to each other. In contrast, in highly collectivistic societies, people tend to be more tightly connected to each other and there is focus on harmony. Given the above, it is advisable for multinationals to apply equity principles (compensate according to performance) in more individualistic societies. In contrast, equality or parity principles (compensate everyone equally) seem to be more sensible for collectivistic countries. In such countries, there is more emphasis on harmony and cohesion, and compensating all employees equally minimizes the risk of conflict.

Few studies have considered compensation practices around the world. The Best International Human Resource Management Practices Project represents one of the most extensive cross-national studies of compensation practices to date.[20] The researchers investigated cross-national variations in compensation practices in several countries (Australia, Canada, China, Indonesia, Japan, South Korea, Mexico, Taiwan, and USA). Respondents were asked a number of questions pertaining to these compensation practices, both in terms of their assessment of the current state of practice and also the extent to which they felt that these practices should be used in the future.

The study showed, for instance, that pay incentives tend to be used relatively modestly in the selected countries. Only China, Japan, and Taiwan had scores above the mean. Furthermore, only one country, South Korea, showed that pay incentives were a significant proportion of total pay. In most other societies, incentives are not as widely used. However, the results also showed some convergence. For instance, it was shown that all countries felt that benefits were an important aspect of any compensation package. Furthermore, all countries felt that compensation should be based more on job performance and other organizational outcomes than on seniority.

A more recent study reveals what job hunters are looking for in jobs. Manpower, the Milwaukee-based staffing giant, surveyed 4,500 job seekers from the leading employment markets, namely Australia, China, Mexico, United Kingdom, and USA. Exhibit 14.5 shows what employees were looking for in the various markets.

As Exhibit 14.5 shows, individuals from the emerging markets of China and Mexico were more likely to use the level of compensation as the most important factor in making career decisions. In fact, 81 percent of the Chinese surveyed valued the level of compensation above the other factors considered. Additionally, both emerging markets respondents also emphasized the benefits offered above the other factors. This is in sharp contrast with the other countries studied where the type of work offered was much more critical.

Given the above, how should a company approach compensation? An MNC with locations in several nations may need several different compensation systems, especially for host country nationals. For each host country, worker compensation levels must match wage levels in the local labor market. Compensation must also meet local minimum-wage rates. Country-level

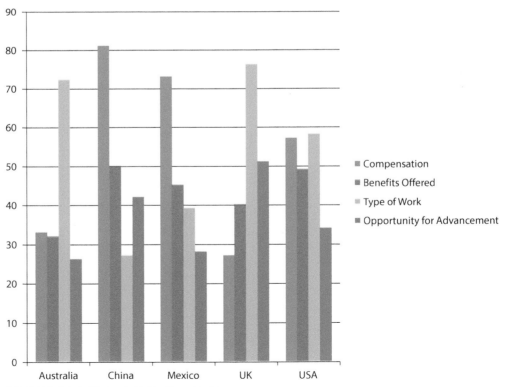

Exhibit 14.5 Selected Factors in Making Career Decisions
Source: Based on Manpower Group, www.manpower.com

comparative compensation data are available from many government, private, and international sources. Information on compensation laws is usually available from host country governments. Furthermore, the studies reviewed in this section show that compensation will remain extremely critical in emerging markets. Multinationals will therefore need to be very strategic about the compensation offered in these markets.

Next, we consider labor relations.

Labor Relations

MNCs often have to take into consideration the labor relations in the various countries where they operate in order to effectively manage human assets. **Labor relations** provide an indication of the relationship between companies and their employees and the degree to which employees influence the company's operations. There are wide variations in the patterns of labor relations in different nations. These differences in patterns stem from cultural factors as well as historical factors. Historical factors, such as the state of technological development during early unionization and the time when governments recognized the legality of unions, influence current union structure and activities. Management's views of labor relations also differ from country to country.

In the US, most unions remain at the regional level. Most local unions associate with some craft, industry, or mixed national union. There are approximately 170 national unions in the United States. Local craft unions tend to represent workers in a local region, while local industrial unions tend to represent workers at the level of the plant. Although most collective bargaining takes place at the local level, in some instances, such as in the automobile industry, unions attempt to make company-wide or industry-wide agreements. However, the US has seen declining union membership. As trade globalizes, local unions are slowly losing their power on workers. Also, management has typically had an upper hand on what unions can do.

In Germany, labor unions are more powerful and have an important influence on what companies do. At the company level, industrial democracy in Germany gives many workers equal representation on the board of directors with those elected by the shareholders. In fact, co-determination, or, in German, *Mitbestimmung*, means that management provides workers with a share of the control of the organization reserved traditionally for management and owners in the US. In Germany, co-determination exists at two levels. At the plant level, workers elect the works council. This group has certain prerogatives supported by law. Some decisions are shared with management, such as selection criteria. Some management decisions can be vetoed, such as reassignment. Finally, management must consult and inform the works council on other decisions, such as accident protection.

How can labor relations affect a multinational's operations? Consider the following IB Emerging Market Strategic Insight.

labor relations provide an indication of the relationship between companies and their employees and the degree to which employees influence the company's operations

South Korea and Labor Relations

South Korea has had a long history of labor unrest and strikes. For a long time, the South Korean government has accepted that strikes are an acceptable ritual of the South Korean business environment. Workers typically strike during the summer and end up with significant raises. Furthermore, many companies have routinely paid the salary of union leaders and authorities have been reluctant to use police force to break strikes. Labor unions in Korea thus have significant political influence. Past and more recent events show that South Korean workers are willing to continue to strike in order to get higher wages and better working conditions.

However, as trade globalizes and competition increases, South Korean companies are starting to find that they can no longer afford to pay higher wages. Frequent disruptions because of strikes have also taken a toll on companies. Consider the case of Hyundai Motors, which has had some form of labor disturbance every year for a significant period of time. In 2006, Hyundai Motors faced a month-long strike, resulting in work slowdown and losses amounting to $1.3 billion. Furthermore, in 2012, rotation of night shift workers was abolished while incentives and wages were increased. These changes were brought about because the bargaining power of labor unions affected Hyundai's operating flexibility. Similarly, steelmaker Posco had to cave in to its workers' demands of higher wages to end a nine-day strike. For the Korean auto industry, such strikes have resulted in significant decreases in exports and losses.

Recent research suggests that South Korean multinationals pay a price for dealing with labor unions. Using data from non-financial firms from the South Korean stock exchange, the study finds that if firms were involved in more unionized industries, their cost of capital was higher. In other words, because of strong labor unions, firms are limited in terms of their ability to restructure operations and even close factories. This lack of operational flexibility means that such firms have to face higher costs of capital.

As such, it is undeniable that South Korean firms face challenges because of the bargaining power of labor unions. To face the strong unions, many South Korean companies are slowly setting up operations in countries with lower wages and more favorable labor relations. For instance, Mando, a Korean car-parts company, now has a factory in Alabama. Mando also has operations in India, China, and Russia. Both Posco and Hyundai either have planned or are planning major operations in India. Samsung also has many plants in China.

Will such movement to other countries lessen the influence of labor unions in South Korea? Many experts argue that continued strikes and wage increases are putting South Korean multinationals at a disadvantage. These experts believe that such changes are inevitable and necessary as such labor unrest continues to present the South Korean economy with a weak spot.

Source: Based on Choe Sang-Hun, 2006, "2 Hyundai companies deal far differently with labor," *New York Times*, July 27, p. C4; I. G. Choi, P. Sohn and J.-Y. Seo, 2015, "The relationship between labor unions' bargaining power and firms' operating flexibility: New evidence from emerging markets," *South African Journal of Business Management*, 46(4), pp. 65–75; Henry Sender, 2006, "South Korea experiences growing pains as its workers strike for bigger slice of prosperity," *Wall Street Journal*, August 14, p. A2.

union membership density
refers to the proportion of workers who belong to unions in a country

Clearly the above shows that labor relations can have significant impact on multinationals. How can a multinational manager assess the extent of labor influence? A strong factor that indicates the degree of labor influence is the **union membership density**. Union membership density refers to the proportion of workers who belong to unions in a country. Exhibit 14.6 shows the union density in selected countries.

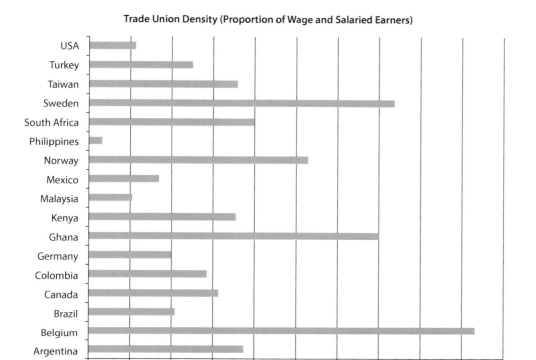

Exhibit 14.6 Union Density for Selected Countries
Source: Adapted from International Labor Organization, 2016, www.ilo.org

As you can see, union membership levels vary around the world. In some societies, such as the Philippines and the USA, union membership levels are relatively low, thereby suggesting minimal influence of labor unions on the multinational's operations. However, it is interesting to note that some emerging markets have high union density rates. For example, the nations of Argentina, Ghana, and South Africa all have high rates. Although these countries have opened themselves to foreign investment, labor still has important influences on company operations. Other countries such as Brazil and Mexico also show the significant influence labor has on company operations. However, emerging markets do not always have high rates. Consider that both Malaysia and the Philippines have relatively low union density rates. In many European countries such as Belgium, Denmark, Sweden, and Norway, the union density levels are high.

Despite the high union membership density in some societies, recent trends suggest that labor unions and their ability to negotiate higher wages are weakening.[21] As the world economy globalizes and there is declining local support for labor unions, more workers are being pressured to accept local wages. The increased emphasis on technological innovation and the willingness of multinationals to start operations in other locations are also decreasing union influence.

Although the influence of labor unions is diminishing, MNCs have no choice but to adapt to local labor practices and traditions when they hire local workers. However, in addition to adapting to local labor laws, multinationals also find other ways to deal with the power of local labor unions. Consider the following BRIC Insight.

In this section, you were exposed to the unique human resource management issues facing any MNC as it tries to hire local workers. However, the multinational also needs to deal with the human resource management issues of those managers who are sent abroad to manage foreign subsidiaries. We therefore consider the unique human resource management issues pertaining to expatriates next.

Dealing With Labor Unions

Most current research on how multinationals deal with labor unions in foreign countries has focused on multinationals from developed nations. However, as more emerging market multinationals expand in other countries, understanding how they deal with local labor unions can provide insights on how to manage labor relations in other countries.

A recent in-depth analysis of Chinese multinationals reveals some strategic insights regarding how to deal with labor unions. An important aspect of appropriately dealing with labor unions is to appreciate the importance of labor unions locally. As such, those multinationals that operated in regions where labor unions were legitimate and powerful made sure to recognize the local unions and to find ways to work with them. The Chinese multinationals wanted to make sure to respect local laws and they therefore respected local trade unions.

However, in some cases where the labor unions were perceived as being too powerful, the Chinese multinationals included in the study would try to find ways to work around such power. For instance, one of the Chinese multinationals in the study avoided collective representation in its India operations by subcontracting the hiring of workers from one of the local hire companies.

Finally, the study also showed that multinationals can use the learning from one market and adapt such lessons to other markets. One of the Chinese multinationals studied applied lessons it learned from operations in the Zambian subsidiary to its new operations in Myanmar. Such application of learned lessons allowed the multinational to start operations smoothly in the new location.

Source: Based on J. S. Zhu, 2015, "Chinese multinational corporations' responses to host country trade unions: An eclectic approach," *Journal of Industrial Relations, 57*(2), pp. 232–249.

Expatriates

expatriate employees employees who come from a different country than where they are working

home country nationals expatriate employees who come from the parent firm's home country

third country nationals expatriates who come from neither the host nor home countries

host country nationals local workers who are hired in the host country where the unit (plant, sales unit, etc.) is located

An MNC's human resource policies must take into account several types of employees in the multinational organization. In the previous section, you learned about human resource practices as an MNC hires workers. However, the MNC may also rely on **expatriate employees,** who may come from a different country from the one where they are working. Expatriates typically belong to the managerial and professional staff rather than to the lower-level workforce and thus present the multinational with unique challenges.

In this section, you will learn about human resource management issues pertaining to expatriates. Expatriates can actually be of different types. Some expatriate employees who come from the parent firm's home country are called **home country nationals.** Others who come from neither the host nor home countries are called **third country nationals.** Finally, local workers may also be hired in the host country where the unit (plant, sales unit, etc.) is located. These workers are known as **host country nationals.**

A basic dilemma facing the MNC pertains to whether it wants to hire host country or home country nationals. Each approach has advantages and disadvantages and is dependent on the multinational's strategy. Hiring host country managers can be advantageous because it offers the multinational the ability to hire someone who has a better understanding of the local cultural and institutional environment. Such knowledge can be valuable to the MNC as it tries to navigate a foreign environment. Host country nationals are usually better able to develop a closer relationship with other local managers and workers and hence identify with the local subsidiary.

However, the host country manager presents the MNC with a big challenge: How can a local person identify and personify with the corporate culture of the company's headquarters?

Because of many multinationals' desire to hire someone who is familiar with the headquarters' corporate culture, many MNCs send home country nationals on expatriate assignments. Despite many multinationals' intentions to use local employees, expatriates will become even more critical in the future. It is now estimated that there are around 8.5 million corporate executives worldwide. And, although the traditional expatriate tended to be senior white male managers in their 40s or 50s, current expatriates tend to reflect the increased diversity of the workplace. Current expatriates tend to be younger (in their 30s), reflecting technical expertise. Furthermore, these individuals can also be women, single women with children, unmarried couples, and even same-sex partnerships.[22] All of these factors contribute to many new challenges that multinationals have to contend with.

Cost of Expatriates

To entice employees to take international assignments as expatriates, the appropriate incentives have to be provided. Often, expatriates are middle- or upper-level management who have to be encouraged to take international assignments. They may be reluctant because they do not want to remove their children from school or may not want to sacrifice their partner's career.[23] As a result, the MNC has to provide significant incentives to encourage its workers to take such assignments and expatriates can be very costly. For instance, total compensation of expatriate managers can often be more than three to four times that of home-based salaries and benefits. As you will see later, as more companies compete, compensation for expatriates is becoming an important source to retain such expatriates.

As you see, expatriates can be very costly in terms of compensation. However, expatriates also incur additional costs that can significantly add to the expatriate cost. For instance, some multinationals provide company cars with chauffeur, country club memberships, paid vacation airfare to the home country, and even a generous expense budget. Another critical cost aspect is the cost of living in a new city. For instance, sending someone to Moscow, Seoul, or Tokyo may entail dramatically higher costs of living than sending someone to Toronto or Prague. Other locations can also add cost of guaranteeing the safety of the expatriate. Consider the following Emerging Market Ethical Challenge.

Expatriates in Terrorism-endangered Countries

EMERGING MARKET
ETHICAL CHALLENGE

As more developed markets become saturated, many multinationals are increasingly looking to focus on emerging markets. These markets tend to often be expanding and more profitable. However, being involved in foreign markets undeniably involves risk. As you saw in Chapter 8, multinationals face political risk as they operate in new markets. Such political risk pertains to all social, political, and economic factors that affect global operations in these countries. One of the most severe of such risks is the potential of violent conflicts and terrorism.

Recent research suggests that there were 10,000 terrorist attacks affecting more than 45,000 victims in over 70 countries. Furthermore, over 75 percent of these attacks occurred in the Middle East and South Asian regions. As more multinationals expand their operations in such regions (e.g., Pakistan, Afghanistan, Saudi Arabia, and Bangladesh), they are exposing their expatriates to such terrorism risks.

Although there is a very small probability that an expatriate will get directly hurt by terrorist attacks, assignments in areas prone to terrorist attacks can still have harmful consequences for the expatriate. Expatriates in areas prone to terrorist attacks can suffer from post-traumatic stress, anxiety, and feelings of insecurity. These issues are further magnified if the expatriate is in a country with his or her family. The expatriate may eventually decide to end the assignment early or may decide to stay but perform poorly.

The consequences of the above can be very costly for multinationals. While you will see that the failure rate for expatriates is typically in the 25 to 40 percent range, it may be around 70 percent for expatriates in terrorism-prone areas. An expatriate leaving an assignment early may jeopardize the entire overseas investment. Additionally, given that expatriates cost around two to ten times a local hire, such expatriates can end up being a significant cost for the multinational.

Source: Based on B. Bader, N. Berg and D. Holtbrugge, 2015, "Expatriate performance in terrorism-endangered countries: The role of family and organizational support," *International Business Review, 24*, pp. 849–860; B. Bader and T. Schuster, 2015, "Expatriate social networks in terrorism-endangered countries: An empirical analysis in Afghanistan, India, Pakistan, and Saudi Arabia," *Journal of International Management, 21*, pp. 63–77; Y. McNulty and K. Hutchings, 2016, "Looking for global talent in all the right places: A critical literature review of non-traditional expatriates," *International Journal of Human Resource Management, 27*(7), pp. 677–728.

Hence, as you can see, operations in terrorism-endangered emerging markets can be very costly. As a starting point, the compensation packages of expatriates are thus dependent on the cost of living in the particular country to which the expatriate is sent. Many multinationals use Mercer Human Resources Consulting's cost-of-living index to determine how much they will pay their expatriates. The index is a measure of the cost of living of American employees assigned to a foreign country. To compute the cost-of-living index, Mercer prices the cost of a two-bedroom unfurnished apartment, a cup of coffee, a fast-food meal, and an international paper. To give you an idea of the relative costs of living in different cities, Exhibit 14.7 shows data on the cost-of-living index in the top sixteen most expensive cities in the Top 50 Cities list compiled by Mercer.

City	Ranking	City	Ranking
Luanda, Angola	1	Tokyo, Japan	11
Hong Kong	2	London, UK	12
Zurich, Switzerland	3	Kinshasa, Congo	13
Singapore, Singapore	4	Shenzhen, China	14
Geneva, Switzerland	5	Guangzhou, China	15
Shanghai, China	6	New York City, USA	16
Beijing, China	7	Victoria, Seychelles	17
Seoul, South Korea	8	Tel Aviv, Israel	18
Bern, Switzerland	9	Buenos Aires, Argentina	19
N'Djamena, Chad	10	Lagos, Nigeria	20

Exhibit 14.7 Cost-of-living Indexes for Selected Cities
Source: Based on Mercer Consulting, www.mercer.com.

As Exhibit 14.7 shows, many of the most expensive cities in the latest survey are found in emerging markets. For instance, the most expensive city is in the African nation of Angola. Mercer reports that although it is an inexpensive city to live in, imported goods and cost of safety makes it one of the most expensive cities in the world. Additionally, many Chinese cities are also in the top 20 most expensive cities. Such data reflect the importance of Chinese cities' contributions to emerging market growth.

As you can see, expatriates can be very costly for multinationals. Furthermore, the expatriate failure rate is very high. Next, we consider some of the reasons for failure.

Expatriate Failure

Across industries, a very large portion of expatriates fail. **Expatriate failure** occurs when the expatriate decides to return to his or her home country before the international assignment is over, failing to meet the expectations of the MNC. Current research points that failure rates are very high, at around 16–70 percent expatriates actually failing, depending on the host country.[24]

Expatriate failure can be extremely costly for companies. Prior estimates suggest that each expatriate failure can cost a multinational around $1 million.[25] Collectively, expatriate failure costs US multinationals over $2 billion per year. Other recent estimates suggest that expatriate failures can cost up to 10 times a local hire.[26] Expatriate failure also results in indirect costs for companies. Such departure may result in loss of opportunities in and knowledge of the foreign markets. Other indirect costs can include loss of market share and damaged relationships with clients and local government officials.

Given such a high failure rate, it is critical to understand why expatriates fail. Reasons for failure can include personal reasons such as inadequate adaptation to the new culture, lack of technical skills to perform the job, or lack of motivation for the new assignment. However, family reasons can also play a prominent role in failure. Sometimes, the family has difficulties adapting to the new culture, or maybe the partner or spouse fails to adapt. In addition, organizational reasons such as a lack of preparation for the international assignment or giving the expatriate an extremely difficult assignment may also account for failure.[27]

As you saw earlier, being assigned in terrorism-endangered countries can add another layer of factors that can contribute to failure. As such, in addition to the many factors discussed previously, expatriates also have to be concerned about safety. Such safety concerns can add a level of stress that may eventually result in disaffection with host country nationals.[28] This stress can also result in poor performance and failure.

An important aspect of the failure to adapt is **culture shock**, which refers to the anxiety or stress that is caused by being in a new and foreign environment and the absence of the familiar signs and symbols of the home country. Culture shock can also cause failure because the expatriate may find the new environment too overwhelming. The added stress and anxiety caused by culture shock may result in poorer performance and less self-worth, thus lessening the expatriate's ability to adapt.

As you can see, because expatriates can be so costly, multinationals need to take every measure to minimize failure. In the next section, you will learn about what can be done to ensure expatriate success.

Ensuring Expatriate Success

What can MNCs do to ensure expatriate success? Recall some of the human resource management functions you read in the earlier parts of this chapter. The MNC needs to ensure that the various functions are applied to the unique situation presented by an expatriate. In this section, the emphasis is on selection and recruitment, which is arguably one of the most critical steps.

expatriate failure occurs when the expatriate decides to return to his or her home country before the international assignment is over

culture shock refers to the anxiety or stress that is caused by being in a new and foreign environment

cultural intelligence
refers to the capacity to adapt and function in a culturally diverse environment

Because expatriate success is so dependent on choosing the right person for the position, the recruitment and selection process is extremely important.[29] While it is obviously critical for the expatriate to have the appropriate technical skills and knowledge to perform the task, possessing such technical skills may not be sufficient if the person does not have the right traits for the job. As such, it is important for the multinational to assess whether the person has **cultural intelligence**, which refers to the ability of the expatriate to adapt well in the new culture and to function well in the new setting. Adaptability relates to an individual's ability to learn from experience and to use new experiences to improve. Prior research suggests that cultural intelligence results in a number of important benefits including the expatriate's ability to sense difference in cultures and to persist to face unfamiliar situations in order to succeed.[30]

emotional intelligence
refers to the ability of being aware of oneself, understanding and relating to others, and being empathetic and managing one's emotions

In addition to cultural intelligence, recent research suggests that expatriates need to have high emotional intelligence. **Emotional intelligence** refers to being aware of oneself, understanding and relating to others, and being empathetic and managing one's emotions. Emotional intelligence is seen as a critical factor in determining how an expatriate can adapt to the new environment. Expatriates who have high emotional intelligence are more likely to relate well with other local managers and can also use emotions to better deal with the situation. A summary of the relevant aspects of both cultural intelligence and emotional intelligence is provided in Exhibit 14.8.

In addition to the qualities in Exhibit 14.8, it is crucial for the MNC to assess the family situation of the expatriate. Research shows that many expatriates fail because the needs of the accompanying family are not taken into consideration. In some cases, the spouse fails to adapt because he or she may feel lonely. While the expatriate has access to a social network through work, spouses are often left with chores such as finding schools for children and can feel alienated. It is therefore important to include the spouse and other family members in the selection process.

Though selection and recruitment are critical steps in ensuring expatriate success, training can also be a major contributor. Training should start even before the expatriate leaves. Many of the cross-cultural training methods you read in Chapter 7 should be followed. The expatriate needs to be given pre-departure training whereby important information necessary upon arrival is provided.[31] Expatriates can also be provided with skills to facilitate adaptation to the new culture. Furthermore, it may also be necessary to train the expatriate in the appropriate language skills. Some knowledge of the host language will enhance the expatriate's ability to communicate with locals and to succeed in the international assignment.[32]

- *Open-mindedness* The expatriate needs to be open-minded about issues and to be receptive to new ideas.
- *Tolerance for difference* The expatriate should have the ability to accept people who are different.
- *Curiosity* The expatriate should be continuously willing to explore.
- *Tolerance for ambiguity* The expatriate should be comfortable with uncertain and new situations.
- *Excellent social skills* The expatriate should be able to relate well to others.
- *Excellent communication skills* The expatriate should be able to communicate well and easily with others.
- *Flexibility* The expatriate should be able to explore new ways of doing things or change the way things are done.
- *Empathy* The expatriate should be able to put himself/herself in others' situations to identify with them.
- *Sensitivity* The expatriate should be able have a high degree of awareness of the local culture and the ability to be sensitive to such local culture.
- *Adaptation* The expatriate should have the capacity to adapt to the new culture and function smoothly in the new environment.

Exhibit 14.8 Components of Cultural and Emotional Intelligence

Source: Based on B. Avril Alizee and Vincent P. Magnini, 2007, "A holistic approach to expatriate success," *International Journal of Contemporary Hospitality Management*, 19(1), pp. 53–64; R. Krishnaveni and R. Arthi, 2015, "An overview of multidimensional factors influencing effective performance of expatriates," *Management*, 20(2), pp. 135–147.

Once the expatriate is in the host country, it is strongly advisable for the MNC to continue the cross-cultural training. In addition, training from locals or other mentors about operating in the host country can be very helpful. Many companies now have mentorship or buddy programs where new expatriates are paired with other expatriates in the host country. They can thus get access to new social networks and learn about potential difficulties relatively quickly.

Many experts also believe that it is important that some training may also be necessary for the family. Offering cultural and other language-training programs may help the family better integrate into the new culture. In fact, the family can also be provided with pre-departure training similar to what is offered to the spouse.[33] Basic transmission of information regarding the customs and norms of the host country is as necessary as other more practical information such as schools or housing details. Companies can also provide some form of career planning for the spouse to ensure that the spouse can easily pursue a career in the new country.

Another component of success is the provision of various forms of organizational support. For instance, by providing training programs, the MNC can show its commitment to help the expatriate succeed. It is also important for the MNC to keep communication gateways open. For instance, the expatriate should be given the opportunity to stay in touch with colleagues and others at home. Such open communication will show that the headquarters care about the foreign operations and how well the expatriate is doing.

Another crucial aspect of expatriate success is compensation. The MNC needs to provide the necessary incentives to motivate the expatriate to succeed. Components of the compensation plan can include premium allowances for accepting postings in international locations, hardship allowances for postings in dangerous locations, relocation and home allowances to provide for the cost implications of moving. Many MNCs are also providing other supplementary benefits such as medical coverage and pensions. Taxes are also a key issue in compensation packages, as expatriates may sometimes face taxation in both the host and home countries.

A final aspect of expatriate success is dealing with repatriation. Expatriates typically face the **repatriation problem**, representing the difficulties that managers face in coming back to their home countries and reconnecting with their old job. Furthermore, expatriates may also experience **reverse culture shock**, where on returning they experience significant challenges in reintegrating their domestic environment. For example, returning expatriates can experience significant stress related to their children facing new expectations at school. Also, they may need to navigate a new social environment where they have to make new friends. Finally, the returning expatriate may also face significant challenges on encountering a new work environment.[34]

These repatriation difficulties can be solved with proper preparation and planning by the expatriate and the company. For instance, the MNC can provide some training for the return. After being gone for a few years, things may have changed at home and it is crucial for the expatriate to be prepared to come back. Often, an important component of such training is to manage the returning expatriate's expectations. Returning expatriates generally expect to be rewarded with a promotion and an environment where their international skills can be utilized. A multinational would be well advised to provide an environment where such expectations can be met. If such expectations are not met, it is very likely that the expatriate may leave the organization upon return.

A survey of the practical literature suggests that the repatriation process needs to be managed.[35] In a study of expatriates returning to New Zealand, the most frustrating part for these expatriates was when their newly acquired global skills were not taken advantage of. These returning expatriates have tremendous skills and multinationals need to plan ahead to ensure that such skills are used effectively. Returning expatriates are most satisfied when such global skills are used.

As you can see, multinationals can implement many programs to ensure a smooth experience for the expatriate.

repatriation problem the difficulties that managers face in coming back to their home countries and reconnecting with their old job

reverse culture shock refers to the significant challenges returning expatriates experience as they return from their international assignment

The Future: Non-traditional and Women Expatriates?

As mentioned at the beginning of this chapter, multinationals are seeing an increased proportion of non-traditional expatriates. While the typical expatriate used to be a white male senior manager in his 40s or 50s, multinationals are now increasingly hiring expatriates who have non-traditional characteristics such as being younger, single, or married couples without children or even same-sex partners.[36] One important aspect of such non-traditional expatriates includes women executives, single women with children, female breadwinners, etc. It therefore becomes very critical for multinationals to design programs to attract and retain such non-traditional expatriates.

Despite the increase in demand for expatriates, the number of females in expatriate positions in the early 2000s was at around 2–15 percent of all expatriate positions.[37] More recent data suggest that women now form around 19 percent of international assignments.[38] However, such levels are surprising, given the scarcity of female employees at the highest level. However, many MNCs tend to be reluctant to post women in expatriate positions. Some MNCs are simply not interested, while others assume that women will face prejudice once in the foreign country. Consider the following Emerging Market Ethical Challenge.

Women Expatriates in China

EMERGING MARKET
ETHICAL CHALLENGE

Despite the growing demand for talented expatriates, reports show that only 19 percent of expatriates are women. Experts attribute this underrepresentation to many factors. For example, only 22 percent of multinationals seem to have systems in place to formally select individuals for individual assignments. This may therefore mean that biases against women may lead to fewer women being selected for such jobs. Furthermore, the fact that many women still shoulder the bulk of family duties such as taking care of children, etc. also implies that women may also be self-selecting themselves out of such jobs.

An additional factor often mentioned is the lack of acceptance of women expatriates in the countries they work in. A recent study of Chinese women expatriates provides some insights on how devastating the lack of acceptance of locals can be. In that study, the researchers examined the prejudice of host country nationals against women expatriates and found that such prejudice can result in poorer performance. Such prejudice can also result in lowering the women expatriates' self-efficacy. In other words, prejudice against women expatriates can also result in lower belief among these women that they can succeed in their international assignments.

Hence multinationals have an ethical obligation to create an environment whereby women expatriates are not only selected but also have chance of succeeding. Multinationals are advised to develop formal selection and recruitment programs to encourage women to consider global assignments. Furthermore, host country nationals should be trained to welcome and appreciate women expatriates. Multinationals may also want to provide more short-term assignments to make it easier for women expatriates to accept such assignments.

Source: Based on Brookfield Global Relocation Services, 2016, "Female expatriates continue to be underrepresented," www.brookfieldgrs.com/; S. Jie and J. Fuming, 2015, "Factors influencing Chinese female expatriates' performance in international assignments," *International Journal of Human Resource Management, 26*(3), pp. 299–315.

There are, however, other factors that are simply seen as fiction. For instance, Adler[39] found that many companies simply assume that women are not interested in international assignments or that managers are reluctant to send women abroad. But, such assumptions are mere myths. In fact, women are as interested and equally successful in global assignments.

Although these myths may persist in some organizations, it is clear that the future will see a rapidly growing number of female expatriates. Such reasoning is logical given that women have some advantages compared to men. For instance, women are more likely to excel in relational skills, a major factor in expatriate success.[40] Women report that local male managers can be more open in communication with a woman than with a man. Local men, even from traditional cultures, can talk at ease with a woman about an array of subjects that include issues outside the domain of traditional "male only" conversations. In other cases, just in being unique, female expatriates tend to be more visible and thus more sought after. Furthermore, women may sometimes have cultural predispositions that are more compatible with local cultures. For instance, Varma, Toh, and Budhwar[41] have shown that female expatriates are preferred in India, where collectivistic traits such as nurturance and collaboration are more valued. It is therefore likely that Indian home country workers prefer US female expatriates relative to male US expatriates, who may seem too aggressive.

What can MNCs do to encourage female expatriates? In addition to the suggestions provided in the Emerging Market Ethical Challenge discussed earlier (e.g., train home country nationals to respect women expatriates, etc.),[42] if necessary, the perception that women are not willing to take international assignments has to be changed. Managers need to provide equal opportunity for both genders to explore expatriate opportunities. Additionally, every effort should be made to provide potential female expatriates with mentors and networks of other female expatriates. This will provide potential candidates with an idea of expectations and potential challenges. Finally, MNCs are also strongly advised to address dual career issues.

Chapter Review

In this chapter, you read about international human resource management. As a multinational expands its operations to emerging markets, it has to manage its human assets to ensure that it keeps its ability to be competitive. Human resources are critical to enable a multinational to implement and realize its strategic objectives. International human resource management deals with managing the human resource functions at an international level. The chapter considers the unique circumstances pertaining to workers as well as more upper-level expatriates.

In the section pertaining to workers, you learned how the various human resource management functions of recruitment, selection, training, performance appraisal, and compensation differ from country to country. Specifically, you read about how both cultural and institutional aspects affect these functions. The chapter also discusses some of the ways these differences can be addressed with a special focus on emerging markets.

In the section on expatriates, you learned about the unique challenges facing MNCs as they send upper-level employees on international assignments. You read about the high costs of expatriates and also the high level of failure. The chapter also suggested some of the things companies do to ensure expatriate success. In the final section, you read about the situation facing women as they embark on international careers. However, you also learned about the scarcity of talented employees and how more women will fill such positions in the future.

As more companies go international and hire individuals from different countries, they will face important challenges with regards to the human resource management function. If these multinationals want to get the best out of their employees, they will need to deal with these employees appropriately. This chapter presented you with the many challenges and solutions to deal with such human resource management functions.

Discussion Questions

1   Discuss the human resource management functions. How is international human resource management different from domestic human resource management?

2   What is recruitment and selection? How do US companies typically approach recruitment and selection? How are these functions different in emerging markets?

3   Compare and contrast US performance appraisals with performance appraisal practices in more collectivistic countries.

4   What is compensation? How is compensation around the world different from US compensation practices?

5   What are expatriates? Why are expatriates so costly for multinationals?

6   Discuss some of the important challenges facing multinationals as they send expatriates on international assignments. How can a multinational better prepare expatriates to succeed?

7   What are some of the important traits expatriates need to have to do well on their international assignments?

8   Discuss the current situation regarding female expatriates. What can companies do to encourage and support their women expatriates?

International Business Skill Builder

Choosing a Plant Location

Step 1: Assume you are the owner of a small business or find a small business that has international operations.

Step 2: You are interested in opening a plant in a foreign location or in assisting the small business in making a plant location decision. You will need to hire employees to operate the plant.

Step 3: Consult the appropriate sources (Mercer Consulting, International Labor Organization, Towers Perrin) to provide the small business with the appropriate advice regarding hiring. Provide information regarding compensation, labor relations, performance appraisal, etc., in the selected countries.

Step 4: Considering four possible destinations for the new plant, provide comparative advice regarding each country. Justify the best alternative.

Chapter Internet Activity

Go to the World Bank "Doing Business" project website at **www.doingbusiness.org/data/exploretopics/labor-market-regulation**. Examine the "Employing Workers" measure. What information does it provide to human resource managers? Discuss how the World Bank arrives at the measure. Select ten countries and compare their employing workers' indexes. What do you learn?

Key Concepts

- ☐ Compensation
- ☐ cultural intelligence
- ☐ culture shock
- ☐ emotional intelligence
- ☐ expatriate employees
- ☐ expatriate failure
- ☐ home country nationals
- ☐ host country nationals
- ☐ international human resource management (IHRM)

- ☐ labor relations
- ☐ performance appraisal
- ☐ recruitment
- ☐ repatriation problem
- ☐ reverse culture shock
- ☐ selection
- ☐ third country nationals
- ☐ training and development
- ☐ union membership density

CASE 14

An American Expat in Costa Rica

As his plane lands at the Santa Maria International Airport in San Jose, Costa Rica, Ed Moore reassures himself that he made the right decision in accepting his first international assignment in this Central American country. The new job will be a promotion, the first time Ed will be entirely responsible for an entire plant, and it will give him international experience, which he hopes to use to continue his advancement in the company.

Ed Moore has worked for his present employer, Jestin Apparel, for 16 years. Ed is viewed as a loyal employee and he prides himself on the fact that he has worked for Jestin longer than he has been married to his wife, Susan. Susan and their two children (Eddie, age 10, and Jessie, age 13) are not as enthusiastic about the idea of living in Turrialba, a rather isolated town about a two-hour drive from San Jose. Although Turrialba is in a beautiful area of the country and offers abundant hunting and fishing opportunities for Ed, Susan worries about the ability of the children to adapt to the isolation. In fact, since the children do not speak Spanish, it will be necessary for Eddie and Jessie to attend school in San Jose, which requires a long bus ride daily. Both Ed and Susan want their children to become "citizens of the world" and they both feel this opportunity may be good for personal development. Although the family vacationed in Europe once before, their international experience was very limited and none of the Moore family members speaks another language.

Ed will be the new plant manager for the Costa Rican manufacturing facility of Jestin. This plant sews together pre-manufactured garments and exports the finished product back to the United States. The previous plant manager relocated to San Salvador to open a new, larger facility for Jestin. Most of the 230 employees are young females, although a number of young men and older women are also employed at the plant. The workers receive an hourly wage which is considerably higher than the average wage in Costa Rica. By most reports the workers are happy with their jobs at Jestin. Turnover at the plant is mainly due to young women getting married and starting a family, or young men moving to the capital for better wages.

Although the quality and efficiency of the plant are considered acceptable by management, Ed has been instructed to try and improve both areas. Ed is known as a rather tough manager, who feels that the best way to motivate employees is through a combined program of threats and incentives. Corporate management felt that Ed's somewhat autocratic style of management would be effective in Costa Rica.

Susan was employed in the United States as an assistant human resources manager, even though she had no formal training in that area.

CASE 14 cont'd

She enjoyed her job and she was hoping that she would be able to work in Costa Rica in a similar capacity. The Turrialba plant already had a bilingual HR manager who was familiar with Costa Rican labor laws and regulations; however, it was felt that perhaps Susan could first learn Spanish and then assist the HR manager. Ed's salary as plant manager will be more than their combined incomes in the United States, and the family will be provided with free housing, a maid, and company provided transportation. The family will live in extreme luxury by local standards.

As the plane touches down in San Jose, Ed remembers the trip the family made to Costa Rica three months earlier. The company had sent the family to Costa Rica to preview the country and to acquaint them with Costa Rican culture. The Moore's enjoyed the cultural tours and the whitewater rafting experiences, however, the children still protested against the move. Leaving friends in the United States is not easy, and they know that they will be giving up the comforts they have become accustomed to in the United States. Ed hopes the assignment will only be for a couple of years, although no plans have been made for his repatriation back to the United States.

As the plane comes to a halt at the gate, Susan looks at Ed and the worry in her face tells him that not all the Moore's are confident that the decision was a good one.

CASE DISCUSSION POINTS:

1   How significant a factor will family happiness be when it comes to Ed's success in this new job?
2   How do you think the Costa Rican employees will respond to Ed's management style?
3   Was Ed the best choice for the position? What criteria should be used in selecting expatriates?

Case prepared by Charles A. Rarick

Notes

1   A. Bailey, 2016, "Emerging markets—has HR got it right?" Chapman CG Newsletters.
2   V. Sinha and P. Thaly, 2013, "A review of changing trends of recruitment practice to enhance the quality of hiring in global organizations," *Management, 18*, pp. 141–156.
3   G. W. Bohlander, S. Snell and A. W. Sherman, 2001, *Managing Human Resources*, Cincinnati, OH: South-Western.
4   G. W. Bohlander, S. Snell and A. W. Sherman, 2001, *Managing Human Resources*, Cincinnati, OH: South-Western.
5   International Social Survey Program (ISSP), 1999/2000, *International Social Survey Program: Work Orientations II, 1997* [computer file], Ann Arbor, MI: Inter-university Consortium for Political and Social Science Research.
6   G. Hofstede, 1991, *Cultures and Organizations*, London: McGraw-Hill, pp. 99–100.
7   V. Sinha and P. Thaly, 2013, "A review of changing trends of recruitment practice to enhance the quality of hiring in global organizations," *Management, 18*, pp. 141–156.

8   David Stern, Yingquan Song and Bridget O'Brien, 2004, "Company training in the United States 1970–2000: What have been the trends over time?" *International Journal of Training and Development*, 8(3), pp. 191–209.

9   T. K. Darwish, S. Singh and G. Wood, 2015, "The impact of human resource practices on actual and perceived organizational performance in a middle eastern market," *Human Resource Management*, 55(2), pp. 261–281.

10   M. E. Van Buren and S. B. King, 2000, "ASTD's annual accounting of worldwide patterns in employer-provided training," *Training and Development*, Alexandra, VA: ASTD, pp. 1–24.

11   ASTD, 2013, State of the Industry. www.td.org/Publications/Research-Reports/2013/2013-State-of-the-Industry

12   Chris Brewster, Geoff Wood, Michael Brookes and Jos Van Ommeren, 2006, "What determines the size of the HR function? A cross-national analysis," *Human Resource Management*, Spring, 45(1), pp. 3–21.

13   Jonathan Katz, 2007, "Worlds of difference," *Industry Week*, December, pp. 39–41.

14   T. S. Rath, M. Mohanty and B. B. Pradhan, 2015, "Career advancement of women bank managers in India: A study in State Bank of India," *Vilakshan IXMB Journal of Management*, 12(1), pp. 79–96.

15   G. Hofstede, 1991, *Cultures and Organizations*, London: McGraw-Hill.

16   R. M. Steers, Y. K. Shin and G. R. Ungson, 1989, *The Chaebol: Korea's New Industrial Might*, New York: Harper Business.

17   Jie Shen, 2005, "Effective international performance appraisals: Easily said, hard to do," *Compensation and Benefits Review*, 37(4), pp. 70–79.

18   A. Shrivastava and P. Purang, 2016, "Performance appraisal fairness and its outcomes: A study of Indian banks," *The Indian Journal of Industrial Relations*, 51(4), pp. 660–674.

19   Michael Segalla, Dominique Rouzies, Madeleine Besson and Barton A. Weitz, 2006, "A cross-national investigation of incentive sales compensation," *International Journal of Research in Marketing*, 23, pp. 419–433.

20   J. M. Geringer, C. A. Frayne and J. F. Milliman, 2002, "In search of 'best practices' in human resource management: Research design and methodology," *Human Resource Management*, 41, pp. 5–30.

21   Jelle Visser, 2000, "Trends in unionisation and collective bargaining," *International Labour Office*, September, pp. 1–18.

22   Y. McNulty and K. Hutchings, 2016, "Looking for global talent in all the right places: A critical literature review of non-traditional expatriates," *International Journal of Human Resource Management*, 27(7), pp. 677–728.

23   *The Economist*, 2006, "Special report: Travelling more lightly—staffing globalization," 379, pp. 83, 84, 99.

24   B. Bader and T. Schuster, 2015, "Expatriate social networks in terrorism-endangered countries: An empirical analysis in Afghanistan, India, Pakistan, and Saudi Arabia," *Journal of International Management*, 21, pp. 63–77.

25   R. H. Sims and M. Schraeder, 2005, "Expatriate compensation," *Career Development International*, 10(2), pp. 98–108.

26   B. Bader and T. Schuster, 2015, "Expatriate social networks in terrorism-endangered countries: An empirical analysis in Afghanistan, India, Pakistan, and Saudi Arabia," *Journal of International Management*, 21, pp. 63–77.

27   Guilherme Pires, John Stanton and Shane Ostenfeld, 2006, "Improving expatriate adjustment and effectiveness in ethnically diverse countries: Marketing insights," *Cross-Cultural Management*, 13(2), pp. 156–170.

28   B. Bader, N. Berg and D. Holtbrugge, 2015, "Expatriate performance in terrorism-endangered countries: The role of family and organizational support," *International Business Review*, 24, pp. 849–860.

29   Alizee B. Avril and Vincent P. Magnini, 2007, "A holistic approach to expatriate success," *International Journal of Contemporary Hospitality Management*, 19(1), pp. 53–64.

30   B. Bader, N. Berg and D. Holtbrugge, 2015, "Expatriate performance in terrorism-endangered countries: The role of family and organizational support," *International Business Review*, 24, pp. 849–860.

31 Alizee B. Avril and Vincent P. Magnini, 2007, "A holistic approach to expatriate success," *International Journal of Contemporary Hospitality Management*, 19(1), pp. 53–64.

32 R. Krishnaveni and R. Arthi, 2015, "An overview of multidimensional factors influencing effective performance of expatriates," *Management*, 20(2), pp. 135–147.

33 J. Teague, 2015, "Corporate preparation for the cross-cultural adaptation experience of the accompanying expatriate spouse," *Journal of International Business Research*, 14(2), pp. 139–151.

34 David C. Martin and John J. Anthony, 2006, "The repatriation and retention of employees: Factors leading to successful programs," *International Journal of Management*, 23(3), pp. 620–631.

35 D. Ellis, 2015, "The ex-expats are here: Management considerations for this growing workforce," *Human Resources*, April/May, pp. 26–27.

36 D. Ellis, 2015,"The ex-expats are here: Management considerations for this growing workforce," *Human Resources*, April/May, pp. 26–27.

37 H. Harris, 2004, "Global careers: Work–life issues and the adjustment of women international managers," *Journal of Management Development*, 23(9), pp. 818–832.

38 Brookfield Global Relocation Services, 2016, "Female expatriates continue to be underrepresented," www.brookfieldgrs.com/

39 N. Adler, 1984, "Expecting international success: Female managers overseas," *Columbia Journal of World Business*, 19(3), pp. 79–85.

40 N. Adler, 1993, "Women managers in a global economy," *HRMagazine*, September, pp. 52–55.

41 Arup Varma, Soo Min Toh and Pawan Budhwar, 2006, "A new perspective on the female expatriate experience: The role of host country national categorization," *Journal of World Business*, 41, pp. 112–120.

42 S. Jie and J. Fuming, 2015, "Factors influencing Chinese female expatriates' performance in international assignments," *International Journal of Human Resource Management*, 26(3), pp. 299–315.

CHAPTER 15

E-commerce and the MNC

After reading this chapter you should be able to:

- Understand what e-commerce is and its importance in today's business environment and specifically in emerging markets.

- Define the forms of e-commerce and understand the importance of e-commerce.

- Appreciate global e-commerce and the key global e-commerce issues.

- Learn about how to build a successful e-commerce strategy.

- Understand cyber and e-commerce security.

International Business   *Preview IB Emerging Market Strategic Insight*

E-commerce in China and India

As global developed markets slow down, many are looking to emerging markets for growth. For instance, China's e-commerce grew by nearly 600 percent between 2010 and 2014. It is now the largest e-commerce market in the world. Much of this expansion was made possible by local companies. For instance, Alibaba, valued at $184 billion in 2016, created a system to encourage people to buy online. Because of the uncertainties of online purchases, Alibaba created Alipay that holds the shopper's payment until the shopper receives the order. This therefore guarantees that the shopper will not get duped in the presence of institutional voids.

Experts see India as the next big e-commerce market. Though people are poorer than in China and its infrastructure worse, there are many changes that point to optimism. For instance, per capita income in 2025 is expected to be twice of that from 2014. Additionally, two thirds of Indians are younger than 35 and many of them have mobile phones. Such phones will provide access to online markets. Additionally, the proportion of smartphones as a percentage of mobile phones increased from 1 in 5 to 1 in 4 from December 2014 to June 2015. These changes will likely result in 1 billion Indian online consumers by 2020.

Despite the optimism, the Indian market presents many challenges. Consider that few consumers have credit cards. Delivering products is also very challenging. Indian companies cannot rely on a well-oiled distribution network. Additionally, the market is not very well regulated thereby posing additional challenges for foreign multinationals. Consider the difficulties faced by Facebook when they decided to establish their "Free Basics" program in India. The "Free Basics" initiative provides free access to Facebook and a number of other online programs to users on their mobile phones. Facebook is now providing this service in around 36 countries. Unfortunately for Facebook, its program had many critics in India and it was banned by the Indian authorities. The authorities deemed that Facebook would create an unfair marketplace because the free service forced users to use those services that they recommend. This could come at the expense of smaller companies.

Source: Based on *The Economist*, 2016, "Can't give it away," January 9, p. 55; *The Economist*, 2016, "The great race," March 5, pp. 19–21.

The Preview IB Emerging Market Strategic Insight describes the importance of emerging markets to e-commerce today. Both the Chinese and Indian markets are expected to grow tremendously over the next few years. At the same time, many foreign multinationals are having significant difficulties getting established in these markets because of the many challenges of operating in them. In contrast, local firms are excelling because of their superior knowledge of these markets.

These and countless other examples provide evidence of the importance of e-commerce in today's business environment. The Internet economy is growing at a tremendous pace—faster than any other business trend in history. Such growth is even more pronounced in emerging markets. No multinational is immune to its effects and companies ignoring e-commerce do so at their own risk. As you will see later, companies are being created solely on the Internet platform and are having significant influences on their respective industries almost immediately. E-commerce therefore presents tremendous opportunities as well as significant challenges for businesses. Successful companies are the ones that will be able to take advantage of e-commerce opportunities while tackling the challenges. Tackling such challenges are even more difficult in emerging markets.

This chapter will provide you with an understanding of the dramatic influence of the Internet and e-commerce on business operations. You will first learn about the basic structure of the Internet economy and the many forms of Internet transactions. You will then read about how the Internet is shaping the globalization phenomenon and its impact and influence in emerging markets. You will also read about the many ways e-commerce is being used by multinationals in their operations and the significant opportunities and challenges presented to multinationals as they use the Internet. You will also learn about the many unique challenges in implementing e-commerce cross-culturally. One of the key challenges facing multinationals with respect to the use of the Internet is cybersecurity. This chapter will also present to you the many challenges associated with building a secure online presence. Finally, you will also learn some of the key steps in building a successful global e-commerce strategy with a special emphasis on emerging markets.

E-commerce: Definitions, Types, and Importance

e-commerce
use of the Internet to buy or sell products and services

E-commerce can be defined as the use of the Internet to buy or sell products and services. These goods or services include those delivered offline, such as FedEx shipping a book purchased through Amazon.com to a customer anywhere in the world. Alibaba, the Chinese online multinational, is another example of a company that provides extensive services to facilitate e-commerce. Alibaba also helps Chinese consumers purchase products globally by providing assistance with listings, marketing, and customs assistance.[1] Other online products also include goods and services delivered online, such as downloaded computer software. As you will see below, e-commerce can take place between individual buyers or corporations.

B2C
business-to-consumer transactions

B2B
business-to-business online transactions

C2C
consumer-to-consumer business transactions

C2B
consumer-to-business online transactions

There are four main types of e-commerce. The first is the business-to-consumer transactions such as buying books from Amazon.com. The acronym **B2C** is commonly used to refer to these forms of purchases. The second type, known as **B2B**, or business-to-business transactions, represents selling among businesses. B2B transactions make up 70 to 85 percent of current e-commerce business. In addition to these e-commerce models, there exist two other forms of business transactions that take place over the Internet. For instance, eBay is a global player in the **C2C** (consumer-to-consumer) business of auctions. Anyone can sell something online and place bids. Finally, another form of business transaction through the Internet is consumer-to-business or **C2B**. Examples of these firms include price-comparison websites such as www.addall.com, which searches online bookstores throughout the world to provide price comparisons and shipping and delivery information.

All types of e-commerce are important in emerging markets. However, the following Emerging Market Brief shows how disruption of a C2B platform was problematic in Brazil.

WhatsApp in Brazil

EMERGING MARKET BRIEF

Facebook-owned WhatsApp is a mobile communications technology that allows users to exchange messages if they are connected to the Internet. However, they do not need to pay texting or other sms (short message service) fees. It is now an important aspect of communications in many emerging markets and disruption can be very disastrous. Consider the recent ban in Brazil. Although WhatsApp started as a cheap and convenient means for friends to text each other, it quickly become an important tool for C2B transactions. WhatsApp allows many types of businesses such as food-trucks and hawkers to list their products while also accepting orders from consumers. Unfortunately, recent regulatory changes in Brazil have made it easier for judges to block the service. A Brazilian judge ordered mobile phone companies to suspend WhatsApp for 72 hours because the company did not provide the needed information regarding a drug investigation. Fortunately, an appeals judge was able to overturn the suspension of services well before the 72 hours. However, the disruption was very problematic for the many businesses dependent on WhatsApp.

Source: Based on *The Economist*, 2016, "Faulty powers," May 7, pp. 32–32.

The above shows the importance of C2B businesses in emerging markets. In fact, all types of online transactions are critical. But how important is e-commerce generally? Recent trends suggest that e-commerce is growing at an amazingly fast rate globally. Consider Exhibit 15.1 and Exhibit 15.2, showing the penetration and growth of the Internet around the world.

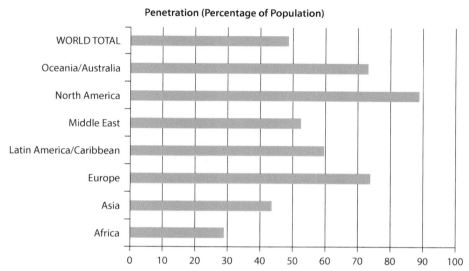

Penetration (Percentage of Population)

Exhibit 15.1 Internet Penetration Around the World
Source: Based on www.Internetworldstats.com

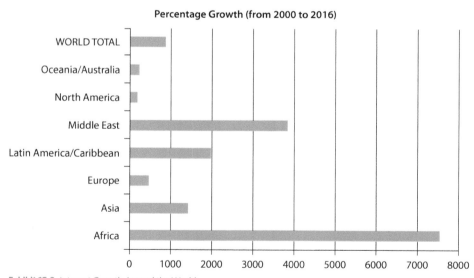

Percentage Growth (from 2000 to 2016)

Exhibit 15.2 Internet Growth Around the World
Source: Based on www.Internetworldstats.com

Several important trends can be inferred from both Exhibits. First of all, an important trend is an assessment of the potential in these various geographic regions. Consider Exhibit 15.1, showing that Internet penetration seems fairly saturated in the more developed nations. Europe, North America, and Oceania/Australia all have penetration rates of 70 percent and higher with North America having a penetration rate of 89 percent. However, the emerging markets present significant potential. Africa has the lowest penetration rate of 29 percent of the total population. Furthermore, the regions of Latin America and Asia both have relatively low penetration rates. On the basis of penetration alone, the Exhibit shows that the Internet still has the potential to reach a large number of new Internet users in Latin America and the Middle East. Such figures also point to the opportunities presented by the Internet globally.

When the above data are coupled with Exhibit 15.2, the growth of Internet usage between 2000 and 2016 shows the tremendous potential offered by emerging markets. Africa has enjoyed a growth of 7520 percent over the 2000 to 2016 period. Consider the following IB Emerging Market Strategic Insight.

E-commerce in Africa

IB EMERGING MARKET
STRATEGIC INSIGHT

As the earlier discussed data show, Internet growth in Africa has been tremendous. As the middle class grows, more people are able to afford the Internet and to participate in online transactions. An important part of the enthusiasm for Africa's middle class is that it is so small and even small growth of the middle class will provide extensive opportunities. Rapid developments in mobile technology are also providing many new potential ventures in new business models. For instance, Nairobi-based M-Kopa can now provide loans to customers to buy its products using pre-loaded apps on mobile phones. Because many Africans are more likely to own mobile phones, use of the technology to promote e-commerce is popular.

Despite these opportunities, experts also note many potential barriers. Similar to the emerging markets of India and China, the use of credit cards is not as popular in Africa. Companies have therefore to find alternative ways to get paid. Additionally, many African nations suffer from a lack of a postal database and less than reliable delivery services. The road network and other infrastructure is not always well developed and therefore getting products to consumers is not always easy.

In spite of such challenges, some companies are taking up the task of expanding e-commerce operations in Africa. Consider the case of Nigerian-based Jumia, striving to be the African Amazon. It currently has operations in around 10 African countries and is adapting to local realities. For its operations in Ivory Coast, it found out that people prefer to pay cash on delivery rather than using their mobile phones. It therefore collects payments when the product is delivered. It also found that importing and delivering all products meant that it had to deal with local customs and unnecessary delays. It now collects payments but works with local firms to have these firms send the products to their warehouse for delivery. It also found that it could not rely on private delivery firms in the Ivory Coast and now has its own contractors.

Source: Based on *The Economist*, 2016, "Special Report, Business in Africa: On the move," April 16, pp. 13–15; *The Economist*, 2016, "Special Report, Business in Africa: Virtual headaches," April 16, p. 14.

Growth in Internet usage in other emerging areas in the world such as Asia, the Middle East, and Latin America ranged from 1445 percent to 3842 percent between 2000 and 2016. Even in areas such as Europe and North America, growth has been lower but steady. Such trends suggest that more individuals are getting access to the Internet, thus presenting tremendous opportunities to multinationals. These trends also point to the importance of emerging markets as e-commerce opportunities.

While the growth of Internet usage provides evidence of the increased importance of e-commerce, MNCs will also have to pay attention to e-commerce because of its potential to help companies become more competitive. E-commerce allows companies not only to find new customers but also to find new ways to improve their operations. This is especially relevant for emerging markets. While many Western multinationals have attempted to enter these markets to take advantage of the growing customer base, local companies have been more successful. Consider, again, the case of Alibaba. While Amazon has struggled to get established, Alibaba continues to benefit from the dramatic growth in Chinese spending. Rather than merely facilitating e-commerce, Alibaba is now playing a big role shaping the market. It is now building service centers in remote areas to facilitate trade among consumers in such areas. In India, other companies are working not only to develop better logistics to facilitate deliveries but are working to improve the financing infrastructure.[2] Such efforts reflect the huge potential presented by emerging markets. Global e-commerce can thus help companies reduce costs. For instance, e-commerce can reduce transaction costs associated with payments, ordering, and invoicing by allowing more effective data storage and manipulation.[3] Such information can also be more effectively shared with employees, customers, and retailers. B2B e-commerce has also helped retailers reduce inventory costs by letting wholesalers handle inventory and provide shipping services.

Finally, e-commerce can help companies build customer loyalty. A website can provide readily accessible information that is not possible with more traditional markets. Many companies such as Best Buy and Circuit City now provide online product demos. Such features provide additional information that can help customers make better purchase decisions.

As you can see, because of its many benefits to individuals and businesses, e-commerce will continue its tremendous growth in the future. Next, we consider the structure of the Internet and e-commerce.

Internet and E-commerce Structure

Before you read about the key e-commerce issues and how they affect MNCs, it is important to first understand the structure of an e-commerce website. According to Chu and colleagues, e-commerce websites have evolved from single buyer–seller interactions or repositories of information to more complex multiple exchanges between buyers and sellers.[4] It is therefore important to understand the many components of e-commerce websites.

At a basic level, e-commerce websites include participants. Participants can be registered or licensed to use the website. The management of the website also plays an important role. The website management decides the environment of the website ("boundary and its general business nature").[5] This defines whether the website is presented merely as a merchant site (i.e. seller of products) or as another form, such as a portal or broker. The website management also decides on the scope of the website—i.e. what relationships the website has with its host.

Another crucial aspect of e-commerce is the core functions that e-commerce websites perform. According to Chu et al., e-commerce websites perform four key functions. These include **transaction incubation**, which refers to the process of setting up a relationship between the participant and the website. For instance, websites such as Facebook.com or MySpace.com require that participants register before their access can be validated. The **transaction negotiation** function refers to the facilitation of the purchase decision by the participant. For instance, one can review products on Amazon.com by browsing through the product offerings and then making a decision about which product to purchase. The **transaction formation** process pertains to the phase where the transaction is finalized. In such cases, participant payment is processed and approved and confirmation of purchase is sent to the buyer. Finally, in the **transaction management** phase, the company manages the various activities linked to

transaction incubation process of setting up a relationship between the participant and the website

transaction negotiation facilitation of the purchase decision

transaction formation process where purchase is finalized

transaction management management of various activities linked to transactions

transactions. In this phase, the company can integrate data collected at the various steps to facilitate e-business processes. For instance, in this stage, the purchase decision can be matched with inventory control for re-order decisions.[6]

Finally, an important critical development in e-commerce is the development of platforms. **Platforms** are exchange markets whereby buyers and sellers can interact under the rules of the platform owner.[7] Examples of prominent platforms include Uber, the taxi ordering service, Facebook, Google, and even Apple. These companies have created new business models that have left traditional firms reeling.[8] An important characteristic of platforms is that the companies involved are able to gather large amounts of data that can be converted into customer intelligence. Such information can then be used to provide better services to customers.

Platforms are quickly becoming critical elements of e-commerce. To give you more insights on the presence of platforms worldwide, Exhibit 15.3 shows the number of platform companies by region.

platform
exchange markets whereby buyers and sellers can interact under the rules of the platform owner

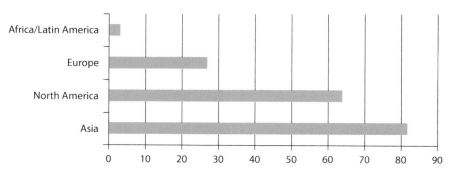

Number of Platform Companies (by region)

Exhibit 15.3 Number of Platform Companies by Region
Source: Based on P. C. Evans and A. Gawer, 2016, "The rise of the platform enterprise: A global survey," www.thecge.net/wp-content/uploads/2016/01/PDF-WEB-Platform-Survey_01_12.pdf

As Exhibit 15.3 shows, a much larger number of platform companies are from Asia. The survey showed that platforms are also critical in emerging markets. In fact, out of the 82 platform companies from the Asian region, 64 are from China. The rest of the companies are from India, Japan, Malaysia, etc. However, it should be noted that the US platform companies have much higher valuation compared to other platform companies. This reflects the importance of US companies to the platform industry.

Now that you have read about the various important components of e-commerce websites, you will learn about the power of e-commerce to allow companies to go global. You will also read about the many important cross-cultural e-commerce issues.

E-commerce and Globalization

The increases in information exchanges and efficiency through the Internet and e-commerce have made it possible for companies to reach customers worldwide and to become global companies. However, the Internet is also enabling the emergence of a new form of multinational called **born-global firms**.[9] As you saw in earlier chapters, many companies tend to operate in the domestic market and gradually expand to foreign markets. However, born-global firms tend to adopt a global view of markets and develop competitive advantage to succeed in the various markets from the day they are started. Research into born-global firms suggests that the key

born-global firms
companies that operate globally from the day they are founded

success factors for success in both Western contexts and emerging market contexts seem fairly similar. Born-globals emerge if companies have a global vision from the start and have managers with international experience. Such companies have an innovation culture and tend to also have an international business network. Additionally, they also tend to have international market knowledge as well as an entrepreneurial mindset. A study of Chinese born-globals suggests that such factors are also influential in how these emerging market companies go global.[10] But it is undeniable that the Internet economy has greatly contributed to this development. However, a pro-internationalization government culture and understanding of local political conditions are also important.[11]

The Internet and e-commerce are not encouraging solely the creation of born-global firms. Many smaller and medium-sized companies are taking full advantage of e-commerce to expand their operations. Why is it easier to pursue e-commerce opportunities today? Many of the initial barriers to e-commerce are falling and e-commerce is becoming more cost-effective. According to Heilemann[12] and others[13] several important reasons account for the growth of e-commerce:

- *Extremely cheap hardware* Computers, servers, and many other pieces of e-commerce hardware are commodities that can be acquired for very little. For instance, while a server used to cost as much as $60,000 over ten years ago, servers can now be purchased for $1,000.
- *Cheap software* Companies can now rely on open-source software to develop their service. Much free software, such as Linux and MySQL, now allows companies to develop their e-commerce presence without exorbitant costs.
- *Access to talent worldwide* Most companies can now access the vast pool of programmers available in India, Romania, and Russia. While such programmers were previously available only to larger multinationals, many smaller companies can now easily tap into these employees.
- *Cheaper Internet worldwide* Many countries are seeing increased availability and decreased price of the Internet. In fact, the OECD sees broadband development as a critical aspect of the Internet and e-commerce.[14] Broadband is a combination of digital technologies that allows rapid transmission of data and other digital services, often simultaneously. It is seen as a major reason for people adopting information and technology products and services, and as prices have come down more people are adopting broadband. See Exhibit 15.4 for the growth of broadband penetration in selected OECD countries between 2004 and 2015. As you can see, broadband penetration is accelerating rapidly in most societies.
- *More targeted marketing* Search engines such as Google have made it easier and more efficient to target potential buyers. Companies do not need to spend large sums of money to reach potential customers effectively.
- *Easier and cheaper to stay in touch with employees worldwide* There are now a large number of tools available for companies to keep their worldwide employees in touch with each other.
- *Increased popularity of blogs and social networking* Many companies are now relying on blogs and social networking sites to better connect with their customers and also build brand loyalty.[15] Consider the case of Air France–KLM's creation of a social networking site called Club China. The site is focused on helping business people do business in China and provides assistance finding translators and even car rentals. This has allowed Air France–KLM to find better ways to serve its customers flying to China. As another example, Facebook is now the world's largest social network and has around 1.65 billion users a month today. Facebook's number of users actually exceeds the Chinese population and these users spend around 50 minutes per day on the site.[16]

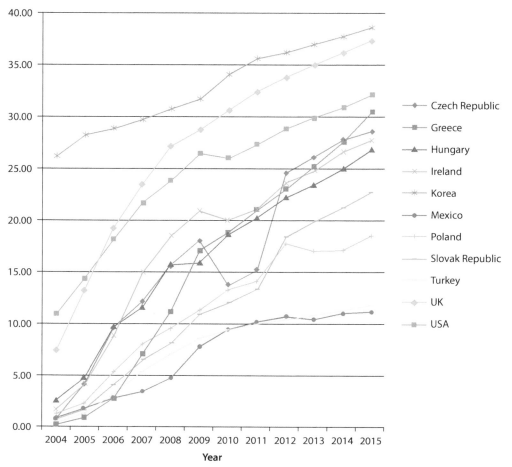

Exhibit 15.4 Broadband Penetration for Selected Countries
Source: Adapted from OECD, 2016.

Growth of e-commerce in emerging markets has been due to a number of other factors.
Consider the following Emerging Market Brief.

E-commerce Growth in Emerging Markets

EMERGING MARKET BRIEF

As you will see later, emerging markets have suffered from a number of barriers that have limited
growth of e-commerce. However, many emerging markets have enjoyed considerable growth
thanks to unique factors in addition to the ones discussed earlier. These include:

■ *Adaptation* While Western-based multinationals have seen local conditions as barriers to the
growth of e-commerce, local companies have seen such barriers as sources of opportunities.
Consider the case of Grofers in India. Indian shoppers typically tend to shop at small
family-owned grocers known as kiranas. These kiranas are often willing to provide loans to
customers and are more than happy to cut and deliver small amounts of fresh food. Grofers

is taking advantage of the network of kiranas by working closely with these family-owned shops. When customers order products, Grofers have their workers get the products from kiranas and deliver such products.

- *Growth in Smartphone Use* While growth of e-commerce in many countries has been made possible because of growing Internet use, many emerging markets have seen a dramatic increase in smartphone use. Smartphone use in many emerging markets is not only creating a new class of consumers but also allowing individuals in these societies to connect and share information.

- *Business Model Improvement* While Western-based companies have developed business models, emerging market multinationals are sometimes improving on such business models. Consider the case of Didi Chuxing, the Chinese response to Uber. Rather than focusing on private-car services like Uber does, Didi Chuxing allows users to select taxis, private cars, shared cars, and even buses. Furthermore, it is making maximal use of its database of users. It has now partnered with a Chinese bank and will soon start offering loans to its drivers. The drivers have income because of the work they perform through the company but may not always have good credit history. Didi Chuxing also intends soon to play the role of matchmaker by allowing drivers and customers to select each other. A partnership with LinkedIn would potentially offer white-collar employees more interesting commutes to work.

Source: Based on *The Economist*, 2016, "E-commerce in India: Local heroes," January 16, pp. 72–73; *The Economist*, 2016, "More than mobility," January 30, p. 57; *The Economist*, 2016, "Special Report, Business in Africa: Fortune favors the brave," April 16, pp. 15–16.

Global E-commerce Opportunities and Threats

As you have read, e-commerce presents tremendous opportunities for companies. E-commerce allows any company to reach customers on a global scale. Customers can browse and shop 24 hours a day, seven days a week. Furthermore, the various technologies you read about earlier show that the Internet and e-commerce are becoming dramatically less expensive and more effective.

However, e-commerce does not present opportunities only in terms of reaching new customers. E-commerce also allows a company to streamline its operations to become more profitable. Inventory can be managed more effectively and employees worldwide can communicate better. Any multinationals can also coordinate more effectively with suppliers to get its supplies in a more timely fashion.

E-commerce is spurring a number of new business models too. For instance, many private tutoring businesses have flourished because anyone can use Skype for free. Instructors can simply call their students to provide more effective instruction. In addition, the examples of platform discussed earlier also show how e-commerce is allowing other business models such as Uber.

According to experts, there are two main types of platforms[17] allowing for different business models. One type of platform, known as transaction platforms, makes transactions possible among individuals and organizations who would find it difficult to find each other in the absence of such platforms. Examples include Amazon, Uber, Ebay, etc. In such cases, businesses that did not exist in the past become possible because of platforms as the latter allows buyers and sellers to transact.

A second type of platform is known as innovation platforms. Such platforms are the base on which other companies build their own products. An example of an innovation platform is the iPhone, which now has thousands of applications that have been built worldwide. Apple has made its technology available to software developers who build new products around such technology.

To give you further insights into where platform companies are located, Exhibit 15.5 shows the top 10 cities where most platforms are located. However, the ordering of the cities reflects the valuation of the companies. As such, San Francisco has the largest number of platform companies with the highest valuation.

As Exhibit 15.5 shows, though US companies have dominated platforms, emerging markets such as China and South Africa have also been important players in the industry. This suggests that the future will see even more competition among companies.

Platforms tend to have unique characteristics that make them different from other e-commerce products. Platforms tend to have more than one group of customers. However, most importantly, platforms tend to have strong network effects. This means that as the number of consumers grows, the platforms become more attractive to other users.

Yet, despite the significant opportunities represented by global e-commerce, there remain significant challenges. For instance, it is expensive to maintain a website on a global level. There exist significant differences across cultures and languages, and the process can be very complicated. Furthermore, if a multinational is selling products, returns and shipping can also

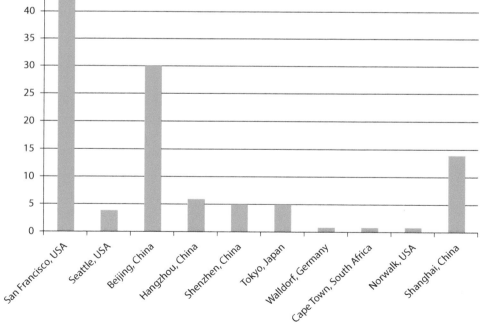

Number of Platform Companies

Exhibit 15.5 Top 10 Cities Where Platforms are Headquartered
Source: Based on P. C. Evans and A. Gawer, 2016, "The rise of the platform enterprise: A global survey," www.thecge.net/wp-content/uploads/2016/01/PDF-WEB-Platform-Survey_01_12.pdf

be very complex. Different countries have different regulations and tax systems in place and multinationals may find it difficult to keep up with payment systems that conform to local regulations. Shipping worldwide can also be expensive. Many online booksellers rely on this mode of transportation as it is much cheaper than air transport. They now have to find cost-effective alternatives or they will likely see sales drop internationally. As you have been reading, when it comes to emerging markets they pose additional challenges. Consider the following Emerging Market Ethical Challenge.

Threats in Emerging Markets

EMERGING MARKET
ETHICAL CHALLENGE

Although emerging markets present tremendous opportunities, there remain significant threats that have made e-commerce challenging. These include:

- Lack of credit—as mentioned in the Preview IB Emerging Market Strategic Insight, the Indian e-commerce landscape is characterized by consumers lacking credit. Credit cards are seldom used. This is also the case in many African nations. Consider that in the Ivory Coast consumers prefer to pay on delivery. Online companies such as Jumia often find that one fifth of all orders are usually returned. This therefore limits the growth in these markets.
- Lack of delivery logistics and infrastructure—many emerging markets suffer from a poor delivery infrastructure. For instance, India has many potential new customers. However, delivering the products may not be easy. In some emerging markets in Africa there is a lack of postal database. Additionally, local postal services may not always be reliable. This therefore adds to the challenges of getting products to potential customers.
- Governmental regulation—as the many examples earlier showed, many emerging markets have new regulations that can take multinationals by surprise. Consider the cases of WhatsApp in Brazil and Facebook in India discussed earlier. A more recent case of governmental regulation applies to Apple in India. The Indian government requires that a foreign company can only sell its products in India if more than 30 percent of the product is sourced locally. IPhones do not meet these requirements and Apple has therefore been banned from selling their smartphones in its Indian stores. This is very damaging to Apple as the Indian smartphone market is growing at 30 percent annually. Apple risks losing out on this growth.

Source: Based on *The Economist*, 2016, "Forbidden fruit," June 4, p. 66; *The Economist*, 2016, "E-commerce in India: Local heroes," January 16, pp. 72–73; *The Economist*, 2016, "Special Report, Business in Africa: Fortune favors the brave," April 16, pp. 15–16.

The previous paragraphs discussed some of the challenges facing any company taking e-commerce cross-culturally. In the next section, we consider some of the key cross-cultural e-commerce issues and the challenges they present. You will also read about solutions to these challenges.

Key Cross-cultural and Global E-commerce Issues

The use of the Internet and e-commerce at a global level presents companies with unique issues and challenges. In this section, you will read about many of these key issues. You will also learn about the ways many multinationals are dealing with these issues.

Cross-cultural E-commerce Adoption and Diffusion

An important component of any company's attempt to go global with e-commerce is e-commerce adoption. **E-commerce adoption** refers to the degree to which companies and individuals are willing to accept the new technologies inherent in performing e-commerce tasks. **E-commerce diffusion**, a related concept, refers to the degree to which e-commerce is spreading and being adopted in different societies. Because the focus for many MNCs is on selling products and services through the Internet in new countries (business-to-consumer, B2C), it becomes critical to understand the factors that encourage B2C in different societies.

Understanding of business-to-business (B2B) e-commerce adoption is also very critical. Experts argue that many emerging markets have environments where e-commerce adoption cannot be taken for granted. However, it is undeniable that e-commerce adoption is very critical especially for small and medium enterprises.[18] Such organizations play a critical role in the economic development of many societies. Understanding the barriers and facilitators of e-commerce adoption in companies is also important.

At a basic level, research shows that e-commerce adoption and diffusion is dependent on the Internet infrastructure and the availability of Internet services at affordable prices.[19] Such findings are not altogether surprising. People are more likely to adopt the Internet if they can afford it. These findings suggest that multinationals may wish to locate their services in places where the Internet is readily available. The Exhibits discussed earlier provide some understanding of Internet penetration and the degree of use by the population, and can be used as the basis for market location decisions.

However, some research also shows that infrastructure and Internet cost alone do not completely explain the degree of e-commerce adoption and diffusion. Cultural factors and institutional factors also play an important role. To better understand e-commerce adoption, it is important to understand the Technology Adoption Model (TAM) developed by Davis.[20] The fundamental premise of the TAM is that acceptance of information technology or e-commerce is dependent on two important factors; namely, the perceived usefulness and perceived ease of use of the technology. When applied to e-commerce, **perceived usefulness** refers to the degree to which an individual believes that using a B2C site will enhance his or her shopping experience[21] while **perceived ease of use** refers to the belief that the use of a B2C website is free of effort. Furthermore, more recent studies also suggest that another factor determining a positive attitude towards acceptance of information technology is the level of social influence. **Social influence** refers to the beliefs of others about the information technology being considered.

To give you an understanding of the TAM model within the context of emerging markets, consider the following Emerging Market Brief.

e-commerce adoption
degree to which companies and individuals are willing to accept new technologies inherent in e-commerce

e-commerce diffusion
degree to which e-commerce is spreading in different societies

perceived usefulness
perception that the use of a B2C site will enhance the shopping experience

perceived ease of use
belief that use of a B2C website is free of effort

social influence
beliefs of others about the information technology being used

SMS Advertising Acceptance in South Korea

EMERGING MARKET BRIEF

As mobile phones grow as an important way for multinationals to reach customers, understanding the reasons why individuals accept short message service (SMS) advertising is important. In an interesting study, researchers studied young American and South Korean mobile phone users and their willingness to accept SMS advertising from companies. Not surprisingly, the researchers found that the TAM model works well. They found that the components of the TAM model applied in both countries and predicted acceptance of SMS advertising. However, the study also showed cross-cultural differences. Specifically, the results showed that South Korean users had generally more positive attitudes towards SMS advertising. This therefore reflects the preference of advertisers in South Korea to prefer SMS advertising. Furthermore, for the South Koreans, the degree of social influence did not impact the attitude towards SMS advertising. Social influence played a bigger role for American mobile phone users. This is also not surprising as South Korea has had a much higher Internet and mobile phone use than the US. South Korean consumers are therefore more likely to accept SMS advertising on a personal level because they have been much more aware of such advertising relative to US customers.

Source: Based on A. Muk and C. Chung, 2015, "Applying the technology acceptance model in a two-country study of SMS advertising," *Journal of Business Research, 68*, pp. 1–6.

As the Emerging Market Brief shows, the TAM model is dependent on the cultural and institutional aspects of a society. For instance, Parboteeah et al.[22] found that the cultural dimensions discussed in Chapter 7 are linked to perceived usefulness of technology. This study found that uncertainty avoidance, which refers to the degree to which people are comfortable with uncertainty, discourages usefulness of technology. Also, more masculine societies, emphasizing work and achievement, viewed technology as being more useful.

Additionally, consistent with Chapter 8 on institutions, the research also found that institutions affect how people see the usefulness of technology. They found that the higher the level of development, the more useful people found technology.[23] To give you more insights on the matter, Exhibit 15.6 shows the average degree to which people perceived the usefulness of technology in making their work more interesting across a large number of countries.

As you can see from Exhibit 15.6, clearly there are differences in terms of how different societies view technology, the Internet, and e-commerce. Many industrialized nations such as Japan, the UK, and Spain see technology as important. However, the most surprising finding is that many of the emerging market economies found in Russia, Poland, and Bulgaria view technologies as extremely important in terms of making work more interesting. Such findings are very important for MNCs. As has been the theme of this chapter, emerging economies have significant potential for e-commerce, and the fact that people view technology as important in these societies is very encouraging for MNCs wishing to expand their operations in these societies.

As discussed previously, understanding e-commerce diffusion and adoption is critical as MNCs decide which markets present the most potential. Next, we consider another crucial cross-culture e-commerce issue—e-commerce consumer trust.

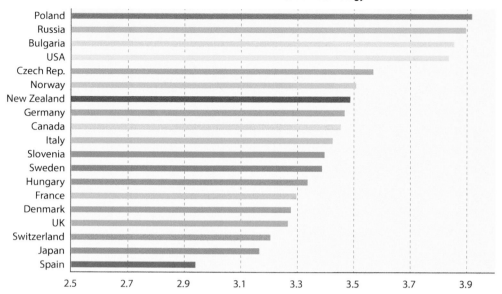

Exhibit 15.6 Perceived Usefulness of Technology in Selected Countries
Source: International Social Survey Program, 2000, *International Social Survey Program: Work Orientations II* [computer file], Ann Arbor, MI: Inter-university Consortium for Political and Social Research.

Cross-cultural Consumer Trust in E-commerce

Consumer trust in e-commerce is seen as a critical factor in influencing consumer adoption of e-commerce.[24] Because the Internet involves significant uncertainty and ambiguity, trust is an important factor in reducing such uncertainty. **Consumer trust in e-commerce** thus refers to the willingness of an online consumer to depend on others, assuming that the other party will deliver as promised. In other words, Internet purchases involve some level of risk whereby purchase consequences have some level of uncertainty. The level of trust refers to the online purchaser's degree of comfort with this uncertainty. Because so many companies are now launching global e-commerce activities, understanding trust in a global environment is very crucial. By understanding what contributes to consumer trust, an MNC can design systems to build trust.

Recent research in the emerging markets of Ukraine and Poland underscores the importance of trust in e-commerce.[25] The researcher noted that although Poland has a much better environment conducive to e-commerce than Ukraine (i.e., stronger technological environment, stronger business environment, more attractive governmental policy), Ukrainians spend three times more on e-commerce relative to their Polish counterparts. A comparative survey of young Ukrainians compared to Poles revealed that Ukrainians are much more trusting of people they meet over the Internet than the Poles. The researcher concludes that this higher level of trust likely explains why Ukrainians spend more on e-commerce.

Research by Teo and Liu suggests that a company's reputation and size have positive effects on consumer trust.[26] In other words, the larger and more well-known a company is, the more likely people will trust the company. Such findings suggest that smaller and lesser known companies need to put forth extra effort to build trust. There is some evidence that consumer trust in e-commerce differs across cultures.[27] Using Hofstede's cultural dimensions as the basis (see Chapter 7), some have argued that more individualist societies are more likely to trust

consumer trust in e-commerce
willingness of an online consumer to depend on others

strangers than more collectivist societies. As you may recall, people in collectivist societies tend to rely on in-group members (friends, family, colleagues) and are more likely to trust these people. As a consequence, one way for companies to build trust in more collectivist societies, such as China and South Korea, is by appealing to the in-group and the "familiar." In fact, it seems likely that local e-commerce companies do better than foreign ones. It therefore makes sense to engage in joint ventures locally if one wants to do well. The BRIC Insight below shows how Alibaba.com built an empire in China.

As you can see from earlier paragraphs, consumer trust in e-commerce is clearly different across cultures. Consider also the cultural dimension of uncertainty avoidance. As you recall from Chapter 7, uncertainty avoidance refers to the degree to which people in a society are comfortable with uncertainty and ambiguity. Clearly, the Internet presents uncertainty, and it is therefore not surprising that people are more wary and less trusting of the Internet in high uncertainty avoidance societies.

Given all of this, what can MNCs do to build trust? One key aspect that contributes to a trustworthy website is e-commerce and cyber security. You will read about what companies can do to make the Internet more secure later. Websites can also be designed appropriately to build trust. A new stream of research suggests that the presence of online characters can build loyalty.[28] In fact, a study in Taiwan showed that different types of avatars can also have an impact on consumer trust. The study showed that different types of avatars (expert versus attractive) can have different impact on cognitive trust (good rational reason for liking the product) or emotional trust (degree of liking of the product).[29] As such, an onscreen character can present a more human aspect of the website, allowing customers to interact and even discuss problems. Onscreen characters can also be tailored to cultural preferences. In a worldwide survey, Luo et al. found that more human-like characters were more effective than cartoon-like characters in being likeable and trustworthy. However, female cartoon-like characters were more effective in terms of website interface.[30]

Jack Ma and Alibaba.com in China   BRIC INSIGHT

Jack Ma is currently one of the biggest players in the e-commerce industry as he is the founder and CEO of Alibaba.com in China. Alibaba.com is seen as the Chinese answer to eBay. Why is Alibaba.com so successful? One can see that Ma appealed to the collectivistic nature of the Chinese in designing Alibaba.com. For instance, for his consumer-to-consumer e-commerce business, he offered instant messaging capabilities to consumers a long time before eBay bought Skype. By allowing buyers to contact sellers through instant messaging, Alibaba offers buyers the ability to get to know the seller to build trust. Furthermore, the Chinese clearly prefer a local company for e-commerce purposes as many of the foreign e-commerce businesses have failed.

Another step Alibaba has taken to encourage people to buy online and to reduce anxiety is through the creation of Alipay. Chinese customers were initially reluctant to buy online as they did not trust that they would receive the products that they purchased. Alipay is an escrow account maintained by Alibaba that keeps the shopper's payment until the shopper receives the product he or she has purchased. This system provided an additional mechanism to ensure that shoppers were comfortable and trusting of online purchases in China.

Source: Based on *The Economist*, 2016, "The great race," March 5, pp. 19–21; J. Heilemann, 2006, "Unlocking the middle kingdom," *Business 2.0*, August, pp. 44–46; K. Hafner and B. Stone, 2006, "eBay is expected to close its auction site in China," *New York Times*, December 19, p. C11.

third party trust seals
retailer associates its
website with another
more reputable and
well-known business

Another way for retailers to build trust is through the use of third party trust seals.[31] **Third party trust seals** are used when a retailer associates its website with another more well-known and reputable company. For example, many smaller retailers tend to show the Better Business Bureau logo on their website to reflect that they can be trusted. This third party seal thus becomes a means by which a new shopper can verify the claims of the retailer through a third party. This can also allow the customer to develop the initial trust to purchase from the website. Recent research suggests that third party trust seals are extremely critical for small retailers.[32] The same research, however, also mentions that too many trust seals can sometimes result in negative purchase intentions for buyers.

**multichannel
integration**
multinational having
both online websites and
physical stores

A final way that multinationals can build trust is by engaging in **multichannel integration**.[33] In other words, a multinational can have both online websites and physical stores. By having both channels, an MNC offers customers the means to freely choose the purchase most comfortable for them. In fact, such multichannel integration is becoming a source of competitive advantage. A key issue with multichannel integration is the degree of integration between the online presence and the physical presence. Teo and Liu suggest that both channels should be fully integrated to get a unified view of customers and to provide a consistent shopping experience.[34]

In this section, you read about cross-cultural consumer e-commerce trust. Another critical aspect of cross-cultural e-commerce is website design. This will be discussed in the next section.

Cross-cultural Web Design

As multinationals increasingly use websites as a way to advertise and sell products globally, more of them are considering the extent to which web design should adapt to local preferences. MNCs need to determine whether they want a **standardized website,** where the company's website is fairly similar in layout and design around the world, or a **localized website,** where the values, appeals, and symbols in the communication content are adapted to the local culture.

standardized website
company's websites
around the world are
fairly similar in layout
and design

The standardized website typically presents the same form of promotion messages translated for the local context. However, there are no other modifications of headings, illustrations, or other sources of information. This form of website is based on the assumption that consumers anywhere around the world share the same needs and wants.[35] The amazing acceptance of the Internet has led to impressive growth, suggesting that standardized websites may be appropriate. For instance, Dell has very minimal website adaptation with websites in 50 countries using 21 different languages. It uses the same layout for the sites in all countries.

localized website
website design and
layout are adapted to fit
local culture

In contrast, the localized approach entails adapting the website and messages to local culture, available media, and industry. Multinationals with localized websites assume that there are significant consumer differences because of cultural and other institutional differences. An MNC must then adapt its website to suit local preferences. McDonald's is a company that localizes its website. A recent study by Wurtz shows that the highly individualistic Swiss and German McDonald's websites display images of individuals listening to music and relaxing (a very individual activity). In contrast, the collectivistic Indian McDonald's website shows a man running with a child in a shopping cart, emphasizing the family ties and group approach typical of more collectivistic societies.[36]

Should MNCs localize or standardize their websites? The answer is, of course, dependent on the nature of the product being sold, consumers, and other factors. Some products, like PCs for instance, do not require much adaptation for the local cultures. However, experts agree that some level of adaptation is critical for most situations. Consider eBay's failure in China.[37] They failed in that market because they did not allow buyers the ability to communicate directly with the seller. Chinese customers prefer to be able to see whether a seller is online and develop trust by interacting directly with the seller. Although eBay made users' seller ratings available,

Chinese customers do not use that information as a basis for trust. As such, the lack of seamless integration of being able to see whether a seller is online and being able to communicate with the seller doomed eBay's efforts in the market. Taobao, a local rival, was better able to adapt their website to such requirements.

If adaptation is needed, how should MNCs approach website adaptation? Recent research suggests that adaptation needs to go beyond mere machine-translated versions of websites.[38] Beyond language adaptation through translation, other issues such as the colors, icons, web page layout, date format, fonts, and so on need to be adapted.[39] Research on culture again provides some insights. For instance, consumers from more masculine societies where work and achievement are emphasized prefer more interactivity from their websites. People in more long-term orientation societies prefer more visual and other emotional appeals.[40] Further research reported by Wurtz shows that the website animation in high context cultures (i.e. where communication is not direct but also includes implicit messages contained in body language and silence) is more centered on people, showing preference for complexity in communication. In contrast, low context culture websites (i.e. where communication occurs primarily through explicit statements through text and speech) are more static and use less animation. Furthermore, navigation on low context culture websites tends to be more linear, whereas high context cultures have more new browser windows opening with less transparent guidance.[41]

A recent study provides further insights into China. Consider the following BRIC Insight.

Cross-cultural Website Challenges in China

BRIC INSIGHT

How should companies adapt their websites in China. A recent study provides a comparison of Chinese and US websites and insights into such adaptation. The authors argue that culture can also be differentiated on the basis of business cultures. Business cultures can be divided into two main components: formal versus informal and deal-focused versus relationship-oriented cultures. China tends to be much more formal and relationship-oriented. In contrast, the US business culture tends to be much more informal and deal-focused.

Given these differences, the author provides for a comparative examination of image analysis (what images are shown on the website) and verbal analysis (what information is shown on the website). Results provide support for the business cultural preferences of the country. For example, the Chinese real estate website tends to show pictures of mostly individuals in the company: a picture of the company president at the top of a mountain, pictures of others around a table, and a picture of a person jogging. These reflect the more formal and collectivistic nature of Chinese society. The company president at the top of the mountain reflects the hierarchy and formality inherent in the society. The picture of the person jogging reflects the company taking care of its workers by encouraging them to exercise. In contrast, the American real estate website shows pictures of houses. This reflects the more deal-oriented nature of the business culture in the US whereby emphasis is on the product and making a deal.

Similar differences are found with regards to verbal analysis. In a comparative analysis of power companies, the author shows that the Chinese company has a website that presents information about the company. All of the tabs are about the company's history, achievements, partnerships, and its service to society. Such characteristics reflect the importance of face in Chinese culture and the need again to display aspects to develop relationships. In contrast, the

American power company's website is more reflective of the services offered by the company. This again reflects the focus of American culture on making the deal. Furthermore, users can quickly find the types of information they need based on required services reflecting the maxim that "time is money."

Source: Based on P. Zhu, 2016, "Impact of business cultural values on web homepage design that may hinder international business," *Journal of Technical Writing and Communication*, 46, pp. 105–124.

Many organizations therefore discover that developing local websites is extremely complex. As the above BRIC Insight shows, adapting websites to the Chinese business culture means building a website that reflects face, hierarchy, people, and power. Understanding how to encourage the website visitor to build relationships based on website characteristics is not easy. Beyond cultural and language sensitivity, they also need to adapt their organizations to the information flow and customer demands created by web locations accessed from anywhere in the world. As such, many multinationals are finding that they are better off outsourcing these functions to specialized companies. One example of such a company is Digital River,[42] which provides all activities (website development and hosting, order management, export and tax management, multi-language customer service, fraud prevention, etc.) needed to maintain localized e-commerce operations.[43]

In the next section, you will read about some of the key steps in building a successful global e-commerce strategy.

Building a Successful Global E-commerce Strategy

In the previous section, you read about the important cross-cultural e-commerce issues. Here, you will learn about some of the key steps in building a successful e-commerce strategy. You will also read about cyber security and the importance of building secure e-commerce operations.

Important Aspects of a Successful E-commerce Strategy

E-commerce strategizing is a new and evolving challenge and its application to the global arena adds more complexity. However, e-commerce has the potential to contribute to profits and competitive advantage for the multinational. It is therefore important for the multinational manager to build on sound, basic strategizing as a prelude to multinational operations. Below you will learn about some of these key aspects.

Experts agree that a successful e-commerce strategy starts with top management.[44] Successful e-commerce is only possible through dynamic and strong leadership coming from the top. At a minimum, the CEO and senior executives should strongly believe in the benefits of an e-commerce approach. As you realize, e-commerce involves strong resource and time commitment. Leaders should have expertise and vision to objectively assess the company's position on e-commerce in order to craft the most appropriate e-commerce strategy.

Beyond expertise, it is critical to assess some of the recent trends to determine the most appropriate strategy. Experts suggest some trends and potential solutions.[45] These include:

- *Speed* One of the most important trends is that customers now want to be able to perform any transaction with speed. Whether a multinational is considering a potential customer or a supplier for supply chain areas, that customer wants to be able to engage in the transaction as efficiently as possible. For the multinational, this suggests that all delays at any step of the process will drive away customers. For instance, if delays occur because of too many approval steps or inappropriate transaction processing, every effort needs to be made to remove sources of such delays.

- *Self-service* Another important trend is the ability for a customer to be able to get self-service at any time. Most of the world is now living in a seven days a week, 24 hours a day, time frame. Everyone believes that they should have the ability to have access to real-time information to make purchases or solve other problems. As mentioned by Garrett and Parrott,[46] consider that Dell provides the ability for customers to order both software and hardware at any point in time. Furthermore, Dell also offers limited technical support without the assistance of a person. How can such services be provided? The website design and data management processes are very important. Websites should be user-friendly and fun. MNCs should also make adjustments to the website based on the popular means of getting Internet access. For instance, movies and other clips should be avoided where broadband is not available.

- *Adaptation* An important success factor you have read about several times in this chapter is the ability for multinationals to adapt to the local needs of customers. The many examples discussed earlier show how a lack of adaptation can lead to failure. In that context, it is important to note that e-commerce can be successful if multinationals are able to market the convenience features of online shopping. However, while convenience in more developed markets implies the ability to shop in shorter periods of time, it may take a more complex dimension in emerging markets.[47] In emerging markets, convenience for consumers often means having an online website that displays product variety. It therefore becomes imperative for the multinational to clearly understand its customers within an emerging market perspective and provide targeted marketing efforts.

- *Customer service* An important trend noted by experts is the provision of superior customer service. Companies can no longer rely on their websites simply as a means of transmitting information. Multinationals are constantly looking for ways to use their e-commerce operations to provide better customer service. Also, as more multinationals become intertwined with other businesses, there is a serious need to coordinate across organizations.

- *Integration of various channels* Most MNCs are facing increased pressure to integrate the various channels through which they operate. For instance, retailers are under increased pressure to coordinate and integrate their online offerings with the store experience. Because of the national and international nature of the Internet, companies are finding that they need to have consistent policies between their online and offline operations. Research suggests that consumers are frustrated when they find that products offered online are not sold in stores, or that prices differ widely across the different channels.[48] Although this issue is not as critical with global websites, multinationals nevertheless need to ensure that a consistent message is being provided across countries.

The above recommendations seem more appropriate for mature markets with well developed infrastructure and processes. But how do companies ensure success in emerging markets. Consider the following IB Emerging Market Strategic Insight.

E-commerce Success in Emerging Markets

While the above recommendations would work well in any market including emerging markets, the latter have several distinctive characteristics that require unique strategies. These include:

- Infrastructure—as discussed earlier, some emerging markets suffer from the lack of proper infrastructure. Product delivery may be challenging because of poor postal facilities or access to Internet may be limited because of lagging infrastructure. The financial infrastructure may also be poorly developed. Multinationals will therefore need to carefully consider such issues and play a bigger role in developing such infrastructure.
- Transaction integrity—many customers in emerging markets may not yet trust the financial infrastructure because they do not have much experience with such impersonal online markets. In addition, many do not have credit cards and banks do not necessarily support online transactions. Successful multinationals will therefore need to approach such markets with caution, building systems with integrity and ensuring that customers can safely undertake financial transactions without any fear.
- First mover—customers in emerging markets have often not yet developed brand preferences. Multinationals that are first movers are therefore in a solid position to develop branding among customers. In fact, a study of around 41 online retailers in the Indian market shows that there are clear first mover advantages. Companies that are first movers in any industry tend to enjoy stronger market share and profitability thereby clearly reflecting the advantages of being first to market and cultivating such markets.

Source: Based on J. Agarwal and T. Wu, 2015, "Factors influencing growth potential of e-commerce in emerging economies: An institution-based N-OLI framework and research propositions," *Thunderbird International Business Review*, *57*(3), pp. 197–215; H. Goparaju, 2015, "A preliminary study of first-mover advantage among e-commerce companies in India," *IUP Journal of Business Strategy*, *12*, pp. 27–45.

As well as the above trends, Epstein suggests that successful global e-commerce companies need to be willing to make significant financial investments if they want to succeed globally.[49] Having a global presence involves dedication of significant effort and resources. If a multinational is not willing to make such investments, its e-commerce operations will likely fail. Such investments need to include adequate financial resources for an IT department and appropriate resources for upgrading the multinational's information systems. It is also important for multinationals to be aware of their limitations in emerging markets and be willing to engage in the appropriate costs using online intermediaries when needed. Local online intermediaries can provide services to enable foreign multinationals to overcome cultural and language barriers.[50] Use of such intermediaries can be an important factor in determining success.

A final important aspect of any successful e-commerce operation is appropriate data management. The Internet and e-commerce provide incredible opportunities for data collection and manipulation. However, if the data are not properly collected and managed, a multinational will lose the ability to take full advantage of such data. Experts[51] suggest the following:

- *Track important data* Customer data can be very important given the potential insights that can be garnered from them. The multinational must ensure that there are systems in place to collect the appropriate information from customer visits. Some companies prefer to focus on number of hits and visits a customer makes to a website. However, the experts argue that the type of interaction a customer has with a website is more critical, as it may reveal information regarding price sensitivity and general appeal of the website.

- *Enter accurate data* A multinational needs to take every step to ensure that the collected information is clean and accurate. For e-commerce operations, it is critical to emphasize to the customer the importance of accurate data. Furthermore, such data can then be compared with other outside sources of data. Additionally, it is important to make sure that the data collected can be matched with visitors to the website. This will ensure a better understanding of previous purchases and future preferences.

- *Maintain data at the lowest level possible* Multinationals should ensure that data are collected at the lowest possible level. For instance, if an MNC is selling various types of products, it is imperative to keep the data at the customer level if possible. Data aggregation is always possible; however, breaking down the data is never possible. For instance, if the multinational combines all sales, it may not be able to analyze purchase patterns by products. Data mining thus becomes very difficult. Finally, it is also strongly advised that data are never destroyed. Data storing means are very inexpensive today and can be done very easily.

- *Protection of privacy* Experts agree that online users in many emerging markets are wary of giving personal data on the Internet. They are not always aware of how the company will use such data. In fact, a recent study in China showed that privacy concerns had a negative impact on trust in wearable technology.[52] Multinationals are therefore well advised to develop systems to protect consumers' data and to also clearly communicate to users how such data will be used.

In this section, you read about some of the key steps in ensuring successful e-commerce operations. In the next and final section, you will learn about one of the most crucial elements of e-commerce—cyber and e-commerce security.

Cyber and E-commerce Security

As businesses and societies increasingly rely on computer technology and the Internet for daily operations, cybercrime is becoming increasingly likely. **Cybercrime** revolves around any crime or other illegal activities using the available computer networks. There are a variety of cybercrimes and these have grown considerably over the last decade. These will be discussed later.

As e-commerce grows in importance, it is undeniable that cybercrime will keep growing too. Cyber security is therefore becoming increasingly crucial for most MNCs. **Cyber security** refers to the challenges and other vulnerabilities the Internet faces as individuals try to exploit and attack weaknesses. While cyber security applies to the Internet, e-commerce security refers to the challenges customers face as they participate in e-commerce transactions. Specifically, **e-commerce security** refers to the degree to which customers feel that their private and personal information can be safeguarded in the hands of online companies collecting such information.

The growth of the Internet and e-commerce on a global basis has led to the creation of several associations to encourage global policy making. In that context, the Global Business Dialogue on e-Society (www.gbd-e.org) is an international government and private company partnership that is examining the key global e-commerce issues to be tackled. It identifies cyber security as one of the most important challenges that needs to be tackled. In fact, it argues that as the Internet and computer software are becoming more interconnected, exploitation of small security holes can lead to catastrophic damage.

cybercrime
crime committed using the available computer networks

cyber security
challenges and other vulnerabilities of the Internet

e-commerce security
degree to which individuals feel that their private information is safe in the hands of companies collecting such information

The Global Business Dialogue on e-Society and others[53] identify the following factors as the major reasons why cyber security is an important issue:

- *Rapid growth of viruses and worms* As more computers are now ever more connected, computer viruses and worms can rapidly copy themselves through e-mails and files, causing serious damage (computer malfunction, Internet slowdown, loss of data, etc.) to the Internet.
- *Hacking* More computers are now vulnerable to attacks from individuals from faraway locations. When hackers break into others' computers, they have the ability to manipulate important data and cause important damage to those data. The authentication and identification processes can become compromised.
- *Spam* The growth of spam or unsolicited mass mailings has become a major annoyance for Internet users. Spam not only reduces employee productivity as they search and delete such e-mails, but it is also slowing down network traffic because of the large amount of spam being sent.
- *Phishing* More Internet users are getting spam where they are requested to submit crucial information, such as credit card numbers and social security numbers, to a website disguised as a legitimate bank or credit card company website. The information collected is then used for fraudulent purposes.
- *Computer attacks and identity theft* Attacks on popular websites are increasing at a very rapid rate. Such attacks have resulted in theft of the credit card numbers of thousands of customers. As personal information gets stolen, the consequences can be very catastrophic, for the individuals involved (e.g. loss of privacy, loss of money, threats) and MNCs (e.g. loss of trade secrets, loss of business opportunities) alike.

Exhibit 15.7 gives you a more complete view on the various types of cybercrimes.

Type	Definition
Spam e-mails	E-mails sent without the receivers' consent. These e-mails often slow down productivity as multinationals have to find ways to filter them out.
Viruses	Computer programs that infiltrate a computer or computer network resulting in either computer malfunction or stealing of information without the users' knowledge.
Phishing	Legitimate looking e-mails or computer programs that trick users to provide key information such as passwords or logins. This information can then be used to access a user's critical accounts such as banking or other financial institutions.
Denial-of-service	The act of flooding a computer network with messages with the intention of crippling a multinational's computer network or computer system.
Malware	The illegal installation of software on a computer that takes control of the computer and provides access to other computers or networks.
Scareware	More multinationals are now having to deal with this where cybercriminals force users to download software that cripples the users' computer systems. The criminals then force the users to pay a fee in return for removal of the scareware.
Fiscal fraud	Infiltration of official financial computer networks with the intent of claiming fraudulent benefits or conduct of online activities for illegal gains.
Carders	Illegal acquisition of credit or other bank card details with the intention to use such information to make purchases or withdraw cash.

Exhibit 15.7 Types of Cybercrime

Source: Based on KPMG, "Cyber crime: A growing challenge for governments," www.kpmg.com/Global/en/IssuesAndInsights/ ArticlesPublications/Documents/cyber-crime.pdf

It is clear that cybercrime will continue growing as the world becomes more interconnected and all aspects of business are done online. Many recent reports underscore the dangers. For instance, a recent study shows that the growth of use of smartphones in e-commerce in India has led to a dramatic increase in the number of 'apps.' Unfortunately, the research shows that around 98 percent of the mobile 'apps' of the top Indian e-commerce companies are vulnerable to online attacks.[54]

China is facing similar challenges with fraudsters focused on the mobile market. Because the systems that have been developed are so new, criminals are taking advantage of their developing nature. One recent study suggests that over 130 million SIM cards in China are not registered. Criminals often use these unregistered phones to commit cybercrime. The Chinese government is now engaged in an effort to register such SIM cards.[55]

What can multinationals do to minimize threats to e-commerce security? At a national level, many countries are taking steps to combat Internet threats. For instance, some countries such as the UK and Japan are setting up computer security incident response teams to provide guidance on how to handle potential Internet threats. Multinationals are being strongly encouraged to partner with such groups for their e-commerce security issues. Countries such as Taiwan and South Korea have increased the punishments associated with cybercrimes such as phishing or hacking. Such punishment is assumed to act as a deterrent for potential cybercriminals. Both the US and Germany have also been active in addressing cyber security issues in a proactive manner.

In addition to the cooperation with governmental authorities described above, multinationals are being encouraged to take appropriate measures to beef up their Internet security. Specifically, most companies need to be concerned about a number of information security issues.[56] These include (1) confidentiality (making sure that private information is protected); (2) availability (ensuring that information is accessible to authorized users); (3) integrity (ensuring that the information collected is accurate and reliable); and (4) authentication (having systems in place to ensure that persons using the systems are legitimate).

Companies are also under increased pressure to protect the privacy of individuals as more and more personal information is being collected, stored, and shared by companies involved in industries such as health care, banking/finance, travel, and the government.[57] In fact, experts suggest that a company can build consumer trust by taking privacy issues seriously. In that context, these experts recommend: (1) taking a consumer mindset when setting the vision for the type of data collected and how they are used—this will ensure that the multinational is aware of consumers' perspectives and will design systems keeping such consumer perspectives in mind; (2) developing privacy policies as a marketing tool—this will make consumers aware of the reasoning behind the privacy policies and ensure that they are communicated well rather than just being a legal tool; (3) making the individual who is responsible for data security and privacy a high level executive—multinationals should be aware of the critical roles played by such an individual; and (4) develop systems across the organization—the threats to all aspects and areas of the organization should be properly assessed and systems implemented to deal with all of these areas.

To ensure a multinational's Internet and cyber security is preserved, experts suggest using firewalls, intrusion detection software, and antivirus shields, whereby systems are in place to keep outsiders from entering private networks.[58] Various companies are specialists in providing technologies to protect a company's network. As more instances of data theft emerge, it is becoming more critical for companies to adequately encrypt the data so that the latter are meaningless if they fall into the hands of criminals. Additionally, to prevent unauthorized access to information, more multinationals are now requiring two-phased authentication processes. Such systems require two forms of identity; namely, a password and some identity token such as a key fob or other device. Many multinationals are also using technology to monitor websites to detect any unusual page requests or other suspicious activity. This will provide some warning if a website is being attacked or is about to be attacked.

Finally, an important but unlikely tool to fight cybercrime is cooperation among companies. Many multinationals are finding that they can learn from each other's mistakes and also share best practices.[59] Several resources such as IBM's X-Force Exchange (https://exchange.xforce.ibmcloud.com/) and Security Colony (www.securitycolony.com/) are portals where multinationals can share best practices of how they dealt with specific threats and intelligence about cybercrime.

An important but indirect challenge of the Internet and e-commerce operations today is e-waste. Consider the following Emerging Market Ethical Challenge.

E-waste in India

EMERGING MARKET
ETHICAL CHALLENGE

E-waste is an incredibly critical problem in most societies today. E-waste refers to the waste generated as old computers and other electronic appliances, such as large and small household appliances, are disposed of when they become old. As societies and companies increasingly rely on computers and other innovative online technology, short product life-cycles of such products are contributing to a massive increase in e-waste. The most recent report shows that the amount of e-waste generated yearly is growing at a rapid pace. Exhibit 15.8 shows the growth of e-waste over the last few years and predicted increases in the future.

Why is such growth in e-waste so disastrous? E-waste from computers, refrigerators, televisions, and mobile phones may contain more than 1,000 toxic materials. Beryllium, cadmium, chromium, and mercury are all chemicals contained in discarded equipment, posing significant health risks as well as environmental challenges. Because these chemicals are not always disposed of properly, they are contributing to an environmental nightmare. Furthermore,

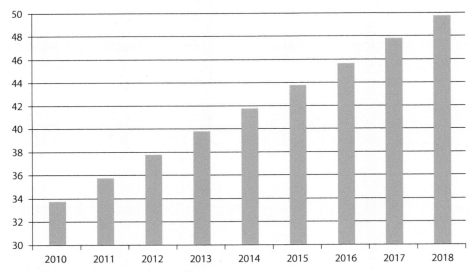

E-Waste Generated (million tonnes)

Exhibit 15.8 E-waste Generated (2010–2018)

Source: Based on United Nations University, The global E-Waste monitor, https://i.unu.edu/media/unu.edu/news/52624/UNU-1stGlobal-E-Waste-Monitor-2014-small.pdf

both India and China have become dumping grounds for old electronic equipment from other more developed countries. Unfortunately, workers in these industries are not properly equipped to deal with these discarded pieces of equipment and the health threat is obvious.

And, although the discarded electronic equipment from more developed countries poses significant risks to India, India is also now facing a domestic battle. As income grows and the price of computers comes down, more Indians can now afford computers. This is generating even more challenges as the greater national turnover in computer technology is contributing to India's e-waste problems. As such, multinationals concerned about the future will find that they need to address the e-waste issue.

Source: Based on S. Gallagher, 2016, "India: The rising tide of e-waste," http://pulitzercenter.org/reporting/asia-india-electronic-waste-toxic-environment; Habib Beary, 2005, "Bangalore faces e-waste hazards," http://news.bbc.co.uk; Ambika Behal, 2006, "Managing Indian e-waste," *Terra Daily*, www.terradaily.com/reports/Managing_Indian_E_Waste.html

Chapter Review

In this chapter you read about the key e-commerce issues facing any MNC today. The chapter first defined e-commerce and described the many types of e-commerce. You also learned about e-commerce structure and the many features making e-commerce a critical aspect of any business today. Multinationals that ignore e-commerce do so at their own peril.

The chapter also discussed some of the key aspects of global e-commerce with a special emphasis on emerging markets. You read about the many factors facilitating e-commerce for any company today. You also learned about the many opportunities and threats facing any company as it takes e-commerce globally. You also read about the unique threats and opportunities facing companies involved in e-commerce in emerging markets. Key cross-cultural e-commerce issues such as e-commerce adoption, cross-cultural consumer trust in e-commerce, and cross-cultural web design were also discussed.

In the final section, you read about the important aspects of any successful e-commerce strategy. You learned about the many important e-commerce trends and possible adaptation to such trends. You also read about how such lessons can be applied to the situation facing emerging markets. An important section of the chapter was also devoted to cyber and e-commerce security. As more computers and networks get connected around the world, it is becoming imperative for companies to assure cyber and e-commerce security. This chapter discussed some possible steps to ensure cyber security. You also learned about e-waste and the challenges it poses for the environment.

As you realize, the Internet and e-commerce will continue to grow in importance in the future. As more people around the world and specifically emerging markets gain access to the Internet, the opportunities presented by the Internet will remain crucial. This chapter hopefully provided you with an understanding of this importance and the many key issues as a multinational or small company takes e-commerce to the global level.

Discussion Questions

1   What is e-commerce? What are the main types of e-commerce?

2   What are some of the ways e-commerce impacts a multinational's operations? Discuss how important e-commerce is for today's company in emerging markets.

3   What are some crucial functions of a website? Discuss the many core functions of a website as a commercial transaction is taking place.

4   What are some of the factors that make e-commerce more accessible to small companies today?

5   Discuss some of the key opportunities and threats of e-commerce in emerging markets.

6   What is e-commerce adoption? What are some of the factors determining e-commerce adoption across cultures?

7   What are some of the factors affecting consumer trust in e-commerce? Discuss some of the ways a multinational can build consumer trust in its global website.

8   How does culture affect cross-cultural website design? Discuss some of the advantages and disadvantages of having a standardized website and a localized website.

9   Discuss three key elements of a successful global e-commerce strategy in the context of emerging markets.

10   What is cyber and e-commerce security? Why is cyber security such a crucial problem for any multinational? Discuss some of the key steps a multinational can implement to maximize e-commerce and cyber security.

International Business Skill Builder

Designing an International Website

As the head of a website development firm, you have been contacted by a company producing dairy products, including cheese among others. The company has determined through market research that there is significant demand from large-scale resellers for its products. The company has also realized that a website in these countries would greatly enhance its market potential.

Step 1: You have been asked to design specific websites for the countries of Brazil, Russia, India, and China (BRIC). Consult appropriate sources and websites in these countries. Provide extensive information regarding the key issues that will need to be considered in creating the websites. Assume that the websites will be used to place orders.

Step 2: Provide the company with information regarding the appropriate web design for each country. Be specific about the web design for each country (i.e. what elements will you use for each country? How will the products be featured?).

Step 3: Consult the US website of a similar company. Provide some information to the company regarding how each country's website will differ from the US website. Provide explanations for these differences.

Chapter Internet Activity

Step 1: You have been asked by a local small company to help them launch a website in a few selected countries. Pick a few countries that you are interested in.

Step 2: Research companies that already have websites in the selected countries. Inform the small company of the unique aspects of these websites.

Step 3: Provide a report to the company regarding specific measures you will need to maintain e-commerce security. Provide detailed information about the potential for cybercrime in the countries.

Key Concepts

- ☐ B2B
- ☐ B2C
- ☐ born-global firms
- ☐ C2B
- ☐ C2C
- ☐ consumer trust in e-commerce
- ☐ cybercrime
- ☐ cyber security
- ☐ e-commerce
- ☐ e-commerce adoption
- ☐ e-commerce diffusion
- ☐ e-commerce security

- ☐ localized website
- ☐ perceived ease of use
- ☐ perceived usefulness
- ☐ platforms
- ☐ social influence
- ☐ standardized website
- ☐ transaction formation
- ☐ third party trust seals
- ☐ transaction incubation
- ☐ transaction management
- ☐ transaction negotiation

CASE 15   BUSINESS > INTERNATIONAL

Alibaba: The Imperial Dragon of E-Commerce

Jack Ma is a man on a mission. The Chinese entrepreneur who founded Alibaba and other companies, wants to change the way business-to-business (B2B) is conducted. He wants to develop a platform to support small and medium-sized enterprises (SMEs). Alibaba, Taobao, and other Ma creations have already begun to make some wonder how this former English teacher, with an unassuming demeanor, has been so successful, and what the future holds for his companies and the future of B2B activity.

The founder of Alibaba, Jack Ma grew up in the Chinese city of Hangzhou, a city known for its beauty. Ma began his work life as a child, acting as a tour guide in order to improve his proficiency in English. Ma's academic skills in math and science were poor; however, he possessed a talent for languages. After graduating from the Hangzhou Normal College, Ma began teaching English. Not satisfied with the salary of an English teacher, Ma began his own translation business. After a trip to the United States and gaining experience with computers and the Internet, Ma created China's first Yellow Pages company. Ma then started Alibaba in his small apartment and has grown the Alibaba Group into a collection of fast-growth companies including Taobao, Alipay, and TMall. While still a humble and frugal man, Jack Ma is building a strong competitive force in the information-based global economy. He is known for not thinking about today or tomorrow, but thinking decades ahead. Jack Ma has a long-term focus which has served him well in becoming China's wealthiest individual. His rise from poverty to prosperity began with a vision, upon which he is constantly expanding. Alibaba is now the largest e-commerce website in the world and has an 80 percent market share of e-commerce in China.

Alibaba is a publicly traded company which initially listed on the Hong Kong Exchange. The initial listing in 2007 had an IPO of $1.5 billion. Having some difficulties with regulators in Hong Kong, in 2014 Alibaba sought to raise additional capital in the United States which resulted in the largest IPO in US history bringing in $25 billion. Alibaba is now mostly owned by investors at 40.3 percent and a bank, SoftBank, at 32.4 percent. Through a previous partnership, Yahoo owns 16.3 percent of Alibaba. Alibaba has some competition in China but the biggest potential competitor to Alibaba might be from the United States. While both Amazon and Alibaba are e-commerce giants, they operate in somewhat different competitive spaces, at the moment. Amazon is a giant retailer, whereas Alibaba acts more as a middle man between manufacturers and business buyers.

The mission of the Alibaba Group is "to make it easy to do business anywhere." The company has a set of core values which include putting the customer first; teamwork; embracing change; acting with integrity;

developing a passion in employees; and a commitment to serving the SMEs of the world. These core values have helped Alibaba become a successful organization by creating a strong and coherent corporate culture. Perhaps the strongest value is the commitment to customers, especially those customer companies in Alibaba's target market. Ma feels strongly that the small and medium-sized companies of the world have been underserved and he hopes to level the playing field with Alibaba.

The Alibaba group consists of several companies, led by Alibaba.com. Additional companies include Taobao—an Internet retail website (similar to eBay); Alipay—a third party Internet payment company (similar to PayPal); TMall—a third party top-end online storefront retailer; Alibaba Cloud—a cloud computing and data management company; Ant Financials—a financial services firm serving small businesses and consumers; Alimama—an online marketing services firm; and other e-commerce related firms.

Core Values of Alibaba

Customer First: The interest of our community of users and paying members must be our first priority.

Teamwork: We expect our employees to collaborate as a team. We encourage input from our employees in the decision-making process, and expect every employee to commit to the team's objectives.

Embrace Change: We operate in a fast-evolving industry. We ask our employees to maintain flexibility, continue to innovate and adapt to new business conditions and practice.

Integrity: Integrity is in the heart of our business as trust is an essential element of a marketplace. We expect our employees to uphold the highest standards of integrity and to deliver on their commitments.

Passion: Our employees are encouraged to act with passion whether it is serving customers or developing new services and products.

Commitment: Our employees have a dedicated focus and commitment to understanding and delivering on the needs of Chinese and global SMEs.

The flagship website, Alibaba.com, is vast and offers a wide variety of products from red onions to red dump trucks. On the site businesses can search by product or country, view pictures and specifics of various products, find company contact information, and in some cases even take a virtual company tour. The site is easy to navigate and offers sellers the opportunity to showcase their goods to the world. While suppliers can join Alibaba for free, many more services are available to suppliers who pay to become Gold Suppliers. Gold Suppliers can showcase an unlimited number of products, get earlier access to potential buyers, receive web templates for storefronts, and have access to performance tools to evaluate consumer activity. The company highlights how SMEs have become more successful through their involvement with Alibaba. One example is Ms. Liang of Yilong Electrical Appliances. According to Liang, "Before we met Alibaba, we had tried several B2B channels but ended up in bad results. Meeting with Alibaba was quite a coincidence. Since our cooperation with Alibaba, we've got orders of about USD 200,000 each year." From the testimonies found on the company site, many SMEs may see the opportunity to greatly expand their business through Alibaba.

Alibaba.com offers a site for businesses seeking customers worldwide. Initially the company acted as a site for Chinese manufacturers to find buyers worldwide but the company has since expanded into other parts of the world catering not only to Chinese suppliers, but also to Indian, Korean, Japanese, and Southeast Asian companies. In addition, suppliers from many other countries have their goods listed on Alibaba. While the company still has a focus on Asian suppliers, Alibaba is moving into Europe and the United States. Ma feels that the business model can work anywhere. He began promoting Alibaba in the United States and feels that his business can not only help sell China goods to the world, but also allow companies to sell their goods to Chinese buyers.

While investors are often concerned about short-term results, Ma insists on a long-term perspective, and his priority list is a bit unusual by Western standards. Ma places customers first, followed by employees, and places shareholders last. He is not concerned about how the investment community feels about his approach saying that people can always choose not to invest if they disagree with his strategy. Ma states that he wants "shareholders" and not "share traders." He wants investors who share his long-term vision for the company.

With a global economic slowdown, sales and profits have slowed at Alibaba. While number of buyers, total revenue, and profits are still growing, the rate of growth is slowing. Alibaba seeks to lure more quality brands from outside China and reduce the problem of counterfeit goods (especially relative to Taobao). There have also been some issues with "fake orders" which are made to increase a supplier's image on Alibaba but are never completed. While some companies would see such an environment as causing a need for reduction, Ma sees it as an opportunity for expansion. Alibaba has recently opened its first office in Australia as the company continues to expand globally. He has also begun to expand in the opposite direction by creating Export to China, a system which allows non-Chinese firms to establish Chinese language storefronts to export their products to China. China's economy has suffered with the rest of the world but its economic growth has remained strong, relative to other countries. There is a strong and growing consumer base in China, and Ma hopes to tap into a part of that growth opportunity as well.

With Alibaba.com as the B2B component, Taobao as the retail equal, and the support functions of Alipay, and other SBUs, the Alibaba Group

CASE 15 cont'd

seems well positioned to change global purchasing practices. Jack Ma's success is based on hard work, a strong customer focus, and a sophisticated knowledge of market needs. He has competed successfully against eBay in China, attributing his success to knowing the Chinese market better, and employing Chinese business practices. As Alibaba seeks to expand globally it will be necessary to maintain this focus and to adapt to the different business and cultural constraints found in the rest of the world.

CASE DISCUSSION POINTS:

1 Are there unique components of Alibaba's e-commerce business model/strategy?
2 Do you think the future of international business will change as more people become familiar with the Alibaba business model? Explain.
3 If Alibaba and Amazon aren't direct competitors yet, how might the business models change in the future which may make them fierce competitors? Who do you think will be more successful and why?

Source: Financial Times, "China's Internet godfather," January 18, retrieved March 25, 2010, from http://news.alibaba.com/article/detail/alibaba/100057565-1-china%2527s-internet-godfather.html; L. Chao, 2009, "How China's Alibaba is surviving and thriving," *Bloomberg BusinessWeek*, April 9, retrieved March 10, 2010, from www.businessweek.com/ magazine/content/09_16/b4127059272628.htm; B. Einhorn, 2009, "Alibaba's next trick: Expanding abroad," *Bloomberg BusinessWeek*, August 6, retrieved March 10, from www.businessweek.com/magazine/content/09_33/b4143049839232.htm; "Alibaba launches ad campaign appealing to would-be entrepreneurs," Auction Bytes: The Independent Trade Publication for Online Merchants, Retrieved March 1, 2010, from www.auctionbytes.com/cab/abn/y09/m08/i10/s04; T. Wang, 2009, "Jack Ma's five-year plan," Forbes.com, retrieved March 28, 2010, from www.forbes.com/2009/05/07/alibaba-jack-ma-markets-equity-china.html; *The Wall Street Journal*, "Alibaba.com weighs forging India e-commerce venture," August 4, retrieved March 20, 2009, from http://online.wsj.com/article/SB124932788653502319.html; http://projects.wsj.com/alibaba/, accessed on July 26, 2016; K. Chu and S. Nassauer, 2016, "Alibaba acknowledges looming challenges," *Wall Street Journal*, March 21; *Forbes*, 2016, "Australia is the next stage for Alibaba's global expansion," July 21.

Case written by Charles A. Rarick and Casimir Barczyk

Notes

1 *The Economist*, 2016, "The great race," March 5, pp. 19–21.
2 *The Economist*, 2016, "The great race," March 5, pp. 19–21.
3 Emin M. Dinlersoz and Pedro Pereira, 2007, "On the diffusion of electronic commerce," *International Journal of Industrial Organization*, 25, pp. 541–574.
4 Sung-Chi Chu, Lawrence C. Leung, Yer Van Hui and Waiman Cheung, 2007, "Evolution of e-commerce web sites: A conceptual framework and a longitudinal study," *Information and Management*, 44, pp. 154–164.

5   Sung-Chi Chu, Lawrence C. Leung, Yer Van Hui and Waiman Cheung, 2007, "Evolution of
    e-commerce web sites: A conceptual framework and a longitudinal study," *Information and
    Management*, *44*, pp. 154–164.

6   Sung-Chi Chu, Lawrence C. Leung, Yer Van Hui and Waiman Cheung, 2007, "Evolution of
    e-commerce web sites: A conceptual framework and a longitudinal study," *Information and
    Management*, *44*, pp. 154–164.

7   *The Economist*, 2016, "The emporium strikes back," May 21, p. 62.

8   *The Economist*, 2016, "Taming the beasts," May 28, pp. 57–59.

9   G. A. Knight and T. Cavusgil, 2005, "A taxonomy of born-global firms," *Management International
    Review*, *45*, pp. 15–35.

10 S. Andersson, M. Danilovic and H. Huang, 2015, "Success factors in Western and Chinese born global
    companies," *iBusiness*, *7*, pp. 25–38.

11 F. C. Ribeiro, M. O. De Miranda, F. Borini and R. Bernardes, 2014, "Accelerated internationalization
    in emerging markets: Empirical evidence from Brazilian technology-based firms," *Journal of
    Technology, Management & Innovation*, *9*, pp. 1–12.

12 John Heilemann, 2005, "Retooling the entrepreneur," *Business 2.0*, *6*(10), pp. 42–45.

13 *The Economist*, 2016, "Taming the beasts," May 28, pp. 57–59.

14 OECD, 2005, *Measuring the Internet Economy*, Paris: Organization for Economic Co-operation and
    Development.

15 Ellen Sheng, 2007, "Corporate connections: Companies find social networks can get people talking—
    about their products," *Wall Street Journal*, January, p. R8.

16 *The Economist*, 2016, "Taming the beasts," May 28, pp. 57–59.

17 P. C. Evans and A. Gawer, 2016, "The rise of the platform enterprise: A global survey," www.thecge.
    net/wp-content/uploads/2016/01/PDF-WEB-Platform-Survey_01_12.pdf

18 S. Kurnia, J. Choudrie, R. M. Mahbubr and B. Alzougool, 2015, "E-commerce technology adoption: A
    Malaysian grocery SME retail," *Journal of Business Research*, *68*, pp. 1906–1918.

19 Alexander Yap, Jayoti Das, John Burbridge and Kathryn Cort, 2006, "A composite-model for
    e-commerce diffusion: Integrating cultural and socio-economic dimensions to the dynamics of
    diffusion," *Journal of Global Information Management*, *14*(3), pp. 17–38.

20 F. D. Davis, 1989, "Perceived usefulness, perceived ease of use, and user acceptance of information
    technology," *MIS Quarterly*, *13*, pp. 319–340.

21 Zhang Pei, Zheng Zhenxiang and Huang Chunping, 2007, "An extended TAM model for Chinese B2C
    websites design," *Journal of Global Information Technology Management*, *10*(1), pp. 51–66.

22 D. V. Parboteeah, K. P. Parboteeah, J. B. Cullen and C. Basu, 2005, "Perceived usefulness of
    technology: A cross-national model," *Journal of Global Information Technology Management*, *8*(4),
    pp. 29–48.

23 D. V. Parboteeah, K. P. Parboteeah, J. B. Cullen and C. Basu, 2005, "Perceived usefulness of
    technology: A cross-national model," *Journal of Global Information Technology Management*, *8*(4),
    pp. 29–48.

24 Thompson S. H. Teo and Jing Liu, 2007, "Consumer trust in E-commerce in the United States,
    Singapore and China," *Omega*, *35*(1), pp. 22–38.

25 J. Wozniak, 2015, "Trust and e-commerce in the Ukraine and Poland in the eyes of young urban
    professionals," *Review of International Comparative Management*, *16*(2), pp. 159–176.

26 Thompson S. H. Teo and Jing Liu, 2007, "Consumer trust in E-commerce in the United States,
    Singapore and China," *Omega*, *35*(1), pp. 22–38.

27 David Gefen and Tsipi Heart, 2006, "On the need to include national culture as a central issue in
    e-commerce trust beliefs," *Journal of Global Information Management*, *14*(4), pp. 1–30.

28 J. T. Luo, Peter McGoldrick, Susan Beatty and Kathleen A. Keeling, 2006, "On-screen characters: Their
    design and influence on consumer trust," *Journal of Services Marketing*, *20*(2), pp. 112–124.

29 H. Lee, P. Shun, T. Chen and Y. Jhu, 2015, "The effects of avatar on trust and purchase intention of
    female online consumer: Consumer knowledge as moderator," *International Journal of Electronic
    Commerce Studies*, *6*(1,) pp. 99–118.

30 J. T. Luo, Peter McGoldrick, Susan Beatty and Kathleen A. Keeling, 2006, "On-screen characters: Their
    design and influence on consumer trust," *Journal of Services Marketing*, *20*(2), pp. 112–124.

31 K. Ozpolat and W. Jank, 2015, "Getting the most out of third party trust seals: An empirical analysis," *Decision Support Systems*, *73*, pp. 47–56.

32 K. Ozpolat and W. Jank, 2015, "Getting the most out of third party trust seals: An empirical analysis," *Decision Support Systems*, *73*, pp. 47–56.

33 Thompson S. H. Teo and Jing Liu, 2007, "Consumer trust in E-commerce in the United States, Singapore and China," *Omega*, *35*(1), pp. 22–38.

34 Thompson S. H. Teo and Jing Liu, 2007, "Consumer trust in E-commerce in the United States, Singapore and China," *Omega*, *35*(1), pp. 22–38.

35 Shintaro Okazaki, 2004, "Do multinationals standardise or localise? The cross-cultural dimensionality of product-based web sites," *Internet Research*, *14*(1), pp. 81–94.

36 Elizabeth Wurtz, 2005, "A cross-cultural analysis of websites from high-context cultures and low-context cultures," *Journal of Computer-Mediated Communication*, *11*(1), article 13.

37 P. Zhu, 2016, "Impact of business cultural values on web homepage design that may hinder international business," *Journal of Technical Writing and Communication*, *46*, pp. 105–124.

38 Nitish Singh, Olivier Furrer and Massimiliano Ostinelli, 2004, "To localize or to standardize on the Web: Empirical evidence from Italy, India, Netherlands, Spain, and Switzerland," *Multinational Business Review*, Spring, *12*(1), pp. 69–87.

39 P. Zhu, 2016, "Impact of business cultural values on web homepage design that may hinder international business," *Journal of Technical Writing and Communication*, *46*, pp. 105–124.

40 N. Tsikriktsis, 2002, "Does culture influence website quality expectations?" *Journal of Service Research*, *5*(2), pp. 101–112.

41 Elizabeth Wurtz, 2005, "A cross-cultural analysis of websites from high-context cultures and low-context cultures," *Journal of Computer-Mediated Communication*, *11*(1), article 13.

42 Digital River, 2016, www.digitalriver.com/

43 *Business Wire*, 2007, "Digital River expands global e-commerce platform with fully integrated physical fulfillment solution," *Business Wire*, March 27.

44 Marc J. Epstein, 2005, "Implementing successful e-commerce initiatives," *Strategic Finance*, *86*(9), pp. 22–29.

45 Marc J. Epstein, 2005, "Implementing successful e-commerce initiatives," *Strategic Finance*, *86*(9), pp. 22–29; Gregory A. Garrett and Gail A. Parrott, 2005, "E-business: Understanding key trends and applying best practices," *Contract Management*, *45*(7), pp. 34–41; Julie Schlosser, 2007, "Engaging with the customer," *Fortune*, *155*(9), p. 28; M. Sundström, M. and A. Radon, 2015, "Utilizing the concept of convenience as a business opportunity in emerging markets," *Organizations and Markets in Emerging Economies*, *6*, pp. 7–21.

46 Gregory A. Garrett and Gail A. Parrott, 2005, "E-business: Understanding key trends and applying best practices," *Contract Management*, *45*(7), pp. 34–41.

47 M. Sundström and A. Radon, 2015, "Utilizing the concept of convenience as a business opportunity in emerging markets," *Organizations and Markets in Emerging Economies*, *6*, pp. 7–21.

48 Colin Beasty, 2006, "Retail's 2 worlds: Tips on integrating online and offline channels," *Customer Relationship Management*, *10*(3), pp. 30–35.

49 Marc J. Epstein, 2005, "Implementing successful e-commerce initiatives," *Strategic Finance*, *86*(9), pp. 22–29.

50 J. Agarwal and T. Wu, 2015, "Factors influencing growth potential of e-commerce in emerging economies: An institution-based N-OLI framework and research propositions," *Thunderbird International Business Review*, *57*(3), pp. 197–215.

51 J. Agarwal and T. Wu, 2015, "Factors influencing growth potential of e-commerce in emerging economies: An institution-based N-OLI framework and research propositions," *Thunderbird International Business Review*, *57*(3), pp. 197–215; Hallie Mummert, 2003, "Best practices," *Target Marketing*, *26*(9), p. 34; Marc J. Epstein, 2005, "Implementing successful e-commerce initiatives," *Strategic Finance*, *86*(9), pp. 22–29; Gregory A. Garrett and Gail A. Parrott, 2005, "E-business: Understanding key trends and applying best practices," *Contract Management*, *45*(7), pp. 34–41; Jim Wheaton, 2007, "The first five commandments of database content management," *Multichannel Merchant*, *3*(2), p. 33.

52 Z. Gu, J. Wei and F. Xu, 2015, "An empirical study on factors influencing consumers' initial trust in wearable commerce," *Journal of Computer Information Systems*, 56, pp. 79–85.

53 KPMG, "Cyber crime: A growing challenge for governments," www.kpmg.com/Global/en/IssuesAndInsights/ArticlesPublications/Documents/cyber-crime.pdf

54 FRPT Research, 2016, "98% of mobile apps of top 50 Indian eCommerce companies vulnerable to security attacks," www.frptresearch.hostoi.com/

55 C. Tutsch, 2016, "Think locally, fight globally," *Computer Fraud and Security*, January, p. 5.

56 L. A. Gordon and M. P. Loeb, 2006, *Managing Cybersecurity Resources: A Cost–Benefit Analysis*, New York: McGraw-Hill.

57 P. Conroy, F. Milwano, A. Narula and R. Singhal, 2014, "A new perspective on data privacy," Westlake, TX: Deloitte University Press.

58 V. Harnish, 2016, "5 immediate ways to fight cybercrime," March 21, http://fortune.com/2016/03/21/business-fight-cybercrime/

59 V. Harnish, 2016, "5 immediate ways to fight cybercrime," March 21, http://fortune.com/2016/03/21/business-fight-cybercrime/

PART FIVE

ETHICAL MANAGEMENT IN THE INTERNATIONAL CONTEXT

CHAPTER 16

Managing Ethical and Social Responsibility in an MNC

After reading this chapter you should be able to:

- Understand the definition of international ethics and corporate social responsibility and the reasons why multinationals are being criticized.

- Understand the three, important global ethical issues, namely labor rights, environmental pollution, and corruption/bribery with a special emphasis on emerging markets.

- Appreciate some of the key approaches to dealing with global ethics.

- Understand how multinational managers can build the socially responsible multinational in emerging markets.

International Ethics in Emerging Markets

As MNCs continue to expand business operations in China and other emerging markets to take advantage of the tremendous opportunities these markets have to offer, they are facing the challenges of tackling corruption in such markets. Experts agree that both developed and emerging markets face business ethics concerns. However, the business environment in many emerging markets tends to facilitate bribery and corruption. Often, such markets have very ambiguous rules governing business ethics. Additionally, the instability will often add to a culture of corruption.

Consider the recent case of Malaysia and the missing $4 billion from the state. The Swiss attorney general recently announced that the amount was misappropriated from the Malaysian government. Hundreds of millions of US$ were found in the prime minister's bank accounts without any solid explanation. Additionally, many businessmen were also involved in the corruption program as they received significant amounts of money from the fund. It is argued that these businessmen helped the prime minister win the 2013 election in return for such favors. It is therefore undeniable that such an environment will likely not encourage ethical practices.

Although some experts argue that corruption is an inevitable aspect of doing business in many emerging markets, recent events suggest that China is very serious about eliminating bribery. For instance, the government has implemented new enforcement programs and procedures to reduce bribery. There is now clearer information detailing what constitutes bribery and the punishment accompanying such illegal activities. Furthermore, a number of officials have been punished in some form or other recently for corruption.

In addition to the complexities inherent in navigating ethics worldwide, MNCs are also under pressure from their home countries to stop such practices. Consider, for instance, the media coverage of the companies recently fined in the US under the Foreign Corrupt Practices Act. The case of Walmart's bribery in Mexico is still attracting significant attention. Clearly, most multinationals are under increased pressure to behave more ethically while also facing the local reality that corruption may be an important part of the business culture. Even when multinationals implement global ethics programs, they are finding that implementing global ethics policies is very difficult. Cultural differences often determine the extent to which local workers will take a global ethics program seriously.

Source: Based on *The Economist*, 2016, "Art of survival; follow the money, if you can," March 5, pp. 33–35; Kenneth J. DeWoskin and Ian J. Stones, 2006, "Facing the China corruption challenge," *Far Eastern Economic Review*, *169*(7), pp. 37–40; M. Kleinhempel, 2015, "Navigating the realities of emerging markets," *IESE Insight*, Fourth Quarter, pp. 32–39.

As you can see from reading the Preview IB Emerging Market Strategic Insight, MNCs are facing increasing complexities as they strive to become better global citizens. On one hand, these MNCs need to understand the local conditions to determine the appropriate way to do business in all of the markets where they operate. Doing business in emerging markets tends to be fraught with the possibility of ethical transgressions. On the other hand, they are facing increasing scrutiny of their business activities and practices. As a result, more MNCs are trying to find the balance between operating effectively locally to stay competitive while at the same time responding to the dramatic calls for better ethical practices.

In this chapter, you will read about global ethics issues. You will learn about the importance for MNCs to implement and enforce ethics programs. The chapter will discuss many of the core ethical issues facing any corporation involved in trade across borders. You will also learn about some of the tools and techniques available to multinationals to enable them to become more ethical citizens.

This chapter contains four major sections all emphasizing emerging markets. In the first section, you will read about the basic definitions of international ethics and social responsibility. You will also learn about why multinationals are being criticized in the context of globalization. In the second section, you will learn about some of the key global ethics issues. This section of the chapter will discuss three main issues, namely labor rights and issues, environmental issues, and finally corruption and bribery. In the third section, you will read about some of the approaches being used to build the global ethical corporation. Finally, in the fourth section, you will learn about the many steps and activities any multinational needs to engage in to become more ethical at a global level.

International Ethics and Social Responsibility

Before you read about international ethics, it is crucial to understand some of the ethical questions managers deal with. Multinational managers at all levels face ethical issues where they have to deal with questions such as: "If we can get cheap child labor overseas, and it is legal there, should we use it because our competitors do?" "Should we refuse to give a bribe to an underpaid government official, and lose the contract to our competitor's weaker product?" "Should we dump our waste in the river knowing well that it will pose pollution risks although it is acceptable in the country?" "Should we pay our female workers less than male workers because that's what all multinationals do?" To give you more insights on the types of questions MNCs ask themselves in the global environment, Exhibit 16.1 shows some of the more typical issues.

• Should safety features of products be removed to make products cheaper in other markets?
• Should child labor be used if it is legal in the country?
• Should local wages be more than what other companies pay?
• Should the MNC dump waste in the waterways in a country if it is legal?
• Should the MNC hire women and allow them to work with men if it is not practiced in the country?
• Should the MNC be responsible for the safety of its workers although it is not required by law in the country?
• Should the MNC exploit local natural resources because it is allowed?
• Should sexual harassment be tolerated because such actions are allowed in the country?
• Should the MNC bribe to get business similar to other companies in the region?

Exhibit 16.1 Typical Ethical Questions for MNCs

As Exhibit 16.1 shows, there are a variety of ethical challenges that a multinational has to deal with. A multinational's approach to dealing with these questions represents its approach to ethics. As such, **ethics** pertains to behaviors or actions that affect people and their welfare. For instance, a decision by managers to knowingly sell a useful but dangerous product or to willingly bribe an official is an ethical decision. In both cases, the decision has important consequences for humans. In the first case, selling the dangerous product can end up hurting customers and perhaps the MNC in the long run. In the second case, provision of a bribe can prevent other companies from legitimately acquiring the business. In both cases, business ethics pertain to an assessment of whether the decision is right or wrong.

> **ethics**
> pertains to behaviors or actions that affect people and their welfare

International business ethics refers to ethical problems faced by multinational managers as they do business with other countries. International business ethics is different from domestic business ethics on a few fronts. International ethics is more complex than domestic ethics because operations take place across borders. Differences in culture and institutions mean that people may not always agree on what is the right way of doing things. However, most importantly, the very large MNCs can have powers and assets that exceed those of some of the nations with which they deal. When using this power, managers in these large and powerful organizations often face challenging ethical dilemmas.

> **international business ethics**
> refers to ethical problems faced by multinational managers as they conduct business with other countries

How powerful are the largest corporations? A comparison of selected countries (based on GDP) and the largest companies in the *Global Fortune* 500 list (based on revenues) shows that many multinationals have revenues that may exceed countries' GDP. Consider Exhibit 16.2

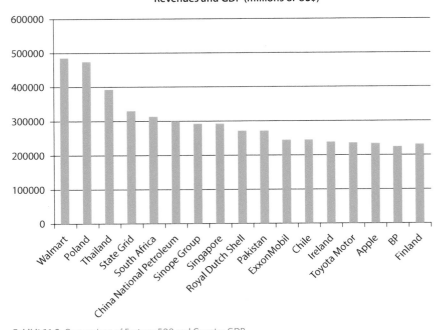

Exhibit 16.2 Comparison of Fortune 500 and Country GDP
Source: Based on *Fortune* 500, 2016, http://money.cnn.com; The World Bank, www.worldbank.org

which provides a comparison of countries based on GDP with some of the USA's largest multinationals based on revenues. As you can see, Walmart's revenues are significantly larger than many countries' gross domestic product. Similarly, as you can see in the graph, China National Petroleum is bigger than the emerging markets of Pakistan and Chile. While the graph only illustrates selected countries and multinationals, it does show that many of the world's largest corporations have significant financial assets to exert power on countries. This power and clout has led many to criticize MNCs.

What is the nature of criticisms against multinational corporations? Some argue that multinationals exploit the natural and human resources in the countries in which they operate. Companies such as Nike, Reebok, and Gap have faced significant criticism because of their labor practices. Additionally, because of their size and financial assets, multinationals have been criticized for using this power to influence governments to get preferential treatment from the government. For instance, some countries give significant tax breaks to encourage investments. Such breaks generally mean the loss of revenue to support important local social programs.

Are these criticisms justified? Some observers argue that multinationals have positive benefits. For instance, Meredith and Hoppough have argued that globalization and the multinationals have lifted around 200 million people out of poverty in China and India.[1] Many argue that as multinationals continue investing, the standard of living is raised and the proportion of the poor decreases. Many countries are seeing dramatic growth in average incomes, and in Asia alone the middle class is expected to be in the vicinity of one billion people within the next few years.

Given the earlier discussed criticisms, many MNCs are going beyond their legal responsibilities and adopting corporate social responsibility programs. **Corporate social responsibility (CSR)** is defined as the responsibility multinationals have to society beyond making profits. That is, social responsibility means that a company must take into account the welfare of other constituents (e.g. customers, suppliers) in addition to stockholders. While you

corporate social responsibility
refers to the notion that businesses have a responsibility to society beyond making profits

saw earlier in this section that business ethics usually concern the ethical dilemmas faced by managers as individuals, corporate social responsibility is usually concerned with the ethical consequences of policies and procedures of the company as an organization. Monitoring the working conditions of your suppliers, paying for the education of the children of workers, and donating money to the local community are examples of corporate social responsibility in action. Multinationals are very aware of the importance of CSR. In fact, recent research suggests that firms that engage in CSR in emerging markets signal to their stakeholders that they can deal with institutional voids.[2] This therefore suggests that firms in such markets send important signals to stakeholders that they possess superior capabilities. Consider the following IB Emerging Market Strategic Insight.

Corporate Social Responsibility in Emerging Markets

IB EMERGING MARKET STRATEGIC INSIGHT

Multinationals worldwide appreciate the importance of CSR in the markets they operate. While the link between CSR and financial performance is still being explored, many experts argue that CSR can add to the brand reputation of any company. This is especially important in emerging markets where MNCs may be unknown and CSR can help enhance a company's legitimacy. Additionally, MNCs may strategically use CSR to understand the bottom of the pyramid consumers to better understand these customers' needs while also contributing to society. It is therefore not surprising that many multinationals now see CSR as a key aspect of their strategy.

An important example of an industry that sees CSR as extremely critical is the pharmaceuticals industry. Companies in these industries often have to structure operations to be advantageous to shareholders while also addressing societal critiques that they contribute to high health care costs. Novartis, the Danish giant pharmaceuticals multinational, often tests its products in India. However, it is very aware that many drugs are not accessible to poorer Indians in rural areas. Novartis therefore implemented a CSR plan that included developing a network of local distributors to make generic drugs available to people in rural areas. This network operates in partnership with NGOs, doctors, and hospitals and also organizes health camps. The program is already successful and has been able to provide improved healthcare access to more than 42 million Indians from around 33,000 villages.

Emerging market multinationals are also very focused on CSR. A recent interview with Japanese and South Korean multinationals also shows that these multinationals saw CSR as a very strategic activity. For example, Samsung developed the "DigitAll Hope" program emphasizing the reduction of the digital divide in Indonesia. Through the program, Samsung is making digital facilities available to disadvantaged Indonesians thereby contributing to society. The Japanese multinational Sharp has developed a "Kids Witness News" program aimed at children. It has implemented the program in many countries. In Indonesia, the program provides children with educational opportunities to develop their creativity and communication skills. The program also develops filming skills of Indonesian children through the use of Panasonic products.

Source: Based on R. Singh, M. Bakshi and P. Mishra, 2015, "Corporate social responsibility: Linking bottom of the pyramid to market development," *Journal of Business Ethics, 131*, pp. 361–373; N. C. Smith, 2016, "From corporate philanthropy to creating shared value: Big pharma's new business models in developing markets," *GFK-Marketing Intelligence Review, 8*(1), pp. 31–35; Y. Park, S. Song, S. Choe and Y. Baik, 2015, "Corporate social responsibility in international business: Illustrations from Korean and Japanese electronics MNEs in Indonesia," *Journal of Business Ethics, 129*, pp. 747–761;

Clearly, the above shows the importance of CSR. Additionally, in this section, you also learned the basic definitions of ethics and international ethics. You also read about why multinational companies are criticized and how CSR can sometimes help assuage these criticisms. In the next section, you will learn about some of these criticisms in more depth by reading about the key global ethics issues.

Key Global Ethics Issues

Multinationals face a multitude of ethical issues ranging from racial discrimination to air pollution to bribery. In this section, you will read about three of the most important global ethics issues multinational managers face. These are labor rights, environmental pollution, and corruption/bribery.

Labor Rights

Labor rights represent one of the most crucial ethical issues multinationals are facing today. In fact, in some countries such as China, workers have very limited rights. Consider the following BRIC Insight.

Labor Rights in China   BRIC INSIGHT

Despite significant economic growth, the average Chinese worker still earns very little and works in very poor conditions. Most workers lack the most basic rights. For instance, although a labor law was mandated in 1994 to give workers the right to a contract specifying salary and employment conditions, many workers do not have such contracts. As a consequence, most workers do not have access to basic rights.

To remedy the situation, the Chinese government is currently considering changing the current labor laws to give new rights to workers. The new law would require mandatory contracts between companies and workers, limits on probationary periods for new workers, provision of severance packages in case of lay-offs, and freedom to both change jobs and create trade unions. However, implementation of these laws will be difficult as China faces an economic slowdown.

Consider the case of many of China's state-owned enterprises (SOEs). As revenues from governmental sources have shrunk because of the economic slowdown, many of the SOEs have been facing difficulties with regards to their financial obligations. Employees are often the ones that suffer from such challenges. For instance, thousands of miners protested in the city of Shuangyashan to demand their wages. Because of weak labor rights, these miners had not been paid for months. Furthermore, many workers are also facing layoffs as these SOEs reduce excess capacity. It is therefore not surprising to see that labor unrest is becoming more prevalent across China. Recent estimates suggest that the number of strikes doubled in 2015 relative to the previous year.

Source: Based on *The Economist*, 2016, "Deep in a pit," March 19, pp. 47–48; Brendan Smith, Jeremy Brecher and Tim Costello, 2006, "Multinationals to China: No new labor rights," *Multinational Monitor*, November/December, *27*(6), pp. 34–37.

As you can see from the BRIC Insight, Chinese workers do not have many rights.[3] Workers generally do not have contracts and are not allowed to form unions. Additionally, workers are sometimes expected to work long hours without overtime pay. Workers can be fired and hired at will and may not have recourse to any form of severance pay.

One of the most important aspects of labor rights is the existence of sweatshops. **Sweatshops** are typically plants where workers work very hard in very poor working environments, often for long hours. Global corporations such as Nike, Gap, Patagonia, and Reebok have all been hit with mainstream criticisms of using workers in sweatshops to produce their products. The media has been paying much more attention to allegations of the use of sweatshops, even in cases where a multinational relies on another party to manufacture the product.

sweatshops
plants where workers work very hard in very poor working conditions

MNCs have also had to deal with allegations of the use of child labor. For instance, multinationals such as Nike and Adidas were in the spotlight for hiring child workers to stitch soccer balls in Pakistan. Though local industrialists prospered as multinationals brought significant business to Pakistan, this prosperity did not necessarily trickle down to soccer-ball stitchers. Additionally, the use of female labor has also resulted in widespread condemnation of sexual discrimination. Women in less developed countries tend to be hired at much lower rates than men for similar occupations. Recent fires in garment factories in Bangladesh have intensified the focus on working conditions in sweatshops.

Multinationals are therefore under increased pressure to monitor labor conditions. Many multinationals have therefore been proactive and are taking many steps to ensure that they do not break labor rights laws. There have not been as many sweatshop headlines lately, and Bernstein attributes the improved labor situation to multinationals taking better steps to respect labor rights.[4] Many large multinationals such as Nike and Gap are now working closely with labor rights organizations to ensure that working conditions in their and their subcontractors' facilities are acceptable.

In addition to self-monitoring efforts, MNCs can also rely on outside organizations for compliance with basic labor rights. International Labor Rights Forum and the Fair Labor Association are both examples of labor rights organizations that have defined labor standards and take care of enforcing these standards. These associations have developed codes of conduct addressing issues such as no child labor or no excessive overtime.[5] These groups monitor plants and provide solutions to alleviate problems and they also work with local communities to protect workers and their rights.

Despite these efforts, it is still necessary for more effort to be expended to reduce violations of labor rights. Many of the major multinationals have not yet cooperated with labor rights organizations to solve labor rights problems. Even those multinationals that work with labor rights groups still have some issues to resolve. Standards vary widely across the two associations mentioned above. Furthermore, there is still no agreement generally on the issue of wages (should a company pay a living wage?), disclosure (should companies freely reveal the names of their factories?), factory inspections (should there be surprise visits?), etc.

As well as multinationals striving to improve working conditions, countries are also taking steps to treat employees more humanely. Consider that many of the emerging nations located in the Middle East Gulf nations have had large immigrant populations involved in many industries. Unfortunately, these workers have had poor rights and are often trapped in contracts with employers. Reforms in the United Arab Emirates (UAE) are now offering workers stronger rights.[6] Workers can now look for new jobs after their contracts expire without the need to request permission from their current employers. Workers are also now allowed to break contracts as long as they give employers fair notice.

In this section, you read about an important global ethical issue—labor rights. Next, we consider environmental pollution. As you saw in Chapter 1, most multinationals are being pressured to become more sustainable and attempts to reduce environmental pollution are becoming important elements of such sustainability efforts.

Environmental Pollution

Multinationals are frequently criticized for ignoring environmental regulations and for polluting the air and the environment. Well-publicized disasters such as the *Exxon Valdez* oil spill and the Union Carbide tragedy in Bhopal, India, have brought the spotlight on multinationals and their roles in less developed countries.[7] More recently, the Volkswagen scandal where the German automaker deliberately manipulated tests to show that its cars were less polluting than they really were has put the automaker in negative light and resulted in losses.[8] In fact, environmental degradation is seen as one of the most pressing and fastest growing problems facing societies, and multinationals are seen to have a significant influence on minimizing such problems.

In developed countries, the media, environmental groups, and the appropriate governmental bodies have tried to pressure multinationals to act responsibly. In such countries, governments have taken measures to enact laws to keep up with potential threats to the environment. As such, governments have systems in place to punish violators while rewarding those companies that act responsibly. Most developed nations have various laws and regulations whereby fines and other taxes are imposed when multinationals break environmental laws. At the same time, companies are also getting benefits by following "green" practices through subsidies and easier bureaucratic processes.

The situation is much more catastrophic in emerging nations. In these countries, multinationals have been more willing to break environmental rules and regulations. Consider the following Emerging Market Ethical Challenge.

Shell Oil and Nigeria

EMERGING MARKET
ETHICAL CHALLENGE

Shell Oil, the Anglo-Dutch oil conglomerate, has been in operation in Nigeria for over 80 years pumping around 39 percent of Nigeria's oil production. Shell Petroleum Development Company of Nigeria has been pumping oil through a network of pipelines in the oil-rich region of the Niger Delta. Unfortunately, the region has experienced significant oil spills over the years. Recent reports suggest that there were around 48,000 tons of oil spilled in the Niger Delta between 2008 and 2014.

The consequences of such spills have been disastrous. Many of the surrounding communities have lost their means of living. Such spills have destroyed the fishing grounds thereby destroying sources of food. Additionally, such oil spills have also destroyed farming and have polluted drinking water. Surrounding communities have therefore lost access to clean drinking water.

Shell has suffered financially as a result of these spills. It will have to pay a $55 million settlement with the Bodo community soon. Additionally, two other communities have also been given permission to sue Shell in the UK for these spills. These lawsuits will test whether multinationals can be held liable in their home countries for events in other countries.

Source: Based on S. Kent, 2016, "Nigerian communities can sue Royal Dutch Shell over Oil Spills, UK court Says," *Wall Street Journal*, March 2, online edition.

As you can see from the Emerging Market Ethical Challenge, Shell has been involved in many spills in the Niger Delta. They have often blamed such spills on local thieves sabotaging the pipelines. However, according to experts, some of these spills have been due to Shell's actions. Why are multinationals often willing to break environmental rules? The reasons for these infractions are numerous. In some emerging nations, the appropriate governments have not kept legislation to combat newer environmental problems. In many cases, the laws tend to be less rigorous and are rarely enforced. And, as you read earlier, multinationals often have assets that may exceed the country's gross domestic product. In some of these cases, the multinationals can simply compensate the relevant government for environmental damage.

Recent events suggest that most emerging market countries are starting to strictly enforce environmental regulation. This is not surprising given that cities in emerging markets tend to have the highest levels of pollution. Exhibit 16.3 below shows the list of 20 most polluting cities in the world.

Exhibit 16.3 shows the level of pollution as measured by particulate matter floating in the air in the top 20 cities worldwide and that all are in emerging markets. Such levels are extremely high and will likely have catastrophic long-term effects if such levels are not controlled. However, many emerging markets are now taking governmental regulation of pollution seriously. For instance, Chao and Oster discuss how studies by Chinese environmental organizations found that around 30 multinationals operating in China violated water pollution rules.[9] Because about a quarter of the Chinese population does not have access to clean water, the Chinese government is taking water pollution issues very seriously. Many companies have been cited for water pollution. Additionally, the Chinese government also sees air pollution as one of the most pressing issues that it needs to address.[10] The Chinese government has implemented many new policies to curb environmental degradation.

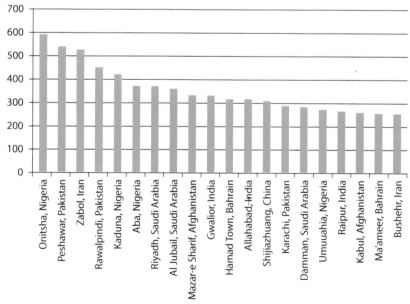

Particulate Concentration (PM10 Level)

Exhibit 16.3 Top 20 Most Polluted Cities, 2016
Source: Based on World Health Organization database, www.who.org

Another issue that is getting significant attention is electronic waste (or e-waste).[11] As mentioned in the previous chapter, the increased reliance on computers in all aspects of life has greatly increased waste as countries tackle challenges of disposing of technological equipment that is rapidly becoming obsolete. Unfortunately, such electronic waste carries significant health and environmental costs if the 1000s of toxic substances are not dealt with properly. It is therefore not surprising to see that India, for instance, has passed several new regulations to deal specifically with electronic waste.

Similar to the labor rights issues, multinationals are realizing that they need to be proactive to deal with the environment. The media is paying much closer attention to the actions of multinationals, and stories of environmental pollution and degradation are frequently publicized. As a consequence, many multinationals are implementing steps to minimize environmental degradation. Later you will read about how multinationals are implementing corporate social responsibility programs to address environmental matters.

In this section you learned about some of the key issues facing multinationals with regards to the environment. Next, you will read about one of the most critical ethical issues facing multinationals today. Specifically, you will learn about corruption and bribery and its prevalence around the world.

Corruption and Bribery

One of the most critical global ethical issues facing multinationals today is corruption and bribery. According to Transparency International (www.transparency.org), an organization dedicated to eradicating corruption, **corruption** is the "misuse of entrusted power for private gain." Corruption occurs when someone receives a bribe and does something that they are legally prohibited from doing. **Bribery** also refers to gifts or payments to someone to expedite a government action or to gain some business advantages.

corruption
process where entrusted power is used for private gain

bribery
gifts or payments to someone to expedite government action or to gain some business advantages

Levels of corruption and bribery vary significantly around the world. In that respect, the Transparency International Corruption Perceptions Index provides an understanding of the degree to which corruption exists among politicians and public officials. The organization collects data from various sources to compile an index that reflects the degree of corruption in society and the relative degree of corruption compared to other societies. Exhibit 16.4 shows the top seven and bottom seven countries based on the 2016 Corruption Index. The index ranks from a score of 100 (no corruption) to 0 (highly corrupt).

A look at Exhibit 16.4 readily reveals one important aspect of the nature of corruption. Corruption tends to be higher in poorer countries. In fact, countries such as Somalia, Sudan, and Haiti are among the poorest in the world and score the lowest on the corruption index. Furthermore, many of these countries are also suffering from wars and other civil unrest. Such findings are not altogether surprising. The trend, though, to be sure, is that more corrupt countries tend to channel funds into high-profile projects such as dams, power plants, etc., at the expense of schools or hospitals. Such corruption leads to the ineffective use of public funds, thereby leading to more poverty. However, Transparency International notes that although wealthier countries tend to be less corrupt, these wealthy countries have not necessarily shown much progress in terms of the fight against corruption. The ultimate measure of effectiveness is movement towards less corruption, and wealthier countries have not necessarily shown such progress. Thus, while poorer countries have a lot to do to reduce corruption, Transparency International encourages wealthier countries to address corruption challenges too.

Corruption and bribery are both attracting lots of attention because of the devastating effects on effective market functions. For instance, as mentioned earlier, corruption often results in waste of public funds, as only expensive and high-profile jobs get funded. Some also argue that companies typically make up for bribery by increasing the contract price by the amount of the

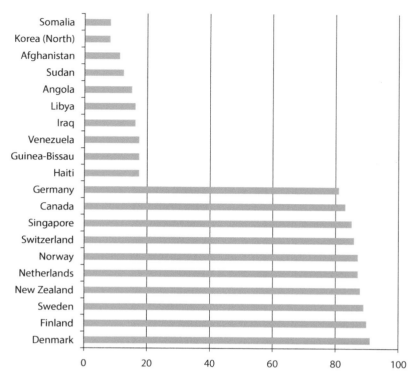

Exhibit 16.4 Top and Bottom Ten Countries on the Corruption Perceptions Index
Source: Based on Transparency International, www.transparency.org

bribe. As such, many emerging countries suffer because they are charged higher prices. Many companies also routinely use poorer quality products or materials to cover for the bribe, thus resulting in inferior products. Furthermore, corruption can result in collusion among firms, thereby resulting in even higher prices. As such, corruption and bribery usually result in higher public spending, lower quality projects, undermined competition, and inefficient allocation of resources.

In addition to these negative effects on the market and quality of products, bribery can also have devastating effects on the effective political functioning and democratic nature of the society. According to Transparency International, corruption and bribery have the worst effects on the "social fabric" of a society. Because of the norms supporting corruption and bribes, most people tend to lose trust in the political system and in politicians. As a result, there is less participation in the democratic process. A weak democratic system supports the election of more corrupt politicians, thereby resulting in a vicious circle.

Bribes can also have dramatic effects on the offending multinationals. Consider the following BRIC Insight.

Petrobas and Bribery

Petrobas, the Brazilian old giant and one of the biggest Latin American entities in terms of revenues, was often considered as the global Latin American multinational star. It was also considered as one of the best Latin American brands and was an important source of pride for Brazil. Additionally, it was seen as a model state-owned multinational that balanced shareholder needs with societal interests.

Unfortunately, this aura came crashing down as a result of recent fraud investigations. Such investigations found that many high-level individuals in the company were funneling Petrobas funds to political parties and Petrobas employees through fake 'Car Wash' companies. Many of these individuals received bribes and other benefits and are being investigated for around $22 billion of suspicious contracts.

The consequences for Petrobas have been quick and severe. The Dow Jones Sustainability World Index immediately removed Petrobas from its prestigious index, thereby resulting in lower share prices. The company has also suffered from budget reductions as well as investment restrictions. Coupled with a general reduction in oil prices, Petrobas' share prices have reduced by 86 percent.

The impact on Brazilian society has been noticeable. Petrobas was involved in many social programs aimed at poverty alleviation and other programs aimed at the arts. The latter included supporting a symphony orchestra and painting exhibitions. After the scandal, Petrobas had no choice but to cut such programs.

Source: Based on L. Casanova, 2016, "Petrobas, the fall of a global Latina star," *Latin Trade*, *24*(2), p. 16.

Given the real and damaging consequences of corruption and bribery, both countries and firms are taking steps to control and eradicate bribery. Several non-governmental organizations have taken steps to fight global corruption. For instance, the OECD has an anti-bribery convention which requires that participants make bribery of officials a crime. Participants are also required to demonstrate that adequate measures are taken to sanction those involved in bribery. This convention went into effect in February 1999 and has been ratified by all OECD members except Slovenia. Additionally, the United Nations Convention Against Corruption, which was adopted in 2003, includes legislation similar to the OECD convention. It requires members to criminalize bribery of government officials. Other regional groups are either implementing or have implemented measures to curb bribery. These include the African Union and the Convention on Preventing and Combating Corruption (July 2003), and the Pacific Basin Economic Council and their Statement on Standards of Transactions Between Business and Governments (November 1997).

One of the most recently passed pieces of legislation is the **Bribery Act** of the United Kingdom.[12] It was passed in 2010 and is seen as one of the most rigorous anti-bribery legislations. Similar to other anti-bribery legislation, it sees bribing to get advantages and bribing foreign officials as illegal. However, it also has provisions to punish companies if they do not have systems in place to prevent bribery. As such, the Act places the burden of proof on companies to show they have the appropriate policies and practices in place to prevent bribery.

The US government has also taken a very strong position on bribery. The **Foreign Corrupt Practices Act** (FCPA), which was passed in 1977, forbids US companies to make or offer payments or gifts to foreign government officials for the sake of gaining or retaining business. It not only applies to US companies but also applies to foreign companies listed in the US. Thus,

Foreign Corrupt Practices Act legislation forbidding US companies from making bribes

while the FCPA is a US legislation aimed at curbing bribery, it is also relevant for foreign emerging market multinationals doing business in the US or listed in the US.

The Foreign Corrupt Practices Act is now being rigorously enforced by the appropriate authorities. For instance, Novartis, the Swiss-based pharmaceuticals, had to pay $25 million to settle bribery charges against its subsidiary in China. Similarly, Hitachi agreed to pay $19 million to resolve charges that it bribed South African officials to get contracts in South Africa. Both of these examples suggest that more multinationals will be scrutinized in the future. To give you further insights on the reach of the FCPA, Exhibit 16.5 shows some examples of the companies fined in the past five years, their nationality, and the extent of their fines.

Although the FCPA makes bribery illegal, it does make some exceptions. Payments made under duress to avoid injury or violence are acceptable. For example, in an unstable political environment, a company may pay local officials "bribes" to avoid harassment of its employees. Smaller payments that encourage officials to do their routine jobs and fulfill their duties are also legal. Payments made that are lawful in a country are also deemed acceptable by the FCPA. Rather than seeking illegal ends, these "grease" payments are acceptable as long as they just speed up or make possible normal business functions, such as necessary paperwork.

An important component of the FCPA for US companies is the law's reason-to-know provision. The reason-to-know provision means that a firm is liable for bribes or questionable payments made by agents hired by the firm. However, if the US firm has neither knowledge of the behavior of the agent nor any reason to expect illegal behavior from the agent, then the US firm has no liability under the FCPA. In contrast, a multinational management is considered "knowing" if: (1) he or she is aware of the high possibility that an illegal act will happen, (2) he or she actually knows an illegal bribe will be given, and (3) he or she perceives that the circumstances make it likely that an illegal bribe will be given.

FCPA Fines (millions of US$)

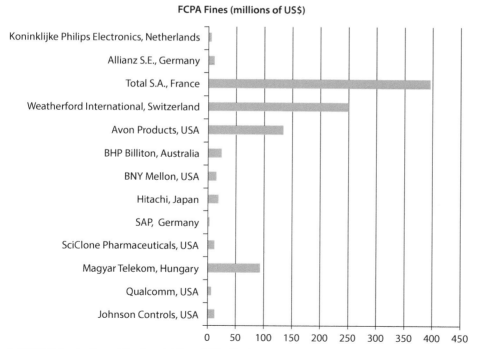

Exhibit 16.5 Foreign Corrupt Practices Act Fines (US$ million)

Source: Based on SEC Enforcement Actions: FCPA Cases, www.sec.gov/spotlight/fcpa/fcpa-cases.shtml

Experts argue that more companies will be prosecuted under the FCPA than in the past. As Exhibit 16.5 showed, companies prosecuted do not necessarily have to be US multinationals. It is therefore imperative for emerging market multinationals to be aware of the FCPA as well as the many other anti-bribery regulations discussed earlier. Even shareholders are considering lawsuits for FCPA violations. As a consequence, companies will need to ensure that their practices respect the FCPA. To give you more insights into the FCPA, Exhibit 16.6, taken directly from the FCPA codes, shows critical aspects of the FCPA.

Prohibited Foreign Trade Practices

It shall be unlawful for *any domestic concern* or for any officer, director, employee, or agent of such domestic concern or any stockholder thereof acting on behalf of such domestic concern, to make use of the mails or any means or instrumentality of interstate commerce corruptly in furtherance of an offer, payment, promise to pay, or authorization of the payment of any money, or offer, gift, promise to give, or authorization of the giving of anything of value to any foreign official for purposes of—

A. influencing any act or decision of such foreign official, political party, party official, or candidate in his or its official capacity, or

B. inducing such foreign official, political party, party official, or candidate to do or omit to do any act in violation of the lawful duty of such foreign official, political party, party official, or candidate, or

C. inducing such foreign official, political party, party official, or candidate to use his or its influence with a foreign government or instrumentality thereof to affect or influence any act or decision of such government or instrumentality, in order to assist such issuer in obtaining or retaining business for or with, or directing business to, any person.

Also prohibited is any offer, payment, promise to pay, or authorization of the payment of any money, or offer, gift, promise to give, or authorization of the giving of anything of value *when given to any person, while knowing* that all or a portion of such money or thing of value will be offered, given, or promised, directly or indirectly, to any foreign official, to any foreign political party or official thereof, or to any candidate for foreign political office, for purposes of A through C above.

Definitions

(1) The term *"domestic concern"* means any individual who is a citizen, national, or resident of the United States; and any corporation, partnership, association, joint-stock company, business trust, unincorporated organization, or sole proprietorship which has its principal place of business in the United States, or which is organized under the laws of a State of the United States or a territory, possession, or commonwealth of the United States.

(2) The term *"foreign official"* means any officer or employee of a foreign government or any department, agency, or instrumentality thereof, or any person acting in an official capacity for or on behalf of any such government or department, agency, or instrumentality.

(3) A person's state of mind is *"knowing"* with respect to conduct, a circumstance, or a result if—
    (i) such person is aware that such person is engaging in such conduct, that such circumstance exists, or that such result is substantially certain to occur; or
    (ii) such person has a firm belief that such circumstance exists or that such result is substantially certain to occur.
    (iii) Knowledge is established if a person is aware of a high probability of the existence of such circumstance, unless the person actually believes that such circumstance does not exist.

(4) The term *"routine government action"* means only an action which is ordinarily and commonly performed by a foreign official in such as obtaining permits, licenses, or other official documents to qualify a person to do business in a foreign country. The term "routine governmental action" does not include any decision by a foreign official whether, or on what terms, to award new business to or to continue business with a particular party, or any action taken by a foreign official involved in the decision-making process to encourage a decision to award new business to or continue business with a particular party.

(5) The term *"interstate commerce"* means trade, commerce, transportation, or communication among the several States, or between any foreign country and any State or between any State and any place or ship outside thereof.

Exhibit 16.6 Critical Aspects of the Foreign Corrupt Practices Act

Exceptions

A. Facilitating or expediting payment to a foreign official, political party, or party official the purpose of which is to expedite or *to secure the performance of a routine governmental action* by a foreign official, political party, or party official.

B. The payment, gift, offer, or promise of anything of value that was made, *was lawful under the written laws and regulations of the foreign official's, political party's, party official's, or candidate's country; or*

C. The payment, gift, offer, or promise of anything of value that was made, was *a reasonable and bona fide expenditure*, such as travel and lodging expenses, incurred by or on behalf of a foreign official, party, party official, or candidate and was directly related to the promotion, demonstration, or explanation of products or services; or the execution or performance of a contract with a foreign government or agency thereof.

Penalties

A. Any domestic concern that violates this section shall be fined not more than $2,000,000 and shall be subject to a civil penalty of not more than $10,000 imposed in an action brought by the Attorney General.

B. Any officer or director of a domestic concern, or stockholder acting on behalf of such domestic concern, who willfully violates this section shall be fined not more than $100,000, or imprisoned not more than 5 years, or both.

C. Any employee or agent of a domestic concern who is a United States citizen, national, or resident or is otherwise subject to the jurisdiction of the United States (other than an officer, director, or stockholder acting on behalf of such domestic concern), and who willfully violates this section, shall be fined not more than $100,000, or imprisoned not more than 5 years, or both.

D. Any officer, director, employee, or agent of a domestic concern, or stockholder acting on behalf of such domestic concern, who violates this section shall be subject to a civil penalty of not more than $10,000 imposed in an action brought by the Attorney General.

E. *Whenever a fine is imposed upon any officer, director, employee, agent, or stockholder of a domestic concern, such fine may not be paid, directly or indirectly, by such domestic concern.*

Exhibit 16.6 Critical Aspects of the Foreign Corrupt Practices Act
Source: US Code, Title 15—Commerce and Trade, Chapter 2B—Securities Exchanges.

In the above section, you read about some of the most crucial global ethics issues. Next, you will learn about some of the key approaches to dealing with global ethical issues.

Dealing With Global Ethics

Here you will read about how the MNC and the individual manager can deal with global ethics. First, you will learn about the multinational's approach to global ethics. In the second part of this section, you will read about how individual managers can approach global ethics.

Multinational Approach to Global Ethics: Ethical Relativism vs Ethical Universalism

Multinationals deal with global ethical issues in two important ways. Some multinationals assume that all cultures are legitimate as a means for people to guide their lives—that is, what people consider right or wrong, pretty or ugly, good or bad, depends on their cultural norms and values. As such, these multinationals practice **ethical relativism**, whereby a multinational manager considers each society's view of ethics as legitimate and ethical. Thus, for example, if bribery is an accepted way of doing business in a country, then it is acceptable for the multinational to follow local examples, even if it would be illegal at home. Thus, for MNCs, ethical relativism means that, when doing business in a country, managers need only follow local ethical conventions.

In contrast, some multinationals practice **ethical universalism**. Ethical universalism holds that there are basic moral principles that transcend cultural and national boundaries. For the

ethical relativism
consideration that each society's views of ethics are legitimate and ethical

ethical universalism
there are basic moral principles that transcend cultural and national boundaries

multinational manager, ethical universalism means that the same ethical standards are applied in all countries in which the multinational operates.

Both approaches present difficulties for multinational managers. Some argue, for instance, that when taken to the extreme, ethical relativism can become "**convenient relativism.**" Convenient relativism occurs when companies use ethical relativism to behave any way that they please, using the excuse of differences in cultures. For instance, a multinational can justify using child labor because it appears to be an acceptable practice in a country. Such logic can be applied to other activities with ethical consequences, such as bribery and pollution.

Extreme ethical universalism also has its problems. Assuming that one can identify universal ethics that all people should follow can lead to a type of cultural imperialism. In other words, multinational employees' managers who assume that they know the ethical ways of behaving can view the moral systems of foreign cultures as inferior or immoral. By assuming that there are universal ethical standards, a multinational may be imposing its own headquarters' culture in the host country.

Which way should multinationals go? Recent studies of firms from 10 Asian emerging markets suggest that these multinationals are adopting ethical universalism. Consider the following IB Emerging Market Strategic Insight.

convenient relativism
taking ethical relativism to the extreme

Emerging Market Multinationals and CSR

IB EMERGING MARKET STRATEGIC INSIGHT

The idea that all multinationals should spend scarce resources on CSR efforts is not necessarily shared by all companies. In fact, evidence suggests that CSR is a relatively new phenomenon in Western societies relative to the long history of the existence of multinationals. However, more recent examples in the media suggest that CSR is now becoming a moral imperative. Multinationals that invest in CSR are expected to develop strong reputation and financial performance as they connect stronger with their stakeholders through CSR programs. It is therefore not unreasonable to argue that CSR is now also becoming an ethically universal principle.

CSR is now becoming more popular in emerging markets. A recent study suggests that emerging market multinationals are also adopting CSR as they embrace ethical universalism. Why would emerging market multinationals see CSR as necessary? A study of sample firms from 10 Asian emerging markets (China, Hong Kong, India, Indonesia, South Korea, Malaysia, Philippines, Singapore, Taiwan, and Thailand) reveals some interesting insights. The authors argue that firms need to signal the effectiveness of their capabilities to their stakeholders. Such signaling is easier in more developed markets where institutions are functioning and stakeholders can easily find information. However, in emerging markets, the presence of institutional voids suggests that stakeholders may not easily have access to information about companies. CSR therefore becomes the means by which stakeholders can assess the superior capabilities of emerging market multinationals.

The study finds that firms that do engage in CSR do have higher market valuation. This suggests that CSR signals to investors and other stakeholders that the emerging market multinational has superior capabilities and adequate resources. In the absence of reliable information from institutions and the media, CSR sends strong positive signals about the worth of a company in such emerging markets.

Source: Based on W. Su, M. W. Peng, W. Tan and Y. Cheung, 2016, "The signaling effect of corporate social responsibility in emerging economies," *Journal of Business Ethics, 134*, pp. 479–491.

Clearly, the above IB Emerging Market Strategic Insight suggests that multinationals are being pressured to adopt ethically universal principles. Next, we consider some of these pressures.

Pressures Supporting Ethical Universalism

Donaldson, an expert in international business ethics, argues that multinationals have a higher moral responsibility than ethical relativism.[13] As such, he suggests that multinationals should follow ethical universalism based on moral languages. **Moral languages** describe the basic ways that people use to think about ethical decisions and to explain their ethical choices. Donaldson further argues that three universal moral languages should provide important guidance to multinationals as they strive to become more ethical.

The three moral languages include avoiding harm (i.e. a multinational should avoid harming its stakeholders), rights/duties (i.e. a multinational has some duties that it needs to fulfill), and the social contract (i.e. the social agreement a multinational has with its employees). These should guide MNCs. He proposes **prescriptive ethics** for multinationals; that is, multinationals should engage in business practices that avoid negative consequences to stakeholders (e.g. employees, the local environment). Though companies keep basic rights, such as profit motive, these rights also carry consequent duties, such as providing a fair wage to local employees. The multinational also has a social contract between itself and its stakeholders. This social contract defines the nature of the relationships. As an example, when a multinational enters a country, it accepts the social contract to follow local laws.

Donaldson believes that these moral languages are most appropriate for managing ethical behaviors among multinationals located in different nations. As such, regardless of their background, companies can agree with their stakeholders on the basic rules of moral behavior. However, for these ideas to work, there must be a code of conduct to guide the multinationals that is independent of national boundaries. Codes are one important component of the global ethical company. In the next and final section, you will read some of the key aspects of building a socially responsible global company and the importance of codes of conduct.

moral languages
basic ways people use to think about ethical decisions

prescriptive ethics
multinationals should engage in business practices that avoid negative consequences

Building the Socially Responsible Company

As has already been mentioned, corporate social responsibility or CSR refers to the idea that businesses have a responsibility to society beyond making profits. In other words, social responsibility means that a company must take into account the welfare of other constituents (e.g. customers, suppliers) in addition to stockholders. Obviously, a socially responsible company has to provide guidance to employees regarding how to deal with ethical dilemmas. The socially responsible company will go beyond merely reacting to ethical situations. Such companies will be proactive in devising systems to ensure that their actions do not affect others negatively.

In this section, you will learn about the many elements of a socially responsible multinational. The first step in building the socially responsible multinational is to understand the impact of one's actions on others. You will therefore read about stakeholder analysis.

Stakeholder Analysis

A socially responsible multinational is one that recognizes and addresses the impact of its actions on its constituents. In that context, any group or entity that is affected by a multinational's decisions or actions is known as a **stakeholder**. There are two main types of stakeholders. **Primary stakeholders** include those who are directly linked to a company's

stakeholder
any group or entity affected by a multinational's decisions

primary stakeholders
those directly affected by a company's decisions

secondary stakeholders
those indirectly impacted
by a multinational's
actions

survival and have important influences on the multinational's strategy. Primary stakeholders include customers, suppliers, employees, and shareholders. In contrast, **secondary stakeholders** tend to be less directly linked to the company's survival. Secondary stakeholders include the media, trade associations, and other special interest groups. However, although secondary stakeholders tend to be less directly linked to the company's survival, they can have disastrous influence if ignored. Consider the following BRIC Insight.

Samarco and the Dam Breaches   BRIC INSIGHT

Samarco, the Brazilian mining company co-owned by Vale and BHP Billiton, was recently involved in one of the worst environmental disasters in Brazil. As part of its operations, it had built several dams to hold the waste from its iron ore mining operations. Two of these dams failed through a process called liquefaction whereby soil becomes saturated with water. The liquefaction process weakened the dams' structure and they ruptured resulting in a catastrophic mudslide. The mudslide covered a rural village killing 19 people in the process. The mud also travelled 400 miles and caused significant damage elsewhere.

Subsequent investigations showed that Samarco did not properly assess the impact of its operations on the surrounding communities, a secondary stakeholder. An expert engineer argues that Samarco was warned of the potential for catastrophe and was asked to strengthen the base of these dams. However, Samarco ignored these warnings and the company was found guilty of negligence. Furthermore, members of the affected communities also claimed that Samarco did not alert them properly of the impeding mudslides. Many of them only heard of the coming mudslide through word of mouth. This also suggests that the company did not have any plan in place should a dam break occur.

This ignoring of secondary stakeholders has been very costly for Samarco. The latter has agreed to pay $1.1 billion in damages to cover for the environmental damages and to compensate the victims. However, this is only a fraction of what the Brazilian government asked originally. It is expected that this disaster will likely be more costly for Samarco.

Source: D. Benyon, 2016, "Brazil dam owners agree pollution package," *Reactions*, March 21, p. 1; P. Kiernan, 2016, "Samarco warned of problems at dam, engineer says," *Wall Street Journal*, January 18, online edition.

As the above BRIC Insight shows, ignoring secondary stakeholders can be very costly. To give you further insights into the impact of stakeholders on a multinational, consider Exhibit 16.7, which depicts the relationships between a multinational and its stakeholders, and potential questions the multinational has to deal with as it interacts with these various groups.

As you can see from Exhibit 16.7, a multinational has the potential to impact many groups through its actions. The socially responsible multinational is proactive in determining potential consequences of its activities and strategies on its stakeholders. However, to be proactive, the multinational needs to address stakeholder issues strategically. One approach is to regularly conduct **stakeholder analysis,** an approach whereby the influence and impact of stakeholders are assessed. Stakeholder analysis begins with an appropriate identification of stakeholders. This step can be facilitated by considering those groups that have the potential to affect or influence the company's survival.

stakeholder analysis
influence and impact of
stakeholders are
assessed

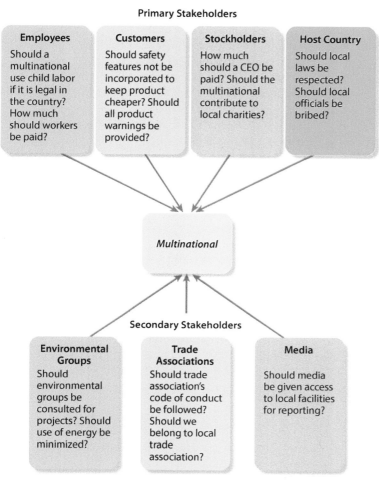

Exhibit 16.7 Stakeholder Analysis

One core component of stakeholder analysis is to understand the saliency of a stakeholder for the organization. This salience can be understood in terms of the power (how likely is the stakeholder to influence the multinational's strategy?), legitimacy (are the stakeholder's claims legitimate?), and urgency (how urgent are the stakeholder's claims?). A multinational manager can identify stakeholders and determine their salience for the multinational. Obviously, the more salient the stakeholder, the more necessary it is for the multinational to determine strategies to address these stakeholders' needs.

Stakeholder analysis thus serves some critical functions for the multinational. By showing its concerns for those it has the potential to affect, a multinational has the ability to show its commitment to corporate social responsibility. Furthermore, by identifying stakeholders, multinational managers are being proactive and can determine who has valid claims on the multinational. Finally, an understanding of stakeholders can help multinational managers determine the best approaches to achieve its multinational goals.

Stakeholder analysis is not always an easy or obvious process. However, conducting the stakeholder analysis is a critical step in terms of building the socially responsible multinational. Another critical aspect of a socially responsible multinational is the creation of a code of conduct. Next, you will learn about codes of conduct.

Codes of Conduct

codes of conduct
specification of
appropriate employee
behaviors and
multinational
responsibilities

According to Kaptein and others,[14] **codes of conduct** (also called codes of ethics) specify appropriate behaviors for employees while also defining the multinational's responsibilities and approaches in terms of its interactions with its stakeholders. Codes of conduct emphasize the norms and values the multinational believes in while it is striving to achieve its business objectives.

Why are codes of conduct important? Codes of conduct announce to all of the stakeholders the ethical values of the multinational. By specifying the appropriate employee behaviors, the multinational also hopes that it can inform its employees of situations whereby unethical behavior may occur. By educating employees about such instances, the multinational hopes that incidences of unethical activities will be reduced. In addition to the above benefits, a properly implemented code of conduct can also help a multinational stay on the legal side and avoid prosecution. For instance, in the US, the appropriate legal rules (i.e. Federal Sentencing Guidelines) typically reduce fines for those companies that have properly enforced codes of conduct. Recent regulations such as the Sarbanes–Oxley Act, enforcing appropriate accounting rules, require multinationals to have codes of conduct.

A study of 210 Indian companies provides more insight on the value of codes of conduct.[15] Managers of the companies were approached and asked to provide their insights on the value of codes of conduct. The findings showed that codes of conduct had three important roles: (1) to help employees become more sensitive to ethical issues, (2) to encourage employees to have stronger ethical intentions, and (3) to encourage ethical behavior. Exhibit 16.8 shows the mean score of managers' perception that the codes of conduct had the mentioned effect.

Which areas should a code of conduct address? The stakeholder analysis discussed earlier provides the basis for deciding this. More salient stakeholders are those stakeholders that have more influence on the corporation. It therefore becomes imperative for the multinational to develop codes of conduct to provide guidance as the multinational and its employees interact

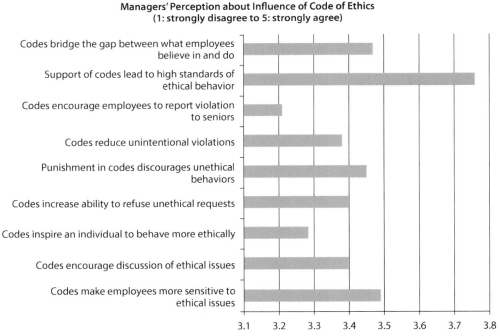

Managers' Perception about Influence of Code of Ethics
(1: strongly disagree to 5: strongly agree)

Exhibit 16.8 Role of Codes of Conduct

Source: Based on A. Mahajan and M. Mahajan, 2016, "Code of ethics among Indian business firms: A cross-sectional analysis of its incidence, role and compliance," *Paradigm, 20*(1), pp. 14–35.

with these salient stakeholders. To give you more insights into the content of codes of conduct, Kaptein investigated the 200 largest corporations in the world. Of these 200 multinationals, only around 52 percent had a code of conduct.[16] Exhibit 16.9 shows the percentage of companies that had different areas mentioned in their codes of conduct.

Although conducted in the 2000s, the study by Kaptein provides some contemporary and important insights into the areas that most multinationals' codes of conduct cover. As you can see, an overwhelming majority of codes of conduct include elements pertaining to the quality of the product and services. This is not surprising given that the multinational's ability to survive depends on its ability to sell quality products and services to its customers. Providing quality products and services is crucial. However, beyond products and services, it is interesting to note that many of the world's largest multinationals' codes of conduct address other issues, such as dealing with stakeholders (transparency, fairness, etc.). These codes of conduct also provide important guidance to employees regarding how to deal with potentially unethical situations, such as use of company property, bribery, etc. Finally, most codes of conduct specify how the multinational will deal with its employees.

Which codes of conduct are perceived as being effective? A study of a number of large Canadian companies suggests that employees view more effective codes of conduct as having a number of characteristics.[17] Specifically, more effective codes of conduct were seen as containing real examples of ethical situations, were easier to read, were relevant, had senior management support, were communicated to employees through training, and had some reporting and enforcement component. While these characteristics may not apply to all multinationals, they provide some guidance as codes of conduct are developed.

Next, you will learn what multinationals can do to successfully implement a code of conduct.

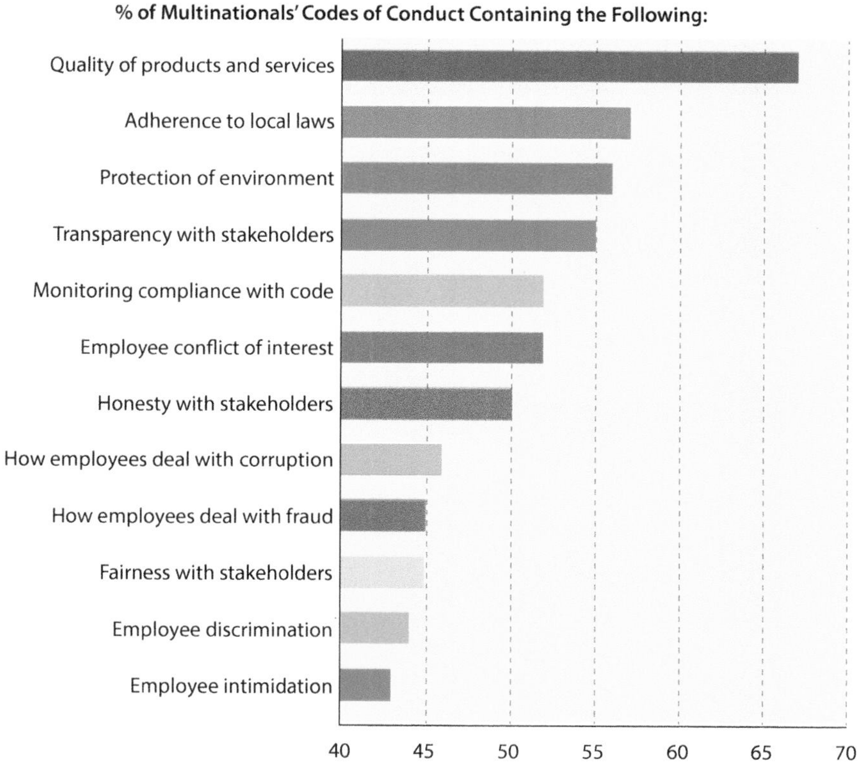

% of Multinationals' Codes of Conduct Containing the Following:

Exhibit 16.9 Content of Codes of Conduct of the World's Largest Corporations

Source: Based on M. Kaptein, 2004, "Business codes of multinational firms: What do they say?" *Journal of Business Ethics*, 50, pp. 13–31.

Successful Implementation of Codes of Conduct

Once a code of conduct has been developed, the standards and rules contained in the code of conduct have to be communicated to employees. In that context, training becomes a crucial tool to inform employees of the appropriate way to deal with stakeholders. Some experts have argued that multinational employees are sometimes unaware of what's ethical and what's not ethical. By training their employees, multinationals can teach employees values and other qualities that matter to the multinationals and their stakeholders.[18]

Beyond training, Adam and Rachman-Moore suggest that there are many methods that can be used to implement codes of conduct.[19] **Formal methods** include using various means of control to ensure that the multinational behaves ethically. In such cases, formal training plays a critical role. However, the multinational can also take a more strategic view of ethics and apply its ethics approach starting with the recruitment and selection process. Potential new employees are carefully screened to ensure that their personal values are consistent with the multinational's expectations. Furthermore, many multinationals have ethics orientation programs that all new employees have to go through. In such orientation programs, employees learn about the company values and how to apply them when they are facing potentially unethical situations. Formal methods work to socialize employees in understanding the appropriate behaviors.

Multinationals can also rely on more **informal methods** to implement codes of conduct. In such cases, the organizational culture can play an important role in ensuring that employees behave consistently with the multinational's expectations. Employees can be pressured to conform to ethical norms by their supervisors or their peers in the multinational. Also, if employees are behaving in ways that are not consistent with the multinational's expectations, superiors or peers can disapprove or reject the employee to show their dissatisfaction with the employee's behavior.

Although formal and informal methods exist to implement codes of conduct, it is important to note that formal training remains the preferred method of informing employees of the correct and ethical behavior. However, this may not be necessarily true for all situations. Consider the following Emerging Market Brief.

formal methods
using various means of control to ensure company is ethical

informal methods
use of organizational culture to train employees to be more ethical

Ethics Training in the Indian IT Sector

EMERGING
MARKET BRIEF

Multinationals use a variety of formal and informal training methods for ethics training. However, multinationals often question the effectiveness of the various methods to determine which methods work best. To help answer this question, researchers recently studied Indian IT professionals to get their views on the use of formal and informal ethics training methods. The researchers studied the impact of such methods on three aspects of ethics training effectiveness: (1) whether the training results in stronger organizational ethical values, (2) whether the training positively affects the employee perception of the importance of ethics, and (3) whether the training positively affected the employee's individual ethical ideologies.

Surveys of IT ethical professionals in a large sample of Indian IT multinationals revealed that both formal and informal methods of training had positive impact on the three measures of effectiveness discussed above. However, the study also showed that the most effective method was a combination of both formal and informal methods. One senior IT professional noted that too much formal training can result in boredom and a lack of interest. Combining it with informal methods will likely make the training more effective.

Source: Based on P. Verma, S. Mohapatra and J. Lowstedt, 2016, "Ethics training in the Indian IT sector: Formal, informal or both?" *Journal of Business Ethics, 133*, pp. 73–93.

As the above Emerging Market Brief shows, for Indian IT multinationals, both formal and informal methods work well. But why should multinationals invest in ethics training? Ethics training can serve many important functions.[20] Ethics training can educate employees about the multinational's expectations as well as the appropriate laws and regulations. Training can also be used to educate employees about the available resources at their disposal should they need advice regarding ethical situations. Furthermore, not all moral issues are clear. Ethics training can also help employees deal with ambiguous ethical situations.[21]

Ethics training can take a variety of forms. Some training can be done in a passive format where employees can learn to respond to ethical dilemmas through self-study, lectures, or reading. Such education can also take place in a regular classroom or in an online environment. However, passive ethics training has been criticized for being static and not being the most appropriate format where participants can learn about dealing with ethical situations. As such, more interactive forms of training where participants are exposed to actual ethical dilemmas and actively participate in such dilemmas are seen as more effective. Many experts argue that ethical decisions are complex decisions that involve focused cognitive reasoning that is only possible with active forms of training.

In this section, you read about the various ways a multinational can implement a code of conduct. In the next section, you will read about ethics monitoring.

Ethics Monitoring and Enforcement

A successful ethics program is not possible without some form of monitoring and enforcement. In other words, a program cannot be effective unless the multinational has some way of measuring performance and progress. Furthermore, some form of enforcement is necessary. Employees need to be rewarded if they are conforming to the multinational's codes and punished if they are violating these codes.

Veral argues that monitoring involves "the most detailed manifestation of specific performance criteria that the multinational has decided to attain."[22] Such monitoring provides valuable benchmarks to assess employee and company achievement of the elements of the code of conduct. For instance, if Nike has a mission of adequately compensating its employees and providing good working conditions, it can set measures that can be assessed. It can, for example, decide to set a goal whereby workers are allowed to work only eight hours per day. Through an audit, Nike can determine what percentage are exceeding this goal. Similarly, any multinational can set a benchmark regarding bathroom breaks or living conditions whereby worker conditions can be assessed.

It is important for a multinational to set goals to determine progress in terms of corporate social responsibility. In addition to such benchmarks, it is also important for any multinational to enforce appropriate ethical behavior through rewards and punishment. As Boudreaux and Steiner discuss, it is important to hold higher level executives to the same standards.[23] Specifically, it is useful to inform directors, officers, and other top managers of the sanctions they face if they break ethical rules or laws. Infractions may result in disciplinary actions involving demotion or discharge. A multinational should also show its commitment to corporate social responsibility by rewarding ethical behavior. Annual meetings can be held to reward employees who have been ethical or who have contributed to making the multinational more ethical.

What specific aspects should a multinational focus on? Recent examination of best practices suggests that multinationals can develop benchmarking processes across all aspects of its operations.[24] Multinationals can also develop systematic processes to determine how well it is doing with respect to business ethics benchmarks. In that respect, Exhibit 16.10 shows some potential data a multinational ethics officer can gather to determine the multinational's benchmarking efforts. Such an exercise can point attention to areas that need attention.

Questions	Yes	Sometimes	No
• The multinational systematically examines its ethics and ethical performance on a yearly basis			
• The multinational benchmarks itself to the industry's business ethics best practices			
• Data are collected from suppliers and customers about ethical performance			
• The multinational tracks unethical behaviors and determines the systematic causes of such behaviors			
• The multinational implements corrective actions when unethical behaviors occur. Employees are dealt with accordingly.			
• Relevant ethical performance information is shared with all key stakeholders including the CEO			

Exhibit 16.10 Best Practices Benchmarking Tools

Source: Adapted from D. Collins, 2016, "Organizational best practices in business ethics: A practical and systematic benchmarking tool," *Business and Society Review, 120*(2), pp. 303–327.

In the next and final section, you will read about some other key elements of a successful, socially responsible multinational.

Other Key Elements of the Successful Socially Responsible Multinational

While the earlier paragraphs discussed some of the major steps needed to build a socially responsible multinational, there are other important guidelines that need to be followed. In this section, you will read about these guidelines as recommended by experts:[25]

- *Setting the example at the top* For a multinational to truly demonstrate its commitment to ethics and ethical behavior, top managers and other top-level executives need to be upholding the same standards. By setting a good example, it is more likely that lower-level employees will behave ethically.
- *Making ethics part of the multinational's strategy* Successful, socially responsible multinationals are the ones whose ethical programs are made part of and integrated into their strategy and vision. All employees need to see how making ethical decisions on a daily basis is connected to the company's strategy and bottom line. Such efforts will ensure that the multinational is living and breathing ethics and is committed to being ethical.
- *Investing financial resources* A successful ethics program requires that a multinational devote the necessary financial resources to support such programs. For instance, new experts in ethics and compliance need to be hired. Business processes may need to be scrutinized and changed to comply with the new ethical direction. These and other efforts require commitment to support the programs through financial investments.
- *Involving all employees* Employees need to be able to voice their concerns and contribute to ethics efforts. By involving as many employees as possible, a multinational has a better chance to determine key ethical areas. Employees are also more likely to buy into such programs if they can participate in devising the ethics program.
- *Communicating* A corporate social responsibility program cannot succeed unless it is communicated regularly and thoroughly to all employees and stakeholders. Employees also need to be given the opportunity to communicate their views regarding the ethical efforts. Multinationals can thus provide communication tools such as 1-800 phone lines, whistle-blowing hotlines, notice boards, and online forums. Managers need to regularly address

ethical issues of great importance. Employees also need to feel that they can voice their ethics-related concerns when necessary.

- *Establish ethical culture* A multinational's ethical codes and other formal aspects will not work if the company does not have values that celebrate ethics. It is therefore critical for the company to devise systems and policies to celebrate ethics. Senior managers should lead by example and compensation and promotion processes should reflect justice and ethics. As such, the company's approach to ethics should be more than just respecting legal obligations.

As has been emphasized in this chapter, the environment of emerging markets is fraught with ethical challenges. Experts therefore suggest the following additional guidelines when operating in such markets: [26]

- *Perform Due Diligence* It is critical for the multinational to conduct a very careful examination of ethical risks. As such, the multinational compliance manager should visit the offices in the emerging market and conduct risk assessments in person. Additionally, rather than rely on foreign colleagues or expatriates, it is highly advisable to spend time with locals to have a better understanding of the ethical environment. Additionally, rather than rely on single sources of information, it is more sensible to consider a variety of sources to get a better understanding of ethical challenges.
- *Consider Local Realities* The environment governing ethics in emerging markets is significantly different from Western markets. Training or other aspects of an ethics program that work in the home country may not necessarily be effective in emerging markets. For example, expecting all suppliers to comply with ethical policies across the supply chain may be more complex in emerging markets. It therefore becomes critical for the multinational to carefully assess cultural and other environmental differences and to design programs to fit such realities. It is also important for the multinational to be flexible and to adapt policies to fit the environment. Applying global codes to all subsidiaries may not be as effective as different subsidiaries may require different training approaches and different policies.

Chapter Review

In this chapter, you read about an area that is becoming increasingly important for multinationals especially when operating in emerging markets. As more attention is paid to the actions of multinationals and the consequences of such actions, it is becoming more critical for these multinationals to become more socially responsible and ethical. In this chapter, you read about the key issues associated with international ethics and social responsibility. In the first section, you learned some basic definitions of international ethics and social responsibility. You also read about why multinationals are being criticized regularly.

The chapter also discussed three important ethical issues facing multinationals today. You read about labor rights and some of the most pressing issues pertaining to labor rights. You read about environmental pollution. Most importantly, you also learned about bribery and corruption and some of the efforts to lower incidences of corruption around the world.

In the third part of the chapter, you read about some of the approaches used by multinationals to deal with global ethics. You learned about ethical relativism and ethical universalism and the associated benefits and dangers of each approach.

In the final section of the chapter, we discussed the many different steps in building the ethical and socially responsible multinational. You read about codes of conduct and successful implementation of such codes. You also learned about the need to monitor and enforce ethics programs. Finally, you read about other key components of any ethics program and some special elements when operating in emerging markets.

Discussion Questions

1   What is international ethics? Why are multinationals increasingly being criticized? Are such criticisms always justified?

2   What is corporate social responsibility? How can a company implement a corporate social responsibility program?

3   Discuss two of the most important ethical issues facing multinationals today.

4   Compare and contrast ethical relativism and ethical universalism. Discuss some benefits and disadvantages of each approach.

5   What are some key elements of a successful ethics program? How do these elements change in emerging markets?

6   Discuss some key components of a code of conduct.

7   What is stakeholder analysis? What are primary and secondary stakeholders? Give some examples.

8   Why do companies need to monitor and enforce ethics? Discuss possible ethical goals of a multinational.

9   Why is building the ethical company more challenging in an emerging market?

International Business Skill Builder

Determining Key Areas of Corporate Social Responsibility

Step 1: Go to the following companies' websites: Mattel Inc. (www.mattel.com), Nike (www.nike.com), and Freeport-McMoRan Mining (www.fcx.com).

Step 2: Locate the company's social responsibility statement or code of conduct.

Step 3: Compile a list of each company's key areas of corporate social responsibility.

Step 4: Identify differences and similarities among these corporate social responsibility priority areas and approaches.

Step 5: Compile a general list of key areas of social responsibility for any multinational.

Chapter Internet Activity

Go to the Transparency International website (**www.transparency.org**). Identify the top ten and bottom ten countries of the latest corruption perception scores. Find out how the index is computed. Find out about some of the possible uses of the corruption perception index scores.

Key Concepts

- ☐ Bribery
- ☐ Bribery Act
- ☐ codes of conduct
- ☐ convenient relativism
- ☐ corporate social responsibility
- ☐ corruption
- ☐ ethical relativism
- ☐ ethical universalism
- ☐ ethics
- ☐ Foreign Corrupt Practices Act

- ☐ formal methods
- ☐ informal methods
- ☐ international business ethics
- ☐ moral languages
- ☐ prescriptive ethics
- ☐ primary stakeholders
- ☐ secondary stakeholders
- ☐ stakeholder
- ☐ stakeholder analysis
- ☐ sweatshops

great pen

Can't be their fault?

what!?!! 100% not fair

CASE 16

BUSINESS > INTERNATIONAL

The Global Problem of E-Waste

A growing problem in the developed economies of the world is what to do with outdated or unusable electronic equipment. Electronic waste, or e-waste, is created when people discard old computers, monitors, printers, televisions, and other electrical equipment. E-waste contains hazardous materials such as lead, mercury, and cadmium. Public landfills generally prohibit the disposal of such hazardous materials due to the potential to cause harmful environmental conditions. Toxic chemicals from the discarded e-waste can seep into underground water and contaminate drinking supplies. With millions of electronic devices such as old computers, cell phones, and television monitors discarded each year in the United States alone, a strong need exists to find a place for these potentially harmful devices.

Computer recycling requires that low wage employees disassemble old computers by extracting the valuable and working parts for reassembly. The so-called "white box" computers are reassembled computers that are sold in developing countries at a much lower price than new ones. By reusing existing computer parts, resources are saved and consumers who might not otherwise be able to afford a computer can purchase one.

Given the labor cost differences between the United States and third world emerging countries, much of the e-waste from the US is shipped to India and China where the cost of recycling is one-tenth the cost of the United States. Unfortunately, the low cost comes at a high price. Safety regulations and worker protection are generally not available in these countries. Workers in the major recycling centers of Guiyu, China and Delhi, India report health-related issues such as respiratory problems and skin irritations. In addition to removing usable parts from old computers, the recycling industry literally burns circuit boards in order to recover valuable silver and gold used in their manufacture. Wiring is dipped into acid vats to remove the plastic covering to salvage the commodity value of the wire. Much of the work is done by women and children from the rural areas, who come to seek work in the cities of China and India. Both of these groups are especially vulnerable to the hazards of toxic substances such as lead. Lead, found in computer monitors and televisions in heavy concentrations can cause lead poisoning in children and often harms and unborn fetus. Compensation for such toxic work is low. Given other employment opportunities, few people would choose to do such work; however, it is often not an option for these workers.

Disposal of e-waste is a lucrative business in the United States, and is expected to increase with even more electronic products being sold each year. In addition, the move to a completely digital television broadcast will produce large quantities of unusable analog sets which will become e-waste. While an old television may be nearly worthless in the United

CASE 16 cont'd

States, a 40 foot container filled with e-waste is worth approximately $5,000 in Hong Kong, the preferred port of entry for such disposables. In order to sell e-waste abroad, US companies must get Environmental Protection Agency (EPA) approval, and the approval of the receiving country before legally shipping their cargo. Enforcement of EPA regulations is, however, difficult. According to one source, "ninety percent of electronics recyclers are cheaters." The United States is one of the few countries in the world that has not ratified the Basel Convention (Basel Convention on the Control of Transboundary Movements of Hazardous Waste) which regulates the movement of hazardous materials, especially from developed to less developed countries.

One proposed solution to the problem is to require electronics manufacturers or retailers to charge a disposal fee at the time of purchase to cover the cost of safely disposing of the product at the end of its usefulness. Or similarly, a recycling fee could be assessed and refunded when the device is returned. As commodity prices drop globally, there is increased pressure to reduce the cost of processing e-waste to extract the precious metals and other components. With an overflowing stock of old computer monitors and other electronic devices in developed countries and a growing population in developing countries needing employment, the hazardous work of recycling is expected to continue to grow.

CASE DISCUSSION POINTS:

1   Who do you feel is most responsible (consumers, manufacturers, American recyclers, foreign governments) for the e-waste problem? Explain your answer.
2   Is it fair for rich countries to dump their e-waste in poor countries? Explain your answer.
3   Can developing countries in any positive way capitalize on the growing stockpile of e-waste?

Source: B. Elgin, B. Grow and E. Gibson, 2007, "The dirty secret of recycling electronics," *Business Week*, November 27; "Growing concerns over India's e-waste," BBC News, November 8, 2008; *Forbes*, 2008, "Heavy metal," October 27; S. Darabshae, 2016, "India struggles to manage E-waste," *MetalMinter*, July 15.

Case written by Charles A. Rarick and Kasia Firlej

Notes

1 Robyn Meredith and Suzanne Hoppough, 2007, "Why globalization is good," *Forbes*, 179(8), pp. 64–68.
2 W. Su, M. W. Peng, W. Tan and Y. Cheung, 2016, "The signaling effect of corporate social responsibility in emerging economies," *Journal of Business Ethics*, 134, pp. 479–491.
3 *The Economist*, 2016, "Deep in a pit," March 19, pp. 47–48.
4 Aaron Bernstein, 2005, "A major swipe at sweatshops," *BusinessWeek*, May 23, 3934, p. 98.
5 www.laborrights.org/ and www.fairlabor.org/

6 *The Economist*, 2016, "Waves of chagrin," April 9, p. 74.

7 Gabriel Eweje, 2006, "Environmental costs and responsibilities resulting from oil exploitation in developing countries: The case of the Niger Delta in Nigeria," *Journal of Business Ethics*, 69, pp. 27–56.

8 *The Economist*, 2016, "Exhaustive analysis," April 30, pp. 58–60.

9 Loretta Chao and Shai Oster, 2006, "Multinationals in China cited for pollution," *Wall Street Journal*, October 30, p. 12.

10 S. Cendrowski, 2014, "Business created China's pollution problem," *Fortune*, April 10, pp. 90–93.

11 A. Borthakur, 2016, "Health and environmental hazards of electronic waste in India," *Journal of Environmental Health*, 78(8), pp. 18–23.

12 Bribery Act 2010, www.legislation.gov.uk/ukpga/2010/23/contents, accessed 2016.

13 T. Donaldson, 1992, "The language of international ethics," *Business Ethics Quarterly*, 2, pp. 271–281.

14 Muel Kaptein, 2004, "Business codes of multinational firms: What do they say?" *Journal of Business Ethics*, 50, pp. 13–31; A. Mahajan and M. Mahajan, 2016, "Code of ethics among Indian business firms: A cross-sectional analysis of its incidence, role and compliance," *Paradigm*, 20(1), pp. 14–35.

15 A. Mahajan and M. Mahajan, 2016, "Code of ethics among Indian business firms: A cross-sectional analysis of its incidence, role and compliance," *Paradigm*, 20(1), pp. 14–35.

16 Muel Kaptein, 2004, "Business codes of multinational firms: What do they say?" *Journal of Business Ethics*, 50, pp. 13–31.

17 Mark S. Schwartz, 2004, "Effective corporate codes of ethics: Perceptions of code users," *Journal of Business Ethics*, 55, pp. 323–353.

18 P. Verma, S. Mohapatra and J. Lowstedt, 2016, "Ethics training in the Indian IT sector: Formal, informal or both?" *Journal of Business Ethics*, 133, pp. 73–93.

19 Avshalom M. Adam and Dalia Rachman-Moore, 2004, "The methods used to implement an ethical code of conduct and employee attitudes," *Journal of Business Ethics*, 54, pp. 225–244.

20 O. C. Ferrell, J. Fraedrich and L. Ferrell, 2014 (10th edn), *Business Ethics: Ethical Decision Making and Cases*, Cengage Learning: Mason, OH.

21 P. Verma, S. Mohapatra and J. Lowstedt, 2016, "Ethics training in the Indian IT sector: Formal, informal or both?" *Journal of Business Ethics*, 133, pp. 73–93.

22 Emre A. Veral, 2005, "Designing and monitoring corporate codes of conduct for multinational corporations," *Business Review*, Summer, 4(1), pp. 145–152, p. 147.

23 Greg Boudreaux and Tracey Steiner, 2005, "Developing a code of ethics," *Management Quarterly*, 46(1), pp. 2–19.

24 D. Collins, 2016, "Organizational best practices in business ethics: A practical and systematic benchmarking tool," *Business and Society Review*, 120(2), pp. 303–327.

25 M. Kleinhempel, 2015, "Navigating the realities of emerging markets," *IESE Insight*, Fourth Quarter, 27, pp. 32–39; Diane Kubal, Michael Baker and Kendra Coleman, 2006, "Doing the right thing: How today's leading companies are becoming more ethical," *Performance Improvement*, March, 45(3), pp. 5–8; Robin Zablow, 2006, "Creating and sustaining an ethical workplace," *Risk Management*, September, 53(9), pp. 26–30.

26 M. Kleinhempel, 2015, "Navigating the realities of emerging markets," *IESE Insight*, Fourth Quarter, 27, pp. 32–39; P. Mandell, 2015, "Four steps to managing compliance in emerging markets," Insidecounsel.com, April, p. 40.

Photo credits

Part IV

Opener © Getty Images

Chapter 9
Opener © Getty Images

Chapter 10
Opener © Thinkstock by Getty Images

Chapter 11
Opener © Thinkstock by Getty Images

Chapter 12
Opener © Thinkstock by Getty Images

Chapter 13
Opener © Thinkstock by Getty Images

Chapter 14
Opener © Thinkstock by Getty Images

Chapter 15
Opener © Thinkstock by Getty Images

Part V

Opener © Shutterstock

Chapter 16
Opener © Thinkstock by Getty Images

Index